Advanced PE & Sport

A level

THIRD EDITION

JOHN HONEYBOURNE

MICHAEL HILL

and HELEN MOORS

Published in 2004 by:
Nelson Thornes Ltd
Delta Place
27 Bath Road
CHELTENHAM
GL53 7TH
United Kingdom

04 05 06 07 08 / 10 9 8 7 6 5 4 3 2 1

A catalogue record for this book is available from the British Library

ISBN 0-7487-7529-3

Illustrations by Angela Lumley, Oxford Designers and Illustrators,
Shaun Williams and Florence Production

Cover image by Image 100

Page make-up by Florence Production, Stoodleigh, Devon
Printed in Great Britain by Scotprint

Contents

Introduction

Physical Education continues to be one of the largest growth subjects at AS and A2 level. Examination board specifications have recently been revised and this edition includes any additional material necessary to fulfil the specifications' requirements. You can be confident in the knowledge that this text covers the content of all the AS and the A2 specifications, including OCR, EDEXCEL, AQA and WJEC. The third edition of this popular and market-leading textbook now has full-colour features making it an even more accessible and attractive must-have resource for students and their teachers.

We have written this book for students to use as a no-nonsense resource. We have all had considerable experience in teaching AS and A level Physical Education, Sports Studies, GCSE Physical Education, BTEC National Sport, GNVQ/AVCE Leisure and Tourism and GNVQ/AVCE Health and Social Care. We have all been senior examiners at A level for three of the four examination boards.

Students and teachers who use this book will realise that the aim is to give only information that is relevant and clearly expressed. This book will give students enough information to pass the AS level examination and the full A level, or to build a portfolio for GNVQ/AVCE work, or to give some of the necessary background for writing assignments for the BTEC Sport qualifications.

The book is clearly set out in Parts and Chapters. Each Part covers the main areas of the subject at AS level and A level and represents the content of all syllabuses in this area at the time of writing. There are seven parts to the book. The first three parts deal with the material relevant to the AS level and the remaining four parts deal with the content of the A2 aspect of the full A level. Part 1 deals with anatomy and physiology. Part 2 covers skill acquisition. Part 3 deals with the social issues in physical education and sport. Part 4 covers exercise physiology. Part 5 covers sports psychology. Part 6 covers the historical development of physical education and sport. Part 7 deals with comparative studies of physical education and sport. There is also an important section in the appendices that deals with the writing of research projects, which some specifications allow.

At the beginning of each chapter, *Learning objectives* clearly state what is to be covered. There are *Activity* boxes, which include ideas to reinforce learning, and *In practice* boxes, which look at the application of theory to practical situations. All of the AS level and A2 examinations and the work required for GNVQ/AVCE and the BTEC National qualifications demand that the student can apply theory to practice. To help understanding we have also included *Definition* boxes, which expand on some key words and phrases. At the end of each chapter there is a list of *Key terms* that need to be learned and understood by the student, along with *Revision* boxes, which will focus students' attention on the key concepts that are important for passing the examination. We have also included a *Revision guide* for each section and *Examination-style questions* that will help to prepare students for the written examinations. There is a *Glossary* of the main key terms at the back of the book, which can again be used for revision purposes.

This is a fascinating and rewarding subject area and should be studied with a view to applying theoretical principles to practical situations. We hope that students and teachers will get maximum benefit from this third edition of the textbook and share our enjoyment of studying and teaching Physical Education and Sport.

This is a book that will not go out of date and will give students the background that is vital for examination success.

John Honeybourne is a freelance Educational Consultant, an OFSTED Additional Inspector and Associate Inspector for the Adult Learning Inspectorate specialising in sport and leisure. An Advanced Skills Teacher Assessor, freelance lecturer and Principal Examiner for a major awarding body, he also runs INSET courses for A Level and AS Level PE and Sport.

Mike Hill is Director of PE at the City of Stoke on Trent Sixth Form College. He has been reviser and Senior Examiner for a major awarding body and is currently Chief Examiner for another leading awarding body.

Helen Moors has taught A level Physical Education since the first pilot examination and until recently at the City of Stoke on Trent Sixth Form College. She has been Senior Examiner, Principal Examiner and question setter for two major awarding bodies. She is currently a freelance education consultant for A Level PE.

Acknowledgements

The authors wish to thank their families for their support and understanding during the writing of all editions of this textbook.

The authors and publishers are grateful to the following for permission reproduce copyright material:

Logos
- British Olympic Association p 163
- Central Council of Physical Recreation p 163
- Maxperformance p 251
- SportsAid p 163
- sports coach UK p 163.

Photo credits
- Action Plus Sports Images pp 262, 273
- Bodleian Library, University of Oxford, Frontispiece engraving of Le Jeu Royal de la Paume from the Annuals of Tennis by Juian Marshall, 1878, (ref. 268 d.41) p 337
- Corel 174 (NT) p 257
- Corel 205 (NT) p 290 (top)
- Corel 341 (NT) p 374
- Corel 337 (NT) p 232
- Corel 423 (NT) pp 83 (right), 290 (bottom)
- Corel 772 (NT) p 116
- Corel 778 (NT) pp 97, 197, 203
- Corel 797 (NT) p 396
- Digital Stock 3 (NT) p 83 (left)
- Digital Vision 11 (NT) pp 160, 249 (left)
- Digital Vision 12 (NT) pp 99, 152 (bottom), 190
- Digital Vision KS (NT) pp 96
- Digital Vision XA (NT) pp 85, 146 (left), 297
- Dundee Art Gallery p 336
- FitnessASSIST, www.fitnessassist.co.uk, Tel: 01978 660077 p 270
- Glyn Kirk/Action Plus Sports Images p 242
- Hulton Getty Picture Library pp 142, 144 (top), 157
- Hypoxico Inc. p 250
- International Fitness Association, www.ifafitness.com p 275 (bottom)
- Mary Evans Picture Library pp 143, 144, 341, 344, 353, 354, 355, 357
- Philippe Millereau/DPPI/Action Plus Sports Images p 263 (top)
- Photodisc 10 (NT) p 125 (right)
- Photodisc 40 (NT) p 20
- Photodisc 41 (NT) p 132
- Photodisc 45 (NT) p 286
- Photodisc 51 (NT) pp 96, 369
- Photodisc 61 (NT) p 125 (left)
- Photodisc 67 (NT) p 271.

All other photographs supplied by Getty Images UK Ltd.

Part 1

ANATOMY, BIOMECHANICS AND PHYSIOLOGY

This part of the book contains:

The following chapters provide an introduction to anatomy, physiology and, in particular, to the systems that play a significant role in the production of skilled human movement – the skeletal, muscular, cardiovascular and respiratory systems. It is important to know both the structure of these systems and how they function, including basic biomechanics, in order to develop a better understanding of how the body works and to appreciate the body's capabilities and limitations in performance of sport.

Introduction to the skeletal system

Learning objectives

- To have a general understanding of the structure of the skeletal system.
- To be aware of the main functions of the skeletal system.
- To know the structure and type of the major joints of the body.
- To know the types of movement that can be produced around each joint.

The skeletal system needs to be studied and understood by any person interested in human movement. The skeletal system provides the system of leverage required for human movement. Each joint is structured in a way that best suits its function, for example the structure of the knee joint allows movement in one plane only. This is because although free movement of the knee is desirable, stability is also needed. The skeletal system provides the basis of attachment for most muscles, enabling them to work together in order to produce efficient and coordinated movement. It helps to provide the strength and stability that is needed in order to stay balanced and upright, and provides protection for many vital organs.

1.1 The skeletal system

The skeletal system is made up of two kinds of tissue: *bone* and *cartilage*.

1.1.1 Bone

There are five different types of bone, which are classified by their shape rather than their size.
1 *Long bones*, such as the femur
2 *Short bones*, for example the metatarsals
3 *Irregular bones*, the vertebrae are examples of these
4 *Flat bones*, for example the scapula
5 *Sesamoid bones*, such as the patella.

Examples of each type of bone are shown in Figure 1.1.

Bone is the hardest connective tissue in the body, mainly because it contains deposits of calcium phosphate and calcium carbonate. Bone acts as a store for calcium, and as a result of regular exercise more calcium is deposited, increasing bone density. The bone matrix also contains *collagen*. Collagen gives bone tissue a flexible strength, allowing it to cope with a certain amount of impact. As you get older the bone contains less collagen and the bone is less dense, resulting in brittle bones that are damaged quite easily. *Hard*, or *compact*, bone makes up the outer layer of all bones, giving them strength. *Cancellous*, or *spongy*, bone is typically found at the ends of the long bones. Cancellous bone is not as dense as hard bone because it contains cavities filled with bone marrow.

1.1.2 Ossification

OSSIFICATION
Ossification is the process of bone formation.

The process of bone formation is known as *ossification*. The skeletal frame is initially made out of cartilage, which is gradually replaced by bone. An outline of the structure of a typical long bone can be seen in Figure 1.2. The ossification process begins in the *diaphysis* (the primary ossification centre) and then occurs in the *epiphyses* (the secondary sites of ossification). A plate of cartilage is left between the diaphysis and each epiphysis; this

Figure 1.1
Classification of bones

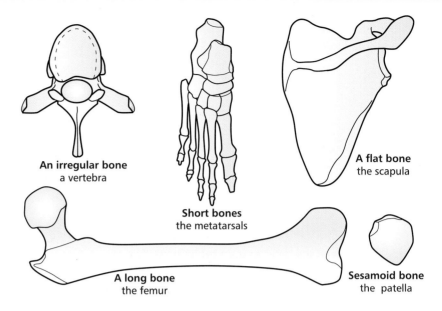

An irregular bone
a vertebra

Short bones
the metatarsals

A flat bone
the scapula

A long bone
the femur

Sesamoid bone
the patella

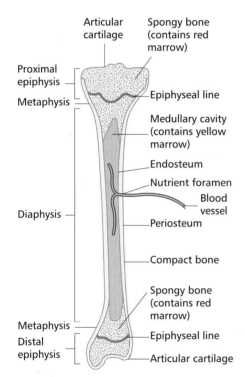

Figure 1.2 *Structure of a typical long bone*

Labels: Articular cartilage · Spongy bone (contains red marrow) · Proximal epiphysis · Metaphysis · Epiphyseal line · Medullary cavity (contains yellow marrow) · Endosteum · Nutrient foramen · Blood vessel · Diaphysis · Periosteum · Compact bone · Spongy bone (contains red marrow) · Metaphysis · Distal epiphysis · Epiphyseal line · Articular cartilage

is where bones grow in length until maturation takes place (endochondral ossification). The plate is known as the *epiphyseal plate* and when growth stops this plate fuses and becomes bone. A long bone also has to increase in diameter; this is achieved by depositing a new layer of bone on the surface. This process is known as *appositional growth*.

in training

As bones do not fully mature until ossification is complete, young athletes can run the risk of damaging the epiphysis and/or the epiphyseal plate. If the epiphyseal plate slips this can result in the hip giving way under the stress of movement and eventually can lead to one leg being shorter than the other. Activities such as swimming (swimmer's shoulder) and tennis (tennis elbow) can put strain on young bones and joints. For this reason plyometric training (see page 266) is not recommended for young athletes.

1.1.3 Cartilage

There are three types of cartilage:

1 *Elastic cartilage*, which is soft and slightly elastic. Examples may be found in the ear lobe and epiglottis.
2 *Fibrocartilage*, which is tough and slightly flexible. This cartilage acts as a shock absorber, helping to prevent damage to the bone. The cartilage between the vertebrae is white fibrocartilage.
3 *Hyaline* or *articular cartilage*, which is solid and smooth. Hyaline cartilage protects the bone from the constant wear and tear of moving and can be found on the articulating surface of bones.

DEFINITION

ARTICULATION

The place where two or more bones meet to form a joint. The articulating surface is the point of contact between the bones.

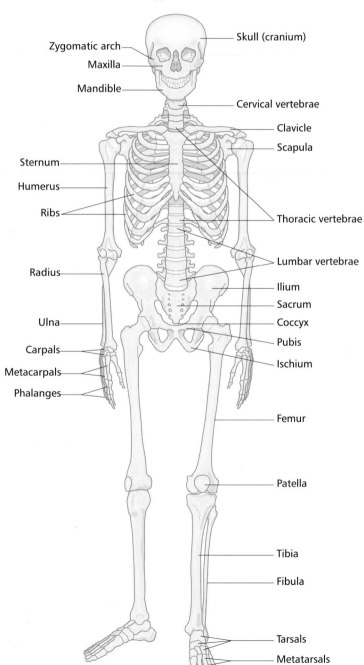

in training

Exercise has a positive effect on bone tissue. It varies the line of stress and stimulates an increase in the amount of calcium salts deposited in the bone, making it stronger.

1.2 The skeleton

The skeleton is made up of 206 bones (Figure 1.3). It comprises the axial skeleton and the appendicular skeleton.

activity

Examine the bones of a skeleton and see if you can classify the following bones: the parietal bone (part of the skull), the ilium (part of the pelvis), phalanges, the sternum, the ulna and the metatarsals.

Figure 1.3
The bones making up the human skeleton

Zygomatic arch
Maxilla
Mandible
Sternum
Humerus
Ribs
Radius
Ulna
Carpals
Metacarpals
Phalanges

Skull (cranium)
Cervical vertebrae
Clavicle
Scapula
Thoracic vertebrae
Lumbar vertebrae
Ilium
Sacrum
Coccyx
Pubis
Ischium
Femur
Patella
Tibia
Fibula
Tarsals
Metatarsals
Phalanges

1.2.1 *The axial skeleton*

This is made up of the skull, the vertebral column, the sternum and the ribs.

1.2.2 *The appendicular skeleton*

The appendicular skeleton is composed of the shoulder girdle, the hip girdle, the bones of the arms and hands and the bones of the legs and feet.

Although for your courses you do not need to know about the individual bones which make up the head and face or the hands and feet, a more detailed knowledge of the spine is useful. This is outlined in Figure 1.4.

in training

The size of an athlete's skeletal frame is largely genetically determined, but exercise and a well-balanced diet can help to ensure proper bone growth.

1.2.3 *Function of the skeletal system*

The skeletal system has four main functions:
* to provide support for the body;
* to provide protection for vital organs;
* to produce blood corpuscles (cells);
* to provide attachment for muscles.

For sport enthusiasts it is the last of these functions which is the most interesting. In order for us to perform the sophisticated movements demanded by many sports, we need a sophisticated system of joints and levers capable of producing a wide range of movements. As you will see, we have been very well designed to do this.

1.3 Joints

Joints can be classified in two ways: by considering their structure, or by considering how much movement they allow.

1.3.1 *Classification by structure*

The following classification of joint by structure should be used.

Fibrous

These joints have no joint cavity and the bones are held together by fibrous connective tissue. Examples are the sutures of the skull bones.

Cartilaginous

Cartilaginous joints also have no joint cavity. There is cartilage between the bones of the joint. Cartilaginous joints may be found between the vertebrae of the spine.

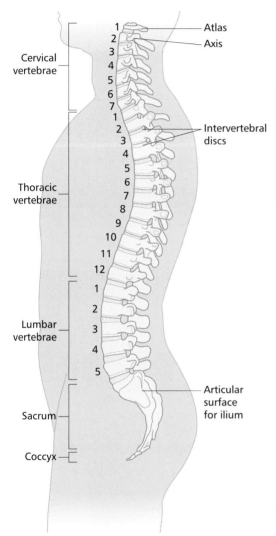

Figure 1.4 *Lateral view of the spinal column*

Synovial

A synovial joint has a fluid-filled cavity surrounded by an articular capsule. The articulating surfaces of the bones are covered in hyaline cartilage. The hinge joint of the knee is a synovial joint.

1.3.2 Classification by movement allowed

When it comes to classifying joints by the movement they allow, the following terms are applied.

Fibrous joint or synarthrosis

This type of joint does not allow any movement. When you consider where these joints occur this makes sense as some parts of the body, such as the brain, need protection. A moveable joint could not provide this protection.

Cartilaginous joint or amphiarthrosis

This joint allows limited movement.

Synovial joint or diarthrosis

A synovial joint allows free movement, or certainly as much movement as the shape of the articulating surfaces permits.

As you may have gathered by now, there always seem to be several types of everything you come across in anatomy and physiology. Joints are no exception. There are six different types of synovial joint – and as these are the joints that allow movement, we need to know more about them.

1.4 Synovial joints

The synovial joints allow movement to take place. How much movement is permitted depends on the shape of the articulating surfaces. Six different joint constructions have been identified. Figure 1.5 illustrates each joint type.

1 *Ball and socket*: a ball-like head fits into a cup-shaped depression – an example of this is the shoulder joint.
2 *Hinge*: a convex surface articulates with a concave surface. The elbow is a typical hinge joint.
3 *Pivot*: part of a bone fits into a ring-like structure. The most well-known pivot joint is the atlas and axis (cervical 1 and 2: see Figure 1.5).

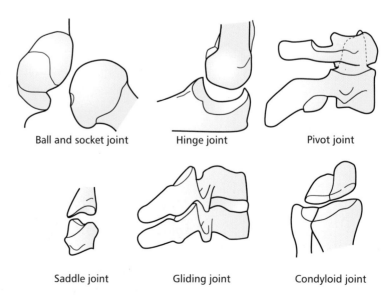

Ball and socket joint   Hinge joint   Pivot joint

Saddle joint   Gliding joint   Condyloid joint

Figure 1.5 *The six types of synovial joint*

4 *Saddle*: a bone fits into a saddle-shaped surface on another bone – the thumb is a good example.
5 *Gliding*: two relatively flat surfaces slide over one another – this may be seen at the articular processes of the vertebrae.
6 *Condyloid*: a convex surface fits into an elliptical cavity – the wrist joint is a condyloid joint.

The six types of synovial joint differ in the amount of movement they allow, but are very similar in structure and share common features. Figure 1.6 highlights the common features of a synovial joint, using the hinge joint of the knee as an illustration.

- The *articular/joint capsule* is a fibrous tissue encasing the joint, forming a capsule.
- The *synovial membrane* acts as a lining to the joint capsule and secretes synovial fluid.
- *Articular/hyaline cartilage* covers the ends of the articulating bones.
- *Synovial fluid* fills the joint capsule and nourishes and lubricates the articular cartilage.
- *Ligaments* are white fibrous connective tissues joining bone to bone, making the joint more stable.
- *Bursa* is found where tendons are in contact with bone. The bursa forms a fluid-filled sac between the tendon and the bone and helps to reduce friction.
- *Articular discs* of cartilage act as shock absorbers.
- *Pads of fat* act as buffers to protect the bones from wear and tear.

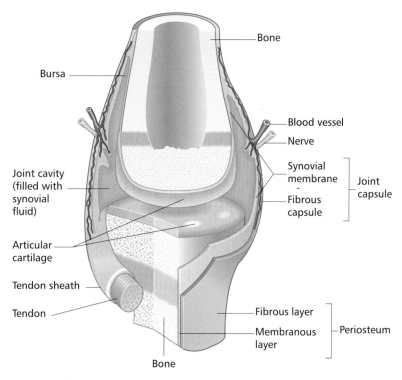

Figure 1.6 *Structure of a synovial joint*

activity

Try to construct a joint by taking the appropriate bones and fastening them together. For example, you could use tape to represent the ligaments and felt or moulding clay for the articular cartilage. If you don't have any bones, improvise!

in training

When organising young children into teams, it is important to match players by size as well as ability, to avoid potential damage to joints due to contact/impact injuries.

1.5 Movement terminology

1.5.1 Movement terms

Later in Part 1 we will look at the structure of some joints in more detail, but here we will consider the range of movement that the body can perform. There are a lot of terms that you need to be familiar with, and you will remember the terms much more easily if you put them into practice.

The terms that you are most likely to use are given below, and are illustrated in Figure 1.7.

* *Flexion*: a decrease in the angle around the joint.
* *Extension*: an increase in the angle around the joint.
* *Abduction*: movement away from the midline of the body.

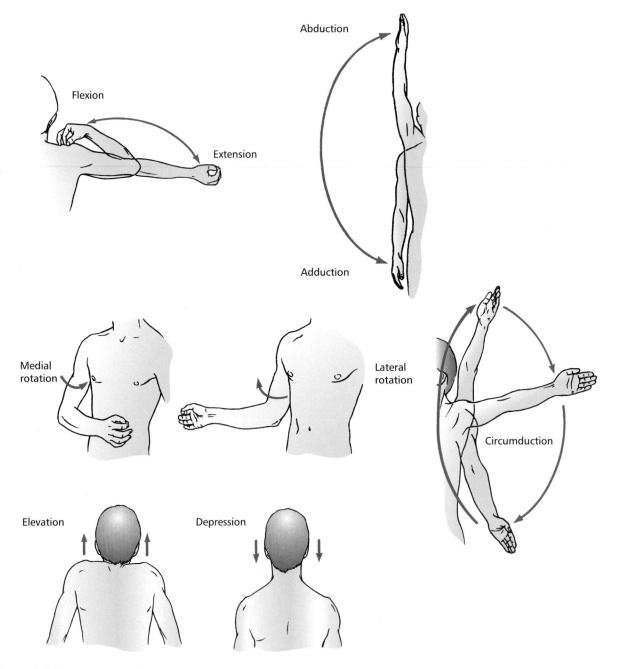

Figure 1.7 *Movement terminology*

- *Adduction*: movement towards the midline of the body.
- *Rotation*: movement of a bone around its longitudinal axis. Rotation can be inward (medial) or outward (lateral).
- *Circumduction*: the lower end of the bone moves in a circle. It is a combination of flexion, extension, adduction and abduction.
- *Lateral flexion*: bending the head or trunk sideways.
- *Elevation*: moving the shoulders upwards.
- *Depression*: moving the shoulders downwards.
- *Plantarflexion*: bending the foot downwards, away from the tibia.
- *Dorsiflexion*: bending the foot upwards, towards the tibia.
- *Pronation*: facing the palm of the hand downwards.
- *Supination*: facing the palm of the hand upwards.

More simply, *flexion* occurs when you bend a limb and *extension* occurs when you straighten it. For example, the movement at the elbow joint when you do press-ups involves both flexion and extension. When performing star jumps, as you move your arms outwards you are *abducting* the shoulder joint and as you bring your arms back to the side of your body you are *adducting* the shoulder joint. As a ballet dancer moves into first position he or she must *rotate* their hip joints laterally. When bowling, a cricketer moves the arm in a full circle – this is *circumduction* of the shoulder joint. Remember: movement occurs around a joint and not a body part, so it is incorrect to say (for example) 'flexion of the leg'. You must refer to the actual joint involved, as in flexion of the hip, knee or ankle joint. Be precise.

When you take part in your next practical session, break down the skills you attempt into simple phases and try to identify the specific movements. It is quite difficult to begin with, but with practice becomes very straightforward. If the joints have a similar structure, then their pattern of movement will be the same: for example, flexion of the hip is the same as flexion of the shoulder joint.

1.5.2 The planes of the body

There are three planes, which relate to the three dimensions of space through which the body or body part can move. Each plane must pass through the centre of gravity. The sagittal or median plane divides the body into left and right halves. The frontal or lateral plane divides the body into front and back, and the transverse or horizontal plane divides the body into upper and lower halves. For example, when you abduct your shoulder joint you are moving through the frontal or lateral plane.

activity

Look back to the list of synovial joints. Working with a partner, locate each of the joints given as examples and determine the types of movement that can take place at each. For example, the elbow joint can flex and extend.

activity

For each of the practical examples given to illustrate the three different axes (right), identify the plane that the body moves through.

In practice

When a body part moves, it moves in a plane and around an axis. The frontal horizontal axis passes horizontally from side to side, e.g. a forward roll. The sagittal horizontal axis passes horizontally from front to back, e.g. a cartwheel. The vertical axis passes vertically from head to toe, e.g. a 180 degree turn. The axis is always at right angles to the plane in which it occurs. In most movement analyses it is easier to work out the axis first and then determine the movement plane.

DEFINITION

HYPOKINETIC DISEASE
Any medical condition caused by a lack of physical activity, e.g. poor posture, high blood pressure.

KYPHOSIS
An abnormal hyperflexion of the thoracic spine (round shouldered).

LUMBAR LORDOSIS
An exaggerated hyperextension of the lumbar spine.

1.5.3 Posture

Posture is the relationship of body parts, whether standing, lying, sitting or moving. Good posture allows a person to function effectively, with very little strain on joints and connective tissue. The amount of muscular work required to remain upright is not great. This is because the ligaments play a vital role in maintaining joint integrity. If a person does not have good posture then the joints become damaged. Lack of physical fitness due to inactivity can contribute to poor posture because of muscular fatigue and weak muscles, and this can lead to more extreme hypokinetic disease.

Key revision points
There are six types of synovial joint: ball and socket, hinge, pivot, gliding, condyloid and saddle. All synovial joints allow some degree of movement and share common features, such as a synovial membrane, synovial fluid, articular cartilage and ligaments.

Key terms

You should now understand the following terms. If you do not, go back through the chapter and find out what they mean.

- Abduction
- Adduction
- Appendicular skeleton
- Articulation
- Axial skeleton
- Cartilaginous joint
- Circumduction
- Extension
- Fibrous joint
- Flexion
- Ossification
- Rotation
- Synovial joint

Progress check

1. List the bones that form the axial skeleton.
2. List the bones that form the appendicular skeleton.
3. What are the functions of the skeleton?
4. Where would you find hyaline cartilage?
5. How may joints be classified?
6. Which category of joint allows free movement?
7. Give an example of a gliding joint.
8. List the common features of a synovial joint.
9. Which features of a synovial joint help increase joint stability?
10. List the movements possible at a ball and socket joint and give a brief description of each movement.
11. What movements can take place at the ankle joint?
12. Name two joints which allow circumduction and give an example in sport of when this movement occurs.
13. The first two cervical vertebrae form a joint. What type of joint is it, and what type of movement does it allow?
14. The range of movement around a joint can be restricted by a number of factors. List three of these factors.
15. Why isn't it advisable for young athletes to do plyometric training?
16. Name a joint that is susceptible to injury when participating in contact sports. Give reasons for your answer.

CHAPTER 2

Joints and muscles

Learning objectives

- To know the bones that articulate at the major joints of the body.
- To be able to identify the muscles that act as prime movers at each major joint.
- To know the type of movement that the prime movers can produce.
- To be able to analyse sporting actions in terms of the joint and muscle used and the movement produced.

A joint cannot move by itself – it needs muscles to manoeuvre the bones into the correct position. Muscles are attached to bones by connective tissue and we refer to the ends of the muscle as the *origin* and the *insertion*. The origin is the more fixed, stable end and the insertion is usually attached to the bone that moves.

When a muscle contracts it shortens and the insertion moves closer to the origin, creating movement around a joint. For example, biceps brachii causes flexion of the elbow. The origin of this muscle is on the scapula and the insertion is on the radius. When the muscle contracts the radius is pulled upwards towards the shoulder, as the insertion moves closer to the origin.

The muscle directly responsible for creating the movement at a joint is called the *prime mover*. There is usually more than one prime mover at a joint, and other muscles can assist the movement. The number of muscles involved depends on the type and amount of work being carried out.

Any sports performer, at whatever level, should have a working knowledge of joint and muscle action. The human body is very complex and is made up of hundreds of muscles acting on numerous joints – see Figure 2.1. As an introduction we will look in more detail at the joints and muscles most involved in the production of gross motor skills.

In practice

A warm-up is useful only if you are warming up the muscles and joints that you are about to use. When preparing a training schedule the exercises you choose should reflect the movement pattern you will be performing in competition.

In practice

When throwing a ball underarm the radioulnar joint is supinated, and when throwing a ball overarm the radioulnar joint is pronated.

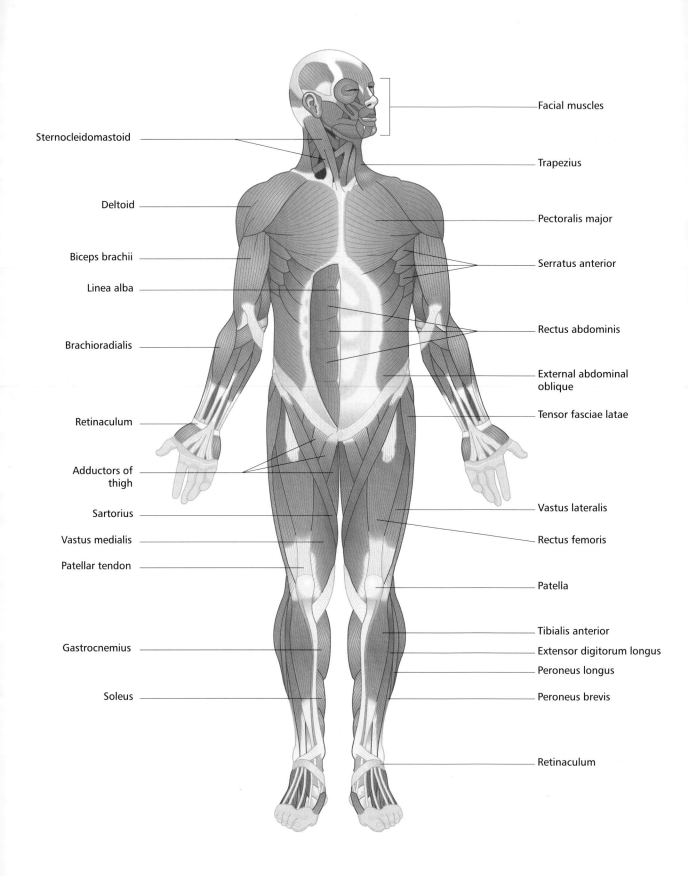

Facial muscles

Sternocleidomastoid

Trapezius

Deltoid

Pectoralis major

Biceps brachii

Serratus anterior

Linea alba

Rectus abdominis

Brachioradialis

External abdominal oblique

Tensor fasciae latae

Retinaculum

Adductors of thigh

Vastus lateralis

Sartorius

Rectus femoris

Vastus medialis

Patellar tendon

Patella

Tibialis anterior

Extensor digitorum longus

Peroneus longus

Gastrocnemius

Peroneus brevis

Soleus

Retinaculum

Figure 2.1a *The muscles of the human body. (a) Anterior view*

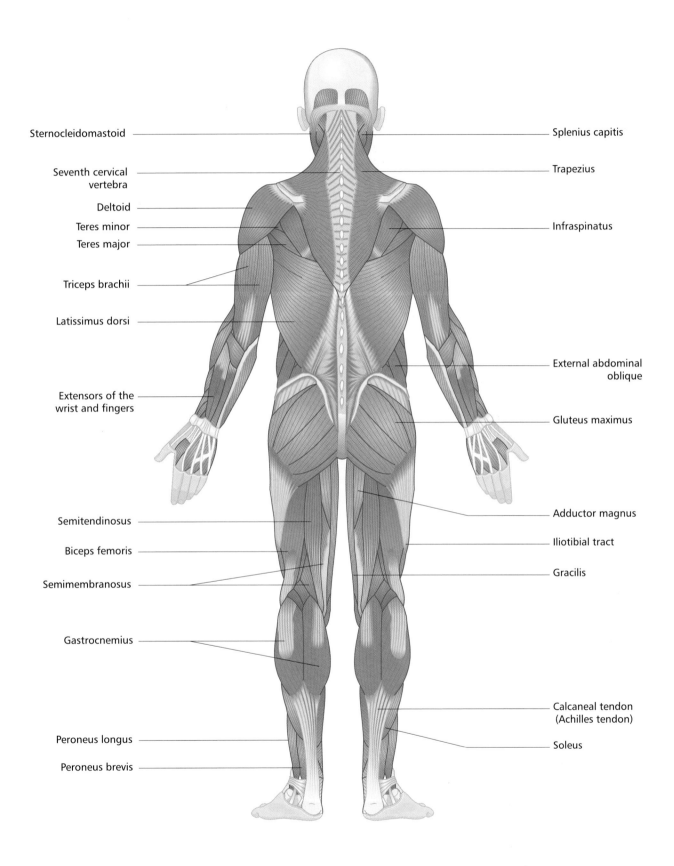

Sternocleidomastoid

Seventh cervical vertebra

Deltoid

Teres minor

Teres major

Triceps brachii

Latissimus dorsi

Extensors of the wrist and fingers

Semitendinosus

Biceps femoris

Semimembranosus

Gastrocnemius

Peroneus longus

Peroneus brevis

Splenius capitis

Trapezius

Infraspinatus

External abdominal oblique

Gluteus maximus

Adductor magnus

Iliotibial tract

Gracilis

Calcaneal tendon (Achilles tendon)

Soleus

Figure 2.1b *The muscles of the human body. (b) Posterior view*

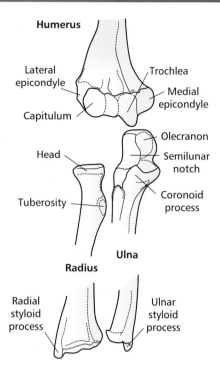

Figure 2.2 *Bony structures of the elbow and radioulnar joints. Surface markings such as bumps and grooves are visible, usually where a tendon inserts or where a joint articulates*

2.1 The elbow joint, the radioulnar joint and the wrist joint

The elbow is a hinge joint, with the *distal* end of the humerus articulating with the *proximal* end of both the radius and the ulna. On the proximal end of the ulna is the olecranon process and this fits into the olecranon fossa on the distal end of the humerus. This feature of the joint prevents the elbow joint from hyperextending. The joint is strengthened by four ligaments. Movement is possible in one plane only, allowing flexion and extension to take place.

Also within the elbow joint capsule the radius articulates with the ulna to form a pivot joint. This radioulnar joint allows pronation and supination of the lower arm (medial and lateral rotation).

Figure 2.2 shows the bones that articulate at the elbow joint.

The movements possible at the elbow and radioulnar joints are shown in Figure 2.3. The muscles that create these movements are outlined in Table 2.1 and illustrated in Figure 2.4. The specific origins and insertions are not given, but a general location of the muscle is provided to help with future movement analysis.

Table 2.1 *Muscles of the elbow joint*

Movement	Prime mover(s)	Origin	Insertion
Elbow (hinge)			
Flexion	Biceps brachii	Scapula	Radius
	Brachialis	Humerus	Ulna
Extension	Triceps brachii	Scapula and humerus	Ulna
	Anconeus	Humerus	Ulna
Radioulnar (pivot)			
Pronation	Pronator teres	Humerus and ulna	Radius
Supination	Supinator	Humerus and ulna	Radius

The wrist is a condyloid joint, where the distal end of the radius and ulna articulate with three of the carpal bones – the navicular, lunate and triquetrum bones. It is a common misconception that the wrist joint can rotate. This is not the case – the wrist joint can only flex, extend, abduct and adduct (and can therefore circumduct). At A level it is not necessary to analyse the movement of the wrist in any

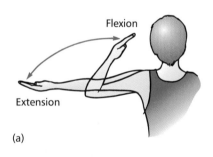

(a)

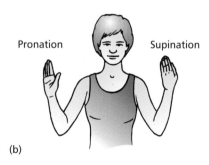

(b)

Figure 2.3 *Movements of the elbow and radioulnar joints. (a) Flexion and extension; (b) right radioulnar joint pronated, left radioulnar joint supinated*

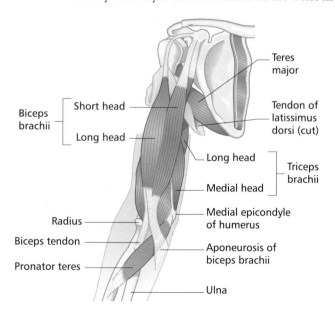

Figure 2.4 *Prime movers of the elbow and radioulnar joints*

DEFINITION

CONDYLE
A large knuckle-shaped articular surface, e.g. lateral condyle of the femur.

HEAD
A ball-shaped articular surface, e.g. the head of the femur.

SPINOUS PROCESS
A long slender projection, e.g. the processes of the vertebrae.

TUBEROSITY
A large rounded surface, for example on the proximal end of the radius.

FORAMEN
A hole, e.g. the vertebral foramen allows the spinal cord to pass through.

FOSSA
A depression, e.g. the olecranon fossa of the humerus.

DEFINITION

PROXIMAL
The proximal end of a bone is the end nearest the centre of the body.

DISTAL
The distal end of the bone is the end furthest away from the centre of the body.

Figure 2.5
The biceps curl

Figure 2.6
The triceps curl

activity

Try to think of a sporting example when each prime mover of the elbow would be in action. For example, during the shot-put elbow extension is caused by contraction of triceps brachii.

great detail, nor is any detailed knowledge of the muscles of the wrist expected. Usually it is sufficient to talk about the muscles collectively as either flexors or extensors of the wrist.

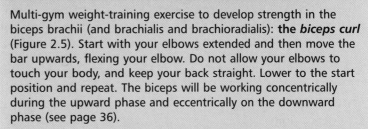

in training

Multi-gym weight-training exercise to develop strength in the biceps brachii (and brachialis and brachioradialis): **the *biceps curl*** (Figure 2.5). Start with your elbows extended and then move the bar upwards, flexing your elbow. Do not allow your elbows to touch your body, and keep your back straight. Lower to the start position and repeat. The biceps will be working concentrically during the upward phase and eccentrically on the downward phase (see page 36).

Multi-gym exercise to develop strength in the triceps: **the *triceps curl*** (Figure 2.6). Flex the elbow and keep your elbows in contact with the side of your body as you pull the bar down towards your thigh until the elbow is extended. Return to start position, keeping your back straight.

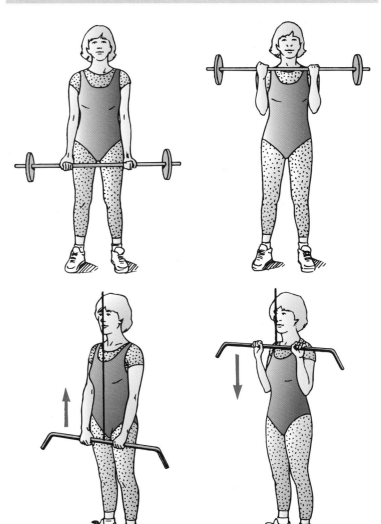

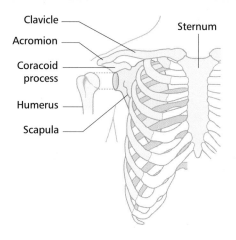

Figure 2.7 *Anterior view of the shoulder girdle*

2.2 The shoulder joint and the shoulder girdle

The structure of the shoulder joint and the shoulder girdle are shown in Figure 2.7.

2.2.1 *The shoulder girdle*

The shoulder girdle is a gliding joint (with slight rotation) where the clavicle articulates with the scapula, usually moving as a unit. We are not particularly aware of the involvement of the shoulder girdle in the numerous arm actions we perform (these are illustrated in Figure 2.8).

The prime movers of the shoulder girdle are outlined in Table 2.2 and illustrated in Figure 2.9.

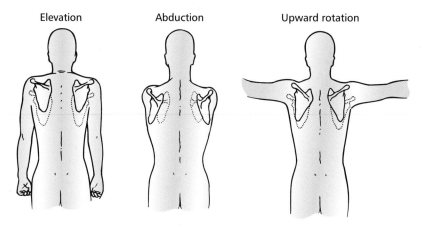

Figure 2.8 *Possible movements of the shoulder*

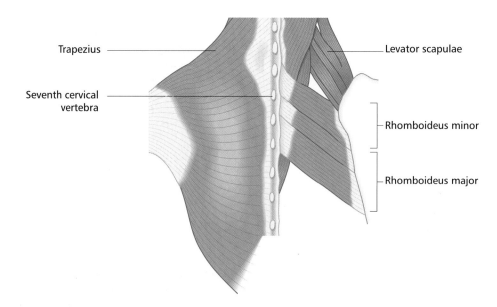

Figure 2.9 *Prime movers of the shoulder girdle*

activity

Work with a partner. Place your hand over your partner's scapula and note what happens when he or she lifts their arms above their head, to the side, etc. You should be able to see that the shoulder girdle can abduct, adduct, rotate upwards and downwards, elevate and depress.

Table 2.2 *Muscles of the shoulder girdle*

Movement	Prime mover(s)	Origin	Insertion
Elevation	Trapezius part one	Skull	Clavicle
Depression	Trapezius part four	Thoracic vertebrae	Base of spine
Upward rotation	Trapezius part two	Ligaments of the neck	Acromion process
Downward rotation	Rhomboids	Cervical and thoracic vertebrae	Scapula
Abduction	Serratus anterior	Side of ribs	Scapula
Adduction	Trapezius part three	Cervical and thoracic vertebrae	Scapula

2.2.2 *The shoulder joint*

The shoulder joint is a ball and socket joint, with the head of the humerus fitting into a very shallow cavity on the scapula called the glenoid fossa. The shoulder joint is the most mobile joint in the body but also one of the most unstable because the shallow cavity gives little support to the head of the humerus. Stability has to be provided by ligaments and muscles. The rotator cuff muscles, namely the subscapularis, supraspinatus, infraspinatus and teres minor are largely responsible for securing the head of the humerus into the glenoid fossa on the scapula.

The movements possible at the shoulder joint are shown in Figure 2.10. They include flexion, extension, horizontal flexion and extension, abduction, adduction, external and internal rotation and circumduction.

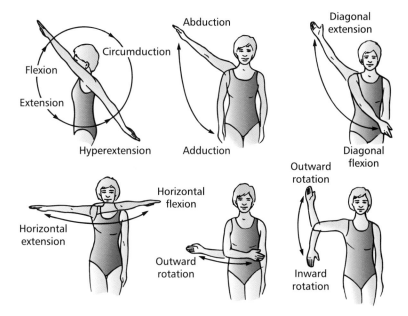

Figure 2.10 *Movements possible at the shoulder joint*

In practice

The rotator cuff muscles will need to be strengthened when athletes repeatedly produce vigorous overhead movements or when they are involved in contact sports such as rugby.

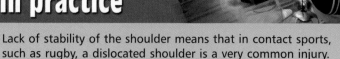

In practice

Lack of stability of the shoulder means that in contact sports, such as rugby, a dislocated shoulder is a very common injury.

For some skills, analysis of the shoulder movement is quite straightforward, for example lifting the arms above the head in preparation for a handstand clearly involves flexion of the shoulder joint and upward rotation of the shoulder girdle. Unfortunately, most of the actions we perform in sport, for example a tennis serve, are a combination of several movements and are therefore quite difficult to analyse. Students at A level are not expected to attempt complex movement analysis – but have a go at the next activity.

activity

Describe the movement pattern at the shoulder and elbow joints during each phase of the javelin throw.

Table 2.3 *Muscles of the shoulder joint*

Movement	Prime mover(s)	Origin	Insertion
Flexion	Anterior deltoid	Clavicle, scapula and acromion process	Humerus
Extension	Latissimus dorsi	Ilium, lumbar and thoracic vertebrae	Humerus
Abduction	Middle deltoid	Clavicle, scapula and acromion	Humerus
Adduction	Pectoralis major	Clavicle, ribs and sternum	Humerus
Inward rotation	Subscapularis	Scapula	Humerus
Outward rotation	Infraspinatus	Scapula	Humerus

Table 2.3 details the muscles and movements of the shoulder joint and the prime movers are illustrated in Figure 2.11.

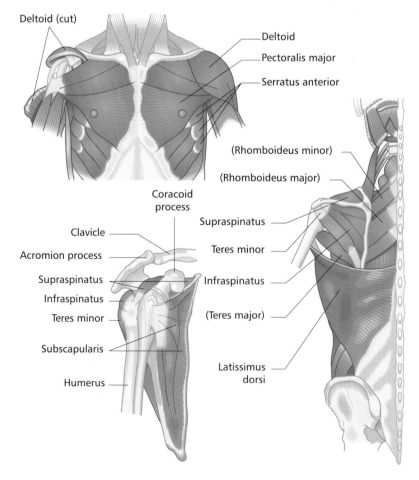

Figure 2.11
Prime movers of the shoulder joint

2.3 The spine

The spinal column has to fulfil many functions. It has to be weight bearing, provide stability and support, act as a shock absorber, protect the spinal cord and allow movement. Although there are five regions of the spine (look back to Figure 1.4 to refresh your memory) we will consider the cervical, thoracic and lumbar regions here, as the sacrum and coccyx are fused together.

The spinal column has three types of joint:
1 A *cartilaginous* joint between the individual vertebrae.
2 A *gliding* joint between the vertebral arches.
3 A *pivot* joint formed by the first two cervical vertebrae (the atlas and axis).

The atlas articulates with the occipital bone of the skull and allows flexion and extension, as in nodding. The atlas and axis articulate and allow rotation, as in shaking your head.

To make the column more stable several ligaments hold the vertebrae together.

in training

Multi-gym weight-training exercise to improve strength in the trapezius and rhomboids: **the *shoulder shrug*** (Figure 2.12). Keeping a straight back, lift your shoulders then roll them back and downwards and forward and up. Make sure that the movement is smooth and controlled.

Figure 2.12
The shoulder shrug

in training

The ***military press*** or ***overhead press*** is a free-weight exercise to improve strength in the deltoid, pectoralis major and triceps brachii (Figure 2.13). Use the overhand grip and with your elbows flexed hold the bar at chest level. Raise the bar above your head, making sure that your elbows are fully extended. Keeping the bar under control, lower the bar back to the starting position.

Figure 2.13
Overhead press

DEFINITION

HYPEREXTENSION

*Continuing to extend a limb beyond
180 degrees.*

FLEXION

*Most flexion occurs in the cervical region,
with some occurring in the lumbar region.
There is little flexion in the thoracic region.*

EXTENSION

*This is quite free in the cervical and
lumbar regions, but very limited in the
thoracic region.*

LATERAL FLEXION

*This takes place in all regions of the
spine but more so in the cervical and
lumbar regions.*

ROTATION

*This is good in the cervical and upper
thoracic regions, but minimal in the
lumbar region.*

2.3.1 *Movement at the spine*

The movements possible at the spine are shown in Figure 2.14. Overall the spine allows flexion, extension, lateral flexion and rotation. The combination of flexion, lateral flexion and hyperextension results in circumduction. Movement is not uniform throughout the three regions and before you read on try to decide which region moves more freely.

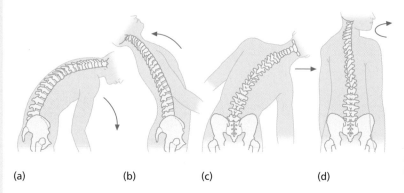

(a)   (b)   (c)   (d)

Figure 2.14 *Movements of the spinal column. (a) Flexion; (b) hyperextension; (c) lateral flexion to the right; (d) rotation to the right*

Table 2.4 outlines the prime movers of the spine. These are illustrated in Figure 2.15.

Although core stability is not included as an aspect of A level study, it is of interest to most athletes. Core stability is the ability of the athlete to maintain correct posture and alignment, particularly in the lumbar spine region, during the production of sporting movements. Correct posture and alignment should help the athlete maximise the effectiveness of his or her technique and reduce the likelihood of injury. The deep muscles of the trunk, e.g. the transverses abdominus and multifidus, support the lumbar spine by stabilising the trunk prior to dynamic activities. As these muscles act as stabilisers they are not required to produce much force, but to be effective they do need to work for long periods of time and therefore need good muscular endurance.

In practice

Core stability should be a key component in the training for all sports. Many top athletes do pilates or Swiss-ball type exercises which are specifically designed to improve core stability.

Table 2.4 *Muscles of the spine*

Movement	Prime mover(s)	Origin	Insertion
Flexion	Rectus abdominis	Pelvis	Base of sternum and ribs
	External oblique	Lower ribs	Pelvis
	Internal oblique	Pelvis	Lower ribs
Extension	Sacrospinalis	Pelvis, sacrum, lumbar and lower ribs	Ribs, base of skull and all vertebrae
Lateral flexion	External oblique	Lower ribs	Pelvis
	Internal oblique	Pelvis	Lower ribs
	Sacrospinalis	Pelvis, sacrum, lumbar and lower ribs	Ribs, base of skull and all vertebrae
Rotation to the same side	Internal oblique	Pelvis	Lower ribs
Rotation to the opposite side	External oblique	Lower ribs	Pelvis

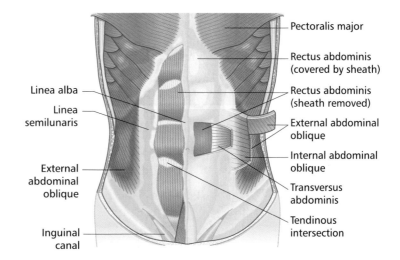

Figure 2.15
Prime movers of the spine

- Pectoralis major
- Rectus abdominis (covered by sheath)
- Rectus abdominis (sheath removed)
- External abdominal oblique
- Internal abdominal oblique
- Transversus abdominis
- Tendinous intersection
- Linea alba
- Linea semilunaris
- External abdominal oblique
- Inguinal canal

activity

In warm-up sessions the muscles of the spine are often neglected. Devise a series of exercises that would involve all possible movements of the spine, and therefore would involve all the prime movers of the spine.

Figure 2.16
The dead lift

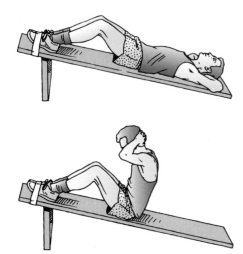

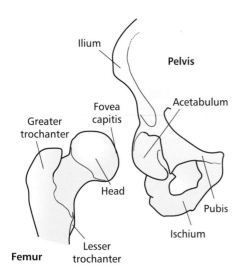

Figure 2.17 *Sit-ups*

2.4 The hip joint

The hip joint is another ball and socket joint, where the head of the femur fits into a deep cavity, called the acetabulum, on the pelvic bone (Figure 2.18). Although it is desirable to have a wide range of movement at this joint, it is perhaps more desirable to have stability. The cavity on the pelvis is much deeper than the cavity on the scapula, so the hip joint is much more stable (but less mobile) than the shoulder joint. The hip joint is also reinforced by extremely strong ligaments, making it much more difficult to dislocate the hip than the shoulder even though they are similar in structure.

Movements possible at the hip include flexion, extension, abduction, adduction, rotation and circumduction – see Figure 2.19.

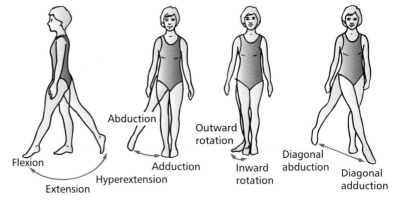

Figure 2.19 *Movements possible at the hip joint*

Figure 2.18 *The hip joint*

in training

Free-weight training exercise to improve the strength of the erector spinae (sacrospinalis): *the dead lift* (Figure 2.16). Start in an upright position, holding the bar in your hands. Bend over, making sure that you keep your elbows and knees extended, until the bar touches the floor. Then return to the start position.

Multi-gym exercise to improve the strength of the abdominal muscles: *sit-ups* (Figure 2.17). Select the angle of the board depending on your fitness level. Start lying on your back, with your knees flexed and hands by the side of your head. Sit up so that your elbows make contact with your knees and then lower your body back to the start position.

activity

Using a goniometer or a 360 degree angle measurer, work with a partner and measure the range of movement possible at both the shoulder and hip joints. Compare your results with those of other people in your group: is there a significant difference between males and females, or between gymnasts and footballers?

In practice

In most gyms people under 16 are not allowed to train using weight-training equipment. This is to prevent any injury to immature joints and muscles. Training using your own body weight is considered to be more than enough overload.

The prime movers of the hip joint are outlined in Table 2.5, and these are illustrated in Figure 2.20.

Table 2.5 *Muscles of the hip joint*

Movement	Prime mover(s)	Origin	Insertion
Flexion	Iliopsoas	Pelvis and lumbar vertebrae	Femur
Extension	Gluteus maximus	Pelvis and sacrum	Femur
Abduction	Gluteus maximus	Pelvis	Femur
Adduction	Adductors longus brevis and magnus	Pelvis	Femur
Inward rotation	Gluteus minimus	Pelvis	Femur
Outward rotation	Gluteus maximus	Pelvis and sacrum	Femur

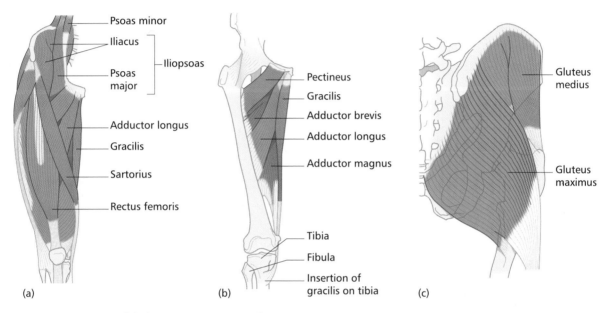

Psoas minor
Iliacus
Psoas major
Iliopsoas
Adductor longus
Gracilis
Sartorius
Rectus femoris
(a)

Pectineus
Gracilis
Adductor brevis
Adductor longus
Adductor magnus
Tibia
Fibula
Insertion of gracilis on tibia
(b)

Gluteus medius
Gluteus maximus
(c)

Figure 2.20 *Prime movers of the hip. (a) Anterior view; (b, c) posterior views*

Figure 2.21 *Hip flexors*

in training

Multi-gym exercise to strengthen the hip flexors: **hip flexors** (Figure 2.21). Support your weight on your forearms and keep your back in contact with the back rest. The start position is with your knees either extended or flexed, but as this exercise can put a lot of strain on the back it is better to have the knees flexed. Flex your hip by raising either one leg at a time or both legs simultaneously and then return to the start position.

activity

Analyse the movements of a hurdler and compare the actions at the hip of the lead leg with the actions at the hip of the trail leg.

2.5 The knee joint

The knee joint (shown in detail in Figure 1.6) is referred to as a hinge joint but it is not a true hinge joint because, although it allows both flexion and extension, it also allows slight medial and lateral rotation (to facilitate full extension and locking of the knee – see Figure 2.22).

The condyles of the femur articulate with the proximal end of the tibia. The patella, attached to the quadriceps tendon, helps to provide a better angle of pull, and is a functional part of the knee joint (Figure 2.23). The fibula is not part of the knee joint and therefore the tibia bears all the weight. The weight-bearing function of the knee is considerable and it is important that the ankle, knee and hip are aligned properly to allow the line of stress to pass through the centre of the knee joint.

The strong ligaments surrounding the knee and the large muscle groups of the thigh help to maintain the most mechanically efficient position.

The prime movers of the knee are outlined in Table 2.6, and illustrated in Figure 2.24.

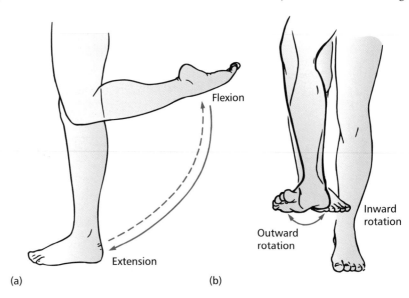

Figure 2.22
Movements possible at the knee joint. (a) Flexion and extension; (b) inward and outward rotation (in a flexed, no-weight-bearing position)

(a)   (b)

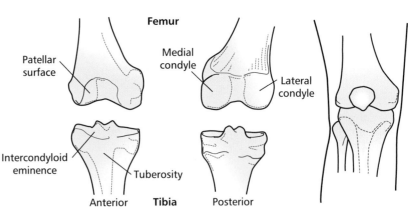

Figure 2.23
Bones of the knee joint

Table 2.6 *Muscles of the knee joint*

Movement	Prime mover(s)	Origin	Insertion
Flexion	Biceps femoris	Pelvis and femur	Tibia and fibula
	Semimembranosus	Pelvis	Tibia
	Semitendinosus	Pelvis	Tibia
Extension	Rectus femoris	Pelvis	Patella
	Vastus lateralis, intermedius and medialis	Femur Femur	Tibia Tibia
Inward rotation	Popliteus	Femur	Tibia
Outward rotation	Biceps femoris	Pelvis and femur	Tibia and fibula

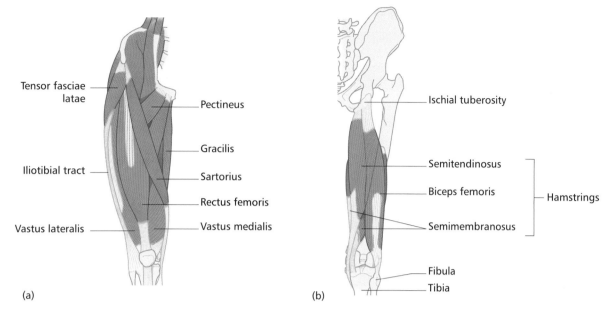

Tensor fasciae latae

Pectineus

Gracilis

Iliotibial tract

Sartorius

Rectus femoris

Vastus lateralis

Vastus medialis

(a)

Ischial tuberosity

Semitendinosus

Biceps femoris — Hamstrings

Semimembranosus

Fibula

Tibia

(b)

Figure 2.24 *Prime movers of the knee. (a) Anterior view; (b) posterior view*

Figure 2.25 *Knee extension*

in training

Multi-gym weight-training exercise to improve strength in the quadriceps: ***knee extension*** (Figure 2.25). Sit on the end of the bench with your knees flexed and your feet placed under the bar. Move your lower leg upwards until the knee is extended, and then lower back to the start position.

The ***hip sled*** (leg and hip press) also works the hip and knee extensors.

Multi-gym weight-training exercise to improve strength in the hamstrings: ***hamstring curl*** (Figure 2.26) Lie on your stomach on the bench with your knees extended and with the back of your ankles under the bar. Lift the lower leg upwards until your knees are fully flexed, and then lower back to the start position.

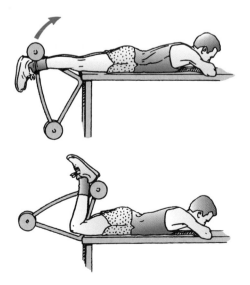

Figure 2.26 *Hamstring curl*

activity

Analyse the three hurdling positions shown in Figure 2.27. Describe the movements taking place at the hip and knee joints and name the prime mover responsible for each movement.

1   2   3

Figure 2.27 *Hurdling*

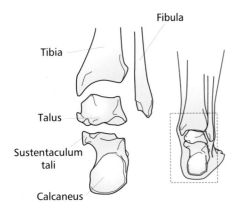

Figure 2.28 *Bones of the ankle and sutalar joints*

2.6 The ankle joint

The ankle joint (shown in Figure 2.28) is a hinge joint, the talus articulating with the tibia and fibula. This allows both flexion and extension – at the ankle this is referred to as *dorsiflexion* and *plantarflexion* (Figure 2.29). As in all synovial joints, ligaments provide additional stability. On the medial (inner) side of the ankle there are five ligaments and on the lateral (outer) side of the ankle there are three ligaments.

Figure 2.30 illustrates the prime movers of the ankle outlined in Table 2.7.

activity

Identify the major prime movers used in either your game or individual activity, and design a weight-training circuit that would improve the strength of each prime mover.

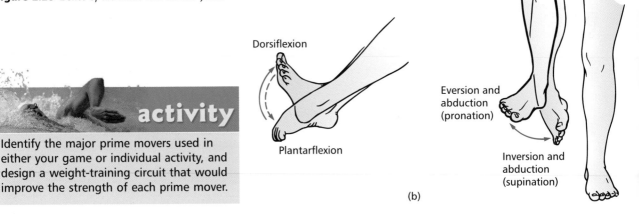

Figure 2.29 *Movements possible at the ankle and tarsal joints. (a) Dorsiflexion and plantarflexion; (b) supination and pronation (tarsal joint only)*

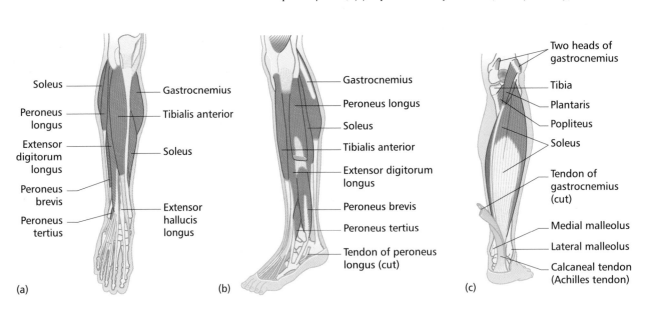

Figure 2.30 *Prime movers of the ankle and foot*

Table 2.7 *Muscles of the ankle joint*

Movement	Prime mover(s)	Origin	Insertion
Dorsiflexion	Tibialis anterior	Tibia	Tarsal bone
Plantarflexion	Soleus	Tibia and fibula	Tarsal bone
	Gastrocnemius	Femur	Tarsal bone

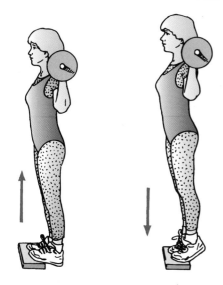

Figure 2.31 *Heel raise*

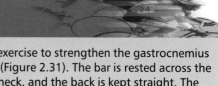

in training

Multi-gym or free-weight exercise to strengthen the gastrocnemius and the soleus: *heel raise* (Figure 2.31). The bar is rested across the shoulders and behind the neck, and the back is kept straight. The balls of your feet should be on a raised ledge – the heels should not be *on* the ledge. Move up onto your toes and then lower your heels to the floor. Return to the start position.

This section of the book is meant only as an introduction to kinesiology. It therefore takes a very simplified view of the joints, and in particular the muscles, used in sporting activities, as a basis for further study. A reading list is suggested at the end of this part of the book.

Key revision points

Movement takes place around a joint and at least one prime mover is responsible for each type of movement that can be produced at a specific joint. You need to know the name and location of the prime mover for each movement possible around the major joints outlined in this chapter.

Key terms

You should now understand the following terms. If you do not, go back through the chapter and find out what they mean.

Condyle
Distal
Foramen
Fossa
Hyperextension
Hypertrophy
Insertion
Origin
Prime mover
Process
Proximal
Tuberosity

Progress check

1 The first two cervical vertebrae form a joint. What type of joint is it and what type of movement does it allow?
2 What regions of the spine allow rotation?
3 Apart from rotation, what movements are possible at the spine?
4 List three functions of the spine.
5 If you broke your fibula would you still be able to walk? Justify your answer.
6 Where would you find the glenoid fossa?
7 Which bones articulate at the following joints:
  a the shoulder
  b the elbow
  c the hip.
8 Name three hinge joints.
9 Does the proximal or distal end of the tibia articulate with the femur?
10 Which of the following statements are true, and which false?
  a Biceps femoris flexes the elbow.
  b Iliopsoas flexes the hip.
  c Latissimus dorsi originates on the radius.
  d Rectus femoris extends the knee.
  e The posterior deltoid abducts the shoulder.
  f Pectoralis major adducts the shoulder.
  g Tibialis anterior dorsiflexes the ankle.
11 Identify a weight-training exercise that would develop strength in the following muscles:
  a biceps brachii
  b quadriceps
  c pectoralis major.

CHAPTER 3

Skeletal muscle: structure, function and control

Learning objectives

- To know the structure of skeletal muscle.
- To know the characteristics of the three muscle fibre types.
- To understand the role of the nervous system in muscular control.
- To be aware of the different functions of muscle.
- To know the different types of muscular contraction.

Muscles produce the force required for movement within the body. The nervous system coordinates the muscular contractions of the muscles to allow us to carry out everyday tasks and bodily functions. Movement can be caused by the contraction of *skeletal muscle*, resulting in the movement of the body or body part. It can be caused by the contraction of *smooth muscle*, resulting in such things as food being moved through the digestive system, or it can be the contraction of *cardiac muscle*, resulting in the movement of blood through the cardiovascular system. This chapter will concentrate mainly on the structure and function of skeletal muscle because of its relevance to the production of movement of the body.

3.1 Muscle tissue

DEFINITION

TENDON
A round cord or band of connective tissue joining muscle to bone.

APONEUROSIS
A fibrous sheet of connective tissue joining muscle to bone or muscle to muscle.

Muscle tissue has four main characteristics: excitability, contractility, extensibility and elasticity. This means that muscles react to a stimulus, contract and apply force, stretch and return to their original length.

There are three types of muscle tissue found in the body:
1. *Cardiac muscle* is a very specialised tissue located in the wall of the heart.
2. *Smooth/visceral muscle* is found in tubular structures such as blood vessels.
3. *Skeletal muscle* is usually attached to bone, or in some cases to other muscles. Skeletal muscle creates movement around a joint, but can also act to hold a body part in a stable position. Unlike cardiac or smooth muscle, skeletal muscle is under voluntary/conscious control – we know what we are going to do and when we are going to do it.

3.2 Structure of skeletal muscle

Skeletal muscle is made up of individual *muscle fibres* (muscle cells) grouped together to form bundles (*fasciculi*), which in turn are grouped together to form the muscle itself (Figure 3.1). Each element of the muscle is covered by connective tissue to help provide shape and add strength. The muscle fibre is covered by the *endomysium*, the fasciculi by the *perimysium* and the muscle by the *epimysium*. More connective tissue, in the form of a tendon or an aponeurosis, joins the muscle to bone or another muscle.

3.2.1 Skeletal muscle fibres

In order to understand how a muscle can shorten we need to take a more detailed look at the structure of each individual muscle fibre. There are lots of terms to remember here, so keep going over the text and referring back to the diagrams – don't expect to understand it first time through.

DEFINITION

Anatomy and physiology can be very confusing because of the vast amount of terminology that has to be learnt. It is useful to know that there are common prefixes and suffixes that can help our understanding of this subject.

For example: epi means upon or on; peri means around; endo means within; myo means muscle.

in training

DOMS (the delayed onset of muscle soreness) is often experienced by athletes one or two days after training or competing. This soreness is usually associated with the discomfort experienced after eccentric strength training. Contrary to popular belief, the pain is not caused by a build up of lactic acid, but is associated with actual structural damage to the muscle. Excessive tension on the muscle causes structural damage to the muscle fibre (Z lines pulled apart) and damage to the sarcolemma, affecting the balance of the cell contents. DOMS can be reduced by avoiding eccentric work early in the training programme and by starting at a low intensity and gradually increasing the stress placed on the muscle.

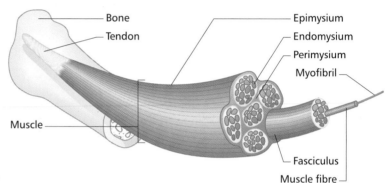

Figure 3.1
The basic structure of a muscle

The muscle fibre is surrounded by a membrane called the *sarcolemma* and within the cell are *myofibrils*, long tubular structures running the length of the muscle fibre. Other organelles of the cell such as the mitochondria are found between the myofibrils. The myofibrils are embedded in the cell's *sarcoplasm* (muscle tissue's equivalent to cytoplasm). Surrounding the myofibrils within the sarcoplasm is the *sarcoplasmic reticulum*, a series of channels that

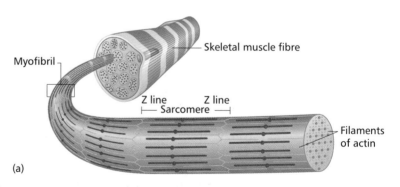

(a)

Figure 3.2
(a) The microstructure of a muscle. Note the striations in the fibre and the myofibril. These are alternating light and dark bands caused by the geometric arrangement of the filaments of actin and myosin
(b) Detail of actin and myosin filaments

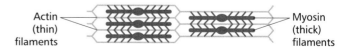

(b)

store and secrete calcium (this is essential for muscle contraction). Also in the sarcoplasm are *transverse tubules/T vesicles* that transmit the nerve stimulus from the sarcolemma into the cell, causing the sarcoplasmic reticulum to release calcium. Figure 3.2 shows the structure of a skeletal muscle fibre.

3.2.2 Myofibrils

Figure 3.3 shows the structure of a myofibril. The myofibrils are an arrangement of separate units connected end on to form long strands. These units are called *sarcomeres* and are the contractile units of the muscle. Within the sarcomeres are two protein filaments called *myosin* and *actin*, the myosin filament being the thicker of the two filaments. The myosin and actin filaments run adjacent to each other but at rest are not attached. The sarcomere is the area between the two *Z lines*, the *I band* contains only the thin filaments of actin, the *H zone* contains only myosin filaments and the *A band* contains both actin and myosin filaments.

When a muscle contracts the actin and myosin filaments slide over each other, rather like a pair of patio doors. As the actin filaments are attached to the Z lines the result is to pull the two Z lines closer together, shortening the sarcomere. This process will be discussed in more detail in Section 3.4.

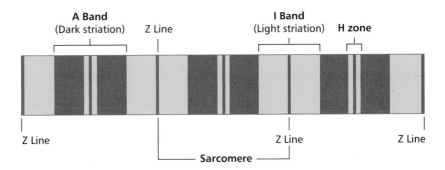

Figure 3.3 *Sarcomeres and myofibril bands*

3.3 Neuromuscular control

All skeletal muscle reacts to an electrical stimulus, which is conducted from the brain to the muscle via nerves. The brain and spinal cord are referred to as the *central nervous system* and nerves that carry information from the central nervous system to skeletal muscle are called *motor* or *efferent* nerves. Motor nerves form part of the *somatic nervous system*, which in turn forms part of the *peripheral nervous system*. Figure 3.4 gives an overall view of the nervous system.

Motor neurones (nerves) are made up of three parts: the *cell body*, the *dendrites* and the *axon*. The structure of a motor neurone is shown in Figure 3.5. Stimuli are received from the central nervous system by the dendrites and passed on via the axon. At the end of the axon is the *axon terminal*, which connects with the motor end plate of the muscle to form the *neuromuscular junction*.

As there are so many muscle fibres it would take a lot of internal 'wiring' to connect them all to a separate motor neurone, so instead one motor neurone branches off and stimulates between 15 and 2000 muscle fibres – this is called a *motor unit*. The number of muscle fibres in a motor unit depends on the type of work the muscle performs and the degree of muscular control required. Once the motor unit is stimulated then all the fibres in it will contract. This is known as the 'all or none' law.

activity

Name a muscle that you think might have motor units containing a lot of muscle fibres and one muscle that may only have a few muscle fibres per unit. Give reasons for your answer.

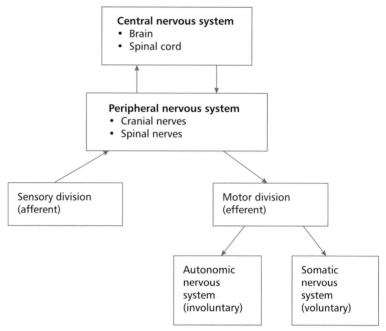

Figure 3.4 *The nervous system*

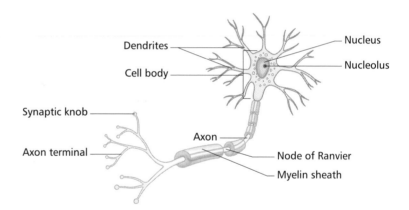

Figure 3.5 *A motor neurone and its structure*

3.3.1 *The nerve impulse*

Information is relayed from the brain to the muscle via a nerve impulse. A nerve impulse is an electrical current running the length of the nerve, starting at the brain and passing down the spinal column to the relevant cell body. The cell bodies of individual motor neurones are located in various regions of the anterior horn of the spinal column. These collections of cell bodies are referred to as *motor neurone pools*. The cell bodies are positioned in relation to the muscle they stimulate, for example the circumflex nerve, which stimulates the deltoid, is found in the fifth cervical vertebra, whereas the sciatic nerve (stimulates biceps femoris) is found in the fifth lumbar vertebra.

The nerve impulse is passed along the axon of the motor neurone. If you refer back to Figure 3.5 you will notice that the axon is covered in a myelin sheath. This sheath is mostly made up of fat and acts to insulate the nerve; however, it is not continuous. Where there is a gap in the myelin sheath there is a node of Ranvier.

The impulse is passed from one node of Ranvier to the next, rather than along the whole length of the axon. This means that the impulse can travel more quickly. This method of nerve impulse propagation is called *saltatory conduction* and the thicker the myelin sheath the faster the nerve impulse can be conducted.

When the impulse reaches the axon terminal the nerve transmits the information to the muscle by releasing a chemical transmitter, called *acetylcholine*, at the neuromuscular junction.

3.4 The sliding filament theory

The muscle responds to a nerve impulse by shortening. The sliding filament theory was put forward to explain how a muscle alters its length.

When a muscle contracts three things can be observed.

1 The I band shortens (the I band is the area in the sarcomere that contains only actin filaments).
2 The A band remains the same length (the A band is the area in the sarcomere that is equal to the length of the myosin filaments).
3 The H zone disappears (the H zone is the area in the sarcomere that contains only myosin filaments).

These three events can be explained by the myosin pulling the actin across so that the two filaments slide closer together, rather than either of the two filaments physically getting shorter.

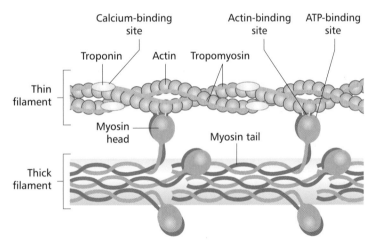

Figure 3.6 *The relationship between troponin, tropomyosis, myosin cross-bridges and calcium*

3.4.1 Cross-bridges

The myosin filaments have small projections called myosin heads, which extend towards the actin but are not actually attached to it. A protein called tropomyosin, bound to the active sites of the actin filament, prevents the myosin heads forming cross-bridges with the actin filament. Another protein bound to actin, troponin, can neutralise the effect of tropomyosin, but only in the presence of calcium (Figure 3.6). When the nerve impulse is transmitted down the transverse tubules it stimulates the release of calcium from the sarcoplasmic reticulum. The troponin is then able to move the tropomyosin from the active site so that cross-bridges form between the myosin and the actin filament to produce acto-myosin. Coupling of actomyosin stimulates the breakdown of ATP, releasing energy. The cross-bridges swivel towards the middle of the sarcomere, pulling the actin over the myosin and making the muscle shorter. More specifically, the myosin head couples with the active site on the actin. The myosin head swivels and collapses and then re-forms on another active site further along the actin, rather like the rowing action in a boat, pulling the actin

along the myosin towards the middle of the sarcomere. When the stimulus from the nerve stops, the calcium ions diffuse back into the sarcoplasmic reticulum and the muscle returns to its normal resting state.

Figure 3.7 summarises the sliding filament theory of muscle contraction.

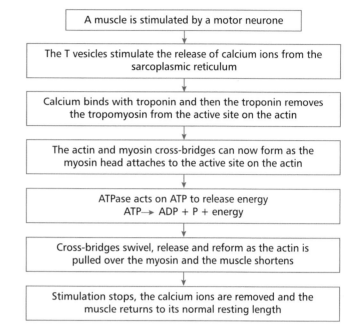

```
┌─────────────────────────────────────────────────┐
│     A muscle is stimulated by a motor neurone     │
└─────────────────────────────────────────────────┘
                         ↓
┌─────────────────────────────────────────────────┐
│  The T vesicles stimulate the release of calcium  │
│   ions from the sarcoplasmic reticulum            │
└─────────────────────────────────────────────────┘
                         ↓
┌─────────────────────────────────────────────────┐
│  Calcium binds with troponin and then the troponin │
│  removes the tropomyosin from the active site on   │
│  the actin                                         │
└─────────────────────────────────────────────────┘
                         ↓
┌─────────────────────────────────────────────────┐
│  The actin and myosin cross-bridges can now form   │
│  as the myosin head attaches to the active site    │
│  on the actin                                      │
└─────────────────────────────────────────────────┘
                         ↓
┌─────────────────────────────────────────────────┐
│        ATPase acts on ATP to release energy        │
│        ATP → ADP + P + energy                      │
└─────────────────────────────────────────────────┘
                         ↓
┌─────────────────────────────────────────────────┐
│  Cross-bridges swivel, release and reform as the   │
│  actin is pulled over the myosin and the muscle    │
│  shortens                                          │
└─────────────────────────────────────────────────┘
                         ↓
┌─────────────────────────────────────────────────┐
│  Stimulation stops, the calcium ions are removed   │
│  and the muscle returns to its normal resting      │
│  length                                            │
└─────────────────────────────────────────────────┘
```

Figure 3.7 *Summary of the sliding filament theory*

DEFINITION

ATP

This stands for adenosine triphosphate. ATP is a form of chemical energy found in all cells. When ATP is broken down to adenosine diphosphate (ADP) and phosphate then energy is released. The enzyme that controls the rate of this reaction is known as ATPase. Remember for future reference that the suffix 'ase' refers to an enzyme.

activity

Try to produce a flow chart showing the chain of events from the start of the nerve impulse in the brain to the point where the muscle releases calcium.

3.5 Types of muscle fibre

Why are some people able to run so much faster than others, while some people may run slower but can keep going for hours? One reason for this is that there are three different types of muscle fibre and any one individual will have a different mix of these fibre types. As the fibres have distinct characteristics this will affect performance in certain sporting activities. The mix of fibres in your physiological make-up is genetically determined.

The three fibre types are referred to as *type I slow oxidative* (SO), *type IIa fast oxidative glycolytic* (FOG) and *type IIb fast glycolytic* (FG). Each muscle contains all three types but not in equal proportions. The fibres are grouped in motor units – you will find only one fibre type in any given motor unit. Usually the proportion of each fibre type found in the muscles of the legs is very similar to the mix of fibre type found in the muscles of the arms.

3.5.1 *Type I slow oxidative fibres*

These fibres are known as *slow twitch fibres* because they contract more slowly than the type II (*fast twitch*) fibres. The myelin sheath of the motor neurone stimulating the muscle fibre is not as thick as that of the fast twitch unit, and this reduces the amount of insulation, slowing down the nerve impulse. Slow twitch fibres do not produce as much force as fast twitch fibres but can easily cope with prolonged bouts of exercise. They are more suited to aerobic work as they contain more mitochondria and myoglobin and have more blood capillaries than fast twitch fibres. Slow twitch fibres have the enzymes necessary for aerobic respiration and are able to break down fat and carbohydrate to carbon dioxide and water. This is a slower process than releasing energy anaerobically but it does not produce any fatiguing by-products.

3.5.2 *Type IIa fast oxidative glycolytic fibres*

The motor neurone stimulating the type IIa fibre has a thicker myelin sheath than the slow twitch fibre, so it can contract more quickly and exert more force. The amount of force produced by the type IIa fibre is greater than the type I fibre because there are more muscle fibres in each motor unit. This fibre type can produce energy both aerobically and anaerobically by breaking down carbohydrate to pyruvic acid, but it is much more suited to anaerobic respiration, which means it can release energy very quickly. The rapid build-up of lactic acid (a by-product of anaerobic respiration) lowers the pH and has a negative affect on enzyme action, causing the muscle fibre to fatigue quickly.

3.5.3 *Type IIb fast glycolytic fibres*

These muscle fibres are also very quick to contract and can exert a large amount of force. They rely heavily on anaerobic respiration for releasing energy as they have very few mitochondria. This means that energy is released rapidly, but also that the muscle fibre is quick to fatigue. The motor neurones supplying this fibre type are large and this increases the contractile speed. The neurone also activates a greater number of muscle fibres meaning that each motor unit can produce much more force than slow oxidative motor units.

Table 3.1 summarises the characteristics of the different fibre types.

in training

It has been generally assumed that the percentage distribution of fibre type is genetically determined and that training would only enhance the capacity of the existing fibre types. More recent research has suggested that fibre type conversion is possible and that with specific training a fibre may adopt the characteristics of another. Type IIa seems to be the most versatile, adopting either more aerobic or more anaerobic characteristics depending on the type of training undertaken. At the moment the research is far from conclusive but watch this space!

activity

Study Table 3.1 and decide which fibre type you think would be predominantly recruited for the following activities: a 5000 m run, a diving save from a goalkeeper, a 400 m hurdle race, and a fast break in basketball.

Table 3.1 *Characteristics of muscle fibres*

Characteristics of muscle fibres	Slow oxidative fibres (type I)	Fast oxidative glycolytic fibres (type IIa)	Fast glycolytic fibres (type IIb)
Structural			
Fibres per motor neurone	10–180	300–800	300–800
Motor neurone size	Small	Large	Large
Type of myosin ATPase	Slow	Fast	Fast
Sarcoplasmic reticulum development	Low	High	High
Functional			
Aerobic capacity	High	Moderate	Low
Anaerobic capacity	Low	High	Very high
Contractile speed	Slow	Fast	Fast
Fatigue resistance	High	Moderate	Low
Motor unit strength	Low	High	High

DEFINITION

AEROBIC RESPIRATION

The complete breakdown of fats and carbohydrate to carbon dioxide and water. This process requires oxygen and releases large amounts of ATP.

ANAEROBIC RESPIRATION

Anaerobic respiration is the partial breakdown of carbohydrate to pyruvic acid. This process does not require oxygen but only releases small amounts of ATP.

MITOCHONDRIA

Organelles in the cell. Aerobic respiration takes place in the mitochondria.

Table 3.2 shows how elite athletes are genetically well suited to their chosen sporting activity. The proportion of fibre type found in their muscles means that they have the potential to match the physical demands of their activity.

in training

Muscular strength usually refers to the maximum force that a muscle can generate in one contraction, referred to as one repetition maximum. Elastic (explosive) strength or power is a combination of strength and speed, and strength endurance is the ability of a muscle to sustain repeated muscular contractions. Every activity demands a different mix of strength components and each athlete should tailor their training to the specific demands of their activity. Athletes will find it difficult to enhance their speed of movement but they can improve their strength. Appropriate training will lead to muscular adaptations that can lead to as much as 100% improvement in strength.

Table 3.2

Athlete	Gender	Muscle	Percentage of slow twitch muscle	Percentage of fast twitch muscle
Sprint runner	Male	Gastrocnemius	24	76
	Female	Gastrocnemius	27	73
Distance runner	Male	Gastrocnemius	79	21
	Female	Gastrocnemius	69	31
Swimmer	Male	Posterior deltoid	67	33
Shot-putter	Male	Gastrocnemius	38	62
Non-athlete	Male	Vastus lateralis	47	53

in training

One widely known strength-training effect is muscle hypertrophy. This hypertrophy is attributed to an increase in size of the myofibrils, with more actin and myosin filaments. More filaments means that more cross-bridges can be formed and therefore more strength can be achieved. Recent research offers another explanation for strength gains as a result of training: *fibre hyperplasia*. Fibre hyperplasia is a term used to describe fibre splitting. It suggests that, instead of every muscle fibre increasing in size, the fibres actually separate first and then increase in size. The research in humans so far is inconclusive, but research involving cats has been verified.

DEFINITION

HYPERPLASIA

An increase in the number of cells in a tissue.

3.6 Muscle function

Muscles can only *actively* contract, so when, for example, biceps brachii is stimulated, it contracts and causes the elbow to flex. In order to straighten the arm we need another muscle to contract to

activity

Identify the muscles that cause flexion and extension of the knee joint and decide which muscles act as the prime mover and which muscles act as the antagonist during both movements.

complete the opposite action. When triceps brachii is stimulated it causes extension of the elbow joint. These two muscles are said to be working as an *antagonistic pair*. The muscle initiating the movement (shortening) is the *prime mover* or *agonist* and the muscle that is relaxing and returning to its original length is the *antagonist*. When you flex your elbow biceps brachii is the prime mover and triceps brachii is the antagonist. When you extend your elbow triceps brachii is acting as the prime mover and biceps brachii as the antagonist. The muscles work as a unit, which requires a high degree of coordination. This coordination is achieved by nervous control. When the prime mover is being stimulated the nerve impulse to the antagonist is inhibited – this is known as *reciprocal innervation*.

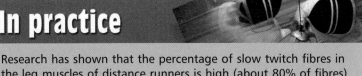

In practice

Research has shown that the percentage of slow twitch fibres in the leg muscles of distance runners is high (about 80% of fibres) and that sprinters have a higher percentage of type IIa and type IIb fibres (roughly 50% and 30%, respectively). This research is by no means conclusive as so many other factors contribute to good sporting performance, but certainly some people are more physiologically suited to some activities than others.

In practice

When you perform an arm curl during a weights session you can feel the tension in the deltoid muscle as it helps to stabilise the shoulder joint.

A muscle may also assist the work of a prime mover at a particular joint, making the movement more efficient. This second muscle is sometimes referred to as a *synergist*. The term can also be used to describe a muscle that acts to counteract an unwanted movement of a prime mover, for example a prime mover that acts around two joints where only one movement is required. Either way, synergistic muscle action is difficult to analyse and is beyond the scope of this book.

The third function of a muscle is to act as a *fixator*. A fixator allows the prime mover to work more efficiently, usually by stabilising the bone where the prime mover originates. The fixator muscle increases in tension but does not allow any movement to take place.

activity

Identify the muscles that act as prime movers and as antagonists when you perform a squat thrust. Identify any muscles that you think act as fixators.

3.7 Types of muscular contraction

There are four different ways that a muscle can contract, reflecting the function that the muscle is performing.

3.7.1 *Isotonic or concentric contraction*

This is the most common form of muscular contraction. It occurs when a muscle is acting as a prime mover and shortening under tension, creating movement around a joint.

3.7.2 *Eccentric contraction*

This is the opposite of concentric action. In eccentric contraction the muscle acting as the antagonist lengthens under tension (usually

In practice

In any activity where you are lowering the body, body part, or an object, muscles will be working eccentrically.

in training

Recent research shows that eccentric training appears to lead to greater hypertrophy in fast twitch muscle fibres than concentric work. See page 266 for plyometric training.

returning to its normal resting length). A muscle contracting eccentrically is acting as a 'brake' to help control the movement of a body part during *negative work*. Negative work describes a resistance that is greater than the contractile strength of the muscle, for example gravity.

When you perform a press-up, starting from the floor, you push your body upwards by extending your elbow joints. Triceps brachii works as the prime mover and contracts concentrically (it shortens under tension), while biceps brachii acts as the antagonist, relaxing and returning to its normal length. During the downward phase (lowering the body) you are performing negative work and triceps brachii, working as the antagonist, contracts eccentrically (lengthens under tension) and helps to control the movement.

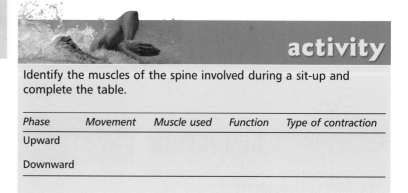

activity

Identify the muscles of the spine involved during a sit-up and complete the table.

Phase	Movement	Muscle used	Function	Type of contraction
Upward				
Downward				

A rugby scrum – muscles are working hard but there is no movement (isometric contraction)

3.7.3 Isometric contraction

The muscle increases in tension but there is no change in its length and therefore no movement. This type of contraction occurs when a muscle is acting as a fixator or when it is working against a resistance that it cannot overcome, for example when two equally strong packs collide in a rugby scrum.

3.7.4 Isokinetic contraction

During this type of contraction the muscle shortens and increases in tension while working at a constant speed against a variable resistance. The muscle works throughout the full range of movement but this can be achieved only by using isokinetic weight-training equipment.

3.8 Gradation of contraction

There is just one more term to introduce: *gradation of contraction*. Put simply, this refers to the strength of contraction exerted by the muscle. Gradation of contraction depends on:

1 The number of motor units stimulated (*recruitment*). If only a few of the motor units within the muscle are stimulated obviously the strength of contraction will be weak. For maximal contraction to occur all motor units must be stimulated.

2 The frequency of the stimuli (*wave summation*). For a motor unit to maintain a contraction it must receive a continuous string of impulses. Usually a frequency of 80–100 stimuli per

Strength gains are not purely a product of hypertrophy or hyperplasia; neural adaptations make a significant contribution in terms of early strength development. Research has concluded that training helps synchronisation of the recruitment of motor units and increases the number of motor units recruited. In order to achieve maximum strength all motor units involved must be recruited at the same time – obviously an increase in the number of units innervated will increase the amount of strength produced.

second is required. Slow twitch muscle fibres have a lower threshold for activation than fast twitch fibres and so tend to be recruited first.

3   Timing of the stimuli to various motor units (*synchronisation* or *spatial summation*). If all the motor units are stimulated at exactly the same time then maximum force can be applied. If, however, a muscle needs to work over a long period, fatigue can be delayed by rotating the number of motor units being stimulated at any one time.

Key revision points

Skeletal muscle creates movement by actively contracting and shortening. The muscle is stimulated by a motor neurone. This stimulation results in each individual sarcomere decreasing in length as the actin and myosin filaments slide over each other. The nature of the contraction produced is a result of the fibre type recruited, the number of fibres stimulated, and the frequency and timing of the stimuli.

Key terms

You should now understand the following terms. If you do not, go back through the chapter and find out what they mean.

Actin
Antagonist
Axon
Fasciculi
Fixator
Myofibril
Myosin
Myosin cross-bridges
Prime mover
Sarcomere
Sarcoplasmic reticulum
Transverse tubules

Progress check

1   Name the two types of connective tissue that attach muscle to bone and muscle to muscle.
2   List four common features of muscle tissue.
3   Why do muscles work in antagonistic pairs?
4   What is the difference between a muscle fibre and a myofibril?
5   What is a sarcomere?
6   Name the two protein filaments responsible for muscle contraction.
7   Sketch and label a diagram showing the structure of a sarcomere.
8   Explain the role of the sarcoplasmic reticulum in muscle contraction.
9   What are the three fibre types found in skeletal muscle?
10   Give four characteristics of each fibre type found in skeletal muscle.
11   Give an example in sport to show when each muscle fibre type would be used.
12   What is the relationship between fibre type distribution and athletic performance?
13   What is the role of a fixator?
14   When would a muscle contract eccentrically?
15   What is meant by gradation of contraction?
16   What is the transmitter substance at the neuromuscular junction called?
17   What is meant by reciprocal innervation?
18   What is the 'all or none' law?
19   What effect does the myelin sheath have on propagation of nerve impulses?
20   What is meant by the term DOMS?
21   What adaptations occur after a period of strength training?

The mechanics of movement

Learning objectives

- To know the three orders of levers.
- To understand the effect of the length of lever and the angle of pull on the movement produced.
- To be familiar with and able to apply Newton's laws of motion.
- To understand the effects of the centre of gravity on balance and rotation.

An ability to analyse movements is extremely helpful to both performer and coach. The ability to identify the joints and muscles involved in a movement and their roles enables development of a suitable training programme. Even though an athlete may work out regularly using weights, he or she may not be exercising the correct muscles, or might be working them concentrically when some eccentric work is also needed. A basic understanding of the principles of movement can help to identify and correct problems with technique. This chapter provides a brief introduction to the mechanics of movement and shows how this knowledge can be applied to help improve sporting performance.

4.1 Levers and their function

When we think of levers, crowbars and wheelbarrows spring to mind rather than ulnas and femurs. The skeleton forms a system of levers that allows us to move. A *lever* is a rigid bar that rotates around a fixed point (a *fulcrum*) and is used to apply force (*effort*) against a *resistance*. In the human body the bones are the levers, the joints the fulcrums, the muscles act as the effort and the weight of the body part, plus anything that it holds, is the resistance.

A single body part, such as an arm, can also act as a lever, providing it works as a rigid unit. Figure 4.1 shows the lever system of the forearm.

A lever has two functions:
- to overcome a larger resistance than the effort applied
- to increase the distance a resistance can be moved by using an effort greater than the resistance.

In other words, a lever provides strength or improves the range of movement. The strength and range of movement of a muscle depend on the position of its insertion (where the effort is applied) relative to the joint it moves (the fulcrum). The greater the distance

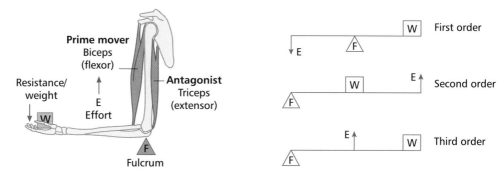

Figure 4.1 *The lever system in the forearm*

Figure 4.2 *Classes of lever*

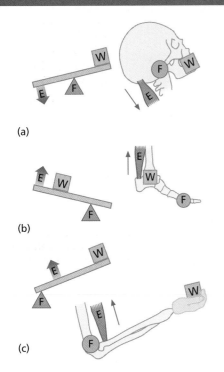

(a)

(b)

(c)

Figure 4.3 *First- (a), second- (b) and third-order (c) levers in the human body*

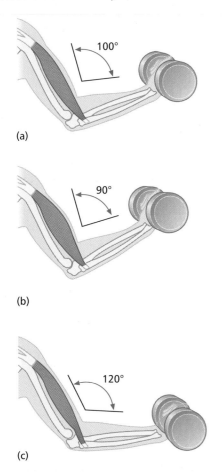

(a)

(b)

(c)

Figure 4.4 *Each joint has an optimal angle of pull (where the force is applied). Biceps brachii has an optimal angle of 100° (a). Decreasing or increasing the joint angle reduce the amount of force produced (b, c)*

between the joint and the muscle insertion, the more strength can be generated; the closer the insertion is to the joint the better the range of movement will be.

The type of lever formed by the joint and the surrounding musculature affects the movement produced, but two related factors also need to be considered: the angle of pull and the length of the lever. These will be described below.

4.2 Classification of levers

A lever can be defined as first-order, second-order or third-order. The three classes of lever are illustrated in Figure 4.2. This classification is based on the relative positions of the fulcrum (joint), effort (muscle insertion) and resistance (body part or external weight).

4.2.1 First-order levers

A first-order lever is organised like a set of scales, with the fulcrum between the effort and the resistance. The head is a good example of the action of a first-order lever in the body when the head and neck are being flexed and extended, as in nodding (see Figure 4.3 (a)).

4.2.2 Second-order levers

When the resistance lies between the fulcrum and the effort a second-order lever is produced. When you raise up on to your toes (plantar flexion of the ankle) you are using a second-order lever. Where the toes are in contact with the floor is the fulcrum, the resistance is at the ankle joint where the body's weight is transferred to the foot and the effort is produced at the position on the ankle where the Achilles tendon inserts onto the calcaneus (see Figure 4.3 (b)).

4.2.3 Third-order levers

In a third-order lever the effort lies between the fulcrum and the resistance. This is the most common form of lever in the human body. In terms of applying force this is a very inefficient lever, but it allows speed and range of movement. An example within the body is the forearm during flexion (see Figure 4.3 (c)).

4.3 Angle of pull

This refers to the position of the insertion of the muscle relative to the position of the joint, measured in degrees. The angle of pull changes continuously as the limb is moved and these changes have a direct effect on the efficiency of the muscle's pulling force. The most efficient angle of the joint, for most joints, is between 90 degrees and 100 degrees. A decrease or increase in this joint angle results in a reduction in the force that can be applied. Structures within joints can act as pulleys to increase the angle of pull and therefore the efficiency of the muscle. For example, the patella, attached to the quadriceps tendon and the patellar ligament, acts as a pulley at the knee joint. A muscle works most effectively as it nears an angle of pull of 90°–100° (Figure 4.4) and where it is not advantageous the only solution is to increase the strength of the muscle.

A combination of levers is used in batting

in training

The muscle's potential to generate force is dependent on several factors:

- how many motor units are recruited
- the type of motor units recruited, e.g. fast glycolytic fibres
- the length of the muscle when recruited
- the angle of pull
- the speed of contraction.

If an athlete wants to produce maximum force in a biceps curl the optimal angle of the joint needs to be 100 degrees. Biceps brachii should be stretched 20% before the contraction and the speed of the concentric muscle contraction should be quite slow.

activity

Choose three hand-held weights that you consider to be light, manageable and heavy. Using Figure 4.4 as a guide try to lift each weight using a different angle of pull. Discuss your results with others in your group.

4.4 Length of lever

The longer the lever the greater the change in momentum, and consequently change in velocity, that can be imparted on an object. This can be an advantage in sports in which you hit objects, for example a squash ball can be hit harder when the elbow joint is fully extended rather than flexed; the use of a racket lengthens the lever arm further. To generate a much greater overall force the effects of several levers can be combined, as in batting in cricket where the trunk, upper arm, forearm and bat all work together as one unit.

activity

Contrast the length of club and stroke technique used in golf at the tee shot with that used in the approach to a short putt. Your answer should make reference to the choice of joint, joint action and lever arm length.

4.5 Force

Forces can be used to make something move, stop something that is already moving or to prevent something from moving altogether. A force might be internal or external. In the human body, muscles act as internal forces, whereas the effect of gravity is external.

Different golf shots use different joint actions and lever lengths

NEWTON

One newton is the force required to produce an acceleration of one metre per second on a mass of one kilogram.

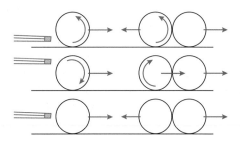

Figure 4.5 *Applying a force slightly off-centre will cause spin*

The effect that a force has on a body is influenced by three factors.

1 *The size, or magnitude, of the force* is measured in newtons (N) or in pounds. The magnitude of the force refers to the weight of a body, which is a product of its mass and the external force of gravity. A muscle's force is determined by the size and number of the fibres contained within any one muscle.

2 *The direction of the force.* If a single force is applied to a body through its centre of gravity the body will move in the same direction as the force.

3 *The position of application of the force.* Applying the force slightly off-centre will produce angular motion, e.g. hitting a snooker ball off-centre will create spin (see Figure 4.5).

In sport, a performer must gauge how much force to apply in any given situation. If you are performing a closed skill, for example a free throw in basketball, you are at an advantage in that the amount of force, the direction and the application of the force required are the same each time you perform the throw. Therefore practice can lead to a habitual response. In open skills the situation will vary each time and errors can be made – a footballer not connecting with the ball correctly will cause it to veer off to one side, a hockey player with an enthusiastic backswing applying too much force to the ball will over-hit a pass. Errors can be rectified very quickly if a coach is able to point out the basic mechanical weaknesses in a technique.

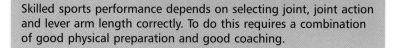

In practice

Skilled sports performance depends on selecting joint, joint action and lever arm length correctly. To do this requires a combination of good physical preparation and good coaching.

4.6 Newton's laws of motion

Motion (movement) will occur only if a force is applied; most movement of the body is caused by the internal force created by the muscles. Motion occurs either in a straight line (linear motion) or around an axis (angular motion). Isaac Newton formulated three laws of motion, which can be applied to sports performance.

4.6.1 Newton's first law of motion (law of inertia)

This law states that:

'a body continues in its state of rest or of uniform motion unless a force acts on it.'

A body or an object is said to be in a state of inertia and a force must be applied to it before any change in velocity can occur. The greater the mass of a body the more force is required to overcome its inertia. You can throw a 5 kg weight further than you can throw a 10 kg weight using the same force.

MASS

Mass is the quantity of matter a body contains.

In practice

A medicine ball has greater inertia than a tennis ball and therefore more force is needed to alter its speed.

4.6.2 *Newton's second law of motion (law of acceleration)*

This law states that:

'the acceleration of an object is directly proportional to the force causing it and is inversely proportional to the mass of the object.'

The speed that a person can throw a tennis ball is proportional to the amount of force applied by the muscles. It also depends on the inertia of the ball.

In sport we often refer to the *momentum* of an object. This is a product of velocity × mass. A defender in hockey usually uses a heavier hockey stick than a forward because it allows him or her to transfer more momentum to the ball, and consequently to hit it further. Momentum can also be built up and transferred from one body part to the rest of the body, resulting in more force – for example, swinging the arms backwards and forwards before take-off transfers momentum to the rest of the body for a vertical jump.

activity

Perform a vertical jump with no preparatory arm swings. Note the height of the jump and then perform the jump using your arms to build up momentum. Compare the two heights.

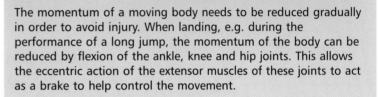

in training

The momentum of a moving body needs to be reduced gradually in order to avoid injury. When landing, e.g. during the performance of a long jump, the momentum of the body can be reduced by flexion of the ankle, knee and hip joints. This allows the eccentric action of the extensor muscles of these joints to act as a brake to help control the movement.

4.6.3 *Newton's third law of motion (law of reaction)*

This law states:

'for every action there is an equal and opposite reaction.'

When an object exerts a force on a second object, the second object exerts an opposite and equal force back on the first. The most common sporting illustration of this law is when an athlete pushes back against the starting blocks at the beginning of a sprint race (exerting a force on the blocks), causing the opposite and equal reaction of being pushed forward out of the blocks. When in mid air it is possible to move one body part to cause another body part to react in opposition; for example in trampolining a half twist is achieved by swinging the arms to the right, rotating the rest of the body to the left.

4.7 Centre of gravity

The centre of gravity, sometimes referred to as the point of balance, is the point in an object where all its mass is concentrated. The centre of gravity of a performer is continually changing as the body position changes. As the centre of gravity is the point of balance of the body we commonly refer to performers being 'balanced' or 'off-balance'. A gymnast plainly displays good balance when performing a handstand (Figure 4.6), but balance is a less obvious requirement of most sports and we often refer to a games player as being 'well balanced'. Therefore balance has both a static and dynamic dimension.

Figure 4.6
Good balance is displayed when performing a handstand

DEFINITION

CENTRE OF GRAVITY

The centre of gravity of an object is the point at which the mass of the object is concentrated. It is sometimes referred to as an object's point of balance.

Figure 4.7 *In some body positions the centre of gravity is located outside the body*

In a uniformly shaped body (such as a snooker ball) the centre of gravity lies at its geometric centre, but the centre of gravity of a non-uniform body is determined by the distribution of its mass and density. When standing upright the centre of gravity of most people is in the hip region, the centre of gravity for males being slightly higher than that for females. As the body's position changes so does its centre of gravity – in some cases it may even be located outside the body (see Figure 4.7).

4.7.1 Maintaining balance

To be in a state of balance the centre of gravity must be over the area of support. For example, when you stand upright the area of support is your feet. The larger the area of support, the easier it is to maintain balance. Lowering or raising the centre of gravity will affect stability. By raising your arms above your head you are redistributing your mass, and your centre of gravity will move higher up your body. When you learn to do a headstand you are encouraged to form a triangle with your head and hands because this position forms a large area of support, making it easier to balance. In the early stages of learning to do a headstand, you bring your legs into a tuck position and hold the balance, rather than extend your legs vertically. It is relatively easy to balance in the tuck position as the centre of gravity is lowered, increasing stability. However, as the legs are extended the centre of gravity is raised, making the position less stable and consequently more difficult to perform.

activity

Rank the gymnastic positions shown in Figure 4.8 in order of stability and difficulty.

4.7.2 Use of the off-balance position

Occasionally a performer needs to become off-balance. A sprinter in the 'set' position holds his or her body so that the line of gravity is as close as possible to the edge of the area of support. On the

Figure 4.8

'go' signal the sprinter moves out of the area of support, causing loss of balance – literally he or she falls forwards. A new area of support now needs to be established.

As mentioned previously, when a force is applied in line with the centre of gravity this will result in linear motion, but when a force is applied out of line with the centre of gravity or the centre of rotation, then rotation will occur. This is known as eccentric force and is used extensively in gymnastics and trampolining. For example, in order to produce a forward somersault in a gymnastic routine the centre of gravity must be displaced in front of the feet.

4.8 Movement analysis

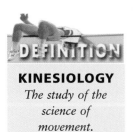

DEFINITION

KINESIOLOGY
The study of the science of movement.

To complete an anatomical and mechanical analysis (kinesiological analysis) of a motor skill you need to be able to:
1 Describe the skill and its purpose.
2 Evaluate the performance in terms of:
   a the joint action, muscle action and function, and
   b the mechanical principles applied.
3 Correct faults where applicable.

The following analysis of the take-off phase of the standing broad jump is an example of the detail required at A level and shows how the basic principles of mechanics can be applied to sporting performance.

4.8.1 Description

The standing broad jump is a forward jump to cover as much horizontal distance as possible. The performer takes off from both feet and lands on both feet.

4.8.2 Joint and muscle action during take-off

Table 4.1 *Joint and muscle action during take-off*

Joint	Joint type	Movement observed	Main muscle involved	Muscle function	Type of contraction
Elbow	Hinge	Extension	Triceps brachii	Prime mover/agonist	Concentric
Shoulder	Ball and socket	Flexion	Anterior deltoid	Prime mover/agonist	Concentric
Shoulder girdle	Gliding	Upward rotation	Trapezius part 2	Prime mover/agonist	Concentric
		Abduction	Serratus anterior	Prime mover/agonist	Concentric
Spine	Gliding and cartilaginous	Extension	Sacrospinalis	Prime mover/agonist	Concentric
Hip	Ball and socket	Extension	Gluteus maximus	Prime mover/agonist	Concentric
Knee	Hinge	Extension	Quadriceps group	Prime mover/agonist	Concentric
Ankle	Hinge	Plantarflexion	Soleus	Prime mover/agonist	Concentric

4.8.3 Mechanical principles involved in take-off

• The application of force at take-off needs to be in line with the centre of gravity. If it isn't the performer will jump slightly to one side and the horizontal distance jumped will be less.
• The speed of projection depends on the total impulse (force × time) generated at take-off. This is the combination of the forces exerted at the ankle, knee, hip and shoulder joints. How strongly and quickly the musculature around these joints can contract affects the distance jumped. Careful timing of joint action is essential, because if joints act out of sequence the overall force that can be applied will be reduced. For the standing broad jump the hips should initiate the movement, followed by the shoulders, knees and ankles.
• The amount of force that can be generated at take-off will increase the upward reaction force (Newton's third law).

activity

Observe the action of an athlete who performs a good standing broad jump, and compare it with a person who performs a relatively poor standing broad jump. List any major differences between the two techniques.

- Preparatory swings of the arms and flexion of the knees will help to overcome inertia (Newton's first law).
- Momentum can be increased by swinging the arms forwards and upwards at take-off (Newton's second law), adding to the overall force of the movement.

Key revision points

A basic kinesiological analysis needs to include three features: a description of the skill; an evaluation of both the joints and muscles used and the mechanical principles applied; and identification and correction of any faults.

Key terms

You should now understand the following terms. If you do not, go back through the chapter and find out what they mean.

Angle of pull
Angular motion
Application of force
Centre of gravity
Fulcrum
Inertia
Kinesiology
Length of lever
Lever
Linear motion
Magnitude of force
Momentum
Reaction force
Resistance

Progress check

1   Give examples within the body of a first-order lever, a second-order lever and a third-order lever.
2   What two functions can a lever perform?
3   Which type of lever allows the greatest range of movement?
4   Give an example from sport, other than batting in cricket, where the effects of several levers are combined to form one unit in order to generate more force.
5   What is the optimum angle of pull for a muscle?
6   What is the advantage of lengthening the lever arm?
7   How can a person raise their centre of gravity?
8   What benefit is gained by lowering your centre of gravity?
9   Give an example from sport where a performer might deliberately lower their centre of gravity.
10 Why is it easier to perform a headstand than a handstand?
11 What benefit does an athlete gain by performing preparatory swings with the arm before throwing the discus?
12 What happens if a force is applied in line with an object's centre of gravity?
13 Describe the three factors that determine the effect that a force will have on a body.
14 Complete a kinesiological analysis of a vertical jump.
15 What stance should you adopt when catching a medicine ball? Give reasons for your answer.
16 Why should you bend the joints of the legs when landing from a jump?

CHAPTER 5

Structure and function of the heart

Learning objectives

- To know the structure of the heart and be able to describe the flow of blood through the heart.
- To describe and explain the structure and function of the conduction system of the heart.
- To understand the relationship between stroke volume, heart rate and cardiac output.
- To be able to describe how the body regulates heart rate.
- To be aware of the effects of exercise on heart rate.

The heart forms part of the *cardiovascular system*; 'cardio' meaning heart and 'vascular' meaning the circulatory networks of the blood vessels. The cardiovascular system ensures constant distribution of blood to the body to help meet the demands of the body's tissues. During exercise the role of the cardiovascular system is extremely significant, in that the efficiency of this system helps to determine the amount of oxygen that can reach the cells. Figure 5.1 gives an overview of the cardiovascular system.

The heart acts as two completely separate pumps. The pump at the right side of the heart sends deoxygenated blood to the lungs and the pump on the left side sends oxygenated blood round to the body's tissues. The two sides of the heart are separated by a muscular wall called the *septum*.

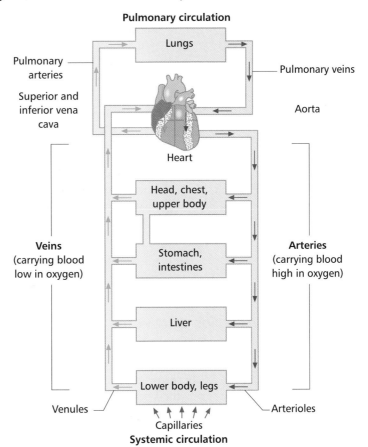

Figure 5.1
Simplified diagram of the circulation of blood around the body

5.1 Structure of the heart

THORACIC CAVITY

The thoracic cavity is the area surrounded by the ribs and bordered by the diaphragm. The thoracic cavity is separated into two halves by the mediastinum.

The heart is about the size of a closed fist and lies within the *pericardial cavity*. The pericardial cavity forms part of the *mediastinum*, which in turn forms part of the thoracic cavity.

The heart is made up of four chambers. The two top chambers are the *atria* and the bottom two are the *ventricles*.

The close proximity of the heart to the lungs means that the right side of the heart has very little work to do compared with the left side. This is reflected in the size and shape of the heart, as the left side is larger.

The heart is surrounded by a closed sac known as the *pericardium* and is bathed in pericardial fluid within the pericardium. As the heart is continually moving, this fluid is needed to reduce the effects of friction on the heart wall (Figure 5.2).

The heart wall is made up of three different layers.

- The *endocardium* is the inner layer. It is made up of very smooth tissue to allow uninterrupted flow of blood through the heart.
- The *myocardium*, the middle layer, is made up of cardiac muscle tissue. Cardiac muscle cells are similar to skeletal muscle cells in that they appear striated but they are highly specialised. Cardiac muscle cells have a single nucleus and contain many mitochondria (Figure 5.3). This is because the heart needs a good supply of ATP to avoid fatigue. Unlike skeletal muscle cells, cardiac muscle cells are connected by intercalated discs. This connection allows a coordinated wave of contraction to occur when the heart muscle is stimulated.
- The *epicardium* is the outer layer of the heart and also forms the inner layer of the pericardium. The outer layer of the pericardium is made of strong fibrous tissue that helps to protect the heart.

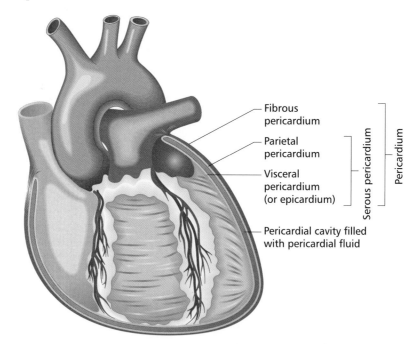

Figure 5.2
The pericardium

5.1.1 *Arteries and veins of the heart*

Numerous blood vessels are attached to the heart, bringing blood to the heart or taking blood away from it (Figure 5.4). Blood enters the heart via the atria and exits through the ventricles. To be more precise, the inferior and superior *venae cavae* bring deoxygenated blood from the body to the right atrium and the four *pulmonary veins* bring oxygenated blood from the lungs to the left atrium. The *pulmonary artery* carries deoxygenated blood from the right ventricle to the lungs and the *aorta* carries oxygenated blood from the left ventricle round the body.

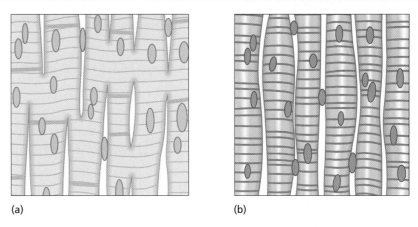

(a)   (b)

Figure 5.3 *Cardiac (a) and skeletal (b) muscle. Note how both muscle types are striated but only cardiac fibres are connected by intercalated discs*

The heart itself requires a good blood supply and the *coronary artery*, which branches from the aorta, distributes oxygenated blood to the heart through an extensive network of capillaries. Deoxygenated blood is returned by the veins of the heart directly into the right atrium through the *coronary sinus*.

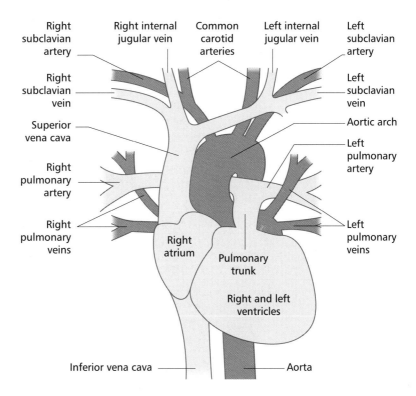

Figure 5.4 *External view of the heart, showing the major blood vessels. The vessels shown in red carry oxygenated blood*

5.1.2 Chambers of the heart

As already mentioned, the two pump units of the heart are separated by a muscular wall called the septum; each unit has an atrium and a ventricle. The atria have relatively thin muscular walls as the force needed to push the blood from them into the ventricles is quite small. The ventricles, as the mechanism pumping blood around the whole body, need much thicker, stronger, muscular walls. The wall of the right ventricle usually exerts

In practice

The closing of the valves creates the heart sounds that can be heard through a stethoscope. The sound is described as 'lubb dupp', the 'lubb' corresponding to the closing of the atrioventricular valves and the 'dupp' to the closing of the semilunar valves. A muffled sound usually indicates a malfunction of one of the valves and is known as a heart murmur.

a pressure of 25 mmHg, whereas the left ventricle exerts a pressure of about 120 mmHg at rest (mm of mercury are used to express the amount of pressure). This difference is because the right ventricle pumps blood only as far as the lungs, but the left ventricle needs to provide sufficient force to carry the blood round the systemic circulation.

5.1.3 *Valves of the heart*

The flow of blood through the heart needs to be regulated so that blood flows only in one direction. Four valves inside the heart help to control blood flow through the heart – two separating the atria from the ventricles and two in the arteries carrying blood from the ventricles. The valves operate only one way and when properly closed prevent backflow of blood. The valves between the atria and the ventricles are known collectively as the *atrioventricular valves*, the valve between the right atrium and right ventricle is the *tricuspid valve* and that between the left atrium and the left ventricle is the *bicuspid valve*. Blood flowing from the atria into the ventricles pushes the valves open, and they are closed by thin connective tissues called the *chordae tendineae*. The chordae tendineae are attached to the papillary muscles, which are attached to the walls of the ventricle. When the ventricles contract so do the papillary muscles, causing the chordae tendineae to tighten and preventing the valves from collapsing inwards.

The *aortic valve* is found between the left ventricle and the aorta and the *pulmonary valve* lies between the right ventricle and the pulmonary artery. These two valves are known collectively as the *semilunar valves*. Ejection of blood from the ventricles forces the semilunar valves open. When the ventricles relax backflow of blood is prevented because the semilunar valves, like the atrioventricular valves, operate in only one direction. The internal structure of the heart is shown in Figure 5.5.

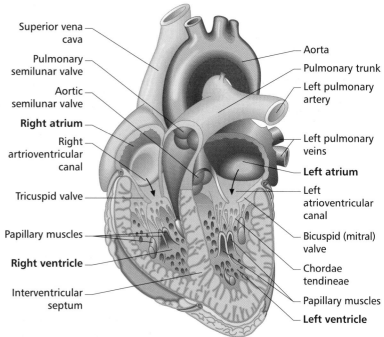

Figure 5.5
Internal structure of the heart

in training

After a period of endurance training changes to the left ventricle are the most significant. The interior volume of the left ventricle increases, allowing greater filling during diastole. The left ventricular wall also increases in size and the hypertrophy of the ventricular wall increases the contractility of the muscle. This means that more blood can be ejected out of the heart during systole.

activity

Borrow a stethoscope and, working in pairs, try to pick up your partner's heart sounds.

activity

On a copy of Figure 5.5 illustrate the flow of blood through the heart. Then complete the flow chart below to show the journey of a red blood cell through the heart and the circulatory systems.

Inferior and superior venae cavae → ? → Tricuspid valve → ? → ? → Pulmonary artery → Lungs → ? → Left atrium → ? → Left ventricle → ? → ? → Tissues of the body → Inferior and superior venae cavae.

5.2 Flow of blood through the heart and the cardiac cycle

Deoxygenated blood flows into and fills the right atrium from the superior and inferior venae cavae. At the same time, oxygenated blood enters the left atrium via the pulmonary veins from the lungs. As the left and right ventricles relax and ventricular pressure drops, blood flows from both atria into them. The atria contract to ensure that the ventricles are completely filled. The ventricles then contract (when this happens the atrioventricular valves close to prevent backflow of blood into the atria) and the blood is pushed out of the ventricles through the semilunar valves into the pulmonary artery and the aorta. When the ventricles relax the semi-lunar valves close, preventing backflow. The atria relax and begin to fill again – and the whole process repeats itself.

This process is known as the *cardiac cycle* and at rest takes approximately 0.8 seconds. The cardiac cycle involves rhythmic contraction and relaxation of the heart muscle. The contraction phase is known as *systole* and takes about 0.3 seconds at rest, the relaxation phase (*diastole*) lasts roughly 0.5 seconds at rest. Note: these terms are usually used to refer to the contraction and relaxation phases of the *ventricles*.

5.3 The conduction system of the heart

The muscular pump of the heart needs a stimulus to make it contract. Unlike skeletal muscle, cardiac muscle needs to create a wave-like contraction so that the atria contract before the ventricles. An added problem is that blood needs to flow downwards from the atria into the ventricles and then flow upwards out of the aorta and pulmonary artery. The system of nerves that stimulate the heart is shown in Figure 5.6.

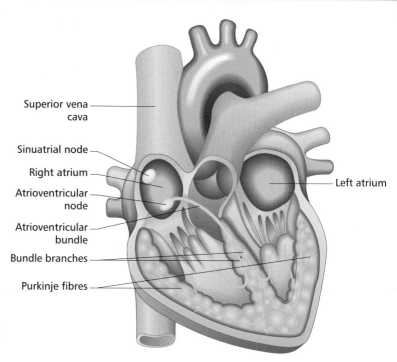

Figure 5.6
The conduction system of the heart

The wave of contraction is initiated by a specialised node in the wall of the right atrium, called the *sinuatrial* (SA) *node* or *pacemaker*. The SA node is controlled by the autonomic nervous system (the regulation of the heart rate will be discussed later in this chapter). The nerve impulse spreads through the cardiac muscle tissue, rather like a 'Mexican wave', as all of the muscle fibres are interconnected. This causes the atria to contract, pushing the blood into the ventricles. The impulse then spreads over the ventricles from the bottom (the *apex*) of the heart. This is achieved by a second node sited in the atrioventricular septum, known as the *atrioventricular* (AV) *node*. The impulse travels across the atria to the AV node and then down a specialised bundle of nerve tissue in the septum (the *bundle of His*). The nerve impulse is carried to the apex of the heart, where the specialised fibres branch out into smaller bundles, called *purkinje fibres*. The purkinje fibres extend upwards and across the ventricles, causing the ventricles to contract and push blood up and out of the heart. Once the ventricles have completely relaxed another impulse is initiated at the SA node and the cycle is repeated.

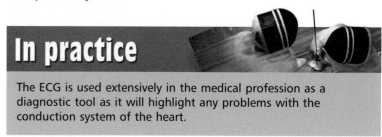

In practice

The ECG is used extensively in the medical profession as a diagnostic tool as it will highlight any problems with the conduction system of the heart.

5.3.1 *The electrocardiogram*

The electrical activity of the heart's conduction system can be measured by electrodes on the skin of the chest. The information is recorded in the form of a trace such as that illustrated in Figure 5.7.

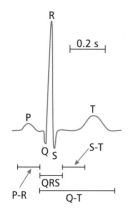

Figure 5.7 *Some of the important events on an ECG*

This trace is an *electrocardiogram* (also known as an ECG). The P wave occurs just before the atria contract, the QRS complex occurs just before the ventricles contract and the T wave corresponds to repolarisation of the ventricles before ventricular diastole.

5.4 Cardiac output

The amount of blood the heart manages to pump out per minute is known as the cardiac output ($\dot{Q}$). The cardiac output is a product of the stroke volume × heart rate.

$\dot{Q} = SV \times HR$

Heart rate (HR) is the number of times the heart actually beats per minute and the stroke volume (SV) is the amount of blood ejected by the ventricle at each contraction.

DEFINITION

STROKE VOLUME

The volume of blood pumped out of the heart by each ventricle during one contraction.

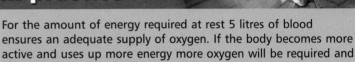

In practice

For the amount of energy required at rest 5 litres of blood ensures an adequate supply of oxygen. If the body becomes more active and uses up more energy more oxygen will be required and the cardiac output will increase.

The stroke volume is measured in millilitres of blood per beat and the heart rate is measured in beats per minute, giving a cardiac output in litres per minute.

Stroke volume can vary due to the following factors:
1 How much blood is being returned to the heart (venous return).
2 How far the ventricles will stretch (remember that muscle tissue is elastic).
3 The contractility of the ventricles.
4 The pressure in the main arteries leading from the heart.

The first two factors relate to how much blood can enter the ventricles and the last two relate to how much blood can be ejected from the heart during systole.

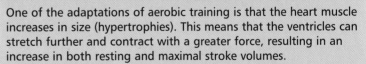

in training

One of the adaptations of aerobic training is that the heart muscle increases in size (hypertrophies). This means that the ventricles can stretch further and contract with a greater force, resulting in an increase in both resting and maximal stroke volumes.

At rest the average stroke volume is 70 ml and the average heart rate 72 beats per minute, giving an overall cardiac output of just over 5 litres/min.

DEFINITION

HYPERTROPHY

Growth of a tissue through an increase in cell size.

The resting heart rate of an individual can vary greatly, although we all need to produce roughly the same cardiac output at rest. If

DEFINITION

END-DIASTOLIC VOLUME

The amount of blood in the ventricles just before the contraction phase (systole).

The heart subjected to regular exercise does not have to beat as often as an untrained heart to produce the same cardiac output at rest. This also means that the maximum cardiac output will increase.

A person's maximum heart rate is estimated as being 220 minus their age, so the maximum heart rate of an athlete aged 20 will be about 200 beats per minute. The maximum SV reached during exercise increases with training – from 110–120 ml per beat for an untrained male to 150–170 ml per beat for an endurance athlete.

a person does a lot of aerobic work (prolonged periods of submaximal exercise) their resting pulse rate often drops to 60 beats per minute or lower. In order to produce the same cardiac output, the stroke volume must increase to compensate for this drop in heart rate.

$$\dot{Q} = SV \times HR$$
$$5 \text{ litres} = ? \times 60 \text{ (beats/min)}$$

By rearranging the equation,

$$SV = \dot{Q}/HR$$
$$= 5 \text{ litres}/60$$
$$83 \text{ ml}$$

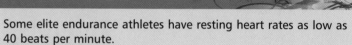

in training

Some elite endurance athletes have resting heart rates as low as 40 beats per minute.

In this case the stroke volume increases to about 120 ml per beat. In effect, it is the increase in SV that produces the drop in heart rate, and not the other way round, because as the heart gets used to regular exercise it gets bigger (undergoes hypertrophy) and stronger.

This means that the *end-diastolic volume* of the ventricle increases (it can physically hold more blood). The ventricle is thus capable of stronger contraction and is able to push more blood out per beat.

In exceptional cases the maximum cardiac output can be as high as 40 litres.

	HR × SV		$\dot{Q}$
Untrained:	200 × 120 ml	=	24 litres
Trained:	200 × 170 ml	=	34 litres

This is an obvious benefit because more oxygen can be delivered to the working tissues, enabling them to work harder or for longer periods of time.

The 5 litres of blood pumped out of the heart at rest is circulated around the body. The proportion of the cardiac output distributed to the particular organs is shown in Table 5.1.

Table 5.1 *Distribution of blood to the vital organs*

Organ	Percentage of cardiac output at rest
Bone	5
Brain	15
Heart	5
Kidney	25
Liver	25
Muscle	15
Skin	5
Other	5

activity

Take the resting pulse of all the members of your group and discuss the amount and type of exercise that each person participates in. Is there a relationship between exercise and resting heart rate?

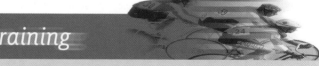

in training

Cardiac output at rest remains relatively unchanged as a result of endurance training. In contrast, the maximum cardiac output after endurance training shows a marked increase. This increase is due to the big increase in maximum stroke volume.

When the body starts to exercise the distribution of the blood changes. The main change is that about 85% is now channelled to the working muscles. The flow of blood to the brain is maintained, but flow to the kidneys, liver and the gastrointestinal tract decreases. The effect of exercise on the cardiac output and blood distribution may be seen in Figure 5.8.

5.5 Control of heart rate

Unlike other muscle tissue the heart initiates its own action potentials automatically at the SA node, resulting in rhythmic contractions of the heart. The contractions are at regular intervals but their timing is altered by two extrinsic factors and one intrinsic factor:

1 neural control
2 hormonal control } extrinsic factors
3 intrinsic control.

Of these, neural control is the most important control mechanism.

Figure 5.8
Effect of exercise on cardiac output and blood distribution

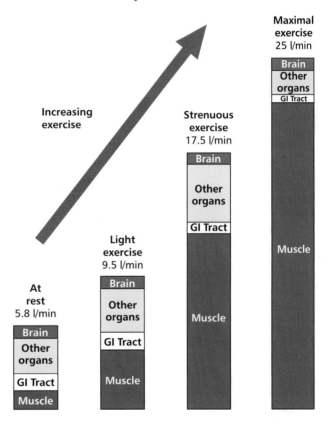

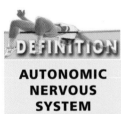

DEFINITION

AUTONOMIC NERVOUS SYSTEM

The autonomic nervous system is made up of sensory nerves and motor nerves. The motor nerves are referred to as the sympathetic and parasympathetic nerves. The autonomic nervous system is under involuntary control.

5.5.1 Neural control

Figure 5.6 shows that the SA node (the pacemaker) in the wall of the right atrium is controlled by the autonomic nervous system. Two nerves stimulate this node: the *sympathetic cardiac accelerator nerve*, which speeds up the heart rate, and the *parasympathetic vagus nerve*, which slows it down.

Overall control of the two nerves is coordinated by the cardiac control centre in the medulla of the brain. The cardiac control centre is stimulated by:

* muscle receptors in the muscles and joints that stimulate the cardiac control centre at the onset of exercise
* chemoreceptors in the muscle that respond to changes in muscle chemistry, such as a rise in lactic acid
* emotional excitement

- changes in blood pressure, detected by the baroreceptors in the aorta and carotid arteries – for example a decrease in blood pressure will result in an increase in heart rate and stroke volume
- chemoreceptors in the aorta and carotid arteries that respond to changes in oxygen, carbon dioxide and pH levels.

5.5.2 *Hormonal control*

Adrenaline is secreted from the adrenal glands into the bloodstream and stimulates the SA node, causing an increase in heart rate. Adrenaline also increases the strength of contraction produced by the myocardium (heart muscle).

5.5.3 *Intrinsic control*

When any muscle gets warmer the conduction of nerve impulses seems to speed up – this is also true of heart muscle. The heart rate of a warm heart increases, and a drop in temperature reduces the heart rate. In addition, during exercise the amount of blood returning to the heart (the venous return) is increased, stretching the cardiac muscle more than usual. This stimulates the SA node and increases the heart rate – it also increases the force of contraction. The relationship between an increase in venous return and an increase in stroke volume is known as *Starling's law*.

5.6 Exercise and control of heart rate

The heart rate needs to increase during exercise in order to increase the supply of oxygen to working muscle and to remove waste products such as carbon dioxide and lactic acid. Before you even begin to exercise your heart rate will start to increase. This *anticipatory rise* in heart rate is caused by the release of adrenaline acting directly on the heart and the impact of emotional excitement on the medulla. As soon as exercise begins the heart rate rises rapidly, mainly due to a nerve reflex response, initiated by the muscle receptors, that stimulates the cardiac control centre. Also within the muscles chemoreceptors respond to the increase in lactic acid and other chemical changes by sending messages to the cardiac control centre to increase heart rate. As the body continues to exercise the heart muscle begins to get warmer and venous return increases, increasing the heart rate further – see above.

When you stop exercising the muscle receptors stop stimulating the cardiac control centre and the heart rate begins to fall quite rapidly. The activity of the chemoreceptors also reduces and this, combined with the reduced levels of adrenaline, the drop in venous return and the drop in body temperature returns the heart rate to normal within a matter of minutes. Figure 5.9 shows a typical response of the heart to submaximal exercise.

DEFINITION

$\dot{V}O_2$(MAX)

The maximum volume of oxygen that can be consumed and used by the body per unit of time. It is usually expressed as millilitres per minute per kilogram of body weight.

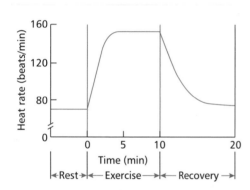

Figure 5.9 *Change in heart rate with submaximal exercise*

in training

Monitoring heart rate is a very good way to monitor exercise intensity. A lot of athletes use a target heart range in order to gauge the efficiency of their aerobic workout. The target heat rate uses the heart rate that is equivalent to the percentage of the $\dot{V}O_2$ (max) that the athlete wishes to train at. This is possible because of the linear relationship between heart rate and oxygen consumption as work rate increases. As the athlete's aerobic capacity improves, the target heart rate range is increased.

in training

Recent research suggests that the stroke volume of an elite endurance athlete does not plateau during exercise, but continues to rise until $\dot{V}O_2$ (max), due to improved ventricular filling caused by an increase in venous return.

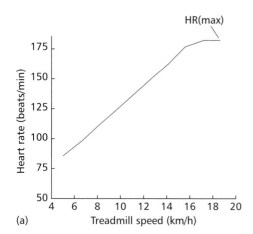

(a)

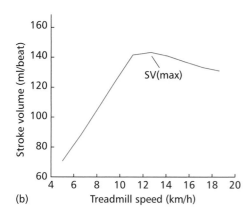

(b)

Figure 5.10 *Changes in heart rate (a) and stroke volume (b) during a progressive treadmill workout*

The heart rate increases in direct proportion to the increase in exercise intensity. Initially the cardiac output increases as a result of both the heart rate and the stroke volume increasing, but maximum stroke volume is achieved during submaximal work and any increase in cardiac output during maximal exercise is due solely to an increase in heart rate. Figure 5.10 shows the changes in both heart rate and stroke volume during a progressive treadmill workout. As the workload is increased the heart rate steadily rises until a maximum heart rate is reached. By this stage most of the energy is being produced anaerobically and you will soon have to stop exercising because of fatigue. If you are working submaximally your heart rate will usually rise until you reach a point where the oxygen delivered to the working muscles is sufficient to release enough energy aerobically to cope with the demands of the exercise. The heart rate will then reach a plateau. This is known as 'steady state' exercise.

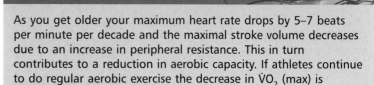

When you stop exercising your heart rate does not immediately return to normal but takes a number of minutes to recover. This is because you need to maintain an elevated rate of aerobic respiration in order to replenish some of the energy stores you have used

during the exercise and also to remove some of the waste products that have accumulated, for example lactic acid and carbon dioxide (Figure 5.9).

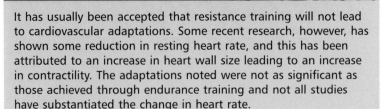

in training

It has usually been accepted that resistance training will not lead to cardiovascular adaptations. Some recent research, however, has shown some reduction in resting heart rate, and this has been attributed to an increase in heart wall size leading to an increase in contractility. The adaptations noted were not as significant as those achieved through endurance training and not all studies have substantiated the change in heart rate.

Key revision points

The heart acts as two separate pumps, distributing oxygenated blood round the body. Deoxygenated blood returns to the heart via the pulmonary and systemic circulatory systems. The heart responds to the demands made on the body when exercising by increasing the heart rate and stroke volume to increase the overall cardiac output.

Key terms

You should now understand the following terms. If you do not, go back through the chapter and find out what they mean.

- Atrioventricular node
- Atrioventricular valve
- Bundle of His
- Cardiac control centre
- Cardiac output
- Diastole
- End-diastolic volume
- Mediastinum
- Myocardium
- Pericardial cavity
- Purkinje fibres
- Semilunar valve
- Sinuatrial node
- Stroke volume
- Systole

Progress check

1. Name the two circulatory systems.
2. Where would you find the pericardium?
3. What centre controls the heart rate and where is it situated in the body?
4. List three factors that directly affect the control centre resulting in a change of heart rate.
5. Which nerve speeds up the heart rate?
6. Describe how the wave of excitation spreads through the heart muscle.
7. Briefly describe the cardiac cycle.
8. Define 'cardiac output' and give typical values at rest and during exercise.
9. How does stroke volume affect cardiac output?
10. Where would you find the papillary muscles? What are their function?
11. List four ways in which cardiac muscle fibre differs from skeletal muscle fibre.
12. What is Starling's law?
13. What name is given to the heart's own blood supply?
14. List three factors that affect cardiac output during the first few moments of exercise and explain what they do.
15. Briefly describe the pathway of a drop of blood through the heart.
16. When someone has trained aerobically for over three months their resting pulse drops. Why?
17. Explain 'steady state' in terms of heart rate and workload.
18. How and when during the cardiac cycle are the heart sounds generated?

6 Structure and function of the vascular system

Learning objectives

- To know the major constituents of blood.
- To describe the structure and function of the arteries, capillaries and veins.
- To know the major arteries and veins of the body.
- To describe the factors influencing venous return.
- To understand the role of the vasomotor centre in regulation of blood flow and blood pressure.
- To know how blood pressure changes within the circulatory system and what changes occur during exercise.

As mentioned in Chapter 5, the blood vessels are part of the cardiovascular system and form the body's transport network. It is essential that a sports performer has an efficient vascular system in order to deliver oxygen and food supplies to the working muscles and to remove waste products such as carbon dioxide. The blood carries all the vital ingredients needed for the muscles to work and the blood vessels form a *closed circulatory network*, allowing distribution of blood to all cells. During exercise there is a dramatic change in the distribution of blood round the body, with up to 85% of the total cardiac output going to the working muscles. The heart, vascular and respiratory systems all work together to coordinate the increase in oxygen delivery needed to cope with the increased demand for energy.

6.1 Constituents of the blood

The blood accounts for about 8% of the total body weight. It is made up of *blood cells* and *platelets* floating in the *plasma*.

The plasma makes up 55% of the blood volume. Approximately 90% of the plasma is water. The following substances may be found dissolved in the plasma:

- salts
- glucose and fatty acids
- blood proteins
- waste products
- enzymes
- hormones
- gases such as oxygen and carbon dioxide.

The blood cells make up 45% of total blood volume. There are three types of blood cell.

Red blood cells (*erythrocytes*) are biconcave discs just small enough to pass through a capillary. These form about 95% of the blood cells. The main function of the erythrocytes is to transport oxygen and carbon dioxide round the body. They contain a protein called *haemoglobin*, which has a high affinity for carbon monoxide, carbon dioxide and oxygen. Haemoglobin is capable of carrying up to four oxygen molecules and transports 97% of the oxygen in the body (the remaining 3% is dissolved in the plasma). Oxygen is carried bound to the haemoglobin as *oxyhaemoglobin*. Haemoglobin can also carry carbon dioxide (about 20% of the carbon dioxide is transported this way, the rest is dissolved in the plasma). However, haemoglobin has highest affinity for carbon monoxide and will

DEFINITION

HAEMATOCRIT

The percentage of blood cells in the total blood volume (95% of blood cells are erythrocytes).

In practice

Cigarette smoke contains carbon monoxide so the oxygen-carrying capacity of a smoker's blood is reduced as the haemoglobin binds to the carbon monoxide. This impairs any performance in aerobic activities until the effects of the cigarette have worn off.

pick up carbon monoxide in preference to either carbon dioxide or oxygen.

White blood cells (*leucocytes*). There are five different types of leucocytes but they basically all have the same function of protecting the body from bacteria, viruses and foreign bodies.

Platelets are small cell fragments that help clot the blood.

in training

One of the advantages of aerobic training is that the total blood volume increases (by about 8% at rest) because the amount of plasma and the number of erythrocytes increase. More erythrocytes means that more oxygen can be transported to the cells, allowing more aerobic respiration to take place. Another way of increasing the number of erythrocytes is to train at high altitude – at higher altitudes the blood oxygen levels decrease, stimulating the body to produce more erythrocytes. A banned performance-enhancing drug called RhEPO (recombinant erythropoietin) artificially stimulates the increased production of red blood cells and is reportedly used by some endurance athletes (see page 249). An untrained male would expect to have a haematocrit of about 43%, but the use of RhEPO can result in a haematocrit of nearer 50%.

6.2 Blood vessels

Five different types of blood vessels in the body link together to form the vascular system. The flow of blood around the body through these vessels is shown in Figure 6.1.

All blood vessels are basically a muscular wall surrounding a central *lumen*, or opening. The walls of the blood vessels (except those of the capillaries) comprise three layers (Figure 6.2).

The *tunica interna* forms the inner lining of the vessel. It contains endothelial cells and collagen.

The *tunica media*, or middle layer, is made up of smooth muscle and elastin fibres. The smooth muscle is stimulated by the sympathetic nerves of the autonomic nervous system.

The *tunica externa* is made up mostly of collagen with some elastin fibres. Vessel walls need to be elastic as they have to cope with large fluctuations in blood volume.

6.2.1 *Arteries and arterioles*

Arteries always carry blood away from the heart. The major arteries in the human body are shown in Figure 6.3. As the arteries branch and become smaller they eventually form arterioles. The largest arteries contain a lot of elastin fibres but as they get smaller the muscular middle layer becomes much thicker and the amount of elastin relatively less. The smaller, more muscular arteries and the arterioles are used to control blood flow. Contraction of the smooth muscle in these vessels narrows their lumen and restricts blood flow.

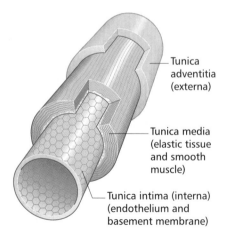

Figure 6.1 *Blood flow through the vessels*

Heart → Arteries → Arterioles → Capillaries → Venules → Veins → Heart

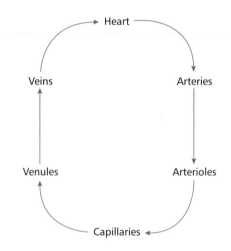

- Tunica adventitia (externa)
- Tunica media (elastic tissue and smooth muscle)
- Tunica intima (interna) (endothelium and basement membrane)

Figure 6.2 *Structure of an elastic artery*

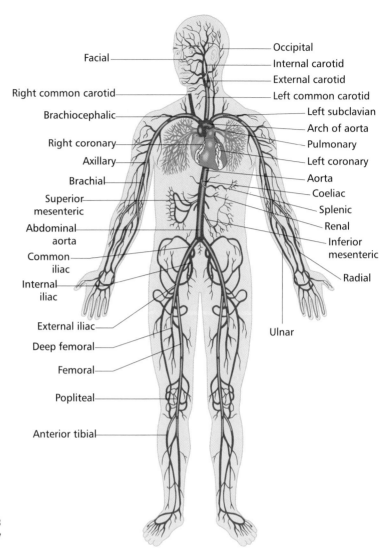

Figure 6.3
The major arteries of the human body

DEFINITION

PRECAPILLARY SPHINCTER

A sphincter is a ring of muscle surrounding an opening. A precapillary sphincter is found between an arteriole and a capillary and can effectively open or close the capillary.

6.2.2 *Capillaries*

The arterioles transport blood to the capillaries. The capillaries are the smallest of the blood vessels and their walls are extremely thin – the exchange of gases and nutrients takes place here. Although capillaries are small they form an extensive network, particularly around skeletal muscle, the heart and the lungs. Capillaries are so small that blood cells can only pass through one at a time. The flow of blood through the capillaries is controlled by *precapillary sphincters*. Capillaries ensure a constant supply of blood to all cells.

DEFINITION

VENOUS RETURN

Flow of blood through the veins back to the heart.

in training

After a period of endurance training there is an increase in capillarisation in the muscle tissue and greater opening of existing capillaries. Both these factors contribute to an increase in blood flow to the working muscle.

6.2.3 *Veins and venules*

Blood flows from the capillaries into the venules. As the venules decrease in number they increase in size and eventually form veins. Veins have much thinner inner and middle layers than arteries and the larger veins contain valves. These valves allow blood to flow only in one direction – back towards the heart – helping venous return.

6.3 Venous return

As we mentioned in Chapter 5, stroke volume depends on venous return. If the venous return decreases, the stroke volume will decrease, reducing the overall cardiac output.

A vein has quite a large lumen and offers very little resistance to blood flow. However, by the time blood enters the veins the blood pressure is low, and active mechanisms are needed to ensure venous return.

6.3.1 *The skeletal muscle pump*

This is the most important mechanism of venous return. When we are moving our muscles contract, squeezing and compressing nearby veins. This action pushes the blood back towards the heart as the valves in the vein allow the blood to flow in one way only, therefore preventing backflow and pooling (Figure 6.4).

6.3.2 *The respiratory pump*

When air is breathed into and out of the lungs the volume of the thoracic cavity changes, creating changes in pressure. During inspiration the pressure around the abdomen increases as the diaphragm lowers to increase the volume of the thoracic cavity. This pressure squeezes the blood in the abdominal veins back towards the heart. During expiration the pressure in the thoracic region increases as the diaphragm and ribs move back to reduce the volume of the thoracic cavity. This has a similar squeezing effect on the veins.

6.3.3 *The valves*

Obviously the valves play an important role in venous return as they direct the flow of blood towards the heart.

Another consideration in venous return is the effect of gravity, especially on veins returning blood from areas above the heart.

6.4 Vasomotor control

The flow and pressure of blood are controlled by the *vasomotor centre* in the medulla of the brain. The vasomotor centre is stimulated by baroreceptors (which respond to changes in blood pressure) in the aorta and carotid arteries. Most blood vessels are stimulated by sympathetic nerves of the autonomic nervous system. Blood vessels receive a continual low-frequency impulse that is known as the *vasomotor tone*. The vasomotor centre controls this stimulus by:

*   increasing vasomotor tone, causing *vasoconstriction* (the lumen decreases in size, resulting in an increase in blood pressure and a reduction in blood flow) or

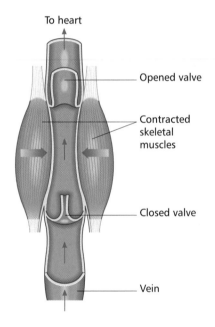

To heart

Opened valve

Contracted skeletal muscles

Closed valve

Vein

Figure 6.4 *The skeletal muscle pump helping blood return to the heart*

DEFINITION

VASOCONSTRICTION

A decrease in the size of the lumen of a blood vessel as the smooth muscle in the tunica media contracts.

VASODILATATION

An increase in the size of the lumen of a blood vessel as the smooth muscle in the tunica media relaxes.

AUTOREGULATION

The local control of blood distribution within the tissues of the body in response to chemical changes.

• decreasing vasomotor tone, causing *vasodilatation* (the lumen increases in size, resulting in a decrease in blood pressure and an increase in blood flow).

As the arterioles have a relatively thick tunica media they are responsible for most of the changes in blood flow and blood pressure.

There is also a degree of local control of blood distribution, called *autoregulation*. The arterioles in some areas of the body react directly to chemical changes in the tissues that they supply. An increased demand by the tissue for oxygen seems to trigger the response of vasodilatation of the surrounding arterioles, as do increases in carbon dioxide and lactic acid.

6.4.1 *The vascular shunt*

During exercise the demand for oxygen from the skeletal muscles increases dramatically and more oxygenated blood must flow to them to meet this demand. The increase in stroke volume and heart rate helps to increase the overall cardiac output and therefore increases oxygen supply, but this in itself is not enough. Blood must also be redistributed so that more goes to the skeletal muscles and less to the other organs. This is known as the *vascular shunt*.

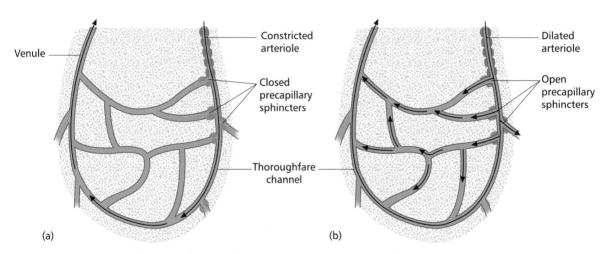

Figure 6.5 *Local blood flow through skeletal muscle (a) at rest; (b) in exercising muscle*

in training

A new vasodilator substance, called nitric oxide, has been discovered. Nitric oxide is produced in the arterioles and an increase in muscular contractions during exercise appears to stimulate its production, which causes the arterioles to vasodilate. Nitric oxide could play a very important role in autoregulation, but a lot more research is needed to fully understand its effects.

The vascular shunt involves two mechanisms:

1 Vasodilatation of the arterioles supplying the skeletal muscles increases the blood flow to them. Vasoconstriction of the arterioles supplying the other organs, such as the kidneys and liver, reduces blood flow to these organs.

2 Opening of the precapillary sphincters in the capillary network supplying skeletal muscle, and closure of the precapillary sphincters in the capillary networks supplying the other organs, increases the flow of blood to the skeletal muscles and decreases flow to the other organs.

The net effect is to substantially increase the percentage of the cardiac output going to the muscles. Figure 6.5 shows the flow of blood through a muscle at rest and during exercise.

The vascular shunt mechanism doesn't only increase blood flow to working muscles. If you are involved in strenuous or prolonged periods of exercise you begin to get hot. The body's response to overheating is to dilate the blood vessels near the skin, increasing the blood flow to the skin and allowing heat to escape from the body.

6.5 Blood flow and blood pressure

Blood, like any other fluid, flows from areas of high pressure to areas of low pressure. The area of high pressure in the human body is the pressure created by contraction of the ventricles, which forces blood out of the heart into the aorta. Blood pressure is equal to blood flow × resistance. The resistance is caused by the friction between the blood and the vessel walls.

During ventricular contraction (systole) the blood pressure at rest for a young adult is about 120 mmHg and during relaxation of the ventricles (diastole) the pressure drops to about 80 mmHg. A doctor normally uses a sphygmomanometer, shown in Figure 6.6, to monitor blood pressure. Blood pressure is usually quoted as systolic pressure 'over' diastolic pressure, for example '120 over 80'. Various factors (such as exercise, stress and pregnancy) can affect blood pressure and the blood pressure varies between individuals. However, a resting blood pressure of 150 over 90 mmHg or above would cause concern because it is indicative of *hypertension*.

DEFINITION

BLOOD PRESSURE

Blood pressure = blood flow × resistance

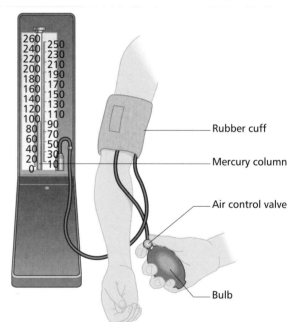

- Rubber cuff
- Mercury column
- Air control valve
- Bulb

Figure 6.6
Measurement of blood pressure using a sphygmomanometer

DEFINITION

HYPERTENSION

The clinical name given to high blood pressure.

activity

Using a sphygmomanometer and a stethoscope attempt to measure your partner's blood pressure. Place the stethoscope over the brachial artery and inflate the cuff to about 180 mmHg, then slowly decrease the pressure. As soon as you detect the sound of the blood through the stethoscope make a note of the pressure: this is the systolic blood pressure. Continue to decrease the pressure until the sound of the blood disappears: this will be the diastolic blood pressure.

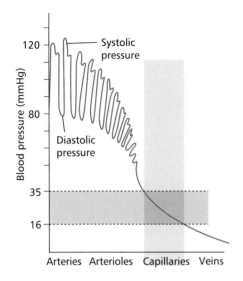

Figure 6.7 *Pressure changes in the systematic circulation*

As blood flows into the large arteries the blood pressure is quite high because they have relatively large lumens and offer little resistance to blood flow. When the blood reaches the arterioles the pressure drops suddenly because the resistance exerted by the vessel walls is much greater. By the time blood reaches the capillaries the blood pressure has dropped to about 35 mmHg. As the blood passes back through the venous system the pressure continues to fall, and is almost zero by the time the blood enters the right atrium (Figure 6.7).

The arterioles play a significant role in regulating blood pressure. By changing the diameter of the lumen (vasoconstriction or vasodilatation) of these vessels their resistance can be increased or decreased, which in turn increases or decreases the blood pressure.

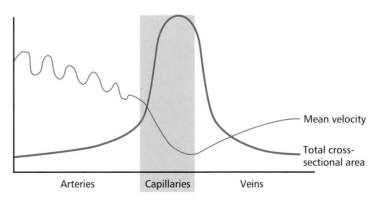

in training

Endurance training has very little effect on resting or exercise blood pressure when the athlete's blood pressure is normal (approx. 120 over 80 mmHg). There is some reduction in blood pressure after endurance training when the athlete is slightly hypertensive to start with.

6.6 Velocity of blood flow

At rest a blood cell will take about a minute to be carried round the circulatory system, but the velocity of the blood flow is far from constant as it passes from one vessel to another. The velocity of the blood flow is affected by the cross-sectional area of the blood vessels. Blood travels through the aorta at about 40 cm/s. As it travels through the smaller arteries and arterioles the *total* cross-sectional area of these vessels increases (although the cross-sectional area of the individual vessels decreases, there are a great many of them), decreasing the velocity of the blood. The greatest *total* cross-sectional area is found in the capillary network as there are so many capillaries. In the capillary network the velocity of the blood is only 0.1 cm/s, slow enough to allow exchange of gases, nutrients and waste products. The blood then flows back through the venules and veins, where the *total* cross-sectional area decreases, resulting in an increase in velocity. The relationship between blood velocity and total cross-sectional area of the vessels is shown graphically in Figure 6.8.

Figure 6.8
The velocity of blood flow varies inversely with the total cross-sectional area of the vessel

6.7 Effects of exercise on blood pressure and blood volume

Overall, systolic blood pressure tends to increase during exercise. The vasodilation that occurs in skeletal muscle causes a drop in blood pressure because of the decrease in resistance, but the cardiac output increases significantly and negates the effect of this vasodilatation. During exercise there is very little change in diastolic pressure; diastolic pressure only increases during isometric work because of the resistance to blood flow caused by the contracting muscle.

After a period of exercise it is much better to perform a series of cooling-down activities rather than to stop abruptly. If you do stop suddenly the blood 'pools' in the working muscles. During heavy exercise about 85% of the cardiac output is distributed to working muscle. The skeletal pump mechanism is largely responsible for maintaining venous return and if you stop exercising the venous return will instantly drop. The knock-on effect is that less blood enters the heart during diastole which means that the stroke volume will be much lower. The overall result is a drastic reduction in blood pressure causing the performer to feel dizzy and sick (Figure 6.9).

Blood volume can change during exercise, but whether it increases or decreases depends on the type of activity and the fitness of the individual. A decrease in volume is mostly caused by plasma moving out of the capillaries into the surrounding tissues. This increases the viscosity of the blood and therefore increases the peripheral resistance. After a period of aerobic training the usual trend identified is an increase in blood volume. This is of great benefit to athletes as it increases their capacity to carry oxygen.

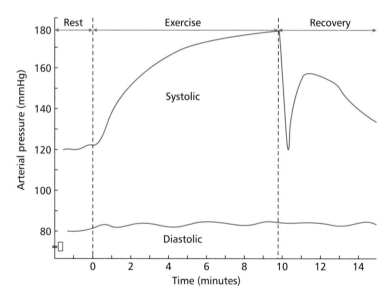

Figure 6.9 *Systolic and diastolic blood pressure during exercise and recovery*

Key revision points

Five different types of vessel form the closed circulatory network that distributes blood to all cells. The distribution of the cardiac output is controlled by the vasomotor centre and is achieved by altering the flow and pressure of the blood. This is mainly brought about by opening or closing of the arterioles and the precapillary sphincters.

You should now understand the following terms. If you do not, go back through the chapter and find out what they mean.

Arteries
Blood pressure
Capillaries
Erythrocyte
Haemoglobin
Leucocyte
Lumen
Precapillary sphincter
Sphygmomanometer
Vascular shunt
Vasoconstriction
Vasodilatation
Vasomotor tone
Veins
Venous return

Progress check

1   Describe how the different blood vessels link together to form the circulatory system.
2   Give one structural and one functional difference between arteries, capillaries and veins.
3   What is the role of haemoglobin?
4   What is meant by venous return?
5   Describe three factors that help maintain venous return.
6   What is the average resting blood pressure?
7   What happens to blood pressure when you start to exercise?
8   If you have a heart problem, or suffer from high blood pressure, what kind of exercise should you avoid?
9   Why does the velocity of the blood change as it passes through the vascular system?
10   Which vessel is mostly responsible for the control of blood flow and blood pressure?
11   What is a precapillary sphincter and what function does it perform?
12   How does smoking affect your capacity for transporting oxygen?
13   Why is it important to perform cooling-down exercises?
14   Name the three layers that form the wall of a blood vessel.
15   What is one of the effects of training at high altitude?
16   What is the function of the vasomotor centre?
17   During exercise a lot more blood is distributed to the working muscles. How is this achieved?
18   What effect does endurance training have on blood flow?

The respiratory system

Learning objectives

- To be able to describe the structures of the respiratory system.
- To understand the process of respiration.
- To describe and explain the mechanics of breathing, both at rest and during exercise.
- To know the definitions and capacities of the pulmonary volumes and how these volumes change with exercise.
- To be able to describe the control mechanisms of the respiratory system.

In order to stay alive we need a continuous supply of oxygen. We use oxygen to break down food to release energy and produce carbon dioxide as a waste product. We need continually to take in oxygen from the air and expel carbon dioxide into the air. This process of exchanging gases is known as *respiration*. Respiration involves all of the following processes:

- Physically moving air into and out of the lungs – *ventilation*.
- The gaseous exchange that takes place between the lungs and the blood – *external respiration*.
- Transport of gases in the blood.
- Exchange of gases between the blood and the cells, known as *internal respiration*.

'Respiration' is also used to describe the process occurring in the mitochondria that uses oxygen to produce ATP. This is usually referred to as *cellular respiration*. The respiratory system has to coordinate with the actions of the cardiovascular system to ensure adequate delivery of oxygen to the cells and efficient removal of carbon dioxide from the cells.

7.1 Structure of the respiratory system

Air taken from the atmosphere passes through several structures before it reaches the bloodstream (Figure 7.1).

7.1.1 *The nose*

Air enters the body through the nose where hairs and mucus help to filter it. The air is also warmed.

7.1.2 *The pharynx*

Air passes from the nose into the pharynx. Both food and air pass through the pharynx. At the bottom of the pharynx air is directed through the larynx and food is directed down the oesophagus.

7.1.3 *The larynx*

The larynx is commonly known as the 'voice box' as it contains the vocal folds. A flap of elastic cartilage, the *epiglottis*, covers the opening of the larynx during swallowing and prevents food entering the lungs.

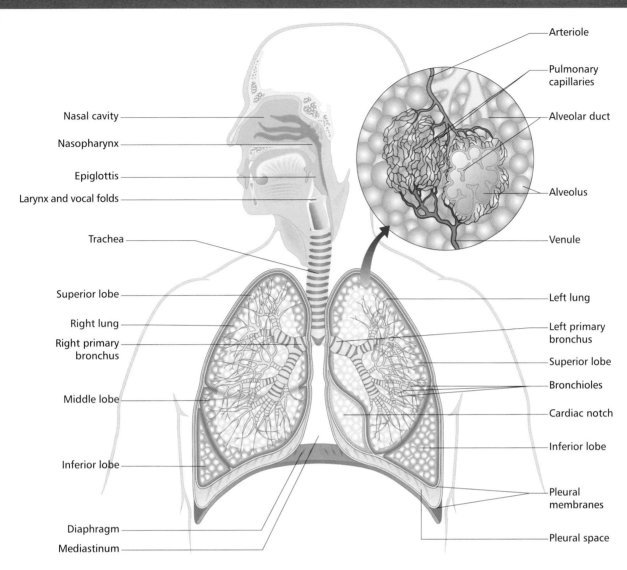

Figure 7.1 *The respiratory system*

7.1.4 *The trachea*

The trachea (or windpipe) is just over 10 cm long and is kept open and protected by C-shaped pieces of cartilage. The trachea is lined with mucus-secreting and ciliated cells. These cells remove foreign particles by pushing them back up towards the larynx. The trachea divides at the bottom to form the left and right bronchi.

7.1.5 *Bronchi*

The right bronchus enters the right lung and the left bronchus enters the left lung. From there the bronchi subdivide to form smaller branches called bronchioles. This structure is known as the *bronchial tree* and carries the air deep into the lungs.

7.1.6 *Bronchioles*

The walls of the bronchioles, unlike those of the bronchi, are not reinforced with cartilage but do contain smooth muscle. When this smooth muscle contracts, as occurs during an asthma attack, it can create severe breathing difficulties. The bronchioles continue to divide, forming *terminal bronchioles* that supply each lobule of the lungs. The terminal bronchioles merge into *respiratory bronchioles* that lead to alveolar air sacs, which contain the alveoli.

7.1.7 *Alveoli*

The alveoli are minute air-filled sacs. There are approximately 300 million alveoli in the lungs, providing a total surface area similar to that of a tennis court. The walls of the alveoli are extremely thin and are surrounded by capillaries. External respiration takes place here (Figure 7.2).

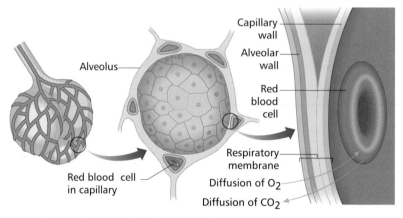

Figure 7.2 *The exchange of oxygen and carbon dioxide between an alveolus and capillary bed*

7.2 The lungs

DEFINITION

LOBULE

Lobules are subdivisions of each lobe of the lung and contain terminal and respiratory bronchioles, alveoli and blood vessels. They are enveloped in sheets of elastic connective tissue.

The two lungs lie in the thoracic cavity. The right lung has three lobes and the left lung two. The heart nestles between the lungs in the mediastinum. Each lobe of a lung is further divided into lobules, which are completely separate units.

Each lung is surrounded by a serous membrane, known as the *pleural membrane*, which lines the *pleural cavity*. The outer layer of the membrane is called the *parietal pleura* and is attached to the wall of the thoracic cavity. The inner layer is known as the *visceral pleura* and covers the lungs.

The pleural cavity contains *pleural fluid*, which holds the two membranes together and acts as a lubricant, reducing friction.

The lower part of the lung is bordered by the *diaphragm*, which separates the thoracic cavity from the abdominal cavity. The diaphragm is a sheet of skeletal muscle and plays an important role in the mechanics of breathing. The lungs receive deoxygenated blood from the heart via the right and left pulmonary arteries and return oxygenated blood to the heart via the pulmonary veins. The lungs' own supply of oxygenated blood is delivered by the bronchial artery.

7.3 Pulmonary ventilation

DEFINITION

SEROUS MEMBRANE

Serous membrane forms the lining of cavities within the body and secretes serous fluid.

Movement of air into and out of the lungs is known as *pulmonary ventilation*. Taking air into the lungs is called *inspiration* and moving air out of the lungs is called *expiration*. The amount of air moved per minute (the minute ventilation, $\dot{V}_E$) varies, depending on the amount of work being performed. As more work is done more energy is required, increasing the demand for oxygen, and so the rate of pulmonary ventilation increases.

At rest, the average rate of breathing is 12–15 breaths per minute and the average amount of air taken in or out per breath (the tidal volume) is 0.5 litres, giving a minute ventilation of 6–7.5 litres per minute.

$$\dot{V}_E = \text{Frequency} \times \text{Tidal volume}$$

At rest,

$$\dot{V}_E = 12 \times 0.5 \text{ litres}$$
$$\dot{V}_E = 6 \text{ litres.}$$

activity

Working in pairs, count how many breaths your partner takes in a minute. Why is it difficult to count your own rate of breathing and what does this imply about the breathing mechanism?

During strenuous exercise the volume of air breathed increases dramatically – up to 180 litres is not uncommon for male athletes. This increase is achieved by increasing the rate and depth of breathing. For example:

$$\dot{V}_E = \text{Frequency} \times \text{Tidal volume}$$
$$= 45 \times 3.5 \text{ litres}$$
$$= 157.5 \text{ litres}$$

In practice

The response of the breathing mechanism to exercise is very similar to the heart rate response (see Chapter 5).

in training

After a period of training pulmonary ventilation will, if anything, be lower at rest, because external respiration becomes more efficient. On the other hand, maximal values increase tremendously. An elite endurance athlete will normally be able to ventilate a maximum of about 180 litres/min. This increase is a combination of an increase in tidal volume and an increase in the rate of respiration.

activity

Complete as many sit-ups as you can in a minute. Get your partner to count the number of breaths you take in one minute after completing your exercise. Continue to monitor your rate of breathing until it returns to normal.

DEFINITION
MINUTE VENTILATION, $\dot{V}_E$
The amount of air taken into or out of the lungs in one minute. It is calculated by multiplying the number of breaths taken by the amount of air inspired or expired in one breath.

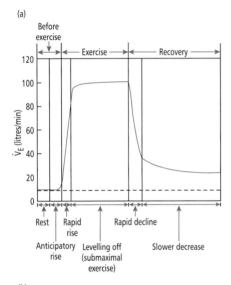
(a)

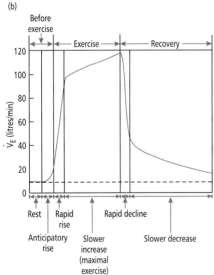
(b)

Figure 7.3 *The changes in ventilation rate during (a) submaximal and (b) maximal exercise*

As with the heart, there is an *anticipatory rise* in ventilation rate, followed by a steep increase and a plateau (during steady-state exercise) or a steady increase to maximum (during maximal exercise). Recovery after exercise shows a substantial initial drop then a gradual levelling off to normal ventilation rates (Figure 7.3).

7.4 The mechanics of breathing

In order for air to move into the lungs the pressure of air within the lungs must be lower than the pressure of air within the atmosphere. The greater the pressure difference is, the faster the air will flow into the lungs. This is because air always moves from an area of high pressure to an area of low pressure. By changing the volume of your thoracic cavity you can alter the pressure of air in your lungs. Reducing the volume will increase the pressure within the alveoli; increasing it will decrease the pressure within the alveoli. The muscles involved in ventilation are shown in Figure 7.4.

Table 7.1 *Summary of the muscles used in ventilation*

Ventilation phase	Muscles used in quiet breathing	Muscles used in laboured breathing
Inspiration	Diaphragm, external intercostals	Diaphragm, external intercostals, sternocleidomastoid, scalenes, pectoralis minor
Expiration	Passive	Internal intercostals, abdominals

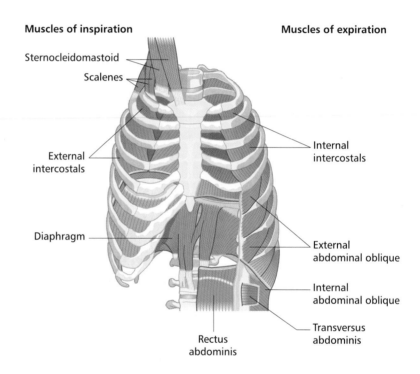

Figure 7.4
The muscles involved in ventilation

7.4.1 *Inspiration*

During inspiration the volume of the thoracic cavity must be increased so that the pressure of air within the lungs is lowered. The pressure of atmospheric air is about 100 kPa (760 mmHg) and during inspiration the pressure within the alveoli is lowered to 99.74 kPa (758 mmHg), causing air to move into the lungs.

During quiet inspiration reduction of pressure in the thorax is achieved in part by contraction of the diaphragm. Usually dome-shaped, the diaphragm flattens during contraction, increasing the volume of the thoracic cavity. At the same time the external *intercostal muscles* contract, pulling the ribs upwards and outwards and helping to increase the volume of the thoracic cavity.

When exercising, three more inspiratory muscles are involved as the rate and depth of breathing increases: *sternocleidomastoid* lifts the sternum and *scalenes* and *pectoralis minor* both help to further elevate the ribs. As the parietal pleura is attached to the wall of the thoracic cavity and the visceral pleura is attached to the lung tissue, the lung tissue is stretched as the thoracic cavity increases in size.

7.4.2 *Expiration*

During quiet breathing expiration is passive. The diaphragm and external intercostal muscles relax, reducing the volume of the thoracic cavity and the lung tissue recoils to its normal position. This increases the pressure within the alveoli so that it exceeds atmospheric pressure and forces air out of the lungs.

When exercising, expiration becomes active as air has to be forced out of the lungs quickly and effectively. The internal intercostal muscles help pull the ribs back downwards and inwards and the abdominal muscles contract, helping to push the diaphragm back upwards. The net result of this is to reduce the volume of the thoracic cavity (Figure 7.5).

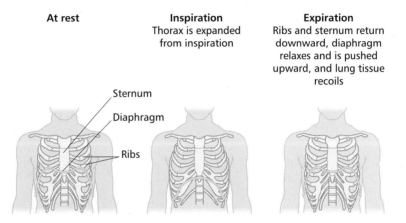

At rest

Inspiration
Thorax is expanded
from inspiration

Expiration
Ribs and sternum return
downward, diaphragm
relaxes and is pushed
upward, and lung tissue
recoils

Sternum

Diaphragm

Ribs

Figure 7.5 *The process of inspiration and expiration*

7.5 Respiratory volume

If you breathe normally for a few seconds and then at the end of expiration try to force more air out of your lungs, you will find you are able to breathe out a lot more air. Equally, if you breathe in normally and then continue to inhale as much air as possible you can take in considerably more air. This suggests that we have a 'working' volume of air that we ventilate normally, with a reserve volume available if we need it. This allows a great deal of flexibility in the amount of exercise we can perform, as we have the capacity to increase our ventilation in line with the increase in demand for oxygen. A normal healthy individual can easily ventilate more than enough air for any activity; the limiting factor is the amount of oxygen we can actually transport and use.

Several lung volumes have been identified (Table 7.2) using a spirometer to measure them. Figure 7.6 shows an example of the trace that a spirometer produces. Lung volumes are measured in litres, ml or dm^3. Table 7.3 shows the differences in lung volumes between an average male and an elite endurance runner.

Table 7.2 *Lung volumes*

Volume	Resting value (ml/dm³)	Definition
Tidal volume	500/0.5	The amount of air breathed in or out of the lungs in one breath
Inspiratory reserve volume	3100/3.1	The amount of air that can be forcibly inspired in addition to the tidal volume
Expiratory reserve volume	1200/1.2	The amount of air that can be forcibly expired in addition to the tidal volume
Vital capacity	4800/4.8	The maximum amount of air that can be forcibly exhaled after breathing in as much as possible
Residual volume	1200/1.2	Even after maximal expiration there is always some air left in the lungs to prevent them from collapsing
Total lung capacity	6000/6.0	The vital capacity plus the residual volume

Table 7.3 *Respiratory rates and volumes*

Respiratory rates and volumes	Average male	Elite endurance runner
Pulmonary ventilation at rest	7 l/min	6 l/min
Maximum pulmonary ventilation	110 l/min	195 l/min
Tidal volume at rest	0.5 l	0.5 l
Maximum tidal volume	2.75 l	3.9 l
Vital capacity	5.8 l	6.2 l
Residual volume	1.4 l	1.2 l

In practice

When you start to exercise, your 'working' volume (tidal volume) increases at the expense of your inspiratory reserve volume and your expiratory reserve volume, which decrease. You only rarely use your full vital capacity – for example, when taking a deep breath before swimming under water. Your tidal volume is usually increased in conjunction with an increase in breathing rate – it is not efficient to take fewer breaths and breathe to capacity.

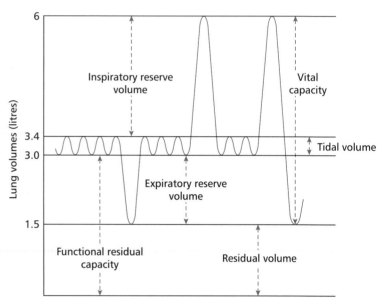

Figure 7.6 *Spirometer tracing, showing the main lung volumes of a normal adult male*

in training

Endurance training does not result in enormous changes to lung volumes. There is a slight increase in vital capacity at the expense of a reduced residual volume. Tidal volume appears to be unchanged at rest but does show an increase during maximal exercise.

Lung volumes differ with age, sex, body frame and aerobic fitness – but, as already mentioned, in most cases pulmonary ventilation is not a limiting factor in sporting performance.

To summarise,

Vital capacity = Tidal volume + Inspiratory reserve + Expiratory reserve

Total lung capacity = Residual volume + Vital capacity

activity

- If, when you are resting, you inspire 500 ml and inhale every six seconds,
- if, when you forcibly exhale to a maximum having just breathed out, you blow out another 1850 ml,
- if, when you fill your lungs to capacity and breathe out as much as you can, you exhale 4300 ml,

what would be your:

1 vital capacity
2 inspiratory reserve volume
3 expiratory reserve volume
4 minute ventilation?

7.5.1 *Asthma and pulmonary efficiency*

Asthma is becoming increasingly common and many elite and highly successful athletes are asthma sufferers. Asthma attacks occur when the smooth muscle of the bronchiole contracts, restricting the movement of air into the lungs. During an attack the mucous membranes also swell, further aggravating the situation. The person experiences anything from a shortage of breath to a feeling of fighting for breath. In most cases this contraction is triggered by an allergic reaction (for example, to dust or pollen). There is also a form of asthma that is exercise induced, in which an attack happens either shortly after exercise or up to six hours later. Factors that seem to influence exercise-induced asthma are:

* *The temperature and humidity of the inspired air*. Cold dry air is more likely to cause an adverse response than warm, moist air.
* *The type of exercise*. Running seems to set off an attack more readily than either cycling or walking. Swimming is less likely to trigger an attack as the inspired air is usually warm and moist (if in an indoor pool).
* *The time lapse between the last medication and the start of exercise*. It is best to keep an inhaler to hand and use it at the first signs of breathing complications.

To help reduce the likelihood of an attack the athlete suffering from asthma should always warm up thoroughly before exercising. The athlete should avoid exercising in cold, dry conditions and should consider cross-training (e.g. instead of running, go for a swim). If the air is cold a scarf can be worn around the lower part of the face to help warm it and retain moisture. Exercise sessions should generally be short in duration and the intensity kept submaximal. It should, however, be stressed that asthma sufferers can safely take part in all sports – although it is not considered advisable for an asthma sufferer to go scuba-diving.

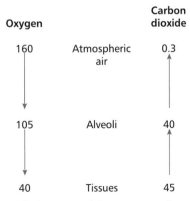

DEFINITION

PARTIAL PRESSURE

The partial pressure of a gas is the pressure it exerts within a mixture of gases.

7.6 External respiration

So far we have looked at how air is moved in and out of the lungs but we now need to consider the gaseous exchange that happens at the lungs' surface.

Gases flow from an area of high pressure to an area of low pressure. The term *partial pressure* is often used when describing the process of respiration: this refers to the pressure that a particular gas exerts within a mixture of gases and is linked to the concentration of the gas and the barometric pressure. At sea level the barometric pressure of air is 760 mmHg. Oxygen makes up 21% of air so oxygen in the atmosphere exerts a partial pressure of roughly 160 mmHg (21% of 760). By the time air reaches the alveoli the partial pressure of the oxygen has reduced to only 105 mmHg, but the partial pressure of oxygen in the alveoli is significantly higher than the partial pressure of the oxygen in the blood vessel surrounding the lungs, which is only 40 mmHg. This is because oxygen has been removed by the tissues so its concentration in the blood is lower, and its partial pressure is lower. The difference between the two pressures (105 – 40) is known as the *concentration gradient* or *diffusion gradient*. Oxygen will move from the area of higher pressure to the area of lower pressure

Partial pressure (mmHg) in:

Oxygen		Carbon dioxide
160	Atmospheric air	0.3
105	Alveoli	40
40	Tissues	45

Figure 7.7 *Summary of the movement of gases during external respiration*

in training

The drop in the partial pressure of oxygen at altitude makes it difficult to train aerobically at the same intensity as at sea level, resulting in detraining. This is because the diffusion gradient between the alveoli and the capillaries is reduced so that the haemoglobin is not fully saturated with oxygen. Therefore the amount of oxygen being supplied to the working muscles is also reduced. In addition the temperature drops and the air is much dryer so athletes can also suffer from dehydration. For more information on altitude training refer to Chapter 23.

DEFINITION

BUFFER

A substance (e.g. haemoglobin) that combines with either an acid or a base to help keep the body's pH at an optimal level.

(down the diffusion gradient) until there is a state of equilibrium. The greater the diffusion gradient is, the faster the diffusion will take place.

In the same way, carbon dioxide diffuses from the capillaries into the alveoli. The partial pressure of carbon dioxide in the alveoli is only 40 mmHg but it is 45 mmHg in the capillaries. Therefore carbon dioxide flows into the air in the alveoli and is expired.

A summary of the movement of the respiratory gases is given in Figure 7.7.

7.7 Internal respiration

The process described in the last section is reversed at the tissues because the cell is continuously using oxygen to produce ATP. This means that the partial pressure of oxygen is lower in the tissues than in the blood so it diffuses into the cell. At the same time, carbon dioxide is being produced continuously by the cell. This results in a higher partial pressure of carbon dioxide within the cell than in the blood, so it diffuses into the blood.

The lungs are designed to ensure that gaseous exchange takes place as quickly and effectively as possible. The most significant factor in terms of diffusion is the difference in the partial pressures of the gases, but the following factors all contribute to the efficiency of the process:

- the respiratory membrane is extremely thin
- the length of the diffusion path is very short
- the total surface area available for diffusion is very large.

7.8 Transport of respiratory gases

7.8.1 *Oxygen*

Oxygen diffuses into the capillaries, where 3% dissolves in plasma and about 97% combines with haemoglobin to form oxyhaemoglobin (see Chapter 6). Haemoglobin, when fully saturated, can carry four oxygen molecules and this happens easily at sea level where the pressure gradient between the alveoli and the blood is high. At the tissues the oxygen dissociates from the haemoglobin because of the relatively low pressure of oxygen in the tissues.

7.8.2 *Carbon dioxide*

Carbon dioxide is transported in one of three ways: 7% dissolves in plasma and 23% combines with haemoglobin; the remaining 70% dissolves in water to form carbonic acid. In the plasma this dissociates to hydrogen ions and bicarbonate ions. Hydrogen ions create a more acidic environment and the body needs to regulate the acid–base balance of the body by neutralising or buffering its effects. This is achieved by combining the hydrogen ions with haemoglobin, as haemoglobin acts as a major buffer within the blood:

$$CO_2 + H_2O \longrightarrow \underset{\text{(carbonic acid)}}{H_2CO_3} \longrightarrow \underset{\text{(bicarbonate ion)}}{H+ + HCO_3^-}$$

in training

An excess of hydrogen ions decreases the body's pH and interferes with ATP production and muscle contractility. Some athletes who perform in highly anaerobic events take sodium bicarbonate to help increase their plasma bicarbonate levels, in order to improve the blood's buffering capacity. This in turn enables the body to remove carbon dioxide and lactic acid more effectively during high-intensity workouts and therefore offset fatigue.

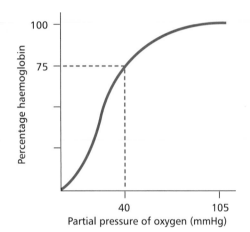

Figure 7.8 *The oxyhaemoglobin dissociation curve at 38°C and pH 7.4*

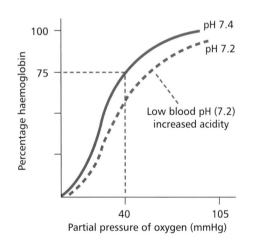

Figure 7.9 *Effect of pH on haemoglobin saturation – the Bohr effect*

7.8.3 *Haemoglobin saturation*

The relationship between oxygen and haemoglobin is often represented by the oxyhaemoglobin dissociation curve (Figure 7.8). The level of saturation of oxygen to the haemoglobin is affected by several factors.

* The *partial pressure of oxygen* influences the saturation of haemoglobin with oxygen. The partial pressure of oxygen at sea level is always high enough for full saturation of haemoglobin in the lungs. When the blood arrives at the tissues the partial pressure of oxygen drops, causing the oxygen to dissociate from the haemoglobin and diffuse into the cell. At high altitude the change in barometric pressure causes the partial pressure of oxygen to drop. This means that the haemoglobin is not fully saturated at the lungs and the oxygen-carrying capacity of the blood is decreased. This can cause problems for an athlete working at altitude.
* As *body temperature* increases the oxygen dissociates more easily from the haemoglobin.
* The *partial pressure of carbon dioxide*. As this increases, the dissociation of oxygen from haemoglobin increases. During exercise the amount of carbon dioxide produced by the cells increases, which helps to increase the diffusion of much-needed oxygen into the cell.
* *Change in pH*. As more carbon dioxide is produced the concentration of hydrogen ions in the blood increases, lowering the pH. A drop in pH causes oxygen to dissociate more easily – this is known as the *Bohr effect* and is shown in Figure 7.9.

A combination of these factors means that as we start to exercise the rate of diffusion of oxygen into the cells accelerates and helps to maintain a good supply of oxygen to the working tissues.

7.9 Control of breathing

Two factors are involved in the control of breathing:
* neural control
* chemical control.

7.9.1 *Neural control*

The respiratory centre in the medulla of the brain controls breathing. This centre is made up of two main areas.

- The *inspiratory centre* is responsible for the rhythmic cycle of inspiration and expiration.
- The *expiratory centre* is inactive during quiet ventilation. When the rate and depth of ventilation increases (detected by stretch receptors in the lungs) the expiratory centre inhibits the inspiratory centre and stimulates expiratory muscles.

Neural control of breathing is summarised in Figure 7.10. In most circumstances the nervous regulation of breathing is involuntary. The respiratory centre sends out nerve impulses via the phrenic and intercostal nerves to the respiratory muscles. The muscles are stimulated for a short period, causing inspiration. Then, when the stimulus stops, expiration occurs.

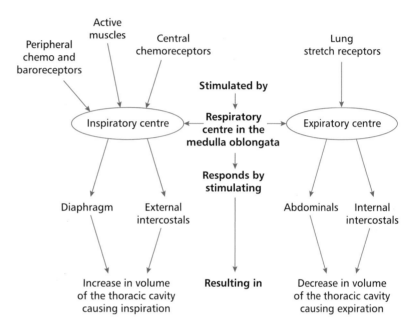

Figure 7.10
Neural control of breathing

The respiratory centre responds mainly to changes in the chemistry and temperature of the blood. The most significant factor is an increase in hydrogen ions in the blood (lowering of blood pH), which occurs when the amount of carbon dioxide being produced by the cells increases. This increase is detected by the respiratory centre and results in an increase in the rate and depth of breathing. A rise in body temperature will cause an increase in the rate of breathing but does not affect the depth of breathing.

Other factors influencing neural control of breathing include:
- A large drop in oxygen tension. This is monitored by the chemoreceptors in the aorta and carotid arteries and results in an increase in the rate and depth of breathing.
- A rise in blood pressure, monitored by the baroreceptors in the aorta and carotid arteries, resulting in a decrease in ventilation rate.
- Proprioceptors in the muscles responding to movement stimulate the respiratory centre, increasing the rate and depth of breathing.
- The respiratory centre can also be affected by higher centres in the brain, for example emotional influences.

The lungs have a safety mechanism to make sure that they are never over-inflated. Stretch receptors located in the walls of the bronchi and bronchioles respond during excessive respiration by sending messages to the respiratory centre to inhibit inspiration. This is known as the *Hering–Breuer* reflex.

The response of the respiratory system to exercise should never really be considered in isolation – if a change occurs in the respiratory system then similar changes usually occur in the cardiac and vascular systems. For example, an increase in blood temperature will cause an increase in heart rate, an increase in ventilation and dilation of the vessels supplying the skin and working muscles. The response of all three systems is coordinated to ensure efficient delivery of oxygen and removal of carbon dioxide and other waste products.

Key revision points

The amount of air required by the body varies considerably, depending on the amount of oxygen used by the cells. This is why we have a 'working' volume of air (tidal volume) plus a reserve volume available (inspiratory and expiratory reserve volumes). The respiratory control centre works in conjunction with the cardiac control centre and the vasomotor control centre to ensure a coordinated response to oxygen demand and delivery.

Key terms

You should now understand the following terms. If you do not, go back through the chapter and find out what they mean.

Alveoli
Bohr effect
Diffusion gradient
Expiratory reserve volume
External respiration
Inspiratory reserve volume
Internal respiration
Minute ventilation
Partial pressure
Pleural membrane
Pulmonary ventilation
Respiratory centre
Tidal volume
Vital capacity

Progress check

1   Define respiration.
2   List the respiratory structures that air passes through from the nose to the alveoli.
3   How is air filtered?
4   Define pulmonary ventilation.
5   What is the relationship between minute ventilation, respiratory frequency and tidal volume?
6   What happens to minute ventilation during exercise?
7   Draw a graph to show the response of the respiratory system to 10 minutes of submaximal exercise followed by a five-minute recovery period.
8   How does the movement of the ribs and diaphragm affect the volume of the thoracic cavity?
9   Which inspiratory muscles are used only during laboured breathing?
10 Describe the pressure changes that cause air to move into and out of the lungs.
11 What is meant by the term partial pressure?
12 List the ways that oxygen and carbon dioxide are transported in the blood.
13 What factors influence the oxygen saturation of haemoglobin?
14 Explain what is meant by the Bohr effect and describe what effect it has on the transport of oxygen during exercise.
15 How is respiration regulated during exercise?
16 Define tidal volume, inspiratory reserve volume and expiratory reserve volume.
17 What effect does exercise have on these three volumes?
18 Complete the following equation:
    Tidal volume + Inspiratory volume + Expiratory reserve = ?
19 Why might an athlete take sodium bicarbonate?
20 Identify the changes that occur to the lung volumes after a period of endurance training.

Further reading

Glen F. Bastian. *An Illustrated Review of Anatomy and Physiology*. 1: The Skeletal and Muscular Systems. 2: The Cardiovascular System. 3: The Respiratory System. Harper Collins College Publishers, 1994.

C. Clegg. *Exercise Physiology and Functional Anatomy*. Feltham Press, 1995.

R.J. Davis, C.R. Bull, J.V. Roscoe and D.A. Roscoe. *Physical Education and the Study of Sport*. Wolfe Medical Publishers, 1991.

D. Davis, T. Kimmet and M. Auty. *Physical Education: Theory and Practice*. Macmillan, Australia, 1986.

E. Fox, R. Bowen and M. Foss. *The Physiological Basis for Exercise and Sport*. Brown and Benchmark, 1989.

W. Kapit and L.M. Elson. *The Anatomy Colouring Book*. Harper Collins College Publishers, 1993.

H.G.Q. Rowett. *Basic Anatomy and Physiology*. John Murray, 1975.

R.R. Seeley, T.D. Stephens and P. Tate. *Essentials of Anatomy and Physiology*. Mosby Year Book Publishers, 1995.

Clem W. Thompson. *Manual of Structural Kinesiology*. Times Mirror/Mosby College Publishing, 1989.

Peter Walder. *Mechanics and Sport Performance*. Feltham Press, 1994.

J.H. Wilmore and D.L. Costill. *Physiology of Sport and Exercise* 2nd edition. Human Kinetics, 1999.

R. Wirhed. *Athletic Ability and the Anatomy of Motion*. Wolfe Medical Publishers, 1989.

Part 2

SKILL ACQUISITION

In this part of the book we will investigate how we learn movement skills associated with physical education and sport. The process of motor learning can only be understood by studying the nature of skill and its characteristics. The more we know about a particular skill, the better we are placed to devise teaching strategies to teach that skill. The importance of fundamental motor skills is stressed because these are the building blocks of future skill learning. We will also look in detail at theories related to the learning of skills. There are no 'watertight' theories about learning because the human brain is such a complex organ, but this part highlights the relevant theories widely accepted by sports psychologists. Finally, this part deals with theories related to the teaching of skills. Effective teaching is dependent on a number of factors, including the personality, level of knowledge and ability of the teacher. To optimise the learning environment the teacher or coach must consider the research underpinning good practice – including the structure of training sessions, the type of guidance given and the possible teaching styles that can be adopted.

CHAPTER 8

Skill and its characteristics

Learning objectives

- To be able to explain what we mean by the term skill and the importance of fundamental motor skills.
- To be able to differentiate between skill and ability.
- To be able to understand task analysis and to classify skill in a number of different ways.
- To understand what is meant by individual, coactive and interactive skills.
- To link our ideas to practical situations.

Are skilful people born that way or do they learn their skills? It seems that the answer is probably a mixture of both. We all have abilities that are thought to be predetermined genetically and these dictate our potential to be skilful. The acquisition of fundamental motor skills is probably undervalued in a child's early development. It is crucial that we are aware of what we actually mean by skill and whether we can affect future performance. The classification of skill is not an exact science, but for us to teach and learn skills we must analyse the task to be performed so that we fully understand how to put movements into action. There may for instance be common actions needed for a range of different skills. If this is the case, then once we have identified these common actions, we can teach them or learn them so that we can transfer them between skills and activities.

8.1 The concept and nature of skill

MOTOR SKILL

An action or task that has a goal and that requires voluntary body and/or limb movement to achieve the goal.

FUNDAMENTAL MOTOR SKILLS

Skills such as throwing a ball or jumping or kicking a ball. We learn these skills at a young age, usually through play, and if they are learned thoroughly, a child can move on to the more sophisticated actions that are required in sport.

We learn fundamental motor skills at a young age

For the activity (left), you probably thought of *fluent*, *coordinated* and *controlled* and phrases like '*seems effortless*', '*looks good*' and '*good technique*'.

We often comment that an experienced sportsperson is 'skilful', but what do we actually mean by the word 'skill'? We use it to describe a task such as kicking a ball, but often we use it to describe the overall actions of someone who is good at what they do. There are two main ways of using the word 'skill':

- to see skill as a specific task to be performed
- to view skill as describing the quality of a particular action, which might include how consistent the performance is and how prepared the performer is to carry out the task.

When we see top-class sportsmen and sportswomen we are often struck by the seemingly effortless way that they perform, and it is not until we try to perform ourselves that we realise just how difficult it really is! We know that these performers are very fit but they don't seem to exert themselves and we are aware that whatever the skill – whether it is a somersault in gymnastics or a perfectly timed rugby tackle – the end product looks good and is aesthetically pleasing. A skilled performer knows what he or she is trying to achieve and more often than not is successful, which is annoying if you are their opponent! A beginner, or novice, will seem clumsy and slow and will lack control. The novice will also tire quickly and expend more energy than is necessary.

When an accomplished hockey player, for instance, performs a skilful pass, he or she shows a technically good movement. This movement is called the *motor skill*.

A skilled hockey player needs both motor skills and perceptual skill

8.1.1 *Fundamental motor skills*

Fundamental motor skills are skills such as throwing, catching and running. These skills are important because they provide the basis for other skills. Without acquiring the fundamental motor skills, it is unlikely that a person would be able to excel in a sports activity. These skills provide the platform on which we can build the more advanced skills demanded in our sports. Acquisition of these essential skills also helps us to follow a lifestyle that is healthy. As we get older, we may draw on many fundamental motor skills to follow

If a tennis player often serves 'aces' in a match, we would label that player as skilled. If we watched him over a number of matches and he continued to serve aces, we would be more justified in labelling him as skilled. A squash player whom we might regard as skilled would anticipate where the ball is going to land and would put herself in a position to receive the ball early so that she could hit it early, thus putting her opponent at a disadvantage.

DEFINITION

PERCEPTION

A complex concept that involves interpretation of stimuli. Not all stimuli are perceived and what is perceived depends on past experience and attention ability. For a detailed explanation of perception see the section on Information Processing on page 104.

lifetime sports, such as golf. Acquiring fundamental motor skills can help children build their self-esteem and make them more accepted in group 'play' situations.

The player also has to assess the position of the opponents and the players on the same team and will have to decide where to pass the ball and how hard to pass it. This interpretation of information or stimuli is called *perception* and the skill required is called *perceptual skill.*

For skill acquisition to take place the person also needs *cognitive skills*. These skills are intellectually based and are linked to working out or solving problems; they underpin verbal reasoning. These skills are often seen as innate, although there is considerable debate among psychologists as to how intelligence is acquired and whether there is only one or many ways that people can show intelligence. For instance, is a football player showing intelligence when he selects a particular skill to be used in a particular situation?

Definition

When we talk of skill, we usually mean a combination of perceptual, cognitive and motor skills.

Skilled performers are not born with most motor skills already programmed in their minds – they have to learn them in a number of different ways. The ways in which we learn skills are investigated in Chapter 9.

'Skill' has been defined in the following way:

> A skilled movement is one in which a predetermined objective is accomplished with maximum efficiency with a minimum outlay of energy.

Key revision points
The main characteristics of skilled movement: learned, goal directed, predetermined goals, consistent achievement, economy of movement, efficiency, coordinated, precise, aesthetically pleasing, fluent, controlled. Motor skills involve fundamental movement patterns and perceptual and cognitive skills.

Your own sport will require fundamental motor skills, more advanced motor skills and perceptual skills. Highlight a few examples of both.

The abilities of balance, strength and flexibility are necessary before you can perform a headstand. A frisbee catch needs the underlying abilities of hand–eye coordination and perceptual awareness.

8.2 Ability

We often talk about improving our own abilities and those of other people, but we probably usually mean 'skills' rather than 'abilities'. Skills are, as we now know, learned and involve often pre-planned movements that are goal directed. To carry out skills, we need certain underlying factors such as strength and hand–eye coordination. These factors are known as *abilities*.

Certain skills require specific abilities

activity

List the abilities required for the following sports: tennis, rugby, snooker, golf, netball.

Our abilities are largely determined genetically – they are *natural* or *innate* – and they tend to be enduring characteristics. This is bad news for some of us who would like to get to the top of our sport but who don't have the natural ability to do so because, no matter how hard we try, we may never reach those giddy heights. We simply may not have the necessary innate qualities. However, research has revealed that some abilities can be enhanced to a certain extent, especially in early childhood.

In the activity (left) you may have listed hand–eye coordination for tennis, strength for rugby, fine motor control for snooker, flexibility for golf, and speed for netball. All of these abilities are found in most sports but their importance to the execution of skills and techniques varies with the particular sport. It would be nice to suppose that there is a general 'sporting ability' which underpins most sports, but research to date does not support this. Several specific abilities help form the foundation for certain sporting skills – two of the most important are *psychomotor* and *gross motor* abilities.

Certain skills require specific abilities or sets of abilities but most motor skills involve the abilities of strength, speed and coordination.

A study for the National Aeronautics and Space Administration in the USA by Parker *et al.* (1965) identified basic perceptual-motor abilities classified into four categories:

1 Fine manipulative abilities:
   a   arm–hand steadiness
   b   holding arm and hand steady while fully extended
   c   wrist–finger speed
   d   making rapid, repetitive tapping movements
   e   finger dexterity
   f   manipulating small objects with fingers
   g   manual dexterity
   h   manipulating large objects with hand.
2 Gross positioning and movement abilities:
   a   position estimation
   b   reaching for specific locations without use of vision
   c   response orientation
   d   making appropriate directional response to non-spatial stimulus
   e   control precision
   f   making fine, controlled positioning movements
   g   speed of arm movement
   h   making discrete, rapid arm movements
   i   multi-limb coordination
   j   using hands and/or feet simultaneously
   k   position reproduction
   l   repeating discrete arm–hand movement without aid of vision.
3 System equalisation abilities:
   a   movement analysis
   b   differentiating target velocity and acceleration
   c   movement prediction
   d   integrating target motion components to estimate future target position
   e   rate control
   f   control vehicle having first-order system dynamics
   g   acceleration control
   h   control vehicle having second-order system dynamics.

DEFINITION

PSYCHOMOTOR ABILITY
Our ability to process information regarding movement and then to put our decisions into action. Psychomotor abilities include reaction time and limb coordination.

GROSS MOTOR ABILITY
Ability involving actual movement – strength, flexibility, speed.

4 Perceptual–cognitive abilities:
   a   perceptual speed
   b   making rapid visual comparisons of display elements
   c   time sharing
   d   dividing attention among several displays
   e   reaction time
   f   responding as rapidly as possible to discrete signal
   g   mirror tracing
   h   using mirror-image display to perform directional hand–arm movements.

Fleishman (1964) developed a 'taxonomy of human perceptual motor abilities'. His results were based on perceptual motor tests given to many different people. After his experiments he identified 11 measurable perceptual motor abilities:

1   multi-limb coordination, e.g. the coordination of arms and legs in the high jump
2   control precision, e.g. the fine-tuning of muscular actions in a snooker shot
3   response orientation, e.g. quick decision making about the type of pass to be made in hockey
4   reaction time, e.g. processing information quickly to choose a shot in cricket
5   speed of arm movement, e.g. moving the arm rapidly in the javelin throw
6   rate control, e.g. change speed and direction accurately to track the target in clay pigeon shooting
7   manual dexterity, e.g. well-directed arm/hand movements in catching a frisbee
8   finger dexterity, e.g. finger control in darts throwing
9   arm–hand steadiness, e.g. precise arm/hand movement in crown green bowls
10 wrist, finger speed, e.g. wrist/finger speed in spin bowling
11 aiming, e.g. aiming in archery.

Physical proficiency abilities (gross motor abilities) include:
• static strength, e.g. prop forward in rugby
• dynamic strength, e.g. press-ups
• explosive strength, e.g. long-jump take-off
• trunk strength, e.g. strength of trunk muscles used in gymnastics
• extent flexibility, e.g. flexing and stretching back muscles in trampolining
• dynamic flexibility, e.g. repeated trunk flexing movements in toe touching
• gross body coordination, e.g. coordination of several parts of the body in motion as in a cricket bowler
• gross body equilibrium, e.g. maintaining balance without visual cues in a rugby scrum
• stamina, e.g. capacity to sustain maximum effort in a marathon race.

Others may include: dynamic and static balance, visual acuity and tracking, eye–hand coordination.

There are also intellectual abilities to be considered such as memory abilities and speed/accuracy in making perceptions and solving problems, all of which can be important in the performance of motor skills in sport.

In some skills, abilities which contribute to performance early on in the learning process, during the cognitive stage of learning, are not necessarily the same abilities that contribute to later performances. Fleishman (1964) comments:

> Abilities can be thought of as capacities for utilising different kinds of information. Thus, individuals who are especially good at using certain types of spatial information, make rapid progress in the early stages of learning certain kinds of motor tasks, while individuals sensitive to proprioceptive cues do better in tasks requiring precise motor control.

8.2.1 *The general and specific views of abilities*

Top sportspeople are popularly thought to possess an overall single ability to perform well. Many researchers believe in many different specific motor abilities, but if these abilities were very closely related then a 'general' motor ability could exist. Some individuals seem to be very good at many different sports, which seems to back the idea of a general motor ability. The presence of a general motor ability could be explained by viewing the performer as having a high degree of prowess in *groups* of abilities. For example, a good all-round sportsperson may have good balance, speed and hand–eye coordination. It would therefore follow that this person is likely to be good at a wide range of sports involving these abilities. However, there is no firm evidence to support the notion that there is such a thing as general motor ability.

Some researchers have looked into ways of predicting athletic prowess after an individual's abilities have been identified. Tests have been performed on young people to find out their abilities and then link these abilities to certain sports. This has not been very successful because different abilities are needed at different stages of skill learning. For instance, good vision and the ability to process information rapidly are important when beginning to learn a complex task, but kinaesthesis is more important in the later stages. Ability tests cannot, therefore, be used to predict accurately sporting prowess.

DEFINITION

KINAESTHESIS

This is the information we hold within ourselves about our body's position. The information comes from receptors found in the muscles, tendons and joints. The term proprioception is often used in the same way.

> ### *Key revision points*
> *We are all born with certain abilities. Before we can be proficient at skills we must have the abilities that help us to perform these skills. There is no single 'general' motor ability but there are many specific abilities – such as manual dexterity or physical strength. A good all-round athlete probably develops through many complex and interlinking factors, such as body type, innate ability, personality, parental support and other socialising factors.*

8.3 Classification of skill

In order to understand fully the nature of a particular skill, we need to analyse it. The traditional way of doing this is by classification, but this can be very unsatisfactory and inaccurate because skills have many characteristics which can change in different situations. For example, catching a frisbee involves large and small muscle movements and involves the catcher adjusting his or her movements according to the varied flight of the frisbee. It is very difficult to classify skills neatly, but to make teaching and learning more effective it is essential that we understand skills fully.

8.3.1 *Analysis of skills*

If we accept that skills cannot be neatly labelled, the best means of analysis is to use a scale or continuum which will illustrate that skills have different characteristics to a greater or lesser extent. The skill in a tennis serve, for instance, has elements of fine muscle movements and gross muscle movements, but we would probably agree that it involves more gross muscle movements. We might place the skill of the tennis serve at X on a continuum like that in Figure 8.1.

Catching a frisbee involves large and small muscle movements

Gross ————— **X** ————————————————————————— **Fine**

Figure 8.1 *Skills should be assessed on a continuum*

Most skill classification systems are based on the view that motor skills are affected by three factors:

1 how precise a movement is
2 whether the movement has a definite beginning and end
3 whether the environment affects the performance of the skill.

The following words and phrases are often used in the classification of skills. Always remember to classify skills according to a continuum because this reflects the true, although complex, nature of skill.

The gross–fine continuum

This is concerned with the precision of movement.

Gross skills involve large muscle movements. These skills are not very precise and include many of the fundamental movement patterns such as walking and jumping. An example of a skill which is predominantly gross is the shot-put.

Fine skills involve more intricate movements using small muscle groups. These skills tend to be precise in nature and generally involve a high degree of hand–eye coordination. An example of a fine motor skill is a snooker shot.

The open–closed continuum

This continuum is concerned with the effects of the environment on skills.

Open skills are affected by the environment and are, therefore, predominantly perceptual. Movements have to be adapted to the environment and the skill is mostly externally paced – for example, a pass in football.

Closed skills are not affected by the environment and are predominantly habitual. Movements follow a set pattern and have a definite beginning and end. These skills tend to be self-paced. An example of a closed skill is a free throw in basketball.

activity

Choose a skill from either soccer or netball and attempt to classify it. Remember to use a continuum. Now analyse the skill or task more closely. Identify the sub-routines and the underlying abilities which are needed for effective execution of the skill.

In practice

A tennis serve is a skill which involves a set pattern of movement. It is not greatly affected by the environment, so it is more closed than open. If the server perceives some movement of their opponent the serve will need some adjustment and therefore there are open elements to the skill – but it still remains predominantly closed.

In practice

A novice rugby player who is about to tackle an opponent is not concentrating fully on the movement of the opponent, but will be distracted by the movement of other players.

The 'pacing' continuum

This is often used in conjunction with the open–closed continuum and refers to the timing of movements.

Self-paced skills. The performer controls the rate at which the skill is executed. Self-pacing involves proaction by the performer. Self-paced skills are usually closed skills – an example is a javelin throw.

Externally paced skills. The environment, which may include your opponent, controls the rate of performing the skill. This type of skill involves reaction and is usually an open skill such as receiving a serve in badminton.

The discrete–serial–continuous continuum

This is concerned with how well defined the beginning and end of the skill are.

Discrete skills have a clear beginning and a clear end. The skill can be repeated but the performer must start again from the beginning. It is a single, specific skill. A penalty flick in hockey is an example of such a skill.

Serial skills have several discrete elements which are put together to make an integrated movement or sequence of movements – for example the sequence of skills in a triple jump.

Continuous skills have no obvious beginning or end – the end of one cycle of movement is the beginning of the next. The skill is repeated as a set pattern, for example cycling.

8.3.2 *Individual, coactive and interactive skills*

Another method of describing groups of skills is to group them according to whether the skill is performed without reference to another player, whether there are others involved (called coactors) or whether the skill is dependent upon interaction with the environment. For example, throwing the javelin is an individual skill, blocking in volleyball is a coactive skill and many skills associated with sailing could be seen as interactive with the environment. However, with any system of classification, it is very difficult to put skills into particular boxes. Skills can be seen as partly individual, partly coactive and partly interactive. The process of analysing is important because it gives us clues to how we should be practising a skill.

activity

Draw an open–closed continuum and place the following skills on it: long-jump, netball catch, hockey penalty flick, pistol shooting, basketball dribble, receiving a serve in badminton, a vault in gymnastics.

activity

Group the following according to whether they are individual, coactive or interactive: bowling in cricket, mountain biking, front-row scrummaging in rugby, stopping the ball in hockey, road racing in cycling, turning in snowboarding, forming a defensive wall in football.

8.4 Task analysis

This involves the teacher of skills understanding what needs to be taught in a detailed way so that a plan of what needs to be taught, when and where can be formulated. The information can be gathered by analysing the skill or task by using the classification systems already described. The analysis should reveal the specific abilities required for a particular skill. These abilities can then be used to develop the *sub-routines* that make up the skill. All of this information can enable coaches and teachers to identify why a particular movement is not being skilfully executed. Once the cause of the problem is isolated then a strategy of eliminating the problem can be put into action.

DEFINITION

SUB-ROUTINES

The elements, or separate movements, that make up a particular skill. For example striking a ball in hockey involves grip, stance, backlift, forward swing, strike and follow through.

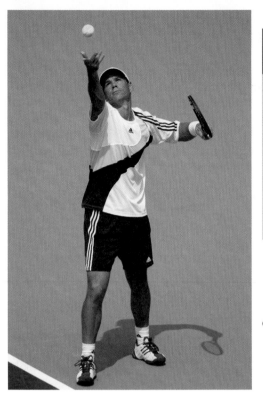

The server uses a pattern of movement but can also perceive the movement of his opponent

In practice

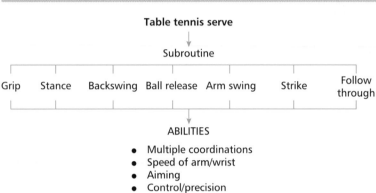

A hockey coach wishes to find out why a particular player cannot flick the ball effectively: she gets no height or speed on the ball and consequently any penalty flick that she may be asked to execute is a hopeless failure! The coach analyses the task, which is the hockey flick. She identifies the sub-routines and the abilities that underpin them and finds out that much of the power needed comes from the transfer of power or momentum from the leg muscles. She plans a training programme to develop strength and power in the player's leg muscles in the hope that this will eventually increase the player's skill in flicking the ball.

Table tennis serve

↓

Subroutine

| Grip | Stance | Backswing | Ball release | Arm swing | Strike | Follow through |

↓

ABILITIES

- Multiple coordinations
- Speed of arm/wrist
- Aiming
- Control/precision
- Rate control
- Static strength
- Trunk strength
- Flexibility

Figure 8.2
Task analysis: a table tennis serve

8.4.1 *Using our knowledge of skill classification*

The coach or teacher and the performer must be able to identify the important aspects of skills. A better understanding of the nature of the task is essential if the task is to be completed skilfully. A knowledge of which stimuli to attend to and which to ignore will help the performer ignore irrelevant information. The coach can also guide the performer towards making the right decisions.

Knowing how to classify skills can help to decide on the type of teaching/learning strategies that will optimise performance – it might be appropriate to split a skill up into its component parts (its sub-routines) if it is serial in nature, or to build strength of large muscles if the skill is predominantly gross in nature. Knowledge of the perceptual requirements of a skill will also help the performer to take in the correct amount and type of information so that there is no *attentional wastage*.

The learning of closed skills is more effective if they are practised repetitively so that the skills become almost 'automatic'. The constancy of the environment makes variable practice unnecessary and often distracting.

When coaching or teaching open skills a variety of situations should be experienced so that the performer can create a number of different strategies to cope with the changing nature of the environment.

DEFINITION

ATTENTIONAL WASTAGE

The performer's concentration can be misdirected to irrelevant cues. This can damage the effectiveness of their performance, and will particularly affect the way a novice learns.

Discrete skills are better taught as a whole rather than splitting them up into sub-routines. Serial skills are better taught by breaking them down into sub-routines. Each sub-routine can then be learned fully before the skill is practised as a whole.

Continuous skills are more effectively practised as a whole so that the kinaesthetic sense of the movement can be retained and the performer can feel the 'true nature' of the skill.

The importance of knowing all there is to know about the skill to be attempted cannot be overstated. It is particularly important at the top level of performance, where only a small difference in technique or tactics can mean the all-important advantage over your opponent.

Coaches who work with performers with disabilities can make important differences to physical performance using their knowledge of skill composition to ensure effective instruction (see Chapter 10).

Knowledge and skill will help to optimise performance

Key revision points

Skills are classified on a continuum. Knowledge of the task/skills gives good insight into movement requirements and teaching strategies. For example, receiving a pass in lacrosse is predominantly perceptual and therefore more of an open skill. A coach would adopt the strategy of giving a player experience in a variety of different situations (see section on schema, page 113).

Key terms

You should now understand the following terms. If you do not, go back through the chapter and find out what they mean.

- Ability
- Attentional wastage
- Cognitive skill
- Continuum
- Discrete, continuous and serial skills
- Fundamental motor skills
- Gross and fine skills
- Gross motor ability
- Kinaesthesis
- Motor skill
- Open and closed skills
- Perception
- Perceptual skill
- Psychomotor ability
- Self-paced and externally paced skills
- Stimuli
- Sub-routines
- Task analysis

Progress check

1 What are the main characteristics of a skilled performer?
2 What is meant by a motor skill?
3 What is a perceptual skill?
4 Give the main differences between skill and ability.
5 Why is there no such thing as general sporting ability?
6 What is meant by the term psychomotor ability?
7 What is meant by the term gross motor ability?
8 Why are ability tests unable to predict sporting prowess?
9 Define kinaesthesis.
10 How could early childhood experiences influence abilities?
11 Why can't we classify skills accurately?
12 What does the term 'continuum' mean in skill classification?
13 What is the gross/fine continuum?
14 Why are open skills predominantly perceptual?
15 If discrete is at one end of a continuum, what should be at the other?
16 Why is a triple jump a serial skill?
17 What is meant by an externally paced skill?
18 How can a skill be a closed skill in an open situation?
19 Why would a teacher or coach split a skill up into sub-routines?
20 How can knowledge related to skill classification help a coach of a disabled athlete?

Theories related to the learning of skills

- To understand the associative and cognitive theories of learning.
- To understand the theory of information processing, including the role of memory.
- To understand the concepts of motor programmes and schema.
- To investigate different types of feedback.
- To understand the role of mental practice in the learning and performance of motor skills.

The human brain is an enormously complex organ and the way in which it receives information, processes it, retains it and then sends messages to our body to move can be explained using a number of different theories and ideas. None of these theories and ideas are watertight but they help to explain in easy terms how our brain operates, particularly when we learn. When we acquire skills we must be motivated to learn and see some benefit in it. In this chapter we will explore the well-established theories of conditioning. We will then investigate why and how we are motivated to learn and how our brains receive and sort information. An important component for learning is our memory. We investigate in simple terms how we remember things and why we forget. As well as practising physically it is important to think about what we are doing and to make sense of our environment. We will be looking into how we mentally rehearse skills and the benefits of such mental practice.

9.1 The associationist or connectionist view of conditioning

The term *associationist* is given to a group of theories related to connecting *stimulus* and *response*. These theories are often referred to as *S–R theories*. An individual is conditioned by stimuli which are 'connected' or 'bonded' to appropriate responses.

A sprinter off the blocks is a response which is closely 'bonded' to the stimulus of the gun

9.1.1 *Classical conditioning*

In classical conditioning an existing S–R connection is replaced by a new bonding. The most famous example of classical conditioning was carried out by Pavlov. Pavlov's experiments with dogs show that pairing an unconditioned stimulus with a conditioned stimulus can eventually result in a conditioned response. Pavlov gave food to his dogs (this is the unconditioned or natural stimulus) and the dogs' natural response (the unconditioned response) was to salivate. Pavlov then rang a bell at the same time as presenting the food. The dogs salivated because of the food, but were unknowingly connecting the arrival of food with the sound of the bell. When the bell was rung again later the dogs still salivated even if no food was presented. The dogs' natural behaviour had now been changed through manipulation of the stimulus – their response became conditioned.

This process is also known as a *conditioned reflex*.

A coach shouts 'now' when it is time for a performer to open out from a somersault

In practice

A coach shouts 'now' to a performer when it is time to open out from a somersault. The performer learns to connect the word 'now' with the kinaesthetic 'feel' of the movement at that exact time. Eventually, the word 'now' becomes redundant because the performer has been conditioned by associating the unconditioned stimulus (kinaesthesis) with the conditioned stimulus ('now') to get the conditioned response (opening out at the right time). In the teaching of motor skills the practice of motor drills, where movements become almost habitual and bad habits are kept to a minimum, is common.

Key revision points

Unconditioned stimulus (food) ⟶ *Unconditioned response (salivation)*

Unconditioned stimulus +
Conditioned stimulus (bell) ⟶ *Unconditioned response*
Conditioned stimulus ⟶ *Conditioned response*

Conditioning is important in the natural environment – for instance, animals learn to recognise other dangerous animals by certain characteristics such as skin colour and avoid coming into contact with them. Conditioning usually allows modification of behaviour to ensure maximum rewards and to avoid punishment. In human behaviour phobias are often the result of conditioning in childhood, including the concept of learned helplessness in sport (see page 300). By punishing their children parents could cause conditioned fear. It has been suggested that when this fear cannot be overcome aggression may result, becoming displaced and directed towards other targets. This may explain aggression in sports performers and some spectators. It is difficult to relate classical conditioning with sports performance, but there are times when a stimulus is manipulated to get a desired response.

activity

Try to think of another example in the teaching of motor skills of a response that has been conditioned using another stimulus. What are the drawbacks of this type of teaching?

The main problem with the 'drill' style of teaching motor skills is that the performer can't gain a real understanding of why he or she is doing something. This lack of understanding can have a detrimental effect on future development of skills.

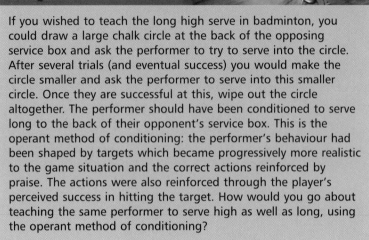

In practice

If you wished to teach the long high serve in badminton, you could draw a large chalk circle at the back of the opposing service box and ask the performer to try to serve into the circle. After several trials (and eventual success) you would make the circle smaller and ask the performer to serve into this smaller circle. Once they are successful at this, wipe out the circle altogether. The performer should have been conditioned to serve long to the back of their opponent's service box. This is the operant method of conditioning: the performer's behaviour had been shaped by targets which became progressively more realistic to the game situation and the correct actions reinforced by praise. The actions were also reinforced through the player's perceived success in hitting the target. How would you go about teaching the same performer to serve high as well as long, using the operant method of conditioning?

9.1.2 *Operant conditioning*

Work undertaken by Skinner revealed that conditioning was more effective through manipulation of behaviour towards a stimulus than through modification of the stimulus. Skinner used a box with a rat inside it. If the rat hit a lever inside the box a food pellet would be released. Through trial and error the rat eventually learned that hitting the lever would produce food. This has become known as *operant conditioning* or *trial and error learning*. Hitting the lever gave food and therefore a reward, which *reinforced* the hitting action. Operant conditioning is concerned with actions being 'shaped' and then reinforced. Conditioning of this type will only take place if reinforcement is present.

Operant conditioning, a process of shaping behaviour occurring. Reinforcement strengthens the S–R bond

DEFINITION

REINFORCEMENT
The process that increases the probability of a behaviour occurring. Reinforcement strengthens the S–R bond.

POSITIVE REINFORCEMENT
A stimulus which increases the probability of a desired response occurring.

NEGATIVE REINFORCEMENT
The stimulus is withdrawn when the desired response occurs.

PUNISHMENT
Giving a stimulus to prevent a response occurring. Not to be confused with negative reinforcement.

activity

Give examples in sport of positive reinforcement, negative reinforcement and punishment.

An example of operant conditioning may be a parent who gives a child a sweet to stop it crying. This reinforces the behaviour and the child cries to get another sweet.

Learning is faster if a reward is given on every occasion – this is known as *complete reinforcement*. Research shows that if a reward is given after a number of correct responses learning takes longer but lasts longer – this is known as *partial reinforcement*. Operant conditioning is commonly used in teaching motor skills.

Rewards are used extensively in skills teaching because they reinforce the type of behaviour required, but there are problems associated with the use of rewards.

In practice

A hockey player who has been drilled to perform a particular penalty flick may become predictable and demotivated by inhibition. Practice should be stopped for a while – perhaps new strategies should be discussed and practised later.

New targets should be set and the practice resumed.

activity

Choose a sport and, using Thorndike's laws, state how you would teach a specific closed skill.

Key revision points
Operant conditioning/trial and error learning is a process which involves modification of behaviour. Behaviour is shaped and then reinforced. For conditioning to take place, reinforcement must be present but partial reinforcement is more effective in the long term than complete reinforcement.

9.1.3 *Thorndike's 'laws'*

Thorndike developed a theory based on strengthening the S–R bond. He developed some 'laws' which he thought should be taken into consideration when trying to match a response to a particular stimulus.

Law of exercise

Repeating or rehearsing the S–R connections is more likely to strengthen them. If the desired response occurs, reinforcement is necessary.

Law of effect

If the response is followed by a 'satisfier', then the S–R bond is strengthened. If the response is followed by an 'annoyer', then the S–R bond is weakened. This means that pleasant outcomes are likely to motivate the performer to repeat the action.

Law of readiness

The performer must be physically and mentally able to complete the task effectively.

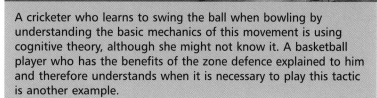

In practice

A cricketer who learns to swing the ball when bowling by understanding the basic mechanics of this movement is using cognitive theory, although she might not know it. A basketball player who has the benefits of the zone defence explained to him and therefore understands when it is necessary to play this tactic is another example.

To find out more about drive theory, turn to page 101.

To find out more about drive reduction, turn to page 101.

DEFINITION

INTERVENING VARIABLES
Mental processes occurring between the stimulus being received and the response.

9.1.4 *Hull's drive theory*

Hull pioneered the 'drive theory'. He stated that if the S–R bond is to be strong a performer must be motivated to do well. He warned against too much repetition of practice, because he thought that it could lead to 'inhibition', which would demotivate the performer and weaken the S–R bond. The inhibition, or drive reduction, can be overcome after a rest interval or when new and more motivating goals are determined.

9.2 Cognitive theories of learning

The cognitive theories go beyond the associative or S–R theories. Many psychologists feel that there are *intervening variables*.

A wide variety of experience in childhood can have
enormous benefits in future skill learning

Cognitive theories are concerned with thinking and understanding rather than connecting certain stimuli to certain responses. Trial and error has no place in cognitive theory. It is sometimes known as *insight learning*.

Kohler used chimpanzees to illustrate this concept. The chimpanzee was placed in a cage with a box and a banana was hung from the roof of the cage. The chimp could reach the banana only by standing on the box once placed underneath the banana. Only one in seven chimpanzees was able to solve this problem without help. Problem solving of this kind involves memory, because chimpanzees who had previous experiences of boxes seemed to be able to solve the problem quicker.

According to cognitive theorists, we are continually receiving information from our surroundings and we work out what has happened using our memories and by our previous knowledge and general understanding (or perception). This cognitive view is often known as *Gestaltist* theory. The word 'gestalt' means 'entirety' or 'wholeness of form'. The Gestaltists think that we perceive objects as a whole, rather than a collection of parts.

The cognitive view lends support to 'whole practice' teaching, rather than part practice – playing the game, so that the participants understand what is required, is more effective than simply learning skills separately, according to the cognitive approach. Giving young children lots of sporting experiences may also help with their future learning and motor development because the child can draw from these experiences to understand a problem and then solve it – gaining insight into the learning process.

activity

To illustrate that you understand the differences between the S–R (associative) approach and the cognitive approach, create two different training practices for teaching the front crawl in swimming. Try to integrate both approaches by creating a third training session.

Key revision points
The Gestaltists formed the cognitive theory of learning, which involves understanding a problem to give insight into learning. Insight is facilitated by past experiences. This is the 'highest' form of learning, and needs mental reasoning and intelligence. Practical applications of this theory include using a whole approach to skill learning, rather than to split a skill into parts, and giving many different sports experiences to children, which allows the learner to develop problem-solving and decision-making skills. Cognitive theory could be used as an argument against didactic, command approaches to skills teaching.

9.2.1 *Social learning theory*

Many examples of human behaviour have been copied from others. As children we were all aware of our elders and their actions, habits and attitudes. Those we view as being high status to us, or 'significant others', are much more likely to be copied than those who we regard as relatively unimportant.

Human beings like to be accepted by others

Human beings like to be accepted by others and to be part of a group. We observe and copy behaviour because it helps us to be part of a group and be more socially acceptable. This process is called *social learning*. We can relate this type of learning to the acquisition of motor skills. We copy the skills performed by others because we are motivated to achieve success and because of our drive to be accepted by others. The coach or teacher could be viewed as a 'significant other', and therefore as a role model he or she is copied.

9.2.2 *Observational learning*

In observational learning the person who is being observed is the *model*. What we learn depends not only on what we see but also on the identity of the model. Social learning is not just about imitating actions – it is also about adopting moral judgements and patterns of social organisation.

In a classic study by Bandura (1973), young children were exposed to a display of adult aggression. The children saw, in isolation from one another, an adult attacking a life-size doll (a 'bobo doll'). When each child was given a similar opportunity to imitate this behaviour, many of them showed patterns of behaviour similar to those they had observed in the adults. This study demonstrated several important points.

1 If the model shows behaviour that is more *appropriate* according to social norms, it is more likely to be copied. For example aggressive male models are more likely to be copied than aggressive female models.

2 The *relevance* of the model's behaviour is also important. Boys are more likely to imitate the aggressive model than girls,

Observational learning depends on the competence, status and attractiveness of the model

because boys, through socialisation, see aggressive behaviour as being relevant to them.

3 The *similarity* of the model to the child (age, sex) is also important.

4 Warm and friendly adults are more likely to be imitated by children than aggressive and unfriendly ones.

5 Models whose behaviour is *reinforced* in some way by significant others are more likely to be copied.

6 More *powerful* models are more likely to be imitated.

7 If a model's behaviour is *consistent*, it is more likely to be copied.

Social learning through observation and imitation is very relevant to physical education and sport. Many of us find ourselves in situations where we can influence the views and behaviour of others, especially children – this may be because we are in a position of authority or because we are good at a particular sport. Top sports people sometimes forget that they are avidly watched by many young viewers who will try to copy their every move – they are *role models*, whose behaviour is seen as acceptable and preferable to others.

When teaching skills, it is the demonstration process which is particularly important. According to Bandura (1973), copying or modelling can affect our performance through four processes, shown in Figure 9.1.

activity

Suppose you are a teacher or a coach needing to demonstrate a skill, or series of skills. Taking the research findings mentioned above into account, use the concept of observational learning to plan your demonstration. Who is going to demonstrate and how? Give reasons for your choices.

Observation → Attention → Retention → Motor reproduction → Motivation → Performance

Receiving and processing stimuli | **Athletic performance**

Figure 9.1 *Bandura's analysis of observational learning*

- *Attention.* To be able to imitate a demonstration, the performer must pay attention to the demonstration and focus on important cues (this is called cueing). The amount of attention paid will be influenced by the perceived attractiveness of the model, the competence of the model and the status of the model. The personal characteristics of the observer (such as personal attention span) and the incentives that are present are also important influences.

- *Retention.* The observer must be able to remember the model that is presented. Therefore he or she needs to create a mental picture of the process (see Chapter 10). Mental rehearsal can improve retention of this mental image.

- *Motor reproduction.* The observer must be physically able to imitate the skill being observed. Demonstrations should therefore be matched to the capabilities of the observer. Feedback during future practices would be important if motor reproduction is eventually to match the model.

- *Motivation.* The level of motivation of the observer is crucial if they are going to imitate the performance. External reinforcement of the model will increase the motivation to imitate it.

There are important links between observational learning and aggression – see Chapter 25.

9.3 Motivation

Motivation is extremely important because without it there is no reason for anyone to want to acquire motor skills. There needs to be a drive to learn and achieve success. The study of motivation has been wide, and it could take a whole book to cover each aspect of motivational research in any detail. There is a more detailed treatment of this subject area and its importance to sports psychology in Chapter 25.

Sage (1974) stated that motivation is 'the internal mechanisms and external stimuli which arouse and direct our behaviour'. This definition has three key points.

1 Motivation involves our *inner drives* towards achieving a goal.
2 Motivation depends on *external pressures* and rewards that we perceive in our environment.
3 Motivation concerns the *intensity* (often referred to as our *arousal level*) and the *direction* of our behaviour.

9.3.1 *Intrinsic motivation*

Intrinsic motivation is a term used for the internal drives to participate or to perform well. Such drives or emotional feelings include fun, enjoyment in participating and the satisfaction that can be felt through playing a particular game. Personal accomplishment and a sense of pride are also intrinsic factors, as well as the physical feeling of well-being when exercising (sometimes referred to as *muscular sensuousness*). The motivation to participate and to perform well in sport can come from internal drives or from external pressures

Intrinsic motivation involves enjoyment of the activity

activity

Choose a sports activity or hobby that you are involved in and write down all the reasons why you participate. Next to each write either 'external' or 'internal', depending on whether you feel that the reason is a result of inner drives or external pressures. You will see that it is not a clear-cut exercise – some external pressures lead to inner drives and vice versa.

In practice

A child who learns to swim and who enjoys swimming can be motivated to swim further by receiving swimming badges. After a time, when the child has achieved the full range of badges, he could lose interest in swimming because he may feel that there are no more rewards to be had. This is an example of rewards assuming too much importance. The intrinsic motives of the swimmer have mainly been lost because there is no longer a sufficient reason to continue. A similar example could also enhance intrinsic motives. The young swimmer may experience more enjoyment in swimming because of the inner drive to achieve something worthwhile (a badge), which may give a lifelong love of swimming.

Extrinsic motivation often comes from external rewards

Instructors who wish to optimise the effects of intrinsic and extrinsic motivation should involve performers in goal-setting and decision-making. An athlete who shares in planning a training programme will view success with a sense of personal achievement.

To find out more about reinforcement, turn to page 94.

9.3.2 *Extrinsic motivation*

External factors can be extremely powerful in determining whether we want to learn a particular skill and whether we want to perfect it. External factors often come in the form of rewards such as medals, badges and prizes. The pressures from other people can also be extrinsic motivators – some young people participate in a particular activity to please their parents, for instance, or you may continue to play for a team once you have lost interest, simply to not let the team down.

As we know, reinforcement from others can ensure that an action is repeated. This is relevant to extrinsic motivation – rewards act as the reinforcers.

9.3.3 *Relationship between intrinsic and extrinsic motivation*

There has been much debate among sports psychologists about whether external rewards undermine or enhance intrinsic motives.

The need to win could be seen as both intrinsically and extrinsically motivating. The performer could be striving for success in order to gain a sense of satisfaction or to achieve recognition. In nearly all cases motivation is a mixture of both. Weinberg (1984) makes the key point that 'rewards do not inherently undermine intrinsic motivation.' Many people feel that it is not the presence of extrinsic rewards that motivates but rather the way the performer perceives the reward. In other words, performers should put rewards into the proper perspective and the people that have influence over the performer (coaches, teachers or parents) must be aware that the performer's perspective can be influenced greatly by their own. If there is too much emphasis on winning the performer will concentrate only on that goal and will not think about the pleasure of taking part.

9.3.4 *Theories related to arousal levels*

Motivation is related to the intensity and direction of behaviour. *Arousal* represents the intensity aspect of motivation. The effects of arousal can be positive or negative. The physiological effects of arousal, which occur along with the psychological reactions, include an increase in heart rate, breathing and production of sweat. In this chapter we are concerned with the psychological reactions. High arousal can cause us to worry and become anxious, which is a negative aspect if it is not controlled. Raising arousal level can also cause a state of 'readiness' to perform – this is largely a positive aspect and can enhance performance.

As a performer's arousal level increases (often referred to as getting 'psyched up') the state of readiness and expectation increases, but if the level of arousal gets too high a performer can lose concentration and feel over-aroused, which we may refer to as being 'stressed out'. This relationship between arousal and performance is often explained through the *drive theory*, the *inverted U theory* and the *catastrophe theory*.

Drive theory

This was first developed by Hull in 1943. The modified drive theory (Spence and Spence, 1968), represented in Figure 9.2, sees the relationship between arousal and performance as linear: performance increases in proportion to arousal. A very high arousal level would result in a high performance level. Hull saw that performance depends on how a dominant learned response is intensified. Learned behaviour, according to Hull, is more likely to occur as the intensity of the competition increases. Spence and Spence (1968) adapted Hull's theory and the formula often used to explain this theory is

$$P = f(H \times D)$$

where P represents performance, f the function, H habit and D drive.

If the dominant learned response is correct then the performance will be enhanced. The dominant response for a beginner, however, may be an incorrect action and if this was intensified performance levels would actually decrease.

Drive may well be reduced if the individual loses motivation (see Chapter 10 for details of reactive inhibition and drive reduction).

Inverted U theory

This theory is more popular among sports psychologists, although it does have drawbacks because of its simplicity. It was first put forward by Yerkes and Dodson (1908) and has since been applied to sports situations. According to this theory, as arousal level increases so does the level of performance – but only to an optimum point, which occurs usually at moderate arousal level. Once past a moderate arousal level, performance decreases. Participants in sport can become anxious if they are over-aroused and their performance usually suffers. This theory fits many observations of sports performers, although it needs modification to apply it to different types of activities, skill levels and personalities.

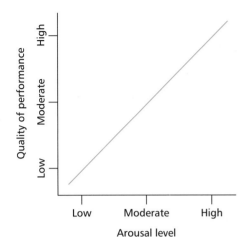

Figure 9.2 *The relationship between arousal and performance: drive theory*

DEFINITION

DRIVE REDUCTION

An individual may be motivated to complete a task, which can be seen as a 'drive'. When that drive is perceived as being fulfilled, then the drive is reduced. If the individual feels that he or she is performing to the best of their ability, the performance may well become habitual and the performer sees no reason to be motivated or 'driven' to do better. Problems can occur if the performer thinks that there is no need to drive to improve, even though there may well be room for much improvement.

REACTIVE INHIBITION

This is a phrase that arises from the work of Hull and his drive theory (1943). A performer of a motor skill may think that they have done their best and reached their goal (e.g. high percentage of effective serves in volleyball), and this causes them to stop trying so hard or 'inhibits' their effort. This can lead to a decrease in performance.

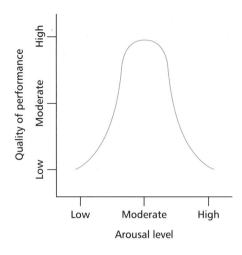

Figure 9.3 *The relationship between arousal and performance: inverted U theory*

In practice

A novice is best taught basic skills in a low-arousal environment. It is better if no one else is watching and if competition is not applied in the early stages of learning.

Types of activities

If the activity to be performed involves many fine controlled movements, then the arousal level of the performer needs to be fairly low for optimum performance. Pistol shooters and archers, for example, go to great lengths to control their emotional arousal levels. If the activity is much more gross, such as weightlifting, arousal levels need to be fairly high to expend so much dynamic strength. Rugby forwards have often been seen 'psyching themselves up' before a match.

Skill levels

If the performer is highly skilled, many movements are controlled by motor programmes. Many of their actions need little conscious attention and therefore they can cope with higher levels of arousal. A performer who has low skill levels will need to attend to many details related to movement and consequently will need to consciously process much more information. If the arousal level is even moderate, a novice may lose concentration or become anxious, and so a low level of arousal is likely to produce optimum performance.

Personality

Personality types who enjoy high levels of excitement and are generally more extrovert can cope in a high-arousal situation. People who are more introverted are generally more likely to perform well under low-arousal conditions. This is backed up by the link between the reticular activating system and personality.

Catastrophe theory

There is much anecdotal evidence to support the view that as arousal increases there is a sudden and dramatic drop in performance. We see many top sports people 'go to pieces' in the big events. The inverted U hypothesis shows only a steady decline in performance when arousal is raised above the moderate level. Catastrophe theory (Jones and Hardy, 1996) shows a much more dramatic decline in performance – hence its name. The theory takes into account that our anxiety can be of two types: *somatic anxiety* (anxiety experienced physiologically, such as sweating) and *cognitive anxiety* (anxiety experienced by the mind – for example, worry about failing). These two types of anxiety interact with each other, with cognitive anxiety being the most crucial in determining the performer's reactions to high levels of stress. These two types of anxiety are dealt with in more detail in Chapter 27. The catastrophe theory is a complex multidimensional theory which concludes that increases in levels of cognitive anxiety will help performance if somatic anxiety is low. So if the body is relaxed but the performer is feeling anxious then this anxiety can help to improve performance.

If there is an increase in cognitive anxiety and somatic anxiety is high then performance will decline.

If there are high levels of cognitive anxiety and there is a continuous increase in somatic anxiety or physiological arousal then performance can suddenly deteriorate – a 'catastrophic' response.

We see many top sportsmen and women 'go to pieces'

In practice

Bird and Horn (1990) showed that female softball players had sudden and major decreases in performance levels and many mental errors when their cognitive anxiety levels were high.

The 'in zone'

DEFINITION

RETICULAR ACTIVATING SYSTEM (RAS)

This is located in the central core of the brainstem and maintains our levels of arousal. It can enhance or inhibit incoming sensory stimuli. According to the theories linked to the biological basis of personality, extroverts tend to inhibit the intensity of stimuli and introverts tend to increase the intensity. According to Eysenck (1970), introverts dislike high arousal conditions because their RAS is already stimulated. Extroverts seek high arousal levels because their RAS lacks stimulation.

If after this catastrophic effect, arousal decreases, then performance will once again improve but not back to its originally optimal level. Figure 9.4 illustrates the catastrophe theory.

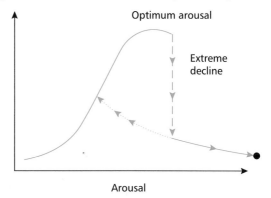

Figure 9.4 *Catastrophe theory*

9.3.5 Peak flow experience

'Peak flow experience' is a phrase that has been used about sportsmen and women who achieve optimum performance levels and associate this with a particular emotional response. Many top athletes describe their feelings when almost nothing can go wrong. They relate that they are 'in the zone', where all that matters is the performance – all else is insignificant. Peak flow experience can be explained by the arousal theories. All the theories related to arousal show that performance is related to the amount of inner drive and self-motivation. There are mental strategies which can help performers achieve this experience, to motivate them to want to repeat it and drive them to achieve their very best.

In practice

Adapted from Sugarman, 1998.
Achieving the 'In Zone' for top performers:

1 Be relaxed. As a top sports performer you do not need very high levels of arousal. You need a balance between wanting to achieve the very best and yet you are relaxed and in control.
2 Be confident. You will have an overall belief that you have great ability. A lapse in performance will not undermine this belief. You will not show fear and you exude pride and confidence. You expect success rather than hope for it.
3 Be completely focused. You will be completely absorbed by your performance. You will not dwell on what has happened before and what may happen in the future.
4 Activity is effortless. You can accomplish often complex and difficult tasks with very little effort. Body and mind are working almost perfectly together.
5 Movements are automatic. This can be related to the motor programme theory visited later in this chapter. There is no real thought that goes into your movement. You move instinctively and there seems to be little conscious thought.
6 Fun. When you are experiencing the flow, the enjoyment is immense. You experience satisfaction and fulfilment. Without this fun feeling you are unlikely to achieve the peak flow experience.
7 In control. You have command over your body and your emotions. You are in charge and you dictate your own destiny.

9.4 Information processing

In this theory the brain is viewed as working like a computer. Stimuli entering the brain are known as *information* or *input*, which is then processed, decisions are made and a response (known as *output*) takes place:

Input → Decision-making process → Output

A more detailed model than this would help us to understand the cognitive processes involved and therefore give us valuable clues to make skill learning more effective. This can be seen in Figure 9.5.

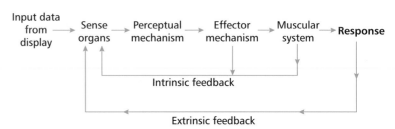

Figure 9.5
Information processing

Models that set out to explain human behaviour are meant only to be illustrative and should not be taken as a factual representation of what actually happens. The environment is constantly changing, as is the nervous system controlling the body's actions. The model of information processing must be taken as dynamic.

To understand what happens at each stage of information processing, we will look at each part of the model from the environment, before information is processed, right through to the feedback immediately after the response.

- The *display* represents the environment surrounding the performer. For instance a basketball player's display might be her opponents, the ball, the basketball, the crowd, the noise and the scoreboard.
- *Sensory input* is the way information is taken in – vision, audition, proprioception, smell, etc.
- The *sense organs* are receptors which pick up the information and transport it to the brain.
- In the *perceptual process* the relevant information is selected, interpreted and then used to make a decision. Memory is also used in the perceptual process. (For more details on selective attention and the role of memory see section 9.5 below.)
- *Decision-making process* or *translatory mechanism*. Once information has been interpreted a motor plan is formed for movement to take place.
- Using the *effector mechanism* the decisions that have been made are put into action and impulses are sent to the muscles for a response to be made. This plan of action may well be in the form of a *motor programme*.
- *Feedback* may be extrinsic via knowledge of results, or intrinsic which arises via proprioception.

Welford (1960) saw the processing elements within the brain, called central mechanisms, as three sub-processors: perceptual mechanisms, translatory mechanisms and effector mechanisms. See Figure 9.6.

In practice

When practising a serve in table tennis, a player would use their short-term memory to store the last shot so that they could compare it with the next to help improvement. The coach may give information to the player, but only a small amount because of the limited capacity of the short-term memory.

DEFINITION

MOTOR PROGRAMME

Sometimes called an executive programme, this is a generalised series of movements stored in the long-term memory that can be retrieved by making one decision.

To find out more about feedback, turn to page 115.

Figure 9.6 *Adaptation of Welford's model of information processing*

The perceptual mechanisms interpret the information, the translatory mechanism makes decisions and the effector mechanism transfers those decisions to the muscles to produce a movement response.

Whiting (1975) included Welford's ideas in a more sophisticated model shown In Figure 9.7. The model includes all the components mentioned before but is seen in relation to its environment. The environment is a constantly changing one for the sports performer so this model is dynamic – in other words many processing functions happen simultaneously and cannot be viewed as a simple flow diagram.

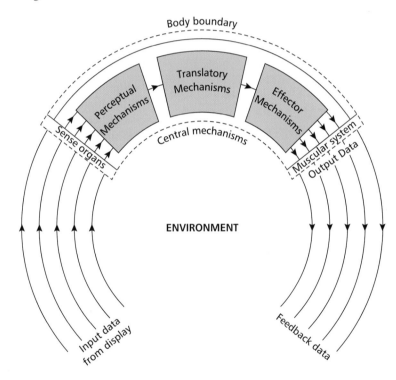

Figure 9.7 *Whiting's model of information processing*

9.4.1 *Stages of information processing*

The whole process of information processing is complex but one way of understanding the process is to divide it into three stages:
1 stimulus identification stage
2 response selection stage
3 response programming stage.

Stage 1: stimulus identification

In this part of the process the sense organs pick up information from the environment and recognise them for what they are. There are aspects of parallel processing which take place in this stage.

Stage 2: response selection

This stage involves making a decision about how to respond to the information that has just been received.

Stage 3: response programming

When the decision to move has been made, the appropriate response is selected. At this stage a motor programme may be used to initiate muscle movement. Some aspects of serial processing occur in this stage.

In practice

Stimulus identification: A netball player who is about to catch the ball detects the movement of the ball, including its speed and direction.

Response selection: The netball player now decides to change direction to get into line with the ball and catch it.

9.4.2 *Serial and parallel processing*

Some of the processes within the information-processing model involve decisions that are *sequential* – one decision follows on from another and affects the next one. Some decisions, however, are simultaneous or *parallel* in nature – in other words, processes are occurring independently from one another. It is generally recognised that if information processing is to be applied to the learning of motor skills there is a mixture of both serial and parallel processing.

Figure 9.8 shows parallel and serial processing.

In practice

In cricket, a batsman may take into account two or more pieces of information, e.g. the flight of the ball and the movement of the players in the field. This can be seen as an example of parallel processing because he has processed the different types of information separately.

In gymnastics a girl performs a handstand to forward roll. She decides to move sequentially into the handstand and then into the forward roll. This can be seen as serial processing in the response programming stage.

9.4.3 *Attentional control*

We explored the debilitating effects of attentional wastage in Chapter 8. Attentional control involves concentration, which is crucial if motivation is to be sustained and skill learning is to be effective. Attention needs to be focused on relevant cues or items of information that are important for the execution of a particular

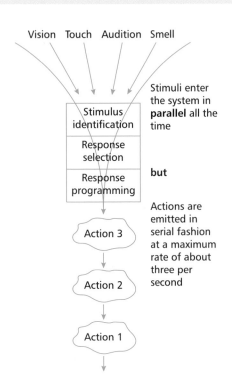

DEFINITION

SERIAL PROCESSING

A type of information processing in which each stage is arranged sequentially, with one stage affecting the next, and so on.

PARALLEL PROCESSING

A type of information processing when two or more processes occur at the same time and one does not necessarily affect the other.

Vision Touch Audition Smell

Stimulus identification

Response selection

Response programming

Action 3

Action 2

Action 1

Stimuli enter the system in **parallel** all the time

but

Actions are emitted in serial fashion at a maximum rate of about three per second

Figure 9.8 *Information processing involves parallel and serial processes*

skill. To enable a performer to reach and stay in the peak flow experience, attentional control is necessary. Nideffer (1976), who is a sports psychologist, stated that there are two types of 'attentional focus':

1 *Broad/narrow focus.* It is broad focus if the player's attention takes into account a lot of information at the same time. A basketball player may well take into account the position of the basket, the position of opponents and the position of his own players. The focus is narrow if the player is concentrating on only one or two important pieces of information or cues.

2 *External/internal focus.* If the focus is external then the player is attending to stimuli originating from the environment. The basketball player would be focusing on the position of a player on the other team. If the focus is internal then the player would focus on his own feelings – for example, how anxious he is at that particular moment.

The control a performer has over the type of attention that is used affects arousal levels and therefore motivation levels. It is important that the performer learns how to control his or her attention. If there is too much information available then the performer is said to have *cognitive overload*.

DEFINITION

COGNITIVE OVERLOAD

A netball player may have just missed a shot at goal. She will have heard the coach shouting instructions at her; she is aware of her own feelings of disappointment; she will be aware of teammates' disappointment and shouts of encouragement. She may well lose concentration because she is overloaded with information. This is often caused by the player being over-aroused.

'Cognitive overload' – mistakes can occur if there is too much information

DEFINITION

REACTION TIME

The time between first presentation of a stimulus to the very start of the movement in response to it.

MOVEMENT TIME

The time between starting and finishing a movement.

RESPONSE TIME

The time between first presentation of the stimulus to completion of the movement (reaction time plus movement time).

activity

Choose a particular sport and imagine you are playing in a particular position. Identify examples of your broad focus, your narrow focus, your external focus and finally your internal focus.

9.4.4 *Reactions*

The speed with which we process information is known as *reaction time*. The process of attending to relevant stimuli, making a decision and responding involves all three of the stages outlined on pages 102–3.

Quick reactions are often crucial if a skill is to be successful

Several factors affect response time:
- whether the reaction involves making a choice
- your age
- your sex
- whether you were expecting the stimulus or not
- previous experience
- how quickly one stimulus follows another
- whether you can anticipate what is going to happen.

Let us look at each of these in more detail.

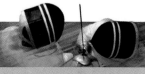

In practice

An example of stimulus–response compatibility could occur in squash, when the position of your opponent's feet indicates that he is going to make a drive down the wall, but he then executes a 'boast' on the side wall. Your reactions may well be slower because the response required is different from the one you were expecting to make.

DEFINITION

HICK'S LAW

Choice reaction time is linearly related to the amount of information that must be processed to resolve the uncertainty about the various possible stimulus response alternatives.

9.4.5 *Hick's law – simple or choice reactions*

A performer will take a lot less time to react to only one stimulus or to a stimulus that requires a simple response than to more than one stimulus or if more than one response is possible. According to *Hick's law*, the more responses that are possible, the longer the reaction time will be.

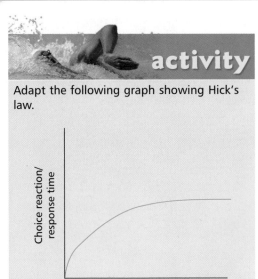

activity

Adapt the following graph showing Hick's law.

Figure 9.9 *Hick's law*

Age

Your reaction time gets quicker, up to an optimum age and then deteriorates.

In practice

Think of situations in your own sport where reactions are important. Identify the stimulus or stimuli which trigger your information-processing system into action. When does the response finish?

Sex

Males have generally quicker reactions than females but the reaction times of females deteriorate less quickly than those of males.

Stimulus–response compatibility

If the response demanded by a stimulus is the one you were expecting, you are likely to react more quickly than if the response demanded is not what you expected.

In practice

An activity involving simple reaction time is the start of a sprint race. The sound of the gun is the only stimulus which needs attention. An example of choice reaction time is waiting to receive a tennis serve – there are several possible responses that could be made to the stimulus of the ball.

Previous experiences

If you have had to react to the same stimulus, or a similar one, in the past your reactions may be quicker, particularly if choice reaction time is involved. Motor programmes may be formed and can be 'run' automatically, cutting down the decision-making requirements.

Psychological refractory period

If a second stimulus follows quite closely behind the first, reaction time is slowed because of the increased information processing time needed. The *single-channel hypothesis* underpins this phenomenon.

Anticipation

As we discussed earlier, a skilled performer seems to have more time available to complete the actions necessary. This is because he or she has drawn on past experience to anticipate what is about to happen, and has processed information before the event actually happened, which saves them time. Anticipation can set a pattern of movement in advance, which can then be used when it is required – this is called *spatial* anticipation. Using anticipation to predict what is about to happen is called *temporal* anticipation.

DEFINITION

SINGLE-CHANNEL HYPOTHESIS

This states that when handling stimuli from the environment the brain can deal with only one stimulus at a time. This is because the brain is thought of as a single-channel organ – it can only deal with one piece of information at a time, which has to be processed before the next stimulus can be dealt with. This is often referred to as the 'bottleneck'.

Anticipation can save valuable time in reaction to a situation

In practice

A basketball player might be able to predict that an opponent is about to make a shot and jumps to block the shot (spatial anticipation). He or she may also use clues given by particular movements of the opponent to predict that a shot is about to be taken (temporal anticipation).

activity

Imagine that you are about to receive a tennis serve. List the cues that you could take notice of to anticipate effectively and cut down your reaction time. Identify the spatial anticipation and temporal anticipation processes.

However, anticipation *can* be wrong and could lengthen reaction time instead of shortening it. The delay could be caused by the psychological refractory period coming into play because the first decision was the wrong one. For example, the basketball player who is perceived to be going for a shot could well be 'faking' the movement.

In practice

'Selling a dummy' is a typical way of delaying an opponent's tackle. The opponent has to clear the initial decision to tackle before dealing with the realisation that a 'dummy' has taken place. This can give a player valuable time to change direction or make an unexpected pass.

Other factors affecting reactions

Other factors, such as the intensity of the stimulus, the presence of warning cues and the type of stimulus/stimuli may also affect the speed of information processing.

9.5 Memory

The memory is very important in processing information. Our previous experiences affect how we judge and interpret information and the course of action we take.

The memory process is very complex and, although there has been much research in this area, it is still not understood fully. It is useful to try to simplify the process by using the information processing approach discussed above. The model in Figure 9.10 seeks to explain the components of memory.

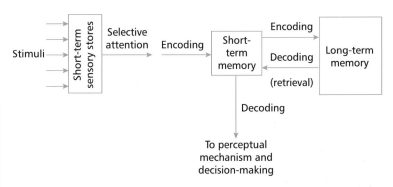

Figure 9.10 *Model representing the memory process*

9.5.1 *Short-term sensory stores*

Information in the form of stimuli enters the brain from the environment. Each store has a large capacity but information is only stored for between a quarter and one second before it is *filtered*. This filtering takes place in the stimulus identification stage. *Selective attention* takes place in the short-term sensory stores.

9.5.2 *Short-term memory*

This has been named the 'workspace' or the 'working memory' because this is where the information is used to decide what needs to be done. Only a limited amount of information can be stored in the short-term memory (research is ambiguous but points to about seven pieces of information) and is only held for a short time (about 30 seconds). To extend the time that the information is stored in the short-term memory, the performer would have to rehearse the information, through imagery or sub-verbal repetition (by talking to yourself). Information can also be held in short-term memory through a process called *chunking*.

DEFINITION

SELECTIVE ATTENTION

In selective attention relevant information is filtered through into the short-term memory and irrelevant information is lost or forgotten. This process is particularly important in sport, where quick reactions depend on being able to concentrate on important information and to shut out distractions.

DEFINITION

CHUNKING

Different pieces of information can be grouped (or chunked) together and then remembered as one piece of information. For example, instead of trying to remember each separate move made by each player in a line-out in rugby or a penalty corner in hockey a player might remember the whole drill as a single number.

Selective attention involves concentration

If information is considered important enough and is rehearsed it can be passed into the long-term memory. This process is called *encoding* the information. Information that is not considered important, or is not rehearsed, is usually lost because it does not go into the long-term memory.

9.5.3 *Long-term memory*

This store of information has almost limitless capacity and holds information for long periods of time. The information which is stored has been encoded (see above). Information is stored in the long-term memory, possibly by associating it with other information or with meaning. Meaningless items are usually not stored for long periods of time. Motor programmes are stored in the long-term memory because they have been rehearsed many times. The process of continued rehearsal leads to a skill being almost automatic and the process of learning by rehearsal is often referred to as 'overlearning'. If you are regularly using particular motor skills you are more likely to remember them – for example, once you have learned to swim you are unlikely to forget.

If you were about to receive a serve in badminton, how would selective attention help you? List the items of information that you would use your short-term memory to process and those you would use your long-term memory for.

> ### Key revision points
> *The memory process is still largely a mystery but simplified models have been developed to try to explain the process. The basic model describes memory as essentially a three-stage process: short-term sensory store; short-term memory; long-term memory.*
> *All information that is selected passes through the short-term memory. The process of chunking (organisation of information) can help a performer deal with larger amounts of information. Items of information need to be rehearsed before they can be stored in the long-term memory.*

9.5.4 *Motor programmes*

Motor control

Levels of motor control dictate the amount of influence the performer's central nervous system has on the control of a motor skill (Marteniuk, 1976). The more the skill is learned, the less feedback information is referred to. The first level described below is much more relevant to the highly skilled performer than the novice which can be identified in level three.

Level 1 of motor control

Movements are almost automatic and reactions are very quick. There is little time to act upon feedback available. The motor programme stimulates the muscles to act in a prescribed manner and is so well rehearsed that it can cause actions to take place that are nearly always exactly the same. There are very few attentional demands. A sports performer can attend or concentrate upon other peripheral stimuli.

Level 2 of motor control

The muscular system receives proprioceptive stimuli, which gives useful information or feedback that can be acted upon immediately to detect and correct errors or to reinforce the correct actions. This is known as *closed loop control*. The 'loop' is closed because any intrinsic feedback is perceived or interpreted quickly and unconsciously.

Level 3 of motor control

This level involves the conscious control of the brain. There is feedback just like level 2, but at this level the muscles and the brain are stimulated with information about the movement. It is a longer process because the brain has to evaluate and assess movements and this loses crucial time in the decision-making process. The coordination of movements is often incorrect at this level because some of the decisions made by inexperienced performers may be wrong.

Open loop control

Motor programmes are generalised series of movements stored in the long-term memory and each is retrieved by a single decision. They usefully explain how we perform very quick actions in sport, especially closed skills. Some almost automatic movements do not seem to be under conscious control – if a decision had to be made about every single muscle action to catch a ball the information processing would take far too long. This kind of control over our actions is known as *open loop control*, and a model of open loop control is shown in Figure 9.11.

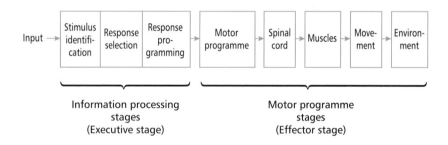

Figure 9.11
Model of open loop control

There is no feedback involved with open loop control. If the environment remains constant and predictable then a motor programme can be used or 'run' effectively.

The more a performer practises a series of movements, the more likely it is that a motor programme will be formed. Most movements that we make in sport are a mixture of open loop control and closed loop control.

Closed loop control

This involves the process of feedback. The feedback for this type of control is internal – information is received from the proprioceptors which detect and correct errors in movement. A model of closed loop control is shown in Figure 9.12.

This theory was proposed by Adams (1971). He states that movements are initiated by a *memory trace*. This triggers an appropriate response that has been stored in the long-term memory.

The *perceptual trace* is then initiated which controls the movement once it has been triggered by the memory trace. The perceptual trace is developed from experiences. When

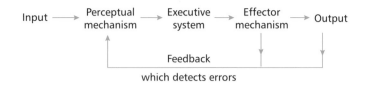

Input → Perceptual mechanism → Executive system → Effector mechanism → Output

Feedback
which detects errors

Figure 9.12 *Model of closed loop control*

In practice

A golfer driving off the tee can feel whether the swing is effective and intrinsic feedback is received. The golfer may alter the action during the swing. Some golfers do not need to look where the ball is going because they can sense whether the swing has been correct. This is closed loop control because the feedback from the player's proprioceptors has been acted upon.

a motor skill is practised, the performer is continuously matching the perceptual trace with feedback. If the feedback tells the performer that the movement matches the perceptual trace then the movement continues. If the feedback tells the performer that there is something wrong because the movement does not match the perceptual trace, then the action is corrected. This process can happen throughout the movement and errors are continuously monitored and movements corrected.

9.5.5 *Schema theory*

Some people feel that the open loop and closed loop theories do not fully explain how we perform so many actions in sport with relatively little conscious control – there simply cannot be enough storage space for so many motor programmes. Under the schema theory a motor programme is seen as only a generalised series of movements that can be modified by taking in information as a skill is performed. The theory usefully explains how we can immediately learn a new skill, and also solves the storage problem. When a movement takes place we perceive information about where we are (knowledge of the environment), what we have to do to perform successfully (response specifications), what the movement feels like (sensory consequences) and what happens when we respond (response outcomes). These items of information, called 'schemas', are then stored and used to update the motor programme when we next want to use it.

In practice

An experienced basketball player probably has developed a motor programme for making a shot at the basket, but will not have a programme for shooting from every possible position on the court or for dealing with every possible position of a blocking opponent. However, he will have had many different experiences from which to draw. These will have become schemas stored in the long-term memory which he can use to modify his shooting programme.

Recall schemas

Recall schemas are the information stored about the production of movement – the environment and the response specifications. The recall schemas start the appropriate movement.

Recognition schemas

These include information stored about evaluating the response – the sensory consequences and the response outcomes. The recognition schemas control the movement.

An experienced basketball player has probably developed a motor programme for the shot

Teachers and coaches who want their students to be successful in a variety of situations must bear the schema theory in mind. If information about many different situations is to be stored, the performer must be exposed in training to as many of these different situations as possible and must be aware of both recall and recognition schemas.

> **Key revision points**
> *Motor programmes are identified as stores of information in the long-term memory. When triggered, they can put into action a whole series of movements. Many movements are initiated with one decision to run a programme – this is known as open loop control. Closed loop control involves intrinsic feedback. Schema theory solves some of the problems that the motor programme theory creates. Schemas are used in a process where programmes are modified or updated. Schemas are built up in the long-term memory by varying practice conditions.*

9.6 Feedback

Feedback involves using the information that is available to the performer during the performance of a skill or after the response to alter the performance. There are several forms of feedback:

- *Continuous* feedback – feedback during the performance, in the form of kinaesthesis or proprioception.
- *Terminal* feedback – feedback after the response has been completed.
- *Knowledge of results* – this is a type of terminal feedback that gives the performer information about the end result of the response.
- *Knowledge of performance* – this is information about how well the movement is being executed, rather than the end result.
- *Internal/intrinsic* feedback – this is a type of continuous feedback that comes from the proprioceptors.
- *External/extrinsic/augmented* feedback – feedback that comes from external sources, for example from sound or vision.
- *Positive* feedback – reinforces skill learning and gives information about a successful outcome.
- *Negative* feedback – information about an unsuccessful outcome, which can be used to build more successful strategies.

Two of these types of feedback are more important than the others in sports performance: knowledge of results and knowledge of performance.

9.6.1 *Knowledge of results*

This feedback is external, and can come from performers seeing the result of their response or from another person, usually a coach or teacher. It is extremely important for performers to know what the result of their action has been. There can be very little learning without this type of feedback, especially in the early stages of skill acquisition.

In practice

A teacher or coach *must* give feedback to the performer – he or she may not be able to detect errors on their own because of limited kinaesthetic awareness. For example, a novice gymnast might not be aware of what a good handstand feels like and therefore feedback related to the end result would help him or her detect errors. The coach could use a video of the performance to show the novice how he performed.

activity

Think of a practical example for each of the types of feedback listed here, using one of the sports that you are involved with.

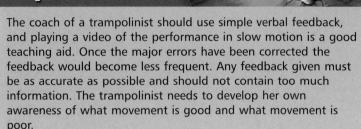

In practice

The coach of a trampolinist should use simple verbal feedback, and playing a video of the performance in slow motion is a good teaching aid. Once the major errors have been corrected the feedback would become less frequent. Any feedback given must be as accurate as possible and should not contain too much information. The trampolinist needs to develop her own awareness of what movement is good and what movement is poor.

A gymnast can gain knowledge of performance through kinesthetic awareness or external feedback

9.6.2 Knowledge of performance

This is feedback about the pattern of movement that has taken, or is taking, place. It is normally associated with external feedback but can be gained through kinaesthetic awareness, especially if the performer is highly skilled and knows what a good performance feels like.

Both knowledge of results and knowledge of performance can help with the motivation of a performer, but if used incorrectly they can also demotivate. Reinforcement, as we discovered earlier in this chapter, is essential for effective skill learning and feedback serves as a good reinforcer. If the movement and/or the result is good then the performer will feel satisfaction, and the S–R bond is strengthened. Knowing that the movement and results are good will help the performer form a picture of what is correct and associate future performance with that picture, image or model.

External feedback should be used with care because the performer may come to depend too heavily upon it and will not develop internal feedback. The type of feedback that should be given depends on the ability of the performer, the type of activity being undertaken and the personality of the performer – different performers respond differently to different types of feedback.

9.6.3 Feedback and setting goals

There is an important link between feedback and setting goals and future motivation and performance. In research carried out by Bandura, 20 cyclists were given performance goals, 20 cyclists received performance feedback but were not set goals, 20 were set goals and received feedback and a further 20 acted as a control group (they were given no feedback and were not set goals). The results of this experiment are set out in Figure 9.13 and show clearly that the effects of feedback are enhanced by goal setting.

When performance is measured and is given to performers as feedback, their motivation can be enhanced and their performance improved. Sports performers often set themselves targets from their previous performances but teachers and coaches can help by constructing performance/goal charts that the performer updates as necessary. These charts serve as feedback on current performance and set clear and progressive targets. This is another useful way of strengthening the all-important S–R bond.

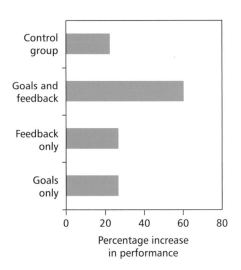

Figure 9.13 *The relationship between performance, feedback and goal-setting*

activity

Give examples of performance feedback. Choose a sport and identify the goals that you might set a novice. How would you link goal setting with performance?

Key revision points

Feedback occurs both during and after movement. The two main types of feedback are knowledge of results and knowledge of performance. Feedback can help to reinforce effective movements and to detect and correct errors. When intrinsic feedback is involved in the detection and correction process, it is known as closed loop control. In order to motivate a performer it is very important to give the appropriate feedback and to set relevant goals.

9.7 Mental rehearsal

This is sometimes called *mental practice* and is a strategy adopted by many sportsmen and women. By mentally rehearsing you form a mental image of the skill or event that you are about to perform. No physical movements are involved in mental rehearsal. Some performers find mental rehearsal easier than others but the ability can be improved with practice. Mental rehearsal is used either to learn a new skill or to improve existing skills. It is important in the cognitive stage of skill learning.

In practice

Before performing the serial skill of a floor routine a gymnast will go through the routine in his mind by creating a mental image of each stage of the routine. Before taking a penalty kick a soccer player may visualise the kick and the desired result. A demonstration will help the novice tennis player to form a mental picture of a serve before actually serving.

9.7.1 Mental rehearsal and skill learning

The cognitive stage of skill learning (identified by Fitts in 1967) involves the performer understanding what is required to perform the skill. This understanding is associated with building a mental image. Mental rehearsal is thought to involve going through possible movements and mentally experiencing the possible outcomes. This process can help to eradicate unnecessary and energy-consuming movements.

For the novice, mental rehearsal may well improve confidence and help to control arousal levels. Research has shown that if a performer concentrates on successful movements rather than unsuccessful ones, a degree of optimism is experienced.

Mental rehearsal can help the performer concentrate

Figure 9.14 *The effects of mental practice on performance*

Figure 9.14 clearly shows the positive effects of mental practice on the performance of a fine motor skill.

By combining physical and mental practice all performers, especially ones who are already skilled, will be able to improve their performance.

In practice

To maximise the effects of mental rehearsal, teachers and coaches should encourage the performer to mentally rehearse successful movements away from the heat of competition. Mental rehearsal should include as much fine detail as possible.
The performer should also be encouraged to mentally rehearse during rest periods between practice sessions.

9.7.2 Mental practice versus physical practice

Many researchers have concluded that mental rehearsal which is combined with physical practice can lead to high performance levels. Physical practice alone has been shown to be less worthwhile than the combination with mental rehearsal. If the skill to be performed is serial in nature (see Chapter 8), then mental rehearsal is particularly important to ensure that the right sequence of movements takes place. Mental practice can help to visualise faults and the correction of those faults, can help with controlling arousal levels and can activate the body to respond to particular cues.

An experiment by McBride and Rothstein (1979) investigated how mental practice affected the learning of a closed and an open skill. All subjects were told to hit a golf ball with a table tennis bat at a 6 foot target that was 10 feet away as a control. The closed skill was also attempted by all the subjects, where they had to hit the ball off a 3 foot high tee. In the open skill condition the subjects had to hit the ball that came at them every 10 seconds from a ball-feeding apparatus. The subjects were divided up into groups:

- Physical practice group – performed the task 40 times.
- Mental practice group – were given a demonstration, had three practice trials and then performed the task mentally 40 times.
- The physical/mental group alternated physical and mental trials.

For both the open and the closed skills the group that combined mental and physical tasks performed better than the other groups, even though the combined group actually performed fewer physical trials than the physical practice group.

In practice

Coaches and teachers should not underestimate the positive effects of mental practice. Fewer physical practices can in fact be better, as long as there is enough good mental rehearsal and preparation.

Key terms

Progress check

You should now understand the following terms. If you do not, go back through the chapter and find out what they mean.

Arousal level
Associationist/connectionist
Classical conditioning
Closed loop control
Cognitive theory
Drive reduction theory
Feedback
Hick's law
Information processing
Insight learning
Long-term memory
Mental practice
Motivation
Motor programme
Open loop control
Operant conditioning
Peak flow experience
Psychological refractory period
Reaction time
Reinforcement
Schema
Selective attention
Serial and parallel processing
Short-term memory
Short-term sensory store
Social learning

1 What is the S–R bond?
2 Why is operant conditioning different from classical conditioning?
3 What is meant by the term reinforcement?
4 What is the difference between negative reinforcement and punishment?
5 Give a practical example, other than the one cited in this chapter, to show operant conditioning in action.
6 What are Thorndike's three laws which help to strengthen the S–R bond?
7 According to Hull, what is wrong with too much repetition in practice situations?
8 What did the Gestaltists say about the learning process? Give a practical example of the cognitive theory in action.
9 Define motivation and give examples of intrinsic and extrinsic motivation.
10 Explain the positive and negative aspects of the relationship between intrinsic and extrinsic motication.
11 Draw a graph to show the drive and inverted U theories.
12 Why is the inverted U theory so much more popular than the drive theory?
13 Draw a detailed information processing model.
14 What are the three stages in information processing?
15 Define reaction time.
16 Choose an example in sport when the time to respond needs to be short. Write down as many factors affecting the performer's response time as you can.
17 Draw a simple model of the memory process.
18 What is meant by the term selective attention?
19 How can a teacher ensure that information is stored in the performer's long-term memory?
20 What is meant by a motor programme?
21 How does schema theory help with the problems of the programme theory?
22 What are the two most important types of feedback and how can they help in future performances?
23 What is mental rehearsal?
24 What are the main effects of mental practice on skill learning?

10 Theories related to the teaching of skills

- To recognise the different stages in the learning process.
- To understand the concept of transfer.
- To be able to investigate the most effective ways of structuring practices.
- To be able to apply different types of guidance to practical situations.
- To be able to identify different teaching styles, along with their advantages and disadvantages.
- To understand the need to adopt different teaching styles in different situations.

The theories related to skill acquisition have been investigated in the last two chapters. In this chapter we apply these theories directly to the teaching process. Effective skills teaching is dependent on the recognition and understanding of the stages that are passed through by the learner. What to include in skills practices is also crucial. It is important for the coach or teacher to include only those skills practices that will benefit rather than hinder the acquisition of motor skills, and this is where the concept of transfer comes in. The personality of the teacher or coach will dictate to a certain extent the way in which they teach skills. There are, however, proven strategies that teachers and coaches can use to optimise the learning process.

10.1 Stages or phases of learning

Fitts identified several different stages in the learning process, although it must be remembered that learning is a complex process and the stages, or *phases* as they were labelled, are not clear cut. However, it is useful to try to identify the different levels of understanding that each phase represents because we are then better able to create successful teaching strategies throughout the learning process.

There are stages that a learner of a skill has to go through

In practice

If a novice badminton player is in the cognitive phase of learning and needs to understand the serve, her teacher could demonstrate the correct technique and highlight important points (this is called *cueing*) so that the player builds up a mental picture of what needs to be done. This 'visualisation' of the movement is more effective if the teaching is simple, clear and concise.

10.1.1 *Phase 1: the cognitive phase*

The cognitive phase is the earliest phase of learning, when the performer understands what needs to be done. There is quite a lot of trial and error in this phase, the beginner trying out certain movements which may be successful or may fail. The successful strategies can be *reinforced* by the performer experiencing success or being told by their teacher that the move has been successful. Unsuccessful strategies should not be dismissed because all experiences can be worthwhile. The performer should understand why failure occurred in order to avoid the same experience in the future. To establish understanding teachers may use demonstrations or other methods of guidance (these are discussed later in this chapter). It is important that relevant cues are highlighted by the teacher and recognised by the performer.

10.1.2 *Phase 2: the associative phase*

In the associative or motor phase of learning the performer practises, and compares or associates the movements produced with the mental image. This is the stage at which feedback occurs and the learner gradually becomes more aware of increasingly subtle and complex cues. During this stage a vast improvement in performance usually occurs. Motor programmes are said to be formed in this phase of learning, although skills have probably not been 'grooved' automatically yet.

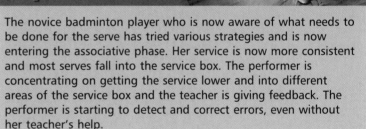

In practice

The novice badminton player who is now aware of what needs to be done for the serve has tried various strategies and is now entering the associative phase. Her service is now more consistent and most serves fall into the service box. The performer is concentrating on getting the service lower and into different areas of the service box and the teacher is giving feedback. The performer is starting to detect and correct errors, even without her teacher's help.

DEFINITION

PERFORMANCE

Performance is only a temporary measurement, which can alter from time to time. It differs from learning in that learning is relatively more permanent.

10.1.3 *Phase 3: the autonomous phase*

This is the final phase of the skill-learning process. Movements are becoming almost automatic, with very little conscious thought. Any distractions are largely ignored and the performer is able to concentrate on more peripheral strategies and tactics. It is said that during this stage motor programmes are completely formed in the long-term memory and reaction time is short. Some performers may never reach this stage or may reach it with only the basic movement patterns. For performers to stay in this phase they must continuously refer back to the associative phase, where practice ensures that motor programmes are reinforced.

In practice

The performer of the badminton serve is now confident and able to perform an accurate serve consistently with the minimum amount of thought. The performer can use more sophisticated strategies such as disguising the nature of her serve, putting her opponent at a disadvantage. She can now also take into consideration more peripheral cues such as her opponent's position on court and, in doubles, the position of the other opposing player.

The skilled performer who is in the autonomous phase can disguise intentions more effectively

Key revision points

Three phases of learning have been identified. In the cognitive phase the learner understands the requirements of the task. There is some trial-and-error learning in this phase. The associative phase is the practice phase in which the learner receives feedback and starts to build motor programmes. In the final, or autonomous, phase execution of the skill is almost automatic. There is apparently little conscious control and the skill is executed speedily. The performer can now concentrate on more complex responses.

10.1.4 Learning curves

You will often hear coaches or performers mention 'being on a learning curve'. This refers to the relationship between practice trials and levels of performance. Strictly speaking, this relationship could be seen as a curve of performance, but the overall picture gives us a rough idea of how much learning has taken place, hence the label – curves of learning.

So curves of learning show an individual's range of performances at particular moments in particular situations. If you were to plot a graph showing your own performances while learning a new skill, you would find that your performances vary quite a lot and that the learning curve would not be very smooth. However, if you took out all of the extremes in performances, you would probably find that a curve of sorts is visible. Obviously, the more trials you record the better indication you will get of the learning that is taking place.

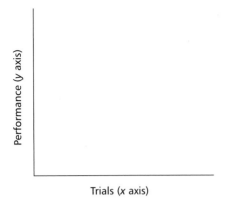

Figure 10.1 *The relationship between trials and performance*

activity

Carry out a simple experiment with a partner. You become the experimenter, your partner becomes the performer. The performer has 20 trials of performing a novel, gross, simple task. Choose a task that can be measured easily after each performance (e.g. throwing a dart with your non-preferred hand at a target, with the greater scores at the centre of the target). Record the scores after each trial and construct a table to show your results. Draw a graph using the axes shown in Figure 10.1.

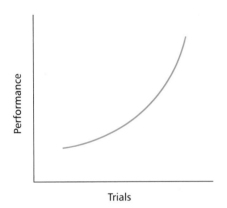

Figure 10.2 *A positive acceleration curve*

POSITIVE ACCELERATION CURVE

This shows that an individual's performances are low in the early stages but increase in later trials (Figure 10.2).

LINEAR CURVE OF LEARNING

This shows that performance is directly proportional to the number of trials. It only occurs over a short period of time and is part of the overall more complex picture of the performance curve.

Figure 10.3 shows a typical curve of learning. Looking at the S-shaped curve you can see that there is an initial period when there is no learning. The performer may fail completely in the early stages of learning a motor skill. At position A you can see a slow rate of improvement over the early trials, when the performer is starting to learn the skill. The curve at A is called a *positive acceleration curve*.

At point B we see a sharp increase in performance levels over a relatively small period of time, indicated by the number of trials. The performer seems to be learning quickly now and consequently the performances are rapidly getting better. This part of the overall picture is called a *linear curve of learning*, which is not a curve at all; rather a straight line showing a short period of proportional improvement.

At point C you can see that there is a slowing down in improvements in performance. This may be because the performer has reached his or her optimum or best possible performance, or could be due to fatigue or lack of motivation to do better. This curve is called a *negative curve of learning*.

The performer then enters into a period, shown at point D, where there is no improvement or a decrease in performance, which is called the *plateau effect*.

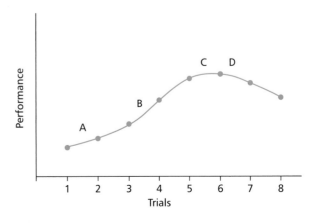

Figure 10.3 *The amount of learning over a given time period*

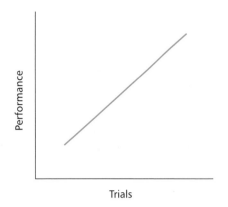

Figure 10.4 *A linear curve*

In practice

When coaching or teaching a novice the tennis serve for instance, be aware that there may be times when improvements could slow – and performance could even get worse. After 20 trials the novice may be getting fewer serves in the serving box than after 10 trials. Give the novice a rest and reassess the goals. Go back to technique and give the novice success again to improve confidence. Make the novice aware of the plateau effect and reassure and encourage. Give plenty of praise when it is earned.

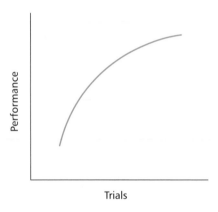

Figure 10.5 *A negative curve*

DEFINITION

NEGATIVE CURVE OF LEARNING

This is when an individual has greater gains in terms of performances earlier, but later there are fewer gains. This is the opposite of the positive curve of learning.

DEFINITION

PLATEAU

There may well be differences or fluctuations from trial to trial but overall there is little or no change in the measured performance. Performances neither increase nor decrease.

The motivation or drive to do well may well have been fulfilled if the performer feels that he or she has made their best possible performance. This is known as drive reduction. This is an aspect of drive theory (dealt with in Chapter 9). This reduction in drive can inhibit the performer to improve and this is referred to as *reactive inhibition*. The concept of drive reduction and the resultant reactive inhibition illustrates well that performance curves are not true reflections of learning.

Reasons for a plateau occurring:
- Lack of motivation by the individual performer. For instance, the practices may lack variety and be boring.
- Physical and/or mental fatigue.
- Perception by the performer that he or she has achieved the goals.
- Lack of rewards, either intrinsic or extrinsic, and therefore loss of interest.
- The performer is not receiving the right information on how to improve.
- The learner feels that the goals are too high for them and therefore becomes demotivated.

Strategies to combat the plateau effect:
- Regular rest intervals.
- New and stimulating rewards.
- Praise and encouragement by the coach or teacher.
- Selective attention employed. Concentration on relevant cues.
- Employment of a positive attitude to improve an individual's skill level.
- Physical and mental training to prepare the performer and to offset the effects of fatigue.
- Setting realistic but challenging goals. For instance, skills could be split up into parts to enable success before going on to more complex movements.
- Being aware of the plateau effect and therefore being prepared to combat it.

INTERTASK TRANSFER

The influence of experience with one skill on a new skill.

INTRATASK TRANSFER

The comparison of different types of practice conditions that may affect the learning of one particular skill.

BILATERAL TRANSFER

The transfer of learning from one limb to another. Learning can be transferred from one muscle group to another through a motor programme (see 9.5.4 above).

PROACTIVE TRANSFER

The influence of one skill on a skill yet to be performed.

RETROACTIVE TRANSFER

The influence of one skill on the learning or performance of a skill that has previously been learned.

10.2 The concept of transfer

Transfer in skill acquisition is the influence of the learning and/or performance of one skill on the learning and/or performance of another. If this influences a skill yet to be learned or performed it is called *proactive* transfer, if it influences the performance of a previously learned skill it is called *retroactive* transfer.

One skill can help in the learning or performance of another, in which case it is known as *positive* transfer, or may hinder the learning or performance of another skill, when it is called *negative* transfer.

It is important that teachers of skills maximise the effects of positive transfer and minimise the negative aspects. Throughout this chapter we will be investigating the best ways of presenting and teaching skills, always bearing in mind the important concept of transfer. In order to do this we must first understand this complex concept.

Teach basic skills first and then build up to more complex actions

activity

Identify whether the following situations are examples of proactive or retroactive transfer, and whether positive or negative transfer are involved.

1 Practising overarm throwing of a ball, then learning the basic cricket bowling action.
2 A novice badminton player spends a day playing tennis, then returns to badminton and finds that many of his shots lack control.

10.2.1 *Basic to complex*

In all areas of education it is common practice to teach basic skills first and then to build upon these skills to achieve more sophisticated skills. In physical education in primary schools, basic

A skill which is highly organised is best practised as a whole but with the support of mechanical or manual aids – like these stabilisers

In practice

To teach a straddle vault in gymnastics, the coach may well use the following sequence of activities:

1 star-jumps with legs wide and straight
2 running with 'two feet take-offs'
3 straddle vault over a partner
4 straddle jump onto a low vault, with support
5 make the vault higher and gradually reduce support.

This encourages transfer of skills in a logical fashion, increases confidence, ensures safety and gives kinaesthetic awareness.

throwing and catching, kicking and striking activities are encouraged so that these basic skills can be transferred to more complex activities such as passing in football and netball or the serve in tennis. Skill teaching is therefore progressive and involves a step-by-step approach from basic 'foundation' actions to more finely tuned complex skills.

10.2.2 Situational influences

Positive transfer is likely to occur only if practice conditions are as realistic as possible. If the response to a training stimulus is not consistent with the response demanded in the real situation, negative transfer could take place and bad habits could be encouraged. For instance, a teacher may use traffic cones to coach dribbling skills in hockey, but the method used to go around the cones is very different from the way a player will go around a real opponent – you don't meet many traffic cones on a hockey pitch! Land drills are often used in the coaching of swimming because it is assumed that positive transfer will take place from the 'dry' situation to the water. However, use of land drills may involve some negative transfer because the different situations have different kinaesthetic experiences. The real situation should be used as much as possible to maximise the transfer effects.

10.2.3 Positive transfer

To ensure that any transfers are helpful, the coach must bear in mind that positive transfer will take place only if the structure and context in which the skills are performed are similar to those used in teaching. Positive transfer is also more likely if the information processing requirements in practice are similar to the ones of the actual skill.

For example, an overarm throw and the tennis serve are both similar skills and therefore positive transfer is likely if the throw is used to learn the serve (the context is not similar but cannot be confused). The information processing requirements are different in some ways – in the tennis serve, for instance, the position of the receiver must be taken into account – but this difference is unlikely to interfere with successful execution of either skill. The 'identical elements theory' (developed by Thorndike in 1914) suggests that the greater the number of components of practice that are relevant to the 'real' situation, the more likely positive transfer is to take place and future responses to be correct. The term 'transfer-appropriate processing' is given to the idea that a new skill might be different from any skill performed before, but if the cognitive, information processing requirements are similar then positive transfer could occur.

It is important to remember that the amount of positive transfer that takes place often depends on how well previously performed skills have been learned. If a skill is broken down and taught in parts, each part must be learned thoroughly before positive transfer can be maximised.

activity

Using your own sport, give examples of skills which could be used to positively influence the learning of new skills. Identify any movement or motor elements which may be useful and also identify similar information-processing requirements.

10.2.4 Negative transfer

Fortunately negative transfer is rare, and mostly temporary. It is more often than not associated with the performer misunderstanding the movement requirements rather than having problems with movement control. Negative transfer must be minimised, and coaches must understand the strategies to avoid it occurring. Negative transfer often occurs when a familiar stimulus requires a new response, particularly if the demands of the new response are so similar to the old demands that the player becomes confused. For example, a tennis player may misjudge her shots when playing indoors because the techniques needed are subtly different from those required in outdoor play. Such problems are usually short lived and, once the performer gets used to the new requirements, normally disappear. If the coach understands that initial performance may be hindered because of negative transfer and draws the performer's attention to the problem, negative transfer can be eliminated.

Key revision points

Transfer in skill acquisition involves one skill influencing the learning and performance of another. Transfer that helps to learn and perform other skills is known as positive transfer. If it hinders other skills it is known as negative transfer. Factors affecting transfer include the structure of practice sessions, situational influences and awareness of possible negative effects. Other types of transfer are listed below:

- *Bilateral transfer – transfer between one limb and another.*
- *Intertask transfer – the influence of one skill on a new skill.*
- *Intratask transfer – the way different conditions in practice can influence the learning of a skill.*
- *Near transfer – when the tasks given in training are very similar to the 'real game' situation.*
- *Far transfer – the training tasks are very different from the 'real game' tasks but give general experiences which could be used in a variety of situations.*

10.3 The structure and presentation of practices

To optimise skill learning, teachers and coaches must create the best possible practice conditions. Using what we learnt of Schmidt's schema theory in Chapter 9, we know that variety in training is very important – not just to build up schema in the long-term memory but also to increase motivation.

For practice to be meaningful and relevant the following factors need to be taken into consideration:

1 The nature of the skills involved – are they open or closed for instance?
2 The amount of technical knowledge needed.
3 The amount of information the performer needs to process.
4 Environmental factors.
5 The previous experience of the performer.
6 The performer's personality and how well they are motivated.

The teacher or coach should analyse carefully the nature of the task involved. A *complex* task involves skills which require a lot of information processing. The perceptual requirements are therefore quite high and the decision-making process depends on feedback and previous experience. The performer needs to understand the task

In practice

In hockey the reverse stick tackle is a complex skill. The information which needs to be processed includes the position and speed of the opponent, the tackler's position, the position of the ball, and an awareness of other players. This skill may be best taught using a slow demonstration, followed by practice at walking pace. The pace of both players may then be increased and then put into a small game situation before coaching within the full game.

In practice

The highly organised skill of cycling would have to be taught as a whole movement, because of the difficulty of splitting it into sub-routines. The use of stabilisers is common; these enable the novice to experience the action safely and effectively. The novice will eventually be able to cycle without the stabilisers, first with manual support and then without any help. The low organisation of the tennis serve is best practised by splitting the skill up into its constituent parts. The throwing action of the arm could be practised first, followed by throwing the ball up, hitting it and following through. Eventually the separate actions could be brought together.

fully and therefore careful explanation is needed. The task may be broken down into easier sub-units and as the performer improves is made more complex, until the complete task can be performed. This technique is most effective in learning open skills, which need high levels of information processing.

The organisation level of the task must also be taken into consideration. A *highly organised task* involves skills that are difficult to split into sub-routines – it is often a continuous skill, such as cycling. A skill which has *low organisation* is easily broken down into its constituent parts – for example the tennis serve involves preparation, throwing up the ball, striking it and finally following through.

The actual structure of the practice session is important when considering the most effective way of teaching skills

10.3.1 Teaching skills using the 'whole' method

In the 'whole' method a skill is taught without breaking it down into sub-routines or parts. If possible this method should be employed more than any other because the player experiences the true 'feel' (or kinaesthetic sense) for the skill, and transfer from practice to the real situation is likely to be positive. The player is also likely to execute the skill fluently and can appreciate the relationships between each part of the movement. If a task is rapid or ballistic in action, the 'whole' method of teaching is best because the components of the skill interact closely with one another.

The golf swing is a good example of this. For the swing to be effective, the action as a whole must be practised because each part of the swing interacts closely with the next. If a motor programme, like a golf swing, is to be built up, then again it is better to practise the movement as a whole.

10.3.2 Teaching skills using the 'part' method

The 'part' method is often used when the skill is low in organisation and can be split up into sub-routines. If the skill is complex this method is useful because it allows the performer to make sense

In practice

A gymnast will benefit from concentrating on one element of a floor routine at a time but must remember that one part of the routine interacts with another. For instance, the way in which he finishes the 'round-off' will affect the start of the back somersault in a sequence.

of the skill and to achieve initial success with basic movements before progressing to the more complex movements. Part practice can also be useful in learning a dangerous skill.

The performer can gain confidence by learning each element of the skill separately and then, when the separate parts are brought together, the performer will have a better idea of the technique involved and be more confident of success. This practice technique is particularly useful when trying to teach serial skills.

10.3.3 *Progressive-part method*

This is often referred to as 'chaining' in the teaching of skills. The skill, usually serial in nature, is broken down into sub-routines which are thought of as the links of a chain. The performer learns one link at a time, then adds on a second link. She practises the two links together, then adds on a third link – and so on, until the links can be practised together as a whole. This process is sometimes referred to as the 'gradual metamorphosis' process.

Many skills are best practised using a mixture of part and whole methods. For instance, a performer may well benefit from trying out the skill as a whole, to get the idea of the complete movement and to understand the interrelationships between the various components. Each component could be practised separately and the skill then brought together and performed as a whole. This mixture of methods highlights weak areas, which can be isolated for more intensive practice.

10.3.4 *The operant method*

This method was described in Chapter 9. It involves 'shaping' behaviour using trial and error followed by reinforcement. The operant method is particularly effective in teaching complex skills. The performer will be able to understand the interrelationships between the components of the skill and also to build strategies for avoiding errors in the future.

10.3.5 *Variable practice*

Practice needs to be varied so that the performer can come into contact with a range of experiences (in line with Schmidt's schema theory, discussed in Chapter 9). Relevant experiences are stored in the long-term memory and can be used to modify motor programmes in the future. With closed skills it is important that practice conditions closely resemble the 'true life' situation. Stimuli that are irrelevant to the closed skill should be varied but those that *are* relevant should *not* be varied.

With open skills, each situation will be different from the last – the conditions, unlike those in closed skills, are not constant. It is essential, therefore, that practice involves many different situations so that the performer can draw from the strategies in long-term memory that he or she has learned in previous practice.

10.3.6 *Massed and distributed practice methods*

The structure of the practice session is important when considering the most effective way of teaching skills. There are many different

In practice

If we take the penalty kick in football as an example, it is clear that the actual conditions of a penalty should be held constant in practice. Stimuli that will vary in the game situation, such as crowd noise, fatigue on the part of the penalty taker and the different pressures associated with the scoreline, must be varied.

In practice

Primary school physical education places emphasis on giving each child a wide variety of experiences, involving gymnastic, dance and game activities. The child then builds a 'bank' of experiences which he or she can draw on when faced with new situations.

activity

Think of a serial skill. Write down how you would break the skill down and use the progressive-part technique to teach it to a novice.

definitions of what is meant by 'massed' and 'distributed' practice, but we will take 'massed' practice to mean practice that involves very short, or no, rest intervals within the practice session. Massed practice, then, is a continuous practice period. 'Distributed' practice involves relatively long rests between trials. The 'rest' intervals could involve tasks that are unrelated to the main practice activity: for example, between basketball drills players could go and play table tennis. It is important to remember the theory of transfer – these rest periods should not involve activities which could lead to negative transfer. Many performers, particularly the experienced ones, use the intervals between activities to practise mental rehearsal, the effects of which have already been discussed.

Research has shown that distributed practice is generally best because massed practice can lead to poor performance and hinder the learning process because of fatigue and demotivation. Massed practice may help learning of discrete skills which are relatively short in duration, but distributed practice is best for learning continuous skills because the player rapidly becomes tired. With tasks that are potentially dangerous, distributed practice is also best because it ensures that physical and mental fatigue does not negatively affect performance and put the performer in danger.

10.3.7 Overlearning

The word 'overlearning' suggests that this is a negative concept but it is usually positive, although in some situations it can be detrimental to skill acquisition. Overlearning is extremely helpful in retention and retrieval of the information needed to perform motor skills.

The definition that is often used for overlearning is 'the practice time spent beyond the amount of practice time needed to achieve success'. This 'extra' practice time can help to strengthen motor programmes and schema. If a skill has been learned so well that it is almost automatic, a performer can concentrate on other variables – for instance, a basketball player may have learned to dribble so well that he or she can direct attention to other aspects of the game, such as the position of colleagues and opponents.

There is, however, an optimal level of practice – too much practice could result in demotivation and fatigue. The teacher or coach must ensure that good performers stay in the autonomous phase of learning by rehearsing skills, but must also be aware of the plateau effect and the costs of doing too much.

Key revision points

Practice sessions must be well planned, taking into consideration the skill to be learned, the performer and the environment. If the skill is complex, with many items of information to process, the skill should be split up into sub-routines and each part taught separately. If the skill is highly organised, and the sub-routines closely interrelated, then it is better to teach as a whole. If the skill is serial in nature, then the progressive-part method may be appropriate. Using this method each section is taught and linked or 'chained' to the next. The operant method of teaching allows learning by trial and error and reinforcement of appropriate responses. Variable practice is important to build up schema in the long-term memory. Massed practice is generally not as effective as distributed practice and involves a practice session with no or very few rest intervals. Massed practice is better for more able performers and can help with overlearning. Distributed practice involves relatively long rest periods. It can help with motivation and delays fatigue. Mental rehearsal is facilitated through this approach. Overlearning generally helps the performer to retain information in the long-term memory. Overlearning helps to ensure that the performer reaches and stays in the autonomous phase of learning.

10.4 Types of guidance in the teaching of motor skills

When a teacher or coach presents a new skill to a student or seeks to develop the skills of an experienced performer he or she needs to decide the best way to transmit the knowledge necessary for effective performance. There are four main types of guidance:

- visual
- verbal
- manual
- mechanical.

The type or combination of types chosen depends on the personality, motivation and ability of the performer, the situation in which learning or development of skills is taking place and the nature of the skill being taught or developed.

10.4.1 *Visual guidance*

Visual guidance is widely used when teaching motor skills. During the cognitive phase of skill learning visual guidance (often a demonstration by the instructor of another competent performer) helps the learner develop a mental image of what needs to be done. Some instructors use videos, charts or other visual aids to build up the 'ideal' picture of what is required to successfully perform a new skill. The demonstration must be accurate so that there is no possibility of the learner building up an incorrect picture. To avoid confusing the learner and overloading him or her with information in the early stages of learning, it is important to concentrate on only a few aspects of the skill. The teacher may therefore only 'cue' the performer onto one or two aspects of the whole movement. One way of ensuring that the learner cues on to the right stimuli is to change the 'display'. The instructor may highlight certain features of the display to help the learner to concentrate on relevant and important information.

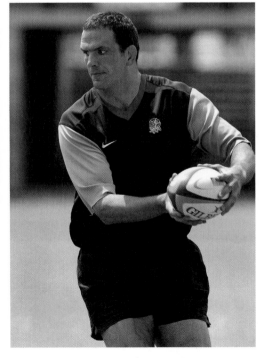

During the cognitive phase of skill learning visual guidance is important for the learner to develop a mental image of what needs to be done

In practice

The following points should be considered before using visual guidance.

- Demonstrations must be accurate and should hold the performer's attention.
- Demonstrations must be repeated but should not be too time consuming.
- Videos can be useful, especially if they have a slow-motion facility, but the student must be able to copy the model presented.
- For a learner to gain maximum benefit, their position during training should be considered. For example, the demonstration of a swimming stroke is best viewed from above on the poolside.
- During the cognitive phase of skill learning visual guidance is important for the learner to develop a mental image of what needs to be done.

activity

Choose a skill from any sport. How would you teach this skill with visual guidance only? Include any ideas about modifying the display.

10.4.2 *Verbal guidance*

This is often associated with visual guidance, being used to describe the action and explain how to perform the activity. Verbal guidance has limitations if used on its own – motor skills are very difficult to describe without a demonstration of some kind. Remember that the instructor is trying to create an image in the learner's mind of what needs to be done. Verbal guidance of the more advanced performer is effective when the more perceptual information, such as tactics or positional play, needs to be conveyed.

In practice

When using verbal guidance the teacher/coach needs to be aware of the following points.

- Do not speak for too long – sports performers have notoriously short attention spans!
- Some movements simply cannot be explained – stick to visual guidance in these cases.
- Direct (or didactic) verbal guidance is better in the early stages to ensure that the learner has a clear idea of what needs to be done.
- Questioning techniques can encourage personal development and develop confidence if handled in the right way – especially for the more advanced performers. Feedback from the performers will also test understanding.

10.4.3 *Manual and mechanical guidance*

This involves two factors:

1 Physical support for the performer by another person or a mechanical device. This is commonly known as 'physical restriction'. An example of this is supporting a gymnast over a vault or the use of a twisting belt in trampolining.

Manual/mechanical guidance can reduce fear in dangerous situations – e.g. arm bands in swimming

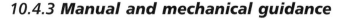

2 The response of the performer being directed physically by another person. This is commonly known as 'forced response'. Holding the arms of a golfer and forcing his or her arms through the movement of a drive is an example of forced response.

In practice

The following points should be considered before using manual or mechanical guidance.

- Manual/mechanical guidance can reduce fear in dangerous situations. For instance, wearing arm bands will help in learning how to swim.
- This method of guidance can give some idea of kinaesthetic awareness of the motion.
- However, it could give unrealistic 'feeling' kinaesthesis of the motion. For example, it is advisable to remove the arm bands as soon as possible to be able to teach stroke technique in swimming.
- The intrinsic feedback received could be incorrect and may instil bad habits or negative transfer.
- There is a reduction in the learner's participation, which could negatively affect motivation.

Key revision points
Visual guidance is used in the early stages of teaching a skill. Demonstrations are the most common form. Important cues must be highlighted through this guidance.
Verbal guidance is not very effective if used on its own, except with very able performers, but with visual guidance it can be very effective, especially to help identify important cues.
Manual and mechanical guidance is important in the early stages of learning. It can help a performer cope with fear and can help with safety. This type of guidance helps to give kinaesthetic awareness but should not be overused.

10.5 Teaching styles related to the acquisition of motor skills

There are many different styles that can be adopted by teachers and coaches. Each instructor has his or her own way of presenting information and the style each chooses depends on several variables.
- The teacher's personality and abilities.
- The type of activity to be taught.
- The ability of those being taught.
- The level of motivation of those being taught.
- The age range of the students.
- Environmental factors.

An effective style takes into account all of these variables. Some teachers are far more extrovert in their approach than others and may adopt a style which is far more open and sociable. Teachers who

Think of some of your instructors. Write down the characteristics they display – are they humorous in their approach? Are they strict? Do they let you have a say in what happens?

Is coaching like acting on a stage?

Think of some teaching/coaching situations where the teacher needs to 'act out' a role, rather than be themselves. Give reasons for your choices. Think of some situations when it is better for the teacher to be truthful about their own thoughts and feelings.

are more introverted may adopt a style which ensures they don't get into situations where they feel uncomfortable. Teachers who are very able physically may adopt a style to use their physical prowess for demonstration purposes. Some teachers are naturally more charismatic than others and so they tend to use a more teacher-centred approach. Coaches need to be aware of their own personality characteristics and abilities before they decide on the approach they will take. Some feel that teaching is an act and that a 'performance' is required – they create an artificial 'persona', masking their own personality and abilities. Others believe that if they act out a role, their pupils will eventually find out and the learning that has been achieved will be devalued. Both arguments are valid, and each individual must decide on the style they will adopt.

The type of activity being taught also has an influence on the style the teacher adopts. For instance, if the activity is dangerous the coach is more likely to adopt a strict, authoritarian style. If the activity is complex and the perceptual demands are high, a more explanatory style will be appropriate. We have already looked at how to analyse and classify motor tasks. Once the instructor has analysed and classified the motor tasks involved, he or she will be in a position to choose an appropriate style of delivery.

The characteristics of the group or individuals being taught is another important element to take into account.

- *Experience* – a novice may need a more direct style to begin with so that he or she gains a clear understanding of what needs to be done. If the individual is experienced, a more consultative or democratic style will allow the individual to give some valuable contributions and share in the decision-making process.
- *Motivation* – if the performers are highly motivated the coach can concentrate on the task rather than attempting to increase motivation. If motivation is low, the teaching style adopted should be more enthusing and reward based.
- *Age* – with very young children a non-threatening style should be adopted, with the emphasis on fun. As the performers get older the emphasis could be more democratic and more responsibility could be shifted onto them. There is nothing worse than the teacher or coach treating responsible adults like children

Environmental situations need to be taken into account when adopting a teaching style!

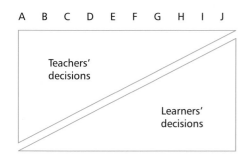

Figure 10.6 *The spectrum of teaching styles*

and not valuing their input. Similarly, too much responsibility should not be placed on young people. A key to successful teaching is to know the characteristics of those who are trying to learn and then to adopt a suitable approach.

- *Environment* – teaching approaches may be affected by the situation. For instance, the weather may dictate the style adopted: a consultative, democratic approach is the last thing that is needed on a cold, wet day! In a dangerous, hostile environment a more task-oriented approach could be called for. Instructors should assess each environmental situation as it arises and adopt the appropriate approach.

10.5.1 *Mosston and Ashworth's spectrum of teaching styles*

In 1986 Mosston and Ashworth identified a range of styles, which are characterised by the amount of decisions that the teacher and learner make in the teaching/learning process. This is shown in Figure 10.6.

When more decisions are made by the teacher, the style is said to be more 'command'. When the learner makes nearly all the decisions the style is said to be 'discovery'. The spectrum includes many styles between these two extremes. At about C or D the style is said to be more 'reciprocal' – this style is characterised by the learners becoming 'teachers' themselves and teaching their peers. This style involves both the instructor and the pupils making decisions. The 'discovery' method is essentially pupil centred; the performers are largely self-motivated and have the experience and creative ability to work largely without help and guidance.

activity

The command, reciprocal and discovery styles are all relevant to the teaching of motor skills. List the advantages and disadvantages of each of these styles.

Successful teachers and coaches are able to adopt a range of styles, depending on the variables identified above. It is important to ensure an enjoyable and productive atmosphere, and motivation can be enhanced if personal achievements are recognised. The teacher should analyse the variables in each situation so that performance and motivation can be optimised.

The best style to use if the teacher has good discipline and the group is large, or if the situation is dangerous, is the command style. This style does not allow social interaction or individual involvement in learning. The learner can simply end up being a clone of the teacher, which may be useful up to a point but does not allow development of new ideas and is not a dynamic process. The reciprocal style of teaching allows more social interaction and encourages a sense of responsibility. Group members must be mature enough to handle the responsibility and have reasonable communication skills. This style is not recommended for complete beginners. The discovery style allows individual creativity but the performer must be well motivated. The instructor must be prepared to step in

The teacher or coach must know what teaching technique motivates each individual in the team if performance is to be optimised

and guide if the performer runs out of strategies or is beginning to develop bad habits. It can be difficult to 'unlearn' incorrect practices, and the learning process could be severely delayed.

Key revision points

There is a range of teaching styles possible. Teachers or coaches should adapt their approach to the type of activity, the age, ability and motivation level of the performer, environmental factors and their own personality and capability. Mosston and Ashworth's spectrum of teaching styles takes into consideration the proportion of decisions made by the learner and the teacher in the learning process. The more decisions that are made by the teacher, the more authoritarian the style. Each style in the spectrum has its advantages and disadvantages and should be chosen, bearing in mind the factors just mentioned. Successful teachers use a wide range of styles, and know how to adapt to changing environmental circumstances and the different needs of performers.

Key terms

You should now understand the following terms. If you do not, go back through the chapter and find out what they mean.

Associative phase
Autonomous phase
Cognitive phase
Distributed practice
Identical elements theory
Learning curves
Manual and mechanical guidance
Massed practice
Negative transfer
Organisation of a task
Overlearning
Part method
Performance curves
Positive transfer
Proactive transfer
Progressive part method
Retroactive transfer
Spectrum of teaching styles
Variable practice
Verbal guidance
Visual guidance
Whole method

Progress check

1. Name the three main stages or phases of learning that were identified by Fitts.
2. What are the characteristics of each of these phases?
3. Why is it important to know what happens in each phase of the learning process?
4. Define what is meant by the term transfer in skill acquisition.
5. Give a practical example of how negative transfer can inhibit effective skill performance.
6. How can a teacher or coach ensure that only positive transfer takes place?
7. What factors must be taken into consideration when structuring a practice session?
8. What is meant by a complex task? Give a practical example.
9. When is it best to use the 'whole' method of teaching a skill?
10. Give a practical example of using the 'part' method of teaching a skill.
11. Why is the 'variable practice' method so important for building up schema?
12. Why is distributed practice usually better than massed practice?
13. What is meant by 'overlearning'?
14. Identify the four main types of guidance.
15. Choose any skill and describe how you would teach it, selecting only one type of guidance.
16. What variables should be taken into consideration when adopting a particular teaching style?
17. Choose one of these variables and justify the 'discovery' approach of teaching it.
18. What could be the problems of adopting a reciprocal approach to teaching?
19. What did Mosston and Ashworth take into account when they developed their spectrum of teaching styles?
20. Give as many advantages and disadvantages as you can for the 'command' style of teaching.

Further reading

J.A. Adams. Closed loop theory of motor learning. *Journal of Motor Behaviour*, 1971.

A. Bandura. *Aggression: A social learning analysis*. Prentice Hall, 1973.

A.M. Bird and A. Horn: Cognitive anxiety and mental errors in sport. *Journal of Sport and Exercise Psychology*, 1990.

D. Davis, T. Kimmet and M. Auty. *Physical Education: Theory and Practice*. Macmillan, 1986.

H.J. Eysenck. *The Structure and Measurement of Personality*. Routledge, 1970.

P.M. Fitts. *Human Performance*. Brooks/Cole, 1967.

E.A. Fleishman. *The Structure and Measurement of Physical Fitness*. Prentice Hall, 1964.

J. Honeybourne. *BTEC National Sport*. Nelson Thornes, 2003.

C.L. Hull. *Principles of Behaviour*. Appleton-Century-Crofts, 1943.

J.G. Jones and L. Hardy, editors. *Stress and Performance in Sport*. Wiley, 1990.

R.A. Magill. *Motor Learning, Concepts and Applications*. Brown and Benchmark, 1993.

R.G. Marteniuk. *Information Processing in Motor Skills*. Holt, Rinehart & Winston, 1976.

E. McBridge and A. Rothstein. Mental and physical practice and the learning and retention of open and closed skills. *Perceptual and Motor Skills*, 1979.

M. Mosston and S. Ashworth. *Teaching Physical Education*. Merrill, 1986.

R.M. Nideffer. Test of attentional and interpersonal style. *Journal of Personality and Social Psychology*, 1976.

J.F. Parker Jr, D.E. Reilly, R.F. Dillon, T.G. Andrews and E.A. Fleishman. Development of tests for measurement of primary perceptual-motor performance. NASA CR p335, 1965.

M. Robb. *The Dynamics of Skill Acquisition*. Prentice Hall, 1972.

G.H. Sage. *Sport and American Society*. Addison-Wesley, 1974.

R.A. Schmidt. *Motor Learning and Performance*. Human Kinetics, 1991.

R. Sharp. *Acquiring Skill in Sport*. Sports Dynamics, 1992.

B.F. Skinner. *Science and Human Behaviour*. Macmillan, 1953.

K. Spence, J. Spence. *The psychology of learning and motivation*, vol 2. London Academic Press, 1968.

K. Sugarman. *Peak Performance. Winning the Mental Way*. Step Up, 1998.

E.L. Thorndike. *Educational Psychology: Briefer Course*. Columbia University Press, 1914.

R.S. Weinberg. The relationship between extrinsic rewards and intrinsic motivation. In: J.M. Silva and R.S. Weinberg. *Psychological Foundations of Sport*. Human Kinetics, 1984.

A.T. Welford. The measurement of sensory-motor performance: survey and reappraisal of twelve years' progress. *Ergonomics*, 1960.

H.T.A. Whiting. *Concepts in Skill Learning*. Lepus Books, 1975.

R.M. Yerkes and J.D. Dodson. The relation of strength of stimulus to rapidity of habit formation. *Journal of Neurological Psychology*, 1908.

Part

3

SOCIOCULTURAL ASPECTS OF PHYSICAL EDUCATION AND SPORT

This part of the book contains:

This part of the book investigates how society can affect the sports performer and how society can be influenced by physical education and sport. In order to understand what is happening today, it is useful to look back at what has happened before and this part deals with historical factors. The terms we use when describing the activities related to sport differ, which can lead to confusion. We encourage readers to analyse these different terms to develop a better understanding of why people get involved in physical education and sport at different levels and the factors which influence and restrict their choices. This part compares physical education and sport in the UK with that of other countries so that we can learn from the experiences of other cultures. Many social issues surround physical education and sport and this part of the book takes an indepth look at the main issues affecting the performer. It is hoped that the reader will base any future decisions and attitudes on careful consideration of the facts surrounding a particular issue, not on hearsay or stereotypes. Discrimination of all forms is unfortunately a feature of our society, in sport as in other aspects. We must strive for equality of opportunity and we hope that this part of the book will help all of us to consider the issues surrounding physical education and sport intelligently and without prejudice.

The origins and study of sport

Learning objectives

- To develop knowledge of the history of sport.
- To be able to discuss the role of the study of sport.
- To be able to define the concepts involved in the study of sport.
- To understand the role that concepts such as outdoor recreation play in society.
- To know the factors that affect sport and recreation in Britain.

DEFINITION

HAKA

A ritual war dance performed by several southern-hemisphere nations before rugby internationals.

Sports are developmental – they develop from *conquest* or from *social hierarchy*. For example, rugby was introduced by the upper classes at Rugby public school in the early 1800s and then spread with the British Empire around the world. The game was taken to western Samoa from New Zealand by plantation farmers and merchants at the beginning of the twentieth century. The western Samoans play the game by the same rules as everyone else, but to them rugby is a *war game* – this is very evident in the ferocity of their tackling. The New Zealand Maoris (and even the national team) play the modern game but have incorporated parts of their own culture into it with the ritual Haka, performed before the game.

In human activity, the invention of the ball may be said to rank with the invention of the wheel

11.1 The origins of sport

The oldest sports were probably gymnastic displays. One of the earliest recorded forms of sport is evident in Minoan Crete – this is bull leaping, in which slaves leapt over the horns of a bull. Records of bull leaping give us a glimpse of the function of this ancient form of sport, mainly as a spectacle with some ritualistic or religious element. To the Minoans the bull symbolised their gods because it was the biggest, most ferocious and strongest animal known to them, and by challenging the bull they honoured their gods. However, bull leaping was also a *test of physique and temperament* – which is the essence of sport. The Minoans did not actually perform the bull leaping themselves – they used servants to represent them. This leads us on to another important element of sport, that of *spectacle*.

In the Haka, the Maoris are really saying 'today we get our own back!'

The modern game of lacrosse originated in a game that the Iroquois Indians of North America played, called baggataway, in which they threw a bag containing the head of an enemy or rival to each other. The South American civilisations had a similar bloody use for the heads of their enemies – ritual games of football, which they played in purpose-built stadiums that can still be seen today. It has been suggested that the great British game of football has its origins in a game called 'Daneshead', played by men who had defeated Scandinavian raiders.

Wrestling originated in Graeco-Roman times. Wrestling was considered as the 'ultimate' sport because it was (and still is) one-on-one and could end in the death of one participant.

These examples point to another characteristic of sport – you often put your life on the line: *there is no sport without risk.*

11.1.1 *Historical links of various sports*

The many sports played today derive from five main historical areas:
• invasion games
• target games
• court games
• field sports
• religious rituals.

Invasion games

These games, such as rugby and football, are warlike games, where the object is to invade the opponent's territory. The origin of these games lies in mob games in which one part of a community played against another part, usually to defend or steal something.

Target games

These games involve use of marksmanship and include sports such as archery, with its clear link to war/defence and also sports such as golf and bowls. The urge to aim and hit targets is almost innate in humans. Think about how you put a piece of scrap paper into the wastebasket – no doubt you screw it into a ball and 'fire' it at the bin.

Court games

Court games originally reflected culture – sophisticated games were thought to represent sophisticated culture. Such games include real tennis, fives, rackets, squash and lawn tennis. The sports are non-contact and mainly individual contests. Because of the sophistication and expense, these games were often confined to the upper classes.

Field sports

Sports such as hunting, shooting and fishing are associated with finding food and survival but also the enjoyment of the chase. The fox was thought of as master of the environment and so a challenge. These sports have also been associated with the upper classes, although the working classes found a similar satisfaction in 'coarse fishing' and in animal baiting.

Games involving ritual

These games included baiting animals, such as bears and bulls, with dogs. The bull was seen as 'bad', man showed his supremacy over the animal, and everybody could own a dog. Baiting the bull before slaughter was often a legal requirement. This is another example of sport reflecting the society in which it exists – but this sport shows an uncivilised society limited in its development.

In bull baiting the bull is tethered and attacked by dogs

11.1.2 *A brief overview of the historical development of modern sport*

Modern sport may be seen to have passed through four stages of development.
1 Popular recreation (before 1800).
2 Public school athleticism (1800–1860).
3 Rationalisation of sport (1860–1919).
4 Twentieth century of sport (1920 onwards).

The transition between the phases represents not only development in sport but also major developments in society.

Popular recreation

In pre-industrial Britain, sports clearly reflected the society. In the main, sports were of two types:
• the sports of the aristocracy – complex and refined, such as real tennis and fencing
• the sports of the peasants – the so-called 'mob' games.

DEFINITION

MOB GAMES

Peasant sports involving large numbers, and few rules, played during the popular recreation phase of sports development – often associated with football-type games.

The mob games and other 'people's' sports were closely associated to the church calendar of holy days and wakes and to the farming year of spring and harvest. These sports were a chance for the people to meet as a community and 'let off steam'. They were not really sport in the modern sense – there were very few (if any) rules, the game being a kind of free-for-all. They were also not played often – sometimes only once a year (for example the annual Ashbourne football game was played once a year on Shrove Tuesday).

Sports involving animals were also popular. Hunting was mostly the domain of the upper classes, and at this time there was still a great deal of 'quarry' available. The royal deer forests are a good example of the exclusivity of this 'sport' – these forests were protected for the sport of the king and those to whom he was pleased to grant a similar privilege. Rigorous game laws were enforced in every county, keeping the common people from catching animals on these lands.

For the lower classes this hunting drive was satisfied by the bloody spectacle of animal baiting. Cock-fighting was a huge gambling sport and bulls, bears and even horses were trained to fight dogs. Special arenas were built to house these events.

Mob football in the Middle Ages

Public school athleticism

At the beginning of the nineteenth century, more public schools began to appear for the upper classes. Very quickly these became an essential element of training to be a gentleman – they were also to play a very important role in the development of modern sport.

Initially the boys took the rural sports into the schools and with some adaptation carried on the sporting traditions of an upper-class gentleman. The games of hare and hounds or cross-country running became substitutes for hunting, but games and sports were increasingly used for educational purposes. Football is the most popular example of this transformation. With its roots in the mob festivals of the populace, football was transformed by public schools into an organised regular game with rules and played an essential role in the education of a gentleman whose destiny was to lead and develop the Empire.

DEFINITION

ATHLETICISM

A term used to describe the character-building values of public school sports during the nineteenth century.

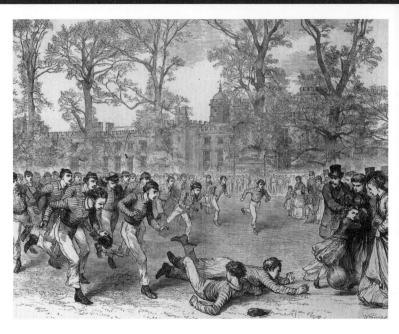

Rugby School – the birthplace of rugby football

Sport was used as social control in the reformation of the public schools, which led to the concept of 'muscular Christianity' – the idea that moral understanding could be developed through athletics.

The public schools were the first bodies to codify sport – to give it rules. This process extended sports and ultimately gave us the concept of sport as we know it today.

Rationalisation of sport

From 1860 onwards the development of sport began to spiral. We can chart the development, codification and administration of all the major sports from this time on. Important changes occurred in society that would determine the image modern sport would portray. It is important that you know a little about the impact of industrialisation and the effect that this had on the people, their work, homes and leisure (a more in-depth investigation can be found in Chapter 30).

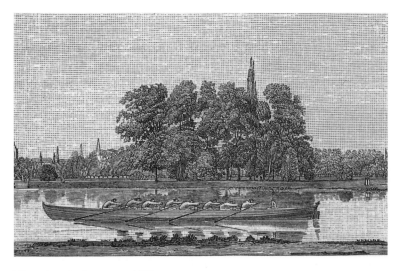

The university boat race, 1829

Most people now lived and worked in urban areas and the influence of the rural elements in sport declined – modern sport is also urban sport.

As boys left their public schools they played an important role in developing sport at the universities of Oxford and Cambridge. They began to unify the various strands and develop national sports, wrote rules and set up governing bodies to oversee these unified sports. These young men then spread their love of games around the world.

Sport in the twentieth century

Several factors have affected the development of sport through the twentieth century. There was a steady move away from participation in sport to the phenomenon of watching sport, initially through spectatorism but increasingly through the media. Spectatorism generated money, which led to professionalism in virtually all sports. Many sports performers are now full-time paid entertainers.

Sport has become a mass consumer spectacle unavoidably linked to commercialism, a point which is discussed further in Chapter 16.

11.2 An introduction to the study of sport

The rest of this chapter involves sociocultural study of the environment in which sports take place. This area is concerned with a family of activities:

- sport
- leisure
- physical recreation
- play
- outdoor recreation
- physical education.

We will take each of these separately and discuss them in their correct contexts. In this chapter we will consider only sport.

11.2.1 *A brief history of sport*

In the middle of the nineteenth century the word 'sport' referred to the 'field' sports of hunting, shooting and fishing which the upper classes enjoyed. Gradually it became more widely applied to all games played in the open air.

Sports (plural) was the name given to a series of athletic contests, often held at rural festivals or gatherings. The Scottish Highland Games and the Basque Games in southern France are good examples of events of this type which still take place.

The modern meaning of sport was born during the industrial revolution at the public schools such as Rugby. Gradually these games were passed on to the lower classes and new pastimes of playing, watching and reading about sport developed. The number of activities that come under the name of 'sport' is ever increasing. Some of the latest additions to this list are speed climbing and mountain biking.

11.2.2 *What is sport?*

We can identify certain characteristics that are shared by all sports.

DEFINITION

SPORT

According to the dictionary 'to sport' means 'to play, or frolic'. A more appropriate definition for this book is 'institutionalised contests, using physical exertion between human beings or teams of human beings'.

activity

Look at the following list of sports and make a list of the characteristics they have in common.

Hockey, rugby, cricket, cycle pursuit, orienteering, netball.

Competitive mountain biking is an example of a modern sport

The essence of sport?

Would you consider the following activities sports?

1 Darts
2 TV's *Super-stars*
3 Jogging
4 Competition ballroom dancing.

SOCIAL CONTROL
Where sport is used to control the masses

The armchair sports enthusiast

From your answers to the activity on page 145, you will have probably discovered the following points:

- they all contain an element of *chance*
- they all involve *competition* between *distinct sides*
- *physically strenuous activity* is involved
- the *clear outcome* has *winners* and *losers*
- games are *spontaneous* and *enjoyable*
- *special equipment* is usually needed to play.

From this list we may develop the hypothesis that all sports must have all of the features in this list.

To check the effectiveness of this hypothesis let us study a particular activity – recreational swimming, for example. Although this activity certainly involves physical exercise and some (very basic) equipment, there is no real competition in swimming a few lengths of a pool. We could argue that there is an element of competition against self, but there are no clear winners and losers, nor any distinct 'sides'. Consequently we may conclude that recreational swimming is not a sport, according to our hypothesis.

Therefore, for a theoretical approach to the study of physical activity, sport can best be defined as an activity that involves competition, which is physically strenuous and enjoyable.

11.2.3 *Why study sport?*

In Britain, sport holds a special place in education and culture. According to Winston Churchill, 'sport was the first of all the British public amusements'. We have a long tradition of sport in Britain. Several sporting events have become national pastimes – Derby Day, the Boat Race, the FA Cup, the Grand National, Wimbledon.

Sport and education
Education has long been associated with sport. Through sport you can learn a lot of life's moral issues and experiences – it also has the advantage of making you healthy!

Sport and social control
Sport has been used to control the masses – a concept called *social control*. If people are playing or watching sport they are not getting themselves into trouble. Social historians have often said that Britain never had a social revolution because its people were too busy playing games!

Britain has a unique position in the history of world sport. Most of the modern games played throughout the world were invented and developed here, and then taken to the extremes of the British Empire.

Sport and international relations
Sport can be used to keep up morale in times of war. For example, the Kuwaiti soccer team toured Britain during the first Gulf War. It can also be used to promote trade and cement allegiances or offer an olive branch to nations that are in conflict with each other. For example, as a means of peace making, a British Army football team played an Afghanistan team shortly after the Afghan conflict.

Sport and the media
Perhaps the best illustration of the importance sport plays in our culture is the amount of time and space the media devote to it. The BBC alone devotes at least 20 hours each week, and most national newspapers dedicate 10–20% of their space to reporting sport.

Key revision points

Sport is a complex concept, the true meaning of which has been distorted by its use in the media. Sport is best seen as any physical activity that includes competition and has a clear winner, and which is strenuous and enjoyable. As Samuel Johnson concluded in 1756, above all, sport is 'tumultuous merriment'.

Ancient sports had the following characteristics: ritual/symbolism, function and spectacle. These elements are still visible in many modern sports. Popular recreation took place in pre-industrial Britain, the games being played having close links to the social background of the players. Sport in public schools was based on the concept of athleticism. Schoolboys adapted the popular games at these schools. Later, schools used sports to develop character ('muscular Christianity') and as a means of social control. A great deal of development and codification of modern sports occurred at universities in the late nineteenth century, which was also a period of great change in society. By the end of the nineteenth century the games ethic was being carried all around the world. In the twentieth century spectatorism, professionalisation and the media have had great influence on sport.

Key terms

You should now understand the following terms. If you do not, go back through the chapter and find out what they mean.

- Athleticism
- Court games
- Field sports
- Haka
- Invasion games
- Mob games
- Popular recreation
- Rationalisation
- Social control
- Sport
- Target games

Progress check

1 Taking Minoan bull leaping as an example, what were the functional aspects of primitive sport?
2 Invasion games have played an important role in Britain's sporting tradition. Suggest reasons for this importance.
3 Why were court games limited to the upper classes in the early years of their development?
4 What are the main characteristics of a sport?
5 What does the New Zealand Haka symbolise?
6 What were 'baiting' sports?
7 Give three examples of activities classified as 'field' sports.
8 Give a historical timescale for our study of popular recreation.
9 In the popular recreation era what were the two main divisions of sporting activity?
10 List the main characteristics of a mob game.
11 How was hunting divided along social lines during the popular recreation era?
12 What role did the public schools play in the development of sport during the nineteenth century?
13 Comment on the origins of 'Hare and Hounds', a game played in public schools during the nineteenth century.
14 Give a historical timescale for our study of the rational phase of sports development.
15 What are the main factors that affected the development of sport in the first part of the twentieth century?

12 CHAPTER

Leisure, recreation and play

Learning objectives

- To develop an understanding of the concept of leisure.
- To be able to discuss the historical development of leisure
- To develop an understanding of the concept of recreation.
- To differentiate between and discuss the use of physical recreation and outdoor recreation.
- To develop an understanding of the concept of play.

Many other terms are used when discussing issues relating to sport and physical education. We will concentrate on the following in this part of the book: *leisure*, *recreation* and *play*. All can be related to physical activity and it is very probable that you have experienced all three. You need to appreciate that an activity can be classified as *any* of these concepts, depending on the context in which it occurs. In terms of preparation for your exam it is important that you can characterise the key points for each of these concepts.

12.1 Leisure

If we listed all the particular things we do in a day, we would probably end up with a very long list. However, most of our activities could be categorised under the following headings:
- work
- bodily needs
- duties
- leisure.

We need to *work* to earn a living. Work consumes a large amount of our time. This definition of work includes related activities such as housework, school and college work, travel to work. Our *bodily needs* include sleeping and eating. *Duties* include the tasks we must perform in relation to family, pets and the home. If we exclude from our day the time required for these three activities we are left with *free time* – this is the time we have available for *leisure*. The average split of a person's daily activities may be represented in a pie chart, as shown in Figure 12.1.

The key to leisure time is that you perform the activities that you *choose* to do. Figure 12.2 shows how the various activities involve choice.

12.1.1 *What exactly is leisure?*

We use the word 'leisure' in two ways:
1 As the period of free time which is left after work.
2 To describe an activity or something we do. A leisure activity is chosen freely.

A great many definitions of leisure are available. Perhaps the best suited to our study are given in the definition box.

Any attempt to fully answer the question 'What is leisure?' reveals it to be a frustrating and elusive concept whose definition changes depending on the context in which it is used. However, leisure does have positive connotations of enjoyment, freedom of choice, self-fulfilment and self-actualisation. These keywords are our criteria for a definition of leisure.

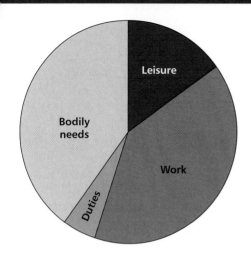

Figure 12.1 *Average split of a person's daily activities*

Make a record of your time over the next few days, put the activities into the categories described above and produce your own pie chart.

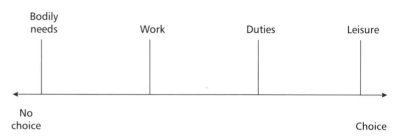

Figure 12.2 *The continuum of choice in activities*

LEISURE

'Time in which there is an opportunity for choice.' (Arnold, 1978). 'An activity, apart from the obligations of work, family and society, to which the individual turns at will, for either relaxation, diversion, or broadening experiences and his spontaneous social participation, their free exercise of his creative capacities.' (Dumazedier, 1967).

WAKE

Initially derived from the ceremony honouring the dedication of the local parish church, extended into first a one-day holiday after the all-night vigil and then in the industrial northern towns to an annual weekly holiday based on the Saint's day of the parish church.

Is housework a leisure activity? To help you answer the question look at the definitions above and the key words we have identified.

12.1.2 *Is leisure a new concept?*

We often hear talk of increasing leisure time and we are said to be living in a leisured society. Increasing automation and development of labour-saving devices, along with the general decline of manufacturing, have meant that most people have more spare time than they used to. However, there has always been leisure time – Roman Britain had 156 'Holy' days (equivalent to our bank holidays), then there were wakes and fairs, half days on Saturdays and other days (e.g. shopkeepers and their half days on Wednesdays). In Sheffield the shop owners formed a sports club so that they could play cricket and football on Wednesday afternoons. They called their club Sheffield Wednesday – a name that is retained by today's professional soccer team.

Leisure has historically been compensation for work done, an escape from drudgery. Clearly the most simple definition of leisure is time away from work. This of course raises the question of what is work – and it is wrong to consider work as only a job one is paid for. Over half of the population are not in paid employment and therefore are not included in the conceptual boundaries of such a definition.

The essence of leisure is that it is not so much the activity but whether it is freely chosen that counts. For example, a person may hate cutting the lawn and will therefore look on it as a duty. However, if she spends hours feeding the grass, talking to it and cutting it so that it resembles a bowling green, this is obviously a freely chosen leisure activity.

Other problems arise when we look at high sport – sport undertaken by top performers. To these people, amateurs and professionals alike, sport is not simply time away from work (it takes up most of their time). Their chance for spontaneous participation in a range of leisure interests is also severely limited. A professional footballer may well be under contract not to take part in any other contact sports or activities such as ice skating because they involve too high a risk of injury.

DEFINITION

RECREATION

According to Lumpkin, 'Recreation refreshes or renews one's strength and spirit after toil.'

Kaplan defines recreation as 'activity voluntarily engaged in during leisure and motivated by the personal satisfactions which result from it . . . a tool for mental and physical therapy.'

Parker says about recreation: 'In its literal sense of re-creation, it may be seen as one of the functions of leisure: that of renewing the self or preparation for work.'

activity

Make a list of your own recreational activities. What do you do to relax and to recuperate?

DEFINITION

SPORT FOR ALL

Physical performance opportunities for all members of the community, with emphasis on participation rather than performance standards.

12.2 Recreation

The word 'recreation' stems from the Latin word *recratio*, which means 'to restore health'. Recreation is an active aspect of leisure, something useful, not simply a time left over after work, duties and so on.

Keywords that are appropriate for recreation include:
- *relaxation* – a chance to escape
- *recuperation* – recovering from stress
- *re-creation* – to be creative.

These are often referred to as recreation's 'three rs'.

In modern life, stress is one of the greatest dangers to health. Worry about work or unemployment, difficulties in the home or in the family can make people ill. Recreation does not usually solve any of these problems but it will enable the individual to relax and 'get away from it all' for a while.

12.2.1 *The history of physical recreation*

The term 'physical recreation' is closely linked with middle-class culture. Its modern usage has been shaped by the public schools and industrial philanthropists of the nineteenth century. In that century people in the middle and upper classes were very concerned about the moral well-being of the working masses – mainly about how the working classes amused themselves in their increasing leisure time. Recreation was considered as positive use of leisure time and the middle classes promoted parks, fresh air, recreation grounds and 'muscular sports' to combat the appeal of the gin palaces and ale houses. Religious movements were also quick to seize on the idea that recreation could be used as a form of social control (keeping the masses in check). This was highlighted by the expansion of church soccer teams, YMCA clubs and organisations such as the Boys' Brigade at the end of the nineteenth century. Holt reports how the Boys' Brigade lured the youth of Glasgow off the corrupting streets by the prospect of 'banging drums, blowing whistles and kicking balls'!

12.2.2 *Physical recreation and outdoor recreation*

Traditionally, *physical recreation* has been used to describe physical activities within the concept of leisure. The term is now better known as 'Sport for All', which describes physical performance opportunities for all members of the community, and places emphasis on participation rather than performance standards.

Outdoor recreation is associated with tradition and the romantic movement. Outdoor recreation usually involves an individual

activity

List the possible rewards that may arise from taking part in a physical recreation under the headings of intrinsic or extrinsic rewards.

DEFINITION

LIFETIME SPORTS

Sports that can be played throughout life, generally ones that can be self-paced or can be adapted.

DEFINITION

HOLISTIC ACTIVITY

Participation involves immersing your whole body in the activity, a complete commitment to the activity.

undertaking a challenging activity in the natural environment. Again, many such activities are available.

12.2.3 *Physical recreation now*

Playing for the sake of playing, or playing sport for intrinsic rather than any extrinsic rewards, is the key to understanding the true meaning of physical recreation.

However, this also accounts for the low status which sport often achieves in our society – if an activity has no external value it serves little function. This is certainly the view of sport that many politicians and leaders adhere to.

Jogging, step aerobics, a knock-up in tennis and visiting a water 'splash' theme pool are all recreational activities. They all involve physical exercise and the participants gain something from doing them. However, they are not sport as we have defined it, because there is no definite outcome, extrinsic reward or stringent organisation.

A new range of activities is developing, associated with this idea of taking part in sporting activities for fun – the 'lifetime sports'. Activities such as badminton and walking can be carried on throughout life, and all generations are being encouraged to get involved. It is hoped that this will break the myth that sport is only for the young – you are not really a veteran at 35, as is currently the rule in sports such as hockey and rugby.

> ### Key revision points
> *Physical recreation is physical activity of a relaxing nature, with limited outcome and organisation. It is a positive use of leisure time, involving an activity worth doing. Physical recreation has a strong link with middle-class moral guidance of the nineteenth century. Intrinsic rewards dominate in physical recreation.*

12.3 Outdoor recreation

In the previous section we defined and discussed the term recreation, and in particular physical recreation. We also identified another term: *outdoor recreation*. This is associated with challenge in the natural environment, but due to the popularity of such activities and the importance the 'great outdoors' plays in our culture the term deserves more detailed investigation.

The simplest and most straightforward definition of outdoor recreation is simply the participation in any enjoyable, *holistic activity* outdoors, where the term outdoors refers to the natural, or at least rural, environment.

12.3.1 *A brief history of outdoor recreation*

The term really developed from two movements that occurred as Britain became an imperial nation and the leading industrial centre of the world in the nineteenth century:
• The naturalist movement
• The romantic movement.

Fishing – Britain's most popular hobby

activity

William Wordsworth (an influential member of the romantic movement) wrote that the Lake District of Cumbria was 'a sort of national property in which every man has a right and would interest anyone who had an eye to perceive and a heart to enjoy'. Do you agree with Wordsworth's idea? What do you think are the advantages and disadvantages of developing outdoor recreation and tourism in such areas?

The challenge of the environment

Both these middle-class cults saw England as 'God's own country' and believed that every Englishman had the right to go out and breathe the fresh air of the country.

Rambling and fishing are our most popular outdoor recreations, and both retain a link with our rural past and the seemingly inherent need to seek out rural roots. The oldest of outdoor recreations, the so-called 'field sports' (a collection of various forms of hunting and other rural pursuits), have in the main been available only to the upper classes.

Rambling, the most popular of modern outdoor recreations, is a much more open activity. It is free and the general development in transport has increasingly opened up the countryside to all. From about the 1850s onwards walking clubs were set up by a variety of organisations. Holt reports how the Manchester YMCA were 'truly muscular Christians', organising weekend rambles of up to 70 miles. Great emphasis was placed on this flight from the rigours of urban life into the more natural pacing of the countryside – a theme the French call *rustic simplicity*. The descendants of these Manchester walkers were no doubt among the working-class ramblers who in 1932 helped cement the status of outdoor recreation with their mass trespass on Kinder Scout – this led to the setting up of our National Parks and to other measures which helped open up the countryside to all.

Cycling followed rambling as a popular form of enjoying the outdoors and has continued to develop – the latest boom being in mountain biking.

Most people now have the use of a car – and this is the way that most of us enjoy some 'fresh air'. Unfortunately, much of the benefits of outdoor recreation seem limited by the fact that few people move more than 200 yards from the car when we do get out into the natural environment.

Some countries have used outdoor recreation as a central part of nation building and even as a political tool. This usually is concerned with fostering a love of the 'Mother country', as seen in the Soviet concept of tourism. The French actively promote 'Le Plein Air' in a country steeped in rural heritage, instilling a love of the outdoors in the young which lasts throughout life. The Americans quest the Frontier Spirit, a concept related to the history of the country and a counter weight to the urban 'win at all costs' society.

12.3.2 *The boom in outdoor recreation*

In recent years there has been a boom in outdoor sports. Activities such as windsurfing and mountain biking have become extremely popular and part of 'fashion' culture. This expansion has been linked to the greater availability of transport, particularly ownership of cars, which has meant that more and more people can get out into the outdoors. Developments in technology and manufacturing have allowed the mass production of cheap equipment (mountain bikes for example), opening these sports up to more and more of the population.

Key revision points
Outdoor recreation involves challenging activities in the natural environment. Most people in Britain partake in some form of outdoor recreation frequently. For most people, the essential element is an escape from the urban environment. The most popular outdoor recreations are walking and fishing.

12.4 Play

One important concept we have not yet looked at and one which has an important part in our society is *play*.

Play is a term with a number of meanings:

- it is an issue in itself, as in *I play*
- it is also part of the morality of sport, as in the phrase *fair play*.

Huizinga suggests that our ability to play has formed the basis for all human cultures and civilisation – humans have always played and it could be argued that many inventions and discoveries have been a product of play. Our children learn about life through play and adults use play to relax and escape from the 'seriousness' of everyday life.

Play is the base from which sport begins. All sports have their origins in play – as children we first play, then move on to more sophisticated games and eventually to sport.

12.4.1 *What is play?*

Play is considered to be a free activity, generally non-serious and outside the maintenance of life. There is certainly a large play element in sport – at the lower level sport is fun and we play to escape and relax. However, the higher you get the more competitive and serious the activity becomes. Sport is not play when there are extrinsic rewards such as money: it becomes too serious.

We can pick out the following keywords that characterise play activities:

- spontaneous
- childlike
- self-fulfilling
- intrinsic.

12.4.2 *The concept of play*

As we have seen above, play is not connected with material interest or profit – so do professional sportspeople *play*?

Play creates an order of its own and often symbolises overtly and covertly aspects of the real world. If we study children at play, it is easy to identify aspects such as competition, dominance and leadership. Gender differences are also obvious: often the boys' football games will dominate the play space, with the girls being confined to the edges.

As mentioned above, we play to learn about life and we usually associate the term with younger people but adults *do* play. Adults play to escape the rigours of work and the stresses of life – paintball or laser arcades are clearly older, if a little more sophisticated, forms of the shooting games that all children play.

activity

List in the terms of play the differences between an amateur and a professional sportsman, using the keywords to help you.

12.4.3 *The functions of play*

What role do play activities have in our lives? It has been suggested that play has three functions:

1 *Biological* – play is an instinctual part of the learning process. It forms a crucial part in the development and refinement of many skills.
2 *Psychological* – play allows us to learn about ourselves; we direct it and it allows us to gain experience. We need to learn how to make decisions and control our emotions and arousal levels, which we usually develop through role play and games when we are young.
3 *Sociological* – play enables children (and to some extent adults) to practise future social roles. We acquire a knowledge of how other people respond to us and how they react to us when we try different roles.

Play also helps to defuse conflict – because of its non-serious nature it can be used to dispel aggression and frustration.

> **Key revision points**
> *Children play to increase their mastery of reality. Adults play to escape from reality. Because of its non-serious quality a number of dimensions of play can be identified:*
>
> *1 Play must be freely undertaken. If constrained it is less playful.*
> *2 Play is non-instrumental. It is an end in itself – you do not play for an outcome.*
> *3 Play generally has its own set of rules and regulations. It is very informal and any rules will be agreed by the participants and may well change during the activity.*
> *4 Play activities involve uncertainty. Play is open ended and has no limits.*

Key terms

You should now understand the following terms. If you do not, go back through the chapter and find out what they mean.

Bodily needs
Duties
Extrinsic rewards
Holistic activity
Intrinsic rewards
Leisure
Lifetime sport
Outdoor recreation
Play
Recreation
Re-creation
Recuperation
Relaxation
Sport for All
Wake

Progress check

1 Our daily activities can be listed under which four headings?
2 Why, for some people, is leisure not free from the obligations of work, family and society?
3 How has the development of labour-saving devices in the home had an effect on leisure?
4 What is the history behind Sheffield Wednesday FC's name?
5 What was a wake?
6 Why is 'time not at work' too simple a definition for leisure?
7 Explain how an activity may be leisure for one person but a duty for another.
8 Why, for professional sports performers, is a definition of leisure difficult?
9 Why is recreation said to be an active aspect of leisure?
10 What therapeutic qualities does recreation have?
11 Why did the upper classes try to promote physical recreation amongst the working classes during the later part of the nineteenth century?
12 How did organisations such as the YMCA and Boys' Brigade use sport?
13 What are intrinsic values in relation to sports activity?
14 Why is badminton a 'lifetime' sport?
15 Why is outdoor recreation a holistic activity?
16 What factors have led to an increase in participation of outdoor sports?
17 Do professional footballers play?
18 Why do adults play? Give some examples of adult play.

CHAPTER 13

Physical and outdoor education

Learning objectives

- To develop an understanding of the concept of physical education.
- To give an overview of the historical development of physical education.
- To have an overview of current developments in physical education and school sport.
- To develop an understanding of the concept of outdoor education.

In this chapter we will discuss the concepts of physical education and outdoor education. These both occur within the education system of the UK. Both have developed over the last century and we will trace this development and investigate the factors which have shaped these concepts today. We will also discuss recent initiatives that have been introduced in an attempt to promote physical activities in schools.

13.1 Physical education

In the UK, physical education takes place only in educational institutions (schools, colleges and universities). It always involves a 'teacher' passing on knowledge to a group of 'pupils' and is almost always concerned with bodily movement. However, it is a wide concept with many different interpretations. Even with the National Curriculum for physical education, no one school's programme is the same as another's. In recent years the academic study of physical education has grown greatly and it is now studied at many levels.

The values developed through physical education are twofold:

- *Practical skills*, which will enable players to take part in a variety of sports.
- *Social skills* such as leadership, discipline and cooperation, which will help an individual develop independence and at the same time produce a love of sport that will continue throughout life and reverse the *post 16 gap*.

Physical education occurs within the school curriculum, although other physical activities may also take place in schools.

The activities actually undertaken vary from school to school, but most of the time is spent on the traditional team games such as football, netball and hockey. Swimming and athletics are the main individual activities and now new innovations such as 'health-related fitness' and the 'lifetime' sports such as badminton and table tennis are gaining in popularity.

DEFINITION

PHYSICAL EDUCATION

The formal inculcation of knowledge and values through physical activity/experience.

POST 16 GAP

It is estimated that after young people leave education over 60% of them will never take part in any physical activities.

activity

The following scenarios may occur in schools, but can you link the correct definition to the scenario?

Scenario	Definition
Impromptu game of football during dinner break	Sport
Playing for school team	Physical education
Attending aerobics club after school	Play
Year 9 football lesson	Recreation

13.1.1 *A brief history of physical education*

Physical education is a modern phenomenon, less than 100 years old. However, its origins go back further than this and it developed from many different strands. Two main pathways can be identified, which developed from the two traditions of education in England in the nineteenth century.

Public school sports education

In the public schools of the upper classes organised games began to appear, at first as spontaneous recreations played by the boys and for the most part disapproved of by the teachers. However, as they became more developed it was recognised that educational objectives could be passed on through participation in games.

Sports became an important feature of all public schools and were regarded as a powerful force in the education of the sons of the upper classes. Team games formed the central core, particularly football and cricket (and rowing at the schools situated near a river). These games were physically strenuous, demanding and relied on cooperation and leadership – all characteristics that a gentleman needed to acquire.

The term 'games cult' has been used to describe the influence of sport in these schools, as have the phrases 'athleticism' and 'muscular Christianity' (see further reading on page 366).

Sports education outside public schools

Outside the public schools, a different type of physical education grew up, springing from several roots: military drill, callisthenics and gymnastics. From these grew the system of physical training, which at the end of the century was adopted in the elementary schools of the lower classes.

From 1902 the government began producing and prescribing a National Syllabus in Physical Training. The 1902 Model Course was composed by the War Office in an attempt to rectify the poor levels of fitness of the lower classes, which had been identified from the performance of recruits during the Boer War (1899–1902). The emphasis of these *drill* exercises was on discipline and obedience – they were aimed at creating a fit, disciplined workforce and army. Drill exercises were compulsory for schoolchildren up to the age of 12 years, and were carried out in the schoolyard with instructions barked out by instructors. Many of the activities involved wooden staves in clear imitation of guns. The instructors were peripatetic, and non-commissioned officers were paid 6d a day by the school to drill the children. This military influence and view of children as 'young soldiers' persisted well into the 1920s.

The course was revised periodically and gradually became a little more educational. The Board of Education took control of the national syllabus and produced a new syllabus in 1904 with revisions in 1909, 1919 and 1933. With each revision the military influence was reduced and slowly 'physical education' grew into something that we would recognise today. However, in 1933 physical education lessons were very formal; instructions were given to teachers in a set of tables and very little variety was allowed. An example of the 1933 syllabus is shown in Table 13.1.

GAMES CULT

The use of team games such as football, rugby and cricket to develop character in public schools.

ELEMENTARY SCHOOL

Free schools for the working classes that gave children an elementary education including reading, writing and arithmetic.

DEFINITION

DRILL

Exercises for working-class children that taught fitness, discipline and obedience.

MODEL COURSE

Set up by the government in 1902 as a response to the poor fitness of working-class soldiers during the Boer War.

activity

Your grandparents could well have experienced some of the above syllabuses. Ask one of them, or another older person you know, about their physical education. Compare this with the physical education lessons your parents experienced and your own physical education programmes.

Table 13.1 *Part of the 1933 syllabus for physical education*

SECTION 1

1. Here, There, Where. Leap-frog practice in threes.
2. 4 Astride jumps with rebound, 4 Skip jumps without rebound.
3. (*Astride*) **Trunk bending downward** with 2 taps forward, 2 backward, 2 pulls on ankles and **Trunk stretching forward** with hands on hips. (1–8). (Latter, with Arm bending upward and Arm stretching upward.)
4. **Upward jumps in threes.** Free Practice. Fig. 39.
5. i. (*Arm Sideways*) **Arm bending and stretching** sideways alternately in one count and two counts
   ii. ([*Astride*] *Arms Crossed*) **Rhythmical Arm swinging** mid-upward (Heels raising). Fig 40
   iii. (*1 Arm Sideways supported at wall*) **Informal Leg circling**.
6. ([*Astride*] *1 Arm Mid-Upward Support*) **Trunk bending sideways** with outer arm raising sideways-upward to touch other hand. (Rhyth.) Figs. 41 and 42.
7. Move to team files, **hopping** with leg swinging forward.
8. (*Knees Full Bend*) **Jump** to 'Astride, Heels Raise' position with arm bending upward or swinging mid-upward.
9. **Riders and Horses.**

SECTION 2

10. (*Kneel Sitting, Trunk Forward, Arms Upward Rest*) **Rhythmical Trunk pressing downward**. (Bench.) Fig. 43.
11. (*Kneel Sitting, Trunk Downward, Forehead Rest*) **Trunk stretching forward** with Elbow swinging sideways. Fig. 44.
12. **Hand-standing**, in pairs, one supporting. (Benches.) Fig. 45.
13. Race round bench twice and mount in 'Knee Raise, Upward end' position. Leg stretching backward with arm stretching upward. Race round twice in opposite direction and repeat balance exercise standing on other leg. (Bench top.)
14. (*Astride High Sitting, 1 Arm Sideways Clenched*) **Trunk and Head turning** to side of raised arm. (Bench.)
15. (*Low Front Support*) **Head turning**. (Benches, 2 high.) Fig 45.
16. Free March on toes, six counts; Knee springing with Knee forward, six counts.
17. (*Front Standing, Trunk Downward, Hands on bench*) **Bouncing up and down**, i.e. pushing off 2 feet and raising hips high. (Benches, 2 high.)
18. **Face vault** with bent knees. (Benches, 2 high.) See Fig 13, page 39.
19. **Running Thro. vault** to High Standing. (Benches, 2 high, and supporters.)

Some examples of exercises in the 1933 syllabus

Physical education in the last 50 years

After 1944 the move towards a free comprehensive education for all was reflected in the development of physical education. The two pathways began to come together, many of the state schools programming both games and physical education into their curriculum. Team games had been adapted by the grammar schools and, with the widespread popularity of sports such as football, became central to all schools. Other activities such as swimming, cross-country and athletics were universally accepted in all physical education programmes.

In the last 30 years physical education has also become an all-graduate profession. Since the introduction of the non-commissioned officers as instructors in the early 1900s the profession has always had a low status in schools, but now the training and career paths of physical education teachers are on a par with those of other subjects. The other great step has been the development of physical education as an academic subject – courses are currently available at GCSE and A level. This has again raised the status of the subject and greatly advanced the study of sports science. We also now have a National Curriculum for physical education, which has given the subject a little more formality and has attempted to bring uniformity to physical education across the country.

The National Curriculum identifies six sport activity areas: games, athletics, gymnastics, dance, swimming and adventure. Schools should offer pupils experience in at least five of the activity areas.

Extracurricular sport (sport outside the actual curriculum) still continues and in most schools is an important part of the school culture. In the main, extracurricular sport involves teams representing the school in fixtures against other schools, but increasingly sports clubs are being used to involve more people in sport. The main problem is that most physical education teachers supervise extracurricular sport in their own time, and are not paid for the extra work. With the increasing demands on all teachers it is difficult to say how long many of them will continue this goodwill activity.

13.1.2 *Current developments in physical education and school sport*

Recent developments have included the development of Top sports programmes in primary schools, the introduction of specialist sports college status in secondary level schools and the developing sports coordinator network. Most of these initiatives have been managed by the Youth Sports Trust and in this section we will investigate their role in both the development and promotion of school-based physical education and school sport.

The Youth Sports Trust, established in 1994, is a registered charity that receives funding direct from the Department of Education and Skills. Its mission is to develop and implement quality PE and sports programmes for all young people aged 18 months to 18 years in schools and their communities. In practice the YST acts as the lead organisation in developing new programmes, working with national agencies such as Sport England as well as private companies such as Nike in the Girls into Sport Project.

The main role of the YST is to manage and promote the Top sports programme and support schools that have applied for or are applying for specialist sports college status. Its main role more recently has been coordinating the school sport coordinators programme.

Top programmes

The Top sports programme has three key features:
- adapted sport-specific equipment that is child friendly
- sport-specific illustrated resource cards to introduce sporting skills
- training and ongoing support for teachers.
  The following programmes are now available for school and community groups to offer. Tops sporting pathway:
- Top Tots: Helping children aged 18 months to three years to experience physical activities and games
- Top Start: Encouraging 3–5-year-olds to learn through physical activity
- Top Play: Supporting 4–9-year-olds as they acquire and develop core skills

NATIONAL CURRICULUM
Issued by the government, this sets out what schools should teach pupils, including physical education.

NIKE'S GIRLS INTO SPORT PROJECT
Programme jointly managed by the YST and Nike to identify reasons for the large numbers of teenage girls dropping out of sport.

EXTRA-CURRICULAR
Activities undertaken in school but outside of normal lesson time – for example, playing for a school team after school.

DEFINITION

DRAGON SPORT

A grass-roots initiative run by the Sports Council for Wales and funded by the national lottery which aims to give primary-school children in Wales greater access to sport. There are seven focus sports, which have been adapted to suit the players' age, ability and skill level. These mini games introduce children to sports coaching, skill development and competitive sport.

- Top Sport: Providing 7–11-year-olds with opportunities to develop skills in a range of sports
- Top Skill: Challenging 11–14-year-olds to extend their sporting skills and knowledge
- Top Link: Enabling 14–19-year-olds to take a lead in the organisation of sport
- Top Sportsability: Creating opportunities for young disabled people to enjoy, participate and perform in PE and sport.

Top programmes are being delivered extensively in England, Scotland and Northern Ireland with over 20 000 schools currently involved. Sport Cymru (the Sports Council for Wales) has developed a similar programme called Dragon Sport.

Sports college status

Specialist sports colleges are one element of the UK government's specialist schools programme set up in 1997. It is planned that by 2005 there will be 250 secondary schools with sports college status in the UK. Schools have to bid for the status in a process which includes raising a considerable sum of money and proving their commitment to the high-quality provision of PE and school sport. If successful the school receives a grant from the government to improve its sports facilities and increase its staff teams. For the following three years the school gets additional funding to help support the school's role in both developing sports excellence in its area and widening participation amongst its partner schools.

School sport coordinators network

Sports colleges are integral to the school sport coordinator programme, another UK government initiative which focuses on improving the quality and quantity of extracurricular sport and inter-school competition. The network is based around families of schools with a sports college at the centre of the network, with school sport coordinators, normally existing PE teachers who are given time off lessons to help manage and coordinate sports fixtures and opportunities in their local schools. They also help develop and extend programmes of sport in primary schools.

The current aim is to set up 150 of these sports families across the UK, incorporating 600 secondary schools and 3000 primary schools.

The other major initiative affecting primary schools is the £150 million of funding (50% from Exchequer funding; 50% from Lotto funding) which the UK government has committed to Space for Sports and Arts. This will enable primary schools to provide new multipurpose sports and arts facilities for children and the wider community.

Key revision points
Physical education takes place only in schools, colleges and universities. In schools a variety of activities can take place – physical education is included within the curriculum and involves learning through practical activities. Modern physical education has developed from two differing systems – the games of the public schools and the drill of the elementary schools. Teaching physical education is now an all-graduate profession and academic courses in physical education are available. Recent initiatives in physical education and school sport include Top programmes, sports college status and the development of school sport coordinator networks.

DEFINITION

OUTDOOR EDUCATION

All those activities concerned with living, moving and learning outdoors.

We discussed earlier the development of both practical and social skills through physical activity. Identify four outdoor activities you have experienced and link them with the type of skills that you may have developed within them.

13.2 Outdoor education

One other activity that takes place in schools that can also involve some form of physical activity is outdoor education. We will look briefly at some of the main characteristics of this concept.

The National Association for Outdoor Education gives the following definition of outdoor education: 'A means of approaching educational objectives through guided direct experience in the environment using its resources as learning materials.' According to Passmore, 'Outdoor education is learning in and for the outdoors.'

Outdoor education is also a concept which has a number of meanings and has been used to embrace all educational activities that take place out of doors. Education out of doors includes many disciplines – geography, biology, history and art as well as physical education. Where do outdoor pursuits fit in? These achieve particular educational objectives: overcoming challenges and the total immersion of one's self in the natural environment.

The definition of outdoor education given in the definition box on this page is probably the best one. It covers all the activities above and involves learning many skills, the learning environment is outside, and preferably in the natural environment.

13.2.1 *The aims of outdoor education*

To heighten awareness of and foster respect for:
- *Self* – by giving yourself a challenge and overcoming that challenge. A good example of this is climbing a rock face.
- *Others* – to gain group experiences, share decisions and work together as a team. Canadian canoeing demonstrates this well.
- *The natural environment* – through direct contact with it.

In outdoor education the emphasis is on holistic experiences and relationships rather than specific skills.

Outdoor education forms some part of most school curricula and is now a stated aim of the National Curriculum. However, in most schools it is only an extracurricular activity. The problems are that outdoor pursuits are very expensive in terms of transport and equipment needed, and many safety precautions must be considered, especially in light of several recent tragedies. Time is another major problem – most schoolchildren have to travel some distance before they can experience the 'natural environment', which makes it very difficult to include such activities within a normal school day. In an attempt to solve these problems, 'trim trails' are being developed – schools are setting up orienteering courses around

If you want to stay afloat and go in a straight line, teamwork is the key

their grounds and artificial climbing walls are being put up in sports halls and playgrounds.

A keyword for outdoor education is *adventure*. In 1984 Mortlock introduced the concept of the 'adventure alternative', believing that we have an instinct for seeking adventure and that outdoor education is one way of fulfilling this drive.

It can be argued that outdoor activities have an advantage over more conventional games in that the decisions that have to be made are much more real. These activities always contain an element of risk because the unpredictability of the natural environment means that there are many uncontrollable (and sometimes life-threatening) factors that need to be taken into consideration. In light of a number of fatal accidents, the UK government has published a new handbook for schools and other organisations who undertake outdoor pursuits activities and other educational visits. All schools must now appoint an educational visits coordinator (EVC) who will check that planning for the trip has been done and a risk assessment has been completed.

Key revision points
Outdoor education is learning in the natural environment. The objectives of outdoor education are the development of the individual through scenarios and experiences that are very novel. Challenge is the essential element, and risk makes the experiences novel.

Key terms

You should now understand the following terms. If you do not, go back through the chapter and find out what they mean.

Dragon Sport
Drill
Elementary schools
Extracurricular
Games cult
Model course
National Curriculum
Outdoor education
Physical education
Post 16 gap
School sport coordinators network
Space for Sports and Arts
Sports college status
Top sport programmes
Youth Sports Trust

Progress check

1   Where does physical education take place?
2   What are the two types of skill that physical education helps to develop?
3   What type of activities tend to take most physical education time in schools?
4   How might a school's physical education programme reverse the post 16 gap?
5   Explain the two pathways that led the development of physical education in UK schools.
6   What led to the introduction of the Model Course in 1902?
7   What were the key characteristics which the 'games cult' developed in its pupils?
8   Why was drill an essential component of elementary schooling in the early part of the twentieth century?
9   Extracurricular sport tends to be elitist. What does this statement mean?
10 What advantages might outdoor education have over normal lessons in the inculcation of social skills?
11 What are the unpredictable parts of the natural environment?
12 In the concept of outdoor education, what does the term 'outdoor' refer to?
13 What are the aims of outdoor education?
14 Why does outdoor education tend to take place as an extracurricular activity in most schools?
15 What advantages do outdoor activities have over conventional games in terms of decision making?

The organisation of sport in the United Kingdom

Learning objectives

- To have an overview of the structure of sport in the UK.
- To know the key organisations in this structure.
- To understand the role of the government in the organisation of British sport.
- To be able to construct a brief historical analysis for the present structure of sport.
- To be able to compare the structure and organisation of sport in the UK with that in other countries.
- To understand the organisation of sport at the local level.

DEFINITION

OPEN OLYMPICS

The modern Olympic Games were set up in 1896, and the International Olympic Committee stated that sports performers should not make a living or any form of profit from sport.

The games were encased in the Olympic Ideal – the important thing was to take part, not win. However, the dramatic rise in performance and needs of the media have led to athletes needing to train all year round and so require money from sport. In the 1980s the Olympics became more open and the rules were altered so that both amateurs and professionals could take part, although the latter will soon dominate as more and more sports become professional.

The development of sport in the UK has not followed a regular pattern. Individuals, groups and clubs have always been free to develop their sport as they liked and the government has never really involved itself directly in the organisation of sport at either local or national level.

Today the *UK Sports Council* has overall responsibility for British sport, with four national Sports Councils overseeing sport in each of the four home countries. In England, *Sport England* has direct responsibility for sporting matters. However, the administration and affairs of each individual sport are controlled by a governing body; there are well over 200 such bodies in the UK.

These governing bodies are all members of the *Central Council of Physical Recreation* (CCPR), a body set up in 1935 to help coordinate sport. The CCPR was superseded (though not replaced) by the Sports Council. The CCPR now has the duty of telling the sports councils how the governing bodies as a group feel about the development of sport.

The governing bodies of sport, for example the Football Association and the Lawn Tennis Association, represent everyone who takes part in their sport and are members of international governing bodies – in these two cases FIFA and the International Tennis Federation. This membership allows British players to take part in international competition.

A governing body may also be affiliated to the British Olympic Association, allowing participation in the Olympic Games. In the past this affiliation was restricted to amateur sports but now the Olympics have become 'open' and many more sports are receiving Olympic status.

An overview of the structure of sports organisation in the UK is shown in Figure 14.2.

14.1 History and background

The administrative structure of British sport has changed little, in general terms, since most of our modern sports and physical activities developed in the late nineteenth century.

To control and codify these increasingly popular activities a number of sporting organisations were established, often with strong ties to the upper classes but particularly to the emerging middle class that had begun to dominate industrial Britain. Elements of this social class hierarchy can still be seen in sport today. The upper classes, who had held power before the industrial revolution, jealously guarded their sporting interests by forming clubs and associations to control participation by more lowly members of society.

Figure 14.1 *Some of the key bodies that organise sport in the UK*

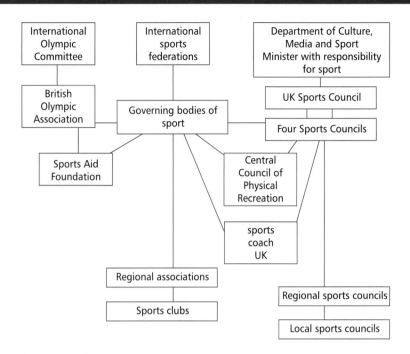

Figure 14.2 *The structure of sports organisations in the UK*

The Jockey Club and the Marylebone Cricket Club are good examples of these upper-class organisations still evident today. The MCC was set up in 1787 and remains an exclusive gentlemen's club. Although its influence is in decline, the MCC is still credited with writing the rules of cricket, selecting England's teams and developing many of the game's traditions. The Jockey Club, set up in 1750, has been the governing body of racing for over 250 years.

The industrial revolution led to the rise of the middle class – the factory owners and entrepreneurs. In the same way as they took over the control of commerce and industry, they also took over control of sport. The middle-class approach to sports administration was a little more democratic; however, they introduced the concept of amateurism into sport, which to a large extent still controls the opportunity to take part in sport. Good examples of governing bodies set up during this time are the Football Association (FA) in 1863 and the Amateur Athletics Association (AAA) in 1880. These national governing bodies appeared in response to the increased participation in sport throughout the country. Generally their task was to establish and maintain the rules of the sport and to organise national competitions.

One characteristic of the British system is that sports are very isolated. The clubs that joined these new governing bodies tended to be single-sport clubs and as a consequence so were the organising bodies. The result was a very decentralised organisation, with individual bodies showing little interest in the affairs of other sporting organisations.

In contrast, in the rest of Europe a more centralised approach developed and organised sport developed 15–20 years later than in the UK. Clubs in France and Germany tend to cater for a number of different sports. This approach encouraged the establishment of multisport federations to coordinate the aims of different sports – an example is the UNSS in France, which has responsibility for sport in all schools in France.

It is only relatively recently that an attempt was made to develop a coordinated approach to sport organisation in the UK. This has centred on the evolution of the CCPR and Sports Council and, more recently, Sport England. However, both of these organisations are concerned with encouraging participation and the provision of facilities rather than actually controlling sport.

The individual sports retain their autonomy – this is the key to understanding the organisation of sport in the UK.

In practice

If you were given the task of reorganising British sport, what areas would you change? What have been the limiting factors in the development of sport in the UK? What have other countries done differently? Try to come up with five major changes, with explanations.

Key revision points

Sport in the UK does not follow a regular pattern and the British government has little control over sport. The UK Sports Council has overall responsibility for sport in the UK – aided by the CCPR. The governing bodies control the affairs of each particular sport – each sport is autonomous. These governing bodies have changed little since their inception many years ago.

14.2 The role of government in the administration of sport in the UK

Despite the popularisation of sport and introduction of universal physical education during the early 1900s, sport and physical recreation have never really been accepted as realms of government responsibility. Since the Second World War, the government has increased its involvement in sport, yet it openly accepted the justification of sport in its own right only during the 1960s.

At various times governments have become involved in control of some parts of the organisation of sport, but this has tended to be only in isolated areas and in response to a problem rather than any planning or development. At the beginning of the twentieth century the government intervened in sport for a while, in order to get the population fit for war (see Chapter 13 for more information on this). Back in 1541, laws were passed to ban all 'frivolous' sports such as football, golf and bowling to make sure that every man under the age of 60 spent his spare time practising archery – a skill needed to defend the country.

The Taylor Report (1990) into the Hillsborough Football disaster prompted government legislation concerning football stadiums in an attempt to stem football hooliganism. The Taylor Report recommended that all Football League grounds should become all-seaters by August 1999. Part of the money required to carry out this massive undertaking was provided through a levy that the government placed on the football pools in 1990, forming the Football Trust – however, most clubs had to bear most of the cost of refurbishment themselves.

DEFINITION

QUANGO

Quasi-Autonomous Non-Governmental Organisations – agencies created by the government to carry out a variety of functions. Quangos have a limited amount of independence.

14.2.1 *The role of quangos in sports control*

Most of the administration and organisation of sport in the public sector is carried out by the various Sports Council *quangos* and local authorities, the latter being the biggest providers of facilities and funders of sport.

14.3 Structure of governmental control

Most of the government's coordination of sport is now undertaken by the *Department of Culture, Media and Sport*. However, sporting concerns do still filter through to other departments, principally the Department for Education and Skills.

14.3.1 *The Department of Culture, Media and Sport*

Although Britain has had a Minister for Sport since the early 1960s, this role has never really risen in status above that of a junior minister, who was a lower member of the Department of the Environment. The many calls for sport to be given cabinet status were ignored. The Sports Council initially planned and campaigned for a Department of Sport and Tourism to be set up, but eventually a coalition with the existing Office of Arts and Libraries was seen as the most effective means of gaining a degree of power.

In 1992 the Department of Heritage was set up and had responsibility for sport and recreation. The new department took up the responsibilities that were previously shared by six government departments and has an extremely varied portfolio, including broadcasting, films, the press, national heritage, arts, sport and tourism. It has two ministers, a secretary of state and a deputy. Sport is further served by a sub-department, the *Sport and Recreation Division*. In 1997 the department was renamed the Department of Culture, Media and Sport.

The major concern of the Department after it was set up was the establishment and development of the National Lottery. The National Lottery was established by an Act of Parliament in 1993 and the first draw was made on 14 November 1994. It followed the pattern developed in many other countries as a means of raising funds for worthy causes, including sport. The five areas of 'good causes' that benefit from the income generated by the National Lottery are:

- sport
- art
- heritage
- charities
- New Opportunities Fund.

Various bodies send bids for funds to the Sports Council, which scrutinises the bids and distributes the money allocated to sport. The amount of money to be distributed by Sport England each year is approximately £200 million. The Sports Lottery Fund has been of tremendous benefit in providing around 3000 new facilities for communities all over the country, with grants worth over £1 billion.

The New Opportunities Fund will provide £125 million to help urban and rural communities create new or enhance existing areas of open space.

activity

Try to find out if any of your local sports bodies have received lottery funding. If any did, how much money did they receive and what was it used for? Information should be available from your local library, council or sports council.

In the summer of 1995 the Prime Minister and the Department of Heritage published a sports policy statement called *Sport – Raising the Game*. This set out the government's proposals for rebuilding the strength of British sport. The main emphasis of these proposals was to recognise the role that schools can play in the development of a sports culture. The publication goes on to outline what the government feels each sector of sport should be undertaking to promote the development of high standards of sport in the country. The other major proposal in the policy statement was that a British Academy of Sport should be set up, similar to the Australian National Institute, which will be a centre of excellence for British sporting talent.

In 1999 Sport England announced its new strategy for the new millennium, entitled 'More people, more places, more medals'. This strategy introduced two new programmes: the Active Sports Programme, aimed at encouraging mass participation, and the World Class Programme, aimed at increasing the standard of England's elite performers. Sport England's plan is to extend the concept of a national academy of sport into a 'national network of 10 elite training centres around England', though their headquarters (known as the UK Sports Institute) is based in London.

In 2002, the UK government produced its latest policy document relating to sport, 'A Sporting Future for All'. It laid out two main objectives for UK sport:

- more people of all ages and all social groups taking part in sport; and
- more success for all top UK competitors and teams in international competition.

The government has identified a number of key issues which it believes need to be tackled if improvements to the UK performance in sport are to be achieved.

- There are not enough opportunities for children and young people to take part.
- People lose interest as they get older, reducing participation and diminishing the pool of talent.
- There are too many obstacles to the progress of those with the potential to reach the top.
- The organisation and management of sport is fragmented and too unprofessional.

14.3.2 *The Sports Council*

This government-funded quango was established in 1965, receiving its Royal Charter in 1972. It is an autonomous body under the Department of Culture, Media and Sport, with a brief to take overall responsibility for sport in the UK.

The Sports Council has four main aims:
1 To increase participation in sport.
2 To increase the quality and quantity of sports facilities.
3 To raise standards of performance.
4 To provide information for and about sport.

In 1994 it was announced that the Sports Council would be reshaped to create two new bodies: the *UK Sports Council* and the *English Sports Council*, rebranded as *Sport England* in 1999. This brings England in line with the other UK nations in that it now has its own Sports Council. The UK Sports Council has a coordinating

activity

Have a look at the sports facilities where you live and look for the Sports Council's emblem. Make an inventory of the facilities the Sports Council has helped to fund in your area.

role, ensuring that all councils work in the same direction, and has responsibility for drugs testing and doping control in all UK sport.

Each council is split further into regional and local sports councils, enabling area-specific planning. Funding for the Council comes from the National Lottery Sports Fund, and Sport England receives £200 million per year. This money is used to run the regional councils, fund campaigns and capital projects and provide information services, although most of it is redistributed to sports governing bodies and institutions as grants to be used for increasing sports participation, building new facilities and setting up recreation programmes.

14.3.3 *The Countryside Commission*

This quango is an independent body which investigates matters relating to the conservation and enhancement of the natural environment, and the provision and development of facilities in the countryside for recreation. You have probably come across the *Country Code*, an initiative set up by the Countryside Commission to teach people how to use and respect the countryside. Its link with sport is to help develop access for outdoor sports and also to manage them so that the landscape is not destroyed.

> ### *Key revision points*
> *The limited role of central government in sports organisation reinforces the decentralised nature of sport organisation in the UK. Most administration in the public sector is left to quangos such as the Sports Council or local authorities. The Department of Culture, Media and Sport has taken charge of sport – its first major job was to develop the National Lottery to help fund sports and charities. The Sports Council has overall responsibility for sport in the UK.*

14.4 The national sports agencies

14.4.1 *An overview*

We have already identified that most sports administration in the UK is carried out by individual governing bodies – these will be discussed in detail in the next section. However, a number of *national agencies* coordinate particular areas of sport, once again characterised by their autonomy and diversity.

Some of these agencies have specific tasks, for example sports coach UK develops coaching expertise and the British Olympic Association coordinates all Olympic matters. Others are more general in their approach, for instance SportsAid is a charitable organisation that helps to fund amateur sports performers, allowing them to compete at international level.

Most of these bodies are funded by the public sector or by voluntary donations – again there is much diversity. In general their role is to advise and provide information rather than administer and organise.

14.4.2 *Central Council of Physical Recreation and British Sports Trust*

This independent voluntary body was set up in 1935, and is the 'voice of the governing bodies' in that it represents the governing

bodies of sport and after consultation passes on their views to the Sports Council and government.

Its greatest success was in establishing the National Sports Centres, specialist centres where our national teams and performers train. Management of these was transferred to the Sports Council and has now moved toward self management.

When the Sports Council was developed in the early 1960s it gradually took over many of the roles of the CCPR. The idea was that the Sports Council would replace the CCPR but the governing bodies, fearing too much government intervention, decided to maintain some independence and the CCPR became a charitable trust. The Sports Council still has some control over the CCPR.

The CCPR now acts as a consultative body to the Sports Council, advising it of the views of the more than 240 individual governing bodies. Its other roles include commissioning reports on sports issues and working in close association with the British Sports Trust. It is funded by a grant from the Sports Council.

In 1998 the CCPR established the British Sports Trust, a wholly owned charity of the CCPR, to fund-raise and then finance the Community Sports Leaders Award.

In a £7 million collaboration between the British Sports Trust, Sport England and the Youth Sports Trust, the 'Step into Sport' initiative will train young volunteers in every local authority and provide a series of opportunities for them once trained, such as developing links with National Governing Bodies.

14.4.3 *The British Olympic Association*

This independent organisation is responsible for all Olympic matters in the UK, primarily entering competitors for the Olympic Games. Other functions include raising funds to enable British performers to compete at the Games and for the transportation, clothing and other expenses involved in sending a British team (up to £4 million). A more general role is to develop interest in the Olympic movement in Britain. It also helps to coordinate any bids to host the games.

The fund-raising role of the British Olympic Association is unique to the UK. In most other countries, even the USA, central government helps to finance the Olympic team – but the British Olympic Association raises all the money itself. This has traditionally been achieved through schoolchildren's sponsored events and donations from the general public and business. Increasingly, more money is being raised through commercial sponsorship, specifically in the use of the Olympic logo (you may have seen the five-ring logo on Mars Bars and cans of Coca Cola).

14.4.4 *SportsAid (formerly The Sports Aid Foundation)*

The Sports Aid Foundation was formed in 1975 by Dennis Howell, then Minister for Sport. This autonomous fund-raising body is managed by a board of governors and trustees and aims to raise and distribute funds to help the very best amateur sports men and women, though it is now mainly aimed at young sports performers, or those who do not qualify for sport lotto funding.

The income required is generated through fund-raising, voluntary donations, National Lottery contributions and commercial sponsorship. In the past international insurance brokers Minet have provided considerable support, although at the moment the biggest contributor is the Foundation for Sport and the Arts.

The Sports Aid Foundation was established to enable our top amateur competitors to train in the same way as many others throughout the world without worrying about finance. Its slogan reinforces this point: 'Giving Britons a Better Sporting Chance'.

To qualify for a national SportsAid grant you must be:
* aged between 12 and 18
* in genuine need, not in receipt of a National Lottery World Class Performance Grant
* a member of a national squad.

Regional grants raised by SportsAid regions are also available to local competitors who are not in receipt of any kind of national grant and have a top six ranking in their sport or are a member of a national squad.

14.4.5 Sports coach UK (formally the National Coaching Foundation)

Established by the Sports Council in 1983, with its headquarters in Leeds, the NCF is run by a small staff under the control of a director. The NCF rebranded itself as Sports Coach UK in 2002. It provides a wide range of opportunities for coaches to improve their knowledge and practice of sport. This function is carried out by regional coaching centres based at higher-education institutions throughout the UK (11 in England, two in Wales, two in Scotland and one in Northern Ireland).

The problem that the Foundation faces is the fact that the UK has such a complex sports structure, mainly due to the autonomy of each governing body (and consequently the coaches). Also most coaches work voluntarily and so don't have the time or the funds to obtain qualifications.

Sports coach UK has two main aims to overcome these problems:
1 To promote education through its coaching courses and awards.
2 To increase knowledge through information centres, its monthly magazine *Supercoach*, videos and its subsidiary (Coachwise Ltd), which provides a service for coaches to purchase books and resources on coaching matters.

Recent major programmes have included *Champion Coaching* and *Coaching for Teachers*.

14.4.6 The English Federation of Disability Sport

This acts as the umbrella organisation for disabled sportsmen and women in the country. Launched in October 1999, the Federation's mission is be the united voice of disability sport in England, influencing organisational policies, practice and structures to promote where appropriate the mainstreaming of disability sport from grass roots to excellence. Operating through a network of 10 regional offices, its other key role is to bring together the seven National Disability Sport Organisations: British Amputee and Les Autres Sports Association, British Blind Sport, British Deaf Sports Council, British Wheelchair Sports Foundation, Cerebral Palsy Sport, Disability Sport England, and the English Sports Association for people with Learning Disability.

The Federation also assists and encourages 'mainstream' sports providers, such as the national governing bodies of sport and local authorities, to include sporting opportunities for athletes with disabilities.

14.4.7 Disability Sport England

Funded though sponsorship and fund-raising, this body's main aim is to promote disability sport in England. It works in a similar way to the mainstream Sport England encouraging mass participation amongst the disabled and highlighting, through campaigns and programmes, the benefits of sport and physical activity for people with disabilities. One of its most successful programmes has been the Mini and Junior Games. These national events are open to all disabled children who compete through regional rounds, culminating in a national final.

14.4.8 British Paralympic Association

The British Paralympic Association was set up in 1989. At the previous 1988 Paralympic Games in Seoul, the Great Britain team was organised by an ad hoc committee made up from the various disability sport organisations. It was decided that a more permanent organisation was required to undertake such a huge task.

The BPA now works in a similar way to the BOA, supporting and helping athletes prepare for games, as well as promoting paralympic sport.

DEFINITION

CHAMPION COACHING
Aimed at developing the performance of 11–14-year-old children through specialist coaching. (This will transfer into the World Class Start Programme over the next few years.)

COACHING FOR TEACHERS
Set up in 1996 in association with the Sports Councils, aimed at encouraging qualified and trainee teachers to take advantage of enhanced coaching opportunities.

AUTONOMOUS
A body is self-governing, making decisions independently without interference from other bodies, including the government.

Key revision points

Sports associations in the UK are autonomous. The national sports agencies offer advice and aid, but have no real control over the organisation of sport in this country. The Central Council of Physical Recreation is the voice of the governing bodies; the British Olympic Association looks after the British Olympic team and matters concerning the Olympics; the Sports Aid Foundation raises money to give amateur sportsmen and women a better chance to compete; and sports coach UK aims to develop the education of coaches. Sport for the disabled is growing and there are now a number of bodies organising sport and physical activity for all categories of disability. The English Federation of Disability Sport attempts to coordinate the many bodies involved and lobby mainstream sport organisations and providers to create more opportunities for people with disability to participate in sport and physical activity.

14.5 The national governing bodies of sport

Most modern sports developed their present form within the last 150 years. As participation in sports began to increase at the end of the nineteenth century and many activities became popular recreations, it became necessary for those taking part to agree to a common set of rules or laws. Until this time there had been many regional variations and it was very difficult for teams from different schools or areas to play against each other.

This need for *codification* led directly to the formation of a governing body within each sport. As Houlihan (1991) concludes, their 'main concern was to harmonise rules and develop a national pattern of organisation'.

It is for this reason that the rules and organisation of each individual sport in the UK lie in the hands of an autonomous national governing body.

14.5.1 Role of the governing bodies

These bodies are responsible for general administration of the sport and the conduct of competitions. They can be very large organisations – 43 000 football clubs are affiliated to the Football Association – or quite small organisations with the responsibility for minority sports, such as the British Water Ski Federation.

The foundation of the system is that clubs become affiliated to their particular governing body. Clubs pay a fee to become members of these bodies, which gives the club the right to vote on sports issues and to take part in sports competitions.

As participation in sport of all kinds has increased, the duties of the governing bodies have become more demanding and their workload has grown accordingly. Today, a number of governing bodies now require full-time administrators to look after their affairs but there is still an emphasis on voluntary work. This reflects the tradition in British sport – committee work and decision making still tends to lie in the hands of unpaid volunteers.

At present there are over 300 national governing bodies in the UK. Their major concerns are:

activity

See if you can find out the names of the national governing bodies for the following sports in the UK: football, rugby union, athletics, tennis, hockey, badminton.

Try to find out the date each body was formed. Can you suggest why these dates are close together?

Figure 14.3 *Local clubs have an input at national and international level*

1 To establish their own rules and regulations.
2 To organise competitions.
3 To develop coaching/leadership awards.
4 To have direct responsibility for sport at the local and national level, as well as representing the sport in international matters.
5 To select teams and competitors to represent the home countries or the UK at international events.

14.5.2 *The structure of the governing bodies*

Single sports clubs tend to be grouped into regional or member associations such as County Associations, whose representatives have an input to the national governing body. This is outlined in Figure 14.3.

Nearly all of the national bodies are members of the international federations for their sport. The international federations decide the rules and regulations of international competition and are responsible for the organisation and administration of major international events and tournaments.

Many bodies in the UK are also linked through membership of the British Olympic Association, which allows a national governing body to enter its members in the Olympic Games.

14.5.3 *Funding*

The national governing bodies draw their income from a variety of sources.
- *Affiliation fees* – membership fees from clubs, associations and individual members.
- *Sports Council grants* – a number of bodies receive grant aid from the Sports Council.
- *Development grants* – for special events/programmes from the Foundation for Sport and the Arts, the National Lottery sports fund or New Opportunities Lottery Fund.
- *Sponsorship* – from commercial companies.
- *Television rights* – TV companies have to pay the governing bodies for the right to televise matches and tournaments.

14.5.4 *Future roles*

With the many changes affecting sport today, the national governing bodies are having to adapt and take on new roles. Professional sport is a now a global industry worth £12 billion of consumer spending in the UK alone and employs 420 000 people.

Media and commercial interests are essential elements of modern sport and the governing bodies need to become more accountable and efficient in their work. Their structure is likely to become sophisticated and they will probably need to employ more full-time staff. Staff will also need a wider variety of skills – media relations and marketing will be essential roles in all sports governing bodies if they are to survive in the twenty-first century.

The other main issue facing many sports is the gap that is developing between elite performers and amateurs. This may result in the top elite breaking away, forming premier bodies and probably securing most of the funding and resources – this has already occurred in football and rugby league.

The UK government, together with the Football Association and FA Premier League, has established a Football Foundation which will channel at least 5% of professional football's television revenues into grass-roots development.

14.5.5 *An example of the structure and responsibilities of a typical governing body: the Amateur Swimming Association*

Affiliated to	International Federation of Amateur Swimming
Headquarters	Freehold offices in Loughborough, Leicestershire
Salaried permanent staff	20
Number of affiliated clubs	1784
Number of members	300 000
Number of registered competitive swimmers	53 000 (each paying an annual fee of £7.50)
Responsible for organisation of	Swimming
	Diving
	Water polo
	Synchronised swimming
Special schemes	ASA education programme for teachers/coaches
	ASA proficiency, life saving, survival awards
	ASA liaison with schools and leisure centres
	ASA contribution to health and safety guidelines
	ASA contribution to medical research
Income	ASA award scheme raises £90 000
	ASA education programme – books, videos, etc.
	ASA Enterprises Ltd – merchandising
	Television fees
	Sponsorship money
	Grant of £632 000 from the Sports Council

Key revision points

The national governing bodies are autonomous organisations. They are responsible for the organisation and codification of their particular sport. Most bodies receive money from Sports Council grants and continue to distance themselves from other sports. However, some are now moving away from their voluntary, middle-class, elite backgrounds and are becoming commercial enterprises.

14.6 Sport at the local level

The Sports Council estimates that one in three people in the UK regularly participate in sports, mostly at the local level. Local authorities are the main providers of sports and recreational facilities, and are financed by the public sector.

However, most of the actual organisation falls within the voluntary sector, with the base level being small, single sport clubs. The role of some local clubs in British sport is shown in Table 14.1.

Table 14.1 *Examples of the role local clubs play in UK sport*

Activity/sport	Number of clubs	Total number of members
Athletics	19 000	110 000
Bowls (outdoors)	3 529	161 672
Football	42 000	1 250 000
Hockey	1 850	80 000
Golf	1 700	238 000
Netball	3 300	60 000
Swimming	1 784	300 000
Tennis	2 432	131 800

activity

Sports clubs tend to be administered and organised by small voluntary committees. There are several key positions that all clubs require: Chairman, Secretary, Treasurer, Coach and Captain. Using a sports club you know, try to find out what each of these people actually does. Summarise the roles in a table.

Sport at the local level consists of many small groups of people taking part quite independently. Clubs are small, the facilities basic and the organisation limited. There is no central organisation at this level to plan and coordinate sport development, again reflecting the autonomy of sport in the UK.

The Sports Council has attempted to tackle this issue by setting up *Local Advisory Sports Councils*. These are independent bodies, made up of local groupings of clubs and other interested bodies. They discuss issues that involve all sports at the local level and pass on their views to the local authorities. However, these bodies are not found in every area and their contribution to the administration of sport is often limited.

14.6.1 *Who provides local facilities?*

Sports facilities at the local level are mostly provided by:
* local authorities
* schools
* private sector.

Local authority provision

Local authorities are the greatest providers of facilities. City, Borough and District Councils provide a vast range of sport and recreational facilities – parks, leisure centres and swimming pools, golf courses, community halls, for example. These centres cater for the needs of the local community, although public sector facilities can also be quite grand, as in Birmingham's National Indoor Arena and Elland Road, Leeds United's stadium, which is owned by Leeds City Council.

There are about 1500 swimming pools and 2000 local leisure centres in the UK but the Sports Council states that the UK is under-resourced and has been campaigning to increase the provision of local sports facilities.

In the past much of the money needed to fund these facilities was drawn directly from central government grants and local taxes (Rates, Community Charge, Council Tax). The main objective of these facilities is to maximise participation in sport so prices are often subsidised, allowing lower admission charges and access to all sections of the community – with concessions for students, the unemployed and other low-income groups. However, local authority budgets have become a lot tighter because central government has been steadily reducing its grants. One of the first areas affected has been the sport and recreational facilities. Admission prices have had to rise and costs have been cut, which has led to the closure of some facilities.

Schools provision

A second major area of facility provision is the education system. Most schools in the UK have a good range of sports halls, pitches and pools. Increasingly these are also being used by the public. The policy of opening up facilities to the public is known as *dual use*. In the main, schools allow their facilities to be used after school, with clubs and organisations paying to use them.

Opportunities for developing dual-use schemes will increase in the future with the recent changes in the financial responsibilities of schools. Local management gives a school's governing body more control over its budget and facilities, which may increase the amount of facilities available.

Commercial fitness centre

DEFINITION

SPORTSMATCH

Sportsmatch is a government scheme that matches pound for pound commercial sponsorship of grass-roots sporting events or activities.

DEFINITION

INSTITUTE OF SPORTS SPONSORSHIP

The trade association for sponsoring companies. Produces a range of printed material to assist companies and sports organisers who want to develop sponsorship programmes.

activity

Make a list of the sports facilities in a three-mile area near you. Find out where the money comes from to fund them and classify each facility as a public sector, private sector or voluntary sector facility.

Private sector provision

This is made up of two main groups: commercial enterprises that provide facilities for the public in return for payment, and companies that provide facilities for their employees.

The role of the first group in providing leisure facilities is growing – the leisure 'boom' of the 1990s has increased demand and many people have seen this as an opportunity to cash in on the leisure trends. These leisure companies tend to cater for specific areas, such as fitness or water sports. Although the facilities provided are usually of a high standard, the prices are also correspondingly high. The development of private sector facilities may encourage a move towards elitism, where only those on higher incomes will be able to afford to take part. The main aim of these companies is to make profit, and there is little emphasis on catering for the needs of the community.

Some companies and businesses provide sports facilities for the use of their employees and families. The company pays all the expenses involved in the upkeep of the buildings, pitches, courts and greens. Often a small membership fee is charged, though many companies provide the facilities free of charge. Companies see this as a way of encouraging people to work for them and of fostering the morale of the existing workforce. Recently many companies have put a lot of emphasis on reducing stress levels in their workforce – this can often be achieved through sporting activities.

Active Sports programme

As part of its millennium strategy, in 1999 Sport England introduced its new Active Sports programme. This programme aims to encourage mass participation amongst young people through funding and support schemes and by bringing together local providers – essentially schools, clubs and community groups.

In order to fulfil this, Sport England and local authorities are issuing lottery money to appoint Active Sports Managers in each local authority area. Their job will be to promote a coordinated approach to grass-roots sport.

A new scheme, the Millennium Volunteers Scheme, was set up as a UK-wide initiative in 2002. This is aimed at 16–24-year-olds who want to volunteer their time for the benefit of others. Millennium Volunteers Scheme projects enable young people to gain experience and recognition while benefiting local community sports groups with enthusiasm and expertise.

Sportsmatch and grass-roots sport

Sportsmatch is the government's grass-roots sports sponsorship incentive scheme, funded by the Department of Culture, Media and Sport through grant aid from Sport England and administered by the Institute of Sports Sponsorship. Receiving around £3.5 million a year, the scheme match funds raised through commercial sponsorship of grass-roots sports organisations. Since 1993 Sportsmatch has encouraged 4000 companies to sponsor projects in 73 sports. An estimated 12 million people have participated in Sportsmatch-backed schemes which in total have put £75 million into grass-roots sport. To coincide with the World Indoor Athletics Championships held in Birmingham in 2003, Norwich Union sponsored a festival of sport for school children. NU's £50 000 sponsorship was matched by £50 000 from Sportsmatch giving the event far wider exposure. The three-day event attracted more than 6000 schoolchildren.

Key revision points

Sport at the local level is carried on by small independent groups arranged in voluntary clubs. Three sectors are involved in the administration and funding of sport at the local level: voluntary, private and public. Local authorities provide most local sports facilities but increasingly private enterprises are providing high-quality facilities.

Key terms

You should now understand the following terms. If you do not, go back through the chapter and find out what they mean.

Active Sports programme
Affiliation
Autonomy
British Olympic Association
Central Council for Physical Recreation
Champion coaching
Coaching for teachers
Codification
Decentralisation
Department of Culture, Media and Sport
Dual use
Elitism
Governing body
Open sports
Private sector
Public sector
Quango
SportsAid
sports coach UK
Sports Councils
Sportsmatch
Voluntary sector
World Class Sports programme

Progress check

1   What problems in the development of sport in the late 1800s led to the formation of national governing bodies?
2   Describe the structure of the CCPR and the role it plays in coordinating sport in the UK.
3   Briefly describe the structure and function of UK Sport
4   Why does a country as small as the UK need regional sports councils?
5   The Sports Council uses the term 'target group'. What does this term mean?
6   What does the phrase 'autonomy of governing bodies' refer to in terms of the structure of British sport?
7   How is sports coach UK aiding sport in the UK's general move towards raising standards in performance?
8   How has SportsAid helped Steve Backley to become an international champion?
9   What is the BOA? What specific role does it play in the organisation of elite sports in the UK?
10 Explain why British sports organisations may be unwilling to accept direct funding from the government.
11 How do the aims and objectives of a public sector facility differ from those of a private sector facility?
12 What are the possible disadvantages of a school developing a dual-use policy with its sports hall?
13 What benefits may a company hope to develop by providing sports facilities for its employees?
14 'Sport for All' is not yet a reality. What sociocultural constraints have hindered its development in the UK?
15 How might the National Lottery increase the opportunity to take part in sport?
16 The UK's decentralised system of sports administration leads to limited funds being spread too thinly. What reforms could be introduced to get better value for money?

The organisation of European sport and global games

Learning objectives

- To look at how sport is organised on a European level and international level.
- To investigate the impact of sport on European life.
- To investigate how sport is used to promote politics and ideals of different countries through global games.
- To know about sports events that have worldwide importance.
- To learn about problems that have occurred in the Olympic Games.

Sport is a universal activity, played around the whole world. In this chapter we will discuss how countries have used sport to further political ideals and show how good *their* country is. This attitude has often affected the most important world sporting events such as the Olympic Games. The organisation of sport at European and international level follows that of the UK. With reduced travel times and the increasing use of satellite broadcasting, sport is quickly becoming a global event. Champions' leagues and World Super Clubs cups appear to be the way that sport is moving forward in the new millennium.

15.1 Sport around the world

Sport is played the world over. Many of the sports that were developed in the UK at the end of the nineteenth century spread around the world and many countries now play sports such as football, rugby and cricket, although some countries have changed such sports slightly and developed their own distinctive games. For example, Australian Rules football and American football are both based on rugby, but they are very distinctive.

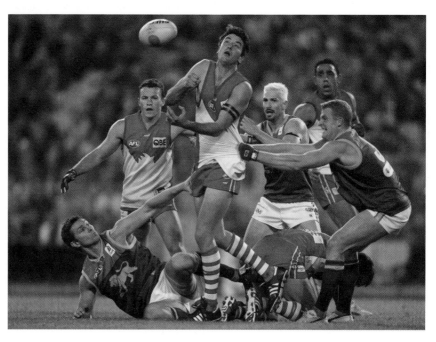

Australian Rules football – a game found only in Australia

activity

Which sports would you link to the following countries? You may put down more than one answer.

USA, Ireland, India, New Zealand, Japan, Canada.

To help you, here are some sports you could think about: ice hockey, Gaelic football, rugby, kabbadi, hockey, American football, sumo wrestling, baseball.

15.2 The organisation of European sport

Sport at a European level follows the decentralised pattern developed in the UK, most individual sports having a European governing body that oversees competition at this level. However, as the European states move closer towards federation more influence comes from the European Commission.

In 1988 the European Commission identified sport as performing five functions throughout the European community:
- educational
- public health
- social
- cultural
- recreational.

European legislation is increasingly affecting sporting practices and activities at both professional and amateur levels, the biggest single impact being the *Bosman case*, which has changed the way professional sport is run throughout Europe.

The European Commission's main role is to consult with sports organisations across Europe to plan for sports development and to identify problems associated with sport. Only in extreme cases will the Commission produce legislation that directly affects sport. For example, sport will be affected by the Commission's decision to phase out from 2001 all forms of tobacco sponsorship and advertising, except on premises where cigarettes are sold.

In an attempt to unify European Sport the Commission now hosts an annual European Conference on Sport, which all sports Ministers from each country attend.

15.2.1 *How European sport is organised*

Over the last half century two different models of sport have developed in Europe:
- an eastern European model
- a western European model.

In the east of Europe sport has tended to be more ideologically orientated. Sport is organised and funded by the state government and has often been used for propaganda purposes.

In western countries sport has developed as a mixed model, where sport is run by both governmental and non-governmental organisations. There is a further division to sport in the western

DEFINITION

BOSMAN CASE

The European Court of Justice recognised in the Bosman case that there is no reason why professional sports people should not enjoy the benefits of the single market – and in particular the free movement of workers. This has resulted in national competitions now being open to any player from a European country. The new legislation also abolished transfer fees if a player is out of contract.

activity

- Can you think of examples of how sport might reflect European identity?
- Does Europe exist as a team in any sports?
- Are there European competitions?
- Can you think of sports that reflect certain member states?

DEFINITION

PROPAGANDA

Using a subject (in this case sport) to get across a political message.

DEFINITION

SPORTING FEDERATION

European equivalent of a UK national governing body of sport.

UEFA

Union Européenne de Football Association, the governing body of European football.

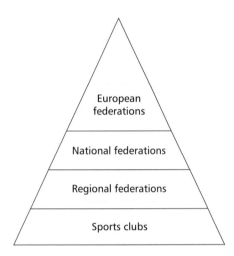

Figure 15.1 *The pyramid structure of European sport*

DEFINITION

FIFA

Federation International de Football Association, the international governing body of football.

DEFINITION

GRASS-ROOTS SPORT

Sport at the bottom of the pyramid.

states – in northern states such as the UK and Germany the government does not regulate sport, whereas in southern states such as France and Spain the government does play a regulatory role.

15.2.2 *The pyramid structure of European sport*

In all member states sports are traditionally organised in a system of national *sporting federations*. Only the top federations (usually one per country) are linked together in European and international federations such as UEFA.

Basically, the structure resembles a pyramid with a hierarchy (Figure 15.1). The pyramid structure implies autonomy at each level, not only on the organisational side but also on the competitive side because competitions are organised at all levels.

Clubs – in all countries the sports club is the basic unit. In the main these are amateur and run within the voluntary system. There are about 545 000 sports clubs in Europe.

Regional federations form the next level. Clubs are members of these organisations. They are responsible for organising regional championships and coordinating sport on a regional level.

National federations, one for each sport, represent the next level. The regional federations are members of these organisations. These bodies regulate all general matters within their sport and represent their sport in European and international federations. They organise national competitions and act as regulatory bodies, dealing with rules and disciplinary matters. As there is only one national federation for each sport, they tend to have a monopolistic position. In each country, for example, there is only one national football federation.

European federations – the top of the pyramid is formed by European federations, which are organised along the same lines as the national federations. Every European federation allows only one national federation from each country to be a member. They organise European championships, administer rules and form the link to international federations such as FIFA.

15.3 The features of European sport

One of the main features of sport in Europe is that it is based on a *grass-roots* approach – the development of sport originates from the level of club. Sport in Europe has traditionally not been linked to state or business.

Sport in Europe is run mainly by non-professional and unpaid volunteers. For them sport is a pastime and a way of contributing to society. In this way European sport differs from that in, say, the USA, where sport is linked to business. In the USA sport is based on a more professional approach and is mainly run by full-time paid people.

15.4 Sport and national identity

The Amsterdam Declaration of 1988 stated that sport has an important social function in forging identity and bringing people together.

Sport represents and strengthens national or regional identity by giving people a sense of belonging to a group, uniting players and spectators. Sport contributes towards social stability and is an emblem for culture and identity.

Can you put your own sport into the European model?

Although globalisation has affected European sport, it can still be seen as one of the last national passions. The EU is keen to promote sport as a means of safeguarding the cultural diversity of Europe (note the importance and support for European soccer championships). Again this differs from the USA, where there is no need for interstate competition.

Football – a game that all European countries share

15.5 The importance of sport in Europe

Traditionally the member states of the European Union have hosted a significantly large percentage of world sports events:
* 54% of summer Olympics
* 50% of football's World Cups.

This is mainly due to history; because Europe saw the start of the industrial revolution it was the first continent to see the development of modern sport. All the major global games have their origins in European initiatives, specifically the Olympic Games and Football World Cup.

Why has Europe been chosen as the host for most major world sporting events? Can you give sporting and cultural reasons?

15.6 Sport For All in Europe

The concept of *Sport For All* first emerged in the early 1960s in Germany and the Nordic countries. In 1968 the *Council of Europe* initiated the setting up of several projects aimed at encouraging mass participation. Its stated aim was to:

> Provide conditions to enable the widest possible range of the population to practise regularly either sport proper or various physical activities calling for an effort adapted to individual capacities.

Growing interest in sport and in the specific development of Sport For All by all European countries led to the adoption of the European Sport For All Charter in 1972. This asserted that 'Every individual has the right to participate in sport' and that 'It is the duty of every member state to support financially and organisationally this ideal'.

*Welcome back – South Africa win the rugby World
Cup (1995) after their return to global sport*

15.6.1 *The implementation of Sport For All in Europe*

The main organisation charged with implementing Sport For All has been the Committee for the Development of Sport (Comité Directeur pour le developement du sport), known as the CDDS.

15.7 Politics in global games

As mentioned above, sport has long been used as a means of proving that one political system is better than another. Part of international sport is that different countries and systems are put in competition with each other.

The best example of this was the USA and the USSR during the 1960s, 1970s and 1980s; the two countries spent huge amounts of money trying to outdo each other in sport. A win at the Olympics, it was said, proved that one political system (capitalism or communism) was better than the other.

Each country also boycotted the Olympics, and they used their power and influence to persuade other countries not to take part in particular Olympics.

Human rights issues have also brought politics and sport together. Human rights are basic entitlements and opportunities that all people should have. In some countries certain types of people are denied these rights – for example, black people under the apartheid system of South Africa (which was abolished in the 1990s). Sport is one area that other countries can use to show their feelings by boycotting sporting events in that country or persuading international sports organisations to ban the country from competition.

Many sports people state that politics and sports should not mix, but it is very difficult for them not to when so many governments actively support and fund the sports organisations in their country. The Olympic Games has been the major focus for these political problems and we will look at this in more detail below.

15.8 Sport on the world stage

Sport is very popular around the world and major events like the Olympic Games and the football World Cup are televised in every country. This is why such events have been the focus for political demonstration. Any person or country that wants to make a point is guaranteed maximum exposure at these events. We have already described how countries and governments manipulate sport and sporting success to their gain. Other, smaller groups have also used the Olympics as a stage on which to make their point to the world. This has meant that the security and safety systems at the Games have to be very complex and are therefore very expensive.

15.9 The Olympic Games

The Olympic Games have their origins in ancient Greece, where they were held every four years as part of a religious ceremony to the god Zeus. At the end of the nineteenth century Baron de Coubertin reintroduced the games (the first being held in Greece in 1896), and set up the International Olympic Committee (IOC)

The Olympics – a global event that attracts audiences around the world

DEFINITION

OLYMPIC OATH

'We swear that we will take part in these Olympic Games in the true spirit of sportsmanship and that we will abide by the rules that govern them, for the glory of sport and the honour of our country.'

FESTOON

The Olympic five-ring symbol, sold to the highest bidders amongst international companies.

and the modern Olympic Games, which are held every four years in a different city.

There are actually two Olympic Games – winter and summer – though it is the summer games that are the most prestigious. De Coubertin's idea was that the games could be used to bring the people of the world together in friendly competition. He hoped that this might help prevent war and develop more international friendship.

The Olympics in the past have been used to promote the good side of sport. All competitors were amateurs, competing purely for enjoyment, and the winner's medal had no real monetary value. Sportsmanship was the central point of the Games, and before competition started all of the athletes took the Olympic Oath.

The IOC organises each games every four years, choosing the host city and coordinating funding. Most of the IOC's income now comes from selling the festoon (the five-ring symbol) to international companies and from television fees.

Each participating nation must have a national Olympic body that takes responsibility for promoting the Olympic ideals in their own country. In the UK this is the British Olympic Association.

15.9.1 *Problems at the Olympics*

Berlin, 1936

This was called the 'Nazi Olympics' and was the first Olympic Games where politics was openly evident. Berlin had been awarded the games in 1931, but by 1936 Adolf Hitler's Nazi party had taken over Germany, and Hitler wanted to use the Games to show the world how powerful Germany and its people were.

Hitler believed in the supremacy of the 'Aryan' race ('true' Germans, blond-haired, blue-eyed and muscular): they would dominate the games and show that the German race was superior to all others. Unfortunately for Hitler, a young black American athlete called Jesse Owens dominated the Games, winning four gold medals. Owens was the only athlete not to receive his gold medals from Hitler, who left the stadium in disgust. Three years later Hitler's aggression led to the start of the Second World War.

Mexico City, 1968

Two main problems affected these Games. Mexico was a very poor country and many people felt that the huge amount of money needed to put on the Games would have been better spent helping to develop the country. Mexican students were the most active in opposition to the Games. They held a number of demonstrations, the final one being 10 days before the Games were due to begin. Over 10 000 people marched to the Square of the Three Cultures in Mexico City. Aware of the impact such a demonstration could have in the world's media so close to the start of the Games, the Mexican authorities reacted strongly, sending in the army to surround the demonstrators. A fierce battle developed, at the end of which 260 people had been killed and several thousand injured. Amazingly, the Games went on with no further trouble.

The next political problem occurred within the Olympic stadium. In America in the late 1960s black civil rights groups had been protesting about the lack of opportunity for black people and the racist attitudes in American society. With the world's media

Tommie Smith and John Carlos giving the Black Power salute at the 1968 Mexico Olympics

watching, two young black American athletes used the medal ceremony to show their support for the Black Power movement. In the 200 m final, Tommie Smith took gold and John Carlos took bronze. As they stood on the medal podium listening to the American national anthem they bowed their heads and each raised one gloved hand in the Black Power salute. Both were expelled by the US Olympic Association and immediately sent home.

Munich, 1972 – the terrorist Games

During the Games, Palestinian terrorists stormed part of the Olympic village, taking several Israeli athletes as hostages. There had long been a serious disagreement between Palestinian groups and the Israeli authorities over the ownership and control of disputed land.

The German police attempted to stage a dramatic rescue but things went wrong, ending in the deaths of nine athletes, a policeman and five terrorists. Many felt that the Games should be abandoned in honour of the athletes killed, but the IOC decided to carry on – so, they said, showing that no terrorist groups could stop the Games.

Montreal, 1976

Again there were two main problems associated with these Games. The Canadian government underestimated the costs and ran out of money before all the facilities were completed. Indeed the Canadian people are still paying via their tax for the 1976 Olympics. After this, the IOC let more commercial companies get involved in the games so that they had financial backing.

The Montreal Games were boycotted by several African countries, who were unhappy that New Zealand had been allowed to compete in the Games even though its rugby team had continued to play against South Africa.

Moscow, 1980

Boycotts also dominated these Games. In December 1979 the Soviet Union had invaded Afghanistan. To show that they did not agree with this, the following countries did not go these Olympics: the USA, Canada, West Germany, Japan and Kenya.

Los Angeles, 1984 – 'tit for tat'

Because the USA had led the boycott of the Soviet Olympics in 1980, the Soviet Union led a boycott of the 1984 Games. No eastern bloc countries competed in these games.

Seoul, 1988

Another Games dominated by the feud between the political systems of communism and capitalism. Korea is a divided country, the north being a communist state, the south capitalist. Seoul (in South Korea) was awarded the Games by the IOC, but North Korea applied to stage some of the events. The IOC refused and North Korea and three other communist countries boycotted the Games.

The 1988 Games were also the first to allow professional performers into the Games, so ending another Olympic tradition. Most of this was to do with the inclusion of tennis as an Olympic sport.

Barcelona, 1992

Generally a very successful Games. No one boycotted the Games and through the development of the commercial side the Games made a profit. South Africa was allowed back into the Olympic movement after abolishing apartheid. The Soviet Union was replaced by the Commonwealth of Independent States and west and east Germany were joined as one team.

Atlanta, 1996 – the centenary Games

These will be remembered for the hype and glamour, a terrorist bomb and the organisational problems that hindered athletes and spectators alike.

Many people felt that the centenary Games should really have gone back to Greece, home of both the ancient Olympics and the first modern games, but the IOC chose Atlanta. Atlanta's other major claim to fame is that it is the home of Coca Cola, the Olympic movement's biggest sponsor.

The Americans claimed that these would be the best Games ever, but problems with transport systems and the very hot weather meant there were lots of complaints. The lowest point of the Games was when a terrorist bomb exploded in the middle of a music concert for athletes and fans in Centenary Park, killing several people and injuring many others.

Sydney, 2000 – the best ever

Perhaps the most successful Olympic Games, excellent organisation and venues coupled with the support of the Australian public. Extensive security and the isolation of Australia meant there were no incidents to report. Though there was concern over athletes using performance-enhancing drugs, the Sydney authorities were determined to crack down on drug abuses and began testing athletes in their training camps which resulted in 43 athletes testing positive and being sent home before the Games began.

Key revision points

Sport at European level follows a decentralised pattern. European legislation is increasingly having an impact on sport – examples include the Bosman case and tobacco sponsorship. There are two basic models of European sport: the eastern European model – state control – and the western European model – autonomous control. Sport throughout Europe follows a pyramid structure. European bodies such as UEFA control the individual sports. These in turn form international bodies (such as FIFA) that control world championships. The 'live' nature of global games can result in their being used as a stage for protest. Sport can be manipulated by states for propaganda purposes.

Key terms

Progress check

You should now understand the following terms. If you do not, go back through the chapter and find out what they mean.

Bosman case
Boycott
European Charter for Sport for All
Festoon
FIFA
Grass-roots sport
IOC
Olympic oath
Propaganda
Sporting federation
UEFA

1   What are the reasons behind the increase in world club competitions?
2   Sport at European level follows a decentralised pattern. What does this mean?
3   Name three of the five functions that the EU believes sport performs in Europe.
4   How does EU legislation affect the provision of sport in Europe?
5   How can sport be used for propaganda purposes?
6   Explain what is meant by the pyramid structure of sport in Europe.
7   What is the role of UEFA in European football?
8   How does the organisation of European sport differ from the organisation of sport in the USA?
9   Explain what a boycott is in the context of sport.
10   Why do global games tend to attract protest?
11   What were de Coubertin's ideals behind the setting up of the modern Olympics?
12   What is the role of the IOC?
13   How does the IOC generate most of the funds it needs?
14   Using examples, describe how some groups of people have used the Olympic Games to stage political protest.
15   How are the EU rules on tobacco sponsorship affecting sport?

16 Sport in society and the pursuit of excellence

Learning objectives

- To understand the role of sport in society.
- To know the way sport reflects the society in which it is played.
- To be able to compare sports in different cultures.
- To understand the concepts of excellence.
- To investigate different strategies in the pursuit of excellence.

The pursuit of excellence is at the forefront of most countries' sports programmes. In this chapter we investigate the role sport plays in different societies. We also investigate the concept of excellence in sport and the methods different countries have used to achieve it.

16.1 Sociological aspects of sport

Sport in the 1990s became a cultural phenomenon of great magnitude, its influence permeating all aspects of our society. Sport is a compulsory element of our education system, it dominates all forms of media and is increasingly becoming an important part of our economy.

Sport can provide a useful focus for studying different societies. Roberts, Sutton, Smith and others have developed the field of *sports sociology*. They foster the view that the games played by a society reflect the values inherent in that society. Sports are also used to teach younger members of the society these values. In other words, sport reflects the society in which it is played.

A particular sport can become an extensive reference for the country or society it is played in. Each game has its own history and pattern of development and this evolution is closely linked to the development, history, geography and values of the country in which it is played.

Take the Gaelic game of hurling as an example. This invasion-type game (see Chapter 11) is only played in Ireland, but is the largest spectator sport in the country. By studying the game we should be able to pick out characteristics of its play and structure that can be linked to the country (Table 16.1). Hurling reflects closely the wider values and traditions in Irish society and remains an important expression of the culture.

Table 16.1 *Linking the characteristics of sport to society – hurling*

Characteristics of sport	Societal links
Robust, physical game	Traditional link with hard/rural work, history of violence
Large pitch	Rural nature of Ireland, allowing traditional large-scale, 'mob' games
Few rules – players can hit, kick or throw the ball	Sport that has retained traditional rules, little change – strong traditional culture
Unique to Ireland	Reflecting Ireland's peripheral geographical position on the edge of Europe – not much mixing. Lack of status meant that, unlike England, Ireland imported rather than exported sports

Hurling – Ireland's national sport

Football also makes an interesting study. All countries play the game of association football to very similar rules, yet it is amazing how different countries impose their own style on this universal game. This is most evident during the World Cup, when we see the flamboyance of the Brazilians clash with the tactical organisation of the German team or the exuberance of the Cameroon team.

Sport is a reflection of society and many issues (such as class, gender and race) have an effect on sport. Sport follows the trends of society and a number of patterns can be identified. These are described below.

activity

This type of analysis can be an interesting way of researching the role sport plays in culture. Try to find some video clips of different sports from other countries and see if you can identify aspects of the country it is played in. Perhaps these questions may help: Why is Australian rules football only played in Australia? How have the West Indies adapted the English game of cricket to suit their own independent culture? What parallels are there between American football and American society?

16.1.1 *Sociological theories*

One recently developed theory is that of *centrality*, which suggests that the dominant roles in sport such as coach, captain, play maker are undertaken by people in the dominant sections of the society in which the sport is played. The sections of the community that are in the minority either numerically or in terms of status, often immigrant or lower-class people, are under-represented in these roles. For example, in American football there are very few Afro-Caribbean quarterbacks and in the UK we have no professional managers in football from ethnic minorities.

Often these anomalies are related to *stereotyping*. This has a great effect in sport on the selection of players and positional decisions. The issue of discrimination in sport is developed further in Chapter 17.

16.1.2 *The role of sport in socialisation*

Socialisation is the way humans adjust to their culture, the process through which we become participating members of society. During socialisation we acquire our personalities and decide on the roles we will take on in later life.

Sport, especially physical education since it is compulsory, is an important vehicle for transmitting the values of the wider society. Physical education is used at school to develop a range of social skills such as cooperation and communication as well as the practical aspects of fitness and motor skills. Sport allows individuals to express themselves and to experiment with different roles and activities.

Sport may also lead to *social mobility* for certain people. In countries where sport is more liberal than the society at large,

underprivileged members of that society can use sport for social recognition and to gain wealth. Sport attracts members of the lower classes because through hard work they can be generously rewarded – and there are many role models to emulate.

16.2 A comparative view of sport

Comparative studies of sport have developed from a sociological base. The emphasis of these studies is on the structure and organisation of sport in other countries and on identifying the aspects we should introduce to our own system. This is an important issue for the present British sports organisation because we would appear to be losing our traditional dominance in international sport.

Emergent cultures select sports and work hard to achieve world status

A truly comparative study would view individual countries, but we will confine our study to just four groupings of countries and the ways they develop sport:
- emergent cultures
- the eastern bloc cultures
- the New World democratic cultures
- the American model.

16.2.1 Emergent cultures

These are the *developing countries,* such as the African nations. In these countries modern sport has often been introduced by previous colonial powers and in the main has replaced the indigenous activities. With their new-found independence, the people have used sport as a process of nation building.

The success of countries such as Kenya in athletics, the West Indies in cricket and Brazil in football has shown that developing countries can take on the developed world and often beat them.

These countries face the problems of limited resources and little infrastructure, but through selection and channelling in only a limited number of sports they are able to compete on the world stage. The model of sports development in these countries is shown in Table 16.2.

Table 16.2 *An emergent model of sport*

Integration	Sport unites the country by bringing together different races, areas and tribes
Defence	National Service gives a chance for selection. The strict regime is suited to training and development of talent
Shop window	Sporting success puts the country onto the world stage
Selection	Concentrate on limited number of sports, usually the ones suited to the environment or the physique of the people

Many emergent countries have now introduced elite sports systems aimed at increasing the chance of gaining gold medals. Often the armed forces act as sports nurseries and screen for sports talent (Kenya is a good example of a country in which the army plays an important role in fostering sports talent).

Performers that do reach an elite level have the opportunity to earn a great deal of money and often move to western countries, where the opportunity to gain higher reward is greater.

16.2.2 *The eastern bloc cultures*

Although now only a historical grouping since the communist system disintegrated in the early 1990s, this culture, dominated by the Soviet Union, is worth study because of the phenomenal sporting success that eastern bloc countries achieved in a short timescale.

In countries such as the Soviet Union and the German Democratic Republic sport was completely state controlled. Every aspect – from selection to training and diet – was coordinated by the central government. The shop window was the objective, although in this case it was the political system that was on show (see Figure 16.1). As Riordan states, 'Every win for the Soviet Union was a win for the Communist system' – and if this win was against an American performer or team, then the political emphasis was maximised.

EASTERN BLOC
Former communist countries found in eastern Europe.

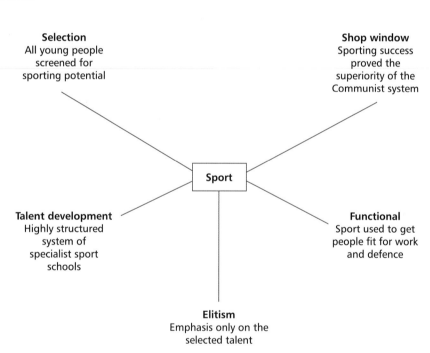

Figure 16.1 *The Eastern bloc model*

In all eastern bloc countries sport played a very important role. Success came as the result of a carefully structured system that tested the entire population and fed the talented through sports schools and training centres to national teams.

Although much of their success has been put down to the widespread use of drugs, this alone would not account for the level and rate of success. Performers in these countries had the best facilities, coaches and support available. Another important point is that sport in these societies reflected the egalitarian ideology of the system, which fostered the idea that everyone in society was equal in status. Although in practice this was not strictly true, in sport everybody had an equal chance of success. If you were identified as having talent in a sport you were selected, no matter what your race or background. This ensured that the state had the widest possible base to select from.

16.2.3 New World democratic cultures

By this title, we mean societies such as Australia, South Africa and New Zealand. These are cultures with European origins and were mostly former British colonies. Most are under 200 years old and, after achieving independence, developed into advanced thriving societies.

In a few sports such as cricket and rugby these countries vie for world honours. Australia in particular is a world leader in an ever-increasing number of sports. South Africa, until recently left out of international sport because of apartheid, is quickly redeveloping its sporting talent and is again emerging as a powerful force in rugby, cricket and athletics.

What these countries have in common, apart from a shared colonial history, is a culture of 'bush ethos'. The environments remain harsh and the people have had to work hard to develop and expand. Being young countries they lack the traditions and history of the Old World and have consequently needed to find new ways of expressing their emotions. Sport has more than filled this role: it is often seen as a substitute for the higher forms of culture in Europe. It is no cliché to say that in these societies sport is a religion.

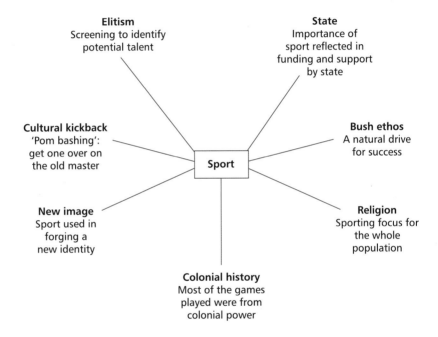

Figure 16.2 *The New World democratic model*

The other drive is again a form of shop window, although here the focus is different. The ambition of all these new cultures is to beat their old colonial powers – in particular England. Their sportsmen and women seem to have an extra edge to their approach, are driven by the win ethic and do not appear to be restrained by our more traditional values and ethics. To them, *winning* is important; it reflects struggle and hard work – the values that are inherent in their societies.

It is interesting to note that a lot of Australia's success can be linked to a Soviet-style programme of state funding and selection. The Australians have made good use of comparative sports study, adapting many successful methods from around the world but predominantly from the old eastern bloc countries.

All young people are now screened for sports talent, the results being fed into a national computer system which then suggests the best sport for the youngster to follow. All talented performers are offered state sponsorship and through the extensive clubs system and chain of national sports centres are nurtured and groomed for international success. The results have been outstanding and as the programme has expanded into football and other sports, Australia can now rightly claim to be a sports superpower.

DEFINITION

SPORTS SEARCH

A sports selection programme used in Australian schools to give children a 'best fit' sport.

DEFINITION

AMERICAN DREAM

The idea of rags-to-riches success, best personified in the Rocky films, where a nobody becomes world champion overnight.

Sports testing

The Australian Institute of Sport has recently introduced a system of sport talent-spotting, which it calls *Sports Search*. Sports Search was originally devised as a way of increasing participation in sport but is now an effective means of identifying talent. It is aimed at children in high school aged 11–15, and it is hoped the project will visit all of Australia's 3200 high schools. Each child will undertake a series of physical tests which will rate them for size, shape, agility, endurance and explosive power. This information will be fed into a computer and each student will be matched to their ideal sport. The school will follow this up by ensuring that each student has the opportunity to take up the sports he or she is best suited to.

16.2.4 The American model

America (according to the Americans) is the world's number one nation in all terms, the superpower in the absence of the Soviet Union, with nobody to beat. America's sports are the most technically advanced in the world, its sports stars are the richest in the world, and in a number of sports the Americans are undisputed world champions. What is interesting is that America's major sports are not really played anywhere else in the world – America is so far ahead that it can hold World Championships in American football and baseball, in which only American teams compete!

Like Australia, the USA has colonial links, but these were cut much earlier in the country's development and for many years the USA developed in planned isolation from Europe. During this time its sports developed, adapted from the old European games but modelled and changed to suit America's new image. In fact so American were these new sports of baseball, gridiron and basketball that even with extensive backing they have never really developed elsewhere.

The sports are high scoring and action packed to maximise their entertainment value. They reflect American culture in that the aim is to win – the win ethic is what drives all American people and this fuels the so-called 'American dream'. The American model is outlined in Figure 16.3.

American football – a sport that reflects the culture in which it is played

Figure 16.3
The United States model

But it is the commercial aspect of American sport which makes it so different. Every level, from professional national teams to the local high-school football teams, is run as a business. The influence of television is total and most sports in the USA rely entirely on the money generated through television deals and advertising revenue. Sports stars in America are millionaires; most professional teams will have a number of players on multi-million dollar annual contracts. Many stars, like Michael Jordan, make even more money through sponsorship deals and endorsements.

There is a flip side to this: sport in the USA is extremely elitist. In athletics, for example, there is not even one amateur club where 'Joe Public' can train. For most Americans sport is something you watch on the television and not something you actually play. The television also dictates the rules – for example, American football has evolved into a constant stop–go staccato pattern to allow companies to screen advertisements every five minutes.

Many of these trends are beginning to filter into British sport, and it may be very difficult for us to prevent Americanisation of our sport.

DEFINITION

AMERICANISATION
Where American trends and attitudes invade traditional culture.

Key revision points
Sport plays an important role in modern societies, reflecting the wider values and traditions of the society. Different countries play different sports, and also play the same games differently. Centrality is a sociological theory which states that the dominant roles in sport are taken by the dominant section of society. Emergent cultures select and channel athletes into a limited number of sports to ensure success. In the eastern bloc cultures the state controls sport for political gain. The New World democratic cultures use sport as a focus of national identity and to gain status over the Old World. In the USA sport is seen as a commercial commodity and is driven by the win ethic. In all cases, the shop window is the aim.

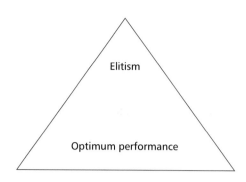

Figure 16.4 *The sports pyramid*

16.3 The pursuit of excellence

Sebastian Coe and his colleagues, in their book *More than a Game*, state that 'Champions are made, not born'. In this section we will discuss how champions are developed and the issues that are related to excellence in sport. Excellence is an important current issue in the UK. Many people have recorded the fall in our sporting standards and in sports such as tennis, where our players were among the elite, we are now slipping down the rankings.

We must first try to define what we mean by 'excellence'. In fact, the word has two meanings, immediately causing a dilemma which we, as sports scientists, need to face. The two meanings can be viewed as two sections of the sports pyramid (shown in Figure 16.4).

activity

What makes a champion? Write down the key factors that create excellence in a performer. Use the following headings to help you: ability, practice, equipment, coaching, sports science support.

16.3.1 *Elitism*

DEFINITION

ELITISM

Activities confined to an exclusive minority, usually the best.

In elitism the emphasis is on a few, the best, performers. The tendency is to look for the most developed and to ignore the rest. We have already seen this approach in the emerging cultures discussed in the previous section. The best example of this approach was seen in the German Democratic Republic, a country with a population of only 16 million which managed to be in the top three for sports such as athletics, swimming and boxing. The whole sports system of this communist country was geared up to selecting and developing champion performers, but this was at the expense of the rest of the population.

16.3.2 *Optimum performance*

DEFINITION

OPTIMUM PERFORMANCE

Sporting excellence should be the target of every individual.

In contrast to elitism, the optimum performance model asserts that sporting excellence should be the target of every individual. The society acknowledges that each person has a potential and that the sports system should help everyone fulfil this objective. This model has been used in physical education in the UK, where the aim has been to try to develop in all participants a feeling of achievement. This is reflected by the vast range of activities we undertake in school and the lack of specialisation.

It has been argued that this system has a great disadvantage in that it will not lead to the development of talent on the level required for international success.

Very few societies are concerned with the optimum performance model because it doesn't bring the short-term responses that they crave or because they do not have the finance or resources to allow every member of the population the chance of success.

If we acknowledge that in the main it is the first model that is most relevant in modern sport then let us investigate more closely the issues in the development of excellence.

16.3.3 Development of excellence

Three key stages may be identified in the development of sporting talent:
1 Selection of talent
2 Development of talent
3 Providing support for performance.

The actual methods used differ from country to country, but increasingly a number of policies are being followed by most. A lot of these have been adapted from the eastern European model of sports excellence, pioneered by the Soviet Union and the German Democratic Republic from the 1950s onwards.

Selection

Selection is the start of this process, identifying individuals with the potential to become champions. The pyramid theory of sports development suggests that the wider the base then the greater the number at the top of the pyramid. The aim of the selection process is to make the base of the pyramid as wide as possible.

In the old Soviet Union this was achieved by screening every child in the education system for sporting potential. At first this would involve gross motor skills but later more specific skill tests, physiological and psychological tests were used to identify talent and channel it into the appropriate sports. This latter aspect is perhaps a debatable issue – many argue that it is wrong for young people to specialise too early because it can lead to problems such as physiological 'burn out'.

The Australian system of screening every child at high school level has been discussed above. In the UK we have tended to keep away from this approach. Performers tend to specialise later in their development, and the general view is that it is still better to develop skills and experiences in a range of sports.

Talent development

Stage two is again a crucial aspect. The children selected are coached, instructed and nurtured to become champions. In many countries this process is achieved through the education system, predominantly in sports schools.

Identifying individuals with talent is a complex business and each sport has distinctively different physical characteristics and capacities that need to be clearly identified.

The UK government's sports policy document, 'A Sporting Future for All', states that there will be a commitment to ensure that all 14–18-year-olds have access to the coaching and support which elite competitors need if they are to be the world champions of tomorrow. The UK government has also asked all national governing bodies of sport to create a national development plan identifying pathways from the grass roots of their sport to the international stage, and integrating the needs of disabled sportspeople.

Sports schools

Sports schools are found in most European countries and are often controlled by the state. They allow young people to develop their sporting potential while continuing with academic studies. They usually have high-quality facilities and specialised staff, the advantage being that students get more time to practise their skills, and the atmosphere of excellence encourages their development.

Andy Cole – a graduate of the FA school of excellence at Lilleshall

DEFINITION

GIFTED AND TALENTED

A government initiative as part of the 'Excellence in Cities' programme which identifies pupils at both primary and secondary school that show potential in either academic subjects or areas such as sport and music and supports them. The school sport coordinators administer the sports strand of the scheme in most areas.

List four advantages and four disadvantages of basing performers in sports schools.

The Soviet Union was the role model in the field of sports schools. After selection, students were filtered up the sports pyramid through city sports schools, regional boarding schools and (the ultimate aim) the national training centre.

In America a slightly different method of development is followed. Sport is viewed as such an important aspect of the American education system that all schools and colleges have extensive sports facilities and place a lot of emphasis on sports success. Students are offered sports scholarships which pay all of their expenses, and they are given a lot of time to practise. The best college players are selected by the professional teams each year during the annual 'draft'.

In the UK the number of sports schools is increasing, but these are still few and of little influence. The best known is the FA school at Lilleshall, where the best 22 young footballers board and spend half a day at a local comprehensive school (players such as Andy Cole and Nick Barmby have progressed through the FA school), and the LTA Tennis School at Bisham Abbey.

The recent introduction of specialist sports status for secondary schools in the UK is a step towards a more national approach to sports excellence at school level. They now form a regional focal point for sports excellence with a particular role in supporting students identified as gifted and talented in sport.

Administration of excellence

The final part of the process is to provide support in terms of administration and funding. If athletes are to be successful they need full support, primarily financial aid to ensure that they don't have to worry about raising the funds to cover their training and competition expenses, which allows them more time to prepare for competition. Again there is wide variation in the method of financial support. In many countries the state funds the top athletes – in Australia, France and the old Soviet Union all top performers are paid grants that allow them to become virtually full-time athletes. In America talented performers are paid scholarships by schools and colleges or athletes are contracted to a professional team. We have already discussed how SportsAid in the UK tries to fund up-and-coming athletes – as yet there is little government input to sports in the UK (see Chapter 14 for more on sports funding).

Modern sports performers also require the support of an ever-increasing range of sports specialists (psychologists, dieticians, physiotherapists), as well as video and computer equipment to help improve technique. In the UK such service is now being developed in a number of National Sports Centres forming a national network, with the United Kingdom Sports Institute (UKSI) as the central focus. The aim is to enable our international performers to use top-quality facilities for training. These now come under the Sports Council's World Class Performance programme, funded by the National Lottery. This Sports Fund has three levels:

- *World Class Start* – programmes aimed at developing talented youngsters.
- *World Class Potential* – assisting with the development of teenagers helping with educational support.
- *World Class Performance* – supporting our elite athletes via financial support and providing top-class facilities through the UKSI.

The funding of UK Sport is prioritised to ensure the most effective use of lottery funds to achieve the overall aim of the UK being one of the world's top five sporting nations. UK Sport has to ensure that the money goes to the sports and individuals most likely to win medals at the Olympics, paralympics and world championships.

- Priority 1 sports – Olympics and paralympics, athletics, cycling, swimming, rowing and sailing.
- Non-Olympic – orienteering, water skiing, gliding, hang gliding.

Most other countries have similar national centres for the use of the national squads.

The national governing body squad systems and the specialist sports colleges excellence programmes are creating a sporting environment in which talent will flourish and progress. UKSI and world-class plans of the national governing bodies of sport will help our best sportsmen and women to compete on equal terms with our sporting competitors on the world stage.

Support for performance

The UKSI network centres, alongside the FA football academies and specialist sports colleges, will provide lifestyle management training and support for talented young performers. Most of this is carried out through the Athlete Career Education (ACE) UK programme, which provides a tailored service that encourages elite athletes to take control of all aspects of their lives. ACE UK enables athletes to identify their personal strengths and supports them to integrate career, education and sporting demands so that they can be successful now and in their life after sport.

The ACE UK programme is modelled on the ACE programme developed through the Australian Institute of Sport. It is a national programme delivered regionally through the UKSI network to promote accessibility.

All elite UK athletes receive an individual athlete assessment with their local adviser in order to identify the athlete's needs and introduce them to the wide range of support that ACE UK has to offer. That could include financial management support, workshops on media training or access to the Olympic and Paralympic Employment Network (OPEN) which helps those athletes in employment with training and work demands.

16.3.4 *Constraints on excellence*

We should now be able to identify aspects of sporting excellence from other societies that we could take and implement in the British sports system with the aim of developing our sports potential – aspects such as setting up more sports schools, introducing state or other sponsorship schemes that will allow our sports performers to be able to train harder and concentrate more on their chosen sports.

However, it is not simply a question of transplanting practices from other societies. As we have already suggested, sport and the way it is administered and developed in a country reflects the values and culture of that country. There are several cultural constraints that explain why we in the UK do not actively encourage excellence in sport.

- *Historical* – we invented most modern sports and retain a status in world sport, so it is not important for us to excel.
- *Geographical* – our population is relatively small, so our pyramid base is much smaller than, say, the USA or China.
- *Ideological* – most of the world sports powers have a very nationalistic approach, where you are playing for the honour and status of your country, but we are patriotic rather than nationalistic. Similarly, we promote the recreational ethic rather than the win ethic, our heroes are Eddie the Eagle and the Frank Brunos of the world. We also tend to feel that winners are arrogant.
- *Socioeconomic* – participation in sport in the UK has been dominated by the middle-class tradition that taking part counts, not winning, and that sport should not be work.

What should we do to develop a more effective programme of sports excellence? The answer is twofold:

1 A large amount of *money* is required to fund such a programme – high-level facilities and equipment, coaches and the extensive back-up require a lot of funding. The National Lottery fund is proving to be a possible source of the money needed.

2 A more coordinated *administration* system is required. At the moment our sports system is too diverse at all levels; we need sports to come together to share aims and objectives for the overall benefit of British sport.

Key revision points

Excellence in sport has two meanings: elitism, which means 'all for the best – forget the rest' or optimum performance, where everyone has the chance to succeed. Most societies emphasise elitism as this produces champions, which can be used as a 'shop window'. There are three major stages in the development of excellence: selection, development and support. There is much diversity in the methods used by different societies.

Key terms

You should now understand the following terms. If you do not, go back through the chapter and find out what they mean.

ACE UK
American dream
Americanisation
Centrality
Culture
Eastern bloc
Elitism
Olympic and Paralympic
    Employment Network
Optimum performance
Social mobility
Socialisation
Society
Sports Search
Sports sociology
UKSI network
World Class Performance
    programme

Progress check

1   In what country is hurling played?
2   Why is sport a useful focus for studying different societies?
3   Explain what is meant by the term 'centrality'.
4   What role does sport play in socialisation?
5   Explain what comparative study is in the context of sport.
6   Give examples of three emergent cultures.
7   How can sport be used for social mobility by emergent athletes?
8   Name two countries that were in the old eastern bloc.
9   Using the eastern bloc as an example, explain what is meant by the term 'shop window'.
10 Give three examples of countries that are classed as New World democratic cultures.
11 What are the moral arguments against the eastern European model of early selection and channelling of young children into a particular sport?
12 Why has a country such as Australia placed so much emphasis on developing sports talent?
13 Explain the Sports Search programme undertaken in Australia.
14 Explain what is meant by 'American dream'.
15 Give examples of how British sport is being Americanised.
16 Explain the pyramid system of sports development. How does it make the development of sporting talent more efficient?
17 What are the two meanings of the term 'excellence'?
18 What are the three stages in the development of sporting talent?

CHAPTER **17**

Factors affecting participation in sport

Learning objectives

- To identify the benefits of regular exercise.
- To understand mass participation in sport.
- To be able to identify discrimination in sport and to understand what causes it.
- To investigate methods of overcoming discrimination.

Sport is a natural part of life, whether you are one of the elite competing for gold medals or just playing for fun and enjoyment. The opportunity to take part in sporting activity should be a basic human right; however, many people suffer constraints that prevent them from taking part. The aim of mass participation is to break down these constraints, whatever they may be, and to encourage as many people as possible to take up sport.

The Sports Council estimates that one in three people in the UK regularly take part in sport. In this chapter we look at the reasons why people take part in sport and recreation and also what constraints may inhibit people from taking part in an active lifestyle.

17.1 Why play sport?

After reading the early sections of this book you should now have some firm ideas about why sport is good for us. It promotes mental and physical health, it is a positive use of spare time and is an important emotional release.

Sport for all will also benefit the country as a whole: people will be fitter so there will be less strain on the health system; they will also be able to work harder and more effectively. Another, less positive, aspect is that people will be fit for war if the need arises.

Everyone should be able to participate in sport

activity

Write a list of specific benefits to a person who regularly plays sport. Your list will contain mainly intrinsic benefits, but there may also be extrinsic benefits for the society as a whole if many of its members participate regularly.

DEFINITION

SPORT FOR ALL CAMPAIGN

This campaign, originally set up in 1972 and still continuing, highlights the value of sport and that it was something to which all members of the community should have access. The campaign initially hoped to increase the opportunities for sport and recreation through developing more facilities, and by informing and educating the public on what was available. More recently the campaign has become more diverse to target groups of the community that remain under-represented in sport. Separate campaigns such as '50+' and 'All to Play For' (aimed at older people) and 'What's your Sport?' (aimed at women) have followed.

In a sporting context there are also other extrinsic rewards – if more people are playing sport the sports pyramid discussed in Chapter 16 will have a wider base.

Many countries have set up mass participation schemes, often state sponsored, to encourage more people to take part in physical activity. Even in the decentralised British sports system, the Sports Council's 'Sport for All' campaign has had considerable state involvement, specifically in its funding.

The phrase 'Sport for All' has now become synonymous with the ideals of mass participation. The Soviet Union used the phrase 'massovost', while in France they have Sport Pour Tous.

The whole emphasis in sport for all should be on promoting the intrinsic value of sport – too many people view sport as either something they had to do at school or something they see on the television which is far too advanced for them to try. The real point is that, as we have mentioned many times, sport is an extremely diverse area, involving many different activities and catering for every shape, personality and level of skill. Perhaps we need to use a few more realistic role models to encourage people to take up activities.

Every Sunday morning well over a million people play football in organised leagues. There are 125 000 voluntary sports clubs in Britain catering for six million members, and many more people regularly take part in sport and recreation outside any structural organisation – be it a kick around in the park or joining the 23% of the adult population that walk two miles or more each week. Mass participation, however, is still not a reality in Britain – even the most generous prediction by the Sports Council puts the figure at one in three of the population. The vast majority of people in Britain do not actively participate and, what is more worrying, the activity levels in young people (who were previously the most active group) are also falling drastically.

We now know that the claim by the Soviet Union that everyone undertook physical activity was a propaganda myth and that sport was confined to the elite. In America, a country with the resources to allow the optimum performance model of excellence discussed in the last chapter, participation levels are low – and falling. If we concentrate on the UK, although we know it is advantageous for us to promote and develop mass participation, the success rate of existing programmes or their overall importance is limited. Again we can use sociocultural analysis to suggest reasons for the failure of mass participation to take off.

17.2 Constraints on mass participation

These may be analysed and classified in the same way as we classified the constraints on excellence in the UK.

- *Historical* – in the past sport has been very closely linked to education, and many people's only sporting experience was through compulsory and often harsh physical education lessons. Many are put off sport for life.
- *Geographical* – many areas of Britain are under-resourced in terms of sports facilities and – equally as important – qualified coaches, teachers and leaders.

Huge numbers of people take part in events such as the London Marathon every year

• *Ideological* – in our culture, sport has always been seen purely as a non-serious recreation: many other more important issues require attention before you turn to sport. Often at school academically bright students are encouraged to move away from sport so that they can concentrate more time on their studies.
• *Socioeconomic* – amateur/voluntary sport has had a rather middle-class image and the fact is that most of us in the UK must 'pay to play'. We have to pay club subscriptions, fees and facility costs, as well as providing our own kit and equipment.

Consequently, although there have been some successes we are still a long way from achieving sport for all. Marathon running has been one success – a previously minority sport involving serious athletes has over the last few years become a true mass participation event. Events such as the London Marathon or the Great North Run have captured the public's imagination and huge numbers of people have taken up running purely for the intrinsic rewards of finishing the course. At the same time, however, these events have remained high quality in terms of excellence, with serious runners racing at the front while thousands plod on behind with the only aim of finishing. Other sports could take many pointers from these events in developing the right formula for mass participation.

activity

Why has running become such a success in terms of getting people involved in physical activity?

Key revision points

Mass participation means maximising the potential for all sections of a community to take part in physical activity. 'Sport for All' is the campaign set up by the Sports Council to foster mass participation in the UK. Taking part in physical activity has many benefits for both the individual and society. Benefits for the individual are classed as intrinsic. Benefits for society are classed as extrinsic. Mass participation is not yet a reality for most countries. A sociocultural analysis can be used to provide some reasons for this.

DEFINITION

DISCRIMINATION

One section of a community is disadvantaged because of certain sociocultural variables.

17.3 Discrimination in sport

In this section we will see again how closely sport reflects the society in which it takes place. In many societies groups are divided by sociocultural variables which lead to *discrimination*.

In the previous section we highlighted the fact that many people do not have equal access to sport, often as a result of discrimination due to a cultural variable.

17.3.1 *Cultural factors*

Five main cultural factors lead to discrimination in sport:
* gender
* class
* race
* age
* ability.

Unfortunately we do not have the space to investigate each of these areas fully, but at the end of Part 3 we suggest further and more specific reading to help students gain a sound grasp of each area. In this chapter we will identify the common variables leading to discrimination in sport and briefly outline the areas highlighted above.

Discrimination can be said to affect the following areas in sport:
* provision
* opportunity
* esteem.

Provision

Are the facilities that allow you to participate available to you? We have already suggested that in the UK there is a shortage of facilities and those that do exist are often sited in particular areas. Living in an inner-city area would discriminate against you because there is little provision in these areas. Equipment is also required, which is often expensive – those on low incomes may be discriminated against unless equipment is available free or can be hired cheaply.

Opportunity

There may be barriers to an individual's participation in an activity. In the UK most sport takes place in the voluntarily run clubs, which are often elitist organisations. Clubs work on membership systems and membership is controlled either by the ability to pay the fees or, in cases such as some golf clubs, election to the club membership. This often closes membership to certain members of the community.

Another consideration for the individual is whether they have the time to play. Women in particular are often faced with this problem. The demands of work and family often mean that women have little leisure time, which accounts in some way for the low levels of female participation in sport.

Esteem

This is concerned with the societal view of individuals. In many cultures societal values dictate that women should not take an active part in sport, or if they do it should be confined to 'feminine' sports such as gymnastics and not 'macho' pursuits such as football or rugby. These judgements are based on the traditional roles men and women have taken in the society and may be very difficult to break.

activity

The British media are still reluctant to devote a lot of space or time to sports such as women's rugby. What cultural constraints may be causing this?

DEFINITION

STEREOTYPE

A group of characteristics that we believe all members of a certain section of society share, usually based on very little actual fact.

SPORTS MYTHS

Stereotypes may lead to myths in sport, and this is where people are discriminated against. Common sports myths are that 'black people can't swim' and that 'women will damage themselves internally if they do the hurdles'. Again, myths are based on very little truth, but often become an important aspect in selection and opportunity.

activity

Try to get hold of a variety of newspapers from the same day and go through the sports pages. Make a record of all the sports covered and the gender they are concerned with. What do you conclude? Look through the television listings for the same day and compile an inventory of how much sport is on – and which gender.

Stereotypes and *sports myths* are also societal variables that lead to discrimination. Often minority groups within a community are labelled as having certain characteristics or traits, and this can lead to them being steered into certain sports or positions and away from others.

One good example in the UK is the current lack of Asian footballers. Much research has been done into this area and programmes are now being set up to try to address the imbalance, but the main problem is that, in our societal view, Asians are not potential footballers.

Stereotypes and myths can become 'self-fulfilling prophecies' – even the people they discriminate against come to believe they are valid and conform to the stereotypes by displaying their appointed characteristics and choosing the sports that fit them. In doing so they are reinforcing society's view. It is only recently that a number of women have broken this system by taking up football and rugby, and it is hoped that the success of the women's England rugby team will start to change the views of society.

Let us now look briefly at the groups identified above and suggest key areas that lead to discrimination.

17.3.2 *Gender*

Each year 33% of all men participate in some form of sporting activity, whereas only 10% of women do. As women make up over 50% of the British population this points to some form of discrimination.

Women's role in society is seen as needing to conform to a set image, referred to as 'femininity', and consequently the amount of and type of sport they play must adhere to this trait guide. There have been many myths about women and sport (see the definition box) and although, thankfully, these have now been largely displaced, many people still hold some faith in them. Other problems concern time – women, due to the demands of work and family, tend to have much less leisure time than men, and even when they do have time they are often physically exhausted.

Women's Sports Foundation

The Women's Sports Foundation founded in 1984 is the only organisation in the UK that is solely committed to improving and promoting opportunities for women and girls in sport at every level. Its key role is informing all about the benefits of an active lifestyle for women and girls. It works with other national agencies to inform, influence ad promote opportunities for females in sport.

Women's Sports Foundation Get Set Go programmes

Run by the WSF, these two-day residential courses are designed to provide a springboard for women into sports leadership. The course includes sessions on communication styles, how to promote yourself, body language, understanding sport and setting your goals.

17.3.3 *Class*

This discrimination is related to the history and tradition of sport. The upper classes have traditionally had the most leisure time, which they filled with exclusive sports such as hunting. The middle classes, which grew up during the industrial revolution, rationalised and then controlled sport, imposing their values, specifically amateurism, on our modern sports. The working classes were allowed to participate in sport, but only after they had finished their work – increasingly, spectatorism filled their time.

The main discriminator is money – sport has always cost money and, although many people now have more disposable income, sports such as polo, golf and tennis still require considerable expense.

17.3.4 Race

The UK is a multicultural nation, with a great mixture of races. A major discriminator is still the colour of a person's skin, and this is an area where stereotypes and myths dominate. We discussed in Chapter 16 the concept of centrality, which affects all minority groups in our culture.

Often there is a double effect, as the minority groups also tend to be in the lower income groups.

Sporting Equals and Racial Equality Charter for Sport

The Commission for Racial Equality has introduced with Sport England a national initiative entitled Sporting Equals. The initiative is working to promote racial equality throughout England. The key focus is to work with sports governing bodies to develop policies and working practices that promote racial equality.

Alongside this campaign the CRE has also introduced the Racial Equality Charter for Sport. This is a public pledge signed by leaders of sport, committing them to use their influence to create a world of sport in which all people can take part without facing racial discrimination of any kind.

17.3.5 Age

In the UK your age is a very important factor in how much sport you play. The General Household Survey found that the age group with the greatest participation in sport was the 16–24-year-olds, with 61%. After this the rate drops dramatically – only 16% of people aged 60 or more take part in any exercise.

In our society sport is definitely the domain of the young, and in many sports you become a veteran at 35! Other societies, such as Japan, encourage participation to continue throughout life, and there are over 70 rugby leagues in Japan. Other programmes, such as masters events and the Golden Olympics, are also attempting to make sport a true 'lifetime' recreation.

Lifetime sports such as golf can be played by all ages

17.3.6 Ability

This covers two areas: your ability in a particular sport and how generally able you are. People with disabilities have, until recently, had little opportunity to take part in sport. Nearly all the facilities were built solely for the able-bodied. Opportunity for disabled sportsmen and women is now increasing and all new sports facilities provide access for people of all abilities. The media have played an important role in this, and events such as wheelchair basketball, the Paralympics and the London Marathon have done a lot to put forward the case of disabled athletes.

Bodies such as the British Paralympic Association and the British Sports Association for the Disabled promote sport for the disabled but they remain a minority and only in a few sports such as bowls can disabled people compete on an equal basis with able-bodied competitors. The International Olympic Committee do now allow a small number of disabled events during the summer Games.

activity

Do a quick survey of your school/college and local sports facilities – do they provide access for differing abilities? When were the facilities built? Is there any correlation between when they were built and the facilities they provide?

Disabled people need to participate in sports as much as able-bodied people

The other area mentioned above – that of your ability in a particular sport – can also prove to be a discriminator. Most clubs/teams are elitist in their structure; they allow only the most talented players, often selected through trials, to play. Those who are not particularly talented are left with few alternatives. In some sports, such as football, it may be possible for less able players to join a 'lower' league such as pub football, and rugby clubs often run social teams.

Even in schools this causes a dilemma. Who do you pick for the school team – the best players, or do you give all those who want to play or attend practices a chance? For many children a chance to play for their school team will be the pinnacle of their sports career. If, as we discussed in the last section, we should be promoting excellence for all, then we should try to give as many people as possible the chance to enjoy sport.

activity

List four advantages and four disadvantages of making your team less elitist and giving as many as possible a chance to take part.

Key revision points

Discrimination in sport arises from sociocultural variables. The five main areas of discrimination are gender, class, race, age and ability. The three elements in sport that are affected by discrimination are provision, opportunity and esteem. Stereotypes have an important influence in sport, affecting access and selection. In sport, stereotypes often lead to myths and self-fulfilling prophecies.

Key terms

You should now understand the following terms. If you do not, go back through the chapter and find out what they mean.

Discrimination
Esteem
Opportunity
Provision
Sport for All
Sporting myth
Stereotype

Progress check

1   What is the aim of mass participation in sport?
2   What benefit would Sport for All bring to the Health Service?
3   'What's your Sport?' was a Sports Council campaign – aimed at whom?
4   How does mass participation fit the concept of the sports pyramid?
5   How many people does the Sports Council claim participate in regular sport?
6   How might a person's experience at school affect their level of participation in sports as adults?
7   What do we mean by the term 'sporting myth'?
8   How can a person's socioeconomic status affect the amount of sport they play?
9   List five cultural factors that may lead to discrimination in sport.
10   Give examples of how provision may cause discrimination.
11   How can a sports club be elitist?
12   What type of sports fit a feminine stereotype?
13   Give examples of sports we might associate with the upper class.
14   Using examples, explain what is meant by stereotyping in sport.
15   How can a person's age affect their access to sport?

CHAPTER 18

Deviance in sport

Learning objectives

- To recognise deviance in sport.
- To investigate the concept of sportsmanship.
- To investigate the concept of gamesmanship.
- To understand the use of performance-enhancing drugs in sport.

Deviance in society is where an individual or group breaks away from the expected norms of the society or drifts away from the structural and functional rules. An example is the criminals who disobey the rules of society.

Sport also has its rules and deviance occurs when participants break these rules. We call this *cheating* and this is an important issue in modern sport. The main concern at present is the vast range of cheating – drug abuse, bribing officials and technological cheating in sports such as Formula One motor racing.

Cheating is not a new concept – we know that the ancient Olympians took tonics to try to improve their performance. Some people would argue that cheating is an important element in sport and that without it sport would be dull.

Sport has many written rules but also *unwritten* rules, and these make investigation of deviance more complicated.

18.1 The concept of sportsmanship

DEFINITION

CHEATING

Breaking the rules of sport.

UNWRITTEN RULES

Sometimes referred to as 'the spirit of the game', unwritten rules are values and ethics which we expect all sportsmen and women to follow.

Sport relies on *sportsmanship*, people conforming to the written and unwritten rules of sport. The idea of *fair play* means that you treat your opponent as an equal and, although you want to beat them, you will do so only by adhering to the rules and a code of conduct that has been developed in the sport through tradition. This includes shaking hands and cheering the other team off at the end of the game.

To cheat not only destroys the game but also detracts from your personal achievement. A win through cheating is a hollow victory as, although you may gain the extrinsic rewards, you will not gain the more fulfilling intrinsic ones.

But is this concept of fair play outdated? It certainly remains an important part of British sport but for many people the overriding factor is to win – at all costs. Governing bodies such as FIFA try to foster sportsmanship by giving out Fair Play Awards. It is interesting to note that at the 1990 World Cup England had the honour of winning the Fair Play Award, but only reached the semi-final – which perhaps reinforces the American cliché that 'nice guys finish last'!

Sport does rely on some form of mutual respect between opponents because often it involves high-speed contact with lethal 'weapons', and to disregard the rules could cause serious injury.

18.2 Gamesmanship

DEFINITION

SPORTSMANSHIP

Conforming to the written and unwritten rules of sport.

The alternative dynamic in sport is known as *gamesmanship*, where you use whatever means you can to overcome your opponent. The only aim here is to win, and for most people it is not a question of breaking the rules – more bending them to your advantage.

activity

Can you write down five ways people can cheat in sport? Why do you think they cheat?

DEFINITION

FAIR PLAY
Treating your opponent as an equal and abiding by the rules of your sport.

DEFINITION

GAMESMANSHIP
Where you use whatever means you can to overcome your opponent.

Many sports stars of the last few years can be classed as 'gamesmen'. For example, John McEnroe used to disrupt his opponent's concentration by arguing and abusing himself, the umpire and people in the crowd.

Deviance in sport is no longer limited to elite able-bodied sport. At almost every level of sport individuals and teams feel a need to bend or break the rules in order to ensure victory. After the 2000 Paralympics the Spanish Paralympic basketball team were ordered to return their gold medals after nearly all of their players were found to have no disability. The Spanish authorities were so keen to bring home a medal to ensure further funding that they openly manipulated registration of the basketball team to allow able-bodied players to participate.

Gamesmanship has now become an acceptable part of modern sport and unfortunately the mood is changing from 'we shall play fairly' to 'if you can't beat them, join them'. The other aspect of gamesmanship is the 'hype' that surrounds the build-up to an event. Primarily for the advantage of the media, this hype is also used by competitors to 'out-psych' or intimidate their opponents.

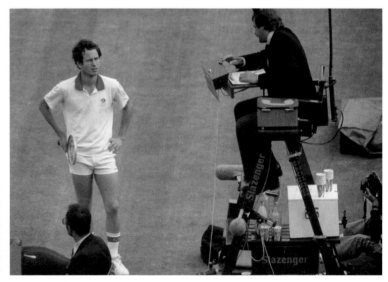

John McEnroe – a sportsman with a reputation for using gamesmanship as a means of winning

18.3 Drugs in sport

Drug abuse has been one of the main areas of deviance in sport during the last few years. It is not clear whether the actual level of drug taking has gone up or whether we now know more about it because testing systems have improved. It is also very difficult to decide where the line should be drawn between illegal and legal substances – many athletes have tested positive but claim that all they took was a cough mixture or other such product which can be bought over the counter.

Drug taking is the ultimate in gamesmanship – taking something to increase your performance and increase your chances of winning. There is a range of performance-enhancing drugs that athletes may take. Most originated as genuine medical treatments but their

Dwain Chambers – suspended from competition for taking drugs to enhance his performance

DEFINITION

PERFORMANCE-ENHANCING DRUGS

Drugs that can improve an athlete's performance.

DEFINITION

STEROIDS

Artificial male hormones that allow the performer to train harder and longer.

DEFINITION

BLOOD DOPING

Removing blood after training at high altitude. The blood is stored and then reinfused shortly before competition in order to improve the aerobic capacity by increasing the number of erythrocytes. Blood doping is very difficult to detect.

side-effects have been used by athletes to improve their athletic performance illegally. The range and availability of these types of drugs is constantly increasing, making control very difficult.

The huge increase in the rewards for winning may have meant that the temptation to take drugs became too great for many athletes to bear. For example, Ben Johnson felt the risk was worthwhile – even though he was stripped of his 1988 gold medal and banned from competition for several years he continued to make money from his fame.

Most media attention has been focused on the use of *steroids*. These artificial male hormones allow the performer to train harder and longer and have been difficult to trace in the past as they are not actually performance-enhancing drugs. Athletes tend to take them in the closed season when they are building up fitness. A breakthrough in detection of these drugs was the decision to test athletes at any time during the year, meaning illegal activity could be detected even in the closed season.

The very fine line between what is legal and illegal causes many dilemmas for both the performer and authorities. A sprinter can legally take ginseng, although it contains substances that have advantageous effects. An athlete can train at high altitude to try to develop the efficiency of their blood system, but *blood doping* is illegal.

A substance is only illegal if it is on the International Olympic Committee's list of banned substances. It may be possible that athletes with access to highly qualified chemists and physiologists may be able to keep one step ahead by taking substances that have not yet been banned.

After the Atlanta Olympic Games in 1996, the American sports magazine, *Sports Illustrated*, undertook an 18-month investigation into drug-taking in elite sport. Its conclusion was that drug use had reached epidemic levels.

> There is a small percentage of athletes who do not use drugs.
> There is a small percentage who use drugs and get caught and there is a very large percentage who use drugs who don't get caught.

At the Sydney Olympic Games in 2000, the IOC worked hard to make the games 100% free of drugs. Some 35 athletes tested positive and were disciplined before the games stated. Most of those caught were from eastern European and under-developed countries. There was a suggestion by many in the international press that these athletes lack the knowledge of how to avoid detection or cannot afford to pay out the thousands of dollars required to buy more sophisticated drugs.

The future

New drugs come on to the scene all the time and this makes it very difficult for organisations such as the International Olympic Medal Commission to keep ahead. New drugs are more sophisticated and harder to detect as they often mimic naturally occurring hormones and chemicals. One of the most highlighted of this new wave of drugs is erythropoietin (EPO). EPO produces a hormone that stimulates bone marrow to produce more red blood cells. It is claimed by scientists to improve an athlete's aerobic performance by up to 15%. Other scientists state that it can have deadly side effects – at night the new red blood cells turn viscous and the heart needs to work harder to move the blood around the body. Some estimates say that 25 athletes have died as a result of taking EPO.

activity

In the table is a list of drugs commonly used illegally in sport to improve performance. Try to find out what effect each has and give some examples of sports in which they might be used.

Substance	Effects	Sport
Amphetamines		
Caffeine		
Anabolic steroids		
Blood doping		
Beta blockers		

18.4 Violence in sport

Violence is also a growing element in modern sport. In some sports the mutual respect that we mentioned above may have disappeared. For example, in rugby we have seen 'stamping', deliberately kicking an opponent on the floor, which often means the victim has to leave the field, in American football the aim of the defence is to 'sack' the quarterback – the more damage you can inflict, the more effective your defence has been – and in soccer we have the 'professional foul' – in which an attacker is deliberately knocked down to prevent him scoring a goal.

Once again it is usually the result that drives such actions; without a key player the opposition is not going to be as big a threat. A professional foul in football may result in a penalty – but there is a chance of the goalkeeper saving it.

Deviance may be occurring more in modern sport as the rewards become so much greater – the win ethic has definitely begun to dominate high-level sport where the result is often seen to justify

Violence in sport is another form of sporting deviance

any means of achieving it. The problem escalates as amateur sports-men – and, more importantly, children – are influenced by what they see professionals doing. Could it be that sporting etiquette is dead and that the gamesman has replaced the sportsman?

Key revision points

Deviance is going against the values and ethics of sport, breaking the rules and codes. Rules can be written or unwritten – the letter or spirit of the game. In cheating, the drive to win overrides the idea of fair play: the recreational ethic of sportsmanship comes up against the win ethic of gamesmanship. Drug abuse – taking chemicals in order to increase performance – is one form of deviance. Violence, also a form of deviance, can also be used to gain an unfair advantage.

Key terms

You should now understand the following terms. If you do not, go back through the chapter and find out what they mean.

Blood doping
Cheating
Fair play
Gamesmanship
Performance-enhancing drugs
Sportsmanship
Steroids
Unwritten rules

Progress check

1. Give three different examples of how people can cheat in sport.
2. Give three reasons why people might cheat in sport.
3. Suggest three methods sports organisations have introduced in an attempt to prevent cheating.
4. Give examples of fair play in sport.
5. Why is a win by cheating said to be a 'hollow' victory?
6. How does FIFA try to promote sportsmanship?
7. Suggest why the occurrence of gamesmanship may have increased over recent years.
8. Give examples of what is meant by the unwritten rules of sport.
9. What is meant by the term 'performance-enhancing' drugs?
10. Give three examples of the use of performance-enhancing drugs in sport.
11. Who decides that a drug is illegal in sport?
12. Explain the use of 'stamping' in rugby.
13. Explain, using examples, what is meant by the term 'professional foul'.
14. Why do gamesmen make bad role models?
15. Gary Lineker was a sportsman, John McEnroe a gamesman. Explain the difference.
16. What incentives make an athlete turn to drugs as a means of improving performance?
17. Cheating in sport means breaking the written and unwritten rules in sport. Explain what these mean.

CHAPTER 19

Sport and the media

Learning objectives

- To understand the role of the media in sport.
- To investigate the link between the media and sports funding.
- To investigate whether televising sport lowers participation.
- To discuss the future role of the media in the development of sport.

'Sport is not a requiem mass. It is entertainment. If you go to a soccer stadium, you see the teams run out and the match. TV gives the viewer a VIP seat . . . Technology enlarges the story you are telling.' (Dave Hill, Head of BSkyB Sport)

The most important influence on sport in the 21st century is the media. Its impact began in the late nineteenth century with the newspapers and extended into radio coverage in the twentieth century. The radio helped to develop major sporting occasions such as the FA Cup and the Derby into essential elements of our culture. In the 1950s television transformed many sports into entertainment packages. In the 1990s satellite added another dimension to sport and made it into a truly global commodity.

19.1 Media and sports funding

MEDIA

A form of mass communication, usually comprising the press, television and radio, although it can also include cinema. The media has a direct influence on the values and morals of a society because it reaches such a large proportion of the population.

The presence of the media has turned sport into a commodity that can be bought and sold. Television companies pay out huge amounts of money to cover sports, and advertisers and sponsors back sport because of the exposure they will get in the media. Individuals train and prepare for sport in the knowledge that the media will give them a stage on which to present their talents – and also gain wealth.

Many sports have either been adapted to suit the needs of television or have changed their structure to attract television coverage. In order to survive a sport needs the media spotlight because without it it will be left behind. In 1994 the Hockey Association paid Sky Television to screen games each week in the hope that it would attract sponsors and other television companies to a sport that has been eclipsed by other games such as rugby and football.

There is a direct link between the funding of sport and the media. Media coverage brings sponsors and advertising to a sport, which are now essential for a sport to remain viable. Companies sponsor sports mainly as a means of cheap advertising, a way of getting into the public's living room. This is referred to as sport's 'golden triangle' and is becoming increasingly essential in the success of sports events. For some companies, like the tobacco firms, sport remains one of the few areas where they can still openly advertise. However, recent European legislation is due to phase out all tobacco sponsorship in the next few years.

SPORT'S GOLDEN TRIANGLE

The association between sports event, sponsorship and the media.

The problem for sports such as hockey is that a vicious circle exists – to attract sponsors you need media coverage, but to gain media coverage you often need the funds to pay performers so they can become highly skilful and make your sport more attractive to the media. This is outlined in Figure 19.1.

The influence the media, and specifically television, has over sport is epitomised by the Olympics. This great event is controlled by American television companies, who pay well over $400 million for the exclusive rights to screen the Olympic Games. This kind of financial influence gives the companies control over many factors – for example, we are now used to having to stay up very late to see key moments such as the 100 m final so that it fits in with the peak viewing time in America.

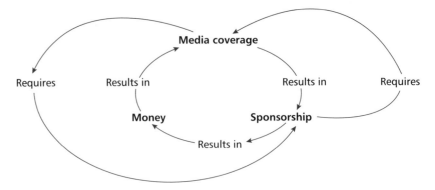

Figure 19.1 *The influence of media coverage on sport*

PAY PER VIEW
*Viewers pay a fee to
watch a particular
programme.*

Other innovations include *pay per view*, where viewers have to pay a one-off fee to their cable or satellite supplier in order to watch a particular sports event. This has already been successfully trialled with both boxing and football and looks set to become a regular feature. Another development is the launch of channels specialising in particular sports or sports clubs – Man U TV is already available to fans and offers them 24-hour programming about their favourite football club.

19.2 Does televising sport lead to lower participation?

Actual participation in sport appears to be falling, and it has been suggested that the amount of sport now available on the television may have influenced this – people don't play sport because they're too busy watching it. However, a number of studies (in particular the Wolfenden Report) have found that, although watching television is our most popular pastime (roughly 25% of our leisure time is spent in front of 'the box'), there is little to link television watching and participation in sport. Indeed, television may actually have a positive effect, in that watching sport on the television often stimulates people to take up sports.

This effect is very noticeable when British teams are successful in world events such as the Olympics. During the last few years ice skating, hockey and curling have all witnessed upsurges in popularity when Britons were seen on the television winning medals.

The one negative effect televised sport does appear to have is on spectatorism, where the lure of a 'live' game on the television and the unpredictability of British weather often makes staying home preferable to going to the stadium. Football clubs can now demand very large fees from television companies (in 1995 Sky paid £70 000 per game for Premiership football), much of which is as compensation for loss of spectators. Cricket and rugby league have also been affected this way.

The media, and the press in particular, have turned sportsmen and women into celebrities, which may be beneficial in terms of potential earnings but which also means that they become 'public figures' and their every move, both on and off the pitch, is scrutinised. There is a general emphasis on sensationalism in the British press where stories (or 'exclusives') are an essential part of the ratings war.

All forms of the media are guilty of concentrating on the critical elements of sport – the action replay questioning an official's decision, or viewing a bad tackle or a violent incident from every possible angle. The use of edited highlights, in which only the goals or action is shown, can also give a rather one-sided view of sports.

Modern technology means that no corner of a sport can remain 'hidden'. We now have cameras in the cricket stumps, in the pockets of a snooker table, on cars, giving the armchair spectator the 'real' view. In some cases this has been very beneficial – many of the deviant practices discussed in the last chapter are more closely scrutinised and many sports now use video evidence to pick out any foul play the referee missed in the heat of the game.

What are the benefits of television technology being made available to sports officials? Are there any disadvantages?

19.3 An analysis

The mass media reflects its culture and may also actually shape that culture in fostering values, particularly in establishing and maintaining stereotypes. In general, the mass media will associate itself with the popular view and in sport this will be represented in the most popular sports.

Even in the quality papers several sports dominate the sports pages – and these will tend to be male-dominated sports often associated with gambling. However, there are some exceptions to this – Channel 4 has successfully introduced a number of ethnic and minority sports to the UK such as sumo wrestling, kabadi, women's football, wheelchair basketball and American football.

Much of the socio-cultural elements in sport we discussed earlier will be evident in the media: there tends to be an emphasis on the dominant culture and its sport, to the detriment of women and ethnic minorities. Sensationalism often feeds on stereotypes and national prejudice. Headlines such as 'We'll Blitz the Frogs' or 'Keagans' Masterplan to Beat Krauts' are blazed across the back pages when our national teams compete. Warlike terminology is often used in reporting sport – you will often see the words 'battle', 'bombarded', 'defence/attack', 'blitzed' and 'sniping' in headlines – perhaps reinforcing sport's historical links with war (see Chapter 11).

Repeat the newspaper analysis you did in section 17.3.2, but this time make up a table showing the amount of space devoted to different sports. Compare a tabloid newspaper with one of the broadsheet papers.

KABBADI

A 'tag' like game, played to a high level in Asia.

SENSATIONALISM

Where the media exaggerates stories about sports stars.

As sports scientists we take a more analytical view than the media. Here are some areas of study you could develop.

Television – BBC 1, BBC 2, ITV 1, Channel 4, satellite channels.
* How is sport presented on each of these channels?
* How will the 'ratings war' and increased rivalry between channels affect sport in the future?

The press – Broadsheet, tabloid, daily, local, weekly, national.
* How does the emphasis on sport reporting differ in each of these types of paper?
* Which papers lean towards sensationalism?
* Do papers provide a balanced view of sport? If not, identify groups that are discriminated against.

The radio – Local, national, BBC Radios 1, 2, 3, 4 and 5, commercial
* How does the emphasis change in each of these stations?
* How does radio's coverage of sport differ from that of the television?

The arts – Literature, painting/sculpture, music, dance, cinema, theatre.
* Can you list any examples of sport represented in these media?
* How is the history of sport linked to the arts?

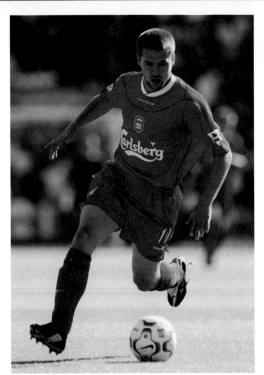

Premiership football – a league exclusive to Sky television though from 2004 the BBC can show edited highlights

DEFINITION

SUPER LEAGUE

The new league competition created by Sky for rugby league.

MERCHANDISING

The sale of commodities such as hats, shirts, mugs and bedspreads that bear the team's name.

19.4 The future

Sport has become an important cornerstone of the media and each side feels it has the upper hand, although it would appear that the media is slowly beginning to take over power in sport. We have already mentioned that the American networks now crontrol the Olympics, and Sky Television has changed football in the UK from a traditional Saturday game into an almost daily event in order to secure maximum viewing potential. In 1990 Sky paid £305 million for exclusive rights to Premiership football for five years. At the time the sale of Sky dishes was low but the capture of England's premier football league led to a huge increase in sales. In 1996 Sky paid a further £670 million to retain its hold on football until the millennium.

In 2000 BSkyB signed a new deal with the Premiership worth £1.3 billion, a fee which led indirectly to a number of footballers earning wages of £100,000 a week, and in 2002 the transfer record was broken when Rio Ferdinand moved from Leeds to Manchester United for £29.3 million.

Rugby league is another sport transformed by satellite television – in 1996 Sky television bought exclusive rights to the game for £85 million, although there were a number of conditions. The game had to forget 100 years of history and change from a winter sport to a summer game to accommodate television schedules. The leagues were restructured to form a *Super League* and new clubs have been manufactured in non-rugby league areas in an attempt to widen the market. To aid the marketing all teams also had to invent nicknames that made them into *merchandising* commodities and in some way broke down the geographical locations of the games – hence we now have the Bulls v the Blue Sox rather than Bradford Northern v Halifax!

There have been, and will continue to be, many positive rewards from this 'media-isation' of sport:

- Modern technology has transformed the way we watch sport – slow-motion and multi-angle approaches extol the aesthetics of every sport.
- It has generated huge interest in every aspect of sport, leading to the development of sports science, academic qualifications and a whole host of books, magazines, videos and films.
- Our modern sports stars are well known and well paid, receiving much-earned rewards for their effort and dedication and generally providing us with excellent role models.

However, if we look at televised programmes such as *Super-stars* or *WWE Wrestling (formerly known as WWF)*, are we seeing the true future of modern sport? Glamour, razzmatazz and the quest for action may kill some sports and ruin others – the wrestlers are very athletic and highly trained performers but they are actors and have lost that essential element that all sportsmen and women possess. In some cases sport may be close to becoming pure entertainment.

Key revision points

The media is a mass communication system made up of the press, television, radio and cinema. The media, and especially television, has been the most influential element in the development of sport over the last century. It plays an important role in the funding of sport by paying to cover sport, by attracting sponsors and advertisers and by making performers into stars who can then attract wealth. Television may stimulate people to take up sport but it may also have a negative effect on spectatorism. The media influences society's views of sport, often fostering and reinforcing stereotypes. It has the power to make or break sports careers. In addition, reports in the media can distort the public's view of sport.

Key terms

Progress check

You should now understand the following terms. If you do not, go back through the chapter and find out what they mean.

Kabbadi
Media
Merchandising
Pay per view
Sensationalism
Sport's golden triangle
Super League

1 In what ways has the increased influence of television affected sport in Britain?
2 'Sport is now a global commodity.' Explain what this term means.
3 Why are sponsors willing to pay out large amounts of money to sports that are seen on television?
4 What role has Channel 4 played in influencing our views of sport?
5 How can the media sensationalise sport?
6 How has rugby league changed to suit television?
7 What effect does the media have in promoting role models?
8 How has the development of media technology helped sports officiate their rules?
9 How might WWE wrestling give us an insight into the future of sport?
10 Why has Sky been prepared to put so much money into Premiership football?
11 What types of sport do newspapers tend to concentrate their coverage on?
12 What role does the media play in the development of stereotypes?
13 Give three examples of the positive effect the media has on sport.
14 Give three examples of the negative effect the media can have on sport.
15 How has the influence of the media in sport affected the earning potential of sports stars?

Further reading

L. Allison, editor. *The Politics of Sport*. Manchester University Press, 1986.

D. Anthony. *A Strategy for British Sport*. Hurst, 1980.

J. Armitage. *Man at Play*. Warne, 1977.

D. Birley. *Sport and the Making of Britain*. Manchester University Press, 1993.

D.W. Calhoun. *Sport, Culture and Personality*. Human Kinetics, 1987.

E. Cashmore. *Making Sense of Sport*. Routledge, 1990.

CCPR. *The Organisation of Sport and Recreation in Britain*. Central Council of Physical Recreation, 1991.

S. Coe, D. Teasdale and D. Wickham. *More than a Game*. BBC Books, 1992.

R. Davis, R. Bull, J. Roscoe and D. Roscoe. *PE and the Study of Sport*, 2nd edition. Mosby, 1994.

Department of National Heritage. *Sport – Raising the Game*. HMSO, 1995

J. Dumazedier. *Towards a Society of Leisure*. Collier-Macmillan, 1967.

J. Ford. *This Sporting Land*. New English Library, 1977.

P. Gardner. *Nice Guys Finish Last*. Allen Lane, 1974.

R. Holt. *Sport and the British*. Oxford University Press, 1990.

B. Houlihan. *The Government and Politics of Sport*. Routledge, 1991.

J. Huizinga. *Homo ludens, a Study of the Play Element in Culture*. Beacon, 1964.

A. Lumpkin. *PE and Sport – A Contemporary Introduction*. Times Mirror, 1990.

T. Mason. *Sport in Britain*. Oxford University Press, 1988.

P. McIntosh. *Physical Education in England since 1800*. Bell and Hyman, 1979.

C. Mortlock. *The Adventure Alternative*. Cicerone Press, 1984.

H.L. Nixon. *Sport and the American Dream*. Leisure Press, 1984.

S. Parker. *The Sociology of Leisure*. Allen and Unwin, 1976.

J. Riordan, editor. *Sport under Communism*. Hurst, 1981.

G.H. Sage. *Power and Ideology in American Sport*. Human Kinetics, 1990.

W.D. Smith. *Stretching their Bodies*. David and Charles, 1974.

Sports Council. *How to Find out About the Organisation of Sport*. Sports Council Information Services, 1993.

Sports Council. *Into the 90's*. Sports Council Information Services, 1988.

Sports Council. *New Horizons*. Sports Council Information Services, 1994.

G. Torkildsen. *Leisure and Recreation Management*, 2nd edition. Spon, 1991.

Websites

www.cre.gov.uk/speqs/

www.olympics.org.uk

www.uksport.org.uk

www.ncf.org.uk

www.youthsporttrust.org

www.sportsmatch.co.uk

www.sports.gov.uk

www.ukathletics.org

www.physicaleducation.co.uk

www.wsf.org.uk

www.lta.org.uk

EXERCISE PHYSIOLOGY

This part of the book contains:

Whereas anatomy, biomechanics and physiology look at the structure and function of the human body, exercise physiology concentrates on the response of the body to exercise. In recent years this area of study has become very popular as teachers and coaches realise the benefits of a more scientific approach to exercise and training. As a consequence of today's increasingly sedentary lifestyles many people are extremely unfit. A knowledge of exercise physiology gives an understanding of the physiological benefits of exercise that can be applied to develop a healthier lifestyle and to significantly improve sporting performance.

CHAPTER 20
Energy

Learning objectives

- To understand the terms energy, work and power.
- To understand the role of ATP in energy production.
- To be able to describe the three methods of ATP production.

The body needs a constant supply of energy in order to perform everyday tasks such as respiration and digestion. When we start to exercise the rate at which our body uses energy increases and the efficiency of the energy supply is one of the major factors determining athletic performance. Production of energy for physical activity has to be able to cope with extreme situations – for example, during a 100 m sprint large amounts of energy are needed very quickly, but during a marathon the energy must be made available over a prolonged period of time. Some people are physiologically better suited to certain activities than others because their bodies are more efficient at releasing energy in a particular way.

DEFINITION

CALORIE

A calorie is the amount of heat energy needed to raise the temperature of 1g water through 1°C. A kilocalorie (kCal) is 1000 calories.

JOULE

1 Cal = 4.2 joules

WATT

A watt is equivalent to the use of one joule per second.

Energy is the capacity or ability to perform work, and is measured in joules or calories.

The more weight-conscious of us avidly study food labels to see how many calories food contains. Basically, the more calories food contains the more exercise we have to perform to burn off the energy provided. If you don't use the energy it is stored until it is required and you put on weight. We are all familiar with this process of energy exchange, but not so familiar with the more technical terms: food (*chemical* energy) is converted into movement (*kinetic* energy) or is stored as fat (*potential* energy).

Work is defined as force × distance, but can be measured in the same units as energy (calories or joules). In most cases the force is equal to the performer's body weight, so if you ran 1500 m you would perform more work and would therefore use up more energy than if you ran 800 m. If two performers run 1500 m, but one is running twice as fast as the other, then the quicker of the two athletes is working harder and is exerting more power. *Power* is work performed per unit of time and is measured in watts.

The way energy is released in the body is quite complicated and in this chapter we give only a very simplified overview of the processes involved. Further reading is suggested at the end of Part 4. There is only one usable form of energy in the body – *adenosine triphosphate* (ATP). All sources of energy, found in the food that we eat, have to be converted into ATP before the potential energy in them can be used.

ATP is a high-energy phosphate compound made up of one molecule of adenosine and three phosphates. The bonds that hold the compound together are a source of quite a lot of potential energy.

ATP = Adenosine–phosphate–phosphate–phosphate

When a compound is broken down (the bonds between the molecules are broken), then energy is released. A reaction that releases energy is known as an *exothermic* reaction. In the body a specific enzyme is used to break down a particular compound – the enzyme used to break down ATP is ATPase. ATP is broken down to adenosine diphosphate (ADP) and free phosphate (P), releasing the stored energy:

ATP → ADP + P + **Energy**

When a compound is built up (or synthesised) energy is needed to restore the bonds between the molecules. A reaction that needs energy to work is known as an *endothermic* reaction. Production of ATP from ADP and P is an endothermic reaction:

ADP + P + **Energy** → ATP

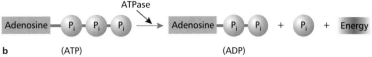

a

b (ATP) (ADP)

Figure 20.1 (a) *The structure of an ATP molecule* (b) *The breakdown of ATP to release energy*

DEFINITION

ELEMENT

An element is a simple substance that cannot be chemically split any further, such as oxygen or carbon.

COMPOUND

A group of elements combined together form a compound, for example carbon dioxide.

MOLECULE

A molecule is a small group of atoms with at least one atom from each element of the compound.

ENZYME

An enzyme is a biological catalyst which acts to bring about a specific reaction.

In practice

Most of the energy in the body (c. 70%) is released as heat energy, which is why we get so hot when we exercise.

The energy released from the breakdown of ATP to ADP and P is converted to kinetic and heat energy.

Once the energy produced from the breakdown of ATP has been used we have a potential problem – what do we do when all the ATP has been broken down to ADP? Energy needs to be put back, in the form of an endothermic reaction, to re-form ATP. There are three ways that this is achieved in the human body.

1 The phosphocreatine system (ATP/PC) or alactic system.
2 The lactic acid system or glycolysis.
3 The aerobic process.

As we cannot afford to run out of ATP all three methods take place very quickly. Each method is good at supplying energy for particular energy demands and duration, allowing us to cope with a variety of situations.

Systems 1 and 2 are *anaerobic* processes: they take place without oxygen. System 3 is *aerobic*: it requires oxygen to work.

20.1 Production of ATP by the phosphocreatine or alactic system

Phosphocreatine (PC) is a high-energy phosphate compound that is found in limited amounts in the sarcoplasm (muscle's equivalent to cytoplasm – see Chapter 3). Potential energy is stored in the bonds of the compound and when the enzyme *creatine kinase* breaks down the phosphocreatine to phosphate and creatine, energy is released:

Phosphocreatine → P + Creatine + **Energy**

In practice

Movements that are fast and powerful rely on the alactic energy system as the predominant method of ATP resynthesis.

A javelin thrower relies on the alactic energy system

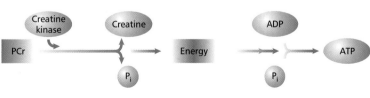

Figure 20.2 *Energy released from the breakdown of phosphocreatine is used to resynthesise ATP*

Creatine kinase is activated when the level of ADP within the muscle cell increases, when our stores of ATP start to diminish. The energy released by the breakdown of PC is used to convert ADP to ATP. The energy has to be liberated by the breakdown of PC before ATP can be formed. This is known as a *coupled reaction*. For every molecule of PC broken down, sufficient energy is released to produce one molecule of ATP. It is important to remember, however, that in any chemical reaction if the potential energy in the chemical bonds of the reactants is greater than that of the products, then energy is released by the reaction. The energy does not actually come from the breaking of the bonds, although this is how it is commonly stated. When the overall reaction is considered the net effect is that energy is released from the breakdown.

The stores of PC in the muscles are enough to sustain all-out effort for about ten seconds, which doesn't really seem very long. However, this is the only system that is capable of producing ATP quickly enough when we are performing activities that demand large amounts of energy over a short period of time, for example a short sprint or a triple jump.

This is because PC is a relatively simple compound that is very easy to break down. Breakdown of PC does not rely on the availability of oxygen and as PC is stored in the muscle cell it is readily accessible as an energy source. This means that energy for ATP synthesis can be obtained extremely quickly from PC and no fatiguing by-products are released.

in training

It is fairly common practice amongst athletes involved in intermittent activities that rely heavily on the anaerobic energy systems to take a creatine supplement. The idea is to artificially boost the amount of creatine stored in the muscle cell to help increase the threshold of the alactic system and to help recovery. As creatine is a naturally occurring substance it is not currently considered to be illegal.

activity

Using a team game of your choice identify three situations where you think that you would rely predominantly on the alactic system as a source of energy.

20.2 ATP production by the lactic acid system or glycolysis

This system is also an anaerobic process taking place in the sarcoplasm, but the energy needed comes from the food we eat. This process involves the *partial* breakdown of glucose – glucose can be fully broken down only in the presence of oxygen. The lactic acid system is sometimes called *anaerobic glycolysis*, as 'glycolysis' simply means the breakdown of glucose. Carbohydrate in the diet is digested to glucose, enters the bloodstream and travels to the muscles and the liver. Glucose is stored in the muscles and liver as *glycogen*.

DEFINITION

GLYCOGEN

A complex chain made up of a number of glucose molecules. It is used as energy storage in muscles and the liver.

Glucose (chemical formula $(C_6 H_{12} O_6)_n$, where *n* can be a very large number) is a much more complex compound than phosphocreatine and therefore stores more energy. Glucose molecules are

added to phosphate groups to form glucose-6-phosphate. This process is known as *phosphorylation* and actually requires ATP for the reaction to take place (Figure 20.3). When glycogen is used the process of phosphorylation does not require ATP to prime the reaction. The following reactions, however, are exothermic and therefore release energy for ATP resynthesis. Glucose-6-phosphate continues to be broken down anaerobically (basically by breaking the molecule in half) by the enzyme *phosphofructokinase*. Phosphofructokinase is activated by a drop in the level of phosphocreatine and by increased levels of calcium (remember that calcium is secreted from the sarcoplasmic reticulum during muscle contraction – see Chapter 3). The glucose is broken down to two molecules of *pyruvic acid*, which is a three-carbon compound. Then, because of the absence of oxygen, *lactic acid* is formed from the pyruvic acid (Figure 20.3). The reason why lactic acid is produced is quite complicated and for a more detailed explanation you should refer to the texts suggested in the further reading section. Very basically, for glycolysis to continue hydrogen ions have to be removed and transported into the mitochondria. This can happen only if sufficient oxygen is available. Under predominantly anaerobic conditions the pyruvic acid has to accept the hydrogen ions instead and lactic acid is formed. The enzyme responsible for this reaction is called *lactate dehydrogenase* (LDH). The net result is that one molecule of glucose ($C_6 H_{12} O_6$) is broken down to two molecules of lactic acid ($2C_3 H_6 O_3$) and enough energy is released to resynthesise two molecules of ATP (or three molecules of ATP if glycogen is used).

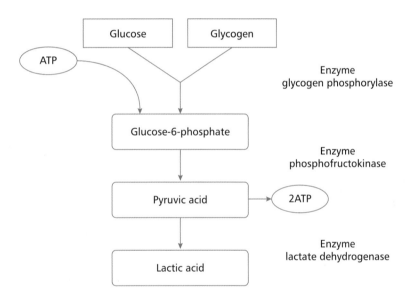

Figure 20.3 *Outline of the lactic acid system of production of energy for resynthesising ATP*

Breakdown of the bonds in glucose releases energy, which is used to synthesise ATP (two molecules of ATP for each molecule of glucose). This is another example of a coupled reaction. It should be remembered that the basic 'ingredients' of each compound are the same: we start off with a large compound containing carbon, hydrogen and oxygen and gradually break it into smaller compounds containing carbon, hydrogen and oxygen, so that as much of the potential energy stored in the original compound as possible is released for ATP synthesis.

The lactic acid system takes longer to produce energy than the ATP/PC system because more reactions have to take place, but it is still a very quick process. Usually this method supplies energy for high-intensity activities for about a minute but it can last longer depending on the intensity of the activity.

The 400 m race is a good example of the possible effects of using this system to the maximum. If an inexperienced runner sets off too quickly, he or she will start to feel the effects of an early build-up of lactic acid and will struggle to reach the finish line. This is because when glycogen is broken down anaerobically, lactic acid is produced. If the lactic acid accumulates it lowers the pH and the drop in pH directly affects the action of phosphofructokinase and the lipoprotein lipase that breaks down fat, so the body's ability to synthesise ATP is temporarily reduced, causing fatigue. The accumulation of lactic acid also interferes with cross-bridge formation within the muscle cell, again contributing to a drop in performance.

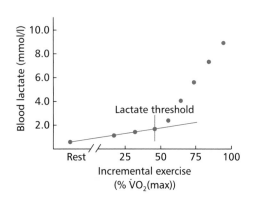

Figure 20.4 *Changes in blood lactic acid concentrations during incremental exercise*

in training

In an untrained person working at 50–60% of their $\dot{V}O_2(max)$ the blood levels of lactic acid begin to increase exponentially. This is unlikely to happen to trained athletes until they are working at 70–80% of their $\dot{V}O_2(max)$. This sudden rise has been attributed to an increase in reliance on the lactic acid system for resynthesising ATP. The point at which this sudden increase begins has been called the *anaerobic threshold* and its occurrence was linked to hypoxic conditions (lack of oxygen). However, the sudden increase in lactic acid could be due to a number of factors such as the reduced rate of lactate removal and the recruitment of fast twitch fibres as well as a lack of oxygen, so it is now referred to as the *onset of blood lactate accumulation* (OBLA) or *lactate threshold* (Figure 20.4).

DEFINITION

OBLA

The onset of blood lactate accumulation is a point during progressive exercise when the blood lactate concentration suddenly increases.

activity

Using a team game of your choice identify three situations in which you think that you would rely predominantly on the lactic acid system for energy.

DEFINITION

LACTATE

Any salt of lactic acid. Lactic acid is produced during anaerobic glycolysis, but it dissociates very quickly to form the salt lactate.

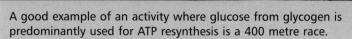
In practice

A good example of an activity where glucose from glycogen is predominantly used for ATP resynthesis is a 400 metre race.

20.3 Production of ATP using the aerobic system

The aerobic system of energy production needs oxygen and, although oxygen is available at the onset of exercise, there is not enough to break down food fuels at a rate that matches the breakdown of ATP, so for immediate energy production the two anaerobic systems are used. However, as soon as we start to exercise our heart rate and rate of ventilation increase and our vascular system distributes more oxygenated blood to the working muscles. Within 1–2 minutes the muscles are being supplied with enough oxygen to allow effective aerobic respiration.

The aerobic system has three stages in which glucose is broken down by a process of oxidation to carbon dioxide and water. These are just about the simplest compounds that can be made from carbon, hydrogen and oxygen, so by breaking the glucose molecule down this far nearly all the energy possible is being released from this compound.

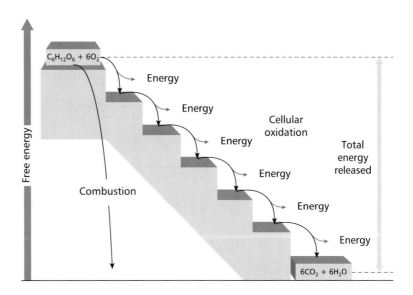

Figure 20.5
The complete breakdown of carbohydrate to carbon dioxide and water

20.3.1 *Stage one: aerobic glycolysis*

Aerobic glycolysis is the same as anaerobic glycolysis: glucose (a six-carbon compound) is broken down to pyruvic acid (a three-carbon compound). However, as oxygen is now present the reaction can proceed further than in anaerobic glycolysis and lactic acid is not produced. The reaction still takes place in the sarcoplasm and the energy yield is sufficient to synthesise two molecules of ATP.

20.3.2 *Stage two: the TCA/citric acid/Krebs' cycle*

The pyruvic acid produced in the first stage diffuses into the matrix of the mitochondria where it is broken down to a two-carbon acetyl group. This combines with coenzyme A (usually shortened to CoA) to form acetyl CoA. A complex cyclical series of reactions now occurs. Put very simply, acetyl CoA combines with oxaloacetic acid to form citric acid, which is changed into a number of different compounds in a series of reactions that produces more energy and results in the regeneration of oxaloacetic acid. The whole cycle can then repeat itself. The cycle is known as the *tricarboxylic acid* (or TCA) *cycle*, the *citric acid cycle* or *Krebs' cycle*.

DEFINITION

COENZYME
A molecule that can carry atoms, transporting them from one reaction to another. An example is coenzyme A.

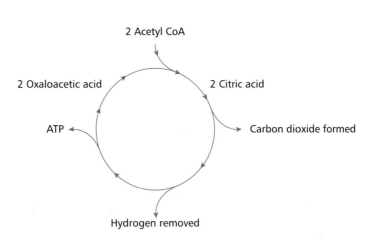

Figure 20.6
The TCA cycle

During the cycle three important things happen:
1 carbon dioxide is formed
2 oxidation takes place – hydrogen is removed from the compound
3 sufficient energy is released to synthesise two molecules of ATP.

A summary of the cycle can be seen in Figure 20.6.

20.3.3 *Stage three: the electron transport chain/electron transport system*

The hydrogen atoms removed during the cycle in stage two are transported by coenzymes to the cristae of the inner membranes of the mitochondria. Here they enter the *electron transport system* and the electrons removed from the hydrogen are passed along by electron carriers, eventually combining with oxygen and the hydrogen ions to form water.

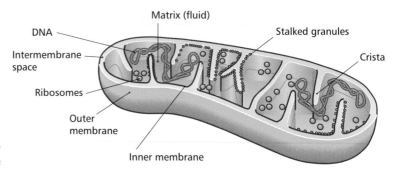

Figure 20.7
Structure of mitochondrion

In an over-simplification of a very complex system, essentially high-energy carbon–hydrogen bonds are being broken (glucose) to form low-energy carbon–oxygen bonds (carbon dioxide) and hydrogen–oxygen bonds (water), and release energy to combine ADP and phosphate to form ATP.

The energy yield from the electron transport chain is sufficient to produce 34 molecules of ATP. This means that the total yield of aerobic respiration (from the three stages combined) is 38 molecules of ATP.

The aerobic system of synthesising ATP is the most efficient in terms of energy produced, and the by-products (carbon dioxide and water) are easily expelled from the body. However, the reactions involved in this system depend on the availability of oxygen and at the onset of exercise and during very intense exercise the oxygen distributed to the cells just isn't enough for the body to rely on this system as a way of replenishing ATP stores. During submaximal exercise the aerobic system is the predominant method of ATP production as oxygen can be delivered at a rate to match the oxygen demand. Unless you run out of carbohydrate, protein and fat stores, this system is unlimited.

in training

Some athletes wear a nasal strip across the bridge of their nose to hold their nostrils open. The intention is to make it easier to ventilate and presumably to get more oxygen into the body. So far there is no evidence that wearing these strips has any effect whatsoever on ventilation.

In practice

The oxidative capacity of a muscle cell will depend on its percentage composition of slow oxidative and fast oxidative fibres, the oxidative enzyme levels and the actual amount of oxygen available.

20.3.4 Summary of the aerobic system of producing ATP

Glucose ($C_6H_{12}O_6$) + Oxygen ($6O_2$) → Carbon dioxide ($6CO_2$) + Water ($6H_2O$) + Energy

Energy + 38 ADP + 38 P = 38 ATP

Stage one, aerobic glycolysis:	2 ATP
Stage two, TCA cycle:	2 ATP
Stage three, electron transport chain:	34 ATP
Total yield:	38 ATP

See Figure 20.8.

So far we have discussed how glycogen stores are broken down aerobically to produce ATP, but both fats and proteins may also be used as fuel for ATP synthesis.

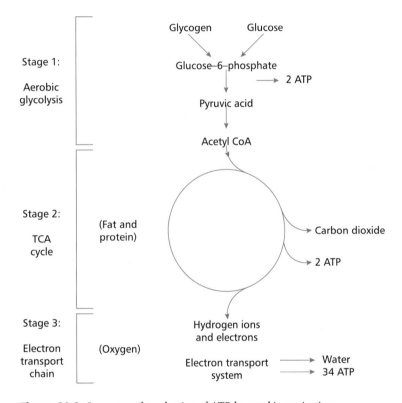

Figure 20.8 *Summary of production of ATP by aerobic respiration*

20.4 Energy from fats

Fat is stored in *adipose tissue* in the form of *triglycerides*. Some fat is stored in the muscle cells and fats are also circulated in the blood.

The breakdown of fat is controlled by enzymes called *lipases* (e.g. lipoprotein lipase) and in the muscle cells the triglyceride is broken down to a two-carbon compound and enters the TCA cycle in a manner similar to the products of glycogen breakdown. Triglycerides contain a lot of high-energy carbon–hydrogen bonds, so when triglyceride is broken down to carbon dioxide and water a lot of energy is released (Figure 20.8). The amount of ATP synthesised by breakdown of fat is much higher than the amount obtained

DEFINITION

TRIGLYCERIDE

A triglyceride molecule is made up of one molecule of glycerol and three fatty acids.

in training

If you add together the body's fat and carbohydrate stores, carbohydrates would account for about 4% of the total stores in terms of weight (estimate based on a small male with average percentage of body fat). In terms of kCal the carbohydrate stores would contribute even less (c. 2%) as fat stores more energy. It is therefore important for athletes to try to conserve their carbohydrate stores and to supplement them whenever possible.

activity

Consider the following activities and decide which would be the predominant energy system used to resynthesise ATP.

1 Resting
2 A 30 m sprint
3 A 2 mile steady-state run
4 A gymnastic tumbling routine
5 A full-court man-to-man defence in basketball followed by a fast break attack.

Remember that the duration and intensity of the exercise dictates which system will be relied on most.

by breakdown of carbohydrate, which makes it a much more economical fuel in terms of energy yield than carbohydrate (Figure 20.9). However, the breakdown of triglycerides requires roughly 15% more oxygen than the breakdown of glycogen, so when the supply of oxygen is limited glycogen stores will be broken down instead of triglyceride stores. The other problem is that the presence of lactic acid inhibits the breakdown of fat, and an increase in insulin will have a similar effect. These factors have serious implications for endurance athletes who are trying to conserve their stores of carbohydrate and maximise the use of their fat stores.

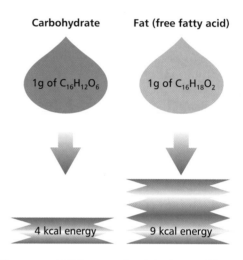

Figure 20.9 *The energy yield from 1g of carbohydrate and from 1g of fat. Though 1g of fat can generate 2.25 times as much energy as a similar amount of carbohydrate, it also takes substantially more oxygen to metabolise fat than carbohydrate.*

20.5 Energy from proteins

Although it *is* possible to use protein as an energy source for ATP synthesis we very rarely do so. Protein is oxidised only when the body is in a state of starvation or near exhaustion. Two-carbon compounds produced by breakdown of proteins also enter into the TCA cycle.

activity

List the advantages and disadvantages of each energy system used to resynthesise ATP.

Key revision points
There are three ways of synthesising ATP from ADP and free phosphate to ensure a constant supply of energy. All three systems work together, the dominance of any one depending on the rate at which energy is used. When the demand for energy is high and immediate then the anaerobic processes are heavily relied on. When the demand for energy is low but sustained then the aerobic process is the main system used.

Table 20.1 *Summary of the energy systems used to produce ATP*

	Alactic system	Lactic acid system	Aerobic system
Site of reaction	Sarcoplasm	Sarcoplasm	Stage 1 sarcoplasm, stages 2 and 3 mitochondria
Presence of oxygen	Anaerobic	Anaerobic	Aerobic
Fuel used	Phosphocreatine	Carbohydrate	Carbohydrate and fat
Active enzyme	Creatine kinase	Glycogen phosphorylase and phosphofructokinase	Glycogen phosphorylase, phosphofructokinase, lipoprotein lipase (fat)
Enzyme activated by	Increase in ADP	Decrease in PC levels, increase in calcium levels	Decrease in insulin levels
Enzyme inhibited by	Increase in ATP levels	Increase in PC, reduction in pH	Increase in insulin, increase in lactic acid
Relative speed of reaction	Very fast	Fast	Slow
Brief outline	PC broken down to creatine, free phosphate and energy, which is used to convert ADP to ATP	Glycogen is broken down to glucose, then to pyruvic acid and then to lactic acid. Energy given off used to produce ATP	Stage 1: glucose broken down to pyruvic acid. Stage 2: cyclic series of reactions producing carbon dioxide. Hydrogen is removed from compounds in the cycle. Stage 3: in the electron transport system hydrogen ions and electrons are recombined with oxygen to make water
By-products	None	Lactic acid	Carbon dioxide and water
Effects of by-products	None	Lowers pH and inhibits action of enzyme	Easily expelled from body
Energy yield (molecules of ATP per molecule broken down)	1	2	Stage 1: 2; stage 2: 2; stage 3: 34
Threshold	Approx. 10 seconds	1–2 minutes, depending on intensity of exercise	Unlimited during submaximal exercise

Key terms

You should now understand the following terms. If you do not, go back through the chapter and find out what they mean.

ATP
Coenzyme
Compound
Coupled reaction
Electron transport system
Endothermic reaction
Energy
Enzyme
Exothermic reaction
Glycolysis
Joule
Krebs' cycle
Power
Watt
Work

Progress check

1 Define the following terms:
   a energy
   b work
   c power.
2 Joules are the units used to express . . .?
3 Watts are the units used to express . . .?
4 What is ATP? Where is it found?
5 How is energy released from ATP?
6 Name the three processes that are used to synthesise ATP.
7 Name the process that relies on the presence of oxygen.
8 What is meant by a coupled reaction? Give an example.
9 Which system is used to produce energy for very short bursts of intensive exercise?
10 During glycolysis glucose is broken down to pyruvic acid and energy is released. How much energy is released per molecule of glucose, and what is it used for?
11 Where in the cell does glycolysis take place?
12 What process takes place in the cristae of the mitochondria?
13 Name and briefly describe the three stages of the aerobic energy system.
14 What is the net energy yield of the aerobic process per molecule of glucose?
15 Which food fuel releases the most energy?
16 When you start to exercise why is carbohydrate broken down rather than fat?
17 During anaerobic glycolysis lactic acid is formed. What effect does a build-up of lactic acid have on the body?

CHAPTER 21

Energy and exercise

Learning objectives

- To understand the concept of the energy continuum.
- To know how the energy systems are regulated.
- To be able to describe the effects of intensity and duration of exercise on energy supplies.
- To appreciate the effect of diet on performance.

We depend on energy to sustain our normal bodily functions and activities, and to understand how our muscles use food to provide the energy for movement is an essential part of exercise physiology. Having enough energy and having the critical mix of fuels available has a dramatic effect on the level of performance that can be achieved. In the previous chapter the three ways of metabolising ATP were discussed. It is the purpose of this chapter to see how interdependent these systems are and how they are used during exercise.

21.1 The energy continuum

In Chapter 20 the three methods of synthesising ATP were looked at in isolation, which tends to give a distorted picture of what actually happens within the cell. We are constantly breaking down food fuels aerobically, and at rest nearly all of our energy is provided this way. As there is no shortage of oxygen the main food fuel used is fat, although carbohydrate is also used.

If we suddenly start to exercise our demand for energy rises rapidly and, although the aerobic system still contributes to ATP synthesis, it cannot provide all the energy required. This is because it takes time to adjust the supply of oxygen to the working muscles. Until it can do so, another system is needed. The phosphocreatine system provides energy for a limited period of time (until stores run out) and the lactic acid system also contributes energy.

We can thus see that in some situations one or other of the systems will contribute nearly all of the energy needed – for example, the aerobic system at rest or the phosphocreatine system during a 60 m sprint. In other situations a 'mix' of all three energy-production systems will be used and the athlete will continually move from one threshold into another system. An example of this occurs during a Fartlek session (see Chapter 24). This continual movement between and combination of the energy systems is known as the *energy continuum* (Figure 21.1).

A 1500 m race represents a mixture of energy sources used, and athletes should reflect this balance in their approach to training.

Aerobic	0%	50%	100%
Anaerobic	100%	50%	0%
Activity	100m sprint	1500m race	Marathon

Figure 21.1 *The energy continuum*

For some activities it is very easy to decide which of the energy systems is involved in the production of energy – for example during a marathon probably 99–100% of the energy will be released aerobically. In other activities it is not quite as clear because many other factors have to be taken into consideration.

A basketball game is usually accepted as being roughly 80% anaerobic, but this depends on several factors, such as:

- the fitness of the player
- the standard of the game
- the tactics being employed, for example a full court press or a zone defence
- the commitment of the players.

Why is it important to identify the role of each energy system in relation to the total energy requirement of an activity? In order to optimise performance an athlete should make his or her training as specific as possible – to them as an individual and to their chosen activity. A knowledge of how intensity and duration of exercise affects the source of energy, along with how each system is regulated, is therefore very important.

activity

Consider the activities shown in the table below. By shading the appropriate areas indicate the involvement of each energy system in supplying the total energy requirements for each activity.

Marathon			
Basketball game			
1500 m swim			
50 m swim			
Hockey match			
Gymnastic floor routine			
Total energy	0%	50%	100%

Compare your answers with those of others in your group.

Discuss any differences in opinion and be prepared to justify your answer. For example, what factors did you consider as significant for each activity when you decided the contribution of each energy system?

In practice

If you weigh 60 kg and go for a 30-minute walk you will use about 90 kCal.

21.2 Exercise and energy supplies

As already mentioned, in order to perform work we need *energy*. Energy is measured in joules or kilocalories. The more work we perform the more energy we need and some activities use up more energy per hour than others (examples are given in Table 21.1).

The amount of energy used is directly related to the amount of oxygen consumed, as the breakdown (oxidation) of glycogen or fat requires a certain amount of oxygen. At rest we consume 0.2–0.3 litres of oxygen per minute (expressed as $\dot{V}O_2$, where $\dot{V}$ stands for

Table 21.1 *Energy requirements for several activities*

Activity	Energy requirement (kCal/h/kg body weight)
Sitting	1
Walking	3
Playing tennis	4–9
Basketball	7–12
Running a mile in eight minutes	12.5

volume per minute and O_2 stands for oxygen). During maximal exercise this can increase to 3–6 litres. This is the maximum amount of oxygen a person can utilise, or the $\dot{V}O_2(max)$.

When a given amount of oxygen breaks down a given amount of fuel, a specific amount of energy is released. It is too difficult to monitor the amount of energy released, but it is possible to monitor how much oxygen is consumed. If you collect the expired air of an athlete you can determine how much oxygen has been used by comparing the percentage of oxygen in the expired air with that of atmospheric air. The amount of energy required to perform an activity can be estimated from the amount of oxygen consumed. When one litre of oxygen is used to oxidise glycogen then 5 kCal are released.

In practice

If during a run you used 0.2 ml of oxygen per kilogram of your body weight per minute and you weighed 70 kg and ran 1500 m, you will have used 21 litres of oxygen. This is the equivalent of expending 105 kCal.

activity

If you weighed 55 kg and you ran five miles in 40 minutes, roughly how many kCal of energy would you have used? Assuming that you are using only carbohydrate to produce energy, approximately how many litres of oxygen would you have consumed during the run?

Although there is no shortage of oxygen in the atmosphere there is a limit to how much oxygen can be taken into the bloodstream and delivered to the muscles. A person's $\dot{V}O_2(max)$ depends on the efficiency of their cardiac, respiratory and vascular systems along with their physiological make up in terms of fibre type. Remember that it is the slow oxidative muscle fibre that works aerobically (Chapter 3). A person may improve their $\dot{V}O_2(max)$ up to 20% by training aerobically, but they still might be more physiologically suited to anaerobic activities.

When sufficient oxygen can't be delivered to the muscles to supply the total energy required aerobically, the anaerobic systems are used. This occurs either at the start of exercise or when the exercise is very intense. The most reliable way of monitoring the contribution of the lactic acid system to energy production is to measure the amount of lactic acid in the blood. A small amount of lactic acid is always present in the blood, but when the level starts to rise rapidly the body is relying heavily on the lactic acid system for energy production.

In practice

The best way to lose weight is to perform any submaximal, continuous exercise for a long period.

in training

In order for endurance athletes to optimise their level of performance they need to increase their lactate threshold. By increasing their lactate threshold they can increase their race pace.

21.2.1 *Carbohydrate compared with fat*

The amount of oxygen available not only has a direct effect on whether energy is released aerobically or anaerobically but also affects the type of food fuel used. The body requires about 15% more oxygen to oxidise fat than to break down carbohydrate. Although fat produces more ATP than carbohydrate, when oxygen is in limited supply the body has to burn carbohydrate. This explains why carbohydrate is the major source of fuel for at least the first 20 minutes of exercise. When activities continue for 45 minutes or more the balance of fat to carbohydrate used changes, with fat being predominantly oxidised after an hour.

This is also the case as the intensity of exercise increases and as an athlete reaches the lactate threshold. The body is struggling to deliver sufficient oxygen to keep pace with the amount of energy required so cannot afford to oxidise fat. Once the lactate threshold has been reached only carbohydrate can be broken down anaerobically, which further depletes the body's store of carbohydrate.

A good way of judging the intensity of an activity is to monitor your heart rate because there is a direct relationship between heart rate and oxygen consumption and therefore exercise intensity. If you intend to exercise for an extended period of time you should not exercise too close to your lactate threshold. You should work at about 75% of your maximum heart rate (this is calculated as 220 minus your age) or about 65% of your $\dot{V}O_2$(max). The body has only a limited supply of carbohydrate, stored in the liver and muscles as glycogen and circulating in the blood in the form of glucose. During exercise glycogen from the liver is broken down to glucose and is transported in the blood to the muscles. During anaerobic energy production this glucose is broken down to lactic acid, which enters the bloodstream and is carried back to the liver where it is converted back to glycogen. This process is known as the *Cori cycle*, and is shown in Figure 21.2.

The production of lactic acid is often considered as having purely a negative effect on performance (as discussed in the previous chapter). It is, however, important to realise that lactic acid can be a very valuable source of energy. There is a hypothesis that the liver is more effective at making glycogen from lactic acid than directly using glucose. Lactic acid is also extensively used by slow oxidative muscle fibres as a preferred fuel. The lactic acid formed in the fast glycolytic muscle fibres either directly enters slow oxidative fibres or enters the blood as lactate and is delivered to the slow oxidative fibres. Here it is oxidised to carbon dioxide and water and the energy released is used to resynthesise ATP (Figure 21.3).

It is possible to severely deplete glycogen stores while performing prolonged periods of exercise like a triathlon. When liver glycogen stores run low the blood glucose is used. If blood glucose levels drop the athlete can suffer from *hypoglycaemia*. This condition can be avoided if the athlete consumes a glucose-based drink during the activity.

Taking a glucose drink or carbohydrate snack shortly before the onset of prolonged exercise will usually have a negative effect on performance, because elevated levels of blood glucose result in an increase in insulin levels. Insulin helps to regulate blood glucose levels by converting excess glucose in the blood to glycogen in the liver. An increase in insulin levels inhibits the enzyme that controls

Glucose
in
blood

Glucose in
muscle

Pyruvic
acid

Glycogen
in
liver

Lactic acid

Lactate
in blood

Figure 21.2 *The Cori cycle*

DEFINITION

HYPOGLYCAEMIA

A condition caused by low blood sugar levels. At best hypoglycaemia can result in loss of concentration and sweating. If blood glucose levels are not returned to normal then the person's condition will quickly deteriorate. In extreme situations this can result in coma or death.

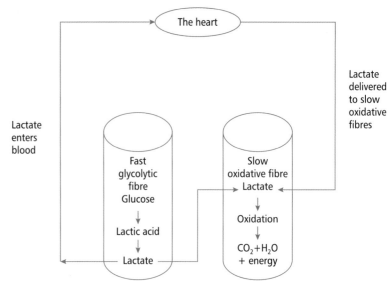

Figure 21.3
Lactic acid is a valuable metabolic fuel

the oxidation of fat, so the body will have to rely more heavily on the breakdown of carbohydrate, depleting stores even more quickly.

There have been lots of studies involving pre-event meals and in particular whether or not carbohydrate should be eaten an hour before an event. Some nutritionists argue that not all carbohydrates cause such a high insulin response and refer to these foods as low glycaemic index foods (an example is lentils). High glycaemic index foods (such as potatoes), on the other hand, *do* raise insulin levels. As with a lot of research, there are many conflicting results and conclusions as to how this really affects performance. It still appears safer to have a high carbohydrate meal a minimum of two hours before the event and to consume a sports drink during the event to avoid an insulin response.

On a similar theme, if an athlete starts a triathlon at a faster pace than he or she can cope with in an attempt to keep up with the leaders, he or she may also encounter difficulties. This is because during the early stages of exercise you rely on anaerobic energy production and if you are working hard lactic acid will accumulate early in the race. Lactic acid also inhibits the enzyme responsible for the breakdown of fat, so you are delaying the use of your most economical fuel. Another related problem is that if you deplete your glycogen stores early in an event you may not have enough left to produce a sprint for home – remember that only carbohydrate can be broken down anaerobically. Pacing in long-distance events is therefore very important.

21.3 Diet and exercise

We need to eat to obtain enough energy to complete our daily tasks; we have to keep pace with our body's *metabolism*.

A term that is commonly used is the *basal metabolic rate* (BMR). The BMR is a measure of the amount of energy we would use if we remained at rest. Our daily intake of food has to cover the BMR plus any additional energy for other activities such as a 20-minute walk to work or a 45-minute game of squash, as well as the more functional activities of the body such as digestion and excretion.

DEFINITION

METABOLISM
The sum of all the chemical reactions that take place within the body.

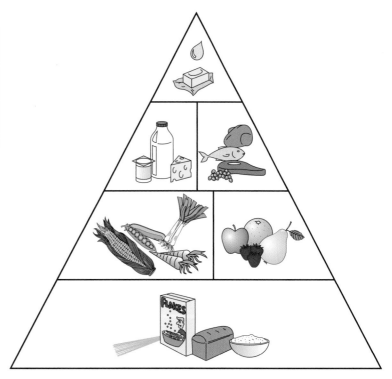

Figure 21.4 *Food pyramid*

Men can usually consume 2800–3000 kCal a day and women 2000–2200 kCal a day without putting on weight. If you are particularly active or train regularly you will probably need to eat 5000–6000 kCal a day. By eating the same amount of energy as you use you will maintain a constant body weight. Metabolic rates vary between individuals, and your metabolic rate will slow down as you get older – so don't expect to eat the same amount of food when you are 40 as you do now and not put on weight.

Body weight is referred to in terms of *body fat* and fat-free weight or *lean body mass*. The body fat is the amount of fat stored in the adipose tissue, the lean body mass being equivalent to the weight of the rest of the body. Men carry an average of 12–15% of their body weight as fat, whereas women carry about 20%. To lose weight we need to lose some of the fat stores and we can achieve this by going on a low-fat diet and by increasing the amount of submaximal exercise we perform. Athletes, particularly endurance athletes, tend to carry far less fat.

A balanced diet contains
- 15% protein
- 30% fat
- 55% carbohydrate.

You also need to make sure that you have enough vitamins and minerals, fibre and water in your diet. If you do a lot of training you might need to increase your carbohydrate intake to 60–65%. After a heavy training session it can take up to 24 hours to fully replenish the glycogen stores, so the following day's training needs to be relatively light.

The choice of food before exercise or competition is very personal, and the psychological benefits of food should be

considered along with the physiological benefits. However, one form of dietary manipulation that has been proved successful is *carbo-loading* or *glycogen loading*. Before an event athletes deplete their stores of glycogen by training on a diet high in protein and fat for three days. Then they do light training on a high-carbohydrate diet for a further three days leading up to the competition. This form of diet significantly increases the stores of glycogen in the muscles and helps to offset fatigue in endurance events. Although this method does work for some athletes it should be noted that some people suffer more psychologically by having their routine changed than they benefit from the carbo-loading.

A more consistent approach is to eat a high-carbohydrate diet all the time. This will ensure that the athlete does not become chronically fatigued during training as a result of low glycogen levels. A high-carbohydrate diet will quickly compensate for drops in glycogen that occur during exercise, prompting full recovery (Figure 21.5).

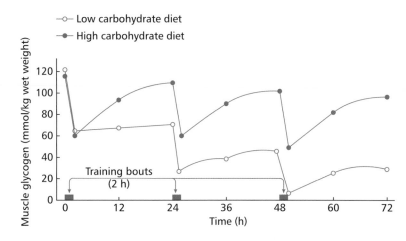

Figure 21.5 *Influence of dietary carbohydrates on muscle glycogen stores*

Marathon running

21.3.1 *Fluid loss and exercise*

Athletes should also consider their fluid intake. As with most things in the body, water balance must be maintained. When an athlete starts to exercise their production of water increases – one of the by-products of the aerobic energy system is water. Unfortunately the amount of water loss (as sweat) also increases in response to the increase in heat production. Overall the body tends to sweat more water than it produces, causing dehydration. Not only water but important electrolytes (such as sodium and chloride) are lost. The combination of water and electrolyte loss means that the athlete's heart rate increases. This is because the plasma volume decreases resulting in a drop in stroke volume. To compensate for the drop in stroke volume the heart rate has to increase to maintain the cardiac output. This circulatory change due to prolonged bouts of exercise is known as the *cardiovascular drift*. The athlete's body temperature also increases, causing distress and fatigue and culminating in a drastic decrease in performance (Figure 21.6).

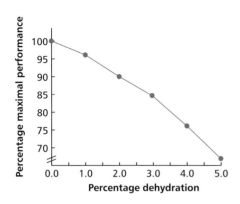

Figure 21.6 *The effect of dehydration on performance*

DEHYDRATION
Loss of body fluids.

in training

The amount of sweat produced by an athlete will be largely down to the athlete's body size and metabolic rate, and the temperature they are working in. Remember to drink *before* you feel thirsty.

CARDIOVASCULAR DRIFT
An increase in heart rate during exercise to compensate for a decrease in stroke volume in an attempt to maintain cardiac output. This will take place only during prolonged bouts of aerobic exercise.

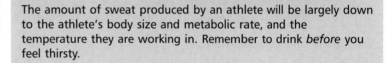

activity

Write down your typical daily diet and try to work out how much carbohydrate, fat and protein you eat. Most food packaging provides extensive nutritional information so you should be able to estimate your calorific intake as well.

21.3.2 *Some food facts*

- Endurance training helps the body to use more fats during submaximal exercise.
- Protein supplements are not needed for body-building, providing a balanced diet is eaten.
- Caffeine helps to mobilise fatty acids in the blood.
- Carbohydrate drinks are not much use for activities that last for less than 40 minutes.
- Any meal before an activity should be eaten at least two hours before the start time and should be high in carbohydrate.
- Go for the 'feel good' factor: if you have a favourite food that gives you a psychological boost, take it.
- Regularly drink small amounts of water or glucose drinks during long endurance events and intermittent exercise to avoid dehydration and hypoglycaemia. Don't wait until you feel thirsty.

FREE RADICAL
A molecule with an unpaired electron, e.g. an oxygen intermediate leaked during the electron transport chain. They are highly reactive and damage tissues.

in training

Endurance athletes have a problem with free radicals that escape from the electron transport chain. These are highly reactive and need to be neutralised by antioxidants. Although the body naturally produces antioxidants, a lot of endurance athletes will take supplementary antioxidant vitamins such as vitamin E.

Key revision points

In most activities we use a 'mix' of all three systems of producing energy. This is reflected in the amount of oxygen we consume and the food fuels we use. By regulating the intensity we work at we can optimise our use of oxygen and fuel supplies to enhance performance.

Key terms

You should now understand the following terms. If you do not, go back through the chapter and find out what they mean.

Aerobic capacity
Basal metabolic rate
Carbo-loading
Cori cycle
Energy continuum
Hypoglycaemia
Lactate threshold
Lean body mass
Threshold
$\dot{V}O_2$(max)

Progress check

1 What is meant by the term energy continuum?
2 List three activities that would predominantly use the aerobic system as a means of energy production.
3 Compare the energy demands of a goalkeeper in football with a midfield player. Estimate the contribution made by each of the three energy systems for both positions.
4 How much oxygen do we consume at rest?
5 Define the term $\dot{V}O_2$(max).
6 How much oxygen is needed to break down sufficient glycogen to produce 15 kCal of energy?
7 When you start to exercise why don't you oxidise fats?
8 How can you estimate your maximum heart rate?
9 What is hypoglycaemia? How can it be avoided?
10 Why should you avoid taking a glucose drink less than an hour before you exercise?
11 Name three foods that are high in carbohydrate.
12 What happens to blood lactate when it reaches the liver?
13 What should a balanced diet consist of?
14 Briefly describe how you would carbo-load before a competition.
15 How can you estimate the amount of energy needed to perform a particular activity?
16 What is a free radical?
17 Explain why the cardiovascular drift occurs during prolonged periods of exercise.

22 The recovery process

Learning objectives

- To understand the role of the energy systems during the recovery process.
- To understand the concept of the oxygen debt.
- To be able to describe the alactacid and lactacid components of the oxygen debt.
- To be able to apply the major concepts of the recovery process to aid training and performance.

During any form of exercise changes occur in the body that need to be reversed once the exercise has stopped. The recovery process involves returning the body to the state it was in before exercise. Exercise provides quite a challenge for the body in that many changes occur that disrupt the internal balance (homeostasis) of the body. Changes such as an increase in lactic acid cannot be allowed to take place without some action being taken to restore the body's preferred pH balance. The body's control mechanisms must react quickly to avoid potentially disastrous consequences. The reactions that need to take place and how long the process takes depends on the duration and intensity of the exercise undertaken and the individual's level of fitness.

22.1 The recovery process

The changes that take place within a muscle cell during a period of exercise are summarised in Table 22.1. We must also consider what is required to reverse these changes. During exercise our demand for energy greatly increases and, not surprisingly, all our energy stores are depleted to some extent. At the same time more of the by-products of respiration have been produced and need to be removed. Energy is needed to reverse these changes.

Table 22.1 *Changes that occur in muscle cells during exercise*

Factor	Levels increased	Levels decreased
ATP		X
Phosphocreatine		X
Glycogen		X
Triglycerides		X
Carbon dioxide	X	
Oxygen/myoglobin stores		X
Lactic acid	X	
Water	X	

DEFINITION

EXCESS POST-EXERCISE OXYGEN CONSUMPTION (EPOC)

The amount of oxygen consumed during recovery above that which would ordinarily have been consumed at rest in the same time.

When we stop exercising our demand for energy returns to its resting level, so why doesn't our cardiac output (calculated as heart rate × stroke volume – see Chapter 5) and our tidal volume (the amount of air breathed in or out in one breath – see Chapter 7) immediately also return to normal? The body continues to take in elevated amounts of oxygen and transport it to the working muscles where elevated rates of aerobic respiration are maintained. So what are we doing with the surplus energy? It is being used to help return the body to its pre-exercise state – this is known as the *oxygen debt* or *excess post-exercise oxygen consumption* (EPOC).

At rest we consume 0.2–0.3 litres of oxygen per minute, which is sufficient to meet the body's demand for energy. During recovery, for several minutes after completing the exercise the body takes in far more oxygen than is actually required.

22.1.1 *The oxygen deficit*

When we start to exercise insufficient oxygen is being distributed to the tissues for all the energy production to be met aerobically. It takes time for the circulatory system to respond to the increase in demand for oxygen and the rate of aerobic respiration in the mitochondria also takes time to adjust. Meanwhile the two anaerobic systems described in Chapter 20 have to be used to satisfy the increased demand for ATP production. This has traditionally been known as the *oxygen deficit* (Figure 22.1).

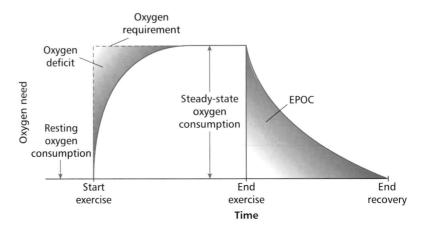

Figure 22.1 *The demand for oxygen during exercise and recovery*

Phosphocreatine stores have to be broken down to phosphate and creatine and the energy produced used to synthesise ATP. Once these stores have been broken down they cannot be built up again until sufficient energy is available to do so during recovery. Glycogen is also being broken down anaerobically, producing lactic acid. The lactic acid accumulates in the blood and lowers its pH, which eventually results in inhibition of the important enzymes controlling breakdown of fats and carbohydrates (lipases and phosphofructokinase). The lactic acid must be removed during recovery so that the blood pH will return to normal. It is important to note that you don't have to actually stop exercising to give your body an opportunity to recover, but the intensity of the exercise has to be significantly reduced.

22.1.2 *The EPOC*

The EPOC, which occurs during recovery, was initially referred to as the oxygen debt. The oxygen debt was made up of two main components:
• the alactacid component
• the lactacid component.

The processes that take place during these components still occur but additional processes have now been highlighted that also contribute to the elevated rate of aerobic respiration during recovery.

The alactacid component

This is the more rapid of the two processes and is involved with restoration of the muscle phosphagen stores (ATP and phosphocreatine). As shown in Table 22.1, the levels of both ATP and phosphocreatine have been depleted as they have been broken down and the energy released has been used.

Both reactions are reversible, provided that energy is made available. During the alactacid component oxygen consumption remains high to allow elevated rates of aerobic respiration to continue. The energy released aerobically is used to continue ATP production and then to re-form the stores of phosphocreatine that were depleted by exercise. The alactacid component uses up to 4 litres of oxygen and takes 2–3 minutes to complete

activity

Using the information in Table 22.2 draw a graph to show the rate of phosphagen restoration during recovery.

restoration after intense exercise. However, the stores are replaced to 50% of normal levels after only 30 seconds of recovery and if the exercise was submaximal replenishment is even quicker. Table 22.2 shows the relationship between recovery time and replenishment of muscle phosphagen.

Table 22.2 *Replenishment of muscle phosphagens after exercise*

Recovery time (seconds)	Percentage of phosphagen replenished
<10	Negligible
30	50
60	75
90	87
120	93
150	97
180	98

As the muscle phosphagen stores provide the energy for short intensive bouts of exercise it is useful to know that the stores can be replenished so quickly. In a game that relies heavily on the anaerobic energy systems, such as basketball, the coach may want to schedule time-outs to help his or her team recover.

The time available may not be sufficient to gain full recovery, but the athlete will be able to offset fatigue as at least some stores will still be available for energy production. Any phosphocreatine stores available will reduce the contribution made by the lactic acid system and will therefore reduce the amount of lactic acid being produced.

In practice

Tennis players are well advised to make the most of the time available when changing ends. Participants in team games have many opportunities during a match to replenish muscle phosphagen stores – for example before a free kick is taken.

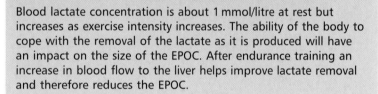

in training

Blood lactate concentration is about 1 mmol/litre at rest but increases as exercise intensity increases. The ability of the body to cope with the removal of the lactate as it is produced will have an impact on the size of the EPOC. After endurance training an increase in blood flow to the liver helps improve lactate removal and therefore reduces the EPOC.

The lactacid component

This is the process responsible for the removal of lactic acid, and full recovery may take up to an hour depending on the duration and intensity of the exercise. Lactic acid accumulates in the working muscles and the blood but may be removed in four ways.

Most (over 60%) of the lactic acid is removed from the cells by using it as a metabolic fuel. Within the muscle and some other organs, such as the heart, lactic acid is converted to pyruvic acid. This reaction requires energy (it is an endothermic reaction) but once it has occurred the pyruvic acid formed enters the TCA cycle and is metabolised aerobically to carbon dioxide, water and energy. The energy needed to convert the lactic acid back to pyruvic acid is made available aerobically because of the elevated rate of respiration during recovery. This is one of the reasons why an active recovery is recommended. The exercise performed during recovery should be submaximal (or you would be producing more lactic acid than you would be removing) and helps to flush the lactic acid out of the fast-twitch muscle fibres.

Other fates of lactic acid are conversion to protein or to glycogen in the muscle and the liver.

in training

Endurance training results in an increase in mitochondria, the oxidative enzymes and the number of capillaries supplying the muscle. This means that when an athlete starts to exercise the rate of aerobic respiration can be activated earlier and more oxygen can be consumed and utilised. The net effect is to reduce the EPOC as the athlete does not have to rely as heavily on the anaerobic energy systems at the onset of exercise.

in training

Anaerobic training increases the buffering capacity of a muscle. This means that the muscle can tolerate higher levels of blood lactate because the lactic acid can be neutralised by the bicarbonate and muscle phosphates. This also allows the athlete to recover more quickly.

Recent studies have suggested that the EPOC isn't entirely dedicated to the removal of lactic acid and the resynthesis of phosphagen stores and that other processes also require an elevated rate of oxygen consumption. As a result the term 'oxygen debt' does not accurately depict what is happening and therefore is no longer used (see Figure 22.1).

The other processes that require additional oxygen that have been identified are:

1 Elevated breathing and heart rates. Carbon dioxide is a waste product that needs to be expelled from the body and this is achieved through increased circulation and respiration.
2 Body temperature. This remains relatively high and therefore keeps respiratory and metabolic rates higher than normal.

Elevated hormonal levels have a similar effect to an increase in body temperature, but when the body stops exercising the levels of noradrenaline and adrenaline (you'll also see these called norepinephrine and epinephrine) quickly drop and therefore may not have a particularly significant role in terms of EPOC. The processes involved that contribute to EPOC are summarised in Figure 22.2.

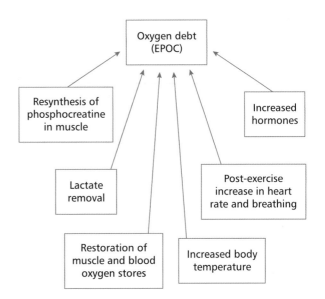

Figure 22.2
Factors that contribute to the EPOC

activity

Select three members of your group to perform three 10 m × 10 m shuttle runs. The first performer is allowed a 10-second recovery between each shuttle, the second performer has 60 seconds to recover and the third performer is allowed 120 seconds. Each shuttle must be timed. Record the shuttle times in a table like the one below.

Performer	Rest interval	Time 1	Time 2	Time 3	Overall drop/increase in performance
Subject 1					
Subject 2					
Subject 3					

Discuss your results in relation to the rest interval allowed and each subject's performance.

Usually 50% of lactic acid can be removed during the first half hour of recovery and 5–8 litres of oxygen is required.

Contrary to popular opinion, lactic acid is not responsible for the muscle soreness and stiffness often felt a day after intensive exercise. This discomfort is more likely to be due to damage to connective tissue and a closer look at technique, muscle strength and warm-up routines may be called for.

22.2 Myoglobin and replenishment of oxygen stores

Myoglobin is found in the sarcoplasm of the cell and is very similar to haemoglobin in that it has a high affinity for oxygen. It acts as a temporary store for oxygen and helps to transport oxygen from the capillaries to the mitochondria. Slow oxidative muscle fibre contains more myoglobin than the other fibres (remember that type 1 fibres produce energy aerobically) and the amount of myoglobin increases with aerobic training, helping to improve the supply of oxygen to the mitochondria.

After intense exercise the myoglobin stores of oxygen are depleted – it takes about 0.5 litres of oxygen and 1–2 minutes to replenish these stores. No energy is required for this process, but it will happen only when a 'surplus' of oxygen is being delivered to the muscles. During recovery the elevated rate of ventilation and heart rate means that additional oxygen is available for myoglobin replenishment.

Myoglobin stores are important because if oxygen is present within the cell then some energy can be produced aerobically and the body does not have to rely solely on the anaerobic systems. This means that valuable stores of phosphocreatine can be maintained for supplying additional bursts of energy – for example for a sprint finish – and that production of lactic acid is slowed down, delaying overall fatigue.

22.3 Glycogen

The stores of glycogen in the body are small relative to the stores of fats and proteins (Figure 22.3).

As glycogen is used as a metabolic fuel for both aerobic and anaerobic work its stores can become depleted very quickly. Certainly, after two hours of intensive exercise the stores are running low. If, for example, you have taken part in a tournament or have completed a triathlon, then you must make sure to replace your glycogen stores. This is achieved very easily – by eating – although it is advisable to eat a high-carbohydrate meal, such as a baked potato or pasta followed by banana pudding and custard. Most of the glycogen is replaced within 10 hours of recovery but complete recovery can take up to two days.

Glycogen stores can be conserved if:
- an athlete learns how to pace him- or herself properly, so that they do not cross their lactate threshold unnecessarily
- the athlete takes any opportunity available to recover muscle phosphagen and myoglobin stores
- he or she regularly takes small amounts of a glucose drink during the exercise.

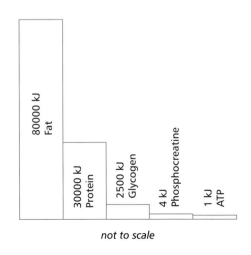

not to scale

Figure 22.3 *Stores in the body*

Aerobic training also improves the body's ability to oxidise fat and therefore helps to conserve glycogen stores during submaximal exercise. If an athlete follows a high-carbohydrate diet and carbo-loads before an event (see Chapter 21), the stores of glycogen in the body will increase. All of these factors combine to enhance overall endurance performance.

Some glycogen is used when an athlete takes part in short periods of intense exercise, but carbohydrate replenishment is not needed during the activity and stores will be replaced shortly after exercise by eating a high-carbohydrate meal. In fact, some of the stores are replaced by the conversion of lactic acid and pyruvate to glycogen (see earlier in this chapter). The energy for this process is made available aerobically during the EPOC.

Triglyceride stores are also used during prolonged periods of activity but because of the large amounts of fat available in the body no other measures need to be taken to replace them other than to eat a normal balanced diet. Similarly, the increased production of carbon dioxide during exercise does not cause any problems. Carbon dioxide enters the blood, by dissolving directly or as carbonic acid in the plasma, or attaching to haemoglobin, and is transported to the lungs and expelled in expiration.

> ## Key revision points
> *The recovery process returns the body to its pre-exercise state. Replenishment of ATP and phosphocreatine stores and removal of lactic acid will take place only when additional energy is available. Elevated rates of respiration during recovery provide the energy for these processes.*

Key terms

You should now understand the following terms. If you do not, go back through the chapter and find out what they mean.

Alactacid component
Elevated respiration
EPOC
Lactacid component
Metabolic fuel
Myoglobin
Oxygen deficit

Progress check

1 What is the purpose of the recovery process?
2 Define the term EPOC.
3 What is the function of the alactacid component of the EPOC?
4 What is the function of the lactacid component of the EPOC?
5 How long does the body take to recover from exercise? Explain your answer fully.
6 What is the role of myoglobin?
7 What factors affect muscle glycogen replenishment after exercise?
8 Why should you cool down actively after exercise?
9 How does the oxygen deficit differ from the oxygen debt?
10 How long does it take to replace 50% of the muscle phosphagen stores?
11 Why is it important to try to replace myoglobin stores during activity?
12 List three opportunities within a game when players can partially or fully recover their muscle phosphagen stores.
13 Outline the process involved in the resynthesis of lactic acid.
14 Name an organ of the body that uses lactic acid as a metabolic fuel.
15 What is the probable cause of muscle soreness after exercise?
16 Why should athletes rest for a day after a particularly intense and prolonged period of exercise?

CHAPTER

23 Principles of training

Learning objectives

- To understand the principles of training.
- To be able to describe the physiological benefits of a warm-up and a cool-down.
- To be able to apply the principles of training and training methods to the development of a personal fitness programme.
- To be aware of the role of ergogenic aids and performance.

It is doubtful that your present state of fitness will match the specific demands of your chosen activity. You can either accept your shortcomings or you can decide to improve your fitness by training.

Most 'recreational' athletes have a very inconsistent approach to training. Usually it takes the form of a couple of frenetic weeks in early January, as penance for excesses over Christmas and as part of yet another New Year's resolution to get fit, and another two weeks before the season starts to make up for the fact that you haven't done anything for the previous three months. Such erratic behaviour has almost no physiological benefit – it just eases your conscience. For training to be effective it should be planned well, and the athlete should follow the basic principles of training. Everyone benefits from training, not just top-class athletes, providing the programme you follow is specifically geared towards your level of fitness and lifestyle.

23.1 The body's response to exercise

The body is continually responding to the demands made on it by the individual and by the environment in an attempt to maintain a stable internal environment, known as *homeostasis*.

The body functions best when body fluids, temperature, oxygen levels etc. are at specific levels. Any change in the body's internal environment usually prompts an immediate response in an attempt to redress the balance.

The internal regulatory systems of the body cause the changes that we experience when we begin to exercise. When we begin to work harder we use up more energy and produce more carbon dioxide. Increases in carbon dioxide concentrations cause an increase in blood acidity, which is an unwelcome change to the body's internal environment. The increase in carbon dioxide is detected by the brain, which responds by increasing the rate and depth of breathing (the respiratory control centre in the medulla of the brain is sensitive to an increase in carbon dioxide levels). This response helps to expel carbon dioxide and to increase the supply of much-needed oxygen.

There are two types of response that the body makes to exercise – short-term physiological responses that occur during exercise and the long-term physiological adaptations that occur as a result of training. Short-term physiological responses are the changes that occur in the body during an exercise session, such as an increase in heart rate, and which return to normal shortly after the period of exercise has finished. Long-term physiological adaptations, sometimes referred to as a *chronic response*, are long-lasting changes that take place in response to training, making the body more efficient at dealing with the demands made on it. A good example is the increase in stroke volume that occurs after a period of aerobic training. This makes the heart more efficient (it supplies more blood per beat) so that it doesn't have to work as hard.

HOMEOSTASIS
Maintenance of a stable internal environment.

241

If no long-term physiological adaptations took place no improvements would be gained and there would be little point in training. The adaptations that do occur are very specific in that they depend on the physiological make-up of the individual and the type of training that he or she performs. A well-planned fitness programme will cause long-term adaptations very quickly, making you fitter, healthier and more able to cope with the demands of your chosen sport.

23.2 The principles of training

The *principles of training* help ensure that sensible, realistic and safe training programmes are developed.

23.2.1 *The principle of overload*

The whole point of training is to improve your level of fitness, but you will improve your level of fitness only if you 'overload' your body. In other words, you make your body work harder than normal by increasing the amount of work it has to perform. The body will then gradually *adapt* to the new level of work and your level of fitness will improve. The physiological adaptations that occur through training are discussed in detail in Chapter 24.

Overload can be achieved by:

1 Increasing the number of times (the *frequency*: F) that you train.
2 Increasing the *intensity* (I) of the activity you are doing, for example running faster or lifting more weight.
3 Increasing the *duration* (time: T) of each individual session, for example go for a 40-minute run rather than a 30-minute run.

23.2.2 *The principle of progression*

Your body will improve only if it is put under stress, but the principle of progression underlines the fact that the amount of overload attempted should be *progressively* made more difficult. The workload should be increased only once some adaptations have occurred, so it is important to monitor your performance closely so that you don't put too much stress on the body too soon. The term *moderation* is often used – meaning that you should be realistic and reasonable about the demands you make of your body. By being over-ambitious you could overtrain and seriously damage your muscular and skeletal systems.

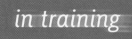

in training

It is always difficult to decide how much overload should be applied and it has been suggested that the training intensity should not be increased by more than 10% a week.

in training

Men and women, in general, have the same response to training.

Getting the overload right in the gym

23.2.3 *The principle of specificity*

Every activity requires a specific mix of fitness components and the training you undertake needs to reflect the contribution made by each component. However, before you attempt any specific training you must have developed a general level of fitness. There is a lot of truth in the saying 'don't play squash to get fit, get fit to play squash'.

Three main factors must be considered:

* *The individual*. Training should be specific to the individual. It is important to assess your initial state of fitness so that the work-load can be estimated accurately. Everyone has limitations, as much of our physical capacity is genetically determined. Being aware of your physiological make-up will help you make the most of your strengths rather than highlight your weaknesses.
* *The activity*. First identify the mix of fitness components required and then identify the major joints and muscles that are used. Make sure that your training uses these joints and muscle groups and try to reproduce the movement patterns that you would use in competition.
* *The energy systems*. Identify the energy systems used during the activity and their overall contribution to total energy expenditure. Make sure that your training reflects the same balance by manipulating the intensity and duration of your work.

23.2.4 *The principle of reversibility*

Fitness cannot be stored for future use and your level of fitness is constantly changing. Any adaptations that take place as a consequence of training will be reversed when you stop training; this is sometimes referred to as *detraining*.

23.2.5 *The principle of variance*

Variety is the spice of life! If you do the same thing week after week it becomes monotonous and boring. The principle of variance is very simple – it suggests that a training programme should include a variety of training methods. This will help to maintain interest and motivation, and makes sure that the loads you work against are varied. It is very easy to develop overuse injuries and if you do not give your body sufficient time to recover you can develop chronic exhaustion.

23.3 Warming up and cooling down

Integral parts of any training session are the warm-up and the cool-down. Both physiological and psychological benefits are to be gained from these two activities. Outlined below are some of the physiological reasons why it is extremely important to warm up and cool down properly.

23.3.1 *The warm-up*

The warm-up helps to prepare the body for the physical exertion to come. By gently raising your pulse you are beginning to increase your cardiac output and your rate of ventilation. Your vasomotor

in training

Aerobic adaptations to endurance training tend to be lost much more quickly than adaptations to strength training during a period of detraining.

Warming up

centre is making sure that more blood is being distributed to the working muscles. The combined effect is to increase the amount of oxygen being delivered to the muscle cells, which will help to reduce the oxygen deficit when you start your activity for real.

The muscle works better when it is warm for several reasons:

- oxygen dissociates from haemoglobin more readily as muscle temperature increases
- the activity of the enzymes responsible for cellular respiration increases, making energy more readily available
- the conduction of nerve impulses is quicker, improving contraction speed and resulting in faster reaction times
- blood vessels within the muscle dilate, further increasing the blood flow
- an increase in muscle temperature allows greater stretch in the muscles and connective tissue, increasing flexibility.

The warm-up has three phases. Phase one involves a continuous, submaximal whole body activity, such as jogging, to gently raise your pulse to about 120 beats/min. This is followed by a stretch session, in which particular attention should be paid to the joints and muscles that will be most active. Recent research has shown that dynamic stretching during the warm-up is much more effective than static stretching in terms of performance benefits and injury reduction. (More information on flexibility can be found in Chapter 24.) Static stretching is more beneficial during the cool-down period when the performer may want to try and increase their range of flexibility. Finally you should specifically rehearse the movement patterns that will be performed, for example performing skill practices.

As well as helping you to prepare mentally and physically for your activity, a warm-up considerably reduces the risk of injury.

23.3.2 *The cool-down*

As mentioned in Chapter 22, your body returns to its pre-exercise state more quickly if you perform light exercise during the recovery period. The increased blood flow helps to flush out waste products

activity

Outline a warm-up session that would be suitable for a 110 m hurdler.

such as lactic acid and carbon dioxide, reducing your overall recovery time. A cool-down also prevents blood pooling – remember that about 85% of the blood volume is distributed to the working muscles and one of the main ways of maintaining blood flow back to the heart is by the skeletal pump mechanism. If muscle action stops suddenly the amount of blood returning to the heart drops dramatically. This in turn reduces the stroke volume and causes a drop in blood pressure, making the athlete feel dizzy and light-headed.

A cool-down allows the muscles to return to their normal temperature slowly because a sudden drop in temperature could cause muscle damage. The cool-down is also a good time to perform flexibility exercises as the muscles are still warm and at their most pliable. In conclusion, a cool-down allows you to physically and mentally relax. It aids recovery and helps to prevent muscle soreness and injury.

23.4 Intensity of training

As mentioned earlier, athletes will develop their fitness only if they overload the system they want to improve. In some cases the amount of work being performed is quite obvious – for example, you can add another weight to the weight stack. For other activities the body's own heart rate response is a good indicator of the intensity of the exercise. Remember, there is a linear relationship between heart rate and oxygen consumption and endurance athletes in particular use target or *training heart rates* to monitor their rate of work.

23.4.1 *Training heart rate*

The intensity of work will depend on your level of fitness. It is important that you work at an intensity that overloads your system, but at the same time keeps you below your anaerobic threshold. Remember that if you go beyond your anaerobic threshold the predominant method of producing energy is the lactic acid system. If you rely heavily on this system lactic acid will accumulate in the tissues and cause fatigue. The training heart rate uses the heart rate that is equivalent to the percentage of the $\dot{V}O_2$(max) that the athlete wishes to train at. The training heart rate can be estimated by using the Karvonen method. To calculate a training heart rate equivalent to 75% of $\dot{V}O_2$(max) the following method should be used:

training heart rate 75% = heart rate at rest + 0.75 (maximum heart rate – heart rate at rest)

Rather than use one target heart rate as a training guide, athletes tend to use a *target heart rate range*. So they may calculate an upper limit range based on 75% $\dot{V}O_2$(max), and a lower limit range of 60% $\dot{V}O_2$(max). Athletes start work at the lower end of the range and gradually progress to the higher limit. As the athlete's aerobic capacity increases they will have to perform at a higher rate of work to reach the training range (Figure 23.1).

23.4.2 *Perceived rate of exertion*

This is another method of monitoring work intensity and is based on the athlete's subjective rating of how hard they think they are

TRAINING HEART RATE
The range of heart rate prescribed to match the training intensity requirements of an athlete. The athlete must remain within this range for training to be effective.

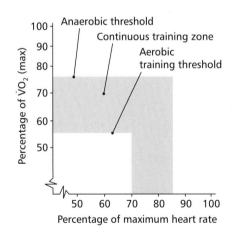

Figure 23.1 *Working within the aerobic threshold*

Calculate your critical training heart rate range using Karvonen's principle. The training threshold is usually about 75% of the athlete's maximum heart rate, but elite endurance athletes can work at 80–85% of their maximum heart rate and still be working aerobically.

During a training session wear a heart rate monitor and note your heart rate response at regular intervals. Before you check your heart rate use the Borg RPE scale to estimate your level of exertion. After the session compare your perceived level of exertion with your actual heart rate response.

working. The Borg RPE scale has a range from 6 to 20, and the athlete's exercise intensity should be between 12/13 (somewhat hard) and 15/16 (very hard). Although this is a subjective measure, if you multiply the numbers of the scale by 10 it corresponds very closely to the target heart rate range with a lower level of 120/130 beats/min and an upper limit of 150/160 beats/min (Table 23.1). The scale is a little difficult to use initially, but with practice can be very accurate.

Table 23.1 *The Borg ratings of perceived exertion (RPE) scale*

Rating	Perceived exertion
6, 7, 8	Very, very light
9, 10	Very light
11, 12	Fairly light
13, 14	Somewhat hard
15, 16	Hard
17, 18	Very hard
19, 20	Extremely hard

23.4.3 *Delayed onset of muscle soreness*

If athletes work at an intensity beyond their level of fitness they run the risk of injury. Some athletes experience pain and discomfort anything from 24 to 48 hours after training. This is known as delayed onset of muscle soreness (or DOMS) and is not, contrary to popular belief, anything to do with lactic acid. Most studies support the view that excessive eccentric muscle action seems to be the main cause of the soreness. During eccentric muscle contraction the muscle fibres are put under a tremendous amount of strain, and this can cause structural damage to the muscle fibre and connective tissue. It can also cause an inflammatory reaction resulting in an accumulation of histamine outside the muscle cells. There is, however, a little truth in the saying 'no pain no gain' as research suggests that over-taxing the muscle stimulates the process of hypertrophy.

23.4.4 *Overtraining*

A common mistake, made particularly by highly motivated athletes, is to put too much strain on the body during training, with too much overload and not enough recovery. Put very simply they over-train. Overtraining for any length of time will ultimately have a negative effect on the athlete's immune system and they will

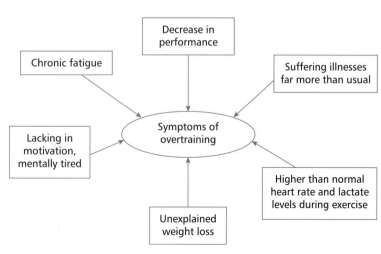

Figure 23.2
Symptoms of overtraining

become ill. There is a fine line between maximising training and overtraining, so athletes must monitor their response to training closely and if they notice any of the symptoms common to over-training they should re-evaluate their training programme and reduce intensity (Figure 23.2).

23.5 Planning a training programme

For training to be properly effective it has to be planned. How precise the planning is depends on how committed the athlete is and what their training goals are. Most people are familiar with the terms off-season, pre-season and the competitive season and different activities are undertaken in each period. Phasing training throughout a year or a specified length of time is known as *periodisation*.

23.5.1 *Off season*

This is usually used for general conditioning work where the athlete tries to keep in shape, or has the opportunity to work on weaker areas of their fitness. Variety is an essential element of this season and quite often the athlete will participate in other sports – a well-known 400 m runner and hurdler used to compete regularly in the Southern Basketball League – to help the athlete mentally relax and enjoy an activity without any pressure.

23.5.2 *Pre-season*

The period leading up to competition is where the training becomes a lot more specific and intense. Workloads will be progressively harder as an attempt is made to fully condition the performer to cope with the demands of the competitive season.

in training

There is often conflict between top athletes and their governing bodies over team selection procedures. If a selection race is held several weeks before a key event, then an athlete may be forced to peak too early, which can have a detrimental effect on his or her performance later in the season.

23.5.3 *Competitive season*

The main focus during this period is to maintain the level of fitness achieved in pre-season training, but in some instances athletes may well be looking to peak in terms of performance in line with specific competition/event dates.

23.5.4 *Macro, meso and micro cycles*

Rather than use the seasonal approach to training some athletes adopt an approach that is similar, known as periodisation. The period of time in question may still be a year but can be altered to suit the goals of the athlete. The athlete will have a training goal for the period, but the period of time will be subdivided into smaller units with each unit having a short-term goal. An athlete using this system will be familiar with three units of time:

1 The *macro cycle* refers to the number of weeks in the period identified by the athlete, which is commonly six or 12 months.
2 The *meso cycle* is a set number of weeks allocated to achieve a short-term goal, commonly 6–8 weeks.
3 The *micro cycle* is usually the training regime for one week, and is repeated for the length of the meso cycle. See Table 23.2.

Another term that athletes will be familiar with is *tapering*. It is not advisable to continue training right up to the competition or event as training does cause damage to the body and does deplete energy stores. So athletes reduce the amount of training they complete as they near the day of the event. Tapering does not have the same effect as detraining – surprisingly, there is usually an improvement in strength and maintenance of $\dot{V}O_2$(max) during tapering as the muscles recover and can produce maximal performance.

DEFINITION

TAPERING

Reducing the amount of training and/or training intensity before a competition day.

23.6 Training programme check list

The content of every athlete's training programme will be different but the framework in which they operate should be very similar. For a training programme to be effective the athlete should pay very careful attention to the principles of training. The following checklist covers most of the essential components needed for a successful training programme.

- Identify the training goal/aim.
- Identify the macro, meso and micro cycles.
- Identify the fitness components to be improved.
- Identify the energy systems involved.
- Identify the main muscle groups that are used.
- Identify the type of contraction employed.
- Be aware of specific movement patterns/neural pathways.
- Evaluate the fitness components involved.
- Determine the modes of training.
- Establish realistic overload.
- Use a training diary to monitor progression.
- Vary your programme to retain interest and motivation.
- Recognise the need for moderation, alternating training and including rest days for recovery.
- Re-evaluate and re-assess goals.

23.7 Performance enhancement

With athletes continually pushing back the boundaries of human performance and with a lot of extrinsic rewards to be gained from winning, it is not surprising that they are continually looking to

Table 23.2 *Periodisation training for strength*

Macro cycle	Meso cycle	Meso cycle	Meso cycle	Meso cycle	Meso cycle
Variable	Phase one: hypertrophy	Phase two: strength	Phase three: power	Phase four: peaking	Active rest
Sets	3–5	3–5	3–5	1–3	General activity
Repetitions	8–20	2–6	2–3	1–3	Or light resistance
Intensity	Low	High	High	Very high	Training
Duration	6 weeks	6 weeks	6 weeks	6 weeks	2 weeks

DEFINITION

ERGOGENIC AID

Any substance or phenomenon that enhances performance.

DEFINITION

ERYTHROPOIETIN

A hormone produced by the kidneys that stimulates the production of red blood cells.

Cyclists are among athletes that use EPO

find new ways of enhancing their performance. Advancements in sports science mean that training techniques are being continually updated but athletes look to *ergogenic aids* to help in their pursuit of excellence. An ergogenic aid can range from the perfectly legal use of creatine to the illegal use of steroids. This chapter intends to examine the use of only a few of the more common and topical ergogenic aids. For more information you should refer to the Further reading section or sites on the internet.

23.7.1 *Erythropoietin*

Erythropoietin (EPO) is a naturally occurring hormone, produced by the kidneys, that stimulates the production of erythrocytes (red blood cells) in the body. EPO can now be manufactured artificially (recombinant erythropoietin, RhEPO) and was initially given to patients with renal failure. When athletes train at altitude the body produces more erythrocytes to compensate for the drop in partial pressure of oxygen. The lower pressure stimulates the release of EPO, which causes an increase in erythrocyte production. The increase is not considerable, however, and athletes are now using RhEPO for more dramatic gains in haemoglobin levels. RhEPO has a very similar effect to blood doping in that it increases the body's oxygen-carrying capacity. Having more erythrocytes means that there is an increase in blood haemoglobin. This in turn increases the haematocrit (the percentage of blood cells in the total blood volume). Ultimately this leads to an increase in $\dot{V}O_2$(max) and an increase in the amount of work that can be performed. Any athlete undertaking endurance events would benefit from taking RhEPO, and top-class cyclists and skiers are among many athletes known to be taking RhEPO. Use of RhEPO is illegal and the IOC classified it as a doping substance in 1990.

23.7.2 *Testing for EPO*

There is now a recognised test for RhEPO. Alongside formal testing, random blood tests are used in some sports. Athletes with an unusually high haematocrit are suspended on health grounds.

The FIS classified RhEPO as a doping substance as early as 1988

Testing for a substance that is found naturally in the body has always caused a problem as every individual tends to have a different amount and establishing a norm is difficult.

23.7.3 *Altitude training*

As athletes are breaking the law by taking RhEPO why don't they train at altitude instead? Unfortunately the problems with altitude training are numerous. It is expensive, and the athlete might suffer from altitude sickness. The drop in the partial pressure of oxygen at altitude makes it difficult to train aerobically at the same intensity as at sea level, resulting in detraining. This is because the oxygen diffusion gradient between the alveoli and the capillaries is reduced so that the haemoglobin is not fully saturated with oxygen. Therefore the amount of oxygen being supplied to the working muscles is also reduced. In addition the temperature drops and the air is much dryer so athletes can suffer from dehydration. Some athletes now sleep at altitude but come down to sea level to train and some countries use specially constructed altitude houses. In these houses the partial pressures of oxygen and carbon dioxide, humidity and temperature can be controlled, without the athlete having to travel anywhere. In fact hypoxic tents are readily available and can be used in the athlete's own home. The athlete can adjust the amount of oxygen in the tent and can very easily imitate the conditions that they would experience at altitude. The acclimatisation that takes place at altitude or in hypoxic conditions results in an increase in red blood cells that in turn leads to an increase in haemoglobin. This increases the oxygen-carrying capacity of the blood. There is also an increase in stroke volume. However, the overall effect on aerobic performance isn't as substantial as that achieved by taking RhEPO.

Hypoxic tent

activity

Calculate the percentage of oxygen in the air at sea level, at 2000 m and at 4000 m. What difficulties do you think an aerobic athlete would experience when performing at altitude without a period of acclimatisation?

Table 23.3 *The effect of altitude on air and oxygen pressures*

Height in metres	Atmospheric pressure	pp oxygen
Sea level	760 mmHg	159.2 mmHg
2000	596 mmHg	124.9 mmHg
4000	462 mmHg	96.9 mmHg

in training

When an athlete is administered RhEPO it is very difficult to predict how many red blood cells will be produced. If the blood viscosity increases too much it can cause clotting and heart failure. If an athlete has a high haematocrit before a race, he or she can have a potentially deadly haematocrit at the end because of dehydration. Several deaths have already occurred as a result of taking RhEPO.

23.7.4 *Blood doping*

Blood doping has the same effect as taking RhEPO. This procedure only really benefits endurance athletes and involves blood being taken from the athlete, frozen and then stored. The athlete's body compensates for the withdrawal by making more red blood cells, and then 5–6 weeks later the stored blood is reinfused and the athlete benefits from a higher-than-normal red blood cell count. This means that the athlete's oxygen-carrying capacity is increased, leading to an improvement in $\dot{V}O_2$(max). Again this is very difficult to detect and, although blood doping is illegal, it is difficult to prove.

23.7.5 *Creatine monohydrate*

Creatine is a naturally occurring substance that can be found in the body and can be supplemented purely by diet. The only problem is that you would have to eat an awful lot of animal products to see even the slightest benefit, so diet is not the solution to supplementation. Creatine can be bought over the counter and its use is perfectly legal (recommended dose approximately 20–30 grams per day, for 5–7 days). Creatine supplementation increases the amount of phosphocreatine stored in the muscles and will therefore increase the threshold of the alactic system. If the creatine is taken with glucose this may enhance the uptake of creatine by the body. More creatine stores will benefit any athlete undertaking high-intensity anaerobic activity, in particular athletes involved in intermittent exercise because the additional creatine helps improve recovery times. Basically, the athlete can work at a high intensity for slightly longer so can train harder, so gains in strength do not come as a complete surprise. Research suggests that taking creatine causes no harmful side-effects, although some athletes have experienced initial weight gain due to water retention.

Creatine monohydrate

23.7.6 *Nasal strips*

Nasal strips are adhesive plastic strips that are worn across the bridge of the nose to hold the nostrils open. They were initially marketed in the early 1990s as an aid to stop people snoring, but were soon used by professional footballers and other athletes. The marketing of the strips suggests that they increase the amount of air that enters the lungs and therefore improve the amount of oxygen that the athlete can take in. Unfortunately, this is not the case – the amount of air that is ventilated by a healthy adult, with or without nasal strips, is not a limiting factor in performance. The only plus factor appears to be that, if an athlete is working in a very hot environment, wearing nasal strips helps to reduce heating of the brain.

23.7.7 *The placebo effect*

Athletes take ergogenic aids to improve performance. In some cases it isn't necessarily about how effective the aid is physiologically, but how effective the athlete *thinks* the aid is. In some strength-training studies athletes have been given a placebo but have been told that it was actually an anabolic steroid. Amazingly, they still made substantial strength gains, in line with athletes who *were* taking the steroids.

A positive mental attitude appears to be the cheapest and the most effective training aid, and is available to all.

Key terms

You should now understand the following terms. If you do not, go back through the chapter and find out what they mean.

Cool-down
DOMS
Long-term response to exercise
Macro cycle
Moderation
Overload
Overtraining
Perceived rate of exertion
Periodisation
Reversibility
Short-term response to exercise
Specificity
Tapering
Training heart rate
Variance
Warm-up

Progress check

1 Briefly outline the principles of training.
2 What happens when you overload a system?
3 Why is it important for overload to be progressive?
4 How can you ensure that your training is specific to your activity?
5 What are the symptoms of overtraining?
6 Give two reasons why training should be varied.
7 List three physiological benefits of a warm-up.
8 List three physiological benefits of a cool-down.
9 What athletes would benefit from taking creatine?
10 How can you calculate your training heart rate range?
11 What intensity can an elite athlete normally train at?
12 How can you avoid suffering from DOMS?
13 What is the difference between detraining and tapering?
14 What is periodisation?
15 What is the difference between a meso and a micro cycle?

24 *Physical fitness*

Learning objectives

- To understand the concept of fitness.
- To be able to identify the different fitness components.
- To know how to evaluate the different fitness components.
- To know the different training methods used to develop each fitness component.
- To understand the physiological adaptations that take place as a result of training.

The fitness industry has exploded over the last few years as people have more leisure time and more disposable income. Most local papers carry pages of advertisements enticing you to 'move it with Mandy', 'step with Sarah', or 'pump iron with Brian' and Lycra-clad examples of bodily perfection encourage you to 'go for the burn' and remind you 'no pain no gain'. Looking beyond all the rhetoric, most people who join a class or visit a gym are attempting to improve their level of fitness for one reason or another. However, one person's concept of fitness may differ considerably from that of someone else.

24.1 What is fitness?

Fitness is the ability to cope effectively with the stresses of everyday life. Fitness cannot be stored so it should be considered as a continuum of fluctuating levels. As everyone's lifestyle (and therefore the stress that they have to cope with) differs, so do their levels of fitness. If you lead a very sedentary life then two or three walks a week will probably be enough exercise to maintain your level of required fitness, but if you play regular competitive sport you will need to train quite hard to maintain the level of fitness needed to perform well.

Fitness should not be confused with *health*, although the two are commonly interchanged. To be healthy means to be in a state of well-being and free from disease – in other words, you are physically, mentally and emotionally in good shape. Being fit can add to your feeling of well-being and make you less likely to suffer from ill health, but fitness only contributes to an overall healthy lifestyle.

Fitness is made up of several components (outlined in Figure 24.1), which can be subdivided into:

- *Health-related* components: aerobic capacity, strength, flexibility and body composition. These contribute towards a healthy body. Everyone would benefit by developing these components of fitness to some degree.
- *Skill-related* components: these include speed, power, balance, reaction time, coordination and agility. The skill-related aspects of fitness are far more appropriate to the sports performer who may wish to develop some of them through additional training.

It is the purpose of this chapter to look in detail at the health-related fitness components and to provide:
- a definition of each component
- methods of evaluating each component
- knowledge of how each fitness component can be improved
- ways of identifying the physiological adaptations that take place as a result of training.

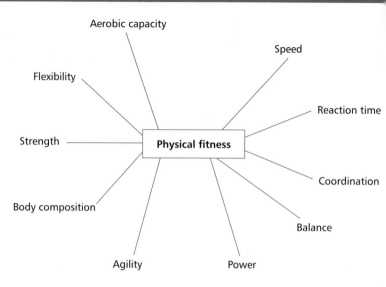

Figure 24.1 *Factors affecting physical fitness*

24.2 Aerobic capacity

The aerobic capacity of an athlete is their ability to take in and use oxygen, allowing participation in prolonged periods of continuous submaximal activities, such as swimming, running, cycling and rowing.

A person's aerobic capacity depends on three factors:
1 Effective external respiration.
2 Effective oxygen transport from the lungs to the cells.
3 Effective use of oxygen within the cell.

Your aerobic capacity therefore depends on the efficiency of your respiratory, cardiac and vascular systems. Your aerobic capacity is mostly genetically determined, for example you will be able to use far more oxygen if you have a high percentage of slow oxidative muscle fibres, but training can improve your aerobic ability. Aerobic capacity is referred to as $\dot{V}O_2$(max). Various values for $\dot{V}O_2$(max), obtained experimentally by Professor Astrand, a famous Swedish sports physiologist, are shown in Tables 24.1 and 24.2.

DEFINITION

$\dot{V}O_2$(MAX)

The maximum volume of oxygen that can be consumed and used by the body per unit of time. It is usually expressed as millilitres per minute per kilogram of body weight.

Table 24.1 $\dot{V}O_2$(max) values for men (ml/min/kg body weight)

Age (years)	Very poor	Poor	Average	Good	Very good
20–29	38	39–43	44–51	52–56	57+
30–39	34	35–39	40–47	48–51	52+
40–49	30	31–35	36–43	44–47	48+
50–59	25	26–31	32–39	40–43	44+
60–69	21	22–26	27–35	36–39	40+

Table 24.2 $\dot{V}O_2$(max) values for women (ml/min/kg body weight)

Age (years)	Very poor	Poor	Average	Good	Very good
20–29	28	29–34	35–43	44–48	49+
30–39	27	28–33	34–41	42–47	48+
40–49	25	26–31	32–40	41–45	46+
50–65	21	22–28	29–36	37–31	42+

A person with a high $\dot{V}O_2$(max) isn't necessarily going to be outstandingly good at endurance events. A much better indicator is

in training

To a large extent an athlete's $\dot{V}O_2$(max) is genetically determined.

the percentage of $\dot{V}O_2$(max) that an athlete can work at for prolonged periods of time without crossing their anaerobic threshold. Elite endurance athletes can usually work at about 85% of their $\dot{V}O_2$(max), but non-athletes will struggle to maintain a workload of about 65% of $\dot{V}O_2$(max). Most male endurance athletes have a $\dot{V}O_2$(max) in excess of 70 ml/min/kg and female endurance athletes have a $\dot{V}O_2$(max) in excess of 60 ml/min/kg.

Table 24.3 lists the differences that gender and age make to $\dot{V}O_2$(max).

activity

Why do you think that the values of $\dot{V}O_2$(max) for men and women differ? Suggest reasons why a person's $\dot{V}O_2$(max) deteriorates with age.

24.3 Evaluation of aerobic capacity

DEFINITION

DOUGLAS BAG

A rubber-lined bag used to collect expired air.

The most accurate way to assess an athlete's $\dot{V}O_2$(max) is under laboratory conditions. The athlete runs on a treadmill and all the air expired is collected in a *Douglas bag*. The athlete works to exhaustion and then the volume and oxygen content of the expired air is measured. We know the percentage of oxygen in atmospheric air so it is possible to calculate how much oxygen has been consumed by the athlete, and therefore to calculate their $\dot{V}O_2$(max).

To measure a person's $\dot{V}O_2$(max) directly relies on the availability of expensive equipment and technical assistance. It is also time consuming, especially if you want to assess the whole of your football or rugby team. Other field tests have been developed that need very little equipment and allow large numbers of athletes to be tested at any one time. The results of these tests may be compared with standardised nomograms or tables to obtain an estimate of the athlete's $\dot{V}O_2$(max). One such test is the *multi-stage*

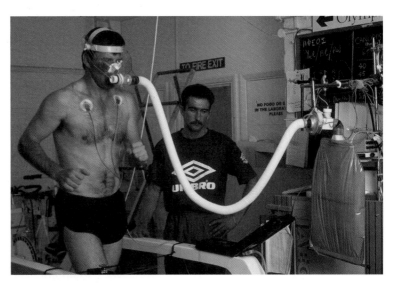

Testing maximal oxygen uptake

Table 24.3 *Differences in* $\dot{V}O_2$*(max) with sex and age*

Sex	Age
Women have a lower maximum cardiac output	Maximum heart rate drops by 5–7 beats per minute per decade
Women have lower stroke volumes due to having a smaller left ventricle	Maximal stroke volume decreases due to an increase in peripheral resistance
Women have a lower blood volume because of a smaller body size	There is a reduced blood flow to active muscles
Women have lower haemoglobin levels	Blood pressure increases at rest and during exercise
Tidal volumes and ventilatory volumes are smaller in women due to body size	Percentage of body fat increases
Women have a higher percentage of body fat	Aerobic capacity decreases by about 10% per decade in inactive people
A $\dot{V}O_2$(max) of 77 ml/kg/min was measured in a female Russian cross-country skier, whereas the highest value for a male cross-country skier is 94 ml/kg/min	Vital capacity and FEV drops with age
Residual volume increases, therefore there is less air that can be exchanged	The overall drop in aerobic capacity is a combination of a decrease in physical activity, weight gain and age-related physiological changes (increased collagen cross-linking leads to less flexibility and a deterioration in elastin makes tissues less elastic)

fitness test, developed by sports coach UK (formerly the National Coaching Foundation), in which an athlete performs a progressive 20 m shuttle run to exhaustion. The level that the athlete reaches is compared with the standard results table. Although this produces only an estimate of the athlete's $\dot{V}O_2$(max) it is a useful guide and can be repeated in future training sessions to monitor progress.

activity

Offer to test the $\dot{V}O_2$(max) of a school team or a local club team using the multi-stage fitness test. Analyse your results in terms of age, sex, frequency and type of training and position. You may need to devise a short questionnaire to supplement your data.

List both the advantages and disadvantages of using the multi-stage fitness test as a method of assessing aerobic capacity.

24.4 Improving your aerobic capacity

In order to improve your aerobic capacity you need to take part in continuous, submaximal activity involving the whole body. Activities such as brisk walking, jogging, running, cycling, swimming and rowing are ideal, as they will all put stress on the cardiovascular and respiratory systems.

The duration of the training session will depend on your initial level of fitness but you should work for a minimum of 12 minutes. This is because for the first couple of minutes of exercise the major contributors to energy production are the anaerobic systems, as your body needs time to adjust to the increased oxygen demand. You need to work long enough to put the aerobic system under stress – if you keep stopping and starting your body will have time to recover and you would not be applying the principle of overload. Usually 30–40 minutes is sufficient for recreational athletes, whereas elite endurance athletes will work for considerably longer periods.

Swimming is a good way to develop your aerobic capacity

A researcher from Finland named Karvonen suggested that we should always train above a point that he called the 'critical threshold' for 20 minutes. The training heart rate range and how to calculate your individual range was discussed in Chapter 23.

The other aspect of overload is frequency, and in order to gain any long-term physiological benefit you need to train aerobically at least twice a week; elite athletes will do at least five sessions a week. You will begin to notice an improvement in your aerobic capacity after 3–4 weeks, but it is recommended that you continue the programme for at least 12 weeks. During that time you need to monitor your performance and increase the overload as and when required. When your heart rate response to the same workload begins to drop, your body has begun to adapt to that intensity of work and you need to increase the workload. Always remain above the critical threshold.

Types of aerobic training include continuous running, Fartlek and interval training.

24.4.1 *Continuous running*

This involves jogging or running continuously at a steady pace. However, any continuous activity can be used – from swimming to step aerobics.

24.4.2 *Fartlek*

Fartlek means 'speed play' in Swedish and the idea of this activity is that the athlete varies the pace of the run and also the terrain they run over. A typical run will include some steady-state running interspersed with sprints and slow recovery work and should include uphill and downhill work. Fartlek involves the athlete working aerobically and anaerobically and it is a much more demanding form of training. Fartlek training helps to improve an athlete's $\dot{V}O_2(\max)$ and recovery process. It is ideal for athletes who need to be able to change pace during an activity and it is also good for games players.

activity

Devise a 30-minute Fartlek session that would be appropriate for your level of fitness. Plan a route near your home or college and attempt the session. If possible, wear a heart rate monitor to assess the intensity you are working at. During steady-state work your heart rate should be above the critical threshold and during the sprints you should raise your heart rate over 180 beats per minute.

An increase in the lactate threshold greatly improves the performance of endurance athletes.

24.4.3 *Interval training*

Interval training is popular because it can be used for both aerobic and anaerobic training. It is a form of training in which periods of work are interspersed with periods of recovery. Four main variables can be manipulated to ensure specificity of training:
1 The duration or distance of the interval.
2 The intensity of the interval.
3 The duration of the recovery period.
4 The number of work/recovery intervals.

Anaerobic training would be based on short-distance, high-intensity intervals and aerobic sessions would involve long-distance, sub-maximal-intensity intervals. If the athlete is concentrating on developing speed the recovery periods need to be long enough to ensure full recovery; if he or she wants to improve their level of endurance and resistance to fatigue the recovery periods need to be shortened accordingly. Interval training adds variety to training sessions and allows quality work to be maintained. The recovery intervals allow some restoration of PC stores and the removal of waste products and therefore the onset of fatigue is delayed, allowing more work to be completed than in an equivalent continuous session.

Interval training can also be adapted for games players by using repetitive skill practices and circuit training. This not only improves fitness levels but also allows practice of individual skills.

Successful interval training depends on the coach or athlete being able to correctly identify the initial fitness level of the athlete, the fitness components required by the activity and the energy systems used in the activity. He or she must then manipulate the four variables to ensure that the interval training session devised is specific to the activity and the athlete.

Examples of intervals used in training:

10 × 60 m @ 8 seconds with 90 seconds recovery
10 × 200 m @ 30 seconds with 90 seconds recovery
5 × 400 m @ 80 seconds with 160 seconds recovery

24.4.4 *Cross training*

Cross training can be interpreted in two different ways:
1 An athlete trains for several sports at the same time, such as a triathlete.
2 An athlete trains more than one fitness component at the same time, e.g. aerobic capacity and strength.

Cross training can be used as a way of varying training and can be a very good motivator, preventing athletes from becoming stale. It can also be used to help avoid injury: after a lot of road running a training session on a cycle might take some pressure off tired weight-bearing joints. Research is still inconclusive as to how effective cross training is; however, it should involve very careful planning and allocation of time and effort.

24.5 Physiological adaptations to aerobic training

As already mentioned, physiological adaptations take place as a result of training. The type of training undertaken determines what

All athletes would benefit from improving their aerobic capacity.

adaptations will take place and every individual responds differently because of their physiological make-up. Remember that our physical capabilities are mostly genetically determined but training will help to maximise our potential.

After following an aerobic training programme for 12 weeks you would probably find your initial training session very easy. A task that once left you tired and out of breath is now accomplished with relative ease – so what has happened? You will have improved your $\dot{V}O_2(max)$, and for that to happen the following adaptations will have taken place.

24.5.1 *The heart*

Hypertrophy of the myocardium

When any muscle is made to work harder it responds by increasing in size. The strength of a muscle relates to its cross-sectional area, so as it gets larger it also gets stronger.

The heart reacts in the same way as any other muscle, and after endurance training is able to contract with more force, enabling it to push more blood out of the heart per beat.

Increase in stroke volume and maximum cardiac output

As the heart increases in size it can hold more blood and the contractility of the myocardium improves. This means that the resting stroke volume of an endurance athlete, along with the maximum stroke volume achieved during exercise, is increased.

During submaximal exercise the heart of an endurance athlete doesn't have to beat as often as that of an untrained individual to deliver the same amount of blood to the working muscle. During maximal exercise the cardiac output will increase, meaning that more oxygen reaches the muscles, helping to improve $\dot{V}O_2(max)$.

For example, a 20-year-old has an estimated maximum heart rate of 200 beats per minute.

Cardiac output = Maximum stroke volume × Maximum heart rate

For an untrained individual	= 120 ml × 200
	= 24 litres
For a trained athlete	= 160 ml × 200
	= 32 litres

Decrease in resting heart rate

The cardiac output required at rest remains the same, as the demand for oxygen is unchanged. As the resting stroke volume has increased the heart doesn't have to beat as many times to produce the same cardiac output, so the resting heart rate decreases.

For example,

Cardiac output = Stroke volume × Heart rate

Before training at rest	= 70 ml × 72
	= 5.04 litres
After training at rest	= 100 ml × 50
	= 5 litres

The combined effect of these changes to the heart means that the heart is far more efficient at pumping blood round the body, helping to distribute more oxygen to the muscles.

DEFINITION

HYPERTROPHY

An increase in cell size leads to an increase in tissue size.

24.5.2 *The lungs*

Maximum pulmonary ventilation

The maximum pulmonary ventilation of endurance athletes is greater than that of untrained individuals due to an increase in the frequency of breathing and the tidal volume.

Respiratory muscles

The respiratory muscles become more efficient with training, making ventilation more efficient.

Lung volumes

After training there is a slight increase in resting lung volumes (apart from tidal volume). This is because you use more of your existing lung capacity.

Diffusion

Diffusion rates improve with training because the increase in lung volume creates a greater surface area, allowing more diffusion to take place.

   These changes don't really have a direct effect on an athlete's $\dot{V}O_2$(max), as healthy lungs are always capable of ventilating more than enough oxygen. Improved ventilation may be linked more to the need to expire the greater volume of carbon dioxide produced due to the increased rate of respiration in the cells.

24.5.3 *Blood*

Blood volume

Blood volume will increase as a result of endurance training. Although most of the increase is due to an increase in the volume of blood plasma, there is also a small increase in the number of red blood cells. This means that more haemoglobin is available, increasing the oxygen-carrying capacity of the blood.

Blood acidity

During submaximal exercise the blood of trained athletes is less acidic because their aerobic system is more effective and they produce less lactic acid. During maximal exercise the reverse is true – as endurance athletes have a greater tolerance to lactic acid, more accumulates in the blood and increases acidity.

24.5.4 *The vascular system*

Endurance training increases the elasticity of the arterial walls, which helps the arteries withstand greater fluctuations in blood pressure. The number of capillaries at the lungs and skeletal muscle increase, helping to improve the rate of gaseous exchange.

24.5.5 *The muscles*

Several changes occur within the muscles, all helping to improve the use of oxygen once it reaches the cell. The muscle itself increases in size and strength (undergoes hypertrophy) and the following other changes also occur.

Myoglobin

The amount of myoglobin in the muscle cell increases, helping to transport oxygen from the capillary to the mitochondria more effectively.

in training

Altitude training will stimulate the production of more red blood cells, increasing the oxygen-carrying capacity of the blood. Any increase though will have disappeared after about two months back at sea level.

Mitochondria

The number of mitochondria increases, allowing greater rates of aerobic respiration and using more oxygen.

Enzyme activity

Increased activity of the respiratory enzymes further adds to the efficiency of the aerobic energy system.

Energy stores

The muscle cell stores more glycogen and triglycerides, plus fat stores are mobilised more efficiently.

24.5.6 *Overall benefits*

The overall effect of all these changes means that the following processes all become more efficient:
* external respiration
* oxygen transport from the lungs to the cells
* use of oxygen within the cell.

These factors lead to an improvement in $\dot{V}O_2(max)$ of up to 20% and therefore significantly improve the performance of activities that rely heavily on the aerobic energy system.

Aerobic activity also has beneficial effects on connective tissue:
* tendons become stronger
* ligaments are stretched, increasing flexibility
* exercise stimulates deposition of calcium to bony tissue, strengthening the bones
* the lines of stress on bone are varied.

Although these last four changes don't affect a person's aerobic capacity, they help to reduce the risk of injury and offset the effects of ageing on connective tissue.

Produce a table summarising the long-term responses of the body to aerobic training.

24.6 Strength

Strength is a general term for applying a force against a resistance. In most team sports the resistance you are working against is your own body weight and, although you are not using your maximum strength, you do need to keep working for long periods of time. In other activities, such as weightlifting, you are applying more force and working to maximum. In sport we therefore need to state more specifically the type of strength being used.

Three types of strength have been identified:
* maximum strength
* elastic strength (power)
* strength endurance.

24.6.1 *Maximum strength*

This is the greatest force the neuromuscular system is capable of exerting in a single maximum voluntary contraction. Men tend to be able to exert a greater maximum strength than women because they have a larger muscle mass – the greater the cross-sectional area of the muscle, the greater the force that can be generated. Fibre type also affects strength, fast glycolytic fibres being able to produce more force than slow oxidative fibres, so once more it is

activity

List three sporting activities where the maximum strength that an athlete can exert is essential for good performance.

in training

Power is the application of both strength and speed and is an essential fitness component in most sports. Again an athlete's power is largely genetically determined as it depends on the athlete's number of fast glycolytic fibres.

down to the genes. Some muscle groups are stronger than others, not only because of their size; muscle shape also plays an important role. The *fusiform* muscle shape (for example the biceps) allows most movement, the *multipennate* shape (such as the deltoid) provides more strength but less movement.

Most people do not need to work on improving their maximum strength as they rarely need to exert maximum strength in everyday life.

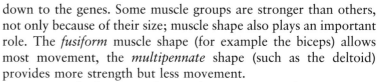

In practice

Any continuous submaximal activity relies on endurance and athletes with a high percentage of slow oxidative fibres will be at an advantage as they can work for prolonged periods of time. Remember that slow oxidative muscle fibres release energy aerobically and do not produce fatiguing by-products.

24.6.2 *Elastic strength or power*

The ability of the neuromuscular system to overcome resistance with a high speed of contraction is called elastic strength or power. This aspect of strength is more appropriate to sport than to general health-related fitness. Elastic or explosive strength is essential for any activities involving sprinting, throwing, jumping or hitting and an athlete needs a high percentage of fast glycolytic muscle fibres to perform well. The motor neurones that stimulate fast-twitch muscle fibres have a thicker myelin sheath than those stimulating the slow oxidative fibres, which speeds up the rate of conduction of the stimulus and therefore the speed of contraction. Power is the application of both strength and speed and is shown as

Power = (force × distance)/time

24.6.3 *Strength endurance*

This is the ability of the muscle to withstand fatigue. This is the type of strength most appropriate to health-related fitness. We are often called upon to do tasks requiring this kind of strength – digging the garden, carrying home the shopping, etc. It is also essential to the sports performer. For example towards the end of a game or when a game goes into extra time, the team whose players have better muscular endurance will be in the more favourable position.

24.7 Evaluation of strength

The easiest way to assess someone's maximum strength is to find out the maximum weight that they can lift in a single contraction. Free weights or a multi-gym can be used and more than one muscle group can be tested. A dynamometer can be used to measure hand grip and leg strength.

A dynamometer

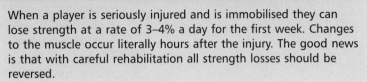

in training

When a player is seriously injured and is immobilised they can lose strength at a rate of 3–4% a day for the first week. Changes to the muscle occur literally hours after the injury. The good news is that with careful rehabilitation all strength losses should be reversed.

activity

Identify the types of strength required to perform the following activities:

1 400 m hurdles
2 triathlon
3 triple jump
4 a diving save by a goalkeeper
5 a routine on the rings.

Lifting to maximum

The vertical jump test

activity

Give three reasons why a cool-down is necessary after the Wingate test.

Endurance can be measured by the sit-up test that has been developed by sports coach UK, but any repetitive exercise such as pull-ups, squat thrusts or dips can be performed over 1–2 minutes and the number performed recorded.

Elastic strength or power is an indication of an athlete's *anaerobic power* or *capacity*. Dynamic activities such as sprinting and jumping require a lot of energy quickly and have to rely predominantly on the alactic and lactic acid energy systems (see Chapter 22). A simple and easy test of elastic strength is the vertical jump, but a more sophisticated test of an athlete's anaerobic capacity is the Wingate test.

24.7.1 *The Wingate test*

This test is performed on a cycle ergometer, and requires maximum effort by the athlete over a period of 30 seconds. The athlete warms up and then the relevant load is added to the bike – for men this load is 0.083–0.092 kg per kg of body weight, for women and children the load is 0.075 kg per kg. As soon as all the weights have been added to the bike the athlete must pedal as fast as possible. Someone must count the number of pedal revolutions for every five seconds of the test. Using the following formula the athlete's power output (in watts) can be calculated.

Output (watts) = Load (kg) × Revolutions (per 5 seconds) × 11.765

The Wingate test is a maximal test and it is very important that the athlete cools down after completing it. A heart rate monitor is not required but as a guide the athlete should cool down until their heart rate has dropped to at least 120 beats per minute.

24.8 Improving strength

In order to improve your strength you need to work against some form of resistance, but in order to make your training programme as specific as possible you need to consider the following:

- the type of strength you want to develop – maximum strength, strength endurance or elastic strength
- which muscle groups you want to improve
- the type of muscle contraction performed – concentric, eccentric or isometric.

The athlete should also:

- follow a general strength conditioning programme before specialising
- exercise large muscle groups before smaller ones
- perform the exercises in such a way as to use the energy system required during the activity
- overload movements that are as close as possible to the movements to be strengthened
- allow appropriate recovery between individual exercises and training sessions.

Any strength training programme refers to the number of *repetitions* and the number of *sets* performed.

The number of repetitions performed will depend on the type of strength being improved. If you are developing maximum strength you may perform only six repetitions per set because you will be working to maximum and will fatigue very quickly. Remember that the fast twitch muscle fibres will be recruited for maximum strength work, and they rely on the anaerobic energy systems and fatigue quickly. If you are developing strength endurance you may do anything from 10 to 20 repetitions per set.

The intensity that you work at will also depend on the type of strength you wish to develop. To develop maximum strength you need to determine the maximum weight that you can successfully lift six times (six repetition maximum: 6RM). As a general guide the session will include low repetitions of high weights. In contrast,

DEFINITION

REPETITION

Repetition is the number of times that an athlete repeats a particular exercise, for example 10 arm curls. The number of repetitions performed is one set.

SET

A set is a certain number of repetitions. Usually three sets are completed in a session.

Improving strength by resistance training

to develop strength endurance the number of repetitions will be high and the resistance will be relatively low (15–20RM).

You might need to develop the strength to hold a particular body position, for example the crucifix position on the rings. In this case the muscles act as fixators and perform an isometric contraction (remember that during an isometric contraction there is an increase in muscle tension, but no movement occurs). It is possible to improve strength using the static resistance method (working isometrically) but you will only improve your strength at the specific joint angle used in training. Most methods of strength training involve concentric and eccentric muscle contraction, where the whole range of muscle movement is improved.

To improve strength you should train two or three times a week and should continue the programme for at least 10 weeks. As with aerobic training, you will begin to notice improvements in your strength due to muscular adaptations after 3–4 weeks. It is important to continually monitor your performance so you can progressively increase the resistance you work against in line with your level of improvement.

Strength can be improved using circuit training, weight training, pulleys and plyometrics.

24.8.1 Circuit training

In circuit training the athlete performs a series of exercises (8–10) arranged in a circuit (Figure 24.2) usually used for general conditioning. The resistance used is the athlete's body weight and each exercise concentrates on stressing a particular muscle group. It is important to order the exercises to alternate the muscles being used and allow for recovery. Typical exercises include press-ups, sit-ups, squat thrusts, step-ups, shuttle runs, star jumps, astride jumps, dips, burpees and pull-ups.

Circuit training can be adapted to include skill training while still developing strength (Figure 24.3); this is ideal for the games player. For example, a basketball circuit might include:
1 a 5 metre shuttle dribbling the ball
2 chest passes against the wall
3 right-handed lay-ups

For your individual and/or team activity identify:

- the types of strength you need to improve
- the major muscles used
- the type of muscle contraction employed.

Arrange the exercises (right) into a circuit, making sure that the major muscle groups being used are rotated to allow recovery.

Sit-ups

Press-ups

Shuttle run

Dips

Figure 24.2
Exercises for circuit training

Figure 24.3
Combining circuit training with skills training

Devise a skills circuit for your team activity that would develop strength endurance.

4 free throws
5 figure-of-eight dribble around two cones
6 rebounding drill (using a crash mat for the landing surface)
7 left-handed lay-ups
8 overhead throw using a medicine ball.

Once you have decided what exercises you are going to perform, you must decide on the length of the work and rest intervals. A typical circuit involves the athlete working to maximum for 30 seconds with a 30-second recovery period. This makes it ideal for working in pairs, with one of each team recording how many repetitions their partner performs in the 30 seconds. If strength endurance is to be stressed it is more appropriate to work for one minute at each station. As a circuit is usually repeated three times in a session you should be realistic about the amount of work you can perform until your level of conditioning has improved.

24.8.2 Weight training

Instead of using the athlete's body weight as the resistance, additional weights, in the form of free weights or a multi-gym, are used. The athlete will perform a number of repetitions and sets at prescribed weights, depending on the type of strength being improved and the athlete's level of fitness. Typical exercises are shown in Table 24.4.

Weight training is good for developing strength, but rarely allows the athlete to reproduce the same movement pattern that is performed during an activity.

Table 24.4 *Typical weight-training exercises*

Exercise	Body part worked
Arm curl	Upper and lower arm
Bench press	Chest
Heel raise	Lower leg
Squat	Back and upper leg

24.8.3 Use of pulleys

To allow an athlete to train against a resistance and still perform the actual movement pattern used in the activity pulleys or flexi cords can be used (see Figure 24.4). This idea is used quite a lot by swimmers and throwers, but can be adapted for most activities. Sprinters quite often run either pulling a tyre behind them or with a small parachute attached to their back. Another method of applying resistance during skill practices is to wear ankle or wrist weights.

24.8.4 Plyometrics

Plyometrics is a form of training that has been developed to improve dynamic strength. It involves jumping, hopping or bounding, in

which muscle groups have to work eccentrically. To be most effective the athlete starts from the top of a bench or box and jumps down. During the landing the muscle groups are working eccentrically, acting as a brake to help control the movement. The athlete should then immediately take off and jump up, performing a concentric muscle contraction (Figure 24.5).

Figure 24.4
Using pulleys to improve strength

Figure 24.5
Plyometrics helps to improve dynamic strength

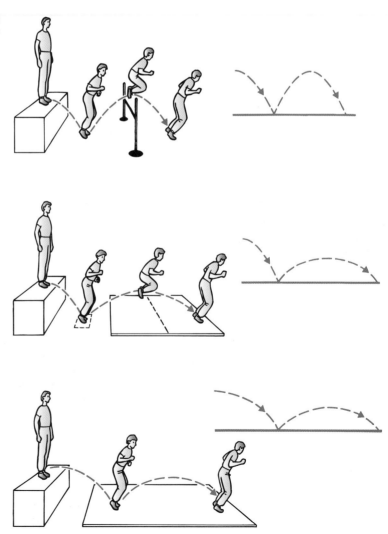

A muscle will contract concentrically with more force if it has been stretched under tension before the contraction (refer to stretch reflex on page 271). This concept can be easily demonstrated with a piece of elastic – the further you stretch it, the more strongly it will recoil; remember that one of the properties of muscle is its elasticity. Any athlete needing to perform explosive movements, for example sprinters, will benefit by doing some plyometric work as this type of training recruits fast glycolytic motor units as well as fast oxidative glycolytic and slow oxidative motor units. An athlete should not attempt plyometric training until a reasonable amount of leg strength has been developed. Moreover young athletes should consult closely with their coach before attempting plyometrics as this type of training puts a lot of stress on the body that may cause injury to immature bones and joints.

24.9 Physiological adaptations to strength training

Different types of strength training will result in different types of physiological adaptations – remember that specificity of training is a very important principle to take into account. Strength endurance programmes will stimulate aerobic adaptations within the muscle cell and also some neural adaptations. It is the adaptations to the nervous system that are largely responsible for the early strength gains experienced by the athlete (Figure 24.6).

24.9.1 *Aerobic adaptations*

Cellular changes to slow oxidative muscle fibres

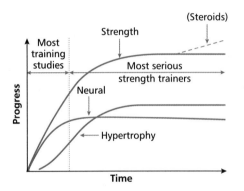

Figure 24.6 *Adaptations to resistance training*

- *Muscle hypertrophy.* The muscle cell actually increases in size with an increase in total protein. The increase in size has also been attributed to *hyperplasia*, which is where the fibre actually splits in two, but as yet research in this area is inconclusive.
- *An increase in the density of mitochondria and myoglobin stores.* As the mitochondrion is the site of aerobic respiration, this means that more energy is available to the muscle, allowing it to work for longer. More myoglobin enables more oxygen to diffuse into the cells and to be transported to the mitochondria.
- *An increase in glycogen and triglyceride stores.* Again, this makes aerobic respiration far more efficient and an increase in aerobic enzyme activity also quickens the process.
- *An increase in capillarisation surrounding the muscle tissue* means that the blood flow to the working muscle is greater, which improves the delivery of oxygen and the removal of carbon dioxide.

Neural adaptations to slow oxidative muscle fibres

- The recruitment of additional motor units means that more strength can be generated.

Training may reduce or counteract autogenic inhibition (the tension threshold of the Golgi tendon organs). Autogenic inhibition is a safety mechanism within the muscle controlled via the Golgi tendon that prevents the muscle exerting more force than the bones and connective tissue can handle. Training appears to reduce the inhibitory effect, allowing the muscle to generate more force.

24.9.2 Anaerobic adaptations

Cellular changes to fast glycolytic and fast oxidative glycolytic muscle fibre

- *Muscle hypertrophy*. The muscle cell increases in size with an increase in total protein. The increase in size has also been attributed to hyperplasia, which is where the fibre actually splits in two, but as yet research in this area is inconclusive.
- *Increased concentrations of ATP and phosphocreatine*. This has the effect of maximising the efficiency of the alactic system, making energy readily available for high-intensity training.
- *Increase in glycogen stores* within the muscle cell, making anaerobic glycolysis more efficient.
- *Increase in tolerance to lactic acid* enables the athlete to work for longer whilst relying heavily on the lactic acid system. The athlete can tolerate greater levels of lactic acid and is able to remove lactic acid more rapidly, which means that they can recover more quickly.

Neural adaptations to fast glycolytic and fast oxidative glycolytic muscle fibre

The adaptations are the same as the changes due to aerobic training, involving improved recruitment and autogenic inhibition. In addition there is some evidence to suggest that the coordination of the neural system gets better, improving the *synchronisation* of motor unit activation. This means that not only are more motor units activated but that they all contract at the same time, generally improving the efficiency of the muscle action.

Refer back to the skills circuit you developed for your games activity. Outline the adaptations you would expect to occur if you followed your programme for three months.

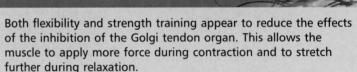

Both flexibility and strength training appear to reduce the effects of the inhibition of the Golgi tendon organ. This allows the muscle to apply more force during contraction and to stretch further during relaxation.

24.10 Flexibility

Flexibility (or static flexibility) is the range of movement possible around a joint and depends on the amount of stretch allowed by the ligaments, joints, tendons and muscles. Dynamic flexibility is slightly different – it is the resistance of a joint to movement. Flexibility has only recently been considered as an important component of physical fitness for all athletes. In the past it was assumed that girls are naturally more flexible than boys and that you need to be flexible to participate in gymnastics or to dance, but that flexibility isn't important for footballers or other male-dominated activities. This attitude has changed considerably – increasing your flexibility aids performance and helps to avoid unnecessary injury.

It is impossible to have the same degree of flexibility around all joints as the joint structure itself limits flexibility, for example a lot of movement is possible at the shoulder joint because it is a ball

and socket joint, but movement at the hinge joint of the knee is more limited. Other factors affecting flexibility are:

- The bony features of the joint – for example, the olecranon process prevents the elbow joint from hyperextending.
- The elasticity of the muscle tissue.
- The length of tendons and ligaments.
- The elasticity of the skin and the amount of adipose tissue.
- The amount of stretch allowed by the antagonistic muscle.
- The temperature of the muscle and connective tissue.
- Age – children are more flexible than adults and you get less flexible as you get older.
- Females are generally more flexible than males.

Increasing body temperature helps to improve flexibility, which is a good reason why an athlete should always warm up. Our range of movement deteriorates as we get older, due to shortening of the connective tissue and general joint degeneration caused by wear and tear.

24.11 Evaluation of flexibility

A widely used test of flexibility is the sit and reach test. The athlete sits on the floor with their legs straight, their toes pointing upwards and their feet in contact with the box. He or she then reaches forward as far as possible and the distance from the toes is measured. The range of joint movement may be measured using a double-arm goniometer or a 360° angle measurer, as shown in Figure 24.7.

Figure 24.7 *The angles of movement can be measured using a double-arm goniometer*

The sit and reach test

activity

Perform the sit and reach test without a warm-up. Thoroughly warm up and perform the test again. Can you suggest any physiological reasons for the difference in performance?

24.12 Improving flexibility

Flexibility is improved by stretching, moving a joint to *just beyond* its point of resistance. Flexibility is limited by the joint itself and the muscles, ligaments and tendons acting on it. We cannot change the bony structures or the type of joint, but we can stretch the soft tissue surrounding the joint. Women have a natural advantage because their body structure allows greater flexibility, but both males and females can significantly improve their flexibility through training.

For improvement to occur a stretch should be held for a minimum of 10 seconds and a mobility session should last for at least 10 minutes. For the best results the body should be warm, so the exercises should be performed after a warm-up or during the cool-down phase of the training session. Flexibility training needs to be undertaken at least three times a week, but improvement is rapid and will be obvious after five or six weeks of training. An athlete should identify the joints where increased flexibility is required and concentrate their efforts on these joints. However, it is not always beneficial to increase the amount of flexibility around a joint as this can lead to lack of stability – and in contact sports this could result in injury.

The muscles and joints have their own safety mechanisms to make sure that joint integrity is maintained. They contain proprioceptors that respond to changes in muscle length and to force exerted. Any athlete who wants to improve their level of flexibility needs to know a little bit about these safety mechanisms in order to make their training more effective.

The muscle contains stretch receptors/muscle spindles that are sensitive to changes in length of the muscle and the rate of change in muscle length. When a muscle is stretched, so is the muscle spindle, and it sends sensory information, which then triggers the stretch reflex. The stretch reflex acts to prevent muscle damage caused by excessive stretch and when activated makes the stretched muscle contract. Equally when a muscle contracts tension is produced within the muscle and this is registered by the Golgi tendon organs. When this exceeds a certain threshold a lengthening reaction occurs and the muscle relaxes; this is known as autogenic inhibition. Proprioceptive, neuro-muscular facilitation (PNF) is a very effective type of training because it uses these two mechanisms to full effect. By forcefully contracting the muscle to be stretched first, it stimulates the lengthening reaction and this allows the body to momentarily override the stretch reflex and the muscle will stretch further than usual.

Types of flexibility training include static and ballistic stretching and PNF.

24.12.1 *Static stretching*

This can be achieved *actively* by an athlete moving into a position that takes the joint beyond its point of resistance, lengthening the soft tissue around the joint. The position is held for a minimum of 10 seconds. In a *passive* stretch a partner is used to move the joint beyond its resistance point and holds the position – see Figure 24.8.

DEFINITION

GOLGI TENDON ORGANS
Provide the central nervous system with information concerning the degree of tension within a muscle.

MUSCLE SPINDLE
Provides information about the changes in muscle length and also the rate of change in muscle length.

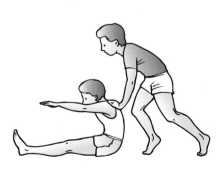

Figure 24.8 *A passive static stretch is performed with the aid of a partner*

Active static stretching

24.12.2 *Ballistic stretching*

This involves the athlete using momentum to move a body part through its extreme range of movement. The exercises involve swinging or bouncing movements, as shown in Figure 24.9. This type of stretching should be undertaken only by athletes who are very flexible, as it is very easy to over-stretch and damage connective tissue. However, the nature of some activities requires dynamic action through a large range of movement, e.g. a tennis serve. This means that some dynamic stretching should be included in the latter stages of the warm-up to fully prepare the body for the activity.

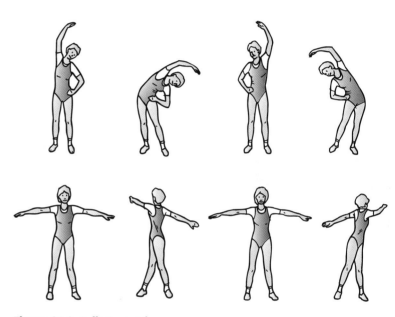

Figure 24.9 *Ballistic stretches*

activity

Design a programme that will improve your flexibility in line with the demands of your individual or team activity.

24.12.3 *Proprioceptive, neuromuscular facilitation (PNF)*

This method of stretching is extremely effective. The athlete moves the joint to just beyond its resistance point and then performs an isometric contraction (a partner can be used to provide the resistance). The muscle is relaxed and stretched again, and will usually stretch further the second time.

24.13 Flexibility adaptations

The soft tissue surrounding a joint (the ligaments, tendons and muscles) can be stretched and their resting or residual length can be increased. This is because they have elastic properties that allow a change in length – providing flexibility training is carried out correctly. In addition the muscle spindle becomes used to the new length and reduces the stimulus to the stretch reflex. There is a much more marked change to muscle tissue than to the connective tissue. Remember that ligaments in particular have a stability function and for that reason are not very elastic.

24.14 Body composition

As mentioned in Chapter 21, your body mass is made up of lean body mass plus body fat. On average men carry 12–15% fat and women 18–20% fat. When people start to carry more fat they become overweight and in some cases obese. This can lead to health problems as the additional weight puts a strain on the cardiovascular system and can cause cardiovascular disease and high blood pressure. Overweight people are less likely to exercise because they get tired very quickly and put a lot of strain on their joints, causing injury and discomfort. If you establish a routine of regular exercise and sensible eating habits when you are young, you are less likely to 'go to seed' as you approach middle age.

In general, most athletes carry less fat than average, mainly because their energy expenditure is quite high and they use their fat stores. Activities such as distance running require lower than average percentage of body fat as less fat leads to much better performance times. Although adipose tissue acts as an energy store it can't directly produce ATP in the same way that muscle tissue can. Therefore you can consider excess adipose tissue as a dead weight that has to be carried around. Each sport has a slightly different ideal in terms of body composition, but in general the less fat the better the performance. As in all things there are some exceptions and athletes involved in contact sports such as American football (particularly defensive linemen) have higher percentages of body fat. Swimmers may also benefit from slightly increased body fat as it provides more buoyancy and helps to minimise body drag.

24.14.1 *Evaluation of body composition*

Skinfold measurement

The percentage of body fat is usually estimated by measuring skin folds at specific sites on the body. Common sites measured include the biceps brachii, triceps brachii, subscapula and suprailiac and usually the sum of the sites selected is calculated and compared against norm tables. A skinfold calliper is needed; the ones made from metal tend to be more accurate than those made of plastic. The person measuring should hold the skinfold, place the calliper

in training

Elite male athletes have been known to have body fat percentages as low as 6%.

Use of skinfold callipers to estimate percentage of body fat

over it and measure the fold in millimetres. Care should be taken not to include muscle tissue.

Many health and fitness texts include nomograms to help you estimate your percentage of body fat, but their validity depends on the accuracy of the measurements taken.

Bioelectric impedance (e.g. bodystat)

Two electrodes are attached to the athlete's ankle, two more are connected to the wrist and a small current is passed through them. The conduction of the current through the body depends on the water and electrolyte distribution. Different types of tissue have different proportions of water and electrolytes and it is more difficult for the current to pass through adipose tissue. The results are based on the amount of impedance and give an estimate of the athlete's percentage body fat. This method is quite accurate and correlates very well with results gained by hydrostatic weighing; however, the equipment needed is quite expensive.

To stay reasonably fit and healthy, athletes and non-athletes alike should be aware of the health-related components of fitness and do the exercise appropriate to maintain an active lifestyle. Many texts outline exercise programmes which are suitable for all ages and standards, but you should select a regime that is realistic and which will fit into your daily routine. Athletes need to be more specific in their approach to fitness because different activities require different mixes of fitness components. A gymnast needs to be very flexible, have good elastic strength and strength endurance, but does not need a lot of aerobic fitness. A marathon runner, on the other hand, needs good aerobic capacity and a lot of strength endurance, but doesn't need to be particularly flexible. An athlete should analyse the requirements of their speciality very closely and make sure that their training reflects the demands that will be made on them.

24.15 Motor/skill-related fitness

The following components are skill related and this section intends to give only a brief outline of each component. More information is available in the texts suggested in the Further reading.

24.15.1 *Speed*

Speed is basically how fast you can move part of your body or the whole of your body, and is measured in metres per second. Speed is an important factor in all explosive sports and activities that require sudden changes in pace (remember that power is work performed per unit of time). How fast you are depends on the percentage of fast glycolytic fibres in particular muscle groups as these fibres receive stimuli more quickly and release energy anaerobically. You need fast reactions to be able to respond to the right cue and also need to be able to select the necessary motor units. Increased speed doesn't always result in an improved performance if you go too quickly and make mistakes.

Evaluation of speed

A 60 metre timed sprint is commonly used to measure an athlete's speed.

Marion Jones, sprinter

24.15.2 Reaction time

This is the time between a stimulus being detected and the first movement made in response to it – for example the time taken between the gun going off and the sprinter starting to move. Reaction time is affected by conduction of the nerve impulse and the speed of muscle contraction, therefore people with a high percentage of fast glycolytic fibres respond more quickly. It also depends on how long you take to process the information, and this can be improved with practice.

Evaluation of reaction time

A number of reaction timers are available. Mostly they involve pushing a button when a light comes on. Pushing the button breaks an electrical circuit and stops a timer, consequently measuring the time it takes to respond to the stimulus.

24.15.3 Agility

Agility is the combination of speed and coordination. It allows you to efficiently change direction and body position at speed, for example a goalkeeper needs to have fast reactions and to be very agile. More emphasis is now being placed on agility and many coaches incorporate ladder drills and other footwork drills into their training sessions to improve agility.

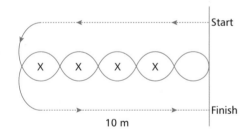

Footwork drills to improve coordination and agility

in training

Ladder drills are incorporated into the training programmes of a wide variety of sports. They are used to increase leg speed, coordination and agility. The drills can be used by athletes of all abilities and range from a basic running pattern through to much more complex drills. The overall aim is to complete the drill as quickly and as accurately as possible.

Evaluation of agility

The Illinois agility run involves an athlete lying face down at the starting line. On the word 'go' they get up and complete the agility course outlined in Figure 24.10 as fast as possible.

Figure 24.10 *Course for the Illinois agility run. X = obstacle*

24.15.4 Balance

Balance is the ability to maintain equilibrium – in other words, something is balanced when its centre of gravity is over its area of support (for more information on centre of gravity refer back to Chapter 4). A balance that is held, such as a headstand in gymnastics, is known as a *static balance*. Balance also has a *dynamic* dimension, as athletes need to retain their balance while in motion. Most games players require good dynamic balance and training programmes are beginning to focus more attention on developing dynamic balance through agility drills and obstacle courses.

Evaluation of balance

A balance board can be used to evaluate balance. This is a circular piece of wood or plastic about 60 cm in diameter with a small hemispherical piece of wood attached to one side as a base. The

Balance board

athlete stands on the board and tries to prevent the sides of the board making contact with the floor. How long the athlete can retain their balance on the board is recorded.

24.15.5 *Coordination*

Coordination involves putting the relevant motor programmes in the right order, and effectively using the neuromuscular system to produce smooth and efficient movement.

Evaluation of coordination

The alternate hand-wall toss is an easy test to administer, requiring little space or equipment. An athlete stands 2 m from a wall, holding a tennis ball in the right hand. He or she tosses the ball underarm against the wall and must catch the ball with the left hand. They then throw the ball from the left hand and attempt to catch it in the right – and so on. The number of successful catches made in 30 seconds is recorded.

SAQ training

SAQ International is a trade mark for a company that delivers awards for sports training to teachers, coaches and athletes. The training is aimed mainly at developing fundamental motor abilities, leading to complete control of the body by the athlete. Therefore the programme focuses on the development of the skill-related fitness components namely multi-directional speed, agility and quickness or acceleration. SAQ International has identified a sequence of training phases to develop the 'fundamentals of good movement competence' that involve a variety of training techniques such as dynamic warm-ups, plyometrics, ladder/agility drills and resistance work.

activity

Complete the following fitness evaluation.

On the table below mark the appropriate rating (1 = very low and 10 = very high) for each fitness component in relation to your present state of fitness and the ideal state of fitness for your chosen activity.

Date
Percentage body fat
Individual sport
Team sport

Fitness component	1	2	3	4	5	6	7	8	9	10
Aerobic capacity										
Flexibility										
Maximum strength										
Strength endurance										
Anaerobic capacity										
Speed										
Balance										
Coordination										
Agility										

The rationale behind fitness testing is not necessarily to compare your performance with others, but to give you an indication of your strengths and weaknesses so that your training can be tailored to your requirements. The tests can be repeated at a later date to monitor improvement.

Key revision points

Physical fitness cannot be stored but must be maintained by following a programme designed with both your physiological make-up and the demands of your sport in mind. Fitness can be divided into health-related components and skill-related components. An athlete should evaluate each component before embarking on a training schedule. The body responds to exercise on both a short-term and a long-term physiological basis. A short-term response, such as an increase in heart rate, takes place during the actual training session and will return to normal shortly after the athlete stops exercising. A long-term response, such as a drop in resting heart rate due to aerobic training, is an adaptation to the body that takes place over a period of time.

Key terms

You should now understand the following terms. If you do not, go back through the chapter and find out what they mean.

Aerobic capacity
Agility
Anaerobic capacity
Coordination
Cross training
Fartlek
Flexibility
Health
Maximum strength
Plyometrics
Reaction time
Strength endurance
$\dot{V}O_2(max)$
Wingate test

Progress check

1 Define health.
2 Define fitness.
3 What is the usual measurement of aerobic capacity?
4 What three main factors affect aerobic capacity?
5 List the four components of health-related fitness.
6 Briefly describe the multi-stage fitness test.
7 List the three different types of strength.
8 Which type of muscle fibres are stimulated when you perform strength endurance activities?
9 What does the Wingate test measure?
10 How is energy released when you are performing dynamic strength exercises?
11 List three factors that limit flexibility.
12 How can flexibility aid performance?
13 What is the difference between static balance and dynamic balance?
14 Identify the main fitness components that are required by:
   a a gymnast
   b a goalkeeper
   c a 400 m hurdler
   d a 10 000 m runner
   e a prop forward.
15 How would the flexibility required by a swimmer differ from that required by a gymnast?
16 Explain what 'Fartlek' means.
17 What four variables can be changed in interval training?
18 What is meant by the term repetition maximum?
19 Explain the general guidelines used when planning:
   a a maximum-strength programme
   b a strength endurance programme.
20 What types of exercise would you be performing in a plyometric session?
21 Explain the difference between a general conditioning circuit and a skill circuit.
22 What is the difference between an active static stretch and a passive static stretch?

Further reading

C. Clegg. *Exercise Physiology and Functional Anatomy*. Feltham Press, 1995.

D. Davis, T. Kimmet and M. Auty. *Physical Education: Theory and Practice*. Macmillan Australia, 1986.

R.J. Davis, C.R. Bull, J.V. Roscoe and D.A. Roscoe. *Physical Education and the Study of Sport*. Wolfe Medical Publishers, 1991.

F. Dick. *Sports Training Principles*. A & C Black, 1989.

E. Fox, R. Bowen and M. Foss. *The Physiological Basis for Exercise and Sport*. Brown and Benchmark, 1989.

R. Hazeldine. *Fitness for Sport*. Gowood Press, 1985.

D. R. Lamb. *Physiology of Exercise, Responses and Adaptations*. Collier Macmillan Publishers, 1984.

W. Paish. *Training for Peak Performance*. A & C Black, 1991.

Peak Performance Magazines. Available by subscription only from Stonehart Leisure Magazines Ltd, 67–71 Goswell Road, London EC1V 7EN.

S. K. Powers and E. T. Howley. *Exercise Physiology. Theory and Application to Fitness and Performance*. McGraw-Hill, 1994.

B.J. Sharkey. *Physiology of Fitness*. Human Kinetics Books, 1990.

J.H. Wilmore and D.L. Costill. *Physiology of Sport and Exercise*, Second edition. Human Kinetics, 1999.

Websites

The Australian Sports Commission www.ausport.gov.au/tophysio.html

Speed, Agility and Quickness International www.saqinternational.com

Sportquest www.sportquest.com/coaching.html

Sports science organisation (New Zealand) www.sportsci.org.

The National Sports Medicine Institute of the United Kingdom www.nsmi.org.uk

Part 5

PSYCHOLOGY OF PHYSICAL EDUCATION AND SPORT

This part of the book contains:

Chapter 25 Individual differences

Chapter 26 Social influences

Chapter 27 Stress and its management

The field of sports psychology is of increasing interest to performers and their teachers or coaches. A performer might have a body that is finely tuned physically for performance, but without mental strength will never reach the top of their sport. Every individual is different, and this part first deals with these differences and how they can affect performance in sport. Every person is affected by other people and their environment. We will be investigating the social influences on the performer of sport and how we can harness the positive aspects and limit the negative ones. Finally, we deal with the concept of stress and how it can help the performer to achieve the best performance possible. Stress is also very destructive in its effects, and we will be studying research related to the management of stress and what this means in practical terms for sports participants and their coaches.

25 CHAPTER

Individual differences

Learning objectives

- To understand what is meant by personality and how it is measured.
- To be aware of the links between personality and performance in physical education and sport.
- To understand how attitudes are formed and the influences upon attitudes.
- To know the links between attitudes, participation and performance.
- To understand what is meant by the term aggression.
- To comprehend what makes performers aggressive.
- To know the ways of harnessing aggression for optimum performance.
- To understand the concept of motivation.
- To understand the different motives held by performers in sport and young people in physical education.
- To be able to describe the links between attribution and motivation.
- To understand the concept of self-efficacy and relate it to participation and performance.

The many differences between individuals make generalisation about human behaviour very difficult and at times false. There are, however, underlying human traits that are common to us all. There are also social and environmental influences that affect our behaviour and we will investigate many of these. Linking individual differences with performance and attitudes in sport is a very complex process and research can often be conflicting. In this chapter we review the main evidence that links our behaviour with our approach and performance in sport. With a greater understanding about why we behave in a particular way, we can get the best out of ourselves and others so that we can enjoy the highest level of performance our abilities allow.

25.1 Personality

The study of personality and its relationship to performance in sport has been wide ranging, and yet solid conclusions are hard to find. To find out whether personality can affect performance in sport, or if sport can actually affect personality, it is important to investigate what is meant by personality and how our personalities are formed.

25.1.1 *Hollander's structure of personality*

Hollander (1971) saw personality as a layered structure (Figure 25.1).
- An inner psychological core, which is not affected by the environment, is where our fairly permanent qualities (such as our basic beliefs and values) reside. This inner core affects the next layer.
- A middle layer, revealing the way we typically or usually respond to certain situations.
- An outer layer called our role-related behaviours. This shows that our typical response may be affected by circumstances. Therefore our behaviour will be completely different at different times and in different situations and may well be quite unlike our psychological core.

The way to get the best from an individual is to get to know them well

Social environment

Role-related behaviours

Typical responses

Psychological core

Figure 25.1 *Hollander's (1971) view of the structure of personality*

DEFINITION

TRAIT

Personality traits are seen as generalisable and behaviour can be predicted in various situations. There is, however, much contradictory evidence with this perspective. The traits most commonly referred to are extroversion, introversion, stability and neurosis. All opposing traits should be viewed on a continuum.

- Around the outer layer is the social environment, which affects our role-related behaviours.

Some psychologists see the central core as controlling and dictating behaviour – what is called the *trait approach*. Those who see the social environment as being the most important take a *social learning* or *interactionist* approach.

25.1.2 *Trait approach, including Type A and Type B personalities*

In psychology there is an approach to personality called the *narrow band* approach. This approach splits personalities into two types: type A is characterised by impatience, intolerance and high levels of stress, type B personalities have a relaxed, tolerant approach, with lower personal stress.

Whether the distinction between type A personality and type B personality is helpful when related to sport is not clear. A study undertaken by Hincle, Lyons and Burke is quite interesting. They identified 96 runners aged between 16 and 66 years as either type A or type B personalities. The runners were compared for levels of competition anxiety, forceful behaviour and response to the challenge of training and racing. The two groups were not significantly different, except type A runners ran more often when they were not motivated than type B runners. This research backs up the argument that one particular personality type is not preferable to another, although the persistence of type A may point towards their behaviour being more aggressive in a sports context.

Cattell (1965) also believed in the trait approach and thought that each individual's personality was made up of a collection of stable traits, which he called personality factors. He constructed a questionnaire called the 16 Personality Factor Questionnaire (16PF). Cattell's approach has gained much credibility in the world of sport. Research using his profiles has revealed differences in the personalities of participants in direct physical contact sports (e.g. wrestling) and those of team players (e.g. American football). There are, however, many flaws in this type of research. For instance, the

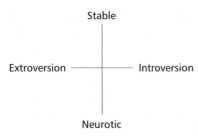

Stable

Extroversion ——————— Introversion

Neurotic

Extrovert: likes social affiliation
Introvert: avoids social contact
Stable: reliable and predictable
Neurotic: extreme emotions and unreliable

Figure 25.2 *Trait dimensions for personality*

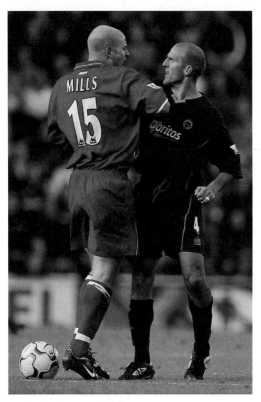

A person's personality may change with the situation

DEFINITION

SOCIAL LEARNING

This involves the way the behaviour of one person is influenced by the behaviour of others. We often observe and imitate others – but only others who are significant to us or whose behaviour is reinforced. There is a comprehensive review of this important theory in Chapter 26.

same subjects given Cattell's questionnaire at different times would give different answers. This type of personality measurement does not take into account differences in situations.

activity

Copy out the two dimensions shown in Figure 25.2 and plot – by drawing an X – where you think your personality profile should lie. Use any well-known personality test, such as Eysenck's personality inventory, and compare the result to your own assessment. Try to account for any possible differences. It might be interesting to repeat the process for a larger sample. Can you see any reliability/validity problems here?

25.1.3 Social learning and personality

Some psychologists think that a person's personality changes with the situation and that the environment (including the behaviour of other people) influences behaviour. This is known as the *social learning* approach. This approach would explain why we are like the people that are of significance to us and why twins that have been separated, for instance, have different personalities. For a more detailed description of the social learning theory see sections 25.3.4 and 26.1.

25.1.4 Interactionist approach to personality

Most sports psychologists feel that both the trait and the social learning approaches have some value – we are all born with certain personality characteristics but some of these can be modified by interacting with the environment. This has resulted in the *interactionist* approach. The interactionist approach agrees that we do have certain traits which appear consistently, but on many other occasions our traits interact with environmental factors in a given situation.

This has been stated simply by Lewin as

B = f(PE)

where B is behaviour, f is the function, P is personality trait and E the environment. This formula is a simplistic but useful way of understanding the interactionist approach. The interaction between personality and the situation determines our behaviour.

25.1.5 Humanistic and psychoanalytical theories of personality

This is a wide and complex area of personality research and a detailed analysis is beyond the scope of this book. However, certain fundamental factors may be of use in our quest for understanding of the relationship between personality and sport.

The humanistic approach to personality focuses on personal growth. It emphasises the importance of free will and an individual's strengths rather than weaknesses. For more information on

DEFINITION

SELF ACTUALISATION

This is the individual's desire to explore and understand the world so that the individual can grow personally and reach their potential.

DEFINITION

ID

The instinctive basis of our personality. It is what drives us to seek to please.

EGO

The logical aspect of our personality.

SUPEREGO

The conscience aspect of our personality. This is dictated to us by the social norms of our culture – in other words, how others in our society expect us to behave.

this approach you should read the works of Maslow (1954). In summary, the humanistic approach states that individuals have a need to *self-actualise* and to strive to realise their potential as human beings.

Rogers (1961) researched the process of trying to reach self-actualisation and stated that individuals like to feel good about themselves, which he called *positive self-regard*. He also hypothesised that we all need the approval of others and he called this *conditional positive regard*.

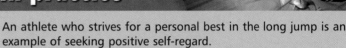

In practice

An athlete who strives for a personal best in the long jump is an example of seeking positive self-regard.

A young swimmer may be attending training because she does not want to let down her parents who have a high regard for her success in the sport. This is an example of conditional positive regard.

Freud's psychoanalytical approach has had a great impact on psychology, and in particular the treatment of psychological disorders. Freud studied individuals in depth and analysed much of what they said and did.

According to Freud, our personalities are made up of the *id*, the *ego* and the *superego*.

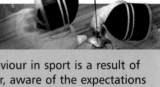

In practice

Freud would see that aggressive behaviour in sport is a result of our instincts (the id). We are, however, aware of the expectations of others and the rules of competition, which tells us that our aggressive antics are wrong (the ego). We therefore find more acceptable ways of releasing our aggressive drives and the superego aspect of our personality directs us to get rid of our anger through 'displacement' – for example, kicking the ball away in football when the referee seemingly makes a 'wrong' decision. The escape of anger and our subsequent feelings of relief is known as catharsis (dealt with later in this chapter).

Freud stated that the ego 'referees' or resolves conflicts between the id and the superego. This approach has particular relevance to aggressive behaviour in sport, and is dealt with later in this chapter.

Eysenck (1970) stated that personality is 'the more or less stable and enduring organisation of a person's character, temperament, intellect and physique which determines the unique adjustment to the environment'. When teaching and coaching individuals it is important that we treat each person as an individual with different feelings and motives. The key to getting the best from each person is to get to know them well.

Personality also involves (among many other factors) how anxious a person becomes in a particular situation and whether he or she can concentrate in any given situation. Gill gives a very good summary of personality:

> Personality is an overall pattern of psychological characteristics that makes each person a unique individual.

25.1.6 *Profile of mood states*

Our personalities are made up of behaviours that are often called *moods*. These are personality states that are related to a particular situation. They are changeable and depend on our environment. The Profile of mood states (or POMS) was designed by McNair, Lorr and Droppleman (1971) to measure the moods of:

* tension
* depression
* anger
* vigour
* fatigue
* confusion.

This profile has been used by sports psychologists to measure the moods of top sportspeople (elite athletes) and unsuccessful sportspeople. Morgan (1979) found that there was a significant difference between the two types of sportspeople. Figure 25.3 illustrates this difference.

Figure 25.3 shows that unsuccessful sportspeople have moods that are fairly consistent (a fairly flat profile). Successful sportspeople, however, show a very different profile. All moods, except anger and vigour, are lower than in unsuccessful sportspeople. The score on vigour is significantly higher, giving an iceberg shape – hence the name *iceberg profile*. Many top athletes have this profile, although it has also been revealed that athletes that are overtrained can revert to the unsuccessful profile.

Using the POMS for selection purposes is dangerous, because moods can be so changeable. It does, however, give an idea of the personality state a person is in at a particular time and this could indicate to the coach that something is wrong. He or she can therefore use intervention strategies – for instance, stress management techniques or motivational techniques if the vigour score is low.

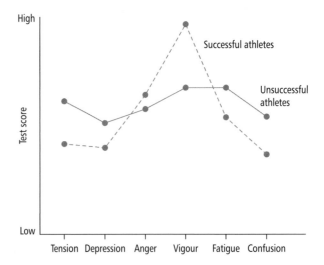

Figure 25.3
Scores for athletes using POMS and illustrating the iceberg principle.

25.1.7 *Measurement of personality*

There are many methods of assessing the personality of an individual (e.g. POMS). All methods have problems with reliability and validity.

Interviews

This method seeks to assess the personality of someone through discussions with them. Projective measures, such as the Rorschach ink-blot test, have been popular with clinical psychologists and psychoanalytical theorists who take the Freudian approach. In this test the subject is presented with an ink blot and he must say what he thinks the picture represents. The responses are then scored and analysed. For example, intelligence is associated with the use of the whole blot and obstinacy is thought to be associated with use of the white space.

Questionnaires

These are sometimes referred to as objective psychological inventories. The use of questionnaires is the most common way of assessing personality. The most common questionnaires used for sports personality research are Cattell's 16PF and Spielberger's Sport Competition Anxiety Test (SCAT). The latter test is discussed in more detail in Chapter 27.

Observing behaviour

The subject is watched and their behaviour characteristics recorded. The validity of this method can be very low – if the subject knows that they are being observed, then that in itself will modify the subject's behaviour. The researcher may be too subjective in analysing what he or she sees. What one person reads into a situation may be completely different from another researcher's assessment. Observation of behaviour can, however, be valuable in conjunction with other research instruments.

activity

Read about the Rorschach ink-blot test in any basic psychology book. Assess its reliability and validity. What value does it have for assessing someone's sporting capabilities?

DEFINITION

RELIABILITY

Reliable research achieves consistency of results after two or more applications of tests.

VALIDITY

There are two types of validity. Internal validity assesses whether the research measures what it is supposed to measure. The research instrument or method must be scientific and unwanted variables that are peripheral (nuisance or confounding variables) are kept to a minimum. External validity assesses whether the results of the research can be generalised to the population as a whole. If the sample used is not representative, then the research has low external validity. Laboratory experiments generally have much lower external validity values than field experiments (which are carried out in real-life situations).

activity

Ask someone to observe with you a person involved in a sporting activity, live or from the television or video. Both of you write down the personality characteristics being displayed (e.g. aggression, extroversion, determination). How can you account for any differences in your assessments?

25.1.8 *Personality research and sports performance*

There is an abundance of research articles on the links between personality and sport – many contradict each other and almost all are too general in their treatment and their conclusions. Many sports psychologists feel that personality traits have little or no bearing on whether someone will be a good sportsperson or not.

Two different groups of psychologists have emerged (Morgan, 1979): the 'sceptical' group, who feel that the study of personality and its link with sport is of little value, and the 'credulous' group, who feel that there is some link between personality, participation and performance in sport.

Various personality tests have been used to screen and select performers for teams but very few coaches would put much

DEFINITION

PROJECTIVE TESTS

Early in the twentieth century, Freud's ideas about the unconscious led to measuring methods that were based on the premise that an individual will reveal their personality characteristics under the appropriate conditions. If the subject is given ambiguous stimuli, according to this approach, he or she will be caught off guard and will reveal their true self.

emphasis on this type of screening alone for selection. The ambiguity of the available research points towards this type of screening being foolhardy.

Some research has been undertaken to study the effects of sport on personality, rather than the other way around. It is often stated that physical education is character-building and that sport can develop social qualities like teamwork, which could then be transferred to other situations. Many outdoor pursuits courses are being marketed as helping to build leadership qualities and teamwork but unfortunately the claims made for these courses are not backed up by valid research – although many people involved in sport would say that it has enriched their lives. A link has been suggested between physical exercise and psychological well-being (Gill, 1986).

Students who are interested should do some further reading about the links between personality and performance. Suggested further reading is listed at the end of Part 5.

There may well be a link between physical exercise and mental health

Key revision points

The trait approach to personality research sees personality as a relatively enduring characteristic which can predict a person's behaviour in a variety of different situations. Traits can be generalised. The social learning approach sees personality as being affected by the environment, including the actions of others. The interactionist approach combines both sides of the argument and can be summarised as B = f(PE). There are many different ways of measuring personality but to be worthwhile research must be reliable and valid. The most valid research instrument (although a combination of many is to be recommended) is the objective questionnaire, which is usually a self-report. Personality research is mostly confusing and many contradictory conclusions have been drawn. It is very dangerous to assume that particular traits suit particular sports. The claims that physical education and sport can affect personality can be backed up anecdotally but there is little scientific evidence to prove the claims.

Prejudice is unfair and decisions are made without adequate or accurate information

activity

Choose an attitude object – a particular sport, or physical education in general. Express your attitude by writing down how you feel about the attitude object. Where have these feelings and beliefs come from?

25.2 Attitudes

We often refer to sportspeople or participants in physical education as having a particular 'attitude', whether positive or negative – but what do we mean by 'attitude'? Attitudes can be seen as a part of someone's personality but they tend not to be regarded as a particular trait. Attitudes are normally directed towards a particular situation, although they are fairly enduring once they have been formed.

Triandis (1977) defines an attitude as 'an idea charged with emotion which predisposes a class of actions to a particular class of social situations'. Mednick (1991) states that an attitude is 'a predisposition to act in a certain way towards some aspect of a person's environment, including other people'.

Whatever definition is chosen there seems to be agreement that we take our attitudes around with us and apply them to particular situations, objects or people. The focus of one's attitude is called the *attitude object*. Attitudes are learned rather than innate and tend to be judgemental. If an attitude is based on false information and is unfair, then it becomes *prejudice*.

25.2.1 *The triadic model of attitudes*

As the name suggests, this model has three elements to it:
1 Beliefs – this is the *cognitive* element.
2 Emotions – this is the *affective* element.
3 Behaviour – this is the *behavioural* element.

This model states that attitudes are formed through influences on these three elements.

Our beliefs are formed through our past experiences and by what we have learned from others. Many of our beliefs are learned from our parents or peers. People who are significant to us are more likely to influence our beliefs.

Our emotional reactions to an attitude object, whether we like or dislike it, also depend on past experiences. If we have previously experienced satisfaction and enjoyment, then if we find ourselves in a similar situation we are more likely to look forward to liking the experience.

Our behaviour is not always consistent with our attitude, for instance we may believe that exercise is good for us and may enjoy participating but we may not exercise very much. We are, however, more likely to behave in a way that reveals our attitude.

In practice

Your attitude to fitness training could be made up of the belief that fitness training will keep you fit and will enhance your body image – this is the *cognitive* element of your attitude. You enjoy fitness training and you have fun being with others who are training with you – this is the *affective* element of your attitude. You go fitness training twice a week – this is the *behavioural* element of your attitude.

A positive attitude can lead to participation

PREJUDICE

This is a prejudgement – someone evaluates a situation before receiving adequate information. It is possible to be prejudiced in favour of something, although psychological research has focused on negative prejudice. Prejudice in a sports context has been seen in crowd behaviour at football matches, for instance. There is a tendency to overvalue the 'in group' and to undervalue the 'out group' and there is pressure for conformity and group cohesion. Allport (1935) stated that prejudice is 'an antipathy based upon a faulty and inflexible generalisation'.

There is continued support for the notion that attitudes are not always linked with behaviour, but the triadic model is still relevant as long as we are not inflexible in its use. All elements must be consistent if an attitude is to be stable and this interdependence is the key to changing attitudes.

25.2.2 *Attitudes and behaviour*

Although the triadic model views behaviour as being closely linked with the other two components, this has not always been evident in observable behaviour. The famous study by La Piere in 1934 is often used to demonstrate the weak link between attitudes and behaviour and although the study is nothing to do with physical education and sport directly, we can apply his findings.

La Piere's study

For two years, during the early 1930s, La Piere travelled around the USA with a Chinese couple, visiting 251 hotels and restaurants. At this period prejudice against the Chinese in America was particularly high, but they were turned away from only one establishment. Six months later La Piere wrote to each of the establishments they had visited and asked if they would accept Chinese customers – 92% indicated that they would not welcome Chinese visitors. There is clearly much inconsistency between attitudes and behaviour.

We can learn from La Piere's study that prejudice can affect behaviour. Attitudes expressed as a behaviour in one context (welcoming the Chinese personally) are different to the attitudes expressed in a written response. In sport, a simplified example could be: a black football player is openly welcomed to the football club but not picked for the team because of racial prejudice rather than ability.

Fishbein's theory

In 1975, Fishbein and Ajzen tried to resolve the problem of the link between attitude and behaviour and demonstrated that only specific attitudes can affect specific behaviours. For instance, a schoolgirl may have a positive attitude to physical education but this may not mean that she participates very often; she also has a positive attitude to specifically playing five-a-side football, and is more likely to participate.

The theory they developed states that the best predictor of behaviour is the individual's 'behavioural intention'. To predict whether a school child is likely to participate in five-a-side football, we should ask her whether she intends to participate. Research has consistently revealed that if a person intends to participate in a particular activity, then they are more likely to do so.

We can learn from Fishbein that if we develop positive attitudes to physical education and sport, participation is more likely because the intention to participate is more pronounced. Fishbein also highlighted the importance of the influences of family and friends and also the environmental setting. If a young person's family supports participation in sport and the facilities are good, then his or her positive attitude to sport is more likely to result in actual participation.

25.2.3 *Changing attitudes*

As a physical educationalist, sports coach or any person involved with promoting the benefits of exercise, you are probably trying to develop positive attitudes and change negative attitudes. Our knowledge of what makes up attitudes and their influences gives us some useful information about how we might go about changing negative attitudes into positive ones.

Persuasion is important in changing attitudes or an element of an attitude. For instance, if you can persuade someone that exercise is fun, then you are on the way to getting them to participate.

The effectiveness of persuasion depends on:
- the person doing the persuading
- the quality of the message
- the characteristics of who is being persuaded.

In order to promote exercise and change the attitudes of those that are 'non-exercisers', the person doing the persuading should have high status. Teachers or coaches have been given authority – a position – therefore they are more likely to be of high status. They may be fit themselves and become role models and they may have good communication/leadership skills. See the later section on leadership (p. 311) for more information.

For persuasion to be successful, the message must make sense and be believable. The information given must be accurate, unambiguous and clear.

The people you are trying to persuade may be intelligent enough to understand the message, but may not accept it. They may put up counter arguments such as 'I haven't got the time to exercise' or 'I might get injured'.

The effectiveness of persuasion depends on the leader, the message and the audience

activity

If you are a student, think of a sport which is not represented in your institution. Seek to persuade the person that has the power (the Head of PE) to run the activity. Think about how you would present your case and the evidence you could use to support your arguments. If you are involved in promoting sport, think of ways in which you can promote physical activity in your local community. Who would front the campaign? What information needs to be put across? Who is your target audience?

In practice

A teacher wants to promote gymnastics to a group of boys. Their attitudes are generally negative because many of them believe that gymnastics is a feminine activity (belief 1). The teacher introduces the class to an older boy, who clearly has high muscle definition and who shows a number of exercises showing strength and courage. The boys are now starting to believe that gymnastics is far more masculine than they previously thought (belief 2). Belief 2 may cause many of the boys to experience dissonance or a disagreement within their own minds. It may take over and dominate belief 1 for many of the boys, whose negative attitude changes to a positive one.

Attitudes towards an activity – for example, gymnastics – can be changed through cognitive dissonance

The most popular theory related to attitude change is Festinger's theory of *cognitive dissonance* (1957). This theory states that all of the three elements involved in an attitude, according to the triadic model, should be consistent if the attitude is to remain stable and the individual to be content. If a change of attitude is desired the individual must experience two or more opposing beliefs. This causes the individual to feel uncomfortable because of the disharmony or dissonance that has been created in the mind. To be comfortable once again, one of these beliefs needs to be dominant, which is where teachers and coaches can influence the attitude of the individual.

25.2.4 *Attitudes associated with physical education and sport*

In physical education, recreation and sport some people possess positive attitudes because:
* they believe in the value of exercise
* they enjoy the activities and have fun or enjoy competition
* they are good at the activity
* they experience excitement because of the physical challenge
* they enjoy the physical sensations and personal expression
* they experience relaxation and see it as an escape from stress (catharsis)
* they see participation as a social norm.

Some have negative attitudes to physical activity because:
* they believe that it is harmful or that they are better off doing other activities
* they dislike the experiences involved
* they lack the physical or perceptual skills necessary for success
* they are frightened of the activity
* they experience stress and anxiety when they participate
* they see the social norm as being non-participation.

Differences in attitudes between boys and girls

Smoll and Schutz (1980) investigated the differences in attitudes towards physical activity between boys and girls. They found that girls were more positive towards the aesthetic activities (e.g. dance). Boys were more positive than girls towards activities that obviously involved physical challenge (e.g. wrestling). It was also found, however, that these attitudes changed over time – showing that attitudes are not necessarily enduring.

activity

Try to account for the differences highlighted by Smoll and Schutz.

Boys and girls are often attracted to different activities because of their attitudes

25.2.5 *Expected behaviour and stereotypes*

There is often enormous social pressure on people to behave in a particular way and to hold certain attitudes. Research has shown that others' expectations of a particular individual can lead to those expectations being fulfilled. A teacher who has high expectations can influence the pupils' expectations and this in turn can motivate them to achieve more. *Stereotyping* can also influence our expectations.

DEFINITION

SOCIAL NORMS

These are behaviours that are deemed 'normal' within a culture and are created through a process called socialisation, which is dealt with later in this part of the book. Some people feel that participation in physical activity is important to be accepted as part of their peer group or in a wider context to be accepted within society. Others may feel that physical activity is not essential for acceptance.

ⓘ To find out more about socialisation, turn to page 306.

DEFINITION

STEREOTYPE

A belief held by a collection of people about traits shared by a certain category of person is called a stereotype. Brown (1981) simply defines a stereotype as 'a shared conception of the character of a group'.

There are many stereotypes in sport, and these can influence our attitudes. For instance, 'boys are no good at dance-type activities or creative movements', 'strength activities are less suited to girls', 'black people are no good at swimming' or 'white people are not so good at sprinting'. These stereotypes are constantly being challenged but they persist and can influence expectations – which, as we have seen, can influence attitudes.

Teachers, coaches and all who try to promote exercise and sport must continue to challenge stereotypes and the prejudice that results from them. Many people have talents that are as yet undiscovered or feel unable to express themselves because of stereotyping. As we have seen, although attitudes do not necessarily predict behaviour, they can certainly influence it.

25.2.6 Measuring attitudes

To find out what type of attitudes are held by sportspeople (and therefore whether the coach needs to reinforce positive attitudes or seek to change the negative ones), attitudes have to be measured. Observation is one method of measuring attitude (this was discussed in the section on personality). The main problem with this approach is that behaviour does not always signify actual attitudes. Some physiological tests may be useful (e.g. testing the heart rate may reveal attitudes to stressful situations). However, most attitude measurement is through *attitude scales*.

The most popular scales are the Thurstone Scale, the Likert Scale and Osgood's Semantic Differential Scale.

We must continue to challenge stereotypes to give equal opportunities

Thurstone Scale

This scale was devised by Thurstone (1931) and includes many statements which reveal attitudes towards a particular attitude object. The respondent has to read each statement and tick the ones that he or she agrees with. A score is then calculated. It is useful if you compare scores with other people.

Likert Scale (1932)

This is a very common method used by psychologists. Like the Thurstone Scale it uses statements, but the respondents state *how much* they agree with the statement on a scale, for instance from 'strongly agree' to 'strongly disagree'. Each respondent is scored and their attitudes revealed.

Osgood's Semantic Differential Scale (1957)

This includes a statement followed by two opposite words, e.g. relaxed and anxious, with a seven-point scale between the two words. The respondent has to circle the value that most closely matches his or her attitude. For example:

Rate how you feel about competition in physical education. Circle the point which describes how you feel.

Good   +3   +2   +1   0   −1   −2   −3   Bad

The researcher then calculates the respondent's attitudes from the completed questionnaire.

Problems with attitude scales

- The respondent might not understand the scale.
- The same statement can mean different things to different people.
- There may be demand characteristics – the respondent could answer in the way he or she thinks they ought to answer.
- The statement itself may influence the individual's response.
- The results may be difficult to relate to sports performance.

DEFINITION

ATTITUDE SCALES

These often list a number of statements, and the respondent has to note how they feel about a particular statement and whether it applies to them by rating how they feel on a scale. The researcher looks at all the responses and then calculates the attitude of that individual.

Key revision points

Attitudes are learned and are made up of beliefs, emotions and the way we behave (cognitive, affective, behavioural) – this is called the triadic model. Prejudice is an extreme form of attitude – it is judgemental and inflexible. Attitudes are not always linked to behaviour but are more likely to be if the attitude is specific towards a specific attitude object. Attitudes can be changed through persuasion and through cognitive dissonance. Attitudes depend largely on previous experience and social learning – we tend to follow social norms. Expectations of behaviour can influence actual behaviour. Stereotyping persists in sport and physical education but is constantly being challenged and equal opportunities are now more realisable.

25.3 Aggression

activity

After reading the following paragraphs on aggression, identify which of the following examples show aggression and which show assertion:

- an athlete shoulder-pushing another on the final bend in a 1500 metre race
- a boxer landing the final knock-out punch
- a rugby forward player punching a member of the opposition in a scrum
- a cyclist in a race cutting up another rider and causing a pile-up
- a squash player smashing her racquet against the wall in frustration
- a football player pulling another player off the ball by the shirt
- a netball player verbally abusing another player.

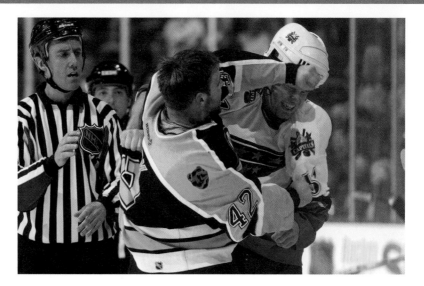

Aggression is the intent to harm outside the rules of the game

The term aggression is used widely in sport but it is important to distinguish between the aggression that is desirable and what is unacceptable. Let us first define what we mean by 'aggression'. Dollard (1939) defined aggression as 'a response having for its goal the injury of a human organism'. Baron (1977) states that 'aggression is any form of behaviour directed toward the goal of harming or injuring another living being who is motivated to avoid such treatment'. Most definitions agree that it is the *intent to harm* which makes an action aggressive. For the purposes of this book we will take aggression as being the intent to harm *outside the laws of the event*. In sport it is often very difficult to distinguish between what is aggressive behaviour and what is not.

Aggressive behaviour that is controlled within the laws of the game is seen as assertion rather than aggression. *Assertion*, instrumental or channelled aggression, is preferable in sport and pure aggression, or reactive aggression, should be discouraged. A player who is aggressive as defined in the previous paragraph is likely to under-achieve, to get injured themselves or to be removed from the game.

25.3.1 *Instinct theory*

This theory views aggression as being a natural response. Aggression is clearly instinctive and is important in the well-being and evolutionary development of the species. Defending the territory is a common expression of aggression in animals. Human behaviour, however, is far more complex and there are problems in relating the animal instinct to the behaviour of a human being. The fundamental problem with the instinct theory is that you would expect all humans (even from different cultures) to display similar tendencies, but this is not so. The major advocate of this theory, after Freud, is Lorenz (1966), who applied the instincts of animals to humans and said that humans generate aggressive energy that needs to be released. Freud stated that aggressive impulses would build up inside an individual and if not released through aggressive acts would become dangerous to the individual's well-being. Lorenz believed that the natural build-up of aggression needs release, either through an antisocial act or via more acceptable behaviour.

The following arguments may be made against this theory:
- early humans were not warriors but 'hunter-gatherers'
- close evolutionary relatives, such as gorillas, would also be expected to be highly aggressive – they are not
- human aggression is often not spontaneous
- human aggression is often learned, and many cultural differences back this up.

Modern psychologists feel that this simplified view is too generalised, that in human aggression more reasoning is involved and that aggression is often a learned response rather than a purely instinctive one.

DRIVE

This is directed, motivated or 'energised' behaviour that an individual has towards achieving a certain goal. The link between drive and motivation is dealt with later in this part of the book.

CATHARSIS

This is the release of frustration which leads to a feeling of well-being – literally 'cleansing of the soul'.

25.3.2 Frustration–aggression hypothesis

This hypothesis was devised by Dollard and co-workers in 1939. It is closely allied to the instinct theory but has more evidence to back it up. The hypothesis states that frustration will always lead to aggression, because any blocking of goals that an individual is trying to reach increases that individual's *drive*, which in turn increases aggression. Aggression, once initiated, will then reduce the frustration, leading to *catharsis*.

Look at the model of the frustration–aggression hypothesis in Figure 25.4. Use an example from sport to explain each part of the model.

Figure 25.4 *The frustration–aggression hypothesis*

Frustration has been seen as one of the causes of aggression

The problem with this theory is that frustration does not always lead to aggression and aggression often occurs with no evidence of frustration. Berkowitz (1974) brings this theory closer to the social learning view when he states that frustration can make an individual potentially aggressive but is not sufficient on its own to cause aggressive behaviour.

Identify practical examples of how a young person might learn to be aggressive in sport. Now write down a few strategies that you could employ to combat this aggression.

25.3.3 Aggressive cue hypothesis

This theory, proposed by Berkowitz (1969), states that when an individual is frustrated there is an increase in their arousal level, which creates a predisposition or readiness for aggression. If aggression is going to occur then, according to Berkowitz, certain stimuli must be present that act as cues for the athlete, who would then associate the cues with having to be aggressive. Figure 25.5 illustrates this theory.

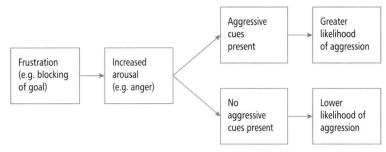

Figure 25.5
The aggressive cue hypothesis

A boxer may see the boxing ring as the cue for aggressive behaviour. List the cues which could trigger an aggressive response for a team player of your chosen sport. As the player's coach, how would you limit the effect of these cues?

An aggressive player can let the rest of the side down

 To find out more about Bandura, turn to Chapter 9 (page 97).

DEFINITION

SIGNIFICANT OTHERS
Those people who are held in high regard by an individual, for instance parents, top sportspeople or influential peers.

25.3.4 *Social learning theory*

Bandura (1973) is one of many who have advocated that aggression is a learned response rather than instinctive. The social learning theory states that we learn by observing the behaviour of others (sometimes known as vicarious processes) and/or by direct reinforcement of our own behaviour. There is more information about Bandura's research in Chapter 26. In sport and physical education, individuals will learn to be aggressive if they see *significant others* being aggressive or if their own aggression is reinforced by significant others.

The social learning theory disputes the idea that we have natural aggressive drives towards goals. This view is known as an optimistic one. If sportspeople can learn aggressive behaviour, then it must be true that they can learn non-aggressive tendencies.

25.3.5 *Eliminating aggressive tendencies in sport and physical education*

The following strategies could be employed to combat aggression.

1 Control the arousal level of the participant via stress management techniques such as relaxation or by focusing attention on the job in hand – this is sometimes called channelling aggression. (More about these types of techniques in Chapter 27.)
2 Avoid situations that initiate aggressive responses – for example by changing the sport or changing positions in the team.
3 Remove the aggressive player completely from the situation – for instance, a basketball coach may substitute an aggressive player out so that he or she can experience a period of calm.
4 Reinforce non-aggressive acts – if a player is successful by being assertive rather than aggressive, then reward him.
5 Show non-aggressive role models and highlight successful sportspeople who are not aggressive.
6 Punish an aggressive participant – for instance, use a fine system or drop the player from the team. The coach and the player could draw up a contract, setting out what would happen if the player lost control and became aggressive during a match.
7 Increase peer pressure to be non-aggressive. If significant others are seen not to reinforce aggressive acts, the aggression may not recur.
8 Give or highlight the player's position of responsibility. Show that aggression could let the rest of the team down.

You may be able to think of other ways of dealing with aggressive players.

To find out more about stress management, turn to page 324.

The motivation to participate and to perform well in sport can come from internal drives or from external pressures

> ### *Key revision points*
>
> *Aggression is the intent to harm outside the rules of the game. Another phrase for aggression is reactive aggression, and channelled aggression is also known as instrumental aggression and assertion. The instinct theory states that aggression is innate and it is natural to express it. Although there may be some truth that there are naturally aggressive responses, the instinct theory has been largely discredited. The frustration–aggression hypothesis is a drive theory, which states that blocking goals can cause frustration to build up. This can then result in aggression which leads to catharsis. This theory seems to be valid if aggression is seen as potential rather than actual. The social learning theory states that we learn to be aggressive by watching significant others being aggressive and also if the aggression of significant others is reinforced. This is known as an optimistic approach. Strategies to combat aggression include internal control of arousal levels, punishment and reinforcement of non-aggressive behaviour. All three of these theories probably have some bearing on why aggression occurs.*

25.4 Achievement motivation

We have already looked at some of the links between personality and performance. One important aspect which needs more detailed investigation is why some people are more motivated to compete than others. Competition is an important aspect in sport, and some people are more competitive than others. *Achievement motivation* is a concept that sports psychologists have developed to link personality to competition.

The theory of achievement motivation is an interaction model, the characteristics of which we have discussed in Section 25.1. According to this, model behaviour is determined by the person's interaction with their environment. Some people have a greater need to achieve ('*Nach*') than others and have what is known as 'approach behaviours'. People at the other end of the scale seem to avoid competitive situations because they need to avoid failure ('*Naf*') and have what is known as 'avoidance' behaviours. Either type of behaviour is more likely to occur when an individual is in an evaluative situation – when someone feels that they are being judged. In sport, evaluation of performance is often occurring and sport is thought to attract more '*Nach*' than '*Naf*' personalities. 'Need to achieve' personalities like a challenge and will take risks.

'*Nach*' personality types are characterised by:
- high task persistence (they stick to the job in hand)
- the ability to complete a task quickly
- a willingness to take reasonable risks
- having a liking for challenging situations
- being able to take responsibility for their actions
- welcoming feedback about their results and their performance.

'Need to achieve' personalities like a challenge and will take risks

'*Naf*' personality types tend to:
- give up easily
- take their time to complete the task or do not complete the task at all
- seek situations that present little challenge
- avoid personal responsibility
- not want to receive feedback about results or performance.

The reasons we give for winning or losing can affect our future motivation

25.4.1 *Application of achievement motivation theory*

Recent work has revealed weaknesses in this view of achievement motivation. It has been suggested that success is interpreted by different people in different ways. Some may see success as beating someone else and showing their superiority – these people are known as 'ego' oriented. Others may see success as being internal, a kind of self-competition (e.g. a personal best is seen as being successful) – these people are known as 'task oriented'. Ego-oriented people are thought to believe that ability is most important for success, whereas task-oriented people regard effort as being more important.

An understanding of the type of motive that drives a particular individual can help to formulate a relevant motivational strategy and improve performance.

Tests have been developed which are claimed to determine the achievement orientation of any individual. An example is Gill and Deeter's sport-specific inventories. These tests can be unreliable and there is no substitute for finding out what motivates someone by talking to them and observing their behaviour in different situations. Most people have a mixture of motives but usually some motives are stronger than others.

25.4.2 **Competitiveness**

This involves the drive or desire to succeed in sports activities. Gill (1986) developed the Sport Orientation Questionnaire (SOQ) that assessed competitiveness, win orientation and goal orientation. Subsequent research using the SOQ not surprisingly showed that athletes are far more competitive than non-athletes but were more concerned with performance than the actual outcome of the event. See link between competitiveness and confidence later in this chapter.

> ### *Key revision points*
> *Achievement motivation is related to a performer's reaction to competition. There are two types of motives – need to achieve (Nach) and need to avoid failure (Naf). Both types of behaviour are more likely to occur in an evaluative situation. Ego-oriented personality types believe that ability is important, but task-oriented people regard effort as more important. Recognition of types of motive can help with motivational strategies such as goal-setting.*

25.5 **Attributions**

Attributions are the perceived causes of a particular outcome. In sport these are often the reasons we give for the results we achieve. For example, a team member may cite the bad weather conditions as a reason for the team losing.

Attributions are important because of the way in which they affect motivation, which in turn affects future performances, future effort and even whether the individual continues to participate. A young person who is told that they failed because they do not have

activity

Think back to your last competitive experience. Write down the reasons that you can think of now for the result you achieved.

Instructors tend to criticise lack of effort and controllable failures

enough ability to succeed is unlikely to try again. If the same individual is given reasons that he or she can work on, such as 'need to try harder', he or she is more likely to continue and to heed the advice.

The model in Figure 25.6 is a well-known representation of the process of attribution. At times inappropriate attributions are given and, for the sake of future success, it is important to change these to ones that are going to be far more helpful. This is known as *attribution retraining*.

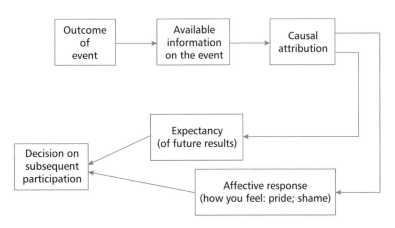

Figure 25.6 *The attribution process*

Locus of causality

	Internal	External
Stable	Ability	Task difficulty
Unstable	Effort	Luck

Stability

Figure 25.7 *Weiner's classification for causal attributions*

Weiner (1979) identified four main reasons given for examination results: ability, effort, task difficulty and luck. He then constructed a two-dimensional model which he called the *locus of causality and stability*. The locus of causality refers to whether the attributions come from within the person (*internal*) or from the environment (*external*). Stability refers to whether the attribution is changeable or unchangeable. Weiner's classification for causal attributions is shown in Figure 25.7.

25.5.1 Attribution theory related to sport

Weiner's model is not sports specific, which causes problems when trying to apply it to sports situations. For instance, task difficulty changes frequently in sport, especially in team games because the opposition changes. Roberts and Pascuzzi (1979) related Weiner's model to sport. They found that the two-dimensional model was still relevant but that far more attributions were given than Weiner's main four. Their model is shown in Figure 25.8.

People who lose tend to attribute their failure to external causes and those who succeed usually attribute their success to internal causes. This is known as the *self-serving bias*. This bias limits the sense of shame due to failure and highlights personal achievement in success. The stability dimension of the model will affect achievement motivation. If the reasons given for winning are stable reasons, the individual is motivated to achieve again. If failure is attributed to an unstable factor the individual is more likely to try again because there is a good chance that the outcome will change.

A third dimension has recently been added to this attribution model – the dimension of *controllability*.

Locus of causality

		Internal	External
Stability	Stable	Ability	Coaching
	Unstable	Effort	Luck
		Unstable ability	Task difficulty
		Psychological factors	Teamwork
			Officials
		Practice	

Figure 25.8 *The attribution model of Roberts and Pascuzzi*

25.5.2 Learned helplessness

This phrase was first used by Dweck in 1980. It refers to a belief that failure is inevitable and a feeling of hopelessness when faced with a particular situation (*specific learned helplessness*) or groups of situations (*global learned helplessness*).

Low achievers often attribute their failure to uncontrollable factors, which can lead to learned helplessness. Dweck saw high achievers as people who are oriented towards mastery and see failure as a learning experience, and who will attribute failure to controllable unstable factors. This fits into Atkinson's model of achievement motivation – the Nach performers are not afraid of failing and will persist with a task until they succeed (see Section 25.4).

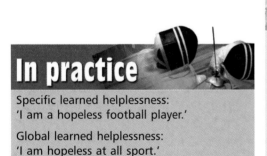

DEFINITION

CONTROLLABILITY

This refers to whether attributions are under the control of the performer or under the control of others. Coaches and teachers tend to praise effort and controllable success and punish or criticise lack of effort and controllable failures. Concentrating on uncontrollable external and stable factors is not of much use if you want to turn failure into success.

activity

Imagine you are a coach of a sports team. Read the following scenarios and write down what attributions you would encourage. Justify your answers by using the theories that we have investigated.

1 Your team won and played well.
2 Your team won but played badly.
3 Your team lost and played well.
4 Your team lost and played badly.

In practice

Specific learned helplessness:
'I am a hopeless football player.'

Global learned helplessness:
'I am hopeless at all sport.'

25.5.3 Attribution retraining

Many attributions that are given are subjective and are therefore not desirable for future progression. For instance, I used to play for a team that constantly blamed the officials for their poor results. Although this helped to draw the team together, they got a bad reputation with most officials and they were not attributing to changeable or (in this case) realistic factors. Attributions often need to be reassessed in order to succeed in the future.

In practice

A person who fails in a task should be encouraged to attribute to controllable unstable factors. For example, a team of 12-year-old girls who have just narrowly lost a hockey match should be encouraged to give attributions such as 'must try harder next week' (these are internal, unstable and controllable).

To help those who have failed and are starting to experience learned helplessness, teachers and coaches should concentrate on the positive attributions. If a performer feels that they lack ability he or she will inevitably fail, but their attribution could be changed to 'having the wrong tactics' or 'slight alteration of technique needed'. The performer may then be disappointed rather than frustrated and will persist with the task rather than avoid it altogether. This process is known as *attribution retraining*.

Key revision points
Attributions are the reasons we give for winning or losing.
Attributions can affect motivation and therefore future performance.
Weiner's model of attribution is two-dimensional, including where the attributions have come from (the locus of causality) and whether they are stable or not (the locus of stability). A third dimension (controllability) has been added, which refers to whether the performer has control over the causes of failure. Low achievers can suffer from learned helplessness, which can be global or specific. Attributing to uncontrollable, stable and internal factors can lead to learned helplessness. Attribution retraining can help to change attributions and minimise the effects of learned helplessness.

Being worried is a natural response and can help to prepare the body for action

activity

Write down the situations in your sport where you feel a low sense of self-efficacy. How do you account for these feelings of low self-confidence?

activity

You would like a fellow student to attempt a high jump but he has low self-confidence. Using Bandura's four factors which influence self-efficacy, state how you would try and raise the athlete's self-efficacy in this situation.

25.6 Self-efficacy

Motivation is often affected by the degree of self-confidence that an individual has. *Self-confidence* is a rather global term which infers a general disposition. According to Bandura (1977) self-confidence can often be specific to a particular situation – Bandura called this *self-efficacy*. This specific confidence can vary from situation to situation and, according to Bandura, can affect performance if the individual is skilful enough. People who expect to be confident in a particular situation are more likely to choose that activity. Conversely, people who expect to have low self-efficacy in a situation will avoid that particular activity.

Our expectations of whether or not self-confidence is going to be high or low may determine the activity we choose, the amount of effort we put into it and whether we stick with the task or give up easily.

25.6.1 *Factors affecting self-efficacy*

Our expectations of self-efficacy depend on four types of information.

Performance accomplishments. These probably have the strongest influence on self-confidence. If success has been experienced in the past, especially if it has been attributed to controllable factors, then feelings of self-confidence are likely to be high.

Vicarious experiences. This refers to what we have observed before. If we watch others perform and be successful, then we are more likely to experience high self-efficacy, as long as the performers we are watching are of a similar standard.

Verbal persuasion. If we are encouraged to try a particular activity, our confidence in that situation may increase. The effectiveness of this encouragement depends upon who is encouraging us and in what ways. Significant others are more likely to persuade us to 'have a go' than strangers.

Emotional arousal. Our perceptions of how aroused we are can affect our confidence in a particular situation. If you have effective strategies to control physiological and psychological arousal levels (perhaps the ability to relax or to use mental rehearsal) then you are more likely to have high self-efficacy. These are illustrated in Figure 25.9.

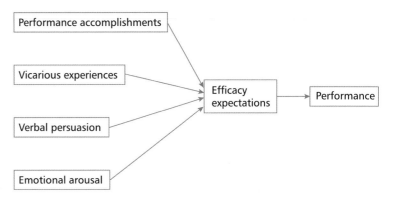

Figure 25.9
Information affecting self-efficacy

In practice

Here are a few strategies that you could use to raise the level of self-efficacy of the athlete in the last activity.

1 Try to give him initial success by lowering the bar to start with, or using some flexi-rope.
2 Demonstrate how it can be done or, if you are much better than him, use someone of similar ability. An actual demonstration (live modelling) can be more effective in raising self-confidence than a video recording.
3 Verbally encourage the athlete. Tell him that he should 'have a go', that you think that he will succeed – even that the mat is nice and soft!
4 Tell him that to be worried is a natural, very positive response because it prepares the body well. Alternatively, teach him some relaxation techniques or how to mentally rehearse the activity (but be aware that this could increase his anxiety).

DEFINITION

SPORT CONFIDENCE

This is the belief or degree of certainty individuals possess about their ability to be successful in sport (Vealey, 1986).

25.6.2 *Vealey's sport confidence model*

Vealey's sport-specific model of sport confidence (1986) investigates the relationship between achievement motivation or competitiveness and self-confidence in sport. The model shown in Figure 25.10 is situation-specific and shows that every sportsperson or athlete has an existing level of sport confidence which is a trait (SC-trait) and a level of competitiveness. The amount of SC-trait and competitive orientation are indicative of the confidence that can be shown in a specific situation in sport (SC-state) or level of self-efficacy during competition. The level of SC-state then dictates, according to this model, the behaviour that is shown and the skill level of the performance. If the athlete has a high level of SC-state then their behaviour is more likely to be confident and well-motivated and consequently performance is likely to improve. If, however, SC-state is low then the athlete's behaviour is likely to be tentative and lacking in confidence and he may therefore turn in a poor performance.

After the performance, again according to this model, either satisfaction or disappointment will prevail. These emotions will then in turn affect the confidence and the competitiveness of the athlete in future performances. Simply put – the more confident you are, the more successful you will be and the more successful you are, the more confident you will be!

In practice

Children should be helped to gain confidence in at least one sport or activity. This will enhance the general perception of sport confidence because the more sports that are experienced the more likely it is for success to be experienced. As the children's personality traits develop, they will experience greater levels of situation-specific sport confidence with new sports and activities. These children will then be much more likely to be motivated to persist in sports activities.

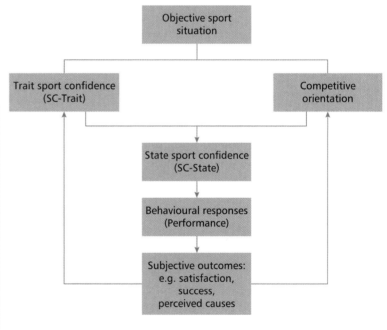

Figure 25.10 *Vealey's model*

Key revision points

Self-efficacy is self-confidence in a specific situation. Expectations of self-efficacy are closely linked to motivation and can affect the choice of activity, the amount of effort expended and persistence at the task. The factors affecting expectations (according to Bandura) are performance accomplishments, vicarious experiences, verbal persuasion and emotional arousal.

Key terms

Progress check

You should now understand the following terms. If you do not, go back through the chapter and find out what they mean.

Aggression
Aggressive cue hypothesis
Assertion
Attribution process
Attribution retraining
Cognitive dissonance
Credulous group
Frustration–aggression hypothesis
Instinct theory
Interactionist
Learned helplessness
Nach
Naf
Prejudice
Profile of Mood States
Psychoanalytical
Reliability
Self-efficacy
Sceptical group
Social learning
Social norms
Stereotypes
Trait
Triadic model
Validity
Vicarious experiences

1 Outline the trait approach to personality research.
2 What approach brings together trait and social learning perspectives?
3 Explain B = f(PE).
4 Using an example from personality research, explain what we mean by validity when we investigate research conclusions.
5 Give a definition of attitudes and describe the triadic model.
6 Do attitudes predict behaviour? Explain your answer using examples from sport or physical education.
7 What makes persuasion an effective way of changing attitudes?
8 Outline the cognitive dissonance theory of attitude change.
9 What is a stereotype? Give an example in a sporting context.
10 Define what is meant by aggression in a sports psychology context.
11 Draw a model to explain the frustration–aggression hypothesis.
12 Using social learning theory, who are we more likely to imitate and why?
13 List five ways of combating aggression in sport.
14 What are the characteristics of a person whose motive is primarily the need to achieve?
15 Why is attribution theory important in sports psychology?
16 Draw Weiner's model of causal attributions and explain it using examples from physical education or sport.
17 What creates learned helplessness and how can it be avoided?
18 Define self-efficacy and, using examples from physical education or sport, list the factors that affect it.

Social influences

Learning objectives

* To understand what is meant by social learning theory.
* To be able to relate social learning to physical education and sport.
* To be able to discover what makes a group or team successful.
* To understand the nature of and qualities related to leadership.
* To know the theories related to leadership styles and be able to apply them to situations in sport and physical education.
* To understand the effects of social facilitation on performance.
* To know how to develop strategies for coping with the effects of social facilitation.

As individuals we all differ, but we often experience similar pressures from the environment. Sportsmen and women take into their sports their own personalities but are also influenced by their culture and other people – players on the same pitch, members of the crowd or family and friends. These social influences can be extremely powerful in motivating us, or even pushing us into places we do not want to go! There are individuals who have been involved in mob violence outside a football stadium who say that they were not really there as individuals, rather the personality of the mob, or an influential leader was to blame. In this chapter we will investigate these social influences and assess how they help or hinder our progress in sport.

26.1 Social learning

In Chapter 25 we came across the concept of social learning. Social learning is a theme which runs throughout psychology. The opposing view, that behaviour is largely a result of innate responses, is also a common theme in psychology. The debate of 'nature versus nurture' is always active in the field of psychology. The social learning view has gained in popularity since the 1980s.

Individuals can lose themselves in the mob

DEFINITION

SOCIALISATION

The process through which children acquire the many behaviours they need to have as adult members of their culture. Socialisation is the process of adopting the norms and values of a culture. Children learn many important responses, including attitudes, values and aspects of self-control, through exposure to their parents and the people around them. Many studies reveal that we learn more from the deeds we witness than from the words we hear. Parents who have the 'do as I say and not as I do' approach often find their children imitating what they actually do.

Most sports activities are set within a social situation, where interaction with others is inevitable. When we investigated the sources of aggressive behaviour (Chapter 25) we learned that observation can lead to imitation. Social learning underpins *socialisation* and therefore dominates all of our behaviours.

Social learning theorists state that we learn by observing other people – this is known as *observational learning*. (See Chapter 9 for more information on observational learning.)

Social learning is often based on copying what we see, especially if that behaviour is reinforced

Key revision points
Social learning is a leading theory to explain human behaviour. In sport nearly all behaviour is set in a social context. Socialisation is the adoption of the norms and values of a culture and is learned mostly in childhood, although it goes on all through life.

26.2 Groups

Group behaviour is of particular interest in physical education and sport because there are many situations where participants and spectators operate within groups. The most common form of a group in sport is the team. To ensure that a team works together well and all the individuals within it maximise their potential, we must understand why and how people work together. The processes within a group and between groups are called *group dynamics* and the relationships within a group are extremely complex because of the many internal and external influences on group performance.

26.2.1 *Group or team formation*

The two main characteristics of a group or team are interaction and the sharing of common goals

The 'forming storming norming performing' theory remains a good explanation of team development and behaviour (Tuckman, 1965).

DEFINITION

GROUP

A group is a number of people who need to communicate with each other in many different ways and who work to some common objective or goal. Therefore a collection of people who just happen to be weight training in the same sports centre is not a group. Shaw (1976) defined a group as 'two or more persons who are interacting with one another in such a manner that each person influences and is influenced by each other person'. Carron (1980) sees a group as having 'a collective identity, a sense of shared purpose or objectives, structured patterns of interaction, structured modes of communication, personal and/or task interdependence and interpersonal attraction'. The model in Figure 26.1 represents this theory.

The progression of the model is as follows:

1 Forming
2 Storming
3 Norming
4 Performing.

Stage 1: Forming

At this stage there is high dependence on the leader for guidance and direction. There is very little agreement on the aims of the team. Each team member's individual roles are unclear and the team leader must be prepared to give strong direction.

Stage 2: Storming

Group decisions are difficult. Team members jostle for position in the team as they attempt to establish themselves in relation to other team members and the leader, who might receive challenges from team members. There is now a clearer focus for the team and they have a stronger sense of purpose, although there are many uncertainties. Cliques form at this stage and there may be power struggles. The team needs to be focused on its goals to avoid becoming distracted by relationships and emotional issues. There needs to be an environment of compromise to enable progress. The leader has a more advisory or coaching role.

Stage 3: Norming

There is now much more agreement and consensus of opinions in the team. Roles and responsibilities are clearer and generally accepted. Decisions that are very important are increasingly made through group agreement. Less important decisions are delegated to individuals or small teams within the group. There is now a much stronger sense of commitment and unity. The team are much more social at this stage and individuals are friendly with each other. There is general respect for the leader and leadership is more likely to be shared.

Stage 4: Performing

The team have more strategies and has a clear vision and clear aims. There is no interference or participation from the leader. There is a focus on achieving goals, and the team makes most of the decisions against criteria agreed with the leader. The team members are trusted to get on with the job in hand with little interference. Disagreements occur but now they are resolved within the team positively and the team makes necessary changes to processes and structure. The team is able to work and be personable at the same time. The team does not need to be instructed or assisted. Team members might ask for assistance from the leader with personal and interpersonal issues.

26.2.2 Cohesion

Cohesion is a term that is widely used when discussing group dynamics. It concerns the motivation which attracts individuals to the group and the resistance of those members to the group breaking up. Festinger (1963) states that cohesiveness is 'the total field of forces which act on members to remain in the group'.

According to Carron (1980) cohesion has two dimensions:

* *group integration* – how the individual members of the group feel about the group as a whole
* *individual attraction to the group* – how attracted the individuals are to the group.

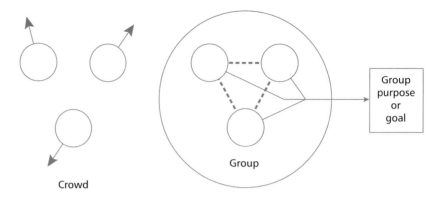

Figure 26.1 *Carron's theory. The broken lines represent group processes such as interaction, personal and task interdependence and communication. The large circle represents a collective identity, while the sense of shared purpose in groups contrasts with the independent behaviour of separate individuals*

In practice

The England rugby union team that won the 2003 World Cup was made up of individuals who had a high regard for all other members of the team and who resisted any break-up of the team after the competition finished. This is an example of group cohesion.

DEFINITION

PROCESS

The interaction behaviours within a group to target resources to group objectives: 'putting it all together'.

Figure 26.1 shows a diagrammatic representation of cohesion.

Widmeyer (1985) saw that these two dimensions could be either *social* motivation or *task* motivation. An individual might want to be part of a team because he likes the personal interaction, or he might want to just play the game and succeed and not be involved in social interaction. Of course, the reasons for joining a group are usually a mixture of these two dimensions, but many people fall on one side or another. For a group or team to be cohesive all members must have similar reasons for being attracted to the team. There has been much debate about whether good performance is a result of a cohesive team or whether a cohesive team develops as a result of good group performance. A team that is on a winning run is nearly always a cohesive team, but a team on a losing streak may also be cohesive, especially if the team members' motives are predominantly social.

26.2.3 *Group performance*

If you bring the best individual performers together you are likely to get the best team, but this is not always the case. It is important to look in more detail at the processes that operate within a team. In 1972 Steiner proposed a model which is helpful when looking at the relationship between the individuals in a group and group performance. Put simply,

Actual productivity = Potential productivity – Losses due to faulty processes

Potential productivity refers to the best possible performance of the group and must take into account the resources available to the group and the abilities of the individual members. Steiner's model proposes that groups fall short of their potential because of *process* faults.

The losses due to process faults are mainly caused by two factors:
1 Coordination problems – if coordination and timing of team members don't match, team strategies that depend on them will suffer, and therefore so will team performance.
2 Motivation problems – if individual members of a team are not motivated to the same extent, they will be 'pulling in different directions' and the potential of the team will not be realised.

Group cohesion can help group performance and performance can help group cohesion

The Ringelmann effect

This arises when the average individual performance decreases as the group size increases. Ingham and colleagues (1974) continued the research of a psychologist called Ringelmann, who found that in a rope-pulling task groups pulled with more force than an individual, but not with as much force as each individual pulling force put together – eight people pulled only four times as hard as one, not eight times as hard. Ingham showed that this loss in performance was due to both coordination and motivational problems but was mainly caused by individuals within the group losing motivation.

In practice

A hockey-team penalty corner drill continues to break down because the timing of the players involved does not match (losses in performance due to coordination fault). A water-polo team are not playing very well because one particular player is not trying very hard (losses in performance due to motivational fault).

DEFINITION

SOCIAL LOAFING

Some individuals in a group seem to lose motivation. It is apparently caused by the individual losing identity when placed in a group. Individual efforts may not be recognised by those who are spectating or by those that are taking part.

In practice

Observe a team game either live or on video. Try to identify any individuals who do not seem to be trying as hard as they should. What are the possible reasons for this?

Latane

Latane (1979) also studied group performance. Latane also found that performance suffered as groups got larger and concluded that both coordination and motivational problems were the main causes. He called the motivational losses *social loafing*.

Social loafing can lead to losses in group performance

Social loafing is undesirable in teams and should be eliminated as far as possible. If lack of identity is the main cause and the individual feels 'lost in the crowd', strategies should be developed to highlight individual performance. Examples of giving credit to individuals in team situations to make them feel important include 'tackle counts' in rugby or the number of 'assists' in basketball. Feedback to individuals about performance can also help to combat social loafing. Support from others in the team can also help – this is known as *social support*. Peer pressure will aid elimination of social loafing and can serve to reinforce individual effort. A team whose players get on well socially will be more cohesive, which also helps to limit social loafing.

To cut down on losses in team performance due to coordination difficulties, individuals should be selected on their interactive skills. Teachers and coaches should also emphasise that good coordination will eventually lead to better performance. Games using small teams, for instance, may help to coordinate the actions of different sets of players within a team.

Key revision points
Groups are characterised by individuals within them interacting and having common goals. A sports team is a typical group and those within it have a collective identity, a shared purpose, patterns of interaction and communication and interpersonal attraction. A team that is cohesive is one where the members are motivated to work together. Team cohesion depends on the motives of team members. Some may be socially motivated, some may be task motivated. A team can become cohesive because of good performance or a cohesive team can help to produce good performance – research is inconclusive on this point! Group performance depends on team coordination and motivation. The Ringelmann effect and research by Latane show that losses in team performance increase as team size increases. Motivational losses can be due to social loafing, which is caused by lack of identity of individuals within a team. Strategies should be developed to limit the effects of poor coordination and lack of individual motivation.

activity

Think of a 'good' leader that you know – a captain, a coach or simply one of your friends. Write down all of the characteristics of this person which contribute to him or her being a 'good' leader.

26.3 Leadership

Leadership is important in influencing behaviour in sport. Team captains, managers, coaches, teachers all need leadership qualities. Barrow (1977) saw leadership as 'the behavioural process influencing individuals and groups towards set goals'. The key words in this definition are *influencing* and *set goals*. Leadership involves personal relationships and affects the motivation of individuals and groups.

An effective leader has a number of qualities; no single quality will ensure effectiveness on its own. Qualities of leadership include:
- good communication skills
- high motivation
- enthusiasm
- having a clear goal or a vision of what needs to be achieved
- empathy (an ability to put yourself in the position of others to understand how they feel)
- good at the sport themselves or having a good knowledge of the sport
- charisma – this is a quality that is difficult to analyse but the person who has charisma is someone who is hard to ignore, has a certain 'presence' and great powers of persuasion.

Some of these qualities may be learned, some may be seen as natural – it is commonly thought that a leader is born, not made.

A leader is likely to be more effective if his qualities match the expectations of the group

Is a leader born or made?

The early instinct theory related to leadership has been called the *great man theory*. This states that leaders are usually male and are born to be leaders because they have certain personality traits. This theory ignores situational factors and interactions with others and on its own has little value. It is, however, still quite a popular view outside psychological research.

Carron (1982) suggested that an individual can become a leader in one of two ways:

1 *Emergent leaders* come from within the group because they are skilful or because the rest of the team selected them.

activity

Outline the advantages and disadvantages of an emergent leader, and a prescribed leader. State which situations would suit which type of leader.

In practice

A team manager's leadership style will be different when talking to the team as a whole before a big match from when she is talking to one member of the team in a training situation (situation characteristics). A captain may adopt different leadership styles with different players, according to the personalities involved (member characteristics). A coach who is extroverted and confident may adopt a dominant leadership style (leader characteristic).

In practice

Coaches and teachers should not rely too heavily on the autocratic approach. It may result in hostility and if the coach is not present the athletes may not take on personal responsibility. A democratic approach may result in less work being done but will increase the positive effects of interaction. The laissez-faire approach should be actively avoided.

2 *Prescribed leaders* are appointed from an external source to a team.

There are advantages and disadvantages in both methods of becoming a leader.

26.3.1 Influences on leadership

The most popular view of leadership is that leaders learn to be leaders through social learning and interactions with their environment. Chelladurai's multidimensional model of leadership, shown in Figure 26.2, is a popular approach to the study of leadership among sport psychologists.

Chelladurai identified three factors that affect leadership.
1 The characteristics of the situation.
2 The characteristics of the leader.
3 The characteristics of the people who are to be led (the group members).

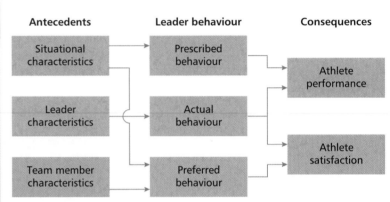

Figure 26.2 *Chelladurai's model of leadership*

The more the elements of this model match each other, the more effective the leadership is likely to be. If the leadership qualities are what the group want and expect, then they are more likely to follow the leader. If the leadership style matches the situation, again leadership is likely to be more effective.

26.3.2 Leadership styles

Many different styles of leadership have been identified, but most fall into two types. One is concerned with the task demands of the group – *task-oriented* leadership – the other is concerned with interpersonal behaviour of the group members – *person-oriented* leadership. These are not mutually exclusive, and effective leadership requires both qualities. Lewin and colleagues (1935) divided leadership into three styles.

Authoritarian leaders are task oriented and are more dictatorial in style. They make most of the decisions and tend to have commanding and directing approaches. They show little interest in the individuals making up the group.

Democratic leaders are person oriented and value the views of other group members. These leaders tend to share decisions and show a good deal of interest in the individuals of the group.

Laissez-faire leaders make very few decisions and give very little feedback. The individual group members mostly do as they wish.

Lewin looked at the styles of leadership that group members preferred. He studied a group of 10-year-old boys attending after-school clubs which were led by adults using the three different styles. Boys with an autocratic leader became aggressive towards each other when things went wrong and were submissive in their approach to the leader. If the leader left the room, they stopped working. Boys with a democratic leader got on much better with each other. They did slightly less work than the group with an autocratic leader but their work was comparable in quality. When the teacher left the room the boys carried on working. With the laissez-faire leader, the boys were aggressive towards each other, did very little work and were easily discouraged.

26.3.3 *Preferred styles of leadership*

Quite a lot of research has been undertaken on the styles of leader that group members prefer. A good leader will not shy away from making unpopular decisions but should consider the preferences of the group when making decisions. Chelladurai listed five categories of leadership behaviour.

Training and instruction behaviour improves performance and emphasises hard training – it is a very structured approach.

Democratic behaviour allows group participation in decision making.

Autocratic behaviour – the coach makes the decisions and stresses his or her personal authority.

Social support behaviour – the coach has concern for individuals and there is a positive and warm atmosphere in the team.

Rewarding behaviour recognises and reinforces good performances.

Chelladurai's results, shown in Figure 26.3, suggest that, from the group members' perceptions, ideal coaching behaviour emphasises skill development, positive feedback and a concern for personal development.

activity

Identify your preferences of coaching behaviour, either as a coach or as a performer. What sort of atmosphere do you thrive in?

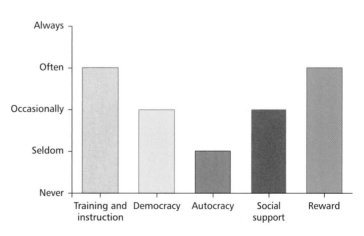

Figure 26.3
Athlete preferences for teaching styles

Your response to the last activity will probably depend on who you are coaching or being coached by and the situation you are in. Some generalisations may be made from the available research findings.

1 Novice athletes prefer more rewards and experts prefer more democratic and social support coaching.

2 Team members prefer more training and instruction, autocratic coaching and rewards. Individual sportspeople prefer democratic coaching and social support.

3 Male athletes prefer a more autocratic style of coaching and females prefer a democratic style.

4 Older athletes prefer democratic coaching, social support and training and instruction. Athletes of all ages seem to value rewards equally.

26.3.4 *Fiedler's contingency model of leadership*

Fiedler (1967) proposed a model which looked at the way the leader interacts with the situation. He used the two classifications of leader for his model that we described earlier – the task-oriented leader (focus on performance) and the person-oriented leader (focus on personal relationships). He saw that the effectiveness of these leaders depends on the *favourableness* of the situation, which itself depends on:

- the relationship between the leader and the group members
- the structure of the task
- the leader's power and position of authority.

The situation is most favourable if the relationships between leader and group members are warm and positive, the task clear and unambiguous and the leader is in a strong position of authority. If a situation is unfavourable the opposites apply.

According to Fiedler task-oriented leaders are more effective in situations that are at the extremes (most favourable or least favourable). Person-oriented leaders are most effective in situations that are moderately favourable.

Leadership is a very complex area because it deals with group dynamics – that, we have already discovered, has many diverse influences. Good leadership can positively affect motivation and performance and bad leadership can inhibit the performance of a team and demotivate individual players.

activity

Which style of leadership would you adopt in the following situations:

- You are introducing yourself as the new coach to a hostile group.
- You would like to bring together a very large group of athletes as a team before a big meeting.
- You are coaching a highly skilled squash player.
- A friendly, successful team of lacrosse players asks you to be their coach.
- A novice weightlifter needs coaching just before the lift.

Give reasons for your answers. (You should take into consideration the three main influences: characteristic of the leader, situational factors, team members' characteristics.)

Good leadership can positively affect team performance

Key revision points
Leadership involves influencing people towards set goals. Leaders may be born or made, but research points to social learning aspects. Leaders can fill positions of responsibility, either by emerging or being prescribed. Effective leadership depends on situational factors, the characteristics of the leader and the expectations and nature of the group members. The main styles of leadership are the authoritarian, task-oriented style or the democratic, person-oriented style. Most leaders have a mix of both but tend towards one or the other. There are preferred styles by sportspeople but again this depends upon situational and group characteristic variables. Fiedler's theory states that the favourableness of the situation must be taken into consideration before adopting a particular style.

26.4 Social facilitation

This has been defined by Zajonc (1965) as 'the influence of the presence of others on performance'. In many physical education and sports settings an audience or a crowd is watching the performers. The effect of this audience and the presence of other performers forms the basis of *social facilitation*. Zajonc's theory is outlined in Figure 26.4.

The earliest study in this area was made by Triplett in 1897. Triplett investigated official bicycle race records under three different conditions:

- alone (unpaced)
- paced against time
- paced in competition with others.

Over different distances performance improved consistently under all three conditions, but paced times tended to be faster than unpaced times. Triplett attributed the increase under paced conditions to a raising of 'competitive instinct' and suggested that the sight of other cyclists 'facilitated' a faster pace.

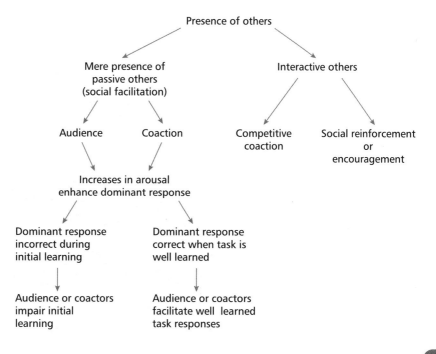

Figure 26.4
Zajonc's theory of social facilitation related to drive theory

An increase in arousal level, caused by the presence of a crowd, can affect performance

DEFINITION

AROUSAL

This is the 'energised state' or the 'readiness for action' that motivates us to behave in a particular way.

Although Triplett's work was far from conclusive, even with his follow-up experiments under laboratory conditions, it pointed the way for others to investigate the effects of the presence of others on performance.

Researchers label the effect of others performing the same activity as the *coaction effect* – the other performers are known as *coactors*. The spectators are known as the *audience*.

Zajonc has more recently identified the following factors as affecting performance:

1 The presence of an audience or coactors increases the arousal level of a performer.

2 This increase in arousal makes it more likely that the performer's dominant response will occur (see the section on drive theory in Chapter 9 for a further explanation of this).

3 If the skill to be performed is simple or if the performer is an expert, the dominant response is likely to be the correct one and performance will improve.

4 If the skill to be performed is complex or if the performer is a novice, the dominant response is likely to be incorrect and performance may decline.

activity

Although Zajonc used the drive theory to back up his arguments, the inverted U theory is also relevant here. Look back at the explanation of this theory, then try to relate it to social facilitation and the concept of high arousal level.

26.4.1 *Evaluation apprehension*

Cottrell (1968) stated that it was not just the presence of the audience or coactors that raised arousal levels and that at times the presence of others had a calming effect, rather than raising anxiety. Cottrell went on to state that arousal level increases only when the others who are present evaluate, or are perceived by the performer to evaluate, the performance. Cottrell labelled this rise in performer's arousal level *evaluation apprehension*.

In practice

The presence of an audience may cause a tennis player, for instance, to be anxious. This anxiety likely to be heightened if the tennis player is inexperienced. If the tennis player also knows that she is being judged in some way (e.g. watched by her parents), her anxiety could increase because of evaluation apprehension.

A performer's anxiety can be increased if he or she thinks the performance is being evaluated

26.4.2 *Effects of social facilitation on performance*

The presence of others will spur some athletes on to greater performances but may 'choke' others, adversely affecting their performance. We have already seen that the psychological effects can be caused by the complexity of the task and the ability of the player, but the situational influences must also be taken into consideration – such as whether the player is playing in familiar surroundings or away from their home base.

26.4.3 *Home/away effects*

Teams win more often at 'home' than they do 'away'. This may have something to do with the nature of the audience – whether they are hostile, whether the team has its own supporters in any numbers, and whether the team feels alienated by the environment. However, it would be very difficult to narrow the effects down to a particular aspect. Some research suggests that playing at home can be a disadvantage – a performer may suffer increased pressure in front of people that he or she knows, or may feel that he or she is being evaluated more as an individual.

The following factors may have some influence on performance.

- High anxiety (type A) individuals perform less well in the presence of others than individuals with a low anxiety trait (type B individuals).
- Extroverts tend to seek situations with high arousal levels (see RAS theory, p. 103), and they therefore perform better with an audience.
- Previous experiences in front of an audience affect future responses. If an individual has failed before in front of an audience, he or she may expect to fail again. Conversely, having been through the experience before may have removed the threat of an audience and future performances may be better.
- Age and gender may have some effect (research is particularly unreliable in this area).

The effects of an audience on performance can be influenced by personal, situational or audience characteristics

- The crowd's knowledge of the sport may increase evaluation apprehension, or the performer may feel supported because of the crowd's well-informed empathy.
- Performing in front of people you know can increase anxiety levels and hinder performance. If the performer is an expert, the presence of peers can increase the sense of pride, thus enhancing the performance.
- The nature of the audience can affect the arousal level of the performer. For example if the crowd is noisy and very competitive, the performer may feel more anxious and possibly more aggressive.
- The physical proximity of the audience can also affect arousal level and in turn affect performance. If the crowd is very close, the performer may feel very threatened (conversely they may feel reassured by the closeness of the crowd).

The negative effects of travel because of the location of the venue can also affect performance, according to research by Courneya and Carron (1992). Since away games involve travel, there seems to be some connection between the amount and type of travel and the negative effects of playing away from home. They concluded that there was some advantage to home teams in major team sports but there were no differences in the level of advantage between USA college and professional sportspeople. The degree of home advantage according to their research findings was also dependent on the type of sport being played. They also suspected that officials tended to favour the home team when making rule decisions.

26.4.4 *Coping with the effects of an audience*

There is no easy way of predicting the behaviour of a sports performer in front of an audience. However, it is very difficult to ignore those who are watching you perform. Many sportspeople try to do exactly that – they try to shut out the audience so that they can mentally prepare for the task in hand, some using imagery techniques, some using relaxation techniques. A number of coaches prepare their athletes to cope with an audience by getting them used to people watching during training.

To find out more about stress management, turn to page 324.

Teachers and coaches should be aware that an audience can impair performance in the early stages of skill learning and so it is best to teach skills in a non-evaluative atmosphere. The athletes must be aware of the negative effects of distractions and must be prepared to deal with the potentially negative reactions of coactors, as well as hostile spectators. Instructors can help by being calm and focused, reassuring the athlete – there may well be a case for decreasing the importance of the event. Other team members also play a part in supporting their fellow players.

Even top sportsmen find it difficult to ignore those who are watching them perform

Whatever strategies are chosen, there is little doubt that all sports performers should be aware of the potentially positive and negative effects of the presence of others during performance.

Key revision points

Social facilitation is the influence of others (an audience or other performers – coactors) on performance. The presence of others raises arousal levels which can have a positive or negative effect on performance. According to drive theory, the dominant response is more likely in high-arousal situations – this will be positive for experts, for simple/gross skills and for extroverts, but negative for the novice, for complex/fine skills and for introverts. The presence of others can cause evaluation apprehension – when there is perceived judgement of performance. Coping strategies should be developed to cope with the negative effects of social facilitation.

Key terms

You should now understand the following terms. If you do not, go back through the chapter and find out what they mean.

Arousal
Coactors
Cohesion
Emergent
Evaluation apprehension
Home/away effects
Nature/nurture
Observational learning
Person-oriented
Prescribed
Process faults
Ringelmann effect
Situation favourableness
Social facilitation
Social learning
Social loafing
Socialisation
Task-oriented

Progress check

1   What is meant by the 'nature versus nurture' debate?
2   Using an example from physical education or sport explain the concept of socialisation.
3   Using Bandura's research explain observational learning.
4   What defines a group?
5   What factors affect group cohesion?
6   Potential productivity of a group depends on what factors?
7   Explain the Ringelmann effect.
8   What is meant by social loafing?
9   How may the effects of social loafing be minimised?
10   What makes a good leader in physical education or sport?
11   In what two ways could a person assume the position of leader?
12   What are the three main influences on the style of leadership?
13   Choose one leadership style and describe it, using an example from sport.
14   What makes a situation favourable according to Fiedler?
15   What leadership styles do different types of participant in sport prefer?
16   Define social facilitation.
17   Draw a model explaining the effects of an audience on a sports participant using drive theory.
18   Using an example from physical education explain what is meant by evaluation apprehension.
19   What are the positive aspects of the presence of an audience?
20   Outline the coping strategies that could be adopted when an audience is present.

Stress and its management

Learning objectives

- To understand the nature of stress.
- To understand anxiety and why it occurs.
- To know the effects of stress and anxiety on performance.
- To be aware of the techniques used to manage stress.
- To understand goal setting and the factors that influence it.
- To be able to apply goal setting to practical situations.

An understanding of the concept of stress is important if it is to be controlled and channelled in the right direction. A great deal of research highlights the negative influences of stress on health. There are direct links between high levels of stress and numerous diseases, many of them fatal. Fitness of the body and fitness of the mind are important if a performer is to reach the highest level in sport, and for beginners to learn new skills. This chapter investigates the nature of stress, how and why it occurs and its links with sporting performance. An important section discusses the management of stress and the many strategies that both teachers and coaches can use to limit its negative aspects.

DEFINITION

EUSTRESS

A type of stress that has a positive effect. The performer actively seeks the thrill of the danger associated with the stressor. A typical activity of this type is bungee jumping.

27.1 The nature of stress

There is much confusion over the terminology associated with stress. We will attempt to clarify the position. Stress can be extremely beneficial to the sports performer – many people say they thrive under stress and some participants even seek stressful situations. This is known as *eustress*.

Stress can also have an extremely negative effect on a performer's readiness to perform and subsequent performance.

The concept of stress can be split into:
- *stressors* – the environmental changes that can induce a stress response
- *stress response* – the physiological changes that occur as a result of stress
- *stress experience* – the way we perceive the situation.

Some people actively seek out stressful situations – for example, bungee jumping

Stressors ———————→ Stress response ———————→ Stress experience

| Environmental changes that create stress, such as crowd noise | Physiological changes, such as raising of arousal level | How we feel about the situation |

Figure 27.1
How we perceive stress

An experience that is potentially stressful is affected by how each of us view that particular experience and so stress is not inevitable. We might view the experience with excitement, as shown in Figure 27.1.

activity

Try to identify what makes you feel under stress in your sport. Do you think that the same stressors will affect someone else the same way? If not, why not?

DEFINITION

STRESSOR

A stressor generally arises when there is an imbalance between the person's perception of the demand being made on them by the situation and their ability to meet the demand.

When we experience stress, according to Lazarus (1984), we judge how threatening the stressor is and then how able we are to cope with the threat. This concept of coping is important when we investigate stress management techniques.

27.1.1 Stressors

In physical education and sport there are many *stressors*. However, an experience that is stressful to one person may not be stressful to another.

Competition itself is a powerful stressor. It puts performers into an evaluative position, and we saw in Chapter 26 that this can cause apprehension. We will look at competitive anxiety later in this chapter.

Conflict, with other players or the opposition, can be a stressor. A sportsperson can bring with them to the sport social stressors from everyday life, causing conflict within the individual about the choices and decisions that have to be made.

Frustration can also be a stressor. When we investigated aggression in Chapter 25, we saw that frustration can build up if we are prevented from reaching a goal. Frustration can be caused by our own inadequacies, by a number of external influences over which we have little control.

Climate can be a stressor. If a sportsperson has to train under very hot or very cold conditions, this can produce a stress experience.

In sport the stressor of being physically hurt (not just through injury but through fatigue that hard training or demanding competition often produces) is very common.

One of the main causes of stress in sport is frustration, which can occur if goals are not reached

(i) To find out more about frustration and aggression, turn to page 294.

activity

List as many stressors as you can think of that sportspeople could experience.

In practice

A golfer has just reached the third tee and is feeling under stress. The stressors include frustration because he made some poor earlier shots, frustration because he was late due to his car not starting and frustration because the people in front of him are making slow progress. How could we help him cope with all this?

27.1.2 *The stress response*

The general adaptation syndrome (GAS) (devised by Selye in 1956) is the most widely accepted theory to explain how our bodies respond to stress. Selye saw GAS as being made up of three stages:

1 The *alarm reaction* involves physiological changes such as increased heart rate, raised blood sugar levels and adrenaline release.
2 *Resistance* – if the stressor is not removed, the body begins to recover from the initial alarm reaction and starts to cope with the situation. Adrenaline levels fall.
3 *Exhaustion* – the body now starts to fail to cope. Blood sugar levels drop and at this stage physiological disorders can develop, such as heart disease.

27.1.3 *The stress experience*

Psychological symptoms are likely to accompany the physiological symptoms of stress identified above. People under stress often feel worried and unable to make decisions. The worry over feeling stressed can cause even more stress and anxiety. Many people who are experiencing stress feel a sense of losing control and not being able to concentrate.

In practice

Experiences of some elite performers (adapted from Jones and Hardy, 1990):

Steve Backley (a javelin thrower) stated that he looked forward to competition and that, for him, stress before a competition is positive. He has been in the position where he has had to impose stress upon himself. His physiological arousal builds up to the competition and he experiences strong physiological changes on the day of competition. 'I'm off to the toilet every 10 minutes, and I'm very active and chattering away.' Steve saw one source of stress as being in a winning position and then someone throwing further than him.

Sue Challis (a trampolinist) became very anxious, even to the point of crying, when she felt under pressure. Her stress levels seemed to be linked to her confidence level at a particular time – if training was going well, her stress levels were consequently low. She described symptoms such as loss of appetite and sleeplessness during her build-up to a competition. She also tended to become mentally exhausted because of her fear of failing. 'On a good run-up to a competition I suffer from panic a week beforehand then I'm all right from then on in – it gets better towards the day.'

Key revision points

Stress can be positive or negative. The process of actively seeking positive stress is called eustress. Stress involves stressors, stress response and stress experience. Coping strategies help us to control the negative effects of stress. Conflict, competition, frustration and environmental factors such as climate are all stressors. The stress response can be explained by GAS, which has three stages: alarm, resistance and exhaustion. The stress experience is characterised by worry and anxiety.

27.2 Anxiety

Anxiety is the negative aspect of experiencing stress and can be caused by worry experienced due to the fear of failing in a competitive situation. Arousal levels are high, due to emotional responses. We may be under intense stress in sports situations because of the importance of winning or because of the presence of a large crowd. Anxiety describes our feelings of being threatened: threat of physical harm, threat to our self-esteem, threat of letting other people down or the fear of being punished.

Some competitors seem to be able to cope with anxiety and remain calm. Others, including some expert performers, can become extremely stressed and even physically ill. Martens (1987) developed the sport competition anxiety test (SCAT) to try to identify performers who were likely to suffer from anxiety in competitive situations. We will investigate what the SCAT tells us about stress later in this chapter.

To find out more about the SCAT test, turn to page 324.

DEFINITION

TRAIT ANXIETY
A trait that is enduring in an individual (also known as 'A trait'). A performer with high trait anxiety has the predisposition or the potential to react to situations with apprehension.

STATE ANXIETY
Anxiety that is felt in a particular situation (also known as 'A state'). There are two types of state anxiety: somatic – the body's response (e.g. tension, increase in pulse rate); cognitive – psychological worry over the situation.

COMPETITIVE TRAIT ANXIETY
A tendency to perceive competitive situations as threatening and to respond to these situations with feelings of apprehension or tension.

27.2.1 *Competitive anxiety*

Martens identified four major factors that are related to competitive anxiety.

1 Individual differences in the way people *interact* with a *situation* (Chapter 26). Important games will generate more anxiety than 'friendly' games.
2 Different types of *anxiety*, which can be treated in different ways. Spielberger (1966) defined *trait anxiety* and *state anxiety*. Performers who have high trait anxiety are more likely to experience high state anxiety in stressful situations but other situational factors can also cause high state anxiety.
3 General or specific anxiety. High A trait performers are likely to become anxious in highly stressful situations but are not equally anxious in all stressful situations: their anxiety levels may vary. Some performers may, for instance, be extremely anxious when in a training situation but in a match, with a large crowd watching, they are not as anxious. Martens identified a particular trait anxiety, which he called *competitive trait anxiety*.
4 The *competition process*. This involves the interaction between personality factors, competitive trait anxiety and the situation. This interaction will affect behaviour and may cause state anxiety.

The Sport Competition Anxiety Test (SCAT)

Martens gave competitors a self-report questionnaire to assess the anxiety they felt during competition. This test measures competitive trait anxiety. The test is reliable and, because it tests tendencies to become anxious about competition, it should be useful in predicting how anxious a performer will be in future competitions – their state anxiety. The results of the SCAT are closely related to the state anxiety a performer feels before competition and is therefore valid in predicting competitive state anxiety (see Figure 27.2).

The SCAT is a personality measure, but it is not just aspects of personality that determine anxiety levels – situational factors also need to be taken into consideration.

Figure 27.2 *Relationship between the situation and personality factors*

Some sportspeople may become extremely anxious in competitive situations

To find out more about catastrophe theory, turn to page 102.

The Competitive State Anxiety Inventory – 2 (SCAU – 2)

Martens and co-workers (1990) created this self-report questionnaire to assess anxiety in a competitive situation. Using this questionnaire they examined three aspects of a sports performer in a competitive situation:

- the respondent's somatic anxiety level
- the respondent's cognitive anxiety level
- the respondent's self-confidence.

Questionnaires are given out a week before, 24 hours before and then only 30 minutes before a competition to assess the anxiety level of the athlete and when that anxiety really 'kicks in'.

Using the SCAT and other questionnaires, it has been found that cognitive state anxiety increases as the competition approaches, although it does not increase immediately before the competition. It has also been found that somatic state anxiety tends to be low leading up to the competition but increases a few hours before.

The effects of both these types of anxiety on performance can be catastrophic (see catastrophe theory in Chapter 9) unless they are controlled.

Key revision points
Anxiety is a negative form of stress. Four factors affect levels of anxiety in competition: individual differences, nature of the anxiety experienced, general or specific anxiety, and the process of competition. There are two types of anxiety: A trait – the enduring characteristic of potential anxiety, and A state – the actual anxiety experienced in a particular situation. The SCAT is a test of competitive trait anxiety and proves that high trait anxiety can lead to competitive state anxiety.

27.3 Stress management

Considerable importance is placed on managing stress to eliminate anxiety and optimise performance. One of the most important factors separating the very best from the merely good is the ability to control anxiety at crucial moments.

Two types of state anxiety have been recognised:

- *Somatic* anxiety (stress response of the body)
- *Cognitive* anxiety (stress response of the mind).

Management of cognitive anxiety can affect the somatic anxiety, and vice versa. Controlling the heart rate by relaxation methods

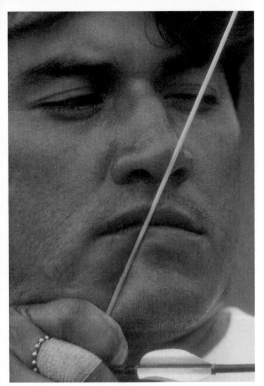

It is important to manage anxiety levels to improve concentration

 To find out more about peak flow experience, turn to page 103.

can make us feel more positive about performing. Positive thinking can, in turn, control our heart rate. Setting goals can affect anxiety levels (we will deal with goal setting later in the chapter).

The zone of optimal functioning is often cited by modern sports psychologists as an important state of well-being. This zone is an emotional response that facilitates top performance and is often referred to as the peak flow experience. This was dealt with in Chapter 9, and we recommend that you return to that chapter as a reminder. Attentional style and control are also discussed in Chapter 9. The following techniques are useful for controlling both types of anxiety.

activity

Visualisation: close your eyes and visualise yourself performing your sport. Try to imagine performing just one skill, such as hitting a forehand in tennis or kicking a ball in football. *Imagery – to escape*: close your eyes and imagine that you are in a comfortable place, such as lying on a deserted beach under the warm sun: mmmm!

27.3.1 *Imagery*

The technique of imagery can help to improve concentration and develop confidence, and to ensure the correct response. Imagery has a number of uses.

* To create a mental picture to get the feeling of movement or to try to capture an *emotional feeling* (see the section on mental rehearsal in Chapter 9).
* To create *pictures of escape* – we could imagine ourselves in a much more relaxed place, like lying on a beach in a far-away place. The creation of mental pictures is called *visualisation*, and many top sportspeople use this method to help them control anxiety.
* To recall *sounds* as well as pictures – to hear the sound of the cricket ball being hit by your bat or the 'swish' of the ball as it goes through the net in basketball.
* To try to *feel* what it is like to perform a skill – a successful tackle in rugby or the exhilaration of running fast.
* Finally, imagery can be used to try to imagine your *emotions* – to feel the happiness and sense of achievement by saving a penalty or holing a putt in golf.

There are two forms of imagery:

* *external* imagery – seeing yourself from outside your body, as if you were in a film
* *internal* imagery – seeing yourself from within.

Internal imagery is probably more effective than external imagery, but most people prefer to use one method over the other. To be effective in using imagery the following points should be taken into consideration.

* Relax in a comfortable, warm setting before you attempt to practise imagery.
* If you want to improve skill by using imagery, practise in a real-life situation.

Positive self-talk can increase confidence and improve performance

Write down three examples of negative self-talk and three of positive self-talk related to:

- technique
- emotions.

- Imagery exercises should be short but frequent.
- Set goals for each session, for example concentrate on imagining the feel of a tennis serve in one short session.
- Construct a programme for your training in imagery.
- Evaluate your programme at regular intervals. Use the sports *imagery evaluation* described below to help you assess your training.

In practice

Imagery evaluation: imagine a situation, providing as much detail from your imagination as possible to make the image as real as you can. Then rate your imagery according to:

1 how vividly you saw the image
2 how clearly you heard the sounds
3 how vividly you felt the body movements
4 how clearly you felt the mood or emotions of the situation.

27.3.2 *Self-instructions/self-talk*

Being positive about your past performances and your future strategies by talking to yourself (no, it is not a sign of complete madness) can help your performance. Many sports performers use negative self-talk: 'I will never get any better'; 'I am going to drop this catch'. Instructions aimed at yourself can be directed towards technique or towards your emotions.

When sportspeople become more anxious they are less able to distinguish between positive and negative thoughts. The negative thoughts become the focus of attention. Negative thoughts, according to Martens (1990), can be placed into five categories:

1 Worry about performance, especially about comparing with others.
2 Inability to make decisions because there is too much going on in your mind.
3 Preoccupation with physical feelings such as fatigue.

Positive thinking helps performance

4 Thinking about what will happen if you lose and the consequences (e.g. disapproval).
5 Thoughts of not having enough ability to do well – too much self-criticism.

As performers become more skilful, they tend not to consciously talk to themselves so much, so it is best to use self-talk in training that is positive. Words or phrases can be used in training to help skill development – in rugby it could be 'fast hands'; in hockey it could be 'steady'.

27.3.3 *Cue utilisation*

Attention and attentional style were discussed in Chapter 9. Attention is more effective if the performer concentrates on cues that are relevant at the particular time: keeping the focus and not being distracted is a feature of a top performer. If cues in the environment are not used effectively then the sportsperson fails to gather relevant information from around the field of play – for instance, a hockey player might not be aware of movements off the ball that will affect her next pass. There is also the danger that the player could be distracted too easily by irrelevant cues such as a person in the crowd shouting at them.

Easterbrook (1959) proposed the *cue utilisation theory*, which states that as the arousal level of the athlete increases, his or her attention narrows. This may have negative consequences, as we have already discussed. This theory can be viewed alongside the inverted U theory (Chapter 9). The optimum level of arousal is seen as being moderate, because this is when the athlete's cueing ignores irrelevant cues but concentrates on the relevant ones. If the arousal levels are too low, then both irrelevant and relevant cues are attended to; if the arousal levels are too high the irrelevant and relevant cues are ignored and consequently there is a drop in performance. (See also catastrophe theory, Chapter 9.)

27.3.4 *Relaxation techniques*

Relaxation mainly controls somatic anxiety but can also control cognitive anxiety. It is useful to go through some relaxation exercises before attempting to train yourself in mental exercises such as imagery. Relaxation can help players adopt a calm and positive attitude before a game, but you do not want to go to sleep! It is important, therefore, to avoid a long session of relaxation just before competition.

Relaxation needs practice, just as mental imagery needs practice, and practices are best if they are progressive.

To find out more about attentional style, turn to page 106.

In practice

Mace (1993) identifies key words that could help top netball players in a variety of situations:

To maintain motivation when winning easily: 'Liven up'; 'Kill'.

When losing or when opponents score: 'Fight'; 'Concentrate . . . think about the strategy to win the game'; 'Let's go'.

When anxiety/tension is affecting performance: 'Stay sharp but steady'; 'Accurate . . . accurate . . . accurate'.

To overcome fatigue: 'Strong'.

Specific position statements: 'Defence'; 'Keep steady' (shooters); 'It's my line'; 'It's my circle'.

In practice

(Adapted from Jones and Hardy, 1990.) David Hemery (athlete) said that just before the Olympic Final in 1968 (he won the gold medal), 'I lay on the bench and the others started jogging around, while I just stayed there, because that was what my plan was, trying to bring my pulse rate down. At will, I tend to be able to relax the whole body without going through the progressive bits.' Hemery went on to explain that this relaxation had come about through relaxation training, which was integral to his other training.

Self-directed relaxation

This needs lots of practice to be effective. The athlete concentrates on each muscle group separately and relaxes it, with help from the coach. Eventually the athlete can perform this without help, or perhaps the aid of a prerecorded tape. The aim of self-relaxation is to take as little time as possible to become fully relaxed so that eventually it will take only a few moments. This time factor is crucial if the athlete is to be able to use the strategy just before or during competition. This technique is effective if the athlete is able to be aware of the muscles to be relaxed – some have more self-awareness than others, although this can be improved over time.

Progressive relaxation training (PRT)

This technique was developed by Jacobsen in 1932 and is sometimes referred to as the Jacobsen technique. It is a much lengthier process initially than self-relaxation but can be very effective. The technique is concerned with learning to be aware of and to 'feel' the tension in the muscles and then to get rid of this tension by 'letting go'.

PRT becomes more effective with practice. The idea is to combine muscle groups, so that eventually the entire body can be relaxed at one time. Although this technique may take longer to master, many top sportspeople have found it most helpful, especially leading up to competition. It has also helped many to achieve a better night's sleep before competition and can be good preparation for imagery exercises.

activity

Sit on the floor with your legs straight out in front of you. Now, tense the muscles of your right leg by a dorsiflex action of your ankle joint (pull your toes up towards your knee using your leg and foot muscles). Develop as much tension as possible and hold it for about five seconds, concentrating on what it feels like. Now completely relax your leg muscles and let your foot go floppy, concentrating on what the relaxed muscles feel like. Now try to relax your muscles even further. How does your leg feel now? It should feel much more relaxed.

Key revision points

Stress management deals with somatic and cognitive anxiety. Imagery helps with concentration and confidence. It can recreate the task about to be performed or can help to visualise successful movements. It can also help the mind escape reality. Imagery can represent sounds, feelings and emotions. There are two forms of imagery: external and internal. Positive self-talk can help with reducing anxiety. In anxious situations athletes are unable to distinguish easily between positive and negative self-talk. Relaxation helps to control somatic anxiety. Relaxation can be self-directed or through progressive relaxation training (PRT). Like all stress-management techniques, PRT becomes more effective through practice.

27.4 Goal setting

The setting of goals is an important strategy to be adopted by teachers, coaches or performers. Goal setting is often used to increase a performer's motivation and confidence. Participants in sport are often faced with complex and threatening situations and may feel anxious. Goal setting can help to alleviate this anxiety and ultimately to enhance performance.

According to Lock and Latham (1985) goal setting can affect performance in four ways:
1 By directing attention.
2 By regulating the amount of effort that is put into a given task.
3 Ensuring effort is sustained until the goal is reached.
4 By motivating people to develop a variety of strategies to reach their goals.

27.4.1 *SMARTER goal setting*

The following points have been made by sports coach UK to make goal setting more effective. If you are a coach, a teacher or a player, you can optimise goal setting by taking them into account.

Think of the word SMARTER!

- S – specific – goals must be clear and specific.
- M – measurable – goals must be assessed and therefore need to be measurable. The more specific they are, the more measurable they are likely to be. Knowing how well you are doing can be motivating and ensures that you remain realistic about future performances.
- A – agreed – goals that coaches and performers have talked about and shared are more likely to be achieved because all interested parties have a common purpose.
- R – realistic – goals must be within the reach of the performer so that motivation remains high. If they are too easy, though, this can be demotivating because the performer may not try as hard.
- T – time phased – goals should be split into short-term goals leading to long-term goals. This step-by-step approach over a period of time ensures that goals remain realistic and achievable.
- E – exciting – goals must be stimulating so that the performer is motivated to continue. Enjoyment is thus a crucial ingredient for achieving goals.
- R – recorded – goals that have been agreed should be recorded so that progress can be monitored. As goals are achieved they can be crossed off, thus motivating the performer to press on towards the next goal.

Setting goals such as a personal best can help to focus on performance rather than the outcome

Goals need to be measurable to be effective

In practice

To help a sportsperson deal with anxiety over the outcome, success may have to be redefined. Personal performance goals may be less stress inducing than outcome goals and will put the participant into a position of control. Emphasis could shift towards more process-type goals. A move away from outcome goals may make losing bearable and less stressful, thus reducing anxiety. Setting goals such as personal bests can help to focus on performance and process-type goals.

27.4.2 Different types of goals

Different types of goals will affect the performer in different ways.

Outcome goals are related to the end result. Sportspeople and their instructors often set goals to win or are concerned with the outcome of the competition.

Performance goals are concerned with performance judged against other performances – perhaps a certain time to be achieved in order to better the last time recorded. Performance goals are related to specific behaviours. Performance goals may affect outcome goals.

Process-oriented goals concentrate on the performer's technique and tactics – in other words, what a performer has to do to be more successful.

27.4.3 Goal difficulty

Research has shown that setting difficult goals leads to better performance than setting medium or easy goals. There is evidence to suggest that goals that are set *just beyond reach* produce a better performance than those that are achieved with ease. If the task to be achieved is complex, with many perceptual requirements, goal setting becomes less effective in the short term, but the strategies that have been tried and failed could be useful in the long term. Generally speaking, goals must be achievable but challenging. If goals are set too easy, motivation will soon decline.

27.4.4 Goal specificity

Clearly defined goals usually lead to better performance. Simply saying 'do your best' is not good enough – targets need to be better defined. Evaluation of goals is also difficult if the goals have not been clearly defined. Sports involving objective measurements, such as time, are easier to make specific, but it is possible to set specific goals in most activities.

27.4.5 Other factors affecting goal setting

Long-term and short-term goals

Achievement of long-term goals is a *progressive* process and must start with achieving short-term goals. Many athletes use realistic target dates to help them achieve their short-term goals. Short-term goals provide a greater opportunity for success, which can reinforce positive feelings, and in turn help to control anxiety levels.

Evaluation

Goals need to be measurable. The measurement of goals will give information about success, in itself a motivating factor, and will give useful information about setting further goals. There is nothing worse for a performer than not knowing how he or she is progressing, so accurate feedback is essential.

Sharing decision making

Goals that are set through negotiation and agreement are far more effective than externally set goals. The participant will have a sense of ownership over the goal setting and will be better motivated to achieve. Goal setting is also likely to be fairer and more realistic if all parties involved have an input.

activity

Write down some long-term goals that you might have related to your sport, your coaching or even your studies. Now try to identify some short-term goals or objectives that might help you achieve your long-term goals. Use all the guidance that was set out in this last section. Are the goals you have set measurable, achievable, specific? Are they outcome goals, performance goals or process-oriented goals?

Key revision points

Goal setting can help motivation, boost confidence and help with anxiety control. There are three different types of goals: outcome goals, performance goals and process-oriented goals. Goals should be challenging, but not too difficult. They should be well defined so that goal evaluation can take place. Long-term goals should be preceded by short-term goals to help with motivation and to control anxiety. Goals must also be measurable for evaluation to take place. If there is a sharing in decisions about goals, then those goals are more likely to be achieved, and anxiety is less likely.

Key terms

You should now understand the following terms. If you do not, go back through the chapter and find out what they mean.

A state
A trait
Anxiety
Attentional style
Cognitive anxiety
Competitive A trait
Competitive State Anxiety
   Inventory
Conflict
Cue utilisation
Eustress
General adaptation syndrome
Imagery
Long-term goals
Performance goals
Process-oriented goals
Progressive relaxation training
Self-directed relaxation
Short-term goals
SMARTER goal setting
Somatic anxiety
Sport Competition Anxiety Test
Stress
Stressor

Progress check

1 Define the term stress and explain what is meant by eustress.
2 Give three examples of typical stressors in a physical education or sports context.
3 Describe Selye's GAS theory of stress response.
4 Define the term anxiety.
5 Using examples from physical education or sport explain what is meant by trait anxiety and state anxiety.
6 What is meant by competitive trait anxiety?
7 Outline the SCAT.
8 Draw a model to show the relationships between competitive trait anxiety, situation and personality factors.
9 What are the two types of state anxiety?
10 Describe the imagery process of stress management. What are the main effects of this process?
11 How do you make imagery more effective?
12 Outline the five categories of negative thoughts, according to Martens.
13 What are the main effects of somatic relaxation?
14 What makes a situation favourable according to Fiedler?
15 What leadership styles do different types of participant in sport prefer?
16 Define social facilitation.

Further reading

G.W. Allport. *Attitudes*. Clarke University Press, 1935.

A. Bandura. *Aggression: A Social Learning Analysis*. Prentice Hall, 1973.

A. Bandura. *Social Learning Theory*. Prentice Hall, 1977.

R.A. Baron. *Human Aggression*. Plenum, 1977.

J.L. Barrow. The variables of leadership. *Academy of Management Review*, 1977.

L. Berkowitz. *Reports of Aggression*. Atherton Press, 1969.

L. Berkowitz. Some determinants of impulsive aggression. *Psychological Review*, 1974.

R.J. Brown and J.C. Turner. *Interpersonal and Intergroup Behaviour*. Blackwell, 1981.

S.J. Bull. *Sport Psychology, A Self Help Guide*. Crowood, 1991.

A.V. Carron. *Social Psychology of Sport*. Mouvement Publications, 1980.

A.V. Carron. Cohesion in sports groups. *Journal of Sports Psychology*, 1982.

R.B. Cattell. *The Scientific Analysis of Personality*. Penguin, 1965.

P. Chelladurai. Multidimensional model of leadership. In: J.M. Silva and R.S. Weinberg. *Psychological Foundations of Sport*. Human Kinetics, 1984.

N.B. Cottrell. *Performance in the Presence of Other Human Beings*. Allyn & Bacon, 1968.

K.S. Courneya and A.V. Carron. The home advantage in sport competitions: A literature review. *Journal of Sport and Exercise Psychology*, 1992.

R.H. Cox. *Sport Psychology Concepts and Applications*. McGraw-Hill, 1998.

B.J. Cratty. *Social Psychology in Athletics*. Prentice Hall, 1981.

M. Csikszentmihalyi. *Beyond Boredom and Anxiety*. Joey-Bass, 1975.

F.L. Deci. *Intrinsic Motivation and Self-determination in Human Behaviour*. Plenum Press, 1985.

J. Dollard. *Frustration and Aggression*. Yale University Press, 1939.

J.L. Duda. The relationship between task and ego orientation. *Journal of Sports Psychology*, 1989.

C. Dweck. The role of expectations and attributions in the alleviation of learned helplessness. *Journal of Personality and Social Psychology*, 1975.

C.S. Dweck. *Learned Helplessness in Sport*. Human Kinetics, 1980.

J.A. Easterbrook. The effect of emotion on cue utilisation and the organisation of behaviour. *Psychological Review*, 1959.

H. Eysenck. *Biological Basis of Personality*. Nature, 1963.

H.J. Eysenck. *The Structure and Measurement of Personality*. Routledge, 1969, 1970.

L.A. Festinger. *A Theory of Cognitive Dissonance*. Harper & Row, 1957.

L.A. Festinger. *Social Pressures in Informal Groups*. Harper & Row, 1963.

F.E. Fiedler. *A Theory of Leadership Effectiveness*. McGraw-Hill, 1967.

D.L. Gill. *Psychological Dynamics of Sport*. Human Kinetics, 1986.

D.L. Gill and T.E. Deeter. Development of the Sport Orientation Questionnaire. *Research Quarterly for Sport*, 1988.

L. Hardy, G. Jones and D. Gould. *Understanding Psychological Preparation for Sport*. John Wiley and Sons, 1996.

J.S. Hinkle et al. Running behaviour. *Journal of Sport Behaviour*, 1989.

E.P. Hollander. *Principles and Methods of Social Psychology*, 2nd edition. Oxford University Press, 1971.

J. Honeybourne. *BTEC National Sport*. Nelson Thornes, 2003.

J. Honeybourne, M. Hill and J. Wyse. *PE for You*. Stanley Thornes, 1998.

A.G. Ingham *et al*. The Ringelmann effect. *Journal of Experimental Psychology*, 1974.

J.G. Jones and L. Hardy, editors. *Stress and Performance in Sport*. Wiley, 1990.

B. Latane *et al*. Many hands make light work. *Journal of Personality*, 1979.

R.S. Lazarus and S. Folkman. *Stress, Appraisal and Coping*. Springer, 1984.

K. Lewin. *A Dynamic Theory of Personality*. McGraw-Hill, 1935.

K. Lewin. *Psychological Theory*. Macmillan, 1951.

R.A. Likert. A technique for the measurement of attitudes. *Archives of Psychology*, 1932.

E. Lock and G. Latham. The Application of Goal Setting in Sport. *Journal of Sport Psychology*, 1985.

K. Lorenz. *On Aggression*. Brace & World, 1966.

R. Mace. *With Netball in Mind*. All England Netball Association, 1993.

R. Martens. Science and sport psychology. *The Sports Psychologist*, 1987.

R. Martens, R.S. Vealey and D. Burton. *Competitive Anxiety in Sport*. Human Kinetics, 1990.

A. Maslow. *Motivation and Personality*. Harper and Row, 1954.

D.M. McNair, M. Lorr and L.F. Droppleman. *Profile of Mood States Manual*. Educational and Industrial Testing Service, 1971.

S.A. Mednick. In: J. Radford and E. Govier, editors. *A Textbook of Psychology*. Routledge, 1991.

W.P. Morgan. Prediction of performance in athletics. In: P. Klavora and J.V. Daniel, editors. *Coach, Athlete, and the Sport Psychologist*. Human Kinetics, 1979.

W.P. Morgan. *Sport Personology*. Mouvement, 1980.

J. Radford and E. Govier. *A Textbook of Psychology*. Routledge, 1991.

C.G. Roberts, editor. *Motivation in Sport and Exercise*. Human Kinetics, 1992.

C.G. Roberts, K.S. Spink and C.L. Pemberton. *Learning Experiences in Sport Psychology*. Human Kinetics, 1986.

K.C. Roberts and D. Pascuzzi. Causal attributions in sport. *Journal of Sports Psychology*, 1979.

C.R. Rogers. *On Becoming a Person*. Houghton Mifflin, 1961.

G.H. Sage. *Sport and American Society*. Addison-Wesley, 1974.

M.E. Shaw. *Group Dynamics*. McGraw-Hill, 1976.

J.M. Silva and R.S. Weinberg, editors. *Psychological Foundations of Sport*. Human Kinetics, 1984.

F.L. Smoll and R.W. Shutz. Children's attitudes towards physical activity. *Journal of Sports Psychology*, 1980.

C.D. Spielberger. *Anxiety and Behaviour*. Academic Press, 1966.

I.D. Steiner. *Group Process and Productivity*. Academic Press, 1972.

L.L. Thurstone. Attitudes can be measured. *American Journal of Sociology*, 1928.

H.C. Triandis. *Interpersonal Behaviour*. Brooks/Cole, 1977.

N. Triplett. In: D.L. Gill, editor. Psychological Dynamics of Sport. *Human Kinetics*, 1986.

B.W. Tuckman. Developmental sequences in small groups. *Psychological Bulletin*, 1965.

R.S. Vealey. Conceptualisation of sport confidence and competitive orientation: Preliminary investigation and instrument development. *Journal of Sport Psychology*, 1986.

R.S. Weinberg. The relationship between extrinsic rewards and intrinsic motivation. In: J.M. Silva and R.S. Weinberg. *Psychological Foundations of Sport*. Human Kinetics, 1984.

B. Weiner. A theory of motivation for some classroom experiences. *Journal of Educational Psychology,* 1979.

W.N. Widmeyer. *The Measurement of Cohesion in Sports Teams*. Sports Dynamics, 1985.

J.D. Willis and L.F. Campbell. *Exercise Psychology*. Human Kinetics, 1992.

B. Woods. *Applying Psychology to Sport*. Hodder & Stoughton, 1998.

R.M. Yerkes and J.D. Dodson. The relation of strength of stimulus to rapidity of habit formation. *Journal of Neurological Psychology*, 1908.

R.B. Zajonc. Social facilitation. *Science*, 1965.

Part

6

THE HISTORICAL DEVELOPMENT OF SPORT

This part of the book contains:

This part of the book will chart the historical development of sport. We will begin our investigation in pre-industrial Britain and look at the sports followed by peasant and court. Many of these activities were the origins of our modern sports.

The next stage of development occurred in the great public schools at the start of the nineteenth century. Here boys adopted the old games, refining them into more formal and regular activities. On leaving school the old boys began to transport their love of games around Britain and the British Empire.

The industrial revolution changed the way people worked and lived and consequently had a major impact on sport. Most people were now living in towns and cities, with less space for sport, and sports had to be adapted to suit the new urban conditions. Changes in working patterns led to all people having more time for leisure and a more regular style of sport developed.

We will finish our investigation into the historical development of sport by following the development of physical education in schools at the start of the twentieth century.

The era of popular recreation

Learning objectives

- To understand the way people spent their leisure time before the industrial revolution.
- To be able to relate how sport of pre-industrial Britain reflected the society of the time.
- To be able to give examples of popular recreations.
- To understand the key characteristics of popular sports and recreations.

After the fall of Rome, we enter a period of history called the Dark Ages. There is little historical evidence to tell us about life during this time, and we can pick up the development of sports only in medieval times. During this period we see the roots of many modern sports, which were played by the peasants in their villages. Leisure time was limited and sports were closely associated with the Church calendar of holy days and festivals. Sports such as mob football were a chance for the entire village to get together and let off steam.

28.1 Life in pre-industrial society

28.1.1 *Societal background*

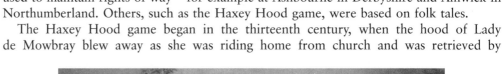

Life in medieval England was short, life expectancy being only about 35 years.

Pre-Christian rituals often involved competitive behaviour – mimicking hunts and fights. From this ritualistic play emerged habits of competition. Many of the mob games played before the industrial revolution have their origins in pagan times. Often ball games were used to maintain rights of way – for example at Ashbourne in Derbyshire and Alnwick in Northumberland. Others, such as the Haxey Hood game, were based on folk tales.

The Haxey Hood game began in the thirteenth century, when the hood of Lady de Mowbray blew away as she was riding home from church and was retrieved by

DEFINITION

HAXEY HOOD

An ancient game still played annually on 6 January at Haxey, Lincolnshire.

A village ball game in pre-industrial Britain

twelve labourers. She was so pleased that she gave a piece of land to the village – known as the 'hoodlands' – and paid for a leather hood that would be competed for every year by twelve men dressed in scarlet.

28.1.2 *The medieval sporting year*

The year began with the spring fertility festivals, although some games took place as early as New Year's Day and Plough Monday (first Monday after Christmas). Most, however, focused on Easter. Shrove Tuesday was a particularly popular day for violent mob games (football, tug of war and animal baiting), before the denials of Lent. May Day was often marked by games in which young men chased women, again concerned with rituals of fertility. Whitsuntide was the high point of the sporting year with much dancing and games. This was a slack time for agriculture, and crops and animals were left to grow. Summer games tended to be gentler – running, jumping, throwing contests. Some, like the Cotswold Games, were not unlike the modern Olympics.

28.1.3 *The population*

In the middle ages, the UK's population was almost totally rural. London (the only substantial town in the twelfth century) had a population of only 20 000. There were 30 'holy' days in a year (as well as Sundays) when sports could be played.

The population was split into two main groups: the gentry and the peasants. These two groups generally kept well apart, though there was some overlap in sport. The land owners had more time for play, less discomfort and better food and housing. Sport for them was used to pass the time and socialise. However, both groups were equally exposed to illness and early death.

28.2 The games of the court and the gentry

The amount of time available, economic and social advantage, and the need to demonstrate their military preparedness made the sporting activities of the ruling classes different from those of the peasants.

The characteristic feature of gentry sport was the horse – a symbol of authority and a practical necessity for travel and war. Knights competed in the tournament, where they practised war skills, as well as providing an entertaining spectacle. These events were only for knights or the nobility, though the peasants and lower classes were sometimes allowed to watch.

When the country was not at war, hunting became the substitute. This was restricted by social status by the game laws – deer were the quarry of only the richest hunters.

The courtly gentleman had to prove himself to be a soldier, but also required manners for a place at court. He had to be aware of classical literature and be skilled in games and other recreations (hunting, riding, wrestling and swordplay – later replaced by fencing). Certain sports were to be avoided (football, skittles) but gambling was a fashionable pastime and stakes grew higher on almost all sports, including bowling, horse races, cock fighting and archery.

DEFINITION

HOLY DAY

A religious festival which gave the people a day off from work. The usual Christian festivals and local saints days were often used for recreation.

Royal tennis – a medieval game that was exclusive to the very rich

DEFINITION

GAME LAWS

Passed in 1390, these laws excluded all artificers and labourers worth less than 40 shillings per year, and any priest or clerk less than £10 a year, from hunting.

Archery and bowls were practised across the social classes, though there is no evidence that different classes played against each other. An act in 1541 sought to reassert class distinction in bowls, closing all public alleys and greens except to gentlemen rated at £100 a year. The lower class were felt not to be spending enough time on archery practice.

28.3 The games and recreations of the populace

The common people's time for sport was often restricted to the holy days. They also had less access to resources and travel, so their recreations had to be localised and using ready-to-hand materials.

Recreations changed through the year. In the winter, mass, violent games were played; in the summer, gentler, more individual and athletic-type activities were followed.

Mass games of football and 'stick' games (such as hurling) were common. These often involved whole villages, and teams were selected on criteria such as 'uppers and downers' or single men against married men. The games were often violent contests with few rules.

In the summer, races and strength contests were more common, and many areas held contests similar to the modern Highland Games.

Recreations involving animals were also popular, though they would be considered very cruel nowadays. People would bet on the outcome of fights between dogs, cockerels, or dogs and bulls and bears – the 'baiting' sports.

Military preparation also formed a part of peasants' recreation. The army needed archers and these were generally recruited from the peasantry. In order to ensure a good supply of fine archers, successive Kings of England (from Richard II in 1388 to Henry VIII in 1541) passed laws making archery practice compulsory and banning other recreations so that archery practice was not neglected. Under these acts, landowners could be punished if they allowed ball games to be played on their land, and further fined if they did not train their servants in the use of a bow and arrow. As the weapons of war developed, particularly gunpowder, the need for archery practice declined and once again the populace was free to pursue other recreations.

28.4 Festivals and the role of the Church

Local festivals were held in addition to the national celebrations of Christmas and Whitsuntide. However, changes in society started to affect sport. By 1600 the population of London had grown to 200 000 and many sports had to be restricted due to lack of space and risk of damage to property.

The Church, and in particular the Reformation, had a great effect on sports in society.

28.4.1 *The Reformation*

The Reformation led to the potent force of Puritanism, whose motto read: 'The gates to salvation can only be opened by what a person believes, thinks or feels during their earthly life'.

DEFINITION

'UPPERS'
Those born or living at the upper end of a village.

'DOWNERS'
People born or living at the lower end of a village.

This had two major effects on sport. First, games played on Sundays and saints days were seen as sacrilegious, so the only possible time available for most people to play sports was removed. Secondly, the belief that sport and games were frivolous and non-productive led to the view that such pastimes were sinful.

This was generally an urban phenomenon – and never really reached the extreme rural areas. Although it lasted only a short time it did have a considerable impact on sport. In particular, it led the way to the decline of the animal sports.

28.4.2 *The Restoration*

The Reformation was followed by the Restoration (the return of King Charles II to power), the decline of the puritans and the return of power and influence to the King – and more so to parliament. This led to relaxation of the constraints against sports and recreations and active Church support for sporting activity. The 'muscular Christians' will be discussed in the next chapter.

To find out more about 'muscular Christianity', turn to page 345.

28.5 Examples of the popular games and recreations of pre-industrial Britain

This section is designed to provide case studies of the type of popular recreational activities undertaken in this era. It is hoped these will give a feel for the structure and function of the sport of the time, whilst giving practical examples. Three sports have been chosen:

* *Real tennis* – a sport confined to the gentry and privileged.
* *Football* – a game of the peasants.
* *Cricket* – a game in which some degree of social mix was permissible.

28.5.1 *Real tennis*

Tennis originated in France and became popular in Britain during the fourteenth century. Kings, nobles and merchants all played it enthusiastically in the courtyards of castles and great houses.

The early tennis courts were often constructed in existing courtyards or quadrangles, leading to a great variation in court dimensions and rules. Some were simply enclosed yards with numerous hazards, or square openings, to deflect the ball. Other courts were more elaborate, with a passage or 'dedans' down one side in which spectators could stand and watch the game. It was this type of court that became the standard form of tennis court.

The 'net' was a rope or cord strung across the centre of the court with tassels hanging down to prevent the ball from passing underneath. Although early players often used a gloved hand to hit the ball, short-handled racquets became the norm. Balls were made of white leather panels sewn together and stuffed with feathers or hair – they were laborious to make and so very expensive.

During the sixteenth century tennis became very popular with the royal court. Courts were built at all the royal palaces, and it is this fashion which led to the name of royal tennis. By the end of the sixteenth century public courts were being built in London, although the cost of their hire maintained the game's exclusivity.

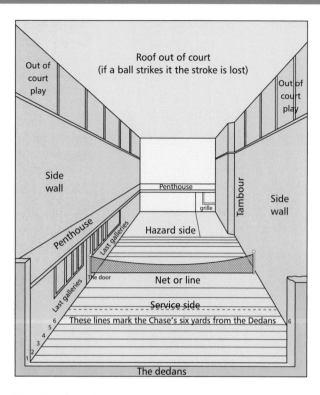

Figure 28.1 *A real tennis court*

28.5.2 *Football*

This was generally a winter activity, being played especially at New Year and Shrovetide celebrations. The Church calendar played an important part in giving time for such recreations. Often referred to as street football, the games were part of local traditions associated with maintaining rights of way. Because the pitch was – quite literally – the street, much damage was done to houses and shops, which led to the decline of these games. In some areas, such as Alnwick in Northumberland, the authorities quickly moved the annual game outside the town into fields. Various kings also attempted to curtail the playing of football as they believed it prevented the populace practising their much-required archery skills.

The following court case from 1576 gives an idea of the form these games took.

> On the said day at Ruyslippe, Middlesex the above named defendants along with many more malefactors to the number of one hundred assembled themselves unlawfully and played a certain unlawful game called football, by means of which unlawful game there was amongst them a great affray, likely to result in homicides and serious accidents.

These games had few rules, though there were distinct teams and goals. Generally games would be between rival parishes: the Alnwick game is fought between the churches of St Michael's and St Peter's. More divisions could be between 'Uppers' and 'Downers', as in the Ashbourne game (see p. 143).

To find out more about mob games, turn to page 143.

28.5.3 *Cricket*

Cricket is a game with ancient origins. There is evidence that the ancient Celts and Romans were playing a cricket-type game, but

Cricket – a game well organised before the industrial revolution

the real history of cricket originated on the Weald of southern England during the early 1700s. Primarily a pastime for shepherds, the components of the game included the short downland grass, a ball of wool to be hit with the crook, and the sheep hurdle (or 'wicket') acting as the target.

By 1750 The Bat and Ball Inn at Hambledon, Hampshire had become the first organised centre for cricket. The game allowed both peasants and gentry to participate, and many early matches were played between the estates of local squires and landowners. Often games were arranged in order to facilitate wagers between the local gentry, as this quote from 1697 highlights:

> The middle of last week a great match at cricket was played in Sussex: they were eleven a side, and they played for fifty guineas a piece.

Cricket is unique in that by 1744 there were published laws of cricket, and it is evident that these were actually a revision of an earlier code. Examples of the 1744 laws include:

> Ye pitching of ye first wicket is to be determined by ye cast of a piece of money.

> When ye wickets are both pitched and ye creases cut, ye party that wins ye toss may order which side shall go in first.

> Ye bowler must deliver ye ball with one foot behind ye Crease even with ye wicket, if he delivers ye ball with his hinder foot over ye bowling crease, ye umpire shall call No ball.

activity

- How does cricket differ from other popular recreations?
- Why do you think it was acceptable for both gentry and peasants to play cricket?
- What societal and cultural factors allowed cricket to develop rules long before most other sports?

Key revision points

Popular recreation took place in pre-industrial society, with most people living in a rural society. The Church calendar allowed regular time for leisure and sport. The social distinction within society between court and peasantry was reflected in the sports each played – peasant sports were mob, informal, large scale and violent; court sports were sophisticated, elite, exclusive and often played on courts. Cricket was one game in which all classes could play side by side. Animal sports were popular, but there was a class distinction – baiting for the lower classes, hunting for the upper classes.

Key terms

Progress check

You should now understand the following terms. If you do not, go back through the chapter and find out what they mean.

- Cricket
- Game laws
- Haxey Hood
- Holy day
- Mob football
- Popular recreation
- Real tennis
- Reformation
- Restoration
- Uppers and Downers

1   What functional role did mob football have in pre-industrial communities?
2   At what time of year were violent mob-type games usually played?
3   What type of focus did May games and activities often have?
4   How did the agricultural year affect the time available for sport?
5   What was a Holy day?
6   In pre-industrial Britain, what two groups was the population split into?
7   How did the social background of a person affect the type of leisure activities they would take part in?
8   Why was the horse so important in pre-industrial society?
9   What type of activities were used as a substitute for war?
10 What effect did the game laws have on leisure pursuits?
11 What sporting activities were played by *all* social classes during the popular recreation era?
12 Why were lower-class activities localised?
13 What were 'baiting' sports?
14 How did the monarchy make sure the people practised their archery skills?
15 What effect did the Reformation of the church have on sports and recreations?
16 Why was real tennis exclusive?
17 Why is real tennis also often referred to as 'Royal' tennis?
18 Give *two* examples of towns or areas that still play mob-type games today.
19 How were teams selected for mob games?
20 In terms of organisation what was unique about cricket?

CHAPTER 29

Nineteenth-century athleticism and the role of the public school

Learning objectives

- To identify the role public school played in the historical development of sport.
- To follow the stages of development of sport in the public schools of the nineteenth century.
- To look at the reasons for the rise of the so-called 'games cult'.
- To look at the education of girls during the nineteenth century.
- To understand the impact of athleticism on society.

In the public schools of the upper classes organised games began to appear, at first as spontaneous recreations and for the most part disapproved of by the teachers. However, as they became more developed it was recognised that educational objectives could be passed on through participation in games.

Sports became a feature of all public schools and were regarded as a powerful force in the education of the sons of the upper classes. Team games formed the central core, particularly football and cricket (and rowing at the schools situated near a river). These games were physically strenuous, demanding and relied on cooperation and leadership – all characteristics that a gentleman needed to acquire.

29.1 The public school

DEFINITION

ENDOWED
Bequeathed permanent income (to help fund a school, for example).

Public school has been defined as:

> an endowed place of education of old standing to which the sons of gentlemen resort in large numbers and where they continue to reside from eight or nine to eighteen years of age.

The schools were termed 'public' because they were not confined by locality: pupils travelled to them from all over the country. They were exclusive as not only travel but also tuition fees had to be paid. By 1810 there were seven boarding schools that fulfilled this definition. This small band of elite schools would have one of the most important impacts on the development of sport. The seven schools were Winchester, Westminster, Eton, Harrow, Charterhouse, Rugby and Shrewsbury.

DEFINITION

FAGGING
Smaller boys had to look after the wants of the senior boys.

At the beginning of the nineteenth century the education in these schools was limited by today's standards. Lessons were almost exclusively 'classical' in their content, with Latin and Greek the mainstays. Facilities were very basic, and the life of the students was brutal and tough. Discipline was maintained by flogging, and bullying and fagging were common.

The schools were often very understaffed. For example, in 1800 Eton had only eight members of staff to teach 550 boys, and in all schools the average number in a class was 70.

29.2 The development of sport in public schools

At the start of the nineteenth century sport was not an element of public-school education that was widely promoted. Headmasters were against sport and spent much of their energy banning the pursuit of such recreations. However, by the middle of the century sports and games had become an essential part in the education of boys of the middle and upper

- What sports might boys have tried to play in school at the beginning of the nineteenth century?
- What features of these popular recreations do you think headmasters might have objected to?
- Can you think of any sports or recreations that might have been acceptable?

classes. In 1800 headmasters felt sport was for 'flannelled fools and muddied oafs', and that education was all about godliness and good learning, but by 1860 games such as rugby, football and cricket had become a central part in the concept of 'muscular Christianity' which now steered public-school education. Headmasters now extolled pupils to 'Play up, play up and play the game'.

29.2.1 *The three stages of development of the games cult*

The change in attitude to sports and games in public schools during the nineteenth century is best viewed as a three-stage progression:
1 The barbarian phase, 1790–1830.
2 The Arnoldian/athleticism phase.
3 The games cult and philistine copies.

The barbarian phase

During this period schools were unruly places, and there was a constant battle between staff and pupils for control. Boys would bring to school the games and recreations they had taken part in at home. These would have included mob games (various forms of football and stick-and-ball games), which were mainly spontaneous and very violent.

Animal sports were also popular – either hunting or baiting/fighting sports. Many schools owned their own packs of hunting dogs and boys were allowed to bring to school fighting cocks and dogs. Many of these events were no doubt linked with gambling, and prize fighting and horse racing, already well established, gave further opportunities for gambling. Sport at this time also had strong associations with inns and hotels and drinking was another vice boys would partake in if allowed. Consequently many schools tried to limit the boys' access to these pursuits. Not surprisingly, boys often resented this, leading to further conflict.

Cricket was more readily accepted by authorities – the game had been codified by the beginning of the nineteenth century and this, coupled with the fact that it was non-violent, made it more suitable as a 'gentry' recreation, The first recorded school match took place in 1796 between Westminster and Eton.

Cricket was one of the few acceptable games in the first phase of public school sport development

This passage from J. Gathone-Hardy's *The Public School Phenomenon* summarises the barbarian phase:

> Games during the eighteenth century and early nineteenth century were extremely popular and much time was spent on them. Minet's 'Journal' is full of cricket scores (one part of the school playing another) and shows that Winchester boys could spend half the day on sport. But the point is that it was entirely left to them. It was not part of school life, and matches or rowing races were always being banned. Games were not played to keep fit or instil virtue like team spirit or to occupy and therefore discipline boys or to sublimate sexual energy. They were played purely for pleasure.

The Arnoldian/athleticism phase

In 1827 Dr Thomas Arnold became headmaster of Rugby School, and he was to have an important influence on the reform of the public schools. Although Arnold's main concern was with the education and control of his pupils, the programmes and rules he introduced had a parallel effect on the reform of games and sports in schools.

His main innovations were to introduce:

- the *house system*, which neatly led to the formation of early sports teams
- *prefects*, who would organise the games and activities of the boys – the first administrators
- *bounds*, whereby games and fights were confined to the school's grounds
- *muscular Christianity*, the idea that there is a close link between Christianity and the concept of sportsmanship
- a *philosophy of character* – games were soon seen as a vehicle of developing character.

Under Arnold's rule, boys were allowed to play sport every day.

It is important to remember that these games were still isolated – travel had not really developed sufficiently to allow schools to play each other regularly, and differences in rules made fixtures difficult. Games evolved in each school that fitted the particular features of the school's buildings and grounds.

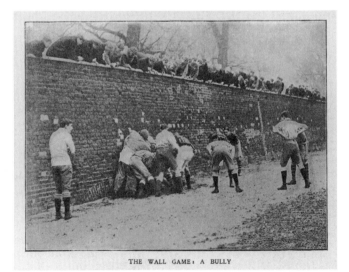

THE WALL GAME: A BULLY

At Eton the wall was used as part of their version of football

activity

Read the following extracts from *Tom Brown's School Days*. It is Tom's first day at Rugby School; his new friend East is showing him around and begins to try and explain the rules of the 'Rugby game'.

'Our House plays the whole of the school at football, and we all wear white trousers to show 'em we don't care for knocks.

'This is one of the goals, the match is for the best of three goals and it won't do you see, just to kick the ball through these posts, it must go over the cross bar; any height'll do so long as its between the posts.'

Tom's respect increased as he struggled to make out his friend's technicalities and East set to work to explain the mysteries of 'off your side', 'drop kicks', 'punts', 'places' and the other intricacies of the great science of football.

'You see this gravel walk running down all along this side of the playing ground and the line of elms opposite on the other? Well they're out of bounds. As soon as the ball gets past them, it's in touch and out of play.'

'And now that the two sides have fairly sundered and each occupies its own ground and we get a good look at them, what absurdity is this? You don't mean to say that those fifty or sixty boys in white trousers, many of them quite small are going to play that huge mass opposite?'

- What aspects of the old mob games survived in the Rugby game?
- What technical developments are evident in the game?
- Can you identify any unique features of the Rugby game?
- Can you identify any character-building virtues evident in the game?

The games cult and philistine copies

The headmaster of Winchester school said in 1870: 'Give me a boy who plays cricket and I can make something of him'. The success of schools such as Rugby led to the cult of games spreading throughout the private education system. Social changes also had an effect. The industrial revolution was now in full swing and creating a new affluent social class (the middle class), so creating a huge market for private education. Middle-class families wanted their sons to be educated as gentlemen and to service this need there was a huge growth of proprietary schools. Matthew Arnold called these the 'philistine' schools. He also identified in the 1860s two groups now making up the upper echelons of British society: the aristocratic class (the traditional gentry, whom he called 'barbarians') and the new middle class whom he called 'philistines'. This social division was also beginning to be evident in the schooling system.

Marlborough School, under the headship of G.E.L. Cotton, and Uppingham, under Edward Thring, are two good examples of the new philistine schools. Cotton had been a junior master at Rugby while Thomas Arnold was headmaster and so transplanted most of the Rugby programme to his new school. This transplantation

was followed by a number of other former Rugby staff and pupils to schools – such as Clifton, Wellington and King Edwards, Birmingham throughout the 1860s.

Thring's influence at Uppingham was slightly different. Although an old boy of Eton, where he had immersed himself in games, he favoured a more holistic approach to school sport. He allowed lessons to finish at midday so that pupils could devote the afternoon to sport. He had a gymnasium built at the school in 1859 and encouraged swimming and athletics because he felt that games were too restrictive and did not appeal to non-athletic boys. However, Thring's ideas did not really catch on in other schools, most preferring to follow the games route.

activity

The later part of the nineteenth century saw a vast expansion in the building of sports facilities at the public schools. Taking rugby as an example, in 1850 Rugby had one fives court and one playing field, but by 1879 Rugby had nine fives courts, two cricket pavilions and pitches, a gymnasium, swimming baths and acres of playing fields.

- What factors might have led to such an expansion in facilities?
- How did the school finance the building of these facilities?
- Why was winning matches against other schools important?

DEFINITION

CLARENDON COMMISSION

A royal commission set up in 1864 to investigate the great public schools.

The Commission reported that boys at Eton devoted more than 20 hours a week to playing cricket.

The games cult is often linked to the Clarendon Commission, a royal commission set up by parliament that gave its first report in 1864. Its role was to investigate the management and programmes of the nine great public schools (Eton, Winchester, Westminster, Charterhouse, St Paul's, Merchant Taylors, Harrow, Rugby and Shrewsbury).

The Committee's main finding was that these schools instilled character in their pupils, many of whom went on to become influential leaders in all walks of life both in Britain and around the Empire. The Commission stated that the system of team games followed by these schools was the main developer of character. Football in particular was singled out as encouraging stamina, courage and the ability to withstand knocks. Cricket was given similar praise.

It is clear from reading the findings of the Commission that by the 1860s most of these schools had really ceased to be academic institutions and were merely sports nurseries. However, the Commission gave games its seal of approval – and so the games cult was formed. All other schools, especially the new middle-class ones, followed the programme promoted by the Commission.

By the end of the nineteenth century school matches had become important social occasions. Parents and old boys came to watch, school magazines reported on matches and even the national papers would cover fixtures. Several fixtures, such as the Eton versus Harrow cricket match, became a national obsession with 10 000 spectators watching the 1863 match.

activity

The following passage by Francis Duckworth sums up the status of sport, and particularly team games, by the end of the nineteenth century.

> Realise the importance of games. It is in football, cricket and rowing that English men get splendid moral training which no other nation gets.
>
> Germany and France overwork their boys . . . nearly always they are stunted and weak. None of them gets that magnificent sporting instinct which is the real foundation of our Great Empire.

- What would this 'character training' be used for in the Empire?
- Why does Duckworth mention Germany and France?
- What common characteristics do football, cricket and rowing have?

29.3 The education of girls

The education of girls lagged behind that of boys. There was very little provision before 1720 when a number of ladies' academies were established. These were boarding institutions catering for only around 50 girls. They taught a little general education but were mainly concerned with teaching 'accomplishments' – dance, sewing, etiquette and a very small amount of physical exercise (mainly the feminine art of marching, which was taught by army sergeants).

The general social view was that there was no need for women to be educated. They were thought to be inferior to men and the only role of girls of the upper classes was to get a husband, which did *not* require a serious education. So what education there was for girls of the upper classes tended to be very vocational. An alternative to school was for a family to appoint a governess, who again would teach mainly etiquette and deportment – and invariably paid no attention to physical exercise apart from dance.

However, in the early nineteenth century the role of women in society began to change. The industrial revolution caused an expansion of the middle classes, creating a potential market for educational entrepreneurs. The first girls' public schools emerged in the mid-nineteenth century – Princess Helena College was set up in 1820 to teach future governesses. Cheltenham Ladies' College (established in 1854) is a better example of a school set up to service the new middle-class market.

Once again it was a royal commission that increased the pace of development. In 1868 the Taunton Commission was set up to examine the schools for boys and girls that had not been covered in the earlier Clarendon Report. Its findings revealed the poor state of education for girls of the upper and middle classes. Following the report parliament passed the Endowed Schools Act in 1869, which allowed the development of many new girls' schools. Many sister schools to existing boys' public schools were established and the more commercial proprietary schools aimed at the middle-class market. These schools joined together to form the Girls' Public

DEFINITION

TAUNTON COMMISSION

Set up in 1868 to review schools not covered by the Clarendon Commission. Included evidence from Miss Buss, Headmistress of North London Collegiate school, and advocated a balanced curriculum that included mental exertion and bodily exercise.

School Day Trust, and copied much of the Clarendon model: houses, prefects and organised games.

Roedean, established in 1881, is a good example. Girls' schools had only the boys' schools to model themselves on: Roedean was modelled on Malvern boys' school and copied exactly its system of houses, dormitories, prefects and organised games. At first these games were not very strenuous. Activities such as croquet, bowls and quoits were preferred, reflecting the wider societal view. Callisthenics and gymnastics did, however, begin to develop.

Pioneers such as Buss, Beale and Osterberg further developed PE programmes for girls. Frances Mary Buss and Dorothea Beale had both been pupils at Queens College, where the virtues of muscular Christianity had been implanted, and went on to become head-mistresses – Buss at North London Collegiate and Beale at Cheltenham Ladies' College. They both promoted sport and games as an essential element in female education but felt that too many boys' games were too rough for girls. At both schools callisthenics and gymnastics became compulsory. The success of these schools and the ladies they produced developed a 'cult' and many other girls' schools followed their lead.

This development created the need for specialist teachers. Although boys' schools tended to solve this through hiring coaches and professionals, girls' schools favoured specialist PE teachers and a number of training colleges were established towards the end of the nineteenth century. Madame Bergman Osterberg was appointed as Superintendent to London Schools in 1881 and set about writing a programme of physical training to be used in the schools. In 1885 she set up a training college in Hampstead to train female PE teachers. The college moved to Dartford in 1895. Other colleges followed: Chelsea in 1898 and Iron Marsh (Liverpool) in 1899.

By the beginning of the twentieth century education for girls had caught up with that of boys – and, it could be argued, in terms of physical education had overtaken it. There were now specialist trained teachers in schools teaching a holistic programme that covered both games and individual activities designed at developing character and physical well-being.

29.4 The impact of athleticism on society

The development of sport through the public school system of the nineteenth century was to have a profound effect on the spread of sport throughout society, both in Britain and throughout the British Empire. It sowed the seeds of the rationalisation of sport, in which sports were codified and regulated by governing bodies, and the boys who left the schools spread the cult of manly games across the world.

Numerous other texts chart this transportation and we feel it is better here to simply summarise the impact these old boys had on society. The further development into the rational phase of sports history will be covered in Chapter 30.

An effective way of summarising this impact is CAT PUICCA.

- C – *colonial*. Many boys took up posts in the colonial service, helping to administer and govern the Empire's many colonies. They took with them their sporting kit. Initially they played amongst themselves but gradually introduced the sports and games to the indigenous populations.

activity

- What type of games could the girls' schools have copied from the boys in the nineteenth century?
- Which of these might have been too rough to adopt?
- Which of these do you think would have been socially acceptable?
- Why did girls' schools, rather than boys' schools, appoint specialist PE teachers?

To find out more about rationalisation of sport, turn to page 356.

- *A – army*. Another career for many boys was as commissioned officers in the armed forces. Initially the officers would use sports as a recreation to fill in long hours, but the social control and moral value of keeping the working-class soldiers occupied were not lost on them. This played an important part in spreading the cult still further.

- *T – teaching*. Many former pupils became teachers, especially in the new expanding proprietary and grammar schools. Often they simply repeated the programme of games and physical recreation they had followed in their schooldays. It was not unusual for sporty teachers to play for the school teams at the end of the nineteenth century.

- *P – patronage*. Supporting sporting events and competitions by providing funding for trophies or land for pitches (and in other ways) was another important role undertaken by old boys.

- *U – university*. This was a very important stage. Cambridge and Oxford chiefly gave young men further time and resources to pursue and refine sporting activities. One major problem though was the plethora of different rules for the various games. In order to allow all to play, compromise rules were required and this was the first step towards the rationalisation of sport.

- *I – industry*. Once they had finished school many boys returned to their fathers' factories and businesses. These were Arnold's 'philistines'. Their love of sport needed an outlet and soon clubs linked to these factories were set up. At first there were some social limits – only managers and office staff could join the teams – but gradually the lower classes were also admitted. Many current football teams – Stoke City, West Ham, Manchester United – were formed in this way.

- *C – church*. Much of the boys' education was religiously based so it is not surprising that many boys took up careers in the Church. Muscular Christianity promoted the use of sport as a vehicle for teaching morals and Christian virtues. Many clergymen used it in its most practical form, encouraging sports and setting up teams both here and abroad. Again there are examples in modern football – Aston Villa, Everton and Wolverhampton Wanderers have church origins.

- *C – clubs*. The first stage for many old boys was to form clubs so they could continue to play their games. The Old Etonians is a good example of this type of club, but many more were also formed.

- *A – administration*. When their playing days were over, many men joined and developed governing bodies for their sports, and helped to formulate national rules.

activity

Thinking about the major world sports, can you find links between the countries that now play them and the influence of the British schoolboys? Try cricket first.

Key revision points

Public schools were endowed, boarding, fee-paying, socially exclusive centres of classical education. The development of sports in public schools went through three stages: barbarian, Arnoldian, games cult and philistine copies. The barbarian phase was characterised by unruly schools, boys in control, mob games and animal sports. The Arnoldian phase introduced the prefect system, sport now being seen as a way of social control and instilling character-building values used in the education of gentlemen. The games cult phase brought middle-class and 'philistine' copies, and the spread of games around Britain and its empire. The Clarendon Commission highlighted good practice, leading to copies of the models in the better schools. Education of girls lagged behind that of boys, being restrained by social constraints. The Taunton Commission and the influence of headmistresses such as Buss, Beale and Bergman Osterberg changed this. Throughout the nineteenth century, games were spread through the British Empire by old boys of public schools.

Key terms

You should now understand the following terms. If you do not, go back through the chapter and find out what they mean.

Bounds
Clarendon Commission
Endowed
Endowed Schools Act
Fagging
House system
Madame Bergman Osterberg
Muscular Christianity
Prefects
Public school
Taunton Commission
Thomas Arnold

Progress check

1 Why were public schools so called?
2 How was discipline maintained in the early public schools?
3 Why at the start of the nineteenth century were many school headmasters opposed to sports and games?
4 What were the three stages of development of public school sport?
5 In the first phase of development, who organised games in public schools?
6 Why were sports involving animals played in schools at the start of the nineteenth century?
7 Which was the only game that was readily accepted in the early schools? Why?
8 How did Dr Arnold change the organisation of Rugby school?
9 Why was it difficult for schools to play each other at sport during the early nineteenth century?
10 What changes in society led to a rise in the popularity of the public schools in the mid 1800s?
11 How and why did the influence of schools such as Rugby spread through the rest of the education system?
12 How did the Clarendon Commission promote the games cult?
13 Which sports did the Clarendon Commission particularly praise?
14 What type of education did ladies' academies offer in the eighteenth century?
15 What societal factors limited the development of female education in the nineteenth century?
16 What role did Miss Buss and Miss Beale play in the development of physical education for girls?
17 How did the teaching of physical education in girls' and boys' schools differ at the start of the twentieth century?
18 How did Madame Bergman Osterberg shape the future of physical education in Britain?
19 What is the link between the public schools and the global spread of sport in the nineteenth century?
20 Outline the origins of some of our present-day professional football teams.

CHAPTER 30

Industrialisation and rational sport

Learning objectives

- To understand the way people spent their leisure time after the industrial revolution.
- To be able to relate how sport in industrial Britain reflected the changes in society.
- To follow the stages of the rationalisation of sport.
- To understand the key characteristics of rational sport.

We can chart the development, codification and administration of all major sports from 1860 onwards. Important changes occurred in society that would determine the image of modern sport. It is important that you know a little about the impact of the industrialisation of British society and the effect that this had on the people, their work, homes and leisure.

After the industrial revolution most people lived and worked in urban areas and the influence of the rural elements from the popular recreation era steadily declined. Modern sport is also urban sport.

30.1 Life in industrial society

DEFINITION

CODIFICATION
The creation and maintenance of rules.

DEFINITION

SABBATARIANISM
Saw Sunday as a holy day of rest, so constraining physical recreations such as sport.

In pre-industrial societies there was little division between work and leisure. Time for sport and recreation was largely determined by the rhythm of the agricultural calendar. Industrialisation changed this, bringing a much clearer distinction between work and leisure.

Factory time meant long shifts – coal and steam power required round-the-clock attention, and people worked 12-hour shifts, which left them little time for leisure. People moved to the towns and cities in their thousands. They had to live within walking distance of the factories and rows of terraced housing sprang up, with little open space. The old common land disappeared under the urban sprawl. Consequently, working-class people had very little active recreation, Sunday was their only day off work, but sabbatarianism decreed that Sunday was a day of rest – which was much needed after working such long hours.

However, recreation did survive: Church holidays were still celebrated and conditions for the workers did improve as the level of industrialisation increased towards the end of the nineteenth century. Employment laws were passed, reducing the hours worked and improving the living conditions of the workers. In parallel with this, the middle and upper classes, who had far fewer constraints, continued to play and promote sports with much vigour.

The industrial period saw the development of sport along very clear social lines. Social class determined how much free time you had and which sports you would pursue.

The upper classes continued to take part in country pursuits. Industrialisation did not really affect their lifestyle or the sports they played. Developments in transport, and especially the railways, allowed people to pursue their sports further afield. The railways opened up areas such as the Lake District and the Scottish Highlands for exploring and hunting.

The middle classes were dominant in developing sport. They continued to promote the games that originated in the public schools, adopted games from the far corners of the Empire and invented new sports and recreations to fill their increasing leisure time. Badminton, hockey and lawn tennis are all good examples of nineteenth-century middle-class inventions.

activity

How did time and space constraints limit the amount of physical recreation the working class could take part in at the start of the industrial period?

DEFINITION

BROKEN TIME PAYMENTS

Clubs paid working-class players the wages they could not earn while playing.

activity

List the type of sports and recreations that the upper, middle and lower classes would have enjoyed during the industrial period.

Working-class people tended to be drawn to sports that could make money – lack of leisure time meant that playing sport often led to the loss of wages, a situation few working people could afford. This led to sports teams in football and rugby paying players 'broken time payments', a development that caused much ill feeling between the classes and led to a further division – a north–south divide (clubs in the north tended to be more open towards paying working-class players). Towards the end of the nineteenth century this led to the development of professionalism in many sports (this will be discussed later in the chapter). Other sports, such as fishing and pigeon racing, allowed working-class men to escape the drudgery of urban industrial life.

Here we can see clearly that sport was reflecting society. Social segregation was an added factor of industrialisation, and culture and recreation mirrored this division – graveyards, trains, seaside resorts, theatre and, above all, sport were all segregated by social class and money.

Battle of the classes – Old Carthusians play Preston North End in the quarter final of the FA cup in 1887. Slowly the working class teams from the north and midlands began to dominate football

30.2 The rural scene

By the mid 1800s Britain had become both an industrialised and a predominately urban society; there was no turning back. In 1881 over 70% of the British population lived in towns or cities. The influence of the rural gentry began to decrease, land values plummeted and the profits from agriculture also suffered. Huge rises in rents for land caused great resentment amongst the remaining rural communities. The demand for food from the cities led to the break-up of many estates and a more commercially oriented farming system began to develop.

Many rural sports suffered from changes in the laws that led to the demise, and in many cases the criminalisation, of popular 'blood sports' such as baiting and cock fighting. However, the law makers overlooked their own field sports, and foxhunting in particular was extremely popular amongst both rural and urban upper classes. Fishing was another country sport that survived, although industrialisation caused a problem – pollution of many rivers and water courses. Social division also occurred here, with the working class confined to 'coarse' fishing and the upper classes having the means to travel further afield to cleaner upland rivers where 'game fishing' had salmon and trout as the prey. The development of the railways opened more and more of the British Isles to the upper classes.

All sports that developed during this industrial phase, whether urban or rural, followed a similar pattern of development. As mentioned in previous chapters, the inspiration came from many sources, including the expanding British Empire. A good example to highlight these stages of development was canoeing.

30.2.1 *Canoeing*

In 1865 a Scot called John MacGregor (nicknamed Rob Roy) visited North America and witnessed the native Americans travelling about in long thin boats propelled by double-bladed paddles – which they called canoes. On his return to London he asked Searles boatmakers in Lambeth to build a replica canoe. Naming the boat 'Rob Roy' he set off to explore the rivers and lakes of northern Europe. MacGregor wrote a book about his adventures – *A Thousand Miles in the Rob Roy Canoe* – which became very popular. Soon Searles were making hundreds of 'Rob Roy' canoes.

Typically it was not long before the new sport received some form of organisation. In 1866 a large number of 'Rob Roy' owners met at the Star and Garter Hotel in Richmond and formed the Canoe Club, and were soon holding their own regatta on the River Thames. MacGregor wrote further books about canoeing down the rivers Nile and Jordan, which led to canoes being exported throughout the British Empire. Canoeing became a sport with worldwide recognition.

Can you identify the following stages of development in the sport of canoeing?

- Formation of clubs.
- A national governing body set up.
- National competition set up.
- Exported to other countries.

Many rural pursuits were adapted to suit the new urban environment. This is a track steeplechase from the 1880s

30.3 Life in town

The needs of industry meant that there was widespread migration of the populace to the growing towns and cities. Although islands of rural tranquillity did survive in some areas, throughout most of Britain – especially the Midlands and the north, southern Scotland and south Wales – the whole geography and culture of society changed.

This urban immigration had a great impact on all aspects of culture: religion was affected as much as sport and leisure. Old ways of playing were not going to survive long in this more liberal, educated and mobile industrialised society. The time available for leisure was also under threat from pressures to get more work done and the expansion of the towns swallowed up what space there was for games and sports.

Sport did survive: the inventiveness of the Victorians led to a period of sports 'genesis', a hotbed of sports development. Between 1860 and 1890 most of today's modern sports were invented and rationalised. There was also a change in geographical dominance away from London and the south-east to the midlands and the north.

The main effect of urbanisation was that there was less chance to play due to limitations on time and space. However, there was a substitute in spectatorism – watching sporting activities, although this was not without its problems. Brailsford (1992) highlights the problems that this could cause: 'What had been feasible in the countryside with a few hundred participants could become a virtual riot when it drew thousands into the streets.'

Pedestrianism was a popular sport at the end of the nineteenth century. Here a working class 'ped' competes against a gentleman 'racer'

activity

- What constraints in industrial towns led to the decline in popular recreations?
- How do you think sport had to adapt to suit this new urban culture?

activity

Look at the picture above.

- Can you identify the 'ped' and the gentlemen?
- How would their reasons for competing differ?

Crowds at horse racing, cricket and boxing matches grew rapidly. The popularity of these sports was aided by the fact that by the beginning of the nineteenth century they had developed governing bodies and standardised rules. Cricket also took advantage of the developing transport network with touring teams, such as William Clarke's All England XI, travelling around the country playing local teams. The development of rail travel also allowed the introduction of cricket's characteristic county structure.

The public house also became an important venue for the industrial classes. Landlords would often promote boxing matches, animal fights and pedestrian races to attract customers. Most pubs also provided facilities and equipment for a range of sports and games: bowls, quoits, fives and rackets. The larger pubs also had football fields and running tracks. Many of the sports offered would have gambling potential – another attraction. Pubs and inns also became the meeting place for sporting associations. Many sports governing bodies were formed in pubs.

activity

Find out where the Football Association and Rugby League were formed.

DEFINITION

PEDESTRIANISM

Walking races between two or more competitors, often for a cash prize.

Time was the great limiting factor for the lower classes' participation in sport. The factory system at the start of the nineteenth century made little provision for leisure; most people worked 12 hours a day six days a week for very poor wages. However, gradually this improved as the factory acts were passed, with half-day holidays being introduced by the mid 1800s, though it would be the beginning of the twentieth century before all occupations were given this free time.

The law makers also had an impact on sport and recreation. Acts were passed to limit cruelty against men and animals, including measures that banned most animal sports. The General Enclosure Act of 1845 made it more difficult to build on open spaces in towns and led the way to the formation of public parks. The Wash House Act 1845 led to urban councils building swimming pools and baths, although their main concern was cleanliness. Swimming and sports such as water polo quickly developed in these new purpose-built facilities.

Another urban addition was the introduction of the enclosed sports arena – entrepreneurs quickly saw the commercial potential of charging people to watch sports on their free half day. The first arenas were built for pedestrianism and football; cricket and rugby were quick to follow. Again publicans led the way in this new venture. The cricket grounds of Lord's and Trent Bridge are good examples of inns using fields originally used in coaching days for sport.

30.4 Organised competition and regular play

Public-school boys and university students sowed the seeds of sports rationalisation in the early 1800s. They developed competition between their houses and colleges, introducing different leagues and cup competitions. Many of these school competitions developed into today's major sporting events – for example, the FA Cup is based on a competition called the Cock House competition that boys at Harrow played in the mid-1800s. It was only natural that on leaving education and forming clubs they would want to continue playing competitively.

Initially fixtures amongst clubs were rather *ad hoc* affairs. Gentlemen's clubs would arrange fixtures on a day and date that suited both parties, and most of these amateur players had no constraints on when and where they could play. The rules played to were also rather informal – games could change at half time from football rules to rugby rules. Generally the home team chose the particular rule and the away team provided the ball – but these did not always work in harmony.

As more and more teams became active, this *ad hoc* arrangement had to change. Clubs began to meet and form associations in order to make matches more regular and to reach compromise over the rules of play. Such meetings ultimately led to the formation of national governing bodies in all major sports by the end of the nineteenth century.

Football is a good example. In 1863, leading figures from the major clubs and schools met at the Free Masons Tavern, Lincoln's Inn Fields, London to finally decide on a common set of rules. This process took many meetings until finally, in December, a vote was

DEFINITION

OPEN CHAMPIONSHIP

Competition open to both amateur and professional performers.

taken to agree on a national set of rules for Association Football. Not all attendees at the meeting agreed, and the members from Blackheath went off on their own to form the Rugby Football Union.

These governing bodies not only governed and controlled their own sport in the UK – due to the status of the British Empire many of our governing bodies became the world's sport regulator. Good examples are the Lawn Tennis Association (tennis) and the Royal and Ancient Club (golf). The competitions these two bodies set up (Wimbledon and the Open Championship) became world-renowned events.

The other major development was that the working classes generally were given Saturday afternoons off, and this consequently became the time for sport. Church and factory teams soon sprang up and many entrepreneurs with an eye for making money set up teams. These teams required regular fixtures and, in order to attract spectators, better players, so clubs began to pay players to play football. The more spectators they attracted the more money there was to pay players and soon an elite group of professional teams from the midlands and north came together to form the Football League in 1888. Cricket's county championship similarly developed into a regular system of fixtures with points and a champion team at the end of the season.

Organised sports festivals became very popular especially during the summer; good examples are the Dover's Games and Much Wenlock Games. Other early Olympic-style sports competitions include the Morpeth Olympic Games in the north-east. The Morpeth Games began in 1873 and included both wrestling bouts and athletic competitions, adding Olympic to their title. The games, unlike the modern Olympics, were only for professional competitors and were last staged in 1958. There were also the Liverpool Olympics, founded in 1862 by Charles Melly the President of the Liverpool Athletic Club, and these catered for a range of sports.

Can you identify rational aspects of sport in the illustration (right)?

The Wimbledon lawn tennis championship, set up in 1877, is a good example of a rational sports event

activity

Football Association   1863
Rugby Football League   1885
Lawn Tennis Association   1888
Badminton Association   1893

Can you find the dates the following bodies were formed?

Hockey Association
Amateur Swimming Association
Amateur Athletic Association
Rugby Football Union

Put these in chronological order. Are there any reasons for this order?

Only 'gentleman amateurs' were allowed to compete, the games were so successful that they attracted over 10 000 spectators and led to the formation of the National Olympian Association which held an Olympic festival at Llandudno in 1866. Both Dr Penny Brookes from Much Wenlock and French aristocrat Baron de Coubertin took on the baton and began formulating a plan to set up an international Olympic movement, culminating in the first modern Olympic Games held in Athens, Greece in 1896.

By the beginning of the twentieth century sport had evolved to match the urban/industrial society. It was now governed by independent bodies who regulated their sport and oversaw competitions, including national leagues and challenge cups. Their net of influence spread far and wide over most of the globe and international competition began. The commercial side of sport was evolving, with professional performers and spectatorism creating commercial clubs and purpose-built sports stadia.

In rational sport few played and many watched – which contrasts directly with the popular recreation of the seventeenth and eighteenth centuries, where many played and few watched.

At the 1908 London Olympics OXO sponsored the Olympic marathon, and flasks full of the drink were handed out to the runners. Both winners of the marathon, Italian Dorando Pietri (who was disqualified as he was assisted over the line) and American John Hayes, took up lucrative contracts to turn professional in the USA. The *London Evening News* sponsored a marathon over the Olympic course in October of the same year, with a first prize of £100. Leading English athlete C.W. Gardiner beat Dorando Pietri for a £100 prize on an indoor track specially laid with coconut matting at the Albert Hall in London.

Key revision points

Most sports were rationalised in the 'hotbed' period – 1860–1890. The industrial revolution led to a change in the way people lived and this was also reflected in the sports they played. Time for sport was governed by social class, and the working classes had to wait much longer for free time than the middle and upper classes. The development of transport allowed inter-town sport competitions and opened up the countryside. Urbanisation meant that only a few people could play, leading to spectatorism and inevitably professionalism. Eventually all the main sports were rationalised – rules were codified and developed nationally. Rational sport became characterised by channelled aggression, stringent organisation, formal rules and regular play.
Pedestrianism was the first sport to switch its contests to a Saturday afternoon to profit from workers with free time on their hands.

Key terms

You should now understand the following terms. If you do not, go back through the chapter and find out what they mean.

Broken time payments
Codification
National governing body
Open championship
Pedestrianism
Rationalisation
Sabbatarianism

Progress check

1   How did industrialisation affect the way people lived?
2   How did industrialisation change the distinction between work and leisure?
3   Why was Sunday not a day available for recreation?
4   What space constraints on sporting activities resulted from industrialisation?
5   What factors improved conditions for the working classes towards the end of the nineteenth century?
6   Why were the middle classes able to play more sport than the lower classes?
7   How did the transport revolution help the upper classes pursue their sporting activities?
8   Give examples of sports invented by the British middle class during the nineteenth century.
9   Where did the inspiration for many of these new sports come from?
10   What were broken time payments?
11   What effect did social class have on choice of sport during the nineteenth century?
12   What type of blood sports were overlooked by the law makers of the nineteenth century?
13   What effect did industrialisation have on the sport of fishing?
14   What was the link between sports rationalisation and the developing British Empire?
15   What happened to the geographical spread of sport after the industrial revolution?
16   During which decades did the so-called 'hotbed' of sport occur?
17   How had the relationship between spectators and performers changed by the end of the nineteenth century?
18   What changes in society led to the development of national governing bodies of sport in the latter part of the nineteenth century?
19   What benefits did leagues bring to clubs?
20   Why were spectators attracted to challenge cup competitions such as the FA Cup (begun in 1872)?

The emergence of physical education

Learning objectives

- To investigate the European origins of physical education.
- To understand the impact of compulsory education on the development of physical education.
- To follow the development of physical education in the United Kingdom.
- To understand the impact of war on the development of physical education.
- To investigate the reasons behind our current system of physical education.

Physical education is a modern phenomenon with a history of less than 100 years. However, its origins go back further than this and it developed from many different strands. Two main pathways can be identified, which developed from the two traditions of education in England in the nineteenth century. In Chapter 29 we discussed the role of the public schools system; in this chapter we will concentrate on state education.

Outside the public schools, a different type of physical education grew up from several roots – European systems of gymnastics, military drill and callisthenics. At the start of the twentieth century these came together to form physical training, which was adopted in the elementary schools for the lower classes. The reasons behind this adoption and the values and characteristics that this type of exercise produced were very different from those of public-school games: physical training produced a fit and obedient workforce. Whereas the public schools produced the nation's leaders, the elementary or state system produced the nation's followers.

To find out more about the public schools system, turn to page 343.

31.1 European roots of physical education

Against the manly diversions of the public-school sports, gymnastics in Britain enjoyed only limited popularity before the end of the nineteenth century. However, in mainland Europe a number of systemised programmes of physical exercise involving gymnastic activities had been developed. They enjoyed widespread popularity and made some inroads into Britain with refugees escaping the numerous social revolutions that occurred in Europe during the nineteenth century.

There were two main influences on this gymnastic development, stemming from two different European countries:

- *German* – based on the work of Gut Muth and Ludwig Jahn.
- *Swedish* – based on the work of Per Hendrick Ling.

The German system had a strong military influence and included marching and rope and ladder climbing. Initially this was the influence that began to filter into Britain – gymnasiums based on the German model were built in London and other cities. P.H. Clias, an officer in the Swiss army, was instrumental in developing these ideas, producing his own version of Gut Muth's exercises. He was appointed to oversee physical training in the British Army and Navy training colleges and was superintendent of gymnastics at Charterhouse School. It was this type of exercise that the newly appointed HM Inspectors of Schools encouraged in 1833.

However, it was the Swedish system of 'drill', inspired by Ling, that had the biggest impact on the development of physical education in Britain. Using the German system as his inspiration, Ling simplified the exercises and reduced the military bias, concentrating more on style and grace. He also paid respect to the classical tradition, emphasising the harmony between body and mind. Ling's system was adopted by many school boards in Britain – most importantly the London School Board, which appointed Madame Bergman Osterberg to oversee this implementation. She played a central role in the development of PE in Britain, establishing the first specialist teacher-training college at Dartford in 1895.

Another uniquely British advocate of gymnastic training was Archibald McLaren who, after studying fencing and gymnastic training in a number of European countries, was appointed by the British army to oversee their physical training systems. He went on to commission his own gymnasium in Oxford in 1858. This became the model for many gymnasiums built by the army and numerous public schools. He also published a number of books and papers on bodily exercise and physical training and therefore further helped to spread the popularity of gymnastic training around the British Isles.

31.2 Schooling for all

In Britain before 1870 there was no national system of elementary education – most provision was fee paying and therefore only children of the upper and middle classes were educated. There was limited opportunity for working-class education, various bodies providing non-fee-paying schools for a limited number of working-class children. The most prolific of these were the British and Foreign School Society and the National Society for Education of the Poor, both of which were dependent on voluntary contributions. Very little sport or exercise was done in these schools and few had playgrounds, though school inspectors did try to encourage some form of physical exercise.

There were two main schools of thought regarding exercise in such schools. Several followed Rousseau's idea of education of the whole person; these practitioners recognised the social training gained from participating in games and physical activities. The second school of thought was those who saw physical drill as a means of developing basic discipline in schools and a paramilitary approach that prepared their charges for future service for the nation.

The working class, with their poor standard of living and long working hours, were unfit and many people began to raise this problem, particularly doctors who were working in urban areas. Mathis Roth was one such doctor. Roth wrote to a number of influential politicians and businessmen asking them to promote the importance of physical exercise for working-class children, maintaining that physical exercise was as important as teaching the 'three Rs'. The army and navy began to reject large numbers of working-class recruits because of their lack of fitness, and this had great influence on the government's decisions concerning education of the working class.

The major breakthrough was the Forster Education Act of 1870, also called the Elementary Education Act. W.E. Forster was Vice President of the Education Department and it was his intention to 'bring English education within the reach of every English home and within the reach of those children who have no homes, covering the country with good schools.' The Act established school boards in every area, and these were responsible for providing schools for all children in their area. The boards were also empowered to establish bylaws that made education compulsory for all children aged between five and 13. This move was further aided by the passing of employment acts which forbade the employment of children under the age of 10. What this Act did was to create a dual system of education in Britain – non-fee-paying state schools and fee-paying private or public schools.

The Forster Act also began the cycle of physical education in British schools. The Act stated that all children should undertake daily sessions of drill under a competent instructor for not more than two hours per week and 20 weeks in the year. This drill would mainly consist of military marching and was often taught by former army sergeants. Often girls were given no physical exercise at all.

In 1871 the London Board decided that all schools under its authority should provide physical training, exercise and drill. The Board also introduced a Drill Certificate for teachers. Although the philosophy was to expand the range of activities offered, the

FORSTER ACT 1870

Made education compulsory for all children between the ages of five and 13 years.

DRILL

Military-style exercise involving marching, carried out in elementary schools after the Forster Act.

DEFINITION

SWEDISH GYMNASTICS

*Drill-type exercises based on the work
of Ling, emphasising style,
grace and movement.*

DEFINITION

DARTFORD COLLEGE

*Established in Hampstead in 1885, this
was the first ever college to train specialist
female PE teachers. The main emphasis was
on practical and teaching skills with
a strong bias towards Ling-style
remedial gymnastics.*

*PE was introduced in the UK in order to get the
population fit in case of war*

military influence remained. However, the popularity of Swedish gymnastics was growing and superintendents employed to promote physical training increasingly pushed this system into the schools. The main pioneer of this movement was Miss Martina Bergman, who was appointed Superintendent of Physical Education in 1881. She set about installing in the London schools a systematic programme of all-round physical exercise based heavily on the work of Ling. Her main concern was with the education of girls; she did not believe in the popular view that strenuous physical activity and femininity were incompatible. She felt that drill was not suitable for girls but Swedish gymnastics was and she created her own training college for female PE teachers, initially based in Hampstead but then moving to Dartford, where the Bergman Osterberg Training College became the first residential college for specialist teachers in physical education.

By the beginning of the twentieth century, although there was now compulsory education for all, physical education was still in a stage of evolution. What was done in the schools depended on the philosophy and membership of the local school boards and, although some (like London and Leeds) promoted the more expansive Swedish style, most still clung stoically to military drill.

31.3 The effects of war

In 1899 Britain began a war in South Africa against a small group of Dutch settlers known as the Boers. By its end in May 1902, the Boer War had made a great impact on Britain's status as an imperial power and caused a knock-on effect in military preparation – and on the system of physical education in state schools.

At the onset of the war it was thought that the Boers, a small band of farmers, would be no match for the might of the British army. However, the Boers fought a guerrilla war of attrition, the like of which the British army had not faced before. The army's poor performance needed explanation back in Britain and the politicians and generals needed a scapegoat. The main accusation was that the working-class recruits were unfit and therefore ill prepared to fight, a point backed up by the increasing number of recruits being rejected by the armed forces. The main reason for this state was thought to be the teaching of Swedish gymnastics in the elementary schools.

In response to this, the Board of Education, in close association with the War Office, issued its Model Course of Physical Training. To implement this policy a former Inspector of Army Gymnastics, Colonel Fox, was appointed Inspector of Physical Training. He introduced barrack square drill to schools through a team of peripatetic instructors, former army sergeants who visited schools drilling the classes.

activity

The *Times* (24 February 1903) reporting on the implementation of the Model Course: 'Compulsory military training in schools was required in order to lay the foundations of a military spirit in the nation.'

What do you think were the advantages and disadvantages of the Model Course?

DEFINITION

THE MODEL COURSE

Established by the government and War Office in 1902, making military drill compulsory in all state schools.

PERIPATETIC INSTRUCTORS

Drill instructors who would visit and instruct at a number of schools in an area.

DEFINITION

1904 BOARD OF EDUCATION SYLLABUS

Replaced the Model Course in an attempt to bring educational values into physical training.

DEFINITION

THE 1909 SYLLABUS OF PHYSICAL TRAINING

Written by the medical department of the Board of Education with an emphasis on therapeutic gymnastics.

THERAPEUTIC GYMNASTICS

Activities that promoted health and resistance to disease and postural defects.

1933 SYLLABUS OF PHYSICAL TRAINING

The last Board of Education syllabus, which differentiated activities for junior and senior pupils.

There were numerous criticisms of the Model Course from the medical profession, National Union of Teachers and the Ling Physical Education Association, all claiming that the military emphasis was too strong and that there was little educational benefit in drill. These protests resulted in a governmental review, consisting of a committee to examine the model course and a number of royal commissions. The committee summarised that the model course was unsatisfactory because it lacked educational development and allowed no differentiation on the basis of age or sex. The committee also drew up a revised syllabus – the 1904 Board of Education Syllabus – which replaced the Model Course, although there was still a strong military bias in the syllabus.

Leading up to 1909, a number of developments occurred that were to have a major impact on physical education. Swedish gymnastics continued to be popular with many school boards and individual schools, both private and state. This was greatly aided by the increasing number of female teachers graduating from the PE training colleges set up by Madame Bergman Osterberg. Colonel Fox himself visited Sweden and was impressed by the systems of physical exercise he witnessed there.

Another important development was the establishment in 1907 of a new medical department within the Board of Education. This new department was given responsibility for physical training in state schools. A new team of inspectors was appointed and they set about examining the current systems of physical training carried out in British schools, in the armed forces and in other European countries. All the new inspectors agreed that the Swedish system was the most suitable for school-age children and in 1909 they produced a new syllabus encompassing Swedish gymnastics.

In 1909 the Board of Education issued a new syllabus – the Syllabus of Physical Training for Schools – which included sections on physiology and hygiene (reflecting the new medical department bias). This syllabus for the first time differentiated between children of different ages, suggesting different activities for infants and older pupils. It allowed more recreational activities (such as dancing, skipping and games) and breaks (there was also mention of therapeutic gymnastics) and was less formal than previous syllabuses. This syllabus represented an almost complete reversion to the Swedish style of physical training prevalent at the end of the nineteenth century. However, there was still a therapeutic core and the large class sizes and lack of space would probably in most cases still have required a drill-style delivery.

The next syllabus, in 1919, followed the horrors of the First World War. From the outset of that war there had been calls for a return to military drill in schools. Many of the public schools heeded this, also setting up cadet corps to aid the training of young officers and soldiers. The state school system, however, rejected such a move, maintaining that children of school age were too young for military training. War yet again was to influence the evolution of physical education – for the first time it brought to the forefront the recreational and morale-boosting characteristics of sports and physical exercise. Such activities were extensively used in the convalescence camps set up for wounded soldiers. The USA was allied to Britain in the war, and links developed between the countries. The popular American 'playground movement' stimulated interest and some adoption on this side of the Atlantic.

The war years were followed by the Depression, and life became very difficult for the lower classes. Throughout these years, though, education continued to develop – the school-leaving age was raised to 14 and new secondary schools were built, many with gymnasiums and playing fields. In 1933 the last Board of Education syllabus was produced – a revised Syllabus of Physical Training for Schools. It had two separate sections, part one suggesting activities for junior-school children (aged 5–11) and part two suggesting activities for children in senior schools (11–14). The emphasis of all activities was now on posture, perhaps reflecting the problems the lowered standards of living during the Depression years had caused. Again games were encouraged and there was one major step away from the drill style of delivery – the introduction of group work, a clear move away from the whole-class, command-style drill exercise.

31.4 Moving and growing

War continued to have an effect on the evolution of physical education. The Second World War (1939–1945) was fought in a more mobile and technological style, which had a knock-on effect on physical training in the armed forces and in education. There was a change of emphasis to initiative training and physical fitness (as opposed to obedience training), extensive use of apparatus and specifically the assault course. The war in the sky also had an impact on society – the threat of bombing led to the evacuation of children from the cities to safer rural areas. After the war the large amounts of 'Blitz' damage also necessitated widespread building of new schools and other civic facilities. New schools were often built with extensive facilities for sport: gymnasiums, playing fields and even swimming pools.

The other major impact was the 1944 Education Act, which made secondary school education available to all children. It also raised the school-leaving age to 15, creating the need for a more mature programme of physical education. The administration of education, both in general terms and in physical education, was realigned – the Board of Education was replaced by the Ministry of Education and PE moved away from the medical department, losing much of its therapeutic bias. The new ministry took the decision that PE teachers should have the same status as all other teachers and therefore training took on a new role. For the first time men were offered specialist courses in PE teacher-training at colleges such as Loughborough, Carnegie, Exeter, Cheltenham and Cardiff.

Post-war educational philosophy also led to a movement away from prescribed syllabuses and in 1952 the Ministry of Education published *Moving and Growing* and in 1954 *Planning the Programme*. All PE teachers received copies. These publications offered advice and suggestions rather than commands and represented the final move towards a child-centred approach to physical education.

DEFINITION

1944 EDUCATION ACT

Made secondary education available to all children.

DEFINITION

MOVING AND GROWING

An advisory physical education publication for primary-school teachers, issued in 1952.

Modern PE is a combination of games from the public schools and physical training from the elementary schools

activity

- What advantages did the schools built in the 1930s and 1940s have over the older schools?
- What effect did the raising of the school-leaving age have on physical education?

Key revision points

Physical education developed through stages: drill; physical training; physical education. Modern PE grew from two main pathways: games from public school, which aimed to develop character and leadership; physical training from elementary schools, devised to develop fitness and discipline. The 1870 Forster Act made education compulsory, but there was limited development of PE due to lack of facilities and space. Gymnastic drill had its origins in the European work of Ling and Gut Muth. The first model course for physical education in schools was written by the War Office in 1902, prompted by the poor health of recruits for the Boer War. This syllabus was revised with a different focus in 1904–1919 and a modern syllabus, taking the best of physical training and introducing PE as a subject in school, was introduced in 1933. Developments during the Second World War lead to an educational and more child-centred approach with the publication of Moving and Growing *and* Planning the Programme.

Key terms

You should now understand the following terms. If you do not, go back through the chapter and find out what they mean.

1904 Board of Education Syllabus
1909 Syllabus of Physical Training
1933 Syllabus of Physical Training
Drill
Education Act 1944
Forster Education Act 1870
Model Course
Moving and Growing
Peripatetic instructors
Swedish gymnastics
Therapeutic gymnastics

Progress check

1   What two pathways can be identified in the evolution of physical education in the UK?
2   Name two European countries that had developed systems of gymnastic exercise by the mid 1800s.
3   What social characteristics did elementary schools aim to produce in their pupils?
4   What influential policies did the London School Board undertake in the mid-1800s?
5   What role did McLaren and his gymnasium play in the development of physical training in the UK?
6   What effect did the 1870 Forster Act have on education in the UK?
7   How did Madame Bergman Osterberg aid the development of specialist teacher training in physical education?
8   Outline the main differences between drill and Swedish gymnastics at the beginning of the twentieth century.
9   How suitable for girls were physical training systems early in the twentieth century?
10   Which war led to the development of the Model Course in 1902?
11   Who was responsible for writing the Model Course and what was the resulting bias?
12   Who taught the Model Course in elementary schools?
13   What were the main criticisms of the Model Course?
14   What role did Colonel Fox play in the development of physical education?
15   What impact did the realignment of responsibility for physical training into the medical department of the Education Board in 1907 have on physical education?
16   What effect did the First World War have on the development of physical education in state schools?
17   How did the 1909 Syllabus of Physical Training allow for differentiation?
18   When was the last Board of Education syllabus in Physical Education written?
19   What were the key effects on education of the 1944 Education Act?
20   How did *Moving and Growing*, published in 1952, differ from earlier syllabuses?

Further reading

D. Birley. *Sport and the Making of Britain*. Manchester University Press, 1993.

D. Birley. *Land of Sport and Glory*. Manchester University Press, 1995.

D. Brailsford. *British Sport – A Social History*. Barnes & Noble, 1992.

R. Brasch. *How did Sports Begin?* Tynron Press, 1986.

R. Cox, G. Jarvie, W. Vamplew (Eds). *Encyclopedia of British Sport*. ABC-Clio Ltd, 2000.

J. Gathorne-Hardy. *The Public School Phenomenon*. Hodder & Stoughton, 1997.

R. Holt. *Sport and the British*. Oxford University Press, 1990.

T. Hughes. *Tom Brown's School Days*. Mayflower, 1857.

R. Hutchinson. *Empire Games – The British Invention of 20th Century Sport*. Mainstream, 1996.

P.C. McIntosh. *Sport in Society*. Watts & Co., 1963.

T. Money. *Manly and Muscular Diversions*. Duckworth, 1997.

J. Rice. *Start of Play*. Prion, 1998.

Websites

British Society of Sports Historians: www.umist.ac.uk/UMIST_sport/bssh.html

Part 7

COMPARATIVE STUDIES OF SPORT

This part of the book contains:

Chapter 32 North America

Chapter 33 Australia

Chapter 34 France

This part of the book investigates sport and physical education in different cultures. This can be used for an in-depth look at sport in a particular culture or as a comparative investigation, identifying similarities in and differences between cultures.

The key to understanding this section is to recognise that sport reflects the culture in which it is being played. Sociocultural differences will have an effect on the way sport is organised and provided, and opportunities to participate may differ between cultures.

Some examination boards require students to undertake a comparative analysis of sport using the UK as the base culture. With this in mind we have written this section to mirror the areas covered in Part 3. Therefore we suggest that you revisit Part 3 to develop a UK perspective.

For each culture we will investigate the sociocultural background then trace the historical development of sport and discuss how sport is organised now. We will also investigate the role that physical education and school sport play in the society and contrast elite and mass sport, before taking a final look at outdoor activities in each culture.

CHAPTER 32

North America

Learning objectives

- To outline the historical and cultural background of North America and recognise the impact this has on sport and physical education.
- To understand the structure and role of physical education and school sport in North American society.
- To understand the structure and role of professional and elite sports in North American society.
- To understand the structure and role of recreational and mass sports in North American society.
- To understand the structure and role of outdoor and adventure activities in North American society.

America's sports are the most technically advanced in the world, its sports stars are the richest in the world, and in a number of sports the Americans are undisputed world champions.

America's population is obsessed with sport – it permeates all aspects of their society and culture. Millions play and watch sport both live and on television; billions of dollars are spent on sport and leisure. Most professional American sport performers are millionaires and clubs are run like commercial companies.

What is interesting is that America's major sports are not really played anywhere else in the world – this is a good example of sport reflecting the culture of a society. America's history and self-belief have established a sports system where it can hold 'world championships' in American football, baseball, basketball and ice hockey in which only American teams compete.

In this chapter we will look at the factors that have shaped America's sporting culture, comparing them with the sports systems in the UK.

DEFINITION

LOMBARDIAN ETHIC

Named after the famous Green Bay Packers' most successful coach Vince Lombardi, who developed the idea that winning is the most important thing.

AMERICAN DREAM

The idea that in the USA anyone can rise from rags to riches.

32.1 Historical and cultural background

The North American continent is a large and diverse environment. The 50 states of the USA and the northern provinces of Canada share a heritage of ancient civilisations transformed by European invasion during the eighteenth and nineteenth centuries and evolution into the ethnic melting pot of the twentieth century. We will concentrate on the sporting and physical education systems of the USA.

Like many countries of the New World, the USA has colonial links, but these were early in the country's development and for many years the USA developed in planned isolation from the rest of the world, and in particular Europe. During this period many of America's sports were adapted from old European games to suit America's new image. In sports such as football and hockey a more robust, glamorous version has developed and distinctively American sports (such as basketball) were invented on American soil. So closely did these sports mirror American society they have never really developed away from America's shores.

Intercollegiate athletics in the USA was born in 1852 with a series of rowing matches between the universities of Harvard and Yale. Although these and other early sporting fixtures were initially organised and funded by interested students, their popularity was such that before long university administrators took control of sport and began hiring

Basketball – a sport invented in the USA

coaches, building athletic programmes and generally treating inter-collegiate sport as a vehicle that could increase the prestige of an institution and attract more new students.

America's sports tend to be high scoring and action packed to maximise their entertainment value. They reflect American culture in that the aim is to win – the win ethic, or Lombardian ethic, is what drives all American people and this fuels the 'American dream' (this idea of rags-to-riches success is best personified in the Rocky films, where a nobody becomes world champion overnight).

The commercial aspect of American sport makes it unique. Every level, from professional national teams to the local high-school football team, is run as a business. The influence of television is total and most sports rely on the money generated through television deals and advertising revenue. Sports stars in America are millionaires – indeed, most professional teams will have a number of players on multi-million-dollar contracts. Many stars, like Michael Jordan, make even more money through sponsorship deals and endorsements.

There is a flip side to this – sport in the USA is extremely elitist. In athletics, for example, there is not even one amateur club where performers can train and compete. Clubs are based in educational establishments such as schools and colleges or professional enterprises. For most Americans, sport is something you watch on the television and is not something most people play after leaving school. Television also dictates the rules – for example, American football has evolved into a staccato stop–go pattern to allow companies to screen advertisements every five minutes.

Many of these trends are beginning to filter into British sport, and it may be very difficult for us to prevent Americanisation of our sport.

32.2 Physical education and school sport

According to Bale (1994), 'It is high school sports . . . which are more important in forging a link between the education system and

Paxon, an American historian, called sport 'the social safety valve that replaced the frontier'. Using sporting examples, explain what you think he meant.

Below is a list of sports currently played in the USA:

American football
lawn tennis
baseball
ice hockey
athletics
basketball
volleyball
golf
soccer
gymnastics

Try to find out about the origins of these sports in the USA and list them under the following headings:

- adapted
- adopted
- invented.

DEFINITION

TRACK AND FIELD

The term used in the USA to mean athletics.

DEFINITION

DRAFT SYSTEM

The system where professional teams select the best college players once a year.

the professional sports' industries.' This is a unique feature of the American sports system. American high schools have the most lavish facilities for sport and receive a level of support from the local community and businesses not found in any other culture. Most schools have large purpose-built stadiums for football, basketball and track and field events, and many thousands of spectators will pay to watch school teams competing.

The level and standard of play are of an unquestionably high standard and the rivalry in the local school leagues is intense, with competitions from local, district and regional levels leading to state championships at school level and national finals for colleges and universities.

The aim of every high-school performer is to reach the 'draft' – the annual recruitment process where professional teams bid for the best college players in the major sports. The draft is a national event covered by all the major television channels; however, the odds of a high-schooler making the draft are very limited – for example, in American football of the 950 000 college-level players only 4.2% go on to play professional football and only 2.2% of the 500 000 college basketball players become professionals.

We can see that the education system in the USA acts as a sports nursery; there is no need for sports schools or academies as every school acts in such a way. In order to fuel this system colleges and some schools offer athletic scholarships to the best performers. These grants, which help to cover board and tuition fees, often run to several thousands of dollars and the best athletes can 'shop around' the various colleges, seeking the best offer.

32.2.1 *Physical education*

Most American children follow a grade system of education, starting in kindergarten at the age of four, moving to elementary school (ages 5–11), junior high (ages 11–14) and finally senior high (14–17), where the aim of all students is to pass the High School Certificate. Education in America is decentralised, with each state and local area within each state having the power to set programmes and curricula. Consequently it is very difficult to give an accurate view of the systems of physical education in American schools. In some states it is not compulsory for students to follow a physical education programme at any grade. However, most elementary and junior high schools provide physical education programmes. In the main it is up to individual departments and teachers to set their physical education curriculum and there are wide variations. The main emphasis appears to be on testing and measuring – an American obsession – and a lot of work is done on fitness and other psychomotor tests. Extra-curricular sport does tend to dominate school sport, and the success of teams and squads tends to take the emphasis away from physical education programmes within schools.

32.2.2 *School sport*

It is in the field of school and college sport that the USA is unique. In sparsely populated areas or less well-off areas, where long distances must be travelled to watch one of the professional National League teams, the school or college team becomes a substitute for community attention.

Most of the USA's top athletes have been nurtured in the college system

The major sports of American football and basketball make vast amounts of revenue for colleges. Attendance at college matches can be greater than for our own Premiership League soccer matches – most college games are watched by crowds of 50 000 all-paying spectators. This gate money is supplemented by television fees (most school and college matches are available on national and local cable stations), donations and fundraising by alumni organisations called booster clubs. This money is used to recruit players for the following season, pay for the best coaches and equipment and to support other sports in the college's athletic programme, such as gymnastics and swimming.

Schools affiliate to their respective State High School Athletic Associations and these in turn belong to the National Federation of State High Schools. These two organisations coordinate and regulate interschool competitions and fixtures. Interschool sport reaches its greatest intensity during grades 11 and 12 (the final two years in high school). Although schools will field teams in a range of sports, most tend to specialise in either American football or basketball. This often follows a geographical pattern, with city schools concentrating on basketball and those in smaller towns playing football.

Those selected to play in high-school basketball and football teams have their timetables altered so that they can train for a number of hours on most school days. Most games take place on a Friday night in order to attract a large community following. School and college teams initially play in local conferences or leagues; the team with the best results at the end of a round-robin tournament then progresses to district and state championships.

32.2.3 Recruitment

At the top level of college sport, NCAA Division 1, college sport is virtually part of the entertainment industry. Games are played in all-seater stadiums and last for several hours. Beside the actual game, cheerleader squads and bands entertain the spectators and food and drink are available.

For the teams to attract paying spectators they need to be successful and one way of achieving success is to recruit the best players. Coaches and scouts working for the college visit high schools across the country, identifying and attempting to recruit players to come to play for their team. To attract players they emphasise the quality of their facilities, the chances of playing in a successful team and therefore a better chance of making the 'draft' – and, of course, the 'athletic scholarship'. The need for success and the drive to fulfil the win ethic can lead to abuses and, although there are strict rules on the recruitment of players, reports of illegal inducements such as cars and apartments are common.

College sport in the USA is controlled by the National Collegiate Athletic Association (NCAA). This organisation was established in 1906 as the Intercollegiate Athletic Association, primarily to bring order to American football. By 1920 it had taken over the control of all sports at college level. There is a considerable amount of pressure on all involved to produce results and these pressures have led to excesses and scandals.

The other pressure is that college sport has become an entertainment attracting huge crowds and national media coverage. This not only requires winning teams but also a high level of performance and razzmatazz.

DEFINITION

TITLE IX

Government legislation in the USA that maintains equality in provision and funding of male and female sport in schools and colleges.

32.2.4 *Men and women in school and college sport*

Both college and school sport have traditionally been dominated by male performers. The role of women has tended to be a supporting one – for example as cheerleaders. However, in the late 1970s Title IX and other federal government legislation went some way to redressing the balance and women's sport is growing fast in school and college. One boom sport is soccer, which is much more socially acceptable as a sport for females in the USA than in the UK, where it has remained the dominant male sport. However, in terms of prestige, power and, above all, money-making potential, it is still some way behind male sport.

32.2.5 *The all-American draft*

The aim of all college athletes in professional sports is the annual draft. This is the mechanism where professional clubs in sports such as American football, basketball and soccer select and offer contracts to the best college players. The event itself attracts huge media interest and most of America sits glued to their TV screens for the couple of days it takes to allocate the players to teams. Just as the colleges select and 'cream off' the best talent from high school, the professional clubs select and recruit the best college players.

Every college game is recorded and analysed by a national office which scores and ranks every player across the country. It is this system that identifies the best athletes that will go forward into the draft. For most professional sports in the USA this is the only route to a contract and again it is a very elitist system with only a very small percentage of college athletes getting this far.

In order to retain as level a playing field as possible in each professional league, the draft works in reverse order with the weakest team from the previous season getting the first pick of the best college athletes. There are a number of rounds to the draft and there is much trading and competition between teams.

32.3 Professional and elite sport

Sport in the USA is run through a decentralised system of autonomous governing bodies with little state or federal intervention. A number of powerful professional sports enjoy considerable support from the American public. These sports are run on a franchise basis and are very commercially oriented, with the main priority of all clubs to make a profit.

The franchise system works on geographical location. Teams must be located at specific distances from other teams to reduce competition and thus establish a monopoly for a team in an area – and so maximise the amount of profit that can be made.

The private sector dominates American sport; there is very little voluntary or public sector provision. Sport relies on gate receipts, media fees and, increasingly, commercial sponsorship. American sports rules maintain that all clubs must be owned by a company and many major businesses own sports teams in America – for example, Annheuser–Busch (which brews Budweiser beer) owns the St Louis Cardinals, McDonalds owns San Diego Padres, and Wrigley Chewing Gum owns the Chicago Cubs. All American

DEFINITION

FRANCHISE

A business agreement set up to maximise profit.

sports teams have a nickname, which makes the team a commodity and its image – say, the Cowboys or the Bulls – can be put on merchandising and is instantly recognised as a trade mark. Companies are prepared to pay huge amounts of money to associate themselves with popular sports and leagues. In 2003 Budweiser was the official beer of the NBA, a status which costs brewers Annheuser–Busch £38 million a year.

Television has played a major role in American sport. Increasingly, sports rely on money from television rights. The huge number of channels available to the American home, especially through cable, means there is a lot of competition. All of the professional sports have rules about televising games, each club having the sole right to televise their game within its own franchise area. 'Blackout' systems also occur where, in order to maximise the number of paying spectators, the game is not screened live. Watching live sport in the USA is still a very popular leisure activity. In 2002 130 million people went to at least one live game.

Table 32.1 *Attendances at live sporting events, 2002*

Sport	Annual total spectators	Average gate
World Series Baseball	72 million	30 000
National Hockey League	20.3 million	16 500
National Basketball League	20 million	17 000
National Football League	16.3 million	66 000

The big American television companies such as NBC or CBS are increasingly dominating world sports events such as the Olympics. Because they have the largest single viewing audience they have a lot of power and financial backing – NBC paid a record US$456 million for the exclusive rights for the Atlanta Olympics in 1996. One of the disadvantages of this is that scheduling of events becomes governed by peak-time viewing in the USA, which means rather unsociable times in other areas of the world. Due to the high level of competition amongst the TV networks, sports can fish around for the highest bidder when negotiating their TV deals. NBA paid a cool US$3 billion to screen NBA basketball games in 2003.

32.4 Recreational and mass sport

American sport has not evolved a sports club system similar to that in northern Europe. Sport tends to be focused on high school, college and professional franchises. There is only limited opportunity outside these spheres to participate in sports. Public parks and open spaces do offer the chance to jog, skate and play touch football or softball, but there is little public-sector sports provision.

One exception to this is 'little league' sport, club leagues for children under 10 run in a number of different sports – Pop Warner Football, Pee Wee Baseball and Biddy Basketball are examples. Teams are run by parents and compete in structured league competitions that mirror the professional leagues, with conferences, play offs and 'superbowls'. There is great emphasis on winning and this has led to some criticism; however, most Americans support the system because they feel that it helps reinforce in children the American way of life.

In many ways commercial spectatorism has replaced the ethic of sport for all in America. After leaving education many people do

Top stars like Michael Jordan make millions from endorsement and commercial sponsorship

DEFINITION

LIFETIME SPORT

A sport that can be played throughout life, generally one that is self-paced or can be adapted.

DEFINITION

ECO SPORT

Recreational activities with little organisation and carried out in the natural environment.

not participate in any sport or physical recreation. There are some exceptions – golf and tennis – but often the facilities for these are associated with country clubs whose membership is very expensive. There has also recently been an upsurge in health and fitness, but again the facilities are provided by commercial companies.

America does support the idea of lifetime sport. In many areas sports and competitions are organised for many different age groups, and 'golden Olympics' are very popular in many states.

32.5 Outdoor and adventure activities

One of the areas that has increased in popularity is the so-called eco sports. Activities such as skiing, backpacking, white-water rafting and mountain biking have boomed in recent years.

The size and beauty of the USA has an important influence on American culture. America is acknowledged as the first country to set up national parks providing access to all citizens. This pride in the 'great outdoors' has remained part of the American Dream and their link to the past and frontier spirit. Much of America's history is closely linked to the outdoors and most of its modern-day urban population yearns to get back to nature – reflected in the recent upsurge in dude ranches and 'city slicker cowboys'.

We would also suggest that these activities are part of a counter-culture, an escape from the elite 'win ethic' culture of most of American sport.

Matching the decentralised administration of the country, there are both national and state parks.

However, due to the presence of large areas of wilderness, there is a degree of central control. Without such stringent control many hikers and other outdoor pursuits enthusiasts could get lost and/or attacked by the native bear population. Movement is restricted and to go into particular areas you must have the correct accreditation or stick to paths/drives – this is policed by an extensive ranger system. Also a comprehensive system of land classification has been set up by the federal government, which classifies all non-urban land depending on the level of wilderness present. Levels run from Class 1 – intensively used recreational areas such as picnic areas – to Class 5 – undisturbed roadless areas characterised by natural,

Rodeo – a truly American sport

wild conditions. The higher the class the less freedom of movement there is and the higher the level of accreditation needed. There is also a Class 6 – historical and cultural sites. These areas receive a high level of environmental protection because, due to America's relatively short history, the people value any building or site of cultural significance.

32.5.1 *Summer camps*

One uniquely American feature of outdoor sport is the annual summer camp that most American children attend between the ages of 6 and 16. Summer camp is an American tradition and there is a lot of pride and importance placed on such activity, families tending to send their children to the camp that the parents and grandparents went to. Although a wide variety of camps is available they all share a number of features:

- they tend to be residential camps set in areas away from towns and cities
- they all have excellent facilities for sport and recreation
- children spend 6–8 weeks there in summer, supervised by counsellors and living together in bunk rooms
- days are spent being coached and competing in a range of sporting activities
- once again, there is huge emphasis on winning; games taking places between teams within the camp and then against teams from other camps.

The climax to the camp is a highly structured inter-camp competition – 'colour war'. The whole camp is split into two teams who then spend seven days in intense competition.

There are thousands of such camps throughout America, catering for all pockets and tastes. Although many offer a general programme, as outlined above, some are more specialised, catering for specific sports and often being sponsored by major sports retailers or for specific interests such as computing or drama – there are even 'fat camps' that help children lose weight. Most of the camps are privately run, parents paying on average £3000 to send their children to camp. However, there are alternatives for the less well-off – church and charity groups run camps where the costs are subsidised, and in some states the government pays for underprivileged children to attend state-run camps.

Key revision points

America is a decentralised society with separate state influence. American sport reflects this, with the private sector dominating. America is a young culture that has used sport for nation building and to reflect their cultural values – to Americans, winning is everything. Olympic success is very important – it is a chance for the USA to gain international prestige through sport. The 'big four' sports (football, baseball, basketball and ice hockey) are confined to the USA, and they hold all-American 'world' championships in these sports. The American education system is very decentralised, and elite school sport dominates. School sport is very important for both the community and as a base of the sports pyramid. Students apply for sports scholarships and the 'draft'. The frontier spirit is evident in outdoor education and the popularity of outdoor pursuits in the USA has been enhanced by the rise in 'eco sports'.

Key terms

You should now understand the following terms. If you do not, go back through the chapter and find out what they mean.

American dream
Booster clubs
Draft system
Eco sport
Franchise
Life-time sport
Lombardian ethic
NCAA
Title IX
Track and field

Progress check

1   What is the 'draft' system in the USA?
2   T-ball is a 'Pee Wee' version of which adult American sport?
3   What is meant by the term 'counter culture'? Give an example of a sport in America that reflects this.
4   In college sport, where does the money required to fund scholarships come from?
5   What is America's equivalent of 'sport for all'?
6   What does Title IX legislate against?
7   Why are high-scoring games so attractive to the American public?
8   Why did America develop sports that were so different from those in Europe?
9   What role do booster clubs play in the financing and promotion of school and college sport?
10   Why is school and college sport so important to communities in America?
11   How do summer camps reinforce the cultural characteristics of America?
12   Why does America need a system of land classification?
13   What role does the media play in American sport?
14   Why is American sport said to be elitist?
15   What is meant by the term 'recruitment' in the context of college sport?
16   How does the franchise system work in American sport?
17   Why has there been a recent rise in the popularity of eco sport in America?
18   How does 'cheerleading' reflect the role of women in American society?
19   The tradition of the 'frontier' is an important part of American culture. How is this reflected in sport?
20   Describe the way America nurtures its future sporting talent.

Learning objectives

- To outline the historical and cultural background of Australia and recognise the impact this has on sport and physical education.

- To understand the structure and role of physical education and school sport in Australian society.

- To understand the structure and role of professional and elite sports in Australian society.

- To understand the structure and role of recreational and mass sports in Australian society.

- To understand the structure and role of outdoor and adventure activities in Australian society.

For a comparatively small population, Australia enjoys an extraordinary degree of success on the sports field and there are few sporting events in which Australia does not excel. Records show that Australia gains more Olympic gold medals per head of population than any other nation. We will investigate the reasons behind this sporting success. This is a contemporary issue because many other nations (including the UK) are looking to Australia for inspiration – and in particular the role of the Australian Institute of Sport, now an acknowledged world leader in the preparation of elite sports performers.

Australia's sporting potential is further enhanced by the fact that it is a 'young' country, in terms of both its culture and its population – nearly half of its population is under the age of 30 (in the UK 50% of the population are over the age of 50). Young Australians are encouraged to train and participate in organised sport before they even start school. Just as in the USA, Little Leagues are extremely popular and dominate the Saturdays of most Australian children, with thousands being ferried by their parents from one sports ground to another.

Australia manages to combine several different sporting concepts from a number of different roots, primarily the UK and America, as well as stamping its own nationhood on its sport – making the kangaroo a world-recognised symbol of high-class sport.

DEFINITION

ABORIGINAL
Indigenous population existing at the arrival of colonists.

33.1 Historical and cultural background

Australia is a nation unique in many ways. It is the only nation that occupies a whole continent; some of its flora and fauna is found nowhere else on Earth; it is the lowest and flattest continent and the sixth largest country in terms of land area. It has a relatively small population of only 18 million, and so one would think that it is a sparsely populated country. In some ways this is true, but Australia is also a land of contradictions and is in fact one of the most urbanised populations – 85% of the population live in only 3.3% of the nation's land area. The original inhabitants of Australia, the Aboriginal people, are one of the oldest civilisations in the world. They arrived in Australia during the Ice Age when Australia was connected to Asia via land bridges. But as the continent moved away from the Asian continent, Australia and its inhabitants were

Australians lead the world in many sports

isolated for several thousands of years, until in the eighteenth century European explorers discovered Terra Australis Incognita ('the unknown southern land').

33.1.1 *A brief history – the empire expands*

In 1788 a British colony was established in Britain's newest acquisition, Australia. This new continent had been charted by Captain Cook 10 years earlier. A fleet of 11 vessels containing 736 convicted criminals, a Governor, some officials and an escort of Royal Marines founded the colony on the eastern coast of Australia in what later became New South Wales. This was the first European settlement of any kind in Australia, an area that was as yet little known about in Europe.

This was quite a gamble by the British government – they knew very little about the area. They considered it important for British interests to establish a trade and shipping base in the Pacific and they believed convicts were the best means of getting a colony started. The colony survived, but only with a great deal of luck.

Transportation was an important part of the British penal system. Convicts had before this time been sent to America, but now the American Revolution and independence meant this country could no longer be used.

By 1852, 160 000 convicts had been sent to Australia. Transportation was the key to the establishment of Australia's two colonies of New South Wales and Van Diemen's Land (Tasmania).

However, there was another side to Australia's colonisation. After the establishment of the first colony, many 'free settlers' also left Britain for Australia. Their numbers increased as the benefits of this new continent were published in Britain. Australia offered the resources of the Pacific, particularly seals and whales, free convict labour and an abundance of land. There were few problems with the native population as the Aborigines were thinly spread out across the country. Sheep farming became Australia's main industry and soon Australian wool became famous around the world. The British government promoted this emigration through its assisted passage scheme. This helped people to cover the costs of travelling to the new colony. The government did this to allow the colonies to develop and grow without convicts.

Free settlements were established in South Australia and Victoria in 1834. This immigration gained pace in the 1850s when gold was discovered in many areas of south-west Australia. By 1861 there were over 1 million white Australians (compare this with the native population – in 1887 there were only 750 000 Aborigines).

Some of the settlers from New South Wales crossed over to New Zealand to use it as a base for voyages into the Pacific and to extend their trade with the Maoris. By 1840 New Zealand had also become a British colony. As elsewhere in the British colonies, the rulers established constitutional arrangements which stated that, although Britain oversaw everything, in the main the white communities were to rule themselves as far as possible. Gradually assemblies were developed to govern these colonies, though assemblies in different parts of the same country were often independent of each other – the Australian colonies did not unite until 1901.

The Commonwealth of Australia was established in 1901 by the union of New South Wales, Victoria, Queensland, South Australia, Tasmania and West Australia.

The main problem was the non-white population of these colonies. Initially Victorian attitudes worked to support the native populations, the idea being that they should be assimilated into colonial culture. The early colonists had a missionary quest to 'civilise' these 'backward' peoples. However, the British government soon relaxed this policy and allowed the white communities to develop as they saw fit, which often resulted in the native populations suffering a great deal of cruelty and persecution.

The Australian colonies witnessed spectacular growth between 1870 and 1918, the population growing rapidly as immigration increased and more people left Britain for the chance to start a new life in Australia. Cities like Sydney and Melbourne matured into classic Victorian cities. In 1901 the Australian colonies formed a union of states. Australia, along with Canada and New Zealand, were very important parts of the British Empire.

DEFINITION

CANBERRA

The national capital of Australia, purpose-built in 1901 and positioned halfway between Sydney and Melbourne. It is also the home of the Australian Institute of Sport.

AUSTRALIAN SPORTS COMMISSION

Set up in 1885 by the federal government, this is the body responsible for increasing participation and developing sports excellence in Australia.

By 1914 these three colonies amounted to one-third of the British population and their national wealth was 40% of Britain's total.

After the First World War, Britain's hold on the colonies began to dwindle and the Balfour declaration of 1926 and the Statute of Westminster (1931) conceded control to the colonies and led to the recognition of Australia's states as governments in their own right. They all remained members of the reformed commonwealth.

Since then, Australia has slowly pulled itself away from Britain and now is more closely associated with Asia (and especially Japan) in terms of trade and industry. Although the British Queen remains Australia's head of state, it is probable that in the future Australia will become a republic.

33.1.2 *Culture*

Although a young country, Australia has used its colonial history to develop and foster high culture. Cities such as Sydney and Melbourne have a wide range of theatres, opera houses, galleries, restaurants and other entertainment facilities. However, it is true to say that sport dominates most Australian households – younger members tend to participate in a range of sports, older members spectate, view and help organise and administer sport. Most of the population live on the low-lying coastal plains running round the south and east coast, and the accessibility of the beach and sea consequently dominate Australian culture. Australian homes are also well endowed with indoor and outdoor space; home-based recreations around the pool and 'barbie' are thus very popular.

33.1.3 *Administration and government*

Australia consists of a number of self-governing states and two areas that have territorial status. The country is governed under a federal system similar to the one that operates in the USA, the main difference being that Australia has maintained its commonwealth status and consequently the British Queen is still its head of state. The system of administration is decentralised. The role of the federal government in Canberra is to oversee national policies, administer the two territories, manage the economy and coordinate Australia's international affairs.

A degree of the old independence of the states is reflected in sport, with different styles of football enjoying popularity in different states. Aussie rules football is the dominant game in Victoria and South Australia, while rugby is more popular in New South Wales and Queensland.

The administration and organisation of sport and recreation in Australia follows this, with each state and territory having a department responsible for sport and recreation and its own elite academy of sport. There is, however, a compromise with a powerful centralising effect from the federally funded Australian Sports Commission and its Institute network.

33.2 *Physical education and school sport*

Physical education is compulsory in all Australian schools, though again there is variation in content and scheduling across the states. Generally speaking, PE is compulsory from kindergarten through to year 11. In year 12 (final year of high school) it is optional but

DEFINITION

MELTING POT

A term used to describe the mixing together or assimilation of different cultures and races, often in education.

DEFINITION

ACHPER

The Australian Council for Health, Physical Education and Recreation; it funds, researches and develops major health-based initiatives and programmes for Australian schools.

many students choose it as part of their High School Certificate. The education department in each state is responsible for all educational matters, though in the case of physical education and school sport they will often work closely with the state's department of sport and recreation.

Just as in America, the high school plays an important part in the development of a national identity. With the recent immigration of large numbers of Europeans and Asians, and the rise in social status of the Aborigines, there is also an element of a 'melting pot' process.

We will concentrate on the programmes run in Victoria's schools.

33.2.1 *Physical education and school sport in Victoria*

In the state of Victoria physical education is compulsory from prep year (kindergarten) to year 10 and is then available as an option in the Victoria State Certificate (VSC), which students take at the age of 17+, and includes practical and theoretical assessment in physical education and sport. The state department is also promoting the concept of a daily physical education programme in its primary schools and most schools now offer this to pupils.

The department is very active and works closely with both schools, teachers and ACHPER.

One of the major initiatives Victoria has introduced is the Fundamental Motor Skills Project. The Victorian Department of Education, recognising the need for a more structured approach to physical education teaching in primary schools, commissioned a programme of research that led to the development of a manual and teaching notes being made available to all Victoria's primary school teachers. The programme recognises the importance that a number of fundamental motor skills play in the development of all sports, and the manual gives teachers the information and skills necessary to correctly teach these fundamental skills to young people. This programme has been very successful and is now being copied by other states.

Other physical education initiatives carried out in Victoria include:

* Sports Person in Schools – run in association with the Australian Institute of Sport (AIS). High-profile performers visit schools to assist in coaching and sports development as well as helping encourage young people to take up sport.
* Inter School Sport – coordinated and funded by the State Education Department. This ensures that all schools – no matter what their location, size or economic situation – can participate equally in state-wide competition. The Victorian state government pledges a budget of A$1.1 million a year to inter-school sport.
* ABC television's 'S'cool Sport', broadcast every Friday evening. This programme reports on school teams, matches and performers, and is very popular amongst Australia's schoolchildren.
* School Sports Awards – a prestigious event in which the state department honours the best school performers, teams and coaches.

AUSSIE SPORT

A programme of sports with modified rules to accommodate all ages and abilities introduced by the Australian Sports Commission in 1986.

ACTIVE AUSTRALIA

A national framework of mass participation that was set up to replace Aussie Sport in 1996.

SALARY CAP

A sports governing body puts a limit on the maximum wage a player can receive from playing their sport.

33.2.2 'Aussie Sport'

Schools in Australia have also had to adapt to pressures from other agencies in terms of physical education. Poor performances by the Australian Olympic Team at the Montreal Olympics of 1976 led to a review of sport and physical education and a lot of the blame was laid on physical education in Australian schools – schools had placed too much emphasis on educational development and not enough on developing sporting talent. The Australian Sports Commission in 1986 introduced a national programme, called 'Aussie Sport', aimed at introducing sport to young people. This programme was offered by schools, clubs and other community groups and dominated the sports education of young people.

Many in education felt that this system placed too much emphasis on winning and competition, and did not enforce the social values that sound programmes of physical education could develop. In 1996 the Australian Sports Commission (ASC) replaced Aussie Sport with a new national participation framework that encompassed sport for young people as well as all societal groups. This programme, called 'Active Australia', aims to focus all relevant bodies throughout Australia in an attempt to encourage mass participation. The programme will be discussed in more detail below.

33.3 Professional and elite sport

Australia followed Britain in its reluctance to accept professionalism in sport – even now, few Australian sports have fully embraced full-time professional status. A good example of this is soccer, a sport that has only recently gained popularity in Australia. Professionalism was allowed for the first time in 1950, which coincides with the expansion of Australia's immigration rules to allow a range of European nationals to start a new life in Australia. These people (Greeks, Italians and Yugoslavs) took to Australia their passion for soccer and had an important impact on the development of soccer. However, Australia can still support only part-time professionals, and it is another Australian sporting trait that there are more Australian soccer players playing abroad than in their home country. Many other Australian sports stars ply their trade on foreign shores, where the level of reward and chance of exposure is greater.

The big two Australian sports – Australian rules football and rugby league – are both fully professional and supported by large audiences (both live and on television), commercial and sponsorship funding as well as public funding in the system of state and national sports academies. However, authorities in both sports have attempted to limit the level of professionalism – and some would say player power – by imposing salary caps.

Professional sports tend to be administered by a hybrid system of British-style governing bodies operating through American-style franchise agreements. In recent seasons the commercial need to expand has led to sports such as rugby league and Australian rules football expanding into areas that have traditionally favoured the other football code.

There is also a strong link between sport and the media in Australia, and the various media corporations play a major role in the promotion and funding of many Australian sports. Sport accounts for 15% of television time in Australia and broadcasting games aids sport by gaining commercial sponsorship.

Various Australian media moguls have had a strong influence on the development of Australian (and ultimately worldwide) sport. Examples include Kerry Packer's repackaging of cricket to suit television audiences in the 1970s and Rupert Murdoch's role in the development of rugby league and the concept of Super League.

Cricket is the most commercial sport in Australia and generates more sponsorship than any other sport. In 2002 mobile phone company Orange paid £8.2 million to become the Australian Cricket teams' main sponsor for five years. Brewers VB paid £1.7 million to sponsor and name the one-day VB series against England in 2003.

TV network Channel 9 currently have exclusive rights to Australian cricket team games in Australia. This gives them considerable power – they decided the dates and venues for the 2003 Ashes series against England.

33.3.1 Olympic sport

It is in Olympic sport that the Australian system excels. Their preparation of athletes is now being copied by many other nations, including the UK. The formation of the Australian Institute of Sport (AIS) in 1981 was a significant move in terms of the nurturing of sports talent and government involvement in sports administration. The lead-up to the formation of the AIS follows a pattern similar to the one that occurred in France at the same time – failure at the 1976 Montreal Olympics led to a national outcry and spurred the federal government to fund and reorganise elite sport. Before 1976 Australian sport was run very much along traditional British lines with autonomous national sporting organisations and little government funding. The Australian government, through its Department of Tourism and Recreation, undertook a thorough review of Australian sport and made good use of comparative study, looking at sporting systems around the globe – specifically at the 'gold medal factories' of East Germany. The conclusion to this review was that Australia needed to develop an elite academy system where its best athletes could train and prepare without worries about funding and finding accommodation. The other main conclusion was the need for a central, federal overview of sport. The result of this was the setting up of the AIS, which was shortly followed by the creation of the Australian Sports Commission (ASC), the body responsible for coordinating the government's sports programmes.

The Olympic Games of 2000 were hosted by Sydney, capital of New South Wales

33.3.2 *The Australian Institute of Sport*

Possibly the best centre for elite athlete preparation in the world, this network of sports academies provides Australia's top performers with the best support. The AIS is funded 95% from federal funds and 5% from commercial sponsorship, with Kellogg's currently a major sponsor. Top athletes receive scholarships to attend the AIS – 500 full-time and 270 visiting scholarships are available each year.

The AIS is not simply one centre. Its main base is in the federal capital of Canberra but due to the vastness of Australia it runs a decentralised programme of outreach centres in each state's capital city.

These state institutes offer elite athletes support through a state-wide network of coaches and support staff. This evolution from a centralised to a decentralised system now sits more comfortably alongside the country's federal/state political administration. This change is also the result of the other key factor in Australia's success, namely that they are continually looking to review and improve their sports systems.

Reviews undertaken by the AIS also concluded that athletes preferred to stay in their local area and that residence at an institute was not always beneficial in terms of either performance or social well being.

States institutes, such as the Victorian Institute of Sport based in Melbourne, are largely non-residential and provide a central location for management, coaches and support services.

33.4 Recreational and mass sport

Equal access to sport has never been a reality in Australia. Sport has followed society in that distinct social groups have enjoyed dominance and freedom at the expense of others. From the formation of the colony there was a severe social hierarchy differentiating colonial from Aborigine, free settler from convict, and this has grown into sociocultural factors (age, gender, race, disability and socio-economic background) that affect access to sports and recreation throughout the world.

In the main, the white Anglo Celts have been the dominant group in both sport and society. Minority groups have had to struggle to compete equally, none more so than the true Australians – the Aborigines and Torres Strait islanders. All this tends to contradict Australia's maxim of a 'fair go for all' and the point of leaving the divided societies of the Old World to begin life in a new culture. On the positive side, Australia is blessed with a young population, a wealth of open space, accessible natural resources such as beach and sea, and (in the most populated south-east) a favourable climate, which all encourages participation in sport and physical recreation. It is also a nation obsessed with sport, which provides most young Australians with their main source of role models, heroes and idols.

Actual participation statistics are inconsistent. Federal government figures suggest that 90% of the Australian population actively participates in sports activities. But, like similar figures for the UK, the inclusion of such wide-ranging activities as walking, cue sports and dancing under the banner of sport make the actual validity of such figures questionable. We do know that there are 6.5 million registered players in Australia, affiliated to over 30 000 sports clubs, and so more accurately we can suggest that around one in three Australians takes part in sport or physical recreation.

Like elsewhere in the developed world, Australian federal and state governments (as well as the sports agencies) are keen to promote sports participation and sharing in the benefits that mass participation brings. A number of programmes and campaigns are attempting to encourage participation. We have already discussed the role of Aussie Sport and noted that this has been replaced by the more extensive Active Australia programme. This national framework, issued by the ASC, requires each state government's recreation department to set up and run programmes and campaigns that follow the guidelines and aims set out in the Active Australia policy document. The aim is to get 'all Australians actively involved in sport, community recreation, fitness, outdoor recreation and other physical activities'.

33.5 Outdoor and adventure activities

Australia has a great range of areas of outstanding natural beauty and its modern integrated transport system makes the outback accessible to all Australians, many of whom make use of it at weekends and holidays. The other main natural resource is the extensive coastline, especially around the main population centres in the south-east. The beach and coast remains the most important recreational facility and related sports and activities such as surfing, fishing and boating are extremely popular.

33.5.1 *Surf lifesaving*

The power and unpredictability of the surf and tides around the Australian coast can cause problems. When sea swimming and surfing became popular in the early 1900s many surfing groups formed themselves into lifesaving groups, the first being at Bondi Beach in 1906. By the early 1920s the various clubs around the coast had come together to form a central body known as Surf Life Saving Australia. To date its members have carried out over 370 000 rescues and in order to promote the skills of lifesaving run many surf lifesaving competitions, culminating in the Australian Surf Lifesaving Championships – an event that is the biggest sporting event in terms of competitors after the Olympics.

33.5.2 *Education for the bush*

The closeness and dangers of the bush means that there is a need to educate Australian children about the outdoors. The exact programmes of outdoor education differ between states, though the emphasis tends to be on environmental education and leisure in the outdoors. The accessibility of surf and sea also means that many schools make use of this free resource, offering students surfing and lifesaving as part of their school curriculum.

Outdoor education is usually labelled 'environmental education' in Australian schools. In the 1980s the federal government initiated a parallel programme called Education for Leisure, setting up residential centres that attempt to give all Australian children a taste of outdoor education through organised field studies.

These centres exist at four levels:
1 Outdoor schools give first-hand experience of environmental and adventure education.
2 Environmental centres exist throughout Australia and focus on environmental studies rather than adventure education.
3 Outdoor pursuit centres form the largest group of field centres staffed by physical education teachers.
4 Outdoor leisure and environmental centres cover a wide range of activities including adventure, environmental and conservation.

As in Britain, however, the decision to send pupils to these camps and centres rests with the individual school and, although the uptake of places is high, not every Australian child gets to visit one of these centres.

There are also private summer camps in Australia and an extensive range of outward-bound centres.

Key revision points

Although Australia is a decentralised society with separate state influence, Australian sport is in the main centrally organised, with the Australian Sports Commission taking a central role in the control and funding of sport. Australia is a young culture that has used sport for nation building and as a substitute for high culture. Failure at the Montreal Olympics in 1976 led to a major review of the sports system and a push to make Australian sport great by a number of initiatives: Aussie Sport, Active Australia, Sports Search, the AIS and state academies. The Australian education system is very decentralised but sport education has its place in programmes for all levels, including Fundamental Motor Skills and the Higher School Certificate. School sport is considered very important for both the community and the base of the sports pyramid, state funding and support. Australia's natural resources are much in evidence and have led to the 'bush culture', a necessity for outdoor education and popularity of outdoor pursuits.

Key terms

You should now understand the following terms. If you do not, go back through the chapter and find out what they mean.

Aboriginal
ACHPER
Active Australia
Aussie Sport
Australian Institute of Sport
Australian Sports Commission
Canberra
Melting pot
Salary cap

Progress check

1 How does the administration of Australia's sport follow a decentralised system?
2 How did transportation shape the development of Australia?
3 How does the structure of Australia's population aid its sporting ambition?
4 How did the development of Australia's sport follow elements of adaptation, adoption and invention?
5 How does football follow a state pattern in Australia?
6 How is the concept of a 'melting pot' reflected in Australia's high schools?
7 What is the philosophy behind Victoria state's Fundamental Motor Skills Project?
8 What role does ACHPER play in the promotion of physical education in Australia?
9 Name and describe the two national programmes the ASC has used to promote sport for all in Australia.
10 What geographical factors may limit the scope of professional sport in Australia?
11 What effect did Olympic failure in 1976 have on the future of Australian sport?
12 What is the function of the AIS?
13 How is the AIS funded?
14 How does the structure of the AIS reflect the decentralising factors of the separate states in Australia?
15 Why is surf lifesaving such a popular recreation in Australia?
16 Why is the beach such an important resource for Australians and their recreation?
17 Why is outdoor education such an important subject in Australian schools?
18 How has the media influenced the development of professional sport in Australia?
19 How does soccer in Australia follow an ethnic pattern?
20 How did the Australian sports authorities use a comparative sports study to aid them in their development of a sports excellence programme?

Learning objectives

- To outline the historical and cultural background of France and recognise the impact this has on sport and physical education.
- To understand the structure and role of physical education and school sport in French society.
- To understand the structure and role of professional and elite sports in French society.
- To understand the structure and role of recreational and mass sports in French society.
- To understand the structure and role of outdoor and adventure activities in French society.

France is geographically three times the size of the UK but has a very similar population and similar history and heritage. It therefore provides an interesting comparative analysis. The differences in geography mean that France has a more rural culture and a lot more space – naturally this is reflected in the sports and pastimes that dominate French society.

France plays many of the sports common in the UK and across the world. It can claim to be the birthplace of cycling, tennis and medieval jousting. It also has retained a handful of sports that are unique to the country – in particular petanque or boules (often seen this side of the Channel as a beach recreation). In France, petanque is a professional sport that attracts large numbers of players, spectators and huge amounts of money from sponsors.

Over the last 20 years the French government has placed a lot of emphasis and funding on developing elite sports squads, which have performed at the Olympics and other global games. At the 2000 Olympics France won 13 gold medals and gained sixth place on the overall medal table; in 1998 the French soccer team became world champions.

The Tour de France – the highlight of France's sporting calendar

34.1 Historical and cultural background

34.1.1 *Cultural influences on French sport*

France has a more rural culture and a lot more space than the UK. It also has a greater variation in climate and topography, allowing a wider variety of sports and recreations. Its extensive coastline and Alpine areas provide many natural facilities available for recreation and leisure.

France has a long tradition of sporting activity. It is the birthplace of the joust, tennis and cycling and, as mentioned above, has its own unique sports such as pelota and boules. There are also some geographical variations – bullfighting is still popular in the regions that border Spain, rugby union tends to be concentrated in the country towns of the south, the Breton region has its form of wrestling. Obviously the Alpine regions concentrate on winter sports and are also major tourist areas.

The French government believes that sport can be used for 'shop window' purposes and therefore puts a lot of support and funding into elite sport, primarily at the National Institute of Sport (INSEP) at Vincennes just outside Paris. There is also a strong government commitment to the health and fitness of the people – Sport Pour Tous is a national scheme set up to promote sport for all.

France has a centralised government and this model of control also covers sport and recreation. The Department of Youth and Sport controls French sport at all levels.

France has a degree of racial assimilation because many of its population originate from its former colonies, mainly those in North Africa. Many immigrants use sport as a ladder for upwards social mobility and France makes good use of this fact when selecting national teams. Zinedine Zidane is a good example: France's World Cup hero is the son of Algerian immigrants.

Although France is a traditional culture with a long history it is also modern and has developed an efficient infrastructure, particularly in communications. Its system of motorways and high-speed rail links make most of the country very accessible, though the centralisation model is repeated with most routes radiating out from Paris like the spokes of a wheel.

DEFINITION

PELOTA

A court game played in the streets in the south of France.

DEFINITION

SPORT POUR TOUS

A national scheme of mass participation.

DEFINITION

DEPARTMENT OF YOUTH AND SPORT

A government department in France with responsibility for all levels of sport.

activity

See how many French sports stars you can name. Make a list of the sports that you think France excels in and look up their record in these sports over the last decade.

Fencing – a sport that originated in France

34.1.2 *A background history of France and its effect on sport*

Sport first developed in France in the middle ages but, as with Britain, this was restricted to the court and the aristocracy. Sport and games were specifically associated with the high culture of the reign of Louis XIV and the two sports that epitomise this era are fencing and royal tennis. Sport at this time was elitist and very artistic in its approach.

This elite culture finally collapsed during the French Revolution, when most court games lost favour. A new approach to sport developed after the revolution. In the Napoleonic period sport became militarised, especially systems of physical education practised in the academies and military schools. This was mirrored by the rise of the French Empire and a great surge in French nationalism. The emphasis was on physical training, with systems based on gymnastic models from Scandinavia and Germany being popular. This emphasis has remained and in French schools physical education is still referred to as 'La Gym'.

However, the revolution did not completely rid the country of its upper-class influence and high culture, and during the nineteenth century there was a resurgence of middle-class sports, much copied from the UK. Aristocrats such as Baron de Coubertin visited and viewed systems of sport throughout Europe and brought back to France many of the sports they had seen. Britain was leading the development of sport, industry and defence and became the most influential culture, particularly spreading the public school games cult that had developed during the nineteenth century.

The ethos of the French Republic is that the state is responsible for the improvement of the general well-being of its citizens. The scope of this ethos then includes sport and physical activity both in schools and in the wider community.

A federal law dating back to 1920 obliges all local authorities and councils to offer facilities for sporting recreation.

34.1.3 *France's role in international sport*

The idea of international sport originated in France – it was de Coubertin who was the major force in the movement that would lead to the establishment of the modern Olympics. As a young man de Coubertin had witnessed the general apathy of the French population towards sport, and felt that much of the blame for this was due to the gymnastics systems of exercise that were popular at the time. In order to investigate alternative systems of exercise he visited public schools in Britain and was greatly impressed with the multitude of football, cricket, athletics and rowing competitions. He could see a clear link between these athletic sports and Britain's success as an imperial power. Baron de Coubertin believed that these sports were a source of physical vigour and national character which enabled Britain to rule its enormous empire. He returned to France determined to propagate such activities in France and to use sport as a means of nation building.

Initially he gathered together the various sporting clubs and organisations that were already established, and persuaded them to turn their attention towards athletic sports. They experienced a huge growth in popularity and membership and very soon many other clubs were set up, many of them adopting British sports such

DEFINITION

LA GYM

What the French call physical education.

DEFINITION

BARON DE COUBERTIN

French aristocrat who brought many British games to France and set up the modern Olympic Games.

activity

Can you track any sports which France may have taken from the British public-school playing fields during the nineteenth century?

as football, rugby and rowing. Having unified the clubs, de Coubertin then began to direct his attention towards international sport, helping to stage the first international football matches in 1892.

Rugby is a good example of a sport developed in France at this period. Although France had its own forms of mob football they took on rugby with great vigour – it appears to be a game that allowed them to flaunt their Gallic flair. Interestingly, cricket never took off in France. Baron de Coubertin also had a wider philosophy, seeing sport as a vehicle in promoting world peace. As an academic he had studied ancient Greece and read with great interest the stories of the Olympic Games. He had an idea that if countries could compete in a festival of sport it could lead to a more harmonious world and at the same time spread the popularity of sport around the globe. Through his tireless lobbying and speaking he managed to persuade a number of European and American sport enthusiasts to join him in re-staging the Olympic Games, and in 1896 the first modern Games were held in Athens.

34.1.4 *French sport in the twentieth century*

As an old imperial power, by 1939 France had the second-largest empire in the world, spreading over four continents. France has maintained strong links with its former colonies in northern Africa, particularly Algeria and Morocco. This is most evident in sport – for example, Said Aouita (the Moroccan athlete) trains in France and is supported by the French government, and many Moroccans and Algerians play soccer and rugby for the French national team. This is a good example of how France as an imperial power differed from Britain – France had a much more liberal colonial policy, allowing all former colonists the right to French citizenship. This has resulted in a very strong allegiance to France although the high levels of immigration have caused some friction in French cities and a strong right-wing fascist political movement has grown up in response to this immigration.

World War Two hit France badly and the German occupancy left France a defeated nation. After World War Two, the French government took an increasing interest in sport and physical recreation and identified two main areas for government intervention:
- Developing elite sports programmes in order to gain international success
- Encouraging sport for all.

Much of the drive for a dynamic sports policy, centrally administered, arose from successive French governments, with strong left-wing/socialist bias which emerged form the resistance movement whose ideal was to make leisure accessible to all French citizens not just the rich and well off. They also saw sport and physical activity as an important vehicle for improving the nation's health and fitness in order that the population could successfully defend against any future invasion by another nation.

In 1945 a government Act enforced the state's right as ultimate power in sport while allowing some delegation of power to the individual sport federations. These central powers were beefed up in Acts of 1975 and 1984, which imposed certain types of common statute on all sporting bodies and highlighted their public-service mission.

The French President after World War II, General de Gaulle, felt, like de Coubertin, that sport could be used to rebuild French pride. However, this was severely hindered by a poor performance at the 1960 Olympics where France failed to gain any victories. De Gaulle was insulted that his vision of French pride and tradition had been besmirched and vowed to ensure that such a tragedy would never occur again. He appointed a Minister of Sport, set up a five-year plan for the provision of facilities (including a national institute) and freed up federal funding to support France's elite athletes. His foundation has produced results – France has achieved better results than its near neighbour Britain over the last four Olympic games.

In the last ten years France's support of elite performance has reaped dividends, culminating in its 13 gold medals at the Sydney Olympics in 2000 and winning the football World Cup in 1998.

Most control of sport lay within the portfolio of the Ministry of Youth and Sports. In 2002 a government reorganisation resulted in a streamlining of departments and all sporting matters are now under the control of the Ministre des Sports (Sports Ministry).

The key to understanding how French sport is run is that the state takes central control at all levels of sport. For example, at club level a mechanism of official recognition (*agrément*) with the Sports Ministry requires all sports clubs in France to hold an annual general meeting, set an annual budget and elect a management committee (unpaid) every four years.

In return, the clubs gain status as 'public utilities' and therefore are able to claim grant aid from the FNDS National Sports Fund (Fonds National pour le Développement du Sport) in proportion to the number of members they have. The FNDS is administered by central government and receives most of it funds form two main sources:

- Loto Sportif (state-run football pools)
- Loterie nationale (national lottery).

Table 34.1 *Comparative European state budgets*

Country	Annual federal sport budget
France	US$1.3 billion
UK	US$132 million
Germany	US$120 million

As opposed to the UK, the French government heavily supports sport and physical recreation. Of all western European countries, France has the strongest government intervention.

In the case of most French sports, the Sports Ministry delegates control and regulation of each particular sport to the National Federation (NGB). However, it retains the right to intervene and take complete control if it feels a sport is not fulfilling its public role.

In football the government delegate power to the French Football Federation (FFF). The FFF is given power by the Sports Ministry to organise, regulate and represent football in France. This includes control of the National Football League (Divisions 1–3) as well as amateur, regional and local divisions. Again the Sports Ministry could at any time withdraw official approval of the federation's status as the national governing body of football.

34.2 Physical education and school sport

34.2.1 Background

The French education system is centralised, meaning that the government administers official instruction. There is a mixture of state and private schools with the majority of private schools being Catholic. Schools and universities are even more academic than in the UK. The aim of most French students is to sit and pass their baccalauréat examination, taken at 18 years, and the higher-education entrance exam. The baccalauréat is a multi-subject exam in which students have to pass all subjects including physical education.

34.2.2 Organisation of physical education

The present organisation of physical education dates from 1967 and the government's official instructions. Mirroring the centralised system of control this is a true national curriculum and one that all schools are required to teach, though lack of facilities and suitably qualified teachers can make this an unattainable aim.

Physical education currently is controlled by the Department of Youth and Sport, which has a wide-ranging remit involving all levels of French sport.

DEFINITION

BACCALAURÉAT

A multi-subject examination, including PE, that is taken before university entrance.

DEFINITION

TIER TEMPS PEDAGOGIQUE

'A third time programme', where primary schools are required to teach six hours of physical education a week.

DEFINITION

TRANSPLANT CLASSES

Outdoor experiences for primary-school children.

34.2.3 *Primary provision*

The revised provisions of 1969 stipulated a more extensive timetable for physical education. The programme *'tier temps pedagogique'* divided the primary curriculum into three equal parts: social, academic and physical.

In theory this should result in primary schools offering six hours of physical education per week. However, there is a lack of supervision to enforce this requirement and, just as in the UK, a lack of facilities and suitably trained teachers further inhibits this programme.

There is provision for extracurricular sport at primary level in the federal organisation Union Sportive de l'Enseignement Primaire (USEP – Primary Schools Sports Union). This organisation aims to promote sport at the primary level and sets up links with local clubs. The other main focus of physical activity at primary level, though one that has been reduced in recent years by lack of funding, is the system of transplant classes. These are outdoor experiences that occur as part of the school curriculum. There are three main focuses, with ski class, sea class and countryside class – ski class being the most popular. The general pattern is that children are transplanted as a class to the natural environment for a week. In the mornings they follow normal lessons; in the afternoons they can take part in a range of outdoor activities.

34.2.4 *Secondary programme*

The secondary school curriculum is prescribed by the official instructions dating from 1967. Called *'la programmation'*, this not only states the time allocation for each subject but also stipulates what should be taught. Consequently (at least in theory) all secondary schools should offer three hours of physical education per week, though again lack of facilities and pressure to fit in other subjects can restrict this. Physical education is a compulsory element of the baccalauréat.

Since 1950 all candidates for the school leaving certificate have had to take a sport and PE test.

In 1984 the test counted for 8% of the total result. But as a result of concerns over the fitness of young people and with an eye to encouraging more potential sporting champions the weighting was increased to 16% of the total result.

Table 34.2 *Schooling in France*

Age of entry	Type	Length of study
6	Primary	4 years
10/11	*Collège* (early secondary school)	4 years
14/15	*Lycée* (upper secondary school)	3 years Baccalauréat

Each school's physical education programme must follow the 'official instructions' on what activities should be taught. In each school the coordinator of PE gets the other teachers together and, using the official instructions, sets up the school's programme. Individual activities such as swimming and athletics tend to dominate the time allocated – this does tend to reflect the available facilities. In de Gaulle's plan after the disappointing 1960 Olympic results most towns were allocated funds to build a swimming pool and an athletics track.

DEFINITION

USEP

Union of Primary School Sport, responsible for coordinating Wednesday afternoon sport in primary schools.

UNSS

National Union of School Sport, responsible for coordinating Wednesday afternoon sport in secondary schools.

To find out more about specialist centres, turn to page 393.

activity

Think about your own school's physical education and sport programmes. How do they compare with the French model?

Draw up a table highlighting the similarities and differences between French and British PE and school sport.

Recently, as in Australia, there has been a change in the direction of physical education teaching. It is now acknowledged that sporting objectives can be best achieved through sports afternoons coordinated by another federal body, the Union National du Sport Scolaire (UNSS – National Union of School Sport). There is now a move towards a more child-centred approach to physical education, and teachers tend to spend more of the lesson time working on an individual basis with students. In most schools physical education is co-educational, girls and boys participating in all sports – including soccer and rugby – together.

34.2.5 *Sports afternoons*

These are considered an official part of the school curriculum and most schools have no lessons on a Wednesday afternoon. The emphasis here is on playing sport and consequently the standard of play is not high. Again there is central control of this feature: USEP and UNSS are given overall control, with regional federations running localised events. The system gives all schools an equal chance of participating in school sport. Schools receive support and funding to enable them to participate. There is some conflict in that, because the system is aimed at mass participation, the level of performance is low and better performers will tend to gravitate towards local clubs who also tend to play junior fixtures on a Wednesday afternoon.

For the elite sports performers in schools there are alternative programmes and specialist centres (which will be discussed in the next section).

34.3 Professional and elite sport

The French are not renowned for being great sportsmen, either as participants or spectators. However, the importance attributed to sport and its growing popularity throughout the country is reflected in the growing numbers of sports clubs and facilities throughout the country.

Over the last 30 years France has consistently been ranked as one of the top Olympic nations. Much of this new-found success resulted from de Gaulle's vision for a new France after the Second World War. As we discussed above, this rebuilding was severely hindered by the poor performance of French athletes at the 1960 Olympics. President de Gaulle set in motion a review and then an overhaul of the sporting system. The control of sport was brought under government influence and now the Minister for Sport, working within the State Department of Youth Sport, has total control of all French sport, including elite preparation and professional organisations.

The government has developed a sound sporting infrastructure that is now paying dividends. A great deal of funding is directed towards sport at all levels but a large proportion is allocated to training elite athletes at a number of national centres. Support for sport occurs at all levels – state, regional and local, creating a clear pyramid structure. All organisations in France work to the same agenda and there is much cooperation.

The state pays for a great many coaches and administration staff, ensuring that they can concentrate all their time and energy on preparing France's top performers.

The route to excellence begins at school, where the programmes of physical education and sports afternoons are used to encourage young people into sport. Those who show promise are channelled towards specialist centres called sports study sections.

34.3.1 *Sports study sections – Les sections sport-etudes*

These are prominent centres for teaching and training of elite young sports performers. They are structured to respond to the sporting needs of the elite, those who have already proved themselves in a particular sport, and – equally importantly – their academic study.
Their exact role is:

> To offer those with sporting hopes, schooling conditions allowing a normal pursuit of secondary courses and the best chance of qualifications, as well as physical training adapted to sport and competition at the top level.

In order to enter these sections, which are attached to normal secondary schools, students must have reached high standard in their sport, passed various medical tests and have attained a reasonable level of academic progress.

The students face a very demanding schedule. They cover the same academic programme as normal students and then have 10–15 hours of sports coaching each week. Some sections specialise in specific sports; others are multidisciplined. They are regionally based, serving the youth in a particular area but, like all things French, they are centrally controlled.

34.3.2 *Institute National du Sport et de L'Education Physique (INSEP)*

At the pinnacle of the French sports pyramid is INSEP, based at Vincennes just outside Paris. Its aim is to provide a national centre of excellence for France's elite athletes. INSEP also acts as an education centre for France's coaches and physical educationalists. The French sports federations have taken the bold step of making it compulsory that any coach working in sport must achieve a nationally accredited qualification through INSEP.

In the main state funded with some commercial sponsorship, INSEP is made up of four departments: research, top level sport, medicine and student education. Backed up with some of the top facilities in the world it is a purpose-built centre with one aim – to win France gold medals. The elite performers are supported by the state with funds that are directed through their sports federations. Elite athletes in France can receive around £1250 a month and if they do win medals for France they are rewarded in cash – a gold medal is worth £32 000, a silver £15 000 and a bronze £10 000. Britain has no system comparable to this.

There are currently around 3500 French athletes classed as elite performers and who are therefore eligible for state funding. Approximately 500 are actually resident at INSEP and this includes a number of athletes from France's former (mainly North African) colonies.

Younger athletes are attached to regional 'mini-INSEPS'. These centres, known in France by the acronym CREPS, were traditionally used to train physical-education teachers but are increasingly being used in the nurture of potential elite athletes.

There are other national centres of excellence available to France's elite, predominately an altitude training centre at Font Romeu in the Pyrenees and La Centre National des Sports de Plein Air at Vallon Pont D'Arc.

The dominant professional sports in France are soccer and rugby. These are run by their separate federations, although the state does have some input into their organisation. The French Football Federation has its own Academy at Clare Fontaine. This centre provides young footballers with top-class facilities and coaches as well as assistance with education and careers. It also acts as a training facility for the national team and a 'university' of football coaching.

Professional sport in France tends to be organised on a smaller scale than its counterpart in the UK; the sparseness of much of France tends to inhibit the level of spectatorism. Individual sports such as petanque can attract large amounts of commercial sponsorship – as they tend to be associated with bars, much of the support comes from alcohol and tobacco firms. The highlights of the French sporting year are arguably the Tour de France cycle race,

CREPS

Centre d'Education Populaire et de Sports are regional centres of sports excellence.

activity

See if you can find any more information about the history and organisation of petanque. Compare this with the development and organisation of bowls in the UK.

which travels around most of France although it tends to be dominated by foreign riders, and a horse race (Le Prix de Les Arcs de Triomphe), when France gets to soak in some of its high culture.

34.4 Recreation and mass sport

Like the rest of Europe, France has enjoyed increasing affluence and shortened working hours and this, coupled with the accessibility of France's open countryside, coast and mountains, means that leisure has boomed over the last decade. Well over six million people belong to French sporting clubs and sports such as tennis are extremely popular. Over four million French people ski on a regular basis.

Once again the government and centralised system of France has had an impact on the provision of sports and recreational facilities. A result of de Gaulle's plan was a concerted effort by national and local authorities to improve local facilities. De Gaulle's dream was that every village and town in France should have a swimming pool, sports hall and a sports stadium. He also believed that a central system of sports administration should be set up to promote a national policy of sport. This means that most urban areas have swimming pools and municipal sports centres. Access to leisure and physical recreation is also enhanced through state support for children's skiing and sailing trips and subsidised holidays for lower-income families.

Sport Pour Tous was set up by the French government to try to promote mass physical recreation. It is similar to the UK's Sport For All campaign in both structure and philosophy.

Although the French sports system is centralised, there are also regional sports councils promoting sport. The French government gives more grants per head of population for sport and recreation than the UK. The public sector provides extensive facilities within the reach of most French people. This government provision was part of de Gaulle's national plan, achieved through local authority provision of facilities for general use – where provided, these facilities are of a very high standard. This appears to have been a deliberate establishment of a structure aimed at maximum participation at local level in order to encourage the development of potential Olympic and world champions.

The aim of the National Plan was to provide enough sports equipment and facilities to meet the needs of the whole population. However, due to budget restraints, this has been achieved only in the building of swimming pools.

Mass participation in France tends to have a health bias, with the Department of Youth and Sport keen to play a major role in developing the health and fitness of the French population. One of the key slogans used – *Sportez-vous bien* – translates as 'Play sport to keep fit'.

In a similar way to the Sports Council in the UK, the French Sports Committee has focused on disadvantaged groups and attempted to make physical recreation available to all. An example of this is an initiative in which 500 *sportez-vous bien* outdoor trails have been built around France, providing a free facility available to all.

A number of ethnic groups in France work hard to maintain their culture and tradition. Although many of them play mainstream sports and represent France, their own ethnic sports play a very

DEFINITION

NATIONAL PLAN
Programme aimed at providing the whole French population with access to sports facilities.

DEFINITION

GOUREN
A form of wrestling practised in Brittany.

'Le plein air' – the outdoors – is an important element in French culture

DEFINITION

CENTRES DE VACANCES
Summer camps for French children, often offering outdoor pursuits and sports.

DEFINITION

HORS LIMITES
The French arm of the Outward Bound movement, which offers opportunities for young people to take part in outdoor pursuits.

important role in the maintenance of their traditions. '*Le plein air*' – the outdoors – is an important element in French culture.

Basques of the south-west have numerous sports including pelota, bullfighting and an annual festival of Basque sport that is similar to the Highland Games in Scotland. The Bretons in the north-west area of France still participate in a form of Celtic wrestling called Gouren.

34.5 Outdoor and adventure activities

France is blessed with a wide range of accessible natural facilities for sports and outdoor recreations. Consequently both outdoor pursuits and tourism are very popular amongst the population. The French authorities are keen to promote '*le plein air*'; that active recreation in the fresh air is an ideal.

The French tradition of life is linked to the countryside, the idea of rustic simplicity and making the most of the natural environment. The French have a greater range of opportunities than the British, with more open space and a greater range of climate and topography. Most French people prefer to take their holidays within France and the choice of beach, skiing, scenic and country holidays can suit most tastes.

34.5.1 Summer camps

The French tend to take an American approach to holidays with parents doing their own thing while children attend summer camps. Called '*centres de vacances*', these have been organised for years by '*comites d'entreprises*', which tend to be made up of the trades unions representing a range of different industries. These raise funds to enable children to take subsidised holidays. There is a range of camps, usually four weeks in length, though children tend to prefer sports-oriented camps – particularly those involving sailing or mountain activities. Increasingly private companies and individuals are also offering camps for both French and foreign children. '*Plein air*' activities are also promoted through education departments, where outdoor education is given a great deal of importance. Not only does this introduce children to outdoor pursuits and sports (which may in turn give France a greater pool of talent for Olympic teams) it also educates children about the beauty and geography of their country. The transplant class system (as mentioned above) has been a central part of this policy, though constraints on funding from government have reduced the scope of this programme in recent years.

Another opportunity to take part in outdoor activities is provided by 'Hors Limites', a branch of the Outward Bound movement. With a purpose-built outdoor pursuits centre at Banassac in the south of France, this organisation promotes an all-round education programme with an emphasis on personal development. Many schools and colleges make use of the movement's courses and facilities.

Excellence in outdoor pursuits is also taken very seriously – it is another chance to promote national pride through sporting success. There are a number of national centres for elite performers including the Centre National des Sports de Plein Air, and these also have the support of the French government.

Key revision points

French sport is centrally organised, with the French government and public sector taking a central role in the control and funding of sport. France is a country with tradition, history and very high culture. Modern sports are a blend of traditional pastimes, British adoptions and outdoor pursuits. President de Gaulle developed a strong sense of nationalism, which was promoted through sport. He organised a push to make French sport great through a number of initiatives such as the National Plan and INSEP. The French education system is very centralised and academic but PE has its place. There are programmes for all levels, including 'tier temps' and a central syllabus. Sports afternoons are very important and are run by USEP/UNSS.

Elite sports provision is through sports study sections. France's natural resources are much in evidence and campaigns, such as 'le plein air', and rustic simplicity are central to French culture. Outdoor pursuits achieve the dual functions of possible medals and mass participation.

Key terms

You should now understand the following terms. If you do not, go back through the chapter and find out what they mean.

Baccalauréat
Centres de Vacances
CREPS
de Coubertin
Department of Youth and Sport
Gouren
Hors Limites
La Gym
National Plan
Pelota
Sport Pour Tous
Tier Temps Pedagogique
Transplant classes
UNSS
USEP

Progress check

1 What is the population of France?
2 What is the French term that relates to mass participation?
3 How does the Tour de France reflect the French attitude towards sport?
4 What do the initials INSEP stand for?
5 What are the reasons behind the French government's support of elite sport?
6 In what type of schools does the Tier Temps programme occur?
7 Which organisation controls extracurricular sport in French secondary schools?
8 What are the three types of transplant class that primary school children can attend?
9 What is the role of the Sports Study Section?
10 Identify three examples showing that the French education system is centrally controlled.
11 Give reasons why outdoor sports are so popular in France.
12 What is the function of Hors Limites?
13 Explain the structure and function of centres de vacances.
14 Give two examples of ethnic sports followed in France.
15 What does the slogan *sportez-vous bien* tell us about the French approach to mass participation?
16 How is the concept of rustic simplicity reflected in French sport?
17 How is the position of Sports Minister in France different from that in the UK?
18 Outline reasons behind the fact that France plays many sports of British origin.
19 Why petanque and not bowls in France?
20 Can you identify any reasons why France tends to excel in individual sports?

Further reading

D. Adair. *Sport in Australian History*. Oxford University Press, 1997.

J. Bale. *Touch Down to Home Base – Sport in the USA*. Altair Publishing, 1994.

H.G. Bissinger. *Friday Night Lights*. Harper Perennial, 1991.

R. Cashman. *Paradise of Sport – The Rise of Organised Sport in Australia*. Oxford University Press, 1995.

G.H. Sage. *American Sport, Power and Ideology*. Human Kinetics, 1990.

R. Smith. *Strikes, Lock outs and Superbowl*. Heinemann Kingswood, 1988.

R. Swanson. *History of Sport and PE in The USA*, 4th edition. Brown & Benchmark, 1995.

W. Vamplew. *Sport in Australia – A Social History*. Cambridge University Press (Australia), 1994.

Websites

www.ausport.gov.au
www.france.net
www.online.fr.insep.entriens

Exam questions: Anatomy, biomechanics and physiology

The questions below are typical of those that you might have to answer in your examination. Try answering each remembering that the number of marks available for each question gives you a clue to the type of answer required.

Maximum possible marks

1 Compare the structure of the hip joint with that of the shoulder joint in relation to joint mobility and joint stability.

4

2 The knee joint is used in the performance of many motor skills. Identify three key features of this typical synovial joint and say how they contribute to the overall stability of the joint.

3

3 a Describe the movements that occur at the ankle, knee and hip joints during the take-off phase of a jump.

3

b For each of these joints, name a prime mover that produces the movement during the take-off phase.

3

4 Using the biceps curl as an example, show how muscles work as antagonistic pairs.

4

5 A person participating in physical activity has to be able to produce a wide range of strength and speed. Explain how the arrangement of muscle fibres into motor units allows the performer to produce various strengths and speeds of muscular contraction.

5

6 Using an example from physical education, show how the functions of either a fast glycolytic fibre or a slow oxidative fibre affect performance.

3

7 The bench press is commonly used to improve the strength of triceps brachii (and other muscles). Identify the type of contraction performed by triceps brachii during the upward phase of the bench press and say how and why the type of contraction changes during the downward phase of this movement.

3

8 Use your knowledge of balance to say why it is easier to perform a headstand than a handstand.

3

9 During a physical education lesson a student takes part in a multi-stage fitness test and manages to reach level 15.

a Draw and label a graph to show the changes in the student's heart rate during the lesson.

4

b Use your knowledge of how heart rate is controlled to explain the changes that would have taken place immediately before and during the fitness test.

6

Maximum
possible marks

10 During exercise it is important to maintain good venous return.
Describe the mechanisms involved in venous return.

4

11 Use your knowledge of the cardiovascular system to explain the
importance of an active cool-down after exercise.

5

12 Define the terms stroke volume, heart rate and cardiac output.

3

13 Identify three factors that affect cardiac output during exercise.

3

14 The medulla oblongata contains the respiratory, cardiac and vasomotor
control centres. These centres are responsible for controlling oxygen
supply. Explain how each control centre responds to an increased need
for oxygen during exercise.

8

15 The velocity of blood changes as it passes through the circulatory
system and the blood moves slowest as it passes through the
capillaries. How is this change in speed achieved, and why does it take
place?

4

16 As you start to exercise, up to 85% of blood flow is redistributed to
the working muscles. How is this redistribution of blood flow
achieved?

4

17 Endurance athletes often train at altitude to help improve their aerobic
capacity. Identify two changes that occur to the cardiovascular system
as a result of altitude training and say how they affect aerobic
capacity.

4

18 After a period of endurance training the heart becomes more efficient.
Identify the changes that take place in the heart as a result of training,
and explain the impact these changes have on stroke volume and
cardiac output.

5

19 Outline the effect that an asthma attack has on the respiratory system.

3

20 As you start to exercise the amount of air that is ventilated by your
lungs increases. Use your knowledge of lung volumes to explain the
changes that take place during exercise.

3

21 Explain how the amount of air ventilated by the lungs is controlled.

4

22 Explain how the exchange of oxygen is achieved between the blood
and muscle cell at rest and how this exchange is accelerated during
exercise.

6

Exam questions: Skill acquisition

The questions below are typical of those that you might have to answer in your examination. Try answering each, remembering that the number of marks available for each question gives you a clue to the type of answer required.

Maximum possible marks

1 Define the terms motor skill, perceptual skill, fundamental motor skill and cognitive skill. Give practical examples to illustrate your answers.

4

2 Choose a motor skill related to sport and classify it using the open/closed continuum. Justify your placement on the continuum.

4

3 Classical conditioning is related to the modification of stimuli. Explain this learning theory and relate it to skill acquisition in sport.

5

4 Reinforcement to ensure learning is at the heart of the operant conditioning theory. Explain, using examples from sport, how reinforcement can help in the learning of motor skills.

4

5 Motivation is important if skill learning is to take place effectively. What is meant by the terms intrinsic and extrinsic motivation? Give examples from physical education to illustrate your answer.

4

6 'The peak flow experience is enjoyed by only the very elite in sport.' Discuss this view by using practical examples.

6

7 Explain each of the elements in the diagram below, using examples from physical education.

8

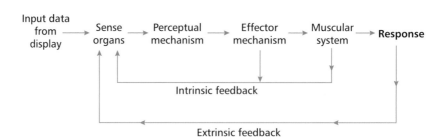

8 Define the terms serial and parallel processing.

4

9 Nideffer (1976) identified two types of attentional focus: broad/narrow focus and external/internal focus. Describe both of these and relate them to examples from physical education.

6

10 Define the terms reaction time, movement time and response time. Using examples from physical education or sport, show how a performer might cut down the time it takes to respond to a particular stimulus.

6

Maximum
possible marks

11 Using a diagram, describe how the memory process affects perception in acquiring motor skills in sport.

6

12 What is meant by a motor programme, and how is it formed?

3

13 Explain, using practical examples, how feedback can motivate a performer.

5

14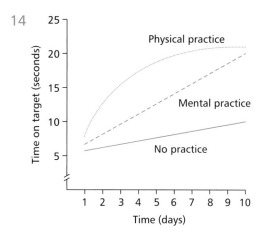
The diagram shows the effects of mental practice on performance. What is meant by mental practice and how do you account for mental practice being so effective?

5

15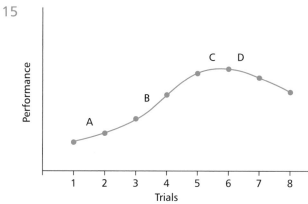
The graph shows the amount of learning experienced over a given period of time. Using the letters on the graph, explain the shape of the graph.

4

16 What is meant by the plateau effect, and how might a teacher or coach seek to combat it in an athlete's performance?

5

17 How would you ensure that positive transfer occurs in skill learning? Illustrate your answer with a practical example.

4

18 What is meant by the whole and part methods of teaching skills? List the advantages and disadvantages of each method.

6

19 When would you use mechanical guidance in the teaching of motor skills? What are the drawbacks of doing this?

5

20 Name three different teaching styles used to teach motor skills, and state when each style is most appropriate.

6

Exam questions: Sociocultural aspects of physical education and sport

The questions below are typical of those that you might have to answer in your examination. Try answering each, remembering that the number of marks available for each question gives you a clue to the type of answer required.

Maximum possible marks

1 Using a practical example, explain the main differences between an activity as a sport and as a physical education. **4**

2 Discuss the idea that the concept of leisure involves the characteristic of escape. **3**

3 What reasons can you give for the rise of the outdoor recreation movement during the industrial revolution of the nineteenth century? **4**

4 'Do professional sports performers play?'
   a Discuss the above question. **4**
   b What constraints in high-level sport might inhibit the concept of play? **4**

5 What is the role of physical education in promoting lifetime sport? **4**

6 What added dimension does outdoor education offer the physical education programme in schools? **4**

7 What constraints limit access to outdoor education in the UK? **6**

8 Sport at the local level is provided by a range of organisations and facilities within the private, public and voluntary sectors. Outline the various types of organisation and facilities at this level. **9**

9 Comment on the role that national sports bodies play in the promotion of Sport for All in the UK. **8**

10 Sport in Europe tends to follow a decentralised pattern. Comment on the meaning of this and suggest historical reasons why this pattern has developed. **6**

11 Traditionally, the member states of the European Union have hosted a significantly large percentage of world sports events. Comment on the cultural and historical reasons for this. **6**

12 Using specific examples, comment on how global games can be used for protest and propaganda purposes. **6**

13 Comment on how the sociological theory of centrality can be applied in sport, using examples in your answer. **4**

Maximum
possible marks

14 Discuss how social mobility can be gained through sport. **3**

15 Why do emergent countries appear to be so successful in global sport? **4**

16 What were the motives for the state control of sport in the former eastern bloc cultures? **4**

17 Comment on the different ways that Australia and the USA have maintained their colonial links with the UK through sport. **6**

18 Can you identify elements of 'Americanisation' developing in UK sport? **5**

19 Give reasons for the importance given to sport in the New World democratic cultures. **5**

20 Discuss the differences between the elitist model of sports excellence and the optimum performance model of sports excellence. **6**

21 Discuss the elements that aid the development of sporting talent. **9**

22 What role can national centres of excellence play in the development of sports excellence? Use specific examples in your answer. **6**

23 Discuss the cultural and socioeconomic constraints that may inhibit the pursuit of sports excellence in the UK. **8**

24 Why should modern societies promote the ideal of Sport for All? Comment on the benefits to the individual and wider society. **6**

25 Discuss the cultural and socioeconomic constraints that may inhibit mass participation in sport in the UK. **8**

Exam questions: Exercise physiology

The questions below are typical of those that you might have to answer in your examination. Try answering each, remembering that the number of marks available for each question gives you a clue to the type of answer required.

Maximum possible marks

1 Describe the lactic acid system of ATP resynthesis. Give an example from physical education when this system is predominantly used. |7|

2 Explain the way in which most ATP is regenerated during a 60 metre sprint. |5|

3 The aerobic system is the predominant energy system used during submaximal work. Describe the processes involved in stages two and three of the aerobic energy system. |6|

4 Using examples from physical education, identify when and why the alactic system would be the body's predominant energy-producing system. |4|

5 Define the term energy and explain the role of ATP within the body. |3|

6 What is the relationship between ATP and PC during a 30 m sprint, and how does this relationship change during a 30-second recovery period? |4|

7 The availability of oxygen determines whether energy is released aerobically or anaerobically and also what food fuel is used. When is carbohydrate used as the predominant food fuel, and why? |4|

8 Using examples from physical education, explain the difference between a short-term physiological response and a long-term physiological adaptation. |4|

9 The body's stores of carbohydrate are limited compared with the amount of fat stored by the body. How might athletes try to maximise their stores of carbohydrate? |4|

10 During physical activity a performer used a 'mix' of the three energy systems to resynthesise ATP. Use examples from physical education to help explain the term 'energy continuum'. |3|

11 The recovery process involves returning the body to its pre-exercise state. Describe the processes that take place during a recovery period. |6|

12 Use an example from physical education to show how knowledge of the recovery process can be used to an athlete's advantage. |3|

Maximum
possible marks

13 Over-reliance on the lactic acid system of energy production will eventually result in muscle fatigue. Explain the effect that lactic acid build-up has on skeletal muscle and suggest why an endurance athlete would want to avoid early build-up of lactic acid.

4

14 Aerobic capacity can be assessed by measuring a person's $\dot{V}O_2$(max). Describe a method of evaluating $\dot{V}O_2$ (max) and discuss three factors that can influence it.

4

15 Why are target heart rate ranges useful when monitoring endurance training?

4

16 Circuit training is often used to improve strength. Give a circuit for one of your chosen activities, giving reasons for your choice and order of exercises.

5

17 After a period of endurance training the body adapts and becomes more efficient. Identify four adaptations that take place as a result of aerobic training, giving reasons why they lead to an improvement in aerobic capacity.

4

18 Explain the importance of a warm-up period before a training session.

4

19 PNF is a popular method of flexibility training. Give an example of this training method and give reasons for its effectiveness.

4

20 Outline an interval training session designed to improve the alactic energy system. Justify your choice of work interval and recovery period.

6

21 Discuss the factors that influence the degree of flexibility around a joint.

3

22 Plyometrics is a form of resistance training. What are the advantages and disadvantages of this form of training?

4

23 Substantial improvements to performance can be gained by following a well-planned training programme. Discuss the factors that you need to consider when designing a training programme.

8

24 Skill circuits as opposed to weight training are often preferred by games players as a means of improving strength. Discuss the advantages of using a skill circuit rather than a multi-gym or free weights.

4

25 The use of ergogenic aids is now widespread amongst elite athletes. In what way does RhEPO enhance performance? Why is it considered to be potentially dangerous?

5

Exam questions: Psychology of physical education and sport

The questions below are typical of those that you might have to answer in your examination. Try answering each, remembering that the number of marks available for each question gives you a clue to the type of answer required.

Maximum possible marks

1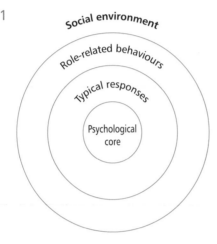

Social environment

Role-related behaviours

Typical responses

Psychological core

The diagram shows Hollander's view of the structure of personality. Using the diagram, and practical examples from sport, explain each element of this structure.

8

2 Discuss the view that personality research can positively affect performance in sport.

6

3 Draw a diagram to show a typical profile of mood states for an elite athlete.

4

4 Name three methods of measuring personality and comment on the validity of each as a research instrument.

6

5 What is meant by an attitude? Using psychological theories, explain how a negative attitude to sport can be changed into a positive one.

5

6 List three theories related to aggressive behaviour and sport. Explain each, giving practical examples.

6

7 As a coach, how would you ensure that performers' aggressive tendencies are channelled so that they are instrumental rather than reactive?

5

8 The 'need to achieve' personality has a much healthier mental state than the 'need to avoid failure' personality type. How would you optimise the 'need to achieve' characteristics?

3

9 Learned helplessness is a dysfunctional aspect of attribution. Explain what is meant by learned helplessness, and give two ways of avoiding it.

5

Maximum
possible marks

10 Define the term self-efficacy and describe how you would ensure that an athlete experiences a high level of self-efficacy.

5

11 Social learning is an important part of socialisation. What is meant by these two terms, and how far is this statement true?

8

12 A team involves a group of people who need to work together well. As a coach, how would you ensure that a team remains cohesive?

5

13 Social loafing is a negative aspect of group dynamics. How does it occur? How would you, as a coach, ensure that there are no 'social loafers'?

6

14 Describe the qualities of a good leader and discuss the view that a leader is born and not made.

8

15 There are two main styles of leadership in sport: task style and democratic style. Describe these styles and explain why you might adopt each of them.

8

16 What is meant by the term social facilitation when applied to sport?

4

17 How do you account for the numerous research findings which reveal that many teams win more often at home than they do away?

4

18 As a sports performer, how might you cope with the effects of a crowd on your performance?

4

19 Identify three main stressors in sport.

3

20 Describe the general adaptation syndrome (GAS) when applied to sport.

3

21 Define the terms trait anxiety and state anxiety. Illustrate your answer with examples from sport.

4

22 Stress management is essential if an athlete is to enter the 'zone of optimal functioning'. Describe in detail one way that an athlete could cognitively manage his or her own anxiety.

5

23 How can goal-setting affect performance?

3

24 What factors should be taken into consideration when setting goals in the sports context?

6

Exam questions: The historical development of sport

The questions below are typical of those that you might have to answer in your examination. Try answering each, remembering that the number of marks available for each question gives you a clue to the type of answer required.

Maximum possible marks

1 Mob games had simple rules. Explain why. How did games manage to function with limited codification? **4**

2 Compare the activities of the gentry and peasants during the popular recreation phase. **8**

3 Why did popular recreations tend to be isolated in terms of participation? **4**

4 During the popular recreation phase of sports development, why was cricket considered acceptable to all classes? **4**

5 What role did the Church play in both the promotion and the eventual curtailment of popular recreations? **5**

6 Explain how, during the popular recreation phase, hunting followed social class hierarchy. **4**

7 'Public schools took football out of the hands of the lower classes and gave it status.' Discuss this statement, explaining the global significance of this new-found status. **6**

8 Outline the technical development of football as it moved from the popular recreation phase into the public school phase. **6**

9 What features of the nineteenth-century public schools facilitated regular sports competition? **5**

10 What important roles did the universities of Oxford and Cambridge play in the development of sports during the nineteenth century? **4**

11 Why was the game of cricket so readily adopted by most public schools? **4**

12 Discuss the reasons why different schools chose different invasion games as their main focus. **10**

13 Comment on how the sociocultural backgrounds of the public schoolboys of the nineteenth century influenced the spread of their games throughout Britain and the British Empire. **12**

Maximum
possible marks

14 How did the changes in work patterns affect sport during the rational phase of sports development?

8

15 How, and why, was the development of working-class sport constrained compared with that of the upper classes?

8

16 What effect did the revolution in transport have on the codification of sport during the rational phase?

4

17 Explain why the rational phase of sports development is characterised by 'few playing, many watching'.

4

18 Using specific examples, explain some of the problems that sports faced as the demands for professionalism from their working-class players increased.

5

19 Comment on the sociocultural factors that led to the creation of most sports governing bodies between 1860 and 1890.

14

20 Comment on the effect that war had on the development of physical education at the start of the twentieth century.

6

21 Explain some of the constraints faced by elementary schools that limited the development of physical education at the end of the nineteenth century.

6

22 What factors might have limited the spread of European gymnastics into Britain during the nineteenth century?

5

23 How were societal needs reflected in the way that different social classes appeared to have been taught different systems and programmes of physical education?

5

24 'Modern PE is a combination of games from the public schools and physical training from the elementary schools.' Comment on the validity of this statement.

6

25 Discuss the view that physical education has been used by the state in the UK as a means of social control.

12

Exam questions: Comparative studies of sport

The questions below are typical of those that you might have to answer in your examination. Try answering each, remembering that the number of marks available for each question gives you a clue to the type of answer required.

Maximum possible marks

1 The USA has been described as 'a land of boundless opportunity in which upward social and economic mobility and success are regularly achieved by the ambitious and hard-working, regardless of their social origins'. Comment on whether this statement is true of US sport.

12

2 Explain the link between high-school and professional sport in the USA.

4

3 Suggest reasons for the huge community interest in high-school sport in the USA.

5

4 Give historical and cultural reasons to explain the fact that the USA holds 'world' sports events in which only American teams are allowed to compete.

5

5 Give examples of how the Olympic movement has been 'Americanised' over recent years.

5

6 Discuss how elements of the 'frontier spirit' manifest themselves in US sport.

5

7 Why are summer schools so popular with American families?

4

8 Compare the access and popularity of outdoor pursuits in the USA and UK.

6

9 Compare the organisation of extracurricular school sport in an average American high school with your own experience of secondary-school sport in the UK. What cultural variations might determine these differences?

12

10 Compare the extreme win ethic with the participation ethic, using examples from school sport in the USA and the UK.

6

11 Describe some of the strategies that Australia has used in an attempt to establish Olympic success.

8

12 What role does the Sports Search programme play in the development of Australia's sporting talent?

4

Maximum
possible marks

13 Compare the organisation of extracurricular school sport in an average Australian high school with your own experience of secondary-school sport in the UK. What cultural variations might determine these differences? **12**

14 Using examples, describe how Australia has adopted, adapted and invented the sports it now plays. **9**

15 Explain why outdoor education programmes take such a central role in Australian schools. **3**

16 Discuss how Australian sports authorities have used comparative study to aid the development of sports excellence programmes. **5**

17 Can you identify any Australian-style programmes being introduced into UK sport? **4**

18 Compare the development of excellence in women's sport in Australia and the UK. **4**

19 The French authorities have established sports study sections in an attempt to develop sports excellence. Describe how these sections operate. **4**

20 Identify examples of central control in the French education system. **4**

21 How do the French sports sections and UNSS compare with attempts to achieve sporting excellence in UK schools? **6**

22 Compare the organisation of extracurricular school sport in an average French high school with your own experience of secondary-school sport in the UK. What cultural variations might determine these differences? **12**

23 What advantages do French children have over their British counterparts in their access to outdoor activities? **4**

24 What are the similarities between Britain and France in the context of joint provision and dual use? **4**

25 Discuss how federal government can influence sport and outline some of the benefits this may bring to a country. **6**

Revision guide: Anatomy, biomechanics and physiology

This guide summarises the most important areas covered in Part 1. By fully understanding everything below you will be better prepared to succeed in your examination.

The skeletal system

There are six types of synovial joint: ball and socket, hinge, pivot, gliding, condyloid and saddle. All synovial joints allow some degree of movement and share common features, such as a synovial membrane, synovial fluid, articular cartilage and ligaments.

- The skeleton is made up of 206 bones, comprising the axial skeleton and the appendicular skeleton.
- The skeleton provides support, protection and attachment for muscles, and produces blood cells.
- There are three types of cartilage: yellow elastic cartilage, white fibrocartilage and hyaline cartilage.
- Ligaments join bone to bone.
- Tendons join muscle to bone.

Joints and muscles

Movement takes place around a joint and at least one prime mover is responsible for each type of movement that can be produced at a specific joint. You need to know the name and location of the prime mover for each movement possible around the major joints outlined in Chapter 2.

- Elbow flexion – biceps brachii; elbow extension – triceps brachii.
- Radioulnar pronation – pronator teres; radioulnar supination – supinator muscle.
- Shoulder flexion – anterior deltoid; shoulder extension – latissimus dorsi; shoulder abduction – middle deltoid; shoulder adduction – pectoralis major; shoulder inward rotation – subscapularis; shoulder outward rotation – infraspinatus.
- Flexion of the trunk – rectus abdominis; extension of the trunk – erector spinae; lateral flexion of the trunk – external and internal obliques.
- Flexion of the hip – iliopsoas; extension of the hip – gluteus maximus; abduction of the hip – gluteus medius; adduction of the hip – adductor longus, brevis and magnus; inward rotation of the hip – gluteus minimus; outward rotation of the hip – gluteus maximus.
- Flexion of the knee – biceps femoris, semitendinosus, semimembranosus; extension of the knee – rectus femoris, vastus lateralis, vastus intermedius, vastus medialis.
- Plantarflexion of the ankle – soleus; dorsiflexion of the ankle – tibialis anterior.

Skeletal muscle

Skeletal muscle creates movement by actively contracting and shortening. The muscle is stimulated by a motor neurone. This stimulation results in each individual sarcomere decreasing in length as the actin and myosin filaments slide over each other. The nature of the contraction produced is a result of the fibre type recruited, the number of fibres stimulated and the frequency and timing of the stimuli.

- 1 A muscle is stimulated by a motor neurone. 2 The T-vesicles stimulate the release of calcium ions from the sarcoplasmic reticulum. 3 Calcium binds with troponin and then the troponin removes the tropomyosin from the binding site on the actin. 4 Actin and myosin cross-bridges can now form as the myosin head attaches to the active site on the actin. 5 ATPase acts on ATP to release energy. 6 The cross-bridges swivel, release and reform as the actin is pulled over the myosin; the muscle shortens. 7 Stimulation stops, the calcium ions are removed and the muscle returns to its normal resting length.
- There are three types of muscle fibre – slow oxidative fibres, fast oxidative glycolytic fibres and fast glycolytic fibres. The percentage distribution of these fibres is genetically determined.
- A muscle can act as an agonist/prime mover, as an antagonist, as a fixator and as a synergist.
- There are four different types of muscle contraction – concentric, eccentric, isometric and isokinetic.
- Gradation of contraction depends on the number of motor units stimulated, the frequency of the stimuli and the timing of the stimuli to various motor units.

The mechanics of movement

A basic kinaesiological analysis needs to include three features: a description of the skill, an evaluation of both the joints and muscles used and the mechanical principles applied, and identification and correction of any faults.

- There are three different orders of lever: first-, second- and third-order levers. The greater the distance between the joint and the muscle insertion, the more strength can be generated. The closer the insertion is to the joint the better the range of movement.

- The longer the lever the greater the change in momentum and consequently the change in velocity that can be imparted on an object, e.g. a squash ball can be hit harder when the elbow is fully extended rather than flexed.
- The angle of pull refers to the position of the muscle relative to the position of the joint, measured in degrees. The angle of pull changes as the limb is moved and this affects the efficiency of the muscle's pulling force. Every joint has an optimum angle of pull.
- The effect that a force has on a body is influenced by: 1 the size of the force, 2 the direction of the force and 3 the position of application of the force.
- Motion (movement) will only occur if a force is applied. Motion occurs either in a straight line (linear motion) or around an axis (angular motion). There are three laws of motion, namely the law of inertia, the law of acceleration and the law of reaction.
- The centre of gravity of an object is the point at which the mass of the object is concentrated.
- The centre of gravity of a performer is continually changing as the body position changes.
- You are in a balanced position when your centre of gravity falls within your base of support. The lower the centre of gravity and the greater the base of support, the more stable a body will be.

Structure and function of the heart

The heart acts as two separate pumps, distributing oxygenated blood round the body and deoxygenated blood to the lungs. Deoxygenated blood returns to the heart via the pulmonary and systemic circulatory systems. The heart responds to the demands made on the body when exercising by increasing the heart rate and stroke volume to increase overall cardiac output.

- Cardiac output = stroke volume × heart rate. At rest it is about 5 litres.
- The cardiac cycle has two phases: systole, when the heart muscle contracts, and diastole, when the heart muscle relaxes.
- There are three mechanisms for controlling the heart rate – neural control, hormonal control and intrinsic control.
- The important components of the conduction system of the heart are the sinuatrial node, the atrioventricular node, the bundle of his and the purkinje fibres.

Structure and function of the vascular system

Five different types of vessel form the closed circulatory network that distributes blood to all cells. The distribution of the cardiac output is controlled by the vasomotor centre and is achieved by altering the flow and pressure of the blood. This is mainly brought about by opening or closing arterioles and pre-capillary sphincters.

- Arteries, arterioles, venules and veins have similar structure. Tunica interna (smooth inner layer), tunica media (smooth muscle layer), tunica externa (collagen layer). Capillaries are only one cell thick to allow diffusion.
- Blood pressure (measured in mmHg) = blood flow × peripheral resistance.
- Blood velocity is directly affected by the total cross-sectional area of the blood vessels. Blood flow slows down through the capillaries as the total cross-sectional area increases to allow diffusion to take place.
- During exercise up to 85% of blood is distributed to the working muscles (the vascular shunt mechanism).

The respiratory system

The amount of air required by the body varies considerably, depending on the amount of oxygen used by the cells. This is why we have a 'working' volume of air (tidal volume) plus a reserve volume available (inspiratory and expiratory reserve volumes). The respiratory control centre works in conjunction with the cardiac control centre and the vasomotor control centre to ensure a coordinated response to oxygen demand and delivery.

- Muscles of inspiration at rest – external intercostals and diaphragm.
- Additional muscles of inspiration during exercise – sternocleidomastoid, scalenes and pectoralis minor.
- Expiration is passive at rest.
- Muscles of expiration during exercise – the internal intercostals, the obliques and rectus abdominis.
- The parietal pleura is attached to the thoracic cavity and diaphragm.
- Lung tissue is made up of millions of air sacs called alveoli, resulting in an extremely large surface area for diffusion.
- Air enters the lungs when the atmospheric air pressure is higher than the pressure of air in the lungs. This is achieved by increasing the volume of the lungs during inspiration.
- In a healthy individual physical performance is not limited by pulmonary ventilation.
- The partial pressure of a gas is the single most important factor that determines gaseous exchange between the alveoli and the capillary and the capillary and the cell.
- The rate of diffusion speeds up during exercise as the diffusion gradient increases, body temperature increases, the partial pressure of carbon dioxide increases and pH drops.

Revision guide: Skill acquisition

This guide summarises the most important areas covered in Part 2. By fully understanding everything below you will be better prepared to succeed in your examination.

The concept and nature of skill

– A motor skill is concerned with movement, and a skilful performer in sport is consistent and follows a good technical pattern.
– Some skills are fundamental to movement in sport, such as throwing and catching a ball. These are the platform on which to build more advanced skills.

Ability

– Abilities are underlying factors that help us to carry out skills in sport. Our abilities are largely determined genetically.
– There are two types of ability: psychomotor ability (the ability to process information – e.g. reaction time) and gross motor ability, which involves actual movement (e.g. speed).

Classification of skill

– To analyse skills we need to classify them. All classifications should view skills on a range of continua.
– Gross skills involve large muscle movements; fine skills involve small muscle movements.
– The open–closed continuum is concerned with the effects of the environment.
– The pacing continuum is concerned with the timing of movements.
– The discrete–serial–continuous continuum is concerned with how well defined the beginning and end of the skill are.

Classical conditioning

– This is concerned with modifying a stimulus to give a conditioned response.
– Pavlov described the process of conditioned reflex.
– This type of conditioning can help performers associate positive feelings, rather than negative ones such as fear, with an event or a particular environment (e.g. swimming).

Operant conditioning

– This involves the modification of behaviour. The work of Skinner is important here.
– Operant conditioning involves shaping behaviour and reinforcing that behaviour.
– Rewards are extensively used in the teaching of motor skills to reinforce correct movements.

Cognitive theories of learning

– These involve intervening variables, which are mental processes that occur between the stimulus being received and the response.
– These theories involve the performer understanding what needs to be done to perform a motor skill. Previous experience is important in this type of learning.
– The Gestaltists (a group of German scientists) established many principles related to cognitive theories of learning.

Motivation

– This involves our inner drives towards achieving a goal, the external pressures we experience and the rewards we receive. It also concerns the intensity and direction of our behaviour.
– Intrinsic motivation is specifically the internal drives to participate and to succeed.
– Extrinsic motivation is concerned with external rewards.
– Arousal represents the intensity aspect of motivation. Its effects can be positive or negative. The correct level of arousal is important if optimal performance is to be achieved.
– The drive theory describes the relationship between arousal and performance as linear. Learned behaviour is more likely to occur as the intensity of the competition increases. The formula often used to describe this theory is $P = f(H \times D)$.
– According to the inverted U theory, optimum performance is reached at moderate arousal levels. Performance will fall under conditions of low or high arousal.
– The catastrophe theory takes into account both cognitive and somatic anxiety factors. The decline in performance under conditions of high arousal is dramatic, rather than the slow decline described in the inverted U theory.

Peak flow experience

– At optimum performance levels many top athletes appear to be in a 'zone' of emotional experience.
– Mental strategies can help to achieve this positive emotional response, which will motivate an athlete and enable them to cope with high levels of anxiety.

Information processing

- This views the brain as working like a computer. Stimuli enter the brain (input), decisions are made and a response occurs (output).
- The stages of information processing – stimulus identification stage, response selection stage, response programming stage.
- Serial processing is a type of information processing in which each stage is arranged sequentially, with one stage affecting the next.
- In parallel processing two or more processes occur at the same time but one does not necessarily affect the other.

Attentional control

- This involves concentration, which is important for motivation and skill learning.
- Nedeffer identified two types of attentional focus: broad/narrow focus and external/internal focus.
- In situations of high arousal there may be cognitive overload, when too much information is available.

Reactions

- Reaction time is important in the execution of skills and is the time between the presentation of the stimulus and the start of the movement. This affects response time.
- Hick's law states that choice reaction time is linearly related to the amount of information to be processed.
- The single-channel hypothesis states that the brain can deal with only one piece of information at a time. It is often referred to as the bottleneck theory.

Memory

- The memory process affects skill learning.
- Selective attention is important in filtering information so that only the important aspects are used.
- Information recently acquired is kept in short-term memory.
- The long-term memory is a store of information that can be used to perform skills. Motor programmes are stored here.
- Motor programmes are associated with open-loop control. They are generalised memories of movements that can be used by making a single decision. No feedback is involved.
- Closed-loop control involves the use of feedback to detect and correct errors in movements.
- Schema are items of information that are used to modify a motor programme. There are two types: recall schema and recognition schema. Variety of practice conditions will ensure the building of schema in the performer's long-term memory and assist in future performances.

Feedback

- This is information available to the performer during and after performance of a skill.
- Knowledge of results and knowledge of performance are the two main types of feedback. These can help with motivation and can reinforce movements.
- Feedback can also be used in setting goals, which can in turn affect future motivation and performance.

Learning curves

- These describe the relationships between practice and performance. Performance is seen as only a temporary measurement; learning is more permanent.
- Types of learning curve include positive acceleration, linear and negative.
- A plateau is a part of a learning curve where there is little or no change in measured performance. Strategies are needed to combat the plateau effect – e.g. regular rest intervals.

Structure of practices

- Practice must be well planned, taking into account the type of skill to be learned and the environment involved.
- If a skill can be split up, each sub-routine could be taught separately. If the skill is highly organised then it is best to teach the skill as a whole.
- Variation in practice will help in the construction of schema.
- Massed practice involves few rest intervals and works best with highly skilled athletes.
- Distributed practice involves rest intervals and can counter the effects of fatigue and the plateau effect. It works best with beginners.

Guidance

- Visual guidance is best used in the early stages of skill learning. Demonstrations are good examples of this type of guidance but should be accurate and highlight important cues.
- Verbal guidance should be used alongside visual and can be used to point out important coaching points.
- Manual and mechanical guidance are important in the early stages of skill learning. They combat fear responses and enable safe practice. Overuse of manual guidance can be detrimental to learning because the performer does not experience the true kinaesthetic feelings of the skill.

Teaching styles

- Teachers and coaches should adapt their approach to the type of activity and the characteristics of the performer.
- Mosston and Ashworth's spectrum of teaching styles states that the more decisions that are made by the teacher, the more authoritarian the approach.
- Advantages and disadvantages of all styles are related to the performer, the teacher and the environment.

Revision guide: Sociocultural aspects of physical education and sport

This guide summarises the most important areas covered in Part 3. By fully understanding everything below you will be better prepared to succeed in your examination.

Conceptual basis of sport

You need to know the meaning of the following terms:
- Sport
- Leisure
- Play
- Physical education
- Outdoor education
- Physical recreation
- Outdoor recreation.

You need to be able to characterise the key points for each of these concepts:
- Sport – physical activity; competition with a clear winner; strenuous and enjoyable.
- Leisure – free time; choice, not work.
- Play – freely undertaken; non-instrumental; informal rules and uncertain ending.
- Physical recreation – physical activity of a relaxing nature; limited organisation and outcome; active form of leisure.
- Physical education – occurs only in school, college or university; learning through bodily movement.
- Outdoor education – learning in the natural environment; novel activities that include challenge.
- Outdoor recreation – challenging activities in the natural environment.

Organisation of sport in the UK

You need to know the role of the following organisations:
- National governing bodies
- Sport England
- The sports councils
- CCPR
- sports coach UK
- BOA
- Sports Aid
- Department of Culture, Media and Sport
- Countryside Commission
- British Sports Association for the Disabled.

Make sure you understand their role in the funding of sport, promoting Sport for All and developing sports excellence.

Sport at the local level is provided by the private, public and voluntary sectors.

Organisation of European sport and global games

- Sport at European level follows a decentralised pattern.
- European legislation is increasingly having an impact on sport. Examples include the Bosman case.
- There are two main European sports models – the western European model (autonomous control) and the eastern European model (state control).
- Sport throughout Europe follows a pyramid structure. European bodies such as UEFA control the individual bodies, which in turn form international bodies that control world championships.
- The 'live' nature of global games makes them a stage for protest and propaganda.

Sport in society and the pursuit of excellence

Sport reflects the wider values and traditions of the society in which it is played.

You need to be able to understand that different cultures approach sport in different ways and you need to be able to characterise the key elements for these different cultural approaches:
- Emergent cultures – select and channel athletes in a limited number of sports to ensure success
- Eastern bloc cultures – the state controls sport for political gain
- New World democratic cultures – use sport as a focus of national identity and to gain international status
- USA – sport is seen as a commercial commodity and is dominated by the win ethic.

Excellence in sport has two meanings:
- Elitism – 'Pick the best; ignore the rest'
- Optimum performance – everyone has the chance to succeed.

Elitism is the most popular model because it creates champions – which bring shop window status.

There are three major stages in the development of excellence:
- Selection
- Development of talent
- Providing support.

Factors affecting participation in sport

Mass participation is maximising the access to sport and recreation for all people.

- 'Sport for All' is a campaign set up by the Sports Council to foster sport for all. Benefits are individual (intrinsic) and societal (extrinsic).
- Discrimination is where one section of a community is disadvantaged because of certain sociocultural variables.
- The five main cultural factors that lead to discrimination are gender, class, race, age and ability.
- The reasons for discrimination can be summarised under three headings: opportunity (have people the chance to play?), provision (where can people play?) and esteem (what will I look like when I play?).

Deviance in sport

- Deviance in sport is breaking the rules and codes, both written and unwritten.
- Sportsmanship – where taking part is the key focus.
- Gamesmanship – winning at all costs is the main focus.
- Examples of deviance include taking performance-enhancing drugs and violence.

Sport and the media

- Media – mass communication, made up of the press, television, radio and cinema.
- Television is now a major influence on sport – funding, fostering popularity and reinforcing stereotypes.

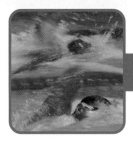

This guide summarises the most important areas covered in Part 4. By fully understanding everything below you will be better prepared to succeed in your examination.

Energy

There are three ways of synthesising ATP from ADP and free phosphate to ensure a constant supply of energy. All three systems work together, the dominance of any one depending on the rate at which energy is used.

When the demand for energy is high and immediate then the anaerobic processes are heavily relied on. When the demand for energy is low but sustained then the aerobic process is the main system used.

- The alactic system uses phosphocreatine (PC), a high-energy phosphate molecule that is stored in the sarcoplasm.
- The energy released by the breakdown of PC is used to rebuild ATP in a coupled reaction. The enzyme creatine kinase controls the rate at which PC is broken down. The system is rapid as it does not require the presence of oxygen, and it is a simple reaction. This system is used during high-intensity, short-duration activities – supplies of PC will provide energy for about 10 seconds.
- The lactic acid system involves the partial breakdown of carbohydrate under anaerobic conditions. The reaction takes place in the sarcoplasm. Glycogen is broken down by glycogenphosphorylase to glucose-6-phosphate and then by phosphofructokinase to pyruvic acid. This in turn is broken down to lactic acid. Sufficient energy is released to resynthesise two molecules of ATP. Phosphofructokinase is activated by a drop in levels of PC and by increased levels of calcium.
- Stage one of the aerobic system is the same as the lactic acid system but the pyruvic acid diffuses into the matrix of the mitochondria. Stage two (the TCA cycle) uses both fats and carbohydrates. Three important things happen during the cycle: carbon dioxide is formed, hydrogen is split from the compound and enough energy is released to resynthesise 2 ATP. Stage three (the electron transport chain) is where electrons from the hydrogen are passed along by electron carriers and the hydrogen eventually combines with oxygen to form water. Enough energy is released to resynthesise 34 ATP.

Energy and exercise

In most activities we use a 'mix' of all three systems of producing energy. This is reflected in the amount of oxygen we consume and the food fuels we use. By regulating the intensity we work at we can optimise our use of oxygen and fuel supplies to enhance performance.

- One gram of carbohydrate will produce 4 kCal of energy; one gram of fat will produce 9 kCal of energy.
- It takes 12% more oxygen to break down fats than it does to break down carbohydrates.
- The energy continuum is a continuum that reflects the type of activity being performed in relation to intensity and duration and the way in which energy for ATP resynthesis is made available.
- Athletes who train at a high intensity on a regular basis should eat a high-carbohydrate diet. Carbohydrate is the primary fuel during high-intensity exercise and energy from carbohydrate can be released three times more quickly than energy from fat.

The recovery process

The recovery process returns the body to its pre-exercise state. Replenishment of ATP and PC stores and removal of lactic acid will take place only when additional energy is available. The elevated rates of aerobic respiration during recovery provide the energy for these processes.

The factors that contribute to excess post-exercise oxygen consumption are:
- Resynthesis of PC in the muscle.
- Removal of lactic acid.
- Restoration of muscle and blood oxygen stores.
- Elevation of heart and breathing rates to help remove elevated levels of carbon dioxide.

The principles of training

The main principles of training include overload, progression, specificity, reversibility and variance. Any training programme should be closely monitored and evaluated and every session should include a warm-up and a cool-down. Training should be specific to the athlete and the sport they participate in but a general fitness programme needs to be completed before any specialisation.

- Overload is achieved by changing the frequency of training, the intensity of training and the duration of training.
- Target training heart rate ranges are used to monitor intensity of exercise because there is a linear relationship between heart rate and oxygen consumption.
- Progression is important – once adaptations have been made overload should be increased but the increase should not exceed 10% of the initial overload.

- Specificity is also important – training should consider the energy system used, the fibre type used, the muscle groups used, the neural pathways and type of contraction.
- Moderation should be followed – athletes should avoid over-training and DOMS by allowing plenty of time for recovery, and should consider tapering before a competition.

Physical fitness

Physical fitness cannot be stored but must be maintained by following a programme designed with both your physiological make-up and the demands of your sport in mind. Fitness can be divided into health-related components and skill-related components. An athlete should evaluate each component before embarking on a training schedule. The body responds to exercise on both a short-term and a long-term physiological basis. A short-term response, such as an increase in heart rate, takes place during the actual training session and will return to normal shortly after the athlete stops exercising. A long-term response, such as a drop in resting heart rate due to aerobic training, is an adaptation to the body that takes place over a period of time.

- Health-related components include aerobic capacity, strength, flexibility and body composition.
- Skill-related components include speed, coordination, reaction time, agility and balance.
- Aerobic capacity is referred to as 'the maximum volume of oxygen that can be consumed and utilised by the body per unit of time'. It depends on the effectiveness of the external respiration process, the effectiveness of oxygen transport from the lungs to the cells and the effectiveness of oxygen use within the cell. Aerobic capacity can be evaluated by the multi-stage fitness test, which gives a predicted value for $\dot{V}O_2(max)$. Training includes continuous running, fartlek, repetition running, spinning, etc.
- Target heart rate ranges can be used to monitor intensity of exercise, and Karvonen's principle can be used to calculate the range. Adaptations occur to 1 the heart (e.g. hypertrophy of the myocardium), 2 the lungs (e.g. increased efficiency of the respiratory muscles), 3 the blood vessels (e.g. increased elasticity of arterial walls), 4 connective tissue (e.g. stimulates increased deposits of calcium to bone tissue) and 5 the muscle (e.g. increased density of mitochondria).

Strength

Strength is a general term for applying a force against a resistance and three types of strength have been highlighted in the book. Maximum strength is the greatest force the neuromuscular system is capable of exerting in a single maximum voluntary contraction. Elastic strength or power is the ability of the neuromuscular system to overcome resistance with a high speed of contraction. Strength endurance is the ability of the muscle to withstand fatigue.

- Maximum strength can be evaluated by finding out the maximum weight that a person can lift in a single contraction. The sports coach UK sit-up test can be used to assess strength endurance and the Wingate test can be used to assess elastic strength.
- Training involves working against some form of resistance and can include circuit training, free weight exercises, multi-gym exercises and plyometrics. A training session is usually divided into repetitions (a number of times that an athlete repeats a particular exercise) and sets (a certain number of repetitions).
- Neural adaptations to training occur first with improved coordination of motor unit activation and recruitment of additional motor units. Hypertrophy of the muscle fibre takes place, along with specific aerobic or anaerobic adaptations depending on the nature of the training.
- Flexibility (or static flexibility) is the range of movement possible around a joint. Increasing flexibility usually improves performance and helps to avoid unnecessary injury.
- There are three main ways to improve flexibility, namely static stretching (active and passive), ballistic stretching and proprioceptive neuromuscular facilitation (PNF).
- Factors that limit flexibility include the type of joint, the resting length of the muscle, body build, muscle temperature, resting length of tendons and ligaments, sex and age.
- For each health-related fitness component you need to know a definition, a method of evaluation, training methods and the physiological adaptations that occur as a result of training.

Revision guide: Psychology of physical education and sport

This guide summarises the most important areas covered in Part 5. By fully understanding everything below you will be better prepared to succeed in your examination.

Personality

- The trait approach involves enduring characteristics which can predict behaviour. Traits can be generalised.
- The social learning theory sees personality as being affected by the environment, including the actions of others.
- The interactionist approach combines both the trait and the social learning approaches. This can be summarised by B = f(PE).
- Personality is often measured by questionnaire, which is usually self report. There are, however, validity and reliability problems with personality measurement.
- Personality research cannot be used very effectively in selection but can give a useful insight into the motivation and stress levels of individual athletes.

Attitudes

- These are learned and are made up of three elements (the triadic model): cognitive, affective and behavioural.
- Prejudice is an extreme form of an attitude because it is judgmental and inflexible.
- Attitudes are not always linked with behaviour but are more likely to be if the attitude is specific towards an attitude object. Attitudes can be changed through the process of cognitive dissonance or through persuasion. Attitudes depend upon previous experience and social learning.

Aggression

- In sports psychology this is the intent to hurt or harm outside the rules of the game.
- The instinct theory states that aggression is innate and it is natural to express it.
- The frustration/aggression hypothesis is a drive theory which states that if goals are blocked frustration occurs. This can lead to aggression.
- The social learning theory states that we learn aggressive behaviour by watching and copying others who are significant to us.
- Strategies to combat aggression include internal control of arousal, punishment and reinforcement of non-aggression.

Achievement motivation

- This is related to a performer's reaction to competition.
- There are two types of motives – need to achieve (Nach) and need to avoid failure (Naf). Both types of behaviour are more likely to occur in an evaluative situation.
- Ego-oriented personality types believe that ability is important but task-oriented people regard effort as more important.
- Recognition of types of motive can help with motivational strategies such as goal-setting.

Attributions

- These are the reasons we give for winning or losing. Attributions can affect motivation and therefore future performance.
- Weiner's model of attribution is two-dimensional, including where the attributions have come from (the locus of causality) and whether they are stable or not (the locus of stability). A third dimension (controllability) has been added, which refers to whether the performer has control over the causes of failure.
- Low achievers can suffer from learned helplessness, which can be global or specific. Attributing to uncontrollable, stable and internal factors can lead to learned helplessness.
- Attribution retraining can help to change attributions and minimise the effects of learned helplessness.

Self-efficacy

- Self-efficacy is self-confidence in a specific situation.
- Expectations of self-efficacy are closely linked to motivation and can affect the choice of activity, the amount of effort expended and persistence at the task. The factors affecting expectations (according to Bandura) are performance accomplishments, vicarious experiences, verbal persuasion and emotional arousal.

Social learning

- In sport nearly all behaviour is set in a social setting.
- Socialisation is the adoption of the norms and values of a culture and is learned mostly in childhood, although it goes on all through life.
- Observational learning is the main way in which we learn behaviour. We observe others and will imitate

- them if the conditions are right. We are more likely to imitate a model if their behaviour is reinforced and he or she is of high status.
- Demonstrations are very important in the acquisition of new skills. Imitation of the demonstration depends on the observer's attention, retention, motor reproduction and motivation.

Groups

- A sports team is a typical group and those within it have a collective identity, a shared purpose, patterns of interaction and communication and interpersonal attraction.
- A cohesive team is one where the members are motivated to work together. Team cohesion depends on the motives of team members. Some may be socially motivated, some may be task motivated.
- Group performance depends on team coordination and motivation. The Ringelmann effect and research by Latane show that losses in team performance increase as team size increases. Motivational losses can be due to social loafing, which is caused by lack of identity of individuals within a team.
- Strategies should be developed to limit the effects of poor coordination and lack of individual motivation.

Leadership

- Leadership involves influencing people towards set goals. Leaders may be born or made but research points to social learning aspects. Leaders can fill positions of responsibility, either by emerging or being prescribed.
- Effective leadership depends on situational factors, the characteristics of the leader and the expectations and nature of the group members.
- The main styles of leadership are the authoritarian, task-oriented style or the democratic, person-oriented style. Most leaders have a mix of both but tend towards one. The preferred style depends upon situational and group characteristic variables.
- Fiedler's theory states that the favourableness of the situation must be taken into consideration before adopting a particular style.

Social facilitation

- Social facilitation is the influence of others on performance. The presence of others raises arousal levels, which can have a positive or negative effect on performance. According to drive theory, the dominant response (this will be positive for experts, for simple/gross skills and for extroverts but negative for the novice, for complex/fine skills and for introverts) is more likely in high-arousal situations.
- The presence of others can cause evaluation apprehension – when there is perceived judgement of performance.
- Coping strategies should be developed to cope with the negative effects of social facilitation.

Nature of stress

- Stress can be positive or negative. The process of actively seeking positive stress is called eustress.
- Stress involves stressors, stress response and stress experience. Conflict, competition, frustration and environmental factors such as climate are all stressors.
- The stress response can be explained by GAS, which has three stages: alarm, resistance and exhaustion.
- The stress experience is characterised by worry and anxiety.
- Coping strategies help us to control the negative effects of stress.

Anxiety

- Anxiety is a negative form of stress.
- Four factors affect levels of anxiety in competition: individual differences, nature of the anxiety experienced, general or specific anxiety and the process of competition.
- There are two types of anxiety: A trait – the enduring characteristic of potential anxiety – and A state – the actual anxiety experienced in a particular situation.
- The SCAT is a test of competitive trait anxiety and proves that high trait anxiety can lead to competitive state anxiety.

Stress management

- Stress management deals with somatic and cognitive anxiety.
- Imagery helps with concentration and confidence. It can recreate the task about to be performed or can help to visualise successful movements. It can also help the mind escape reality. Imagery can represent sounds, feelings and emotions. There are two forms of imagery: external and internal.
- Positive self-talk can help with reducing anxiety. In anxious situations athletes are unable to distinguish easily between positive and negative self-talk.
- Relaxation helps to control somatic anxiety. Relaxation can be self-directed or through progressive relaxation training (PRT). Like all stress management techniques, PRT becomes more effective through practice.

Goal setting

- Goal setting can help motivation, boost confidence and help with anxiety control. There are three different types of goals: outcome goals, performance goals and process-oriented goals. Goals should be challenging, but not too difficult. They should be well-defined so that goal evaluation can take place.
- Long-term goals should be preceded by short-term goals to help with motivation and to control anxiety.
- Goals must also be measurable to allow for evaluation.
- If there is a sharing in decisions about goals, then those goals are more likely to be achieved, and anxiety is less likely.

Revision guide: The historical development of sport

This guide summarises the most important areas covered in Part 6. By fully understanding everything below you will be better prepared to succeed in your examination.

You need to understand that sport has developed through four main phases:
- The popular recreation phase (fifteenth to seventeenth centuries).
- The public-school phase (eighteenth to nineteenth centuries).
- The industrial and rational phase (nineteenth century).
- The emergence of physical education (twentieth century).

You need to be able to characterise the key elements reflected in the sports and games of each phase and understand the societal and cultural reasons for these particular features. You also need to understand the societal, cultural and sporting reasons behind the transitions between phases.

Popular recreation phase – pre-industrial sport

Popular recreation sports were characterised by the following elements:
- localised
- uncoded
- cruel
- courtly/sophisticated
- peasant/mob
- rural
- occasional
- often involving wagering.

The societal background to this phase can be characterised by the following elements:
- Feudal basis of society – people were either land-owning gentry or peasants.
- Rural society.
- Agricultural occupations or cottage industries meant that there were 'slack' times during the year.
- There was lack of law and order in society.
- Life was tough and life expectancy low.

It would be helpful if you could include specific examples of popular recreation activities in your answers. The following are good examples:
- Alnwick game
- Ashbourne game
- Haxey Hood game
- Robert Dover's Cotswold games
- Lutterworth Mob Hockey
- Hurling the Silver Ball.

You also need to recognise some of the reasons why these popular recreations began to be curtailed and suppressed at the end of the seventeenth century:
- Influence of the Church and puritan authorities.
- The need for war preparation – especially archery practice.
- The development of law and order in society.

Nineteenth-century athleticism and the role of the public school

- Public schools were endowed, boarding, fee paying, socially exclusive centres of education.
- The development of sport within public schools went through three stages: **barbarian stage** – characterised by unruly schools, boys in control, mob games and domination of animal sports; **Arnoldian stage** – characterised by the prefect system, sport seen as a method of social control and instilling character-building values, sport now seen as an essential part of a gentleman's education; **games cult phase** – with middle-class/philistine copies and the spread of games around Britain and the Empire.
- The Clarendon Commission highlighted good practice of the 'great' public schools, which further enhanced the reputation of the games cult.
- Education of girls lagged behind that of boys, held back by social constraints. The Taunton Commission and several influential headmistresses promoted athleticism for girls towards the end of the nineteenth century.

Make sure you understand the influence that old boys of public schools had on the spread of games around the world. The mnemonic CATPUICCA on pages 349–50 is a good way of remembering this influence.

Industrialisation and rational sport

Nearly all sports were codified and developed a system of administration from 1860 onwards. You need to be able to chart this phase of sports development and recognise the important changes in society that shaped modern sport.
Key features of this phase:
- The industrial revolution led to a change in the way people lived and for the first time created a regular system of leisure.

- Leisure time was governed by social class and the working class had to wait longer for free time than the upper and middle classes.
- The development of transport systems allowed inter-town competition and greater travel opportunities.
- Urbanisation meant that only a few people could play.
- Gradually spectatorism led to the rise of professionalism in sport.
- By 1890 most sports were rationalised – they were codified and had national status.

Rational sports are summarised by the following characteristics:
- Channelled aggression, stringent organisation, formal rules and regular play.

The emergence of physical education

Physical education developed through three main stages:
- Drill
- Physical training
- Physical education.

Modern PE grew from two main pathways:
- Games from the public school – these developed character and leadership.
- Physical training from the elementary schools – these developed fitness and discipline.

Key features of this phase
- The 1870 Forster Act made education compulsory, but lack of space and facilities limited early development of PE.
- Gymnastic drill had its origins in European systems of exercise.
- The first attempt at a syllabus was the Model Course of 1902, written by the War Office.
- Syllabuses were revised through the period 1904–1919, but the focus on all schemes was PT, with a strong military influence.
- The 1933 syllabus was the first to introduce the idea of PE.
- The experiences of the Second World War led to a more educational and child-centred approach, which was developed further after the 1944 Education Act.

Revision guide: Comparative studies of sport

This guide summarises the most important areas covered in Part 7. By fully understanding everything below you will be better prepared to succeed in your examination.

The key to understanding this section is to recognise that sport reflects the culture in which it is played. Sociocultural differences will have an effect on the way sport is organised and provided. Opportunities to participate may also vary between cultures.

For each of the study cultures you need to know something about these key areas:
- Sociocultural background.
- How the culture and its sports are administered.
- The role physical education and school sport plays.
- The role of outdoor education and outdoor pursuits.
- The culture's policy and philosophy for mass participation.
- The culture's policy and philosophy on elite sport.

The United States of America

A big country, with a big population. Recognised as the only remaining superpower in commerce, politics and sport. Much of American culture is linked with the 'frontier spirit' and spirit of the Wild West. The USA is a melting pot of many races and cultures, and sport is an important outlet for this pluralist approach.

The USA sports model
- The USA follows a decentralised model, with much variation because of the separate state influence.
- The private sector dominates the provision of sport and recreation.

The USA is a young culture that has used sport for nation building and to reflect their cultural values – especially the win ethic and the American dream.
- American sport is dominated by the 'big four', which also tend to be isolated to the USA.

Physical education is characterised by:
- Decentralised administration and programmes.
- Elite school team sport dominates.

School sport is very important for both the community and as a nursery for the professional sports.
- The best students receive athletics scholarships and hope to progress into the draft.

The frontier spirit is evident in outdoor education and the popularity of outdoor pursuits in the USA has been enhanced by the rise in eco sport.

Australia

A vast country with only a small population; however, the majority of the population are urban dwellers. Climate, space and youthful population make sport an important part of the Australian culture.

The Australian sports model
- Although Australia is a decentralised culture with separate state influence, Australian sport is centrally organised.
- The Australian Sports Commission takes a central role in the control and funding of sport.
- Failure at the Montreal Olympics of 1976 led to a major review of the Australian sports system and much use was made of comparative study.
- Many initiatives have been introduced to make Australia great again in sport.

Make sure you know some of the background to the following:
- Aussie Sport, Active Australia, Sports Search, AIS, State sports academies.

Physical education is characterised by:
- A decentralised system but both PE and sport education are given prominence at all levels.
- PE is an optional, but popular, part of the Higher School Certificate.
- In many schools, sport is given major emphasis, is state controlled and given curriculum status.
- A recent innovation in primary schools has been the Fundamental Motor Skills Project.
- Sporting success at school is very important for both the community and base of the sports pyramid.

Australia's natural resources are much in evidence and have led to the 'bush culture'.

All students must experience outdoor education, and accessibility makes outdoor pursuits very popular.

France

A large country in European terms, with a good range of climate and topography, which makes many outdoor pursuits accessible. A traditional country, dominated by high culture – sport has struggled to gain prominence, but quietly France does very well as a sporting nation.

The French sporting model
   – A centralised system with the state and public sector taking a central role in the control and funding of sports.
   – Modern sports are a blend of traditional pastimes, British adoptions and outdoor pursuits.
   – Olympic failure in 1960 and de Gaulle's drive to promote French nationalism have led to an impressive elite sports system.

Make sure you know about initiatives such as the National Plan and the role of INSEP.

The role of physical education in France
   – Centralised system with a very academic focus – but PE is a compulsory part of the baccalauréat.
   – There are PE/sport programmes for all levels, including 'tier temps' and a central syllabus.
   – Sports afternoons are very important and are centrally run by UNSS/USEP.
   – Elite sports provision is developed through sports study sections.

France's natural resources are much in evidence and campaigns such as Le Plein Air and the concept of rustic simplicity are central to French culture.

   Outdoor pursuits achieve the dual function of possible medals and mass participation.

   Make sure you know some of the background to schemes such as the transplant classes and centres de vacances.

Research project guidelines

In most of the examination specifications there is an opportunity to complete a research project as coursework. This is assessed and the results of the assessment go towards your final grade.

Examination boards differ in their requirements for a research project. There are, however, some general guidelines that you would be wise to follow for completing a project. Here are some important tips which will help you to obtain a good grade for your research project.

Projects often have a word limit. For example, for the AQA specification (used to be called a syllabus) at AS level for Sports and Physical Education the word limit is 1000 words. For the full A level (A2) a maximum of 2000 words is required. For the Edexcel specification the project must be between 1500 and 2000 words for AS level and up to 2500 words for the full A level (A2). Make sure that you keep within the limit. Examiners emphasise quality rather than quantity, so do not try to write up to the maximum allowed just for the sake of it. Be sure that you fulfil the minimum requirements.

Each specification has specific requirements. Make sure that you fully understand the structure required for your project. For example:
- **Edexcel** requires: Introduction, Literature review, Method, Results, Discussion/conclusions, Appraisal of the project, Bibliography, Appendices.
- **AQA specifications** require: Abstract, Acknowledgements, Planning, Observation/analysis/evaluation, Literature review, Method, Results, Discussion/conclusion, Bibliography, Appendices.

As you can see there is a great deal of overlap with these requirements, whatever the specifications (syllabus). Your choice of subject is largely dictated by your examination board, so make sure you understand what you can write about and what you cannot write about.

Planning

Include a coherent timetable of how you are going to develop the project and the relevance of the project. If you have to state a hypothesis (a statement about what you think the outcome of the project is going to be), make it clear and to the point, e.g. 'Exercise affects the mood of an athlete'.

The better your planning, the better your project. Do not be afraid of choosing several topics, doing background research and then choosing the one you feel you can cope with most effectively. Remember, the examiners are not expecting groundbreaking research. Keep your project simple!

Abstract

This is a short synopsis or summary of your project. It should contain enough detail for the examiner to know what you did, with whom and what the outcome was. Give a brief statement about your sample if relevant. An abstract should be only about 200 words long.

Literature review

This is demanded by some examination boards. Describe any relevant research or theories from books that deal with your subject. If you find that information about your topic is extremely thin you might be better off choosing another topic. Make sure that you keep a record of the books you have used, along with authors, publication dates and publishers for your bibliography.

Method

You should describe fully your research techniques and your reasons for using them. Be concise. Your procedure should be easily replicated and your research method copied by other people. The structure of the method can vary considerably depending on the nature of your project, but the following format is common:
- Design
- Participants/sample
- Apparatus/materials
- Procedure.

Results

This section should include a clear presentation of the data you have collected. There should be some element of data analysis. Describe how you have analysed the data and include any statistical procedures that you have used. If it is possible, represent your data in chart and graph forms to give a visual representation of the data you have collected.

Discussion / conclusion

This may also involve an appraisal of your study – in other words, you may wish to criticise your project because of the methods you used or to praise your project because the methods worked well.

The results should be discussed in this section and if you have used a literature review you should try to link your results with the material in the review. Do your results agree with other findings or do they show something different?

Conclusions that you draw should relate back to your hypothesis and the aims of your study. Does the study prove your hypothesis or not? If your project does not show that your hypothesis is correct this does not mean that you score lower marks – the process of finding out is the important aspect of your research project.

Bibliography

This should be an alphabetical list by author and should follow the Harvard system. For example, if you used this book for your project you would record:

Honeybourne, J., Hill, M., Moors, H., *Advanced PE and Sport for A Level* (3rd edition), Nelson Thornes, 2004.

Make sure that all the books and journals you have used are included in your bibliography.

Appendices

Materials used in your project (instruction sheets, tally charts, questionnaire responses, etc.) are usually put into the appendices. As you write your project, you can refer to material in your appendices.

Presentation

Just as in life many people judge on first impressions, the same can be said for projects. If a project looks like a professional piece of work, then it is only human nature to assess it as such. Write neatly and legibly – or, better still, word-process your project. If you do use a word processor, make sure that the spacing is either 1.5 or double spaced. A readable font helps – probably 12 point – and ensure that you use the spell-checker! A title page and a contents page referring to numbered pages also help to give the right impression.

Glossary

A state   Anxiety that is felt in a particular situation

A trait   Anxiety which is experienced by a performer caused by a predisposition towards apprehension

Abduction   Movement away from the midline of the body

Ability   Underlying factors which are largely predetermined genetically

ACHPER   The Australian Council for Health, Physical Education and Recreation. Funds, researches and develops major health-based initiatives and programmes for Australian schools

Actin   A protein filament found within the sarcomere

Active Australia   A national framework of mass participation, set up in 1996 to replace Aussie Sport

Adduction   Movement towards the midline of the body

Aerobic capacity   The maximum amount of oxygen that can be taken in and used by the body in one minute

Aerobic respiration   The complete breakdown of fats and carbohydrates to carbon dioxide and water. This process requires oxygen

Affiliation   Payment of a membership/subscription to a club which gives the right to perform and take decisions in the administration of the particular sport

Aggression   In sports psychology this means that there is an intention to harm or injure outside the rules of the game or activity

Alactacid component   Part of the recovery process (oxygen debt) where the muscle phosphagen stores are replenished

American dream   The idea that in the USA anyone can move from rags to riches

Anaerobic respiration   The partial breakdown of carbohydrate to pyruvic acid. This process does not require oxygen

Anaerobic threshold   The point at which the intensity of the exercise leads to a dramatic increase in the anaerobic production of energy

Angular motion   Movement around an axis

Antagonist   A muscle that works in conjunction with a prime mover. As the prime mover contracts, the antagonist relaxes and returns to its original resting length

Anxiety   The negative aspect of experiencing stress. It is the worry that is experienced due to fear of failure

Aponeurosis   A fibrous sheet of connective tissue joining muscle to bone or muscle to muscle

Appendicular skeleton   The part of the skeleton that comprises the upper and lower limbs, the shoulder girdle and the pelvic girdle

Arousal   The energised state, or the readiness for action that motivates a performer to behave in a particular way

Arteries   Blood vessels that always carry blood away from the heart

Articulation   The place where two or more bones meet to form a joint

Assertion   When forceful behaviour is controlled and directed within the rules of the game or activity. In sports psychology this is sometimes known as channelled aggression or instrumental aggression

Associationist theories   Theories which connect or bond a stimulus with a particular response

Associative phase of learning   The second phase of learning, which is when practice takes place and feedback is available

Athleticism   A philosophy of physical, moral and challenging activities that fostered the development of character in young men. A term associated with sport developed in the public schools of England in the nineteenth century

ATP   Adenosine triphosphate. A form of chemical energy found in all cells

Atrioventricular node   A specialised node found in the atrioventricular septum that forms part of the conduction system of the heart

Attentional wastage   When a performer's concentration is misdirected to irrelevant cues

Attributional retraining	A process which helps those who have learned helplessness to attribute to more controllable factors
Attributions	The perceived causes of a particular outcome. The reasons that are given for a particular result
Aussie Sport	A programme of sports with modified rules to accommodate all ages and abilities introduced by the Australian Sports Commission in 1986
Australian Sports Commission	Set up in 1885 by the federal government. The body responsible for increasing participation and developing sports excellence in Australia
Autonomous phase of learning	The final phase of learning, when movements are almost automatic and motor programmes have been completely formed
Autonomous	Self-governing, independent
Autoregulation	The local control of blood distribution within the tissues of the body in response to chemical changes
Axial skeleton	The part of the skeleton that comprises the skull, spine and ribcage
Baccalauréat	A multi-subject examination, including PE, that is taken before university entrance
Basal metabolic rate	How much energy we would use to carry out all necessary reactions if we remained at rest
Blood pressure	Blood flow × resistance. The resistance is caused by friction between the blood and the vessel walls
Bohr effect	A drop in pH causes oxygen to dissociate from haemoglobin more readily
Buffer	A substance, e.g. haemoglobin, that combines with either an acid or a base to help keep the body's pH at an optimal level
Bundle of His	Specialised bundles of nerve fibre found in the septum that form part of the conduction system of the heart
Calorie	The amount of heat energy required to raise the temperature of one gram of water through one degree Celsius
Capillaries	The smallest type of blood vessel. Their walls are only one cell thick. This is where the exchange of gases and nutrients take place
Carbo-loading	Initial depletion of carbohydrate stores, followed by a high carbohydrate diet
Cardiac output	The amount of blood ejected from one ventricle in one minute
Cardiovascular drift	An increase in heart rate during exercise to compensate for a decrease in stroke volume in an attempt to maintain cardiac output
Cartilaginous joint	A joint with no joint cavity but with cartilage between the bones of the joint. Examples are the joints between the vertebrae of the spine
Centrality	A sociological theory which states that dominant roles in sport are taken up by the dominant culture in society
Centre of gravity	The point where all the mass of an object is concentrated
Centres de vacances	Summer camps for French children, often offering outdoor pursuits and sports
Channelled aggression	See Assertion
Chronic response	A long-term physiological adaptation that occurs as a result of training
Circumduction	The lower end of the bone moves in a circle. Circumduction is a combination of flexion, extension, abduction and adduction
Clarendon Commission	A royal commission set up in 1864 to investigate the great public schools
Classical conditioning	An unconditioned stimulus is paired with a conditioned stimulus to create a conditioned response
Codification	Creation and maintenance of rules
Coenzyme	A molecule that can carry atoms, transporting them from one reaction to another
Cognitive dissonance	If an individual experiences two or more opposing beliefs which causes disharmony, then the overall attitude will change to regain harmony
Cognitive phase of learning	The first phase of learning. Involves the performer discovering movement strategies
Cognitive skill	A skill that involves the intellectual ability of the performer
Cohesion	The motivational aspects which attract individual members to a group and the resistance of those members to the group breaking up
Compound	A group of elements combine to form a compound
Concentric	A form of muscular contraction in which the muscle is acting as the prime mover and shortening under tension

Condyle	A large knuckle-shaped articular surface
Connectionist theory	See Associationist theories
Conquest	In a sociocultural sense, where one society takes over another and in doing so imposes its own culture upon it
Cori cycle	The chain of reactions that converts lactic acid back to glycogen
Critical threshold	A training guideline for aerobic work developed by a researcher from Finland called Karvonen. Calculated as resting heart rate + 60% of (maximum heart rate – resting heart rate)
Decentralised	The power of control is spread among many
Dehydration	Loss of body fluids
Dendrite	A process of the motor neurone that carries the nerve impulse from the central nervous system to the cell body
Department of Youth and Sport	A government department in France with responsibility for all levels of sport
Diastole	The relaxation phase of the cardiac cycle
Distal	Furthest away from the centre of the body
Distributed practice	Practice which includes rest periods between trials
DOMS	The delayed onset of muscle soreness experienced one or two days after training
Draft system	The system where professional teams select the best college players once a year
Drill	Military-style exercise involving marching, carried out in elementary schools
Drive	Directed, motivated or 'energised' behaviour that an individual has towards achieving a certain goal
Drive reduction theory	When performance is perceived to be at its optimum, the performer experiences inhibition which demotivates
Drive theory	The relationship between arousal and performance is linear: as arousal levels increase, so does performance
Dual use	Use of a sport/leisure facility is shared by two sectors of the community
Eccentric	A form of muscular contraction in which the muscle is acting as the antagonist and lengthens under tension
Eco sport	Recreational activities with little organisation and natural in focus
Element	A simple substance that cannot be chemically split any further
Elitism	Activities confined to an exclusive minority
Emergent leader	A leader who arises from within the group
End diastolic volume	The amount of blood in the ventricles just before the contraction phase of the cardiac cycle
Endothermic reaction	A reaction that requires energy to be put into it
Enzyme	A biological catalyst that acts to bring about a specific reaction
Epinephrine	A hormone. More commonly known as adrenaline
EPO	Erythropoietin or EPO is a naturally occurring hormone produced by the kidney and stimulates the production of red blood cells in the body. EPO can now be artificially manufactured
Ergogenic aid	Any substance or phenomenon that enhances performance
Erythrocyte	A biconcave disc containing haemoglobin that helps transport respiratory gases around the body. Also known as a red blood cell
Eustress	A type of positive stress that is actively sought by a performer
Evaluation apprehension	A sense of anxiety caused by the performer perceiving that he or she is being judged by those in the audience
Exothermic reaction	A reaction that releases energy
Expiratory reserve volume	The amount of air that can be forcibly exhaled from the lungs in addition to the tidal volume
Extension	An increase in the angle around a joint
External respiration	The exchange of respiratory gases (oxygen and carbon dioxide) between the lungs and the blood
Extrinsic motivation	External factors which influence behaviour, such as rewards
Fartlek	A form of aerobic training. Fartlek means 'speed play'. An athlete varies the pace and terrain of the run
Fasciculus	A group of individual muscle fibres bound together by connective tissue to form a bundle. Plural is fasciculi

Fibrous joint	A joint with no joint cavity and the bones held together by fibrous connective tissue. An example is the sutures of the skull bones
Field sports	Another term for country pursuits such as hunting, shooting and fishing
Fixator	A muscle which allows the prime mover to work more efficiently by stabilising the bone where the prime mover originates
Flexibility	The range of movement possible around a joint
Flexion	A decrease in the angle around a joint
Foramen	A hole in a bone
Forster Act	Passed in 1870. Made education compulsory for all children between the ages of 5 and 13 years
Fossa	A depression in a bone
Free radical	A molecule with an unpaired electron, e.g. an oxygen intermediate leaked during the electron transport chain. They are highly reactive and cause tissue damage
Fulcrum	The fixed point that a lever acts around. In the body the joint acts as the fulcrum
Fundamental motor skills	Skills learned at a young age that are basic to many sports
Fusiform	A muscle shape, where the muscle fibres run the length of the muscle
Games cult	A way of thinking about sports which was exported around the world (see also Athleticism)
Game laws	Passed in 1390. Made hunting of animals exclusively the right of certain social classes
General adaptation syndrome	A way of explaining how our bodies respond to stress. It involves three stages: alarm reaction, resistance, exhaustion
Gestaltists	A group of German scientists who established principles of perception and insight learning
Glycogen	A complex chain of sugars, made up of a number of glucose molecules. Glycogen is the body's main medium for storing carbohydrate
Golgi tendon organ	Provides the central nervous system with information concerning the degree of tension within a muscle
Gouren	A form of wrestling practised in Brittany
Haematocrit	The percentage of blood cells in the total blood volume
Haemoglobin	A protein in red blood cells with a high affinity for carbon monoxide, carbon dioxide and oxygen
Haxey Hood	An ancient game, still played annually on 6 January at Haxey in Lincolnshire
Healthy	To be in a state of well-being and free from disease
Hick's law	The more alternative responses that could be made, the longer the reaction time of the performer
Holy day	A religious festival, which gave people a day off work
Homeostasis	The maintenance of a stable internal environment
Hors Limites	The French arm of the Outward Bound movement. Offers opportunities for young people to take part in outdoor pursuits
Hyperextension	Continuing to extend a limb beyond 180°
Hyperplasia	An increase in the number of cells in a tissue
Hypertrophy	Where an increase in cell size leads to an increase in tissue size
Hypoglycaemia	A condition caused by low blood sugar levels
Imagery	A technique of managing stress. Mental pictures are created in order to escape the immediate stressful situation
Inertia	A body or an object is said to be in a state of inertia and needs a force to be applied before any change of velocity can occur
Insertion	The part of a muscle that is attached by connective tissue to a bone that moves
Insight learning	A performer learns through understanding rather than simply connecting a certain stimulus with a particular response
Inspiratory reserve volume	The amount of air that can be forcibly inspired into the lungs in addition to the tidal volume
Interactionist	Linking of traits with environmental factors. Determines behaviour
Internal respiration	The exchange of respiratory gases (oxygen and carbon dioxide) between the blood and the tissues
Interval training	A form of training in which periods of work are interspersed with periods of recovery

Intrinsic motivation	Internal drives such as emotional feelings
Invasion games	Games in which the aim is to invade another team's territory – for example football
Inverted U theory	As arousal levels increase, so does performance, but only to a certain point, usually at moderate arousal levels. Once past moderate arousal level, performance decreases
Isometric	A form of muscular contraction in which the muscle increases in tension but its length does not alter
Joule	The SI unit of energy. 4.2 joules is equal to one kilocalorie
Kinaesiology	The study of the science of movement
Kinaesthesis	The information that we hold within ourselves about our body's position
Lactacid component	Part of the recovery process (oxygen debt) where lactic acid is removed from the muscles
Lactate	Any salt of lactic acid
LDH	Lactate dehydrogenase is the enzyme responsible for pyruvic acid accepting hydrogen ions and forming lactic acid
Lean body mass	Fat-free weight
Learned helplessness	The belief that failure is inevitable because of negative previous experiences
Lever	A rigid bar that rotates around a fixed point. In the body bones act as levers
Lifetime sports	Sports that can be played throughout life, generally ones that are self-paced or can be adopted
Linear motion	Movement in a straight line
Lombardian ethic	The idea that winning is the most important thing
Mass	The quantity of matter a body contains
Massed practice	A continuous practice period with very short, or no, rest intervals
Maximum strength	The maximum force that can be generated by a muscle in a single contraction
Metabolism	The sum of all the chemical reactions that take place within our body
Minute ventilation	The amount of air taken into or pushed out of the lungs in one minute. It is calculated by multiplying the number of breaths taken by how much air is inspired or expired in one breath
Mitochondrion	An organelle found in the cell where the process of aerobic respiration takes place. The plural is mitochondria
Model course	Established in 1902 by the War Office. Made military drill compulsory in all state schools
Molecule	A small group of atoms with at least one atom from each element of the compound
Momentum	The product of velocity × mass
Motor programme	A generalised series of movements stored in the long-term memory
Motor skill	An action or task that has a goal and which requires voluntary movements
Movement time	The time taken from the start of a movement to its completion
Multidimensional model of leadership	Effective leadership is influenced by the qualities of the leader, the situation and the characteristics of the group members
Multipennate	A muscle shape, where the fibres run off either side of small tendons that are attached to the main tendon
Muscle spindle	Provides information about the changes in muscle length and also the rate of change in muscle length
Myelin sheath	A fatty sheath that covers the axon of a motor neurone
Myocardium	Cardiac muscle tissue that forms the middle layer of the heart wall
Myoglobin	A protein substance found in the sarcoplasm of the cell. It has a high affinity for oxygen and helps transport oxygen from the capillary to the mitochondria
Myosin	A protein filament found within the sarcomere
National Plan	A programme aimed at providing the whole French population with access to sports facilities
NCAA	The National Collegiate Athletic Association is the body that oversees college sport in the USA
Neuromuscular junction	The point where the axon terminal of a motor neurone contacts the sarcolemma of a muscle fibre

Newton	One newton is the force required to produce an acceleration of one metre per second per second on a mass of one kilogram
Nitric oxide	A vasodilator substance involved in autoregulation
OBLA	The onset of blood lactate accumulation, a point during progressive exercise when the blood lactate concentration suddenly increases. Also referred to as lactate threshold
Observational learning	A performer learns by watching and imitating others. The extent of imitation depends upon the significance of those that are being watched (see also Significant others)
Open championship	Competition that is open to both professionals and amateurs
Operant conditioning	Actions are 'shaped' and then reinforced. The behaviour is manipulated, rather than the stimulus
Origin	The part of a muscle that is attached by connective tissue to a stationary bone
Ossification	The process of bone formation
Outcome goals	Goals that are related to the end result or the outcome of competition
Overload	One of the principles of training. A body needs to be made to work harder than normal before any adaptations will take place
Oxygen debt	The amount of oxygen consumed during recovery above that which would have ordinarily been consumed at rest in the same time
Oxygen deficit	When insufficient oxygen is being distributed to the tissues for all the energy production to be met aerobically
Part method of training	A skill is split up into sub-routines for more effective teaching
Partial pressure	The pressure a gas exerts within a mixture of gases
Peak flow experience	The emotional response of an elite athlete whose performance levels are optimal
Pedestrianism	Walking races between two or more competitors, often for cash prizes
Pelota	A court game played in the streets in the south of France
Perception	Interpretation of stimuli as part of information processing
Performance goals	Goals related to performance, which can be judged against other performances
Periodisation	The phases of training undertaken during a specified period of time
Person-oriented leader	A leader who is concerned primarily with the interpersonal behaviour of the group members
Phosphorylation	The addition of phosphate to an organic compound
Plyometrics	A form of training used to develop dynamic strength. Plyometric activities involve jumping, hopping or bounding, to make muscle groups work eccentrically
PNF	Proprioceptive neuromuscular facilitation is a form of flexibility training
Popular recreation	Sporting activities before the industrial revolution
Post 16 gap	The 60% drop-off in participation of sport among young people after they leave school
Power	The work performed per unit of time
Precapillary sphincters	Found between the arteriole and the capillary. A sphincter is a ring of muscle that surrounds an opening and can effectively open up or close down the capillary
Prescribed leader	A leader who has been appointed from an external source to a particular group or team
Prime mover	The muscle that is directly responsible for creating the movement produced at a joint
Private sector	Ownership of a facility is in the hands of private individuals or companies
Process	A prominent projection of a bone – for example, the spinous process of a vertebra
Profile of mood states	The measurement of moods of those who participate in sport
Progression	One of the principles of training. The workload attempted needs to be closely monitored and increased only after some adaptations have taken place
Progressive relaxation training	Concerned with learning to be aware of the tension in the muscles and then to get rid of this tension by relaxing. Developed by Jacobsen
Proximal	Nearest the centre of the body

Psychological refractory period	The delay caused by the increased information-processing time when a second stimulus follows closely after the first
Public sector	A facility in public ownership, usually administered by a local authority
Pulmonary ventilation	The movement of air into and out of the lungs
Purkinje fibres	Specialised nerve fibres found in the ventricles that form part of the conduction system of the heart
QUANGO	Quasi-autonomous non-governmental organisation
Rationalisation	A term associated with the development of sport that occurred during the industrial revolution, resulting in the codification and organisation of modern sport
Reaction time	The time between presentation of a stimulus and the start of movement
Reinforcement	The process which increases the probability of a behaviour reoccurring. Reinforcement strengthens the S–R bond
Reliability	Research that achieves consistency of results after two or more applications of tests
Repetition	The number of times that an athlete repeats a particular exercise
Response time	The time between presentation of a stimulus and completion of the movement
Reticular activating system	A region of the central core of the brainstem which maintains levels of arousal. It can enhance or inhibit incoming sensory stimuli
Reversibility	Any adaptations that take place as a consequence of training will be reversed when you stop training
Ringelmann effect	When the average individual performance decreases with the increase in group size
Romanticism	An artistic movement in the nineteenth century that encouraged all people to get into 'the great outdoors'
Sabbatarianism	The view that Sunday is a holy day of rest
Sarcomere	The smallest contractile unit of a skeletal muscle fibre
Self-efficacy	The degree of self-confidence that is felt in a specific situation
Self-serving bias	A tendency to attribute failure to internal rather than external causes and thus to limit the sense of shame
Shop window	Sport is used to show off a country
Significant others	People who are held in high regard by an individual
Single-channel hypothesis	This states that the brain can only process one stimulus at a time. It is often referred to as the 'bottleneck' theory
Sinuatrial node	A specialised node in the wall of the right atrium, sometimes called the pacemaker, that forms part of the conduction system of the heart
Social facilitation	The influence of the presence of others on performance. These others could be in the audience or performing the same activity (in which case they are called coactors)
Social learning	The influence of others on a person's behaviour, often through observation and imitation
Social loafing	A phenomenon in which some individuals seem to lose motivation in group situations. This may be caused by a lack of personal identity
Socialisation	The process by which humans adapt and grow into their society
Sport pour Tous	A French national scheme of mass participation
Stereotype	A series of characteristics or traits used, often wrongly, to label certain groups in society
Strength endurance	The ability of a muscle to withstand fatigue
Stroke volume	The volume of blood pumped out of the heart by each ventricle during one contraction
Swedish gymnastics	Drill-type exercises based on the work of Ling. Emphasises style, grace and movement
Synovial joint	A fluid-filled joint cavity is surrounded by an articular capsule. The articulating surfaces are covered in hyaline cartilage. An example is the hinge joint of the knee
Systole	The contraction phase of the cardiac cycle
Task-oriented leader	A leader who is concerned primarily with completion of a task rather than interpersonal relationships
Tapering	Reducing the amount of training and/or training intensity prior to a competition day

Taunton Commission	Set up in 1868 to review schools (including girls') not covered by the Clarendon Commission
Tendon	A round cord or bank of connective tissue joining muscle to bone
Thoracic cavity	The area surrounded by the ribs and bordered by the diaphragm. The thoracic cavity is divided into two halves by the mediastinum
Threshold	The point at which the energy system being used is no longer effective in producing energy for ATP synthesis
Tidal volume	The amount of air breathed into or out of the lungs in one breath
Tier Temps Pedagogique	A programme in which primary schools must teach six hours of PE each week
Title IX	Government legislation in the USA to maintain equality in funding and provision of sport in colleges and schools for both males and females
Track and field	What the Americans call athletics
Training heart rate	The range of heart rate prescribed to match the training intensity requirements of an athlete. The athlete must remain within this range for training to be effective
Trait	Linked to personality, traits are generalisable behaviours that are enduring and largely innate
Transfer	The influence that the learning and/or performance of one skill has on the learning/performance of another
Transplant classes	Outdoor experience for French primary school children
Triadic model	Attitudes have three important elements: cognitive, affective and behavioural
UNSS	The National Union of School Sport, responsible for coordinating Wednesday afternoon sport in French secondary schools
USEP	The Union of Primary School Sport, responsible for coordinating Wednesday afternoon sport in French primary schools
Validity	Research that has high internal validity is scientific and keeps unwanted variables to a minimum. Research that has high external validity can be generalised to the population as a whole
Variance	One of the principles of training. A training programme needs to include a variety of training methods to help maintain motivation and to avoid overuse injuries
Vascular shunt	The redistribution of the cardiac output during exercise, taking more blood to the working muscles and less blood to other organs such as the kidneys and the liver
Vasoconstriction	A decrease in the size of the lumen of the blood vessel as the smooth muscle of the tunica media contracts
Vasodilatation	An increase in the size of the lumen of the blood vessel as the smooth muscle of the tunica media relaxes
Vasomotor tone	The continual low-frequency impulse received by blood vessels
Veins	Blood vessels that always carry blood towards the heart
Venous return	The flow of blood through the veins back to the heart
Vicarious experiences	What the performer has previously observed (see also Observational learning)
Vital capacity	The maximum amount of air that can be forcibly exhaled after breathing in as much as possible
$\dot{V}O_2(max)$	The maximum amount of oxygen that can be taken into and used by the body in one minute, expressed in millilitres per minute per kilogram of body weight
Voluntary sector	Facilities run and administered by volunteers
Watt	One watt is the use of one joule per second
Whole method of training	Teaching skills without breaking them down into sub-routines or parts
Wingate test	A cycle ergometer test that measures an athlete's power output in watts
Work	Force × distance

Index

Page numbers in **bold** indicate an illustration or table.